The Blacks in Canada

THE BLACKS IN CANADA

A HISTORY

Robin W. Winks

Second Edition

McGill-Queen's University Press
Montreal & Kingston • London • Buffalo

© McGill-Queen's University Press 1997
ISBN 0-7735-1631-X (cloth)
ISBN 0-7735-1632-8 (paper)

Legal deposit first quarter 1997
Bibliothèque nationale du Québec

Printed in Canada on acid-free paper

First edition published by Yale University Press, 1971

McGill-Queen's University Press acknowledges the support
received for its publishing program from the Canada Council's
Block Grants program.

Canadian Cataloguing in Publication Data

Winks, Robin W., 1930–
    The Blacks in Canada : a history
    Includes bibliographical references and index.
    ISBN 0-7735-1631-X (bound)
    ISBN 0-7735-1632-8 (pbk.)
    1. Blacks – Canada – History. I. Title.
    FC106.B6W55 1997   971'.00496   C96-990097-X
    F1035.N3W5 1997

Designed by John O.C. McCrillis and set in Times Roman type.

*To Honor Leigh and to Eliot,
born after this book was begun,
who nagged it to completion*

Contents

Maps

Preface

Negroes have lived in Canada for nearly as long as in the present United States. In 1628, nine years after a Dutch ship unloaded the first cargo of Africans at Jamestown, David Kirke, the so-called English Conqueror of Quebec, brought a slave boy to the French shores, and Negroes were present in New France and in British North America thereafter. Those who were slaves gained their freedom in 1834, in common with all in the British empire. The black population grew in numbers and sometimes in strength during the next two decades as a result of a substantial influx of fugitives from the United States. Yet other migrations in the late nineteenth and early twentieth centuries brought other black men to Canada. The story of these men—settlers and transients—has never been told in any reasonably full way.

The chief purpose of this book is to examine the history of Negro life in Canada from 1628 to the 1960s, and by so doing to reveal something of the nature of prejudice in Canada. A second purpose is to use the Negro's story as a means of examining some of the ways in which Canadian attitudes toward immigration and ethnic identity differ from the American, as a contribution to the continuing search for a Canadian identity. A third desire is to show the Negro as an actor in the context of an emerging national history, as a person who acts and reacts as well as one acted upon. Finally, since most black men in Canada came more immediately from the United States, or those British colonies that became the United States, this study also is an attempt to inquire into a neglected aspect of Canadian-American cultural relations.

At no time in the twentieth century have Negroes comprised more than a tiny fraction of the Canadian population, and although accurate statistics are virtually impossible to find, the Negro proportion of the population probably is no more than two percent today. For this reason alone, although there are other reasons as well, this chapter of the Negro's story has been ignored by historians of both Canada and the Negro. On the other hand, those Canadians who have made it their special mission to find, to define, or to create a sense of Canadian identity often point with pride to the fact that, when the Negro slave was seeking escape from his servitude after 1850, he sought out freedom "under the lion's paw" in the British provinces. Scores of self-congratulatory newspaper articles appear each year in Toronto, London, Hamilton, and Windsor on the theme of how the slave found freedom in Canada, and an official marker of the Canadian government notes the spot on the banks of the Detroit River where the Underground Railroad is said to have had its terminus. There, the monument proclaims, the fugitive "found in Canada friends, freedom, protection, under the British flag."

Struck by the lack of literature on this aspect of Negro history, I thought it would be instructive to investigate the friends, freedom, and protection thus memorialized. But one could not know how the fugitives were received without understanding something of how British North Americans had dealt with slavery and with the Negro in the two centuries before the fugitives came. Nor could any real assessment be made of the meaning of the fugitive migration for Canadian history without investigating the extent of later Negro assimilation. Slowly, as its three purposes developed clarity, the study became an inquiry into Negro history, Canadian history, and Canadian-American relations. This book is the result.

Some observations may also be helpful in defining what this book does not attempt to do. The writer is not a sociologist, and a graduate degree in anthropology has served chiefly to warn him of the dangers of venturing into other professional fields without a full control of either the discipline or the literature. In deciding to bring this account down to the present decade, and in attempting to generalize about the Negro condition as it is today, one has had to borrow on occasion from that literature, but no sociological claims are made for what is said here.

Nor are many side paths followed which, were one to attempt a "definitive" study, require deeper enquiries. Perhaps one should look more fully into the influence of labor unions in general and of the Brotherhood of Sleeping Car Porters in particular upon the growth of self-awareness among Negro workers. Far more can be written of the West Indian immigrants. A comprehensive study of Negro religious practices in Canada remains for someone interested in church history. Such examples might be multiplied, for judgment on the necessary extent of research into peripherally related areas will differ from scholar to scholar, since one man's thoroughness is another man's pedantry. It is, in any case, intolerable to be given too much information.

Two groups of historians may find this study of some use. Until now, however, the two audiences have been quite distinct. Few Canadian historians can be said to have read extensively in Negro history, and even fewer historians of the Negro can be expected to be familiar with Canadian history. As a result, figures who are daily companions to one group require identification for the other, and documentation must be somewhat heavier than one would otherwise wish. The author can see no way to avoid this, for not all Canadians have heard of Martin R. Delany, nor do all Negroes know of Sir Clifford Sifton. Little more than half of the material gathered has been incorporated directly into the pages of this book, lest data on the Negro swamp data on Canada; and with the thought that someone might wish to pursue various topics further, the body of notes, correspondence, and related papers has been deposited with the Schomburg Collection of Negro History in the Countee Cullen Branch of the New York Public Library.

R. W. W.

London
September 1970

Preface to the Second Edition

The Blacks in Canada was first published in 1971 by Yale University Press
in the United States and Great Britain and McGill-Queen's University Press
in Canada. The book was intended to be a sweeping history, from the
introduction of slavery (and the first slave) into New France in 1628 to the
near-present. Research and writing had been done between 1960 and 1969
and the story the book tells ended in the latter year. The final portions of the
book verged on contemporary history, for the last segregated school had
closed in Ontario in 1965 and until 1968 African-Canadians were denied
burial in some Nova Scotian cemeteries.

My interest in the subject had grown from a variety of influences. As a
teenager I had seen my schoolteacher father dismissed from a position in
rural Colorado because he supported a minority student at a time when few
teachers would do so. Both my parents were quite without racial prejudice,
and I was unprepared, when I went to college, to meet presumably educated
people who clearly held deep racist convictions. As a graduate student in
anthropology (a discipline I left after a Master's degree) I had studied Maori-
pakeha relations in New Zealand and wanted to pursue other inquiries,
though with the methods of the historian, into the nature of race relations in
high technology societies. My doctoral dissertation and second book was on
Canadian-American relations during the Civil War, and my research for that
book had given me some insights into White Canadian attitudes toward
fugitive slaves who had fled to Canada before the war. I was also interested
in how people perceive themselves: I had been struck by a historical plaque
in Windsor, Ontario, which declared that fugitive slaves had found freedom
"under the lion's paw" upon their arrival in British North America, when I
knew that this was not the full story. Finally, the 1960s were a time of ferment
in the United States, and I was interested in the civil rights movement and
curious why, at the time I began my research in 1960, there seemed to be
no similar movement in Canada.

The study began as an inquiry into how fugitive slaves were received in
British North America, what they did when they were on Canadian soil, and
what the answers to these two questions might tell us about Canada. I soon
realized that I could not limit my study in this way, however, for Canadian
attitudes toward Black newcomers had already been shaped in some measure
by earlier Black migrations; nor could I end the story so abruptly, since the
real meaning of events in the mid-nineteenth century was brought to light

only by much later developments. Thus I conceived of a full history from the entry of the first slave until as close as possible to the moment of publication. (That moment was somewhat delayed, for in 1969 I took a leave of absence from my university to serve in the U.S. Department of State, and my frequent travels extended production time to twice the publisher's expectations.)

At the outset I had six distinct goals for *The Blacks in Canada*. I wanted to examine the history and nature of African-Canadian life in Canada, to reveal something of the nature of prejudice in Canada, to inquire into Canadian attitudes toward immigration and ethnic identity, using the Black story as a point of entry, to see how these attitudes differed from American attitudes, to show the African-Canadian as an actor in the emerging national history of Canada, and to deal with a neglected aspect of Canadian-American relations. I was by training a comparative and a diplomatic historian; I was moving away from the latter, but still entertained questions relating to diplomatic history (hence my sixth goal), as I was moving more consistently into the former.

As I soon learned, the story I was to tell was extraordinarily complex. Further, few Canadians were aware of it, and what little was known was frequently wrong. I found that Black Canadians did not appear to have a sense of common identity, which I ascribed to the seven diverse waves of immigration to Canada, each with a different story, requiring the use of different and often widely dispersed sources. To the extent that any of the stories (except for slavery in French Canada, well examined by Marcel Trudel) had already been told, it had been told in isolation. There were the Black slaves brought to Nova Scotia and the Canadas by Loyalists at the close of the American Revolution. There were the Black Refugees who went to Nova Scotia following the War of 1812. There were the Jamaican Maroons. There were the fugitive slaves who fled to British North America from the end of the War of 1812 and during the Civil War, a subject already well begun by William and Jane Pease and Larry Gara. There were Black West Coast businessmen who helped settle British Columbia, particularly Victoria. There were Black farmers who moved to the Canadian plains shortly before World War I. There were the West Indians who after World War II immigrated to the urban centers of Canada. I wanted to learn all I could about each of these groups, these communities, and to relate each story to the others. In the end my research took me to Britain and France, to Jamaica and Sierra Leone, and throughout Canada, and what I had expected to be a four-year enterprise became the all-consuming effort of nine years.

Two books used in some measure as models for *The Blacks in Canada* account for some of its strengths as well as some of its weaknesses. These were Gunnar Myrdal's classic 1944 work, *An American Dilemma: The Negro Problem and Modern Democracy*, on the nature of Black-White relations in the United States, and John Porter's 1965 book, *The Vertical Mosaic: An*

Analysis of Social Class and Power in Canada. At the time both books were powerfully attractive and influential: I derived some of my organizing principles from them and perhaps too readily accepted the idea of Canada as a mosaic of ethnic identities. This accounts for the emphasis placed on "the black tile in the mosaic" in my concluding chapter, and while I still support many of the conclusions reached in that chapter, I no longer think the image is appropriate.

A reader today—indeed, a reader of history any day—must not forget that it is the historian's duty to report on events and attitudes as they were, not as one might wish them to have been. This is a cliché of the historian's trade, and no less true for that. But the present also influences the writing of history and attitudes toward history as a methodology. Society's concerns with what history might provide that is of relevance to today's concerns, even the language of discourse, changes. My research and my writing changed over those nine years, as they have changed even more in the quarter-century since this book was first published.

A case in point is the title of the book. During much of the time I talked with African-Canadians, they preferred to be called Negroes (or even, somewhat to my surprise, coloured); both words occur repeatedly in the tapes and notes from my interviews. But by the latter 1960s terminology was changing. The publisher therefore asked whether we should try to change the language throughout the text from Negro to Black, which was becoming the preferred term. But the book was in production and in the end the publisher felt unable to alter the production schedule to make systematic changes throughout. I responded that nonetheless the title of the book should be changed to its present form. There was some to-and-fro over whether the title should be *Blacks in Canada* or *The Blacks in Canada*, and I held out for use of the definite article as a matter of dignity. As a historian I had no problem with the word Negro in most of the text, since the language reflected the period under discussion, though I was not willing to make any concession to terms that Blacks themselves had always found hurtful or derogatory. After all, I reflected, the National Association for the Advancement of Colored People had not changed its venerable name (though it had buried it in the invariable acronym NAACP). I suggested that we might change running titles to the chapters where appropriate, but this posed other difficulties. Then, as I was reading a short, new essay by a writer I much admired, Ralph Ellison, author of *Invisible Man*, I noted that he had used the term *Negro* throughout his writing. I felt that what was right for Ellison was still right for me: the title would point toward the future, the content, as a work of history, toward the past.

I belabor this point before moving on to what I regard as a genuine weakness of the book simply because I have received so many questions about title and content. The issue of language led some commentators to condemn *The Blacks in Canada*, on occasion I suspect unread, two decades later. But the book was, and is, about Negro Canadians and Black Canadians and Afro-Canadians and African-Canadians. These shifts are significant, and in speech and subsequent writing I have followed them, both as a matter of courtesy and because I accepted the changing sense of self the shifts implied. A book is written in a time, and published at a moment, and were it a political tract perhaps it should shift as the politics shift. But this book is not a political tract.

At the time *The Blacks in Canada* was published, however, some reviewers implied that it was. One reviewer derided my use of "the fashionable epithet 'blacks' in the title"; another imagined that the book was written from a commitment to New Deal Liberalism; another wanted far more "relevant" sociology and anthropology; yet another, apparently unmindful of the fact that I was writing for three audiences—Canadian, American, and Black readers—complained that I explained events and references that no Canadian needed explained.

Despite these observations, the reviews were overwhelmingly favorable. Several reviewers declared that the book would create a new field in Canadian studies; some praised the interpretation, some the research; all remarked upon the extent of primary sources drawn upon. There was general agreement that the book was a good start to a neglected subject and that more books would follow.

More books did follow. Many filled in gaps and corrected errors. Were I to revise *The Blacks in Canada* now, extending its story from 1969 toward the end of the century, there would be much more to say, new perceptions of past events, many significant books and articles to draw upon and to argue with. (I have chosen not to revise the book, for I feel that a new volume of nearly equal length would be required to tell the rich story of the last twenty-five years.) More has been done, and more remains to be done, on the period after World War I. Further research is needed on Black women, on trade unionism, on immigration from Latin America and Africa. Far more must be written on Black writers in Canadian literature; more is needed on the West Indian presence. Despite the detailed account here and elsewhere, there is more to be said about Black settlements in Ontario before the Civil War, about the Ku Klux Klan in Canada, about Africville and Halifax.

Yet if these subjects, and others, remain insufficiently explored, the student of African-Canadian history can rejoice in the outpouring of work that has informed a broadening readership during this quarter-century. Peggy Bristow, Dionne Brand, Velma Carter, Linda Carty, Afua P. Cooper, Agnes Calliste, Daniel Gay, Sylvia Hamilton, Judith S. Hill, Hilary Lawson, Saje Mathieu, Howard and Tamara Palmer, Adrienne Shadd, Bruce Shepard, A.W. Spray, Jonathan Walton, and Dorothy Williams do not appear here. Daniel G. Hill is cited, but his best work was yet to come in 1969. I do not agree with all these authors, and they most certainly do not all agree with me, but there is a clear intellectual interaction between all nonetheless.

What do I think of *The Blacks in Canada* today? No one is the same person after writing a book as before: the struggle to write should change the author. I have written several books since this one, and each has changed me in many ways. I still feel affection toward this book or I would not consent to seeing it reissued; I still feel it contains much research, most of it sound, much of it interesting, a good bit of it significant, and to the best of my abilities all of it true. But of course I recognize the ways in which it speaks from 1969 rather than from the 1990s.

At the time of publication my most formidable critic was James W. St. G. Walker, now one of the leading scholars of African-Canadian history, and then very shortly to publish his own superb work on the Refugee Blacks. He faulted me for not telling "the history of Negro life in Canada" adequately, and he was right. I had, he argued, written a "history of the Black man as an issue in white Canadian life." Because I began with the perspective that racial barriers are wrong—Walker did not suggest that he felt otherwise—I overemphasized the building and the destruction of barriers between Black and other Canadians. (Indeed, I had written most of one chapter in the passive voice, thinking this a stylistically subtle way to show how Black Canadians were acted upon rather than acting, with respect to the subject of the chapter. No reviewer noted my stylistic preciousness, which was just as well, since it lent support to a view that was inherently wrong anyway.) I was particularly taken to task by Walker, but by others as well, for what was felt to be an unsympathetic depiction of Black churches as reinforcers of racial separation. Since these reviewers saw me as that New Deal Liberal whose goal was racial integration rather than the celebration of a separate and prideful identity, they concluded that I was without regard for legitimate Black aspirations distinct from an American melting pot or a Canadian mosaic. Walker concluded that I was "dangerously" suggesting that Blacks themselves, not White racism, were responsible for their unequal position in society.

I did not, and do not, think this, but Walker was correct to point out the ambiguities of my language and analysis. Other commentators since have singled out the chapter on self-help and voluntarism as marked by a critical approach insufficiently understanding of Black culture or of economic and class realities. I believe these criticisms to be just, and were I to approach the subject again, I would do so armored with all the literature that has appeared since 1969, with a wider grasp of the literature of Black identity that was shaping public debate in the 1960s, and with less of the rude Jacksonian democracy that informs and shapes some of the conclusions here.

Of course, if one has influenced the scholarship of others, negatively as well as positively, one may take some pleasure from knowing that what one has done has not proven to be irrelevant to matters of great importance to all of us. The research accomplishment remains real, if the perspective is now dated. One cannot please all critics (some found the story well written, "sharp," "pungent," filled with "dry wit," even "dramatically told," while others found it "dense," "a catalog," "far too academic," and even "flabby"). No book of this scope has displaced it. Dozens of articles have appeared which have drawn upon its documentation (not always with acknowledgment). Were I teaching a course in African-Canadian history today, this is not the book with which I would begin, but I continue to believe that one would arrive at it nonetheless, if only to argue with its perspective and conclusions.

One of those previous reviewers twice called *The Blacks in Canada* "a definitive history." It is not that—no history ever is. But it was a start, a prod, a goad, a reminder to others of a story to be told, enriched, corrected, and extended. It was a beginning, for me and for many readers. My views and the views of those readers have changed, sometimes congruently and no doubt sometimes putting greater distance between us. Yet there is one element in the book I would not change were I to begin again. The reviewer who flatteringly if mistakenly thought the book definitive remarked on the historian's inclination to place too much emphasis on the significance of leadership. I continue to believe that individuals make a difference, and while I fully recognize that class, gender, sexual orientation, environment, and much else narrows the channels in which we all live and make our decisions, I will accept no determinism and will not back away from my conviction that leadership remains basic to all human endeavor.

I wish to thank the many people who, over the years, have corresponded with me about this or that aspect of *The Blacks in Canada*, who have corrected me, provided new sources, and kept me informed as the field has developed. I wish in particular to thank my friend Austin Clarke, son of Barbados, distinguished Canadian novelist, who has acted as a one-man clipping service over the years, and Saje Mathieu, my student, who mixes her criticisms with wit and grace and has drawn my attention to several writers and their articles I might well have not otherwise known about. I also thank the Yale University Press for releasing copyright so that this new edition could become a reality.

New Haven, Connecticut
October, 1996

Acknowledgments

Literally hundreds of academicians, archivists, librarians, local historians, and private individuals have helped me to gather materials, and each cannot be singled out for thanks. Some I have mentioned in the appropriate places in the notes; of many others I must ask that they take this book itself as testimony to my gratitude and as witness to the fact that their aid was not entirely wasted. Foremost among those I must thank are the many Canadian Negroes themselves who, collectively in meetings or alone across cups of tea in their homes, nearly always were responsive, responsible, and interested. What is said here will anger some of those who helped me most, for one must mention some who are still active in their work; but even those with whom I most disagree will, I trust, grant me my conclusions as I grant them the sincerity of their actions.

The Social Science Research Council, through a grant-in-aid of research in 1959–60, enabled me to begin this study; and Yale University, through the award of a Morse Fellowship and supplementary travel funds for research in Canada, the United Kingdom, France, Jamaica, and West Africa, helped me to complete it. The Yale University Library sought out several hundred titles through interlibrary loans and purchased at least as many more titles from its William Inglis Morse fund for Canadiana. I am grateful to these institutions—and to the men who have made them what they are—for their help.

Brief portions of this book have appeared elsewhere. I wish to thank the Princeton University Press and Martin B. Duberman for permission to reprint paragraphs from an essay of mine in his *Anti-Slavery Vanguard: New Essays on the Abolitionists* (1965). *The Canadian Historical Review,* in which, in 1969, an extended version of chapter 12 appeared, and the Canadian Historical Association, to which in 1964 I read a paper derived in part from chapters 3 and 14, also receive my appreciation. This paper has subsequently appeared in the *Dalhousie Review* (1969). Portions of the concluding chapter have been published in *The Journal of Negro History,* vols. 53 (1968) and 54 (1969).

Friends and colleagues have given me much exacting and practical help by reading portions of this study as it progressed. Particular gratitude goes to C. Vann Woodward, Sterling Professor of History at Yale University, who read the entire manuscript in its penultimate version, and to Benjamin Quarles, Professor of History at Morgan State College, who read it in its final form. Professor John Hope Franklin of the University of Chicago, Professor William H. Pease of the University of Maine, Professor Harold H. Potter of Sir George Williams University, and Professor W. L. Morton of Trent University read intermediate drafts of major portions and rooted out numerous infelicities of style and misleading nuances of meaning. Mr. Christopher H. Fyfe of the University of Edinburgh criticized chapters 3 and 5 in an early draft and directed me to most of the manuscript sources used in Sierra Leone, while Professor Edwin Redkey of the University of Tennessee helped by evaluating chapter 11. Dr. C. Bruce Fergusson, Archivist for the Province of Nova Scotia, sought out errors in chapters 2, 3, and 5, and Professor Marcel Trudel of l'Université d'Ottawa read chapters 1 and 2. Dr. Daniel G. Hill of the Ontario Human Rights Commission, and Professor Alexander L. Murray of York University sity gave me access to their unpublished dissertations, while the late Fred Landon, Professor Emeritus of the University of Western Ontario, showed unfailing interest and gave me unlimited use of his own files. Professor George A. Rawlyk of Queen's University was a most helpful commentator on an early paper, and he provided entrée to private records in Halifax, while the Reverends William Oliver and Charles Coleman of that city also aided me in many ways. Mrs. Miriam Swanson and Mrs. Anne Granger typed the final manuscript and cheerfully eliminated a host of split infinitives, dangling participles, and inconsistent spellings. Barbara Folsom of Yale University Press prepared the manuscript for publication. The maps for this volume were made possible by a grant for this purpose from the Provost's Fund. To all, I owe much. That this study will nonetheless retain errors of fact, judgment, and interpretation remains solely my responsibility.

On the occasion of a second printing, I have corrected a small number of typographical and other errors—R. W. W. (March 1972).

A Note on Terminology

Throughout the text *Canada* is normally used to designate the area encompassed by the Dominion of Canada. This term technically is incorrect for many portions of the present Dominion prior to 1867 (and for Newfoundland before 1949). When technical accuracy is required, as in dealing with legal matters, more precise terms are used. *New France* refers to the French colony prior to 1763. The *Maritime Provinces* are Nova Scotia, New Brunswick, and Prince Edward Island; if reference is made to the *Atlantic Provinces,* these three provinces are joined by Newfoundland. Initially, Prince Edward Island was called Isle St. Jean; New Brunswick was part of Nova Scotia until 1784. Toronto was York until 1837. Until 1841, present-day Ontario was Upper Canada and present-day Quebec was Lower Canada; from 1841 to 1867, they were Canada West and Canada East respectively. During both periods they were referred to collectively as *the Canadas,* a term that excluded the Maritime Provinces. The whole of these British possessions were the British North American Provinces and they were, despite the term *provinces,* colonies.

The Crown Colony of Vancouver Island was proclaimed in 1849, and it did not unite with British Columbia until 1866; references to British Columbia prior to the latter date are not meant to include the island. Some Canadians regard *Americans* as inappropriate when applied exclusively to inhabitants of the United States, but the word is so used here. Finally, *Negroes* as used in this study means any people who considered themselves to be Negro, or who were so considered by the law. West Indians are included within the term except where stated otherwise. There is a substantial body of literature which traces the evolution of this word and which suggests that *colored* is a more satisfactory term, while many Negroes today prefer *Afro-Americans* or *blacks.* Since few white Canadians were aware of these controversies, and since many Negroes quite rightly reject *colored* for the value judgment it implies, *Negro* is given its broader, or popular, meaning here, although all of the terms are used, in context.

List of Abbreviations

AHR	*American Historical Review*
BCA	Provincial Archives of British Columbia, Victoria
BM	The British Museum, London
BPL	Boston Public Library
CHA	Canadian Historical Association
CHR	*Canadian Historical Review*
CMS	Church Missionary Society, London
CO	Colonial Office Records, Public Record Office, London
FO	Foreign Office Records, Public Record Office, London
G	Governor General's Records, Public Archives of Canada, Ottawa
HO	Home Office Records, Public Record Office, London
JNH	*Journal of Negro History*
LC	Library of Congress, Washington
MHS	Massachusetts Historical Society, Boston
MVHR	*Mississippi Valley Historical Review*
NA	National Archives, Washington
NBM	New Brunswick Museum, Saint John
OH	*Ontario History*
OHS	Ontario Historical Society
OPA	Ontario Public Archives, Toronto
PAC	Public Archives of Canada, Ottawa
PANS	Public Archives of Nova Scotia, Halifax
PRO	Public Record Office, London
PSHS	Pennsylvania State Historical Society, Philadelphia
RSC	Royal Society of Canada
SPG	Society for the Propagation of the Gospel, London
TPL	Toronto Public Library
WO	War Office Records, PRO

Abbreviations or short titles for less frequently employed depositories, publications, and organizations are established on the occasion of the first usage within each chapter. With most manuscript citations, a date or a folio number is provided—whichever may be most helpful to the reader.

CANADA, with particular reference to the West

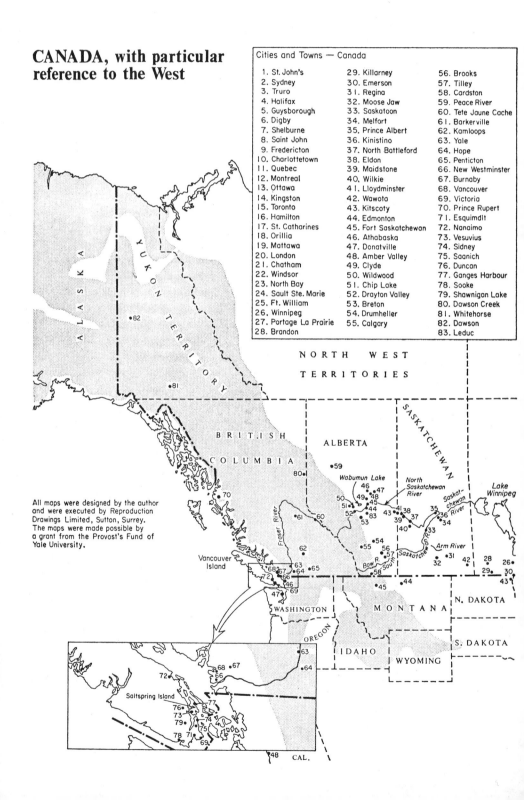

Cities and Towns — Canada

1. St. John's	29. Killarney	56. Brooks
2. Sydney	30. Emerson	57. Tilley
3. Truro	31. Regina	58. Cardston
4. Halifax	32. Moose Jaw	59. Peace River
5. Guysborough	33. Saskatoon	60. Tete Jaune Cache
6. Digby	34. Melfort	61. Barkerville
7. Shelburne	35. Prince Albert	62. Kamloops
8. Saint John	36. Kinistino	63. Yale
9. Fredericton	37. North Battleford	64. Hope
10. Charlottetown	38. Eldon	65. Penticton
11. Quebec	39. Maidstone	66. New Westminster
12. Montreal	40. Wilkie	67. Burnaby
13. Ottawa	41. Lloydminster	68. Vancouver
14. Kingston	42. Wawota	69. Victoria
15. Toronto	43. Kitscoty	70. Prince Rupert
16. Hamilton	44. Edmonton	71. Esquimalt
17. St. Catharines	45. Fort Saskatchewan	72. Nanaimo
18. Orillia	46. Athabaska	73. Vesuvius
19. Mattawa	47. Donatville	74. Sidney
20. London	48. Amber Valley	75. Saanich
21. Chatham	49. Clyde	76. Duncan
22. Windsor	50. Wildwood	77. Ganges Harbour
23. North Bay	51. Chip Lake	78. Sooke
24. Sault Ste. Marie	52. Drayton Valley	79. Shawnigan Lake
25. Ft. William	53. Breton	80. Dawson Creek
26. Winnipeg	54. Drumheller	81. Whitehorse
27. Portage La Prairie	55. Calgary	82. Dawson
28. Brandon		83. Leduc

All maps were designed by the author and were executed by Reproduction Drawings Limited, Sutton, Surrey. The maps were made possible by a grant from the Provost's Fund of Yale University.

Cities and Towns — U.S.A.

1. Portland	17. Utica	33. Galesburg
2. Concord	18. New York City	34. Detroit
3. Montpelier	19. Cleveland	35. Pontiac
4. Boston	20. Sandusky	36. Flint
5. Providence	21. Toledo	37. Lansing
6. Hartford	22. Oberlin	38. Kalamazoo
7. New Haven	23. Columbus	39. Milwaukee
8. Albany	24. Cincinnati	40. Waukesha
9. Ballston	25. Philadelphia	41. Duluth
10. Schenectady	26. Pittsburgh	42. St. Paul
11. Syracuse	27. Harrisburg	43. Pembina
12. Skaneateles	28. Indianapolis	44. Havre
13. Rochester	29. Fountain City	45. Browning
14. Buffalo	30. Fort Wayne	46. Bellingham
15. Niagara Falls ,	31. Chicago	47. Seattle
16. Auburn	32. Springfield	48. San Francisco

Towns — Nova Scotia

1. Glace Bay
2. New Waterford
3. Sydney
4. Louisbourg
5. Tracadie
6. Upper Big Tracadie
7. Guysborough
8. Birchtown II
9. Canso
10. Antigonish
11. Addington
12. Country Harbour
13. New Glasgow
14. Stellarton
15. Trenton
16. Westville
17. Pictou
18. River John
19. Amherst
20. Joggins
21. Springhill
22. Fundy
23. Five Islands
24. Parrsboro
25. Blomidon
26. Truro
27. Onslow
28. Stewiacke
29. Musquodoboit Harbour
30. Porters Lake
31. Dipper's Creek
32. Waverley
33. Dartmouth
34. Preston
35. New Road Settlement
36. Maroon Hill
37. Beechville
38. Beech Hill
39. Middle Sackville
40. Hammond's Plains
41. Halifax
42. Africville
43. Sambro
44. Prospect
45. Chester
46. Mahone Bay
47. Bridgewater
48. Lunenburg
49. La Have
50. Greenfield
51. Liverpool
52. Sable River
53. Ohio
54. Shelburne
55. Birchtown I
56. Barrington
57. Port La Tour
58. Tusket
59. Salmon River
60. Yarmouth
61. Weymouth
62. Weymouth Falls
63. Bear River
64. Cornwallis
65. Digby
66. Clementsport
67. Annapolis Royal
68. Port Royal
69. Granville
70. Bridgetown
71. Paradise
72. Middleton
73. Wilmot
74. Waterville
75. Kentville
76. Wolfville
77. Horton
78. Hantsport
79. Five Mile Plains
80. Falmouth
81. Windsor
82. Newport
83. Whycocomagh

NEW BRUNSWICK

St. John River

Otnabog River

Nerepis River

Loch Lomond

St. Croix River

MAINE

Passamaquoddy Bay

Grand Manan Island

Bay of Fundy

St. Mary Bay

Sissiboo Lake

Rosewoy River

Bedeque Bay

Chignecto Bay

Cobequid Bay

Minas Basin

oMacNutt's Is.
Cape Negro

Cape Sable

THE ATLANTIC PROVINCES

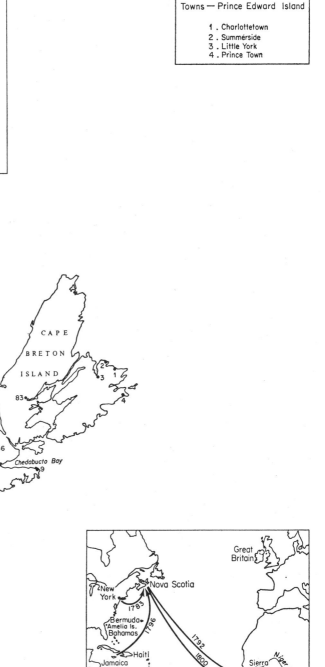

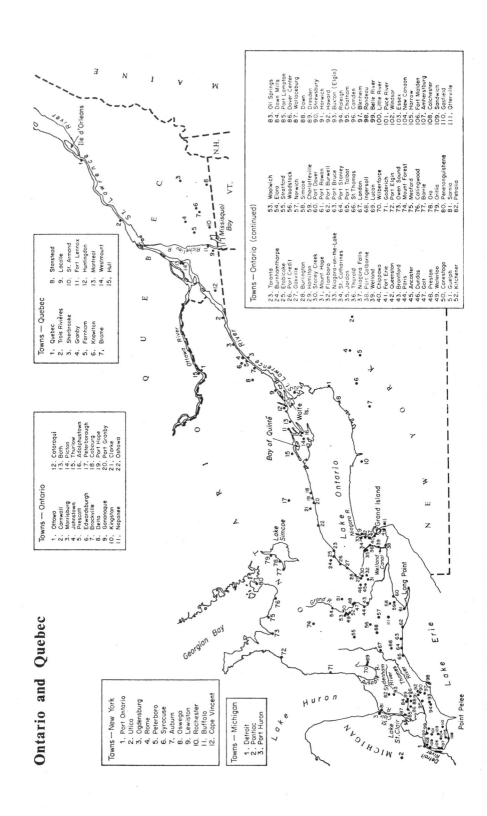

Ontario and Quebec

Towns — New York
1. Port Ontario
2. Utica
3. Ogdensburg
4. Rome
5. Peterboro
6. Syracuse
7. Auburn
8. Oswego
9. Lewiston
10. Rochester
11. Buffalo
12. Cape Vincent

Towns — Michigan
1. Detroit
2. Pontiac
3. Port Huron

Towns — Ontario
1. Ottawa
2. Cornwall
3. Morrisburg
4. Johnstown
5. Prescott
6. Edwardsburgh
7. Brockville
8. Delta
9. Gananoque
10. Kingston
11. Napanee
12. Cataraqui
13. Bath
14. Picton
15. Thurlow
16. Adolphustown
17. Peterborough
18. Cobourg
19. Port Hope
20. Port Granby
21. Clarke
22. Oshawa

Towns — Quebec
1. Quebec
2. Trois Rivières
3. Sherbrooke
4. Granby
5. Farnham
6. Knowlton
7. Brome
8. Stanstead
9. Lacolle
10. St. Armand
11. Fort Lennox
12. Huntingdon
13. Montreal
14. Westmount
15. Hull

Towns — Ontario (continued)
23. Toronto
24. Burnhamthorpe
25. Etobicoke
26. Port Credit
27. Oakville
28. Burlington
29. Hamilton
30. Stoney Creek
31. Mount Hope
32. Flamboro
33. Niagara-on-the-Lake
34. St. Catharines
35. Jordan
36. Thorold
37. Niagara Falls
38. Port Colborne
39. Welland
40. Chippawa
41. Fort Erie
42. Queenston
43. Brantford
44. Paris
45. Ancaster
46. Guelds
47. Galt
48. Preston
49. Oro
50. Conestogo
51. Guelph
52. Kitchener
53. Woolwich
54. Elora
55. Stratford
56. Woodstock
57. Norwich
58. Simcoe
59. Charlotteville
60. Port Dover
61. Port Rowan
62. Port Burwell
63. Port Stanley
64. Port Bruce
65. Port Talbot
66. Port
67. London
68. Ingersoll
69. Lucan
70. Wilberforce
71. Goderich
72. Port Elgin
73. Owen Sound
74. Mount Forest
75. Medford
76. Collingwood
77. Barrie
78. Oro
79. Orillia
80. Penetanguishene
81. Sarnia
82. Petrolia
83. Oil Springs
84. Dawn Mills
85. Port Lampton
86. Dover Center
87. Wallaceburg
88. Dawn
89. Dresden
90. Shrewsbury
91. Harwich
92. Howard
93. Buxton (Elgin)
94. Raleigh
95. Gordon
96. Camden
97. Blenheim
98. Rondeau
99. Belle River
100. Little River
101. Puce River
102. Windsor
103. Essex
104. New Canaan
105. Harrow
106. Fort Malden
107. Amherstburg
108. Colchester
109. Sandwich
110. Gosfield
111. Otterville

The Blacks in Canada

1. Slavery in New France, 1628-1760

"You say that by baptism I shall be like you: I am black and you are white, I must have my skin taken off then in order to be like you." Thus in 1632 did *"un petit nègre"* rebuke the Jesuit missionary Paul Le Jeune for claiming that all men were one when united in Christianity.[1] Father Le Jeune had spoken of an all-embracing truth that he presumed lay behind his ritual; but the Negro boy, the first slave to be sold in New France, already had recognized that, whatever he might be in the eyes of God, in the eyes of man he was different. He was black, and he was a slave.

Olivier Le Jeune,[2] as he was to die, was neither the first slave nor the first Negro in New France, but he was the first of whom there is any adequate record. The Portuguese explorer, Gaspar Corte-Real, had enslaved fifty Indian men and women in 1501 when he put ashore from an inlet in Labrador or Newfoundland;[3] and in 1607 Baron Jean de Biencourt de Poutrincourt, Lieutenant-Governor of Acadia, may have tried to enslave Indians to run his gristmill near Port Royal.[4] An anonymous Negro had died of scurvy at Port Royal the preceding winter, and the Governor, the Sieur Du Gua de Monts, is said to have had a Negro servant, Mathieu de Coste, working in Acadia in 1608.[5] But Olivier Le Jeune is not only the first Negro to whom we can give more than a name, he is the first to

1. Reuben Gold Thwaites, ed., *The Jesuit Relations and Allied Documents: Travels and Explorations of the Jesuit Missionaries in New France, 1610–1791* . . . (Cleveland, 1897), vol. 5, *Quebec: 1632–1633*, pp. 62–65. A copy of the original *Relation*, published in Paris in 1632, is in the John Carter Brown Library, Brown University, Providence. The quotation appears on pp. 58–60.

2. Ida Greaves, "The Negro in Canada," *McGill University Economic Studies*, no. 16 (Orillia, Ont., 1930), p. 9, says the slave's name was Louis, but this appears to be mistaken, as is the date of sale.

3. See H. P. Biggar, ed., *The Precursors of Jacques Cartier, 1497–1534: A Collection of Documents relating to the Early History of the Dominion of Canada* (Ottawa, 1911). Biggar says there were sixty Indian slaves (p. xiv); the source itself refers to fifty (p. 64).

4. Benjamin Sulte, *Histoire des canadiens-français, 1608–1880* (Montreal, 1882), *1*, 66, tells this story, but it is open to considerable doubt and is not confirmed by Adrien Huguet in his *Jean de Poutrincourt, fondateur de Port-Royal en Acadie, vice-roi du Canada, 1557–1615* . . . (Paris, 1932), vol. 44 of Société des Antiquaries de Picardie, *Mémoires*.

5. *Dictionary of Canadian Biography, 1* (Toronto, 1966), 452; hereafter cited as *DCB*.

have been transported directly from Africa, to have been sold as a slave in New France, and apparently to have died a free man.

The *petit nègre* had been brought to New France from Madagascar [6] by the English and given to one of the three Kirke brothers, most probably David. The Kirkes had taken Tadoussac in 1628 and, following a quick voyage to England, had returned to capture Quebec the following year, Champlain surrendering in the summer of 1629. The Kirkes then sold their slave, a child of perhaps six, for fifty *écus* to a French clerk who had agreed to collaborate with them.[7] In July 1632, when the Kirkes abandoned Quebec and, under the terms of the Treaty of Saint-Germain-en-Laye, restored Champlain to power, the clerk wisely chose to sail for England with them. He gave the Negro to Guillaume Couillard, a friend of Champlain who had remained in Quebec throughout the occupation and who already had shown his humanity by adopting two young Indian girls.[8]

Couillard needed help, for he had ten children, a hundred acres of land (twenty under cultivation), and plans to open a flour mill. He appears to have been a benevolent taskmaster. Father Le Jeune, a hard-working and equally benevolent convert from Calvinism who had just arrived to be the superior of the Jesuits in Quebec, began to teach the Negro and an Indian boy; and while the Negro did not learn to read—in later life he signed his name with a cross—he learned his catechism well. In 1633 he was baptized and, as Christianized natives were permitted to do, took the Christian name Olivier (from Olivier le Tardif, the head clerk), and later added Le Jeune in recognition of his teacher. Apparently Couillard set Olivier Le Jeune free, for at the latter's death in 1654 the burial register listed him as a *domestique;* even so, he probably was not free in 1638 when he was put in chains for a day for slandering one of the settlers.[9] When he died he was little more than thirty, and there appears to have been no Negro slave in New France thereafter until the last decades of the century, although *panis* (or Indian) slaves were reported in Montreal in 1670, and Indians on the northwest coast also kept slaves of their own.[10]

6. Father Le Jeune said Madagascar, while a document in the Archives du Séminaire de Québec dated August 20, 1638, suggests the Guinée (Ghana) coast: see Marcel Trudel, *L'esclavage au Canada français: Histoire et conditions de l'esclavage* (Quebec, 1960), p. 3.

7. Thwaites, *Jesuit Relations, 5,* 196–99; or the original *Relation* . . . (Paris, 1633), pp. 121–[22], in the John Carter Brown Library, Providence, R.I.

8. On Couillard, see *DCB, 1,* 236–37.

9. Trudel, *L'esclavage,* pp. 4–5, 19, 214, 230, 248; Pierre-Georges Roy, *Les petites choses de notre histoire* (Lévis, 1923), 5, 42–44.

10. *Mémoires de la Société Historique de Montréal 4* (1869), 200; Iuliíà Pavlovna Averkieva, *Slavery among the Indians of North America,* trans. G. R. Elliott, rev. ed. (Victoria, B.C., 1966), p. 11.

To the small extent that slavery existed in seventeenth-century New France, it was without legal foundation. This was true in the English colonies to the south too, for there the first mention of laws to regulate slavery does not occur until after 1660, and not until the 1720s did English law codes fully confirm that the slave, usually a Negro, was a chattel. For New France each of the steps toward the creation of a legal concept of slavery came roughly half a generation later, and throughout the process there were far more *panis* slaves than Negro, so that the system did not become so inexorably and so quickly intertwined with a single race. French slavery arose from a patchwork of jurisprudence, and eventually it declined in the same way, not under open attack but from the withering effects of unobserved laws, hostile jurists, and disadvantageous political, economic, and social conditions.

Slavery was given its legal foundation in New France between 1689 and 1709, and had the timing been different, the institution might well have taken a firmer hold than it did. Prior to 1663 New France had been a seigneury of the Compagnie des Cent-Associés, administered by the company with an eye to quick profits from the fur trade and fitfully aided by the Society of Jesus as a mission colony. Colonization had been subordinated, and economic rather than social ends had shaped the conventional wisdom of the time. The fur trade required no skilled labor; it required no gang labor either. A full-blown slave system had not been needed, and although the Indians enslaved many of their captives, on occasion selling a *pani* to work as a field hand or as a domestic servant for the French, there had been no economic base upon which slavery could profitably be built and little demand for either slave or *engagé* ("indentured") labor.

When New France was transferred from company to royal control in 1663, this conventional wisdom was broken temporarily and Louis XIV set about building a new colony. Upon the wilderness he imposed an effective form of administration, with a governor who was responsible for external affairs and the military and an intendant who was to maintain law and order, to provide a secure financial basis for the colony and to take charge of internal development. The following year the Coutume de Paris was introduced by a newly created Conseil Souverain, thus bringing local laws into conformity with those of the metropole. Jean-Baptiste Colbert, the Minister of the Marine, encouraged intermarriage between French and Indians so that a new people of one blood might emerge, with their loyalties and their future pinned to the revitalized colony. And for five years Jean Talon, "The Great Intendant," labored to diversify the economy of New France.

Under Talon and his immediate successors the colony was a projection into the New World of a growing, centralized society near the height of its power. Religious orthodoxy was mandatory after the revocation of the

Edict of Nantes in 1685. A local militia began training in Montreal. Talon brought in purebred livestock, tested seed grain, encouraged the development of industry, investigated the fisheries, tapped the filling reservoir of skilled workers, and endeavored to begin trade with the French West Indies. More seigniories were granted, and in order to increase population the state brought in *filles de roi,* gave dowries to the needy and grants to those who went forth and multiplied, and forced bachelors into marriage. Careful censuses were taken to measure the colony's growth in manpower, to gauge the proper use of the skilled immigrants, and to forecast possibilities for new industries and new channels of trade.

During this period of imaginative and expansive thinking, slavery appeared to be one means of increasing manpower. In 1677 Jean-Baptiste de Lagny, Sieur des Bringandières, obtained royal permission to exploit the mines of New France. He soon found that there was too much to do and too few to do it: the fisheries, the mines, and agriculture all offered potential wealth too great for only nine thousand colonists to tap. Consequently, sometime in 1688 apparently, he communicated his conviction to the governor, Jacques-Réné de Brisay, Marquis de Denonville, who in turn and together with the intendant, Jean Bochart de Champigny, that year appealed to France for Negro slaves. "Workers and servants are so rare and extraordinarily expensive," they wrote, ". . . as to ruin all those who attempt to be enterprising. We believe that the best means to remedy this is to have Negro slaves here. The Attorney General of the Council, who is in Paris, assures us that if His Majesty agrees to this proposition, some of the principal inhabitants will have some [slaves] bought for them in the Islands as vessels arrive from Guinée, and he will do so as well." [11]

Denonville was an aggressive governor who already had shown little regard for other races and who was determined to build the economy of New France, at least in some measure, along the lines laid down by Talon. Two years earlier he had sought diligently for two Negro slaves who had escaped from New York, and in 1687 he had seized forty Iroquois whom

11. On Lagny, see Benjamin Sulte, "L'esclavage en Canada," *La revue Canadienne,* n.s., 8 (1911), 318, who gives more prominence to Lagny's letter than do other authors. Extracts from the letters of Denonville and Champigny, dated August 10, October 31, and November 6, 1688, are printed in [Jacques Viger and Louis Hippolyte Lafontaine, eds.], "De l'esclavage en Canada," in La Société Historique de Montréal, *Mémoires et documents relatifs à l'histoire du Canada 1* (1859), 1–2. The translation is my own. Francis Parkman, while engaged in research for *The Old Regime in Canada* (1874) and *A Half-Century of Conflict* (1892), had extracts copied from these and other pertinent documents; the copies are in the Parkman Papers in the MHS. Viger kept his notes in books that he called *Ma Saberdache,* from which he quotes; when Viger died in 1858, Lafontaine carried the work forward. Lafontaine's copies of the documents are in the PAC, Lafontaine Papers, *14,* file 64, fols. 5552–65; the originals are in the Laval University library.

he had invited to a peace conference and had shipped them to France as slaves. Now he was in the midst of a war precipitated by his duplicity. By the end of the year he was to be defeated and, in 1689, recalled by Louis XIV. In 1685 the *Code Noir* had been promulgated for the West Indies, and Denonville reasoned that the *Code,* as well as the slaves, might be brought from the islands to help solve New France's chronic shortage of unskilled labor. In this wish he was helped by the Attorney General, Charles-François-Marie Ruette d'Auteuil, who early in 1689 sent a memorandum to the King in which he argued that slavery would be profitable for New France, since even the expense of clothing the slaves might be turned to advantage: the Negroes could, as the Algonquins did, wear dry beaver skins which, through use, would become *castor gras* of doubled value.[12]

Whether moved by a vision of more productive mines or of prime pelts from black backs, Louis XIV assented on May 1, 1689.[13] In doing so, he rather carelessly limited his remarks to the importation of Negro slaves to help with agriculture, and he cautioned that since these expensive purchases would be coming from a radically different climate, the entire project might well fail should the sudden contrast in environment prove too much for the Negroes. Almost immediately thereafter, the outbreak of King William's War, and Denonville's recall, virtually nullified the royal assent. The King gave a second authorization in 1701,[14] four years after the Treaty of Ryswick. Queen Anne's War, or the War of the Spanish Succession, broke out during the following year, however, once again making sea routes dangerous and transport scarce. Thereafter, the colony was left to its own devices for obtaining slaves, and when, in 1704, Paris declared that colonies existed solely to serve the mother country and should not compete for industry, commerce, or population, New France reverted to an economy based in part upon the declining fur trade, effectively ending any likely need for a large number of slaves.

Nonetheless, slavery continued to grow slowly, for domestic servants

12. Viger and Lafontaine, "L'esclavage," pp. 2–3; Trudel, pp. 20–21; Parkman Papers, *25*, 294, on d'Auteuil; A. Judd Northrup, "Slavery in New York: A Historical Sketch," *83d Annual Report 1900,* New York State Library, Appendix 6: *State Library Bulletin History No. 4* (Albany), pp. 258–59, 275.

13. Several brief summaries of slavery erroneously state that it was authorized in New France by the rescript of 1688, a mistake apparently perpetuated from Hubert Neilson, "Slavery in Old Canada Before and After the Conquest," *Transactions of the Literary and Historical Society of Quebec,* ser. 2, no. 26 (1906), p. 21. It was Louis's reply of 1689 that legalized slavery.

14. Archives de la Province de Québec, Quebec, Ordres du Roi, ser. B, *22:* King to Louis Hector de Callière, governor of New France, and to Champigny, May 31, 1701. On October 5, the governor and intendant reported that they permitted colonists to hold Negro slaves (Parkman Papers, *6,* 238).

and field hands were wanted by the wealthier families, and local authorities tried to give to it a more secure legal base when they could. The word *esclave* itself had not been used in the civil registers of New France before 1694,[15] but thereafter it became increasingly common. Clearly, confusion as to the formal status of the slave and how to give him his freedom lay back of the final step by which slavery acquired its tenuous footing in New France. On April 13, 1709, the intendant, Jacques Raudot, disturbed by the presence of a number of Indians who, despite the widespread assumption that they were slaves by law, were claiming to be free men, read a lengthy *ordonnance* [16] in which he declared that "all the *panis and Negroes who have been purchased and who will be purchased, shall be the property of those who have purchased them* and will be their *slaves."* Anyone who induced a slave to run away from his master was to be fined fifty livres.[17]

But if Raudot were to provide an official statement in support of slavery, official action also was necessary to ensure that those *panis* and Negroes whom their masters genuinely wished to set free might enjoy that freedom. Between 1706 and 1736 the number of slaves who had been given their freedom—or claimed they had—increased rapidly, leading to confusion (especially among the unchristianized who shared the same or similar names) about who was slave and who was free. Accordingly, in the latter year the intendant, Gilles Hocquart, issued a new *ordonnance* that provided for a uniform means of manumission. Verbal agreements were no longer sufficient: to free a slave by gift or by purchase, the owner or purchaser was to obtain a notary's certificate, and all such transactions were to be registered immediately with a royal registry office. Previous manumissions were valid, but none could depart from this procedure after the first of September. Clearly, slavery had grown sufficiently to require records as well as regulation; equally clearly, there was a body of opinion that wished to extend freedom to the slaves, since we may presume that Hocquart's *ordonnance* was in response to a petition, although the initiative may have come not from owners but from freed Negroes and *panis.*[18]

The status of slaves in New France also was regulated by the *Code Noir,* which though never proclaimed in the colony [19] appears to have

15. Trudel, p. 315.

16. Presumably Raudot acted upon a petition or remonstrance from slave-owners, for an *ordonnance* normally arose from a petition addressed to the King or to his representative.

17. Printed in Viger and Lafontaine, pp. 4–5.

18. *Arrêts et Règlements du Conseil Supérieur de Québec, et Ordonnances et Jugements des Intendants du Canada* (Quebec, 1955), p. 371.

19. There is some disagreement on this point. William Renwick Riddell, in "Le Code Noir," *JNH, 10* (1925), 321, n. 1, feels there is "no sufficient ground" for doubting that the code was applied to New France, but the only evidence he gives

been used as customary law. There were, in fact, two codes: the first, of 1685, was limited specifically to the West Indies; a revised code of 1724 applied to the new colony of Louisiana as well. The second code did not depart from the first in any significant way except to forbid intermarriage. The original *Code* was drafted to protect the white man from forms of slave violence: theft, revolt, and escape. Since slaves were not numerous in New France, little attention was given to specific regulations covering such eventualities until a specific case arose, which then was dealt with on its merits and within the spirit of the code. Because gang labor was virtually impossible, and since most Negro slaves in particular were domestic servants, less attention needed to be given to safeguards—either for owner or for slave—with respect to clothing, housing, and working conditions. The memory of Colbert and Talon appears to have lingered, for no steps were taken to prevent intermarriage in New France, and if a white man took a Negro slave wife, she was freed by the act of marriage. Further, by the Coutume de Paris, Negro slaves were chattels (*meubles*), and as personal property they were not attached to the land as serfs but solely to their owners.

Hocquart issued his ordinance partially because, as he said, slaves were deserting their masters almost daily under the mistaken belief that there could be no slavery in France or in her dominions. There had been slaves in France, in fact, from early in the seventeenth century. Slavery, it was true, never had been expressly recognized in France: in 1571, when a cargo of Negroes was landed at Bordeaux for sale, the *parlement* ordered their release because slavery did not exist there; and in 1691 the Minister of the Marine declared that Negroes who were brought into the country would be free upon arrival. But his order did not touch upon the legality of slavery in the colonies. In any case, regulations of this sort were seldom enforced, and slaves did serve government officials, ship captains, soldiers, and planters throughout the century. That de facto slavery existed is proven by the suits for freedom undertaken in the eighteenth century.[20]

---

is dubious. While Neilson ("Slavery in Old Canada," p. 26) asserts that, since the code of 1685 was incorporated in the Coutume de Paris, which received royal sanction as being applicable to all colonies in the New World, it did apply, he appears to confuse the code itself with the Coutume's regulation concerning *meubles*. Trudel (pp. 27, 163, 213, 316) points out that he could find no evidence that the code was promulgated formally.

20. On slavery and attitudes toward slavery in France, see Gaston Martin, *Histoire de l'esclavage dans les colonies françaises* (Paris, 1948); Paul Trayer, *Etude historique sur la condition légale des esclaves dans les colonies françaises* (Paris, 1887); Charles de la Roncière, *Nègres et négriers,* 9th ed. (Paris, 1933); and Shelby T. McCloy, *The Negro in France* (Lexington, Ky., 1961), especially pp. 5–6, 12–14, 22–51. Hilda M. Neatby, *The Administration of Justice under the Quebec Act* (Minneapolis, 1937), pp. 9–11, discusses the validity of the Coutume de Paris in New France.

King and colony were by no means in agreement about slavery, adding to the confusion created by having one set of regulations in France, another—the *Code Noir*—in the Antilles, and a third for New France. A concert of opinion between governor and intendant in 1688 and 1701 had elicited formal approvals of slavery from the King, but by 1716 such a bond of opinion was broken. In October the intendant, Michel Bégon, repeated Champigny's plea: as there were only twenty thousand inhabitants in New France, he wrote, labor was expensive and scarce. If the colony were encouraged to enter into the slave trade, local industry, agriculture, and commerce would improve much as they had in the English colonies to the south. Boston supported a thriving economy partially on slaves, and in New York the land was cultivated by Negroes so that white energies could be directed to trade. In New France, the intendant suggested, Negroes could till the soil, fish for cod, saw timber, build ships, and exploit the iron mines "out of which the King and the colony could derive the greatest advantages" if there were but workers to develop them.

Apparently Bégon anticipated the major objection at its source, for the governor, Philippe de Rigaud, Marquis de Vaudreuil, later wrote in the margin of Bégon's *mémoire* that the climate was too cold and the expense of clothing slaves too great. In prior refutation Bégon pointed out that the climate of Boston and New York was not markedly different and that those Negroes already in New France were in good health. Further, the expense need not be lasting, for the free trade in beaver skins, fresh letters of exchange, and the normal royal funds spent on the colony would provide sufficient revenue. Since in 1716 the slave-trading monopolies enjoyed by the Compagnie de Guinée and the Compagnie du Sénégal were broken by opening the trade to the Guinea Coast to all, Bégon may also have hoped to create in New France a small center for building slave ships. In this he would have been frustrated, however, for the King required that vessels engaged in the Guinea trade should be fitted out exclusively at Bordeaux, Nantes, Rochelle, or Rouen.[21]

Although persistent, without Vaudreuil's support Bégon could accomplish very little. In 1720, one month after the Compagnie des Indes was given a new monopoly over the Guinea trade, Bégon asked the King to send Negroes to work in the hemp market, and he forwarded a memorial in which the inhabitants of New France undertook to buy one hundred and one Negroes from the company at six hundred livres each. In June 1721, the Navy Board informed Bégon that it would have the company carry a cargo of Africans to Quebec, but no action appears to have been

21. *Collection de manuscrits contenant lettres, mémoires et autres documents historiques relatifs à la Nouvelle-France . . .* (Quebec, 1884), *3*, 21.

taken after the Board learned that the Negroes of Sénégal, who might be sent, were worth one thousand livres each in the West Indies.[22]

Other evidence that the intendants, and on occasion the governors, wished to push slavery while the King was reluctant to do so may be found in the circumstances of Hocquart's *ordonnance* in 1736. The intendant apparently had wished to be more sweeping than his statement reveals, for the King told both him and the governor, Charles, Marquis de Beauharnois, that he did not approve of their proposal to decide on the status of *panis* and other slaves by an explicit law, and it was he who ordered that the colony's judges should be content to follow the custom that considered *panis* to be slaves until those masters who wished to do so granted them freedom by notarial deed.[23] Any move to advance the assumption that all Negroes were slaves—as was occurring for Negroes in the English colonies at this time—and thus to formalize their condition along purely racial lines, was thereby blocked.

What, then, were the conditions of the Negro slave in New France? How many slaves were there, and where? An exhaustive inquiry by Professor Marcel Trudel of l'Université d'Ottawa provides us with a remarkably full picture.[24] No exact census of the slave population is possible, of course, but Professor Trudel reached a number of useful conclusions: local records reveal 3,604 separate slaves by 1759; of these, 1,132 were Negroes. In all, there probably were some four thousand slaves in New France; French settlers preferred *panis* but English settlers chose, and after 1759 brought in, substantial numbers of Negroes. *Panis* became a synonym for slave and was occasionally applied to Negroes as well; for the majority of Indian slaves were, in fact, either Pawnees or from closely related tribes. Most of the slaves lived in or near Montreal, where 52.3 percent of the known total were found; 77.2 percent of all slaves lived in

22. See Ordres du Roi, *44*, fols. 3, 528 1/2; *47*, fol. 1242. These are summarized by Edouard Richard in *Report concerning Canadian Archives for the Year 1904* (Ottawa, 1905), App. K, 21, 28, 54. See also Joseph-Noël Fauteux, *Essai sur l'industrie au Canada sous le régime française,* (Quebec, 1927), *1*, 476–77.

23. Ordres du Roi, *63*, fol. 642 1/2, as printed by Richard in *Canadian Archives Report 1904*, p. 211.

24. I wish to thank Professor Trudel, and l'Archives de la Province de Québec, for giving me access to both volumes of his *L'esclavage au Canada français* while it was still in typescript. The first volume was published in 1960; it is based on thorough research in all pertinent local archives, and the following paragraphs are based closely on Professor Trudel's findings. The second volume, "Dictionnaire des esclaves et de leurs proprietaires," has not been published, but its conclusions were incorporated into the first. The major study that I cite, *L'esclavage au Canada français: Histoire et conditions de l'esclavage* (Quebec, 1960), is not to be confused with the condensed edition of the book, *L'esclavage au Canada français* (Montreal, 1963).

towns. Thus few slaves worked in the fields or mines, even though the intendants emphasized agriculture in their requests for Negroes: 22.8 percent of the slaves were field laborers, but only 192 of these were Negroes, since the black man most often was a servant.[25] Perhaps for this reason Negro slaves lived longer—but not long. The average age at death for the *panis* was 17.7 years, for the Negro 25.2 years. Several Negroes lived to be over eighty, while no Indian male reached seventy. Negroes, moreover, were less susceptible to the white man's ills, and especially to smallpox. In 1733, fifty-eight Indians were carried away by the disease but only two Negroes; in 1755, smallpox took fifty-six Indians but only six Negroes; and in the epidemic of 1757 fifty-one Indians and only four Negroes died. But though relatively fewer Negroes died of the pox, many must have borne its marks, for it was a special note of aesthetic quality to advertise that a domestic *"has never had the small-pox."*

Even under English rule considerably more Frenchmen than Englishmen owned slaves as domestics and wharf laborers: 96.7 percent of the owners were French. Trudel traced 1,509 owners, representing 962 different families, of which only 181 were English. More than a quarter of the slaves (1,068) belonged to members of the merchant class, especially among the French; the gentry, the governors, notaries, doctors, and the military also owned slaves, and so too did members of the clergy. On the whole, few possessed more than two or three slaves; only twenty-nine owners held as many as ten slaves each. Interestingly, the Campeau family, who were small-scale traders only, held fifty-seven slaves, more than the far wealthier Lacorne and Lemoyne de Longueuil families.

Generally, these slaves of New France, and especially the Negro slaves, seem not to have been treated badly. They were, after all, expensive and intimately connected to the household as domestics.[26] The protection that was extended to slaves in the Antilles by the *Code Noir* was applied in New France even if the code was not law. Further, the slave, and in par-

25. Trudel, pp. 86, 95, 126–92, 232–56, 264, 284, 317–27. On the mines, see La Societé historique de Montreal, *Mémoires et documents, 2* (1859), Addenda. The first scholarly attempt at constructing a list of slaves was Cyprien Tanguay's in 1887 in his *Dictionnaire Généalogique des Familles Canadiennes* . . . (Montreal), *3,* 603–07, which lists 152 slaves by name. In the typescript version of his study, Trudel himself gives figures other than those contained in his book, for he refers to 3,689 slaves—1,183 of them Negro—and 1,434 proprietors.

26. There are three known pictorial evidences of Negro slavery in New France, and all show domestic servants. Edwin Holgate's oil panel, "Jeune indienne de la Jamïque," actually a Creole girl, hangs in the Quebec Provincial Museum in Quebec city. In the McCord Museum of Canadian History in Montreal there is a watercolor by G[eorge] Heriot, ca. 1806, of a minstrel and two Negro servants. The McCord also has an oil by François-Maleport de Beaucourt, the first native-born Canadian artist of repute, "L'esclave noire," painted in 1786.

ticular Negro slaves, enjoyed certain privileges normally reserved to free men. They could serve as witnesses at religious ceremonies, and apparently they could petition against free persons, as one did in 1727. Slaves who claimed their liberty before the courts had recourse to all the customary processes and, after the English arrived, slaves secured the rights of habeas corpus and trial by jury. Punishment was no more severe for a slave than for a free man. Murder, crimes with violence, and arson could lead to hanging for both, but not invariably so: when a Negress belonging to Mme. François Poulin de Francheville set fire to her mistress's house in April 1734, thereby destroying a portion of Montreal, she was tried and hanged; but in 1781 when a Negro slave assaulted his master, he was imprisoned, not executed.[27]

Mulattoes acquired no legal status of their own, contrary to the growing practice in the Antilles, and they were seldom referred to as such.[28] Although *panis* and Negro slaves lived in the same households, there is little evidence of cohabitation between them. On occasion the French did marry their slaves: Trudel found records attesting to thirty-four marriages with *panis* (usually female, who were preferred for indoor work, and who were said to be especially docile, proximity and temperament thus encouraging interracial sexual relations) and to eleven marriages with Negroes (usually white women with black men). At least 103 children were born from these unions: 84 half-breeds and 19 mulattoes. These children married and in turn had their descendants, and through the generations must have "passed" over to white. Apparently concerned with the thought that Indian and Negro blood was mixed with French Canadian, the historian Benjamin Sulte remarked in 1911 that by such marriages not more than a single drop of the Missouri River had been added to the greatness of the St. Lawrence. But he seems to have neglected those liaisons undertaken without the sanction of the church. Of 573 children of slaves for whom there is adequate record, 59.5 percent were born outside any form of marriage, and while in many cases the parents may have been of the same race, the entry in the registers—*pere inconnu*—no doubt covers many white men too. The French settlers especially were attracted to Indian women, and 75.9 percent of all *panis* children were *batards,* while only 32.1 percent of Negro children were born out of wedlock.[29] That the

27. William Renwick Riddell, "The Slave in Canada," *JNH, 5* (1920), 267; J. Douglas Borthwick, *History and Biographical Gazetteer of Montreal to the Year 1892* (Montreal, 1892), p. 27.

28. On interracial sex and the status of mulattoes, see Winthrop D. Jordan, "American Chiaroscuro: The Status and Definition of Mulattoes in the British Colonies," *The William and Mary Quarterly,* ser. 3, *19* (1962), 182–200.

29. Sulte, "L'esclavage en Canada," p. 324; Trudel, pp. 290–327.

figure is low may, in part, be attributed to the moral influence of the church.

As in other Roman Catholic colonies, the church tended to soften the effects of slavery even as it condoned it. Neither the church nor the state in French territories faced the reality of slavery so readily as in some Spanish and Portuguese lands, but neither did slavery emerge in so hardened and harsh a form as in the English colonies. In Latin areas the Roman-based law codes and a long acquaintance with racial differences served to modify the slave–master relationship and to give it something of the nature of a contract. Slave status was not thought to be inherent in man but was a temporary condition arising from the accident of events. Although Hocquart's *ordonnance* of 1736 implied that proof of his freedom lay with the Negro, the ruling was directed to an immediate administrative problem. In the English colonies, on the other hand, neither the church nor the law codes tempered the conditions of servitude. The colonies placed legal obstacles in the way of manumission in contrast to Hocquart's simple procedure, and the presumption of the law was in favor of slavery as the Negro's natural condition. In most Latin colonies the influence of the Roman Catholic church—which held that the spiritual nature of the slave transcended his temporary status, that he retained a moral personality even in servitude, and that to give a man his freedom was to please God—was added to the moderating effects of long experience and more humane laws and regulations.[30]

Nonetheless, in New France the church appears not to have been active in opposing slavery as such, perhaps because there was less to oppose than in the West Indies and South America. The Jesuits, Dominicans, and Franciscans treated their slaves well and often encouraged manumission, but in New France the Jesuit missionaries were displaced by other bodies—by the Sulpicians in 1657 at Montreal and by the Recollets in 1670 at Trois-Rivières—while Quebec passed into the hands of the secular clergy. While Quebec's able first bishop, the Jesuit François de Montmorency-Laval, owned no slaves, he was replaced in 1688 by Jean-de-la-Croix St. Vallier, who did, as did Bishops Pierre-Herman Dosquet and Henri Marie Pontbriand. Secular priests, religious communities (including the Jesuits), the Ursulines in Louisiana (which was within the diocese of Quebec), the Brothers of Charity at Louisbourg, and the benevolent Mother Marie d'Youville, who ran the Hôpital-Général, all owned slaves. In 1720 religious communities were among those who promised to purchase a hun-

30. See Frank Tannenbaum, *Slave and Citizen: The Negro in the Americas* (New York: Vintage ed., 1963), p. 65, n. 153; Tannenbaum, "The Destiny of the Negro in the Western Hemisphere," *Political Science Quarterly, 61* (1946), 1–41; and in partial contradiction, Charles R. Boxer, "The Colour Question in the Portuguese Empire, 1415–1825," *Proceedings of the British Academy, 1961* (London, 1962), pp. 113-38.

dred Negroes through the intendant, then Bégon. In all the clergy held
at least forty-three slaves.[31]

Only Bishop St. Vallier addressed himself specifically to slavery. In his
Catéchisme of 1702, in which he listed the conditions for admission to
the clergy, he excluded slaves and thus, seven years before Raudot's *ordonnance,* indirectly supported slavery. Further, if one married a *pani* or
Negro in ignorance of his enslaved condition, this ignorance was sufficient
to cancel the marriage. The following year, in France, St. Vallier's *Rituel*
reaffirmed the *Catéchisme* but, with reference to marriage, added that the
interdiction did not apply in "this Kingdom, where all people are free."
Apparently not realizing that the *Rituel* was published in France and that
this phrase applied only to the mother country, some students of the
church quite erroneously have thought that St. Vallier held slavery to be
illegal in the colony.[32] In short, in New France the clergy did not actively
promote slavery, as the Protestant sects of the English colonies were to
do, but neither did the church actively oppose the institution, and there
is no record of any clergyman having spoken out against it.

However, the clergy were scarcely in a position to lead an attack on
slavery. The power of the church declined after the retirement of Bishop
Laval and it was increasingly submissive to the state in temporal matters.
After 1760, with slavery specifically protected by the terms of the treaty
of capitulation between Britain and France, and with Canada under the
same control as the more prosperous, slaveholding colonies to the south,
priests had less opportunity to turn to the attack even had they wished to
do so. Further, they were as susceptible as other men to the racial thought
of the times—thought that even in nonslaveholding France led in 1763 to
a prohibition upon all Negroes, slave or free, who would sail from the colonies to France, in order to prevent any mixing of blood and the debasing
of French culture. Slavery was a social reality, and as such the church accepted it.[33]

Certainly the fact that the church admitted the slave to equality in some
of the sacraments,—baptism, communion, and burial—must have encouraged owners to think of their property in more humane terms than in those

31. See Marcel Trudel, "L'attitude de l'Eglise catholique vis-à-vis l'esclavage au
Canada français," CHA, *Report, 1961, of the Annual Meeting* . . . , pp. 28–34. Also
see Trudel, *L'esclavage,* pp. 38–39, 193–212, 322–23.

32. *Catéchisme du diocèse de Québec* (Paris, 1702), p. 298, and *Rituel du diocèse
de Québec publié par l'ordre de Monseigneur de Saint-Vallier* . . . (Paris, 1703),
p. 326. Trudel, *L'esclavage,* pp. 38–39, comments on the confusion caused by Saint-
Vallier's words.

33. See "The Attitude of the Roman Catholic Church toward the Negro during
Slavery," in W. D. Weatherford, *American Churches and the Negro* (Boston, 1957),
pp. 222–45, and John K. A. Farrell, "Some Opinions of Christian Europeans regard-
ing Negro Slavery in the Seventeenth and Early Eighteenth Centuries," *The Canadian
Catholic Historical Association, Report* (1958), pp. 13–22.

few colonies where slaves no more than horses could fully qualify for the Christian life. No law required that slaves be baptized, but the influence of Christian thought was pervasive and, while owners often waited many years, ultimately four-fifths of all slaves were baptized—largely as Roman Catholics, although 223 were Protestants. (They did not always remain so, as the records of abjurations in Quebec show.) Roman Catholic baptisms were frequently social occasions for the blacks, and in French society the owner often claimed for himself the honor of serving as godfather to his slave, a custom seldom found among the Protestant English. Forty eight slaves (including sixteen Negroes) also received the sacrament of confirmation, and at least twenty slaves were given the sacrament of the Eucharist.[34] When the Christian slave died, he was buried as a Christian. French owners (in contrast to English) often witnessed the act of burial. Marriage was permitted with the master's permission. On occasion the act of consent was accompanied by a clause requiring of each owner that he free his slave.[35] Children born of slave marriages belonged to the mother's master. Neither slave nor free Negroes could take Holy Orders or become a priest.

Custom as well as the church further humanized the master–slave relationship. In many French households slaves took their master's family name after baptism. At least one hundred and ten Negroes acquired Christian names in this way. Given names also were taken from the family—Marie, Joseph, Jean-Baptiste, and Pierre were especially common—while in other slave societies classical names such as Caesar, Pompey, and Jupiter were more common. When seriously ill, slaves were taken to the hospital: the registers of l'Hôtel-Dieu de Montreal show that from 1690 to 1800 at least 525 slaves were hospitalized.

Despite these "humane and familial traits"[36] found in slavery as practiced in New France, the slaves themselves cannot have thought the system so agreeable, for there were numerous attempts to escape, especially

34. Register of Christ Church, William Henry (Sorel), the original of which is in the office of the Protonotaire for Richelieu County, Sorel, P.Q., a copy being in PAC; the book of marriages, baptisms, and burials for Christ Church, Montreal, 1766–95, in the Archives du Palais de Justice de Montréal; PAC, Miscellaneous Documents [hereafter, Misc. Docs.], *16,* no. 124; PAC photostats, "Adjurations of Heresy, Ville de Quebec, 1662–1759," Nov. 8, 1750, p. 16. At least one Jew owned a slave. See Arthur D. Hart, ed., *The Jew in Canada: A Complete Record of Canadian Jewry from the Days of the French Regime to the Present Time* (Toronto, 1926), p. 18.

35. Note, for example, the marriage of Jacques César and Marie, a marriage which was delayed for two years until Marie's owner, Mme. Baron de Longueuil (Marie Catherine Deschambeault), gave her consent to the condition made by the owner of the former, Ignace Gamelin, that the Negroes be freed (Neilson, pp. 29–31).

36. Trudel, *L'esclavage,* pp. 325–26; Hector Berthelot and E.-Z. Massicotte, *Montréal, le bon vieux temps* (Montreal, 1916), p. 35.

by Negroes. Fugitives, and the growing willingness of some of the c
nists to connive with them, led intendant Hocquart to issue an *ordonn*
in 1734 directing all captains and officers of militia to help an owner find
a missing Carib slave and imposing penalties on any who aided his escape.
Thereafter advertisements for runaways normally were accompanied by
warnings to ship captains against carrying them out of the province and
to the public against employing them.[37]

In the period from the summer of 1769 to the summer of 1794, for
example, advertisements for missing slaves were scattered through the
Quebec Gazette. One may presume that there were also many unsuccessful attempts at escape or short-termed flights that did not receive public
notice. In 1769, Joseph, a Negro who spoke French and English, ran away
from Montreal. Slaves escaped in 1771 and 1778, four times in 1779, in
1781, three times in 1783, in 1785, three times in 1788, in 1789, 1790, and
1794. In all but one instance they were Negroes who spoke English,
French, or Dutch, rather than *panis*. One Ishmael ran away from his
owner, John Turner, twice on occasions nine years apart. Indeed, advertisements for runaway slaves were more frequent during this time than
were those for the sale of slaves.[38]

Nonetheless, slaves were sold, of course, often side by side with livestock, since no public market was set apart expressly for their sale. Few
were disposed of by lot—the largest sale was of five slaves in 1743—and
families seldom can have been divided. Most slaves were purchased before
they were twenty years old and remained with one family, to be willed to
the next generation if they survived. In one thirty-year period, only 137
slaves were announced for sale in the newspapers. Under the French, the
average *pani* cost four hundred livres while the Negro brought nine hundred livres; again, the latter's greater expense helped to protect him against
abuse.[39]

37. Lafontaine Papers, fol. 5559; Sulte, "L'esclavage en Canada," p. 325.

38. *Gazette*, July 20, 1769, May 3, 1770, Aug. 15, 1771, Sept. 8, 1774, Feb. 12,
Aug. 20, 1778, July 29, Sept. 23, Nov. 4, 1779, Oct. 4, 18, Dec. 20, 1781, June 12,
July 17, Aug. 14, Nov. 6, 1783, March 4, 25, May 13, Sept. 2, 1784, June 9, 1785,
May 8, June 26, 1788, April 1, Sept. 3, Oct. 1, 1789, April 22, Oct. 28, 1790, Oct. 17,
1793, and May 22, 1794. The whole of this sample falls within the period of the
British administration, after the number of slaves had increased and when public
opinion was turning against slavery, but we have no adequate record of escapes for
the earlier period. Bills of sale for Montreal Negroes are found in the record books
of E. W. Gray, notary, for 1765–76, 1775–85, and 1783–1801, and in the *repertoire
et index* of J.-G. Beeck, notary, 1781–1821 (2 vols.) in the Archives du Palais de
Justice de Montréal. I should like to thank M. Jean-Jacques Lefebvre, the archivist,
for bringing these records to my attention.

39. Seventeen notarial acts preserved in l'Archives de la Province de Québec,
all relating to sales, are printed in *Rapport de l'archiviste de la province de Quebec
pour 1921–1922* (Quebec, 1922), pp. 110–23. These are paraphrased, with some

While slaves were bought and sold internally, there was no international or intercolonial market of substance. Raudot pointed out that his *ordonnance* applied only to New France and did not grant any authorization for an export trade. On occasion, *panis* were sent to the West Indies as punishment, but no trade developed with the other French colonies, and for most of the duration of legalized slavery in New France, trade with the nearer British colonists was prevented by war. Slaves from New York escaped to New France in sufficient numbers prior to Raudot's clarification of 1709 to provoke from the assembly in Albany, in the midst of Queen Anne's War in August 1705, an "Act to prevent the running away of Negro slaves out of the Citty and County of Albany to the French at Canada." The English naturally resented the loss of their property to an enemy, and they feared that the runaway slaves carried military information to Quebec. The act held that any slave found more than forty miles above Albany in the direction of the French frontier would die for a felony. The assembly passed a similar act in May 1745, during King George's War, to be in force during the conflict with France and no longer. When the two nations technically were at peace, the French sought to prevent English goods from being smuggled into New France by prosecuting a number of young men for having relations with Albany through an intermediary in Montreal; such controls applied, of course, to slaves.[40]

Although the settlers preferred Negro to *panis* slaves, the number of Negroes did not grow proportionately. Slaves could neither be bought from nor sold to the West Indies in large numbers because of war and the scarcity of transport, and slaves seldom could be purchased from the British because of war and the suspicion of war. An *édit* of 1727, registered in Quebec the following year, forbade selling to the British in any case. Most Indian traders dealt only in *panis* slaves. One additional source of Negro supply lay open: the spoils of war. On July 23, 1745, the King decreed that slaves from enemy colonies who fled into French territory could be sold and that the proceeds were to belong to his Majesty, as though they were derived from enemy ships or from goods wrecked upon his shores.[41] But such a source was neither dependable nor, when the slaves were carried away during raids into English territory, legal. Since many of the abuses of slavery were associated with the auction block,

---

errors of fact, by William Renwick Riddell in "Notes on the Slave in Nouvelle-France," *JNH*, 8 (1923), 318–25, to which he adds material taken from court proceedings, PAC, pp. 325–30.

40. Northrup, "Slavery in New York," pp. 262–64; William Kingsford, *The History of Canada* (Toronto, 1888), 2, 507; Lulu M. Johnson, "The Negro in Canada, Slave and Free" (M.A. thesis, Univ. of Iowa, 1930), p. 4.

41. Viger and Lafontaine, pp. 6–8. The decree was registered in Quebec in 1748.

slaves in New France thus further benefited from these limitations on the trade.

If slavery in New France was among the most benevolent expressions of the institution in North America, nonetheless it was slavery, with accompanying potentialities toward the dominance of one man, and of one race, over another. That these potentialities were limited in comparison to the English colonies by the lack of trade, the *Code Noir,* customs that grew independently in New France, and to some extent by the church, is clear. The chief limitations on slavery, however, arose less from specific conditions than from the overall nature of French society in the New World and from the unique circumstances of the French experience in Quebec.

Slavery in New France, and later in the British North American provinces, was on the margin of a dynamic world of European expansion. But since New France, in particular, remained upon the margin of that world and was of importance to the metropole after 1704 largely for reasons of diplomacy, there were few opportunities for slavery to prosper. Certainly some of the preconditions necessary to such growth were present: the local inhabitants appeared to favor slavery; governors, intendants, and bishops gave it the stamp of tacit and sometimes of official approval; and labor was chronically scarce during much of the period. Why, then, did the institution fail to grow?

Those who contend that slavery had no chance of survival in New France argue from four considerations, three of which are barely relevant to Canada. Some have remarked that the paucity of evidence about slavery and the clear lack of fully worked-out theories in relation to the institution in the seventeenth and early eighteenth centuries indicates a corresponding lack of interest. Indeed it does, precisely because slavery was increasingly taken for granted: it was accepted as a matter of course, as not opinion-worthy. Subservience was a characteristic of society, and slavery was merely the ne plus ultra of the natural order of things. At the time slavery was introduced into New France, there was no assumption that the condition attached to a single race, and as many of the slaves in Canada were Indians, the first century of slavery gave little opportunity for such a belief to take root. Theoretical justifications for slavery or speculative explanations of racial differences were not necessary. Not until 1765 did a Frenchman attempt to account at length and formally for different races,[42] and by then New France was no more. That there were

42. See the work of the Rouen surgeon, Nicolas le Cat, *Traité de la couleur de le peau humaine,* published in Amsterdam in 1765. However, Hannah Arendt finds the roots of racism in the Comte de Boulainvilliers, a French nobleman who in 1727

different races was accepted without need for elaborate explanations; that some men were slaves and some were not was also accepted; and there was as yet no necessary connection between the two conclusions.

Other writers have maintained, although their case is given little hearing today, that there were natural limits to the expansion of slavery and that colder climates were inhospitable to it. In 1929, Charles W. Ramsdell gave scholarly authority to the arguments offered long before by Stephen A. Douglas and Daniel Webster, who maintained that slavery expanded almost solely on cotton and sugar, which had natural limits, and therefore that slavery could continue to show profits only where there was an abundance of rich land.[43] Clearly cotton and sugarcane could not be grown in the far north, and the land was neither abundant, as laid out, nor rich. But slavery was conditioned not only by soils, topography, climate, and certain assumptions about profits; customs, prejudices, systems of land tenure, and religious beliefs also shaped it. Natural conditions—if by these we mean conditions arising primarily from climate, which was the crux of Ramsdell's argument—did not limit slavery in New France. The limiting conditions were man-made, fortuitous, accidental, and open to change —namely, European diplomacy, patterns of trade, dependence upon the beaver, economically unprofitable seigniories which could not use gang labor effectively, and the persistent authority of the Roman Catholic church.

As we know from innumerable instances, however, people are motivated less by objective realities than by what they believe to be true. Negroes have no marked difficulty in adjusting to cold climates, and they thrive in Canada and the northern United States today, but in 1689 Louis XIV feared that the proposal of Denonville and Champigny would prove useless in the cold. Into the twentieth century Canadians were to argue that slavery, fugitive slaves, and eventually Negroes themselves could have no place in Canadian life because black men were unable to tolerate the cold.

Most relevant to Canada is the question of whether slavery paid or could be made to pay. A strong case can be made to show that it did, or could, in nineteenth-century America.[44] But at the time most observers

was writing of "the right of conquest" and the "obedience always due to the strongest." Consult her "Race-Thinking before Racism," *The Review of Politics, 6* (1944), 36–73.

43. Ramsdell, "The Natural Limits of Slavery Expansion," *MVHR, 16* (1929), 151–71. Frederick V. Emerson had anticipated much of this thesis in "Geographical Influences in American Slavery," *Bulletin of the American Geographical Society, 43* (1911), 13–26, 106–18, 170–81.

44. See Alfred H. Conrad and John R. Meyer, *The Economics of Slavery and Other Studies in Econometric History* (Chicago, 1964); and Harold D. Woodman,

assumed that slavery did not pay, and certainly such was the assumption in the Canadas by the end of the eighteenth century.

François-Xavier Garneau, widely regarded as the founder of "scientific history" in French Canada, gave rise to what became a fifth, unwarranted, and far more sweeping assumption about the failure of slavery to take root in New France: that it never existed. In his *Histoire du Canada,* in 1846, he wrote that the secular authorities and clergy had been opposed to introducing Negro slaves into the colony and that great honor was due the French monarch since, by his skeptical reply to the request from Denonville and Champigny, the King saved Canada from "the grand and terrible plague" of slavery. Soon writers were maintaining that there had been no slavery in New France at all, despite the historical evidence (including that suppressed by Garneau himself), and a new popularly held assumption joined those about climate and cotton to obscure any national memory of French slavery.[45]

"The Profitability of Slavery: A Historical Perennial," *Journal of Southern History, 29* (1963), 303–25.

45. No one can read the first edition of Garneau's work and conclude otherwise than that he wrote deliberately to confuse his readers and to compare a slaveless French to the disadvantage of the British. He must have known of Jacques Viger's research, cited above, for he had been close to Viger's cousin, Denis Benjamin Viger; and had Garneau's third edition not appeared at the same time as the published work of Jacques Viger and Lafontaine, one might assume that he would have modified it, especially since a revision was carried out after his death—presumably in keeping with his instructions—by his eldest son Alfred, in 1882. In this, the fourth edition, the crucial passages were changed to read that the French government wished "not to encourage the introduction of slaves into Canada," that "it is true that there were ordinances as to slavery," that "slavery did not prevail in Canada," and that the "plague [was] unknown under our northern sky"—all of which is true enough. That Garneau falsified the record in his first edition is clear; but several researchers continued to attack him unnecessarily, without noting these changes in the fourth edition.

The earliest corrective was administered by François-Marie-Maximilien Bibaud in *Revue critique de l'histoire du Canada, de M. Garneau* (Montreal, 1855), p. 26, which charged the historian with charlatanism and incompetence. Garneau no doubt felt it appropriate to ignore the work of the son of Michel Bibaud, a Tory-leaning historian who was unpopular in French Canada; Viger and Lafontaine, technically writing anonymously but under Viger's initials, followed in 1859. Neilson (pp. 19–20) was especially hard on Garneau in 1906 on the basis of the unrevised third edition, as was Riddell in 1920 in "The Slave in Canada" (p. 263), in which he used Garneau's first edition. Only Riddell appeared to have noticed the difference in the fourth edition ("Slave in Nouvell-France," p. 317, published in 1923); and in doing so he bent over backwards to make amends for what he regarded as the "heedless" attacks of other historians, including mixing (and distorting) his translations of portions of the 1882 text with those from the text of 1846; Riddell changed the translation he had given in 1920 (see p. 317, n. 2) even while quoting the same text.

For the Garneau texts, see *Histoire du Canada* (1st ed., Quebec, 1846), *2,* 447;

The chief reason slavery gained little hold in Canada arose from the fact that the French remained in possession of the northern tier of the New World while the British were acquiring the West Indies, which could exploit immediately, obviously, and profitably a system of slave labor. To say that slavery could not be adjusted to the economy of New France, even to the fur trade, is to go too far; although to say that it would have been difficult to establish it—that the active intervention of the state would have been required—is correct. Slavery, if not dependent upon, certainly thrived upon one-crop, mass-production, gang-labor economies; and against such, a few beaver hats did not signify. From the outset the Canadians were, to use Edward Gibbon Wakefield's phrase, "earth-scratchers." [46] When all things are equal, free labor is preferable to slave, which is given reluctantly, without skills or versatility, and at a high cost of overseeing time and maintenance. But in most colonies other things were not equal: "When slavery is adopted it is not adopted as the choice over free labor; there is no choice at all." [47] For the seigniors, and for the early Canadian staple trade, there were no options either, since the controlling authority in France made the choice explicit: the economy would continue to be based on the beaver trade, where free labor obviously was more effective than slave.

Did slavery give rise to the prejudice later so clearly expressed in British North America against the Negro? On the whole probably not, for by the middle of the nineteenth century there was little awareness in the provinces of there having been any slavery in Canada at all; prejudice cannot feed upon an assumption of a slave background when that background has been forgotten. While the majority of Negroes in the Canadas of the 1850s were thought to be fugitive slaves, it was well understood that many were free men; yet the free Negroes came to be as much, if not more, the objects of racial prejudice since they did not have the protective advantage of being in need of sanctuary from the slave states. The racial prejudice which was beginning to be apparent at the close of the French period, and which intensified greatly in the following decades, appears to have grown independently of ideas relating directly to slavery. Negroes were inferior not because they had been slaves but because they

---

(3rd ed., Quebec, 1859), *2,* 167; (4th ed., Montreal, 1882), *2,* 167, *3,* 90 n. Andrew Bell, in his translation, *History of Canada from the Time of its Discovery til the Union Year 1840–1* (Montreal, 1860), *1,* 440, published on the eve of the Civil War, modified Garneau's original statement in the direction of accuracy. The whole is an interesting example of how erroneous conclusions about slavery can gain the force of truth for many.

46. Herman Merivale, *Lectures on Colonization and Colonies* (Oxford, 1928 ed.), p. 262.

47. Eric Williams, *Capitalism & Slavery* (Chapel Hill, N.C., 1944), p. 6.

were Negroes. For this reason, and because Garneau and his successors helped to suppress the early history of slavery, the institution in New France had comparatively little impact upon later generations of either Negroes or French Canadians.[48]

Slavery in New France, like freedom, never was a matter of doctrine but rather of pragmatic circumstance and of specific accident. The church modified slavery, thus contributing to an ethical climate, not by positive acts as in Latin America but by taking no action at all. The Protestant churches were to explain the slave condition away through predestinarian arguments or, later, through other forms of fundamentalism; they found slavery a positive good. The Roman Catholic church found in slavery, one feels, an irrelevancy; had it grown in France, the church would have gone along with it; as it died, the church let it. In the French West Indies and in Latin America after 1789, the slave codes were influenced by the spirit of the French Revolution; not so in Canada, where the revolutionary ideals took little root. Inaction, not *égalité,* aided the Negro in the Canadas.

Other local conditions operated to weaken slavery further. Most slaves lived in Quebec, Montreal, and Trois-Rivières; not until as late as 1767, after the Conquest, was slavery established in Presqu'île,[49] for example. The presence of free Negroes, physical proximity to one's masters, the greater possibility of education that town life provided, and the stability of service engendered by marriage customs and inheritance served to limit the social distance between white and black as fostered under rural, plantation conditions. Further, since slaves were not permitted permanently in France itself, and since many of the colonists who held slaves were government officials and military officers who expected to return to France one day, many owners knew that they could not hold their property indefinitely. Only the professional classes had the opportunity, the need, and the continuity of residence necessary to considering slaves as true chattels; since the clergy and the legal profession were uninterested in promoting slavery, any positive defense of it fell to the merchants. They alone could scarcely sustain a genuine case for the institution so long as royal regulations limited local opportunities in commerce and industry. Nor could owners make harsh demands of their slaves, for the slave had two safety

---

48. On the relationship between servitude and racism, see Oscar and Mary F. Handlin, "Origins of the Southern Labor System," *William and Mary Quarterly,* ser. 3, 7 (1950), 199–222; Carl N. Degler, "Slavery and the Genesis of American Race Prejudice," *Comparative Studies in Society and History,* 2 (1959), 49–66; David Brion Davis, *The Problem of Slavery in Western Culture* (Ithaca, N.Y., 1966), pp. 223–61; and Winthrop D. Jordan, *White Over Black: American Attitudes toward the Negro, 1550–1812* (Chapel Hill, N.C., 1968), passim.

49. Robert-Lionel Séguin, "L'esclavage dans la presqu'île," *Le Bulletin des recherches historiques,* 55 (1949), 91–93. Hereafter cited as *BRH.*

valves that operated in his favor: he could escape into the forests which always lay nearby, affording food, cover, and distance, and after 1787 he could escape southwards into the Northwest Territory of the new United States, where slavery was illegal. The frontier was, as one scholar has remarked, a sieve.[50]

The white man as well as the black had occasion to remember that the sieve was there. Colonization of New France was largely voluntary. Only in 1723 did France, over protests from the colony, send a small group of involuntary settlers. Free settlers were more aware of their own responsibilities and of their own worth. They were hierarchical, as were most men in the seventeenth and eighteenth centuries, but on the whole they felt less need to create artificial barriers than did the English colonists, who were of far more mixed origins. Since immigration into New France was slight after the 1680s, population growth depended upon an increased birth rate. No "new men" arrived, no class of eager, growing entrepreneurs demanded a constant supply of new muscle. The social structure of New France did not change as rapidly as that of the American colonies. Even in rural areas no wide gap formed between the habitant and the seignior, and there was no need to acquire slaves as a quick means to status. While owning a slave or two did indicate social standing, it did not create such standing, and in any case, although Negro slaves were preferred to *panis* slaves, the practice of slavery was not yet associated with a single race. Not only did the economy of New France not require—although it could have used—slavery, but the social structure had relatively little use for the slave beyond the purely utilitarian one of providing domestic help.[51]

In the English colonies, on the other hand, the slave trade began to be regularized as early as the 1680s. The effects of successive psychic shocks of capture, transport, and seasoning, together with exposure to the absolute power of the slave-master over an extended period of time may have tended to develop, as Stanley M. Elkins has argued (perhaps too strongly), an indolent, unimaginative, "Sambo type" upon whom preconceived racist assumptions could feed.[52] Not so in New France, where few slaves were

50. Kenneth D. McRae, "The Structure of Canadian History," in Louis Hartz, ed., *The Founding of New Societies: Studies in the History of the United States, Latin America, South Africa, Canada, and Australia* (New York, 1964), p. 225.

51. See Sigmund Diamond, "An Experiment in 'Feudalism': French Canada in the Seventeenth Century," *William and Mary Quarterly*, ser. 3, *18* (1961), 11–19. Hilda M. Neatby, in *Quebec: The Revolutionary Age, 1760–1791* (Toronto, 1966), p. 234, suggests that slaves may have created prejudice against domestic service, but the nature of a frontier economy provides a better explanation for the scarcity of servants.

52. Elkins, *Slavery: A Problem in American Institutional and Intellectual Life* (Chicago, 1959), pp. 81–139.

brought directly from Africa, where there was little trading in slaves, where virtually none were subject to an overseer, and where the Roman-based law, the church, and a longer historical awareness of racial differences continued to soften attitudes towards slavery as an institution and Negroes as a race.

Indeed, slavery hardly became an institution as such in New France. Limited in numbers and in extent, fully legal but not fully practiced, approached only spasmodically and unsystematically as a solution to chronic labor problems that were created in Paris, slave labor was never given a chance by the French in North America. Having neither many defenders nor many detractors, slavery appears to have been an irrelevancy not only to the church but to the state. As an irrelevancy, slavery survived in New France for seventy-one years; only briefly during this time did conditions favor the potential growth of slavery. Between 1663 and 1680 or even 1704, in an expanding New France, slave labor might have been used to considerable advantage; but slavery was not given full legal support until 1709, well after the colony was restored to its classical mercantilist base, and no genuine trial of its adaptability to the needs of New France was ever made. The society and the institution did not grow at the same time or in the same direction; and after 1713, when New France itself fell into decline, the institution declined with it.

But not immediately, as slavery expanded slowly from 1760 under a new regime, and rapidly after 1783 with the arrival of displaced settlers from the rebellious British North American colonies. Slavery was legal for another seventy-four years. In 1760, slavery in Canada was virtually at its midpoint, for the British gave it new life.

2. Slavery, the Loyalists, and English Canada, 1760–1801

By the Treaty of Paris in 1763, France ceded the whole of her mainland North American empire east of the Mississippi to Great Britain. An incidental effect of this transfer of power was the legal strengthening of slavery in Canada. On three occasions explicit guarantees were given to slave-owners that their property would be respected, and between 1763 and 1790 the British government added to the legal superstructure so that a once vaguely defined system of slavery took on clearer outlines.

When Pierre François Rigaud, Marquis de Vaudreuil, surrendered at the Chateau de Ramezay on September 8, 1760, he included in the treaty of capitulation a clause, number 47, which affirmed that all slaves would remain the possessions of their masters, that they might continue to be sold, and that they could be instructed in the Roman Catholic faith. The Commander-in-Chief of the British forces in North America, Jeffrey Amherst, who received the surrender documents, accepted the clause, reserving those slaves who had been taken prisoner by the British during the fighting.[1] On the following day Vaudreuil wrote to the French commandant at Detroit to inform him of the terms of the peace and to instruct him to return any slaves taken from the British during the war.[2] Three years later article 47 was incorporated, virtually without change, into the final treaty of peace. In July 1764, the bedraggled Huron allies of the French made their own peace with Sir William Johnson, the Superintendent of Indian Affairs for New York, and Johnson not only ordered that all "negro's, Panis or other slaves . . . who are British property" should be delivered to the commandant at Detroit, but warned that the Hurons must turn over to the commanding officer any slaves who subsequently might seek refuge with them.[3]

The Treaty of Paris introduced English criminal and civil law to Que-

1. Adam Shortt and Arthur G. Doughty, eds., *Documents relating to the Constitutional History of Canada, 1759–1791,* 2nd ed. (Ottawa, 1918), *1,* 22.

2. Jacques Viger, *Ma Saberdache,* M, I, and quoted in Ernest J. Lajeunesse, ed., *The Windsor Border Region, Canada's Southernmost Frontier: A Collection of Documents* (Toronto, 1960), pp. 88, 275.

3. PAC, Misc. Docs., *21,* no. 47: article 2, July 18, 1764.

bec, depriving slaves of those few protections provided by the informally observed *Code Noir*. But in 1774, with the Quebec Act, Britain restored the earlier French civil law to the province while retaining the English criminal code. The boundaries of Quebec were extended to the Ohio River, bringing under the one administration those few slaves living in the old Northwest. Most important among these were the slaves held at Detroit, increasing in number although, in 1774, slightly short of one hundred in all.[4] In 1791 Quebec was divided into two provinces, and Britain preserved the French laws for Lower Canada while introducing English civil law into Upper Canada. English criminal law was applied in both Canadas.

The English civil and criminal law that was introduced into Quebec in 1763 contained no effective strictures against slavery; indeed, the entire weight of law and custom in the British colonies tended to support the legality of the institution overseas. Lord Mansfield's famous decision, from the Court of King's Bench in the case of Somerset vs. Stewart, which held that slavery could not exist in England itself without specific legislation, did not come until 1772, well after the British administrators in Quebec had made it clear to the French that they would be permitted to retain their slaves. The 47th article of capitulation at Montreal, the same article in the definitive treaty of peace, and George III's proclamation of October 7, 1763, which affirmed those articles, had all given support to the institution. And in the Quebec Act the British Parliament reaffirmed that all His Majesty's subjects within the province could continue to hold and to enjoy their property and possessions. To the east, in Nova Scotia, the General Assembly had given indirect recognition to slavery in 1762 by referring, in an act intended to control the sale of liquor on credit, to "any soldier, sailor, servant, apprentice, bound servant or negro slave." An attempt in 1789 to pass a bill asserting that no one could enslave a British subject "unless they are proved by Birth or otherwise to be bound to Servitude for Life" would fail.[5]

At its first session in 1792, the Parliament of Upper Canada affirmed English law in order to remove certain ambiguities arising out of the act of 1774 and the division of the two Canadas in 1791. When, during the second session in 1793, the Parliament brought in a specific bill to promote

4. Lajeunesse, *Windsor Border Region:*, pp. lxvii–lxviii. Detroit Public Library, Burton Historical Collection: typescript history, "Negroes in Detroit," discusses early slave sales; see also Frederick C. Hamil, "Sally Ainse, Fur Trader," The Algonquin Club, *Historical Bulletin*, 3 (1939), 6. The Census for 1750, which shows thirty-three slaves, may be found in PAC, G 1, *461*, 28. The number of slaves in Detroit rose to 179 by 1782.

5. *Statutes at Large, Nova Scotia* (Halifax, 1805), p. 77; PANS, Unpassed Bills: "An Act for the Regulation of Relief of the Free Negroes within the Province of Nova Scotia."

the abolition of slavery, it was clear that the mere introduction of English common law was insufficient to this end. While public opinion, and not a few antiquarians and local historians, have held that slavery was illegal in the whole of British North America after the Somerset case, this was not so; for Lord Mansfield's decision, whatever it may be that he said,[6] had no legal effect within the colonies.

But the most important legal protection given to slavery by Britain for the northern provinces was contained in an Imperial act of 1790 to encourage immigration into British North America. Britain permitted free importation into North America, the Bahamas, and Bermuda of all "Negroes, household furniture, utensils of husbandry or cloathing." No one could sell such goods for a year after entering the colonies; and furniture, utensils, and clothing were not to exceed in value £50 for every white and £2 for every Negro slave. Free Negroes were not encouraged.[7] All white settlers over fourteen years old were to take an oath of allegiance; children and Negroes, slave or free, were not expected to do so since they were unable to swear.

The British military governor of Quebec, General James Murray, echoed the arguments of Denonville, Champigny, and Bègon, for he hoped to bring more Negro slaves into the reorganized colony. In November 1763, Murray wrote to a friend in New York asking for "two Stout Young fellows" and—so that they might have "a Communication with the Ladys" and be happy—"for each a clean young Wife." While these four Negro slaves were to be his, he saw broader possibilities: "without Servants nothing can be done"; soldiers would be poor laborers, and the French would work for no one but themselves. Murray hoped, "by setting a good Example," to improve agriculture. "Black Slaves are Certainly the only people to be depended upon, but . . . they should be born in one or other of our Northern Colonies, [as] the Winters here will not agree, with a Native of the Torrid Zone." For the right Negro slaves he would "begrudge no price." [8] Wishing to conciliate the French and to create a colony loyal to the British Crown, Murray appears to have allowed French customs and codes to govern slave relations as before. In effect, slavery continued under the British as under the French.

6. The famous words credited to Mansfield, "The air of England has long been too pure for a slave and every man is free who breathes it," do not appear even in Capel Lofft's reports on the Court of King's Bench. The quotation is, in fact, from John Lord Campbell, *The Lives of the Chief Justices of England* (London, 1849), 2, 418.

7. PAC, Misc. Docs., *16*, pt. 2: act of Aug. 1, 1790.

8. PAC, James Murray Papers, Letter Books, *2*, 15–16: to John Watts, Nov. 2, 1763.

There were Negroes, and slavery,[9] on the eastern seaboard as well. French blacks had been involved in the unsuccessful defense of Louisbourg in 1745, and among the common laborers there in 1747 was a free black laborer, Quash, who received the same pay as his thirty-five white coworkers did, and two free Negro masons.[10] In 1749 the British government offered passage, provisions, muskets, and ammunition to settlers, and free Negroes were included; in 1750 fifteen or more were victualed at Halifax. When the Nova Scotian government opened parcels of the original French lands to settlers from New England in 1759, blacks again were given the same opportunities to come as whites.[11]

The first clear references to slaves occur in 1752. A "negro servant" named Orange was mentioned in a will; and in May an entrepreneur and victualler to the navy at Halifax, Joshua Mauger, advertised several Negro slaves for sale.[12] A Halifax merchant and magistrate, Malachy Salter, asked his wife to buy a Negro boy for him while she was in Boston in 1759, confessing that he was "obliged to exercise the cat or stick [against one of his two slaves] almost every day." [13] Negro slaves were introduced to Liverpool by 1760, to the New Glasgow region in 1767, and to Bridgetown, Amherst, Onslow, and Cornwallis by 1770. In that year Henry Denny Denson of Falmouth held five and possibly as many as sixteen slaves at his Mount Denson home.[14] "A boy and a girl, about eleven years old; likewise a puncheon of choice cherry brandy," were offered for sale in 1760; and in 1769 an auction was held on the beach at Halifax to sell

9. In 1686 one of the settlers at Cape Sable was La Liberté, "le neigre," possibly an escaped slave from the English colonies, and as we have seen, there may have been a slave at Port Royal as early as 1606. Louisbourg's Governor Isaac Louis Forant owned a Martinique man in 1739–40. See PANS, 2, "French Documents relating to Acadia," vol. 1, no. 28; and Archibald M. MacMechan, *A Calendar of Two Letter-Books and One Commission-Book in the Possession of the Government of Nova Scotia, 1713–1741,* Nova Scotia Archives, publication no. 2 (Halifax, 1900), pp. 100, 102, 104–05.

10. LC, America, British Colonies, MSS: "Military Affairs at Louisburg in New England 1747," a pay and general record book.

11. PANS, 32, Nov. 28, 1750; *Report, Board of Trustees of the Public Archives of Nova Scotia . . . 1941* (Halifax, 1942), pp. 23–43; Lorenzo Johnston Greene, *The Negro in Colonial New England, 1620–1776* (New York, 1942), p. 83.

12. *Halifax Royal Gazette,* May 15, 1752.

13. Quoted in T. Watson Smith, "The Slave in Canada," *Collections of the Nova Scotia Historical Society for the Years 1896–98, 10* (1899), 7.

14. *Saint John Telegraph,* May 27, 1884; Norman L. Nicholson, "Rural Settlement and Land Use in the New Glasgow Region," *Geographical Bulletin,* no. 7 (1955), p. 45; James F. More, *The History of Queens County, N.S.* (Halifax, 1873), pp. 125–26; John V. Duncanson, *Falmouth—A New England Township in Nova Scotia, 1760–1965* (Windsor, Ont., 1965), p. 32.

"two hogsheads of rum, three of sugar and two well-grown negro girls, aged fourteen and twelve." By 1767 there was at least one slave on the Saint John River, a "rascal negro" who, according to his owner, "cannot be flattered or drove to do one-fourth a man's work." [15] In 1768 alone, 2,217 Negro slaves valued at £77,595 sterling were imported into the British provinces of North America, Newfoundland, Bahama, and Bermuda; and while most of these probably went to the Bahamas, many did not. In 1788 "robust able black men" were at work in the Newfoundland fisheries; for thirty-four sloops from Bermuda, each carrying eight to twelve men—three quarters of whom were Negro slaves—arrived at the banks early in the spring. Although at first not feared as competitors because of the widespread belief that Negroes could not stand the climate, they soon excelled the locals at the catch, abandoning the banks only for lack of any place to dry their fish.[16]

The Loyalist migration to the faithful British lands in North America brought the first really major influx of Negroes to the maritime areas, however. Some of the Loyalists had owned large plantations in the rebellious colonies, with household slaves and field hands. Others had owned little more than the clothes on their backs. Loyalists came from all colonies, all professions, and all levels of society, having in common only a conscious commitment to their Crown and a general respect for property. Many took slavery for granted, and those who owned slaves found important work for them to do in the new land—clearing fields, chopping wood against the long winters, and building ships.

Five results of this influx of Loyalists are clear. The number of slaves increased rapidly. The defense of slavery received a number of vocal and well-informed advocates. Negro slaves virtually supplanted *panis* slaves, even in Quebec. Because many of the slaves came from larger plantations where they had been trained to specific skills, the variety of work done by Negroes was greatly expanded. Since a number of the Negroes were freedmen, slave and free Negroes now lived side by side.

But in time the effect of the Loyalist and Negro immigration was the reverse of the initial trend. The slaves, given the example of free Negro agricultural settlers nearby, cannot have continued to assume that black skins automatically decreed servitude. Many of the Loyalists found that they could not afford to maintain gangs of fifty or more field hands, and

15. *Halifax Royal Gazette*, Nov. 1, 1760; Smith, "Slave in Canada," p. 10; Riddell, "Slave in Canada," pp. 298–99.

16. BM, Additional Manuscripts (hereafter, Add. MSS), 15,485: "Exports and Imports of North America, 1768–9," pp. 28, 32; Daniel Woodley Prowse, *A History of Newfoundland, from the English, Colonial, and Foreign Records* (London, 1895), pp. 345–47, 416–18.

that once the land was cleared it was not sufficiently productive to require an extensive labor force. Since the Loyalists came from several colonies, they tended to apply to their slaves a pastiche of their previous practices and laws, but without specific enactments; and in doing so, they seem almost always to have applied the softer, less formal of the regulations. Slaves were baptized, given some education, and kept together as families, whatever the practices may have been in the colonies to the south. Most important, a number of the Loyalists already had been moving toward antislavery positions; and once they resettled, they tended to look upon slavery as too closely associated with the new Republic which they had cause to hate. Although the Loyalists temporarily gave new numbers and new strength to slavery in Canada, within two decades those same Loyalists had all but ended the practice.

Judging slavery to be a major weakness of the rebellious southern colonies, the British offered emancipation to all slaves who, during the Revolution, volunteered to serve with their forces. Britain hoped to get thousands of laborers in this way, and also slowly to strangle the southern economy. Fewer slaves accepted the call than the British had hoped, however, and since slaves were valuable property, many British officers were unable to resist the temptation to sell them in the West Indies. In Quebec, too, the desire to turn a small fortune led to illegal seizures, betrayals, and unjust enslavements; but since the numbers dealt with along the northern frontier were small, the problem was also small.

The line between slaves who surrendered to British officers, and slaves who were captured and thus taken to be the legitimate spoils of war, was one too thin to draw at times. While Montreal was still in French hands, at least one free Negro who had been taken prisoner at Fort William Henry was sold in Montreal as a slave. In 1778 some men stationed in Quebec with the Light Infantry Chasseurs of Brunswick took away and sold a slave belonging to a French merchant, Joseph Despin; and later that year a Negro who had been captured by "the Yankys," twice petitioned the new governor, Frederick Haldimand, for a clear grant of his freedom. In 1780 a number of slaves captured in Kentucky were brought into Quebec via Detroit and sold, although at least ten apparently belonged to a Loyalist; and near Detroit Indians continued to seize Negroes for themselves. In New York two Loyalist groups, the Royal Regiment of New York and Colonel John Butler's Queen's Rangers, together with Indian allies, took a number of slaves as spoils, to sell in Montreal and on the Niagara peninsula; in one raid on Ballston, New York, in 1781, seven or more Negroes were captured. In 1787 a man held by Captain Johan Jost Herkimer, who had settled on the Bay of Quinté after the war, complained that, although he had escaped from the rebels in New York and had served the King, he was kept as a slave; and a Negro with Richard Cartwright, Colonel Butler's former secretary, also told of being enslaved illegally. Indeed, as Captain John Monroe, who was in charge of the expedition against Ballston,[17] later was to declare, "he never considered these captured negroes as ordinary prisoners of war and consequently did not report to the Commander-in-Chief or any other Commanding officer," for selling Negroes was "customary." It is, therefore, impossible to know how many slaves were carried into Quebec during the Revolution.[18]

The Governor, Sir Frederick Haldimand, wished to know. After an unsuccessful attempt to have a group of illegally seized slaves returned at Detroit to their Loyalist owner, in 1781 Haldimand ordered Sir John Johnson, a Loyalist from New York who, together with Butler, had organized many of the raids into rebel territory, to report to him on "all Negroes who have been brought into the Province by Parties in any Respect under your Directions whether Troops or Indians." Johnson himself had owned slaves, including one who had loyally buried his master's silver plate when the Johnson family estate was confiscated, and he had brought fourteen with him. (Sir John's ability to work with Indians was to lead, two years later, to his appointment as Superintendent-General of Indian Affairs.) He filed a census return in July—far too quickly to be credited with anything approaching accuracy—in which he accounted for the disposition of only fifty slaves.[19] But Haldimand cannot have hoped for a true accounting, for Negroes sought refuge in the province throughout the Revolutionary War, and most quite naturally claimed to be free men; nor could effective controls be applied to the sale of slaves around Detroit, especially of those taken captive by marauding Indians, although Haldimand tried to block unauthorized slave entry into the colony. The Negroes

17. Ballston appears as Ball's Town and Bolston in several references. Neilson ("Slavery in Old Canada," p. 38) and Viger and Lafontaine, "L'esclavage" (p. 22), give Monroe as Munro; and they may be correct, although the oath of Randel Huet, in the Porteous Papers, McCord Museum, McGill University, March 9, 1761, uses Monroe. There are other variations in spelling place-names; either those most commonly accepted by contemporaries, or those now used for purposes of identification, are employed throughout this book.

18. WO61, Jeffery Amherst Papers: Thomas Hancock to Amherst, Sept. 8, Dec. 21, 1761; CO5/66, 447, and CO323/23, 79: Court of Enquiry, March 11, 1786; Brome County Historical Society, Knowlton, P.Q.: Eastern Townships Papers, Feb. 16, 1779; PAC, Misc. Docs., *16,* pt. 2: deposition, John Mittelburger vs. Patrick Langan, June 10, 1787, and statement by Monroe-Munro, July 16, 1788; PAC, Internal Correspondence, Quebec, 1788: "Grievances of the Loyalists of Sorel, Cataracoui, etc.," pp. 66, 74.

19. BM, Add. MSS 21,763, fol. 369: "Return of Negroes, brought into Canada by Scouts and sold at Montreal," n.d.

had one advantage over whites taken captive by the Indians, however: if the latter might be slain, Negroes were kept alive because they could be sold.

During the war, the British employed Negroes against the enemy in many ways. In the army they were boatmen, woodsmen, general laborers, buglers and musicians. One corps, the Black Pioneers, was formed entirely from free Negroes. Sir Henry Clinton encouraged slaves to desert rebel masters and promised them their freedom if they did so. To regularize such offers, late in the war Sir Guy Carleton, then commander-in-chief of the British troops in North America, guaranteed that all slaves would be free who, upon seeking refuge behind British lines, made formal claim to British protection; and as he supervised the massive evacuation of Loyalists and troops from New York in 1783, he sought out places to which these Negroes might go. The great majority of them were resettled in the British West Indies, and others temporarily in East Florida, but many—slave and free—went to the remaining British provinces in North America.

A final settlement between Britain and the United States had to wait until terms were agreed upon between Britain and France, but in the meantime hundreds of former slaves, who had taken refuge with the British and thought themselves free, now lived in fear of return to and punishment by their putative owners. Carleton decided to transport them elsewhere, promising that if doing so infringed the final treaty, the British governor would compensate the owners; and he ordered that a register should be kept on the name, age, occupation, and former owner of all Negroes. Not all masters were opposed to this arrangement, for in the northern states many preferred the promised compensation to the slaves. In any case, as Carleton pointed out in defense of his decision, the Negroes would have found other ways of getting out of New York "so that the former owner would no longer have been able to trace them," thus losing any chance of compensation. Because of Carleton's registers, we have a clearer record of Negro movement by sea into Nova Scotia at the end of the Revolutionary War than for any other major Negro migration into British North America.

General Washington met with Carleton in May of 1783 to discuss how American property should be preserved, with particular reference to Negro slaves. Carleton insisted that those Negroes who had taken advantage of the proclamations issued in their favor during the war should be embarked if they wished to be, and admitted that some already had been. Washington apparently stood upon the letter of the Provisional Articles of the previous November, the seventh of which had stipulated that "His Britannic Majesty shall with all convenient speed, and without causing any destruction, or

carrying away any Negroes, or other property of the American Inhabitants, withdraw all his Armies." In the interim between the date of the
Provisional Articles and the conclusion of the British treaty with France,
Carleton had arranged for the evacuation. He now insisted that those
Negroes who had come to the British lines were, by their act, free and
therefore did not fall within the terms of article seven which, although
it referred only to Negroes and not to slaves, nonetheless clearly meant
only those Negroes who were slaves—a condition they lost upon their
formal application for freedom before the British. Washington insisted
that the provisional article was binding on this point and that it had prohibited carrying away any Negroes at all, to which Carleton is said to
have responded that "no interpretation could be sound, that was inconsistent with prior Engagements of the Faith and honor of the Nation,
which he should inviolably maintain with People of all Colours and
Conditions." If Britain shared Washington's view, Carleton added, his
registers would make full compensation possible: "the Slave would have
his liberty, his Master his Price, and the Nation support [of] its honor."
Ultimately they agreed that an American should help oversee the em-
barkation, and from May until November of 1783, Washington's aide-de-
camp stood by in New York as hundreds of Negroes embarked for Nova
Scotia.[20]

Despite Carleton's decisive stand, which was approved by Lord North
in August, an air of indecision and expediency hung over the preparations
for evacuation from the American colonies, since deep into 1782 no one
had known which ports in North America Britain might ultimately retain.
In August, 4,230 whites and 7,163 Negroes were gathered in Charleston,
South Carolina, awaiting transport; and while most expressed a desire to
be taken to either Jamaica or St. Augustine, they continued to mill about
uncertainly, not wanting to "bind themselves now to any specific spot."
Not until March of 1783 did Carleton order the commissary at Halifax
to issue provisions for an advance body of 259 white adults, 65 children,
and 24 slaves who were to be sent from this group in South Carolina.

20. The British contentions are set out in the BM, Chatham MSS: bundle 343,
pp. 71–72, a report endorsed September, 1819, but prepared in 1794. The British continued to insist that compensation could be paid only for "such Negroes as were
not emancipated by Proclamation in the course of the War, *if any such instances
can be assigned*," leaving the burden of proof to the former owners. The American
version of the May meeting appears in LC, George Washington Papers, *220,* no. 71,
May 6. Lord North's approval of Carleton's decision is in the PRO, Headquarters
Papers of the British Army in America (commonly, Carleton Papers), *51,* North to
Carleton, Aug. 8, 1783. The confusion over transporting the Negroes is discussed
in Benjamin Quarles, *The Negro in the American Revolution* (Chapel Hill, N.C.,
1961), pp. 163–77.

Many of the whites and Negroes who were sent to Jamaica and East Florida were unable to find work, and faced with the prospect of supplying them with provisions long beyond the allotted time, Carleton transferred some of them to Nova Scotia as well.

Between April 15 and November 30, 1783, Carleton's commissioners at New York inspected every vessel bound for Nova Scotia, save for two that failed to comply with regulations, to learn how many Negroes were being carried away. In the first two weeks they accounted for 328 Negro men, 230 women, and 48 children, all free in British eyes, as well as several slaves accompanying white Loyalists. In June, when the two recalcitrant vessels were inspected upon arrival in Nova Scotia, 165 more free Negroes were registered. They continued to arrive in Nova Scotia in such numbers that in some sections they outnumbered the whites, and by the end of November the British and American commissioners had accounted for 2,714 free Negroes who had gone to the one colony, and an additional 286 were cleared for Nova Scotia in November in the absence of the Americans. Of these three thousand free Negro migrants, 1,336 were men, 914 were women, and 750 were children. Carleton's figures did not include the Loyalists' slaves or the few Negroes who left before mid-April.[21]

Most of the Negroes taken into Quebec were slaves, the property of Loyalist owners fleeing the rebel states, and Carleton's registers can tell us nothing of them. There were slaves in virtually all of the Loyalist settlements, however—along the Bay of Quinté, for example, the Harmen Pruynses from New York, Richard Cartwright at Cataraqui, the Everett family, and Major Peter Van Alstine, who helped found Adolphustown, owned perhaps ten or more each, while several other families brought one or two. John Stuart, Episcopal missionary to the Mohawk Indians, took his slaves with him, as did Captain Justus Sherwood, one of the founders of Johnstown. Thomas Fraser at Fraserfield possessed several slaves, and there were a number at Delta in Leeds County, kept on an island in a

21. Carleton Papers, *46:* Alexander Leslie to Carleton, Aug. 10, and return of Loyalists at Charleston, Aug. 13, 1782; *57:* return of refugees arrived at East Florida, Dec. 23, 1782; *64:* Frederick Mackenzie to Brook Watson, March 4, 1783; *66:* memorial, Charles Ogilvie et al. to Carleton, April 8; *77:* Henry Knipschild to Carleton, Aug. 13; *78:* Robert Morse to H. E. Fox, Aug. 23; *79:* Fox to Carleton, Aug. 26; and reply, *81,* Sept. 15; *83:* James Peters to Carleton, Oct. 5; *92:* petitioners of Norfolk and Princess Anne counties, Va., April 28, all 1783; and *55,* Book of Negroes, pp. 90–104. On occasion the Carleton Papers are cited as "Royal Institute Papers," "Williamsburg Papers," or "Dorchester Papers." A copy of the Book of Negroes is in the PANS, but it contains minor errors; PAC holds a more accurate copy (American MSS, *12,* Sundry Letters). American versions of several of the returns are in the NA, Papers of the Continental Congress and Washington Papers.

lake. The pioneers of Camden and Edwardsburgh were slave-owners. Peter Russell, William Jarvis, James and Robert Isaac Dey Gray, Peter Robinson, and others who were to figure prominently in the early political history of Upper Canada all held slaves in substantial numbers.[22] Russell is said to have owned ninety-nine Negroes, which is unlikely, and his friend Matthew Elliott brought between fifty and sixty.[23] The principal chief of the Six Nations, Joseph Brant, who settled on the Grand River, seventy miles northwest of Niagara, also kept slaves at his estate.[24] The family of William Davis, from North Carolina, arrived with a grandfather clock, some peach stones, some carpet, and "several faithful slaves." In the Niagara district alone—where the first slave arrived in 1782—an estimate put the slave population (now chiefly Negro, although a few *panis* remained) at nearly three hundred in 1791.[25]

Many slaves were also taken into the relatively rich lands east of Montreal, soon to be known as the Eastern Townships. One carried his master on his back while the family treasure was drawn up-river in boats; others carried precious seeds, books, the family Bible, and their own young children. Crossing over from New York to Missisquoi Bay in 1782, Colonel Philip Luke brought several slaves who helped fell trees, build houses and barns, clear stumps from the fields, and thus make the tiny

22. PAC, MS Group 10, E II-1-8: list of inhabitants of Edwardsburgh (showing fifteen slaves), and Record Group 19, C35, *1*, Misc. Records: victualing lists for Ernestown and Adolphustown, provision list for Lake Township, and return of families, Cataraqui; Horace Hume van Wart, "The Loyalist Settlement of Adolphustown," *The Loyalist Gazette, 2* (1932), 2; Thomas W. Casey, "Early Slavery in Midland District," Lennox and Addington Historical Society, *Papers and Records, '4* (1912), 12–17; Thaddeus W. H. Leavitt, *History of Leeds and Grenville, Ontario, from 1749 to 1879* . . . (Brockville, Ont., 1879), pp. 20–21; Mrs. W. T. Hallam, *Slave Days in Canada* [Toronto, 1919], pp. 3–4; Gerald E. Boyce, *Historic Hastings* (Belleville, Ont., 1967), pp. 34–35; Roy F. Fleming, "Negro Slaves with the United Empire Loyalists in Upper Canada," *Ontario History, 45* (1953), 27–29; William Renwick Riddell, "An Official Record of Slavery in Upper Canada," OHS, *Papers and Records, 25* (1929), 393–97.

23. A search for Russell's will in the Surrogate Office of the County of York and at Osgoode Hall, Toronto, proved fruitless. Riddell, "Slave in Canada," credits Elliott with "more than 50 slaves" on p. 326, n. 17, and on p. 333 with "some sixty."

24. One of Brant's visitors in 1797 reported much later having seen many slaves who had been taken prisoner during the war: Jeromus Johnson to William L. Stone, Dec. 1, 1837, in Stone, *Life of Joseph Brant-Thayendanegna: Including the Border Wars of the American Revolution* . . . (New York, 1838), *2,* xliv. One slave, Sophia Pooley, was alive in Galt in 1854. In 1801 Russell planned to sell a slave to Brant, but there is no record of whether he did or not: OPA, Russell Papers, Elliott to Russell, Oct. 8, 1801, Jan. 2, 1802, and reply to first, Oct. 31, 1801.

25. Smith, "Slave in Canada," p. 40; Richard D. Merritt, "The Davis Family of Mount Albion: A Loyalist Sketch," Head-of-the-Lake Historical Society, *Wentworth Bygones, 7* (1967), 33–38.

settlement of St. Armand possible, so that Luke might get on with an ashery and his business as a general merchant. And since Vermont had outlawed slavery in 1777, those who remained there were forced to sell quickly elsewhere, including across the line into Quebec.[26] In 1784 a census of slaves for what was to become Lower Canada showed only 304,[27] but this number was low, and since manumissions were gaining ground and more slaves were being brought in throughout the year, one may assume the presence of a substantially larger number of Negroes.

But by far the greatest number went to Nova Scotia, and there the majority were free men. Thinking themselves Loyalists, many felt entitled to the same benefits that a grateful King gave to his white subjects. Their descendants, and the descendants of the corps of Black Pioneers, were to remind themselves much later that they, too, were of Loyalist strain; and they would be no more eager to cooperate with non-Loyalist Negroes who arrived from other sources and under other compulsions than United Empire Loyalists in Upper Canada were willing to make common cause with the rude Irish immigrants of the 1840s. Legally secure in all rights except for the vote, these free Negroes wished to stand apart from the enslaved.

Not entirely apart, however, for like their slave brethern, they had not chosen to come to the barren, rocky lands of Nova Scotia. Transported from New York and Charleston harbors, accustomed to the warm lands around Chesapeake Bay or the fertile soils back of the Hudson River, most had been field workers before they became free by seeking out the British lines; they knew relatively little about farming the thin soils of their new home and almost nothing about how to employ their energies, their time, or their talents to help themselves. Unless they had served actively in the British forces with the Black Pioneers, they received substantially smaller allotments of land than the white settlers did, and when the first company of 1782–83 reached Nova Scotia they found that neither land nor provisions were ready for them, despite promises that they would receive grants in common with the Loyalists and rations and seed for three years. Consequently, the chief military engineer in Halifax put a number to work repairing barracks, and few went directly onto the land. With no long history of freedom from which to draw sustenance, a reservoir of varied skills, and organizing experience, they were to compare unfavorably

26. NBM, William O. Raymond Scrapbooks, F29, p. 112; "Nigger Rock—St. Armand," Missisquoi County Historical Society, *Fourth Report* (1908–09); "St. Armand Negro Burying Ground," Brome County Historical Society roneod paper (1959), pp. 1–2; text of talk, "Negro Burying Ground at St. Armand," loaned by Marion L. Phelps, Cowansville, Que.; and Archives du Palais de Justice de Montréal: William Ward, sale to P. W. Campbell, April 26, 1785.

27. *Report on Canadian Archives, 1889* (Ottawa, 1890), p. 39.

with the white settlers when they did take up their small and often inconveniently located grants.

In nearly every case the black settlers were segregated. In Annapolis County seventy-six free Negroes received grants in 1785; all were of a single acre, all in Digby or its township, and none were wharf lots. At the same time, white settlers received from one hundred to four hundred acres throughout Annapolis County. In 1789, in Clements, 148 of 184 went to Negroes; all but one of the warrants was for fifty acres, the allotment usually accorded to white women who were heads of families. However, although the warrants were surveyed, the transactions on them were seldom completed, many of the grants not being confirmed. In Shelburne County, grants of fifty acres each were made on McNutt's Island in 1785 to four different groups of Negro pilots (sixteen in all), as well as to a single pilot, Joseph Restine; while 177 warrants were issued for from ten to forty acres to 178 Negroes, all in Shelburne Township, in 1787. In the same year, seventy-four Negroes who had originally been settled at Chedabucto Bay under Thomas Brownspriggs were granted forty acres each in Tracadie, in Sydney (now Guysborough) County; and eleven grants, ranging from ten to fifty acres (with a single grant of a hundred acres) were made in Preston Township in Halifax County. Whites in the township, which was notably rocky, received from one to two hundred acres. Only the blacks who remained on Chedabucto Bay or who settled in Preston Township were not wholly segregated, and in the latter the pattern of grants tended to have much the same effect.[28] Ultimately, most of these Negro settlers were to fail, dispersing widely outside their original compact settlements, drifting into conditions that approached peonage, particularly in Preston and Tracadie, and becoming unwilling charges upon the nearby white communities and upon the province.

The Black Pioneers were considered to be disbanded as soon as they embarked from New York, and thus they were not entitled to either pay or clothing upon arrival in the province. Many did not get away until snow had begun to fall on the Hudson, and they arrived at Annapolis and on the Saint John River very late in the season. Carleton knew that they would suffer from the weather for not having had time to build adequate houses, and in October he ordered that special stores be sent to them and that temporary shelters be built. He wanted the corps of

28. Marion Gilroy, comp., *Loyalists and Land Settlement in Nova Scotia*, PANS Pub. no. 4 (Halifax, 1937), pp. 7–29, 43–54, 89–115, 119–44. On the trials of Tracadie, see George A. Rawlyk, "The Guysborough Negroes: A Study in Isolation," *The Dalhousie Review, 48* (1968), 24–36. Note that the Guysborough Road School, mentioned in the article, is near Halifax, and not in Guysborough County.

pioneers to be given one acre each in Shelburne or Annapolis Royal and twenty acres of farmland; and if they settled too far from either to use town lots, he hoped to see their grants increased to a hundred acres of land.[29] Most, in fact, received fifty acres or less and no town lot, after a delay of three years.

But other Negroes had reached Port Roseway quite early, beginning on May 4, 1783, and they and the white settlers had time to prepare for winter well before it came. Shelburne, as Port Roseway was renamed, was expected to be something of a model community for resettlement of the Negroes, and in truth it began as such. Seldom were its Negroes called "slaves," for the British commissioners in New York were conscious of the fact that slaves, so designated, could become a source for future controversy with the United States; so they were enrolled in the registers as "servants," a term owners in Shelburne continued to use even when selling them later. Relations in the first fifteen months of settlement were harmonious between white and black and between slave and free.

The slaves tended to be concentrated in the hands of a few owners. Captain Andrew Barclay and his company of 55 adults brought 57 servants, 36 of whom were owned by four families; Charles Oliver Brueff, a goldsmith from New York, had fifteen; Stephen Shakespeare held twenty, as did James and Alexander Robertson from Pennsylvania, who launched the *Royal American Gazette* in Shelburne. The slaves continued to live with their masters in Shelburne, while nearly all of the free Negroes lived in a predominately black community of their own, Birchtown (or, as often spelled then, Burchtown), which straggled along the Northwest Arm of the Roseway River some three to six miles away and where most of the grants of land made to Negroes in Shelburne County were concentrated. By 1787 there were approximately two hundred Negro families in Birchtown, and perhaps half had built houses and begun to improve their lands. Another seventy families lived in the northern division of the township. In July of 1784 a muster of blacks in Shelburne accounted for 1,521. But Negroes continued to arrive, including 194 from St. Augustine, and informal estimates (a bit too generously) placed the total Negro population of the county, slave and free, at four thousand by 1787.[30]

29. Carleton Papers, *83:* Mackenzie to Fox, Oct. 10, 11, 1783; *87:* David Hurd to Carleton, n.d. [Nov., 1783?]; and PAC transcripts, *6:* Carleton to Fox, Oct. 21, 1783.
30. PANS, Letters of Lieut. Gov. to Sec. of State, *47,* 85–88; Carleton Papers, *75:* Governor John Parr to Carleton, July 25, 1783; *An Abstract of the Proceedings of the Associates of Doctor Bray, for the year 1787* ([London], 1787): report of Stephen Blucke, Dec. 22, pp. 34–35; William Francis Ganong, ed., "Historical-Geographical Documents relating to New Brunswick," *Collections of the New Brunswick Historical Society,* no. 8 (1909), pp. 226-30; R. R. McLeod, "Historical Sketch of the Town of Shelburne, Nova Scotia," *Acadiensis, 8* (1908), 38, 42; T. Watson Smith, "The

The muster book for the Port Roseway Associates provides a partial picture of Negro settlers at Shelburne and Birchtown.[31] In January 1784, there were 4,700 Loyalist settlers, 1,191 disbanded white soldiers, 1,485 free Negroes, and 1,269 servants, largely Negro slaves—something like 2,700 Negroes and 5,900 whites—at Port Roseway. Among the slaves, men outnumbered women three to one; but among the free Negroes, men were only half again as numerous as women. At Birchtown, in the first muster in July, there were 44 heads of families; the average age of 42 male heads of families was thirty-one, the average age of 40 females was twenty-nine, and the average age of 29 children was just under eight. Of the wives, 4 were under twenty-one and the youngest was sixteen; of the husbands, 2 were under twenty-one. The largest family had five children. There were only 2 settlers over sixty, both women. Among the occupations listed were ropemaker, boatbuilder, farmer, chimney sweep, carpenter, sawyer, sailor, and seamstress—although most Negroes were unskilled laborers. The majority were from the southern states. In August another company of free settlers arrived, and their muster in September showed 35 males of an average age of thirty-five, 34 females of an average age of thirty, and 39 children who averaged seven years of age. Many couples had no children; of those who did, the average number was 3. The same occupations were found, together with caulker, cook, pilot, and pedler.

Many former slaves, apparently freed upon arrival in Nova Scotia, continued to work as hired or, on occasion, indentured servants to their former masters. One hundred and thirty-eight white families in and near Birchtown employed or owned 396 servants; sixty of these families kept only a single servant, while Oliver Brueff now had sixteen. Subsequent musters for other companies confirm this pattern: most of the free Negro settlers were of age, still in their prime, with modest families and some skills. The stereotype of child marriages, large families, burdensome grandparents, and total lack of skills, does not apply. Thus Negro labor was useful to the white inhabitants, and when Shelburne grew into the largest and most prosperous community in the province, with an estimated population of eight thousand in 1785, Negroes were instrumental to that growth.

Neither the economic boom nor the harmony between whites and blacks lasted for long. Almost from the outset white settlers, and Andrew Barclay

Loyalists at Shelburne," *Collections of the Nova Scotia Historical Society for the Year 1887–88, 6* (1888), 74–77; Lorenzo Sabine, *Biographical Sketches of Loyalists of the American Revolution* . . . (Boston, 1864), *2*, 220, 487.

31. PAC, Port Roseway Associates, 1782–83, Minute Books of Proceedings: "Muster Book of Free Blacks of Birch Town," 1784, pp. 107–22, 172–208.

in particular, had tried to gain possession of the better Birchtown lots, and in July 1784, an "Extraordinary mobb, or Riot" [32] descended upon the community. Hundreds of disbanded white soldiers, still in possession of their arms, had become increasingly unruly when they found that they either could not find work, since the residents of Shelburne preferred to employ free Negroes at lower wages, or that they had to accept work at rates competitive with Negro labor. They directed their anger at the free Negroes of Birchtown who consistently underbid them, and went rampaging through the settlement, pulling down some twenty Negro houses. The government surveyor, Benjamin Marston, who had encouraged the use of Negro laborers and resisted the whites' efforts to acquire their land, had to be given military protection and was spirited away to Halifax. Troops helped to restore order, and Governor John Parr visited Shelburne where, as he reported, he found the public peace greatly disturbed. He asked that a frigate be stationed at the port to avert further incidents and to remain until a vessel might be placed there on a more permanent basis.[33]

Relations between Shelburne and Birchtown did not return to the harmonious ways of the previous year. Shelburne was an insecure base for the settlers, for it was too far from the closely knit political control of Halifax and too near to potential American incursions. The soil proved unyielding, and the low cost of land led to widespread speculation and the alienation of much acreage. By the end of the decade many of the original Loyalist settlers had moved on toward Liverpool, Yarmouth, and Tusket, taking their slaves with them, and numbers of the free Negroes had followed. Increasingly, Shelburne came to depend upon the uneven rum trade with the West Indies, in which the community could not compete with Massachusetts; and when Britain's renewed war with France in the 1790s cut off much of the West Indies from Shelburne's merchants, the town declined steadily.

The physical and economic decline was accompanied by further strains on racial harmony. The government stopped issuing rations in 1787, and several owners freed their slaves rather than provide for them. Two years later the local Overseers of the Poor asked Halifax to free the settlement from a "burden it cannot bear," for the blacks of Birchtown were living "in the most distressing circumstances"; only food from the Overseers had forestalled starvation—food which could not be given another year be-

32. D. C. Harvey, ed., *The Diary of Simeon Perkins, 1780–1789* (Toronto, 1958), p. 238.
33. PANS, *136*, Letter Book: Parr to Sir Charles Douglas, Aug. 31, Sept. 2, 1784; Harry Young Payzant, *People: A Story of the People of Nova Scotia* (Truro, [1935]), pp. 193–94; W[illiam] O. Raymond, "The Founding of Shelburne: Benjamin Marston at Halifax, Shelburne and Miramichi," *Collections of the New Brunswick Historical Society*, no. 8 (1909), pp. 226–35, 240, 265–66.

cause whites, who took priority, were also in need. Persistent rumors that free Negroes were being carried off to sea and sold in the West Indies demoralized the black community,[34] while the legal, local market for slaves was so insecure that at least one was sold for a hundred bushels of potatoes. In 1789 the town fathers passed an ordinance requiring that handbills should be printed warning Negroes against holding their "dances and frolicks" in Shelburne itself; and by the first decade of the new century both Shelburne and Birchtown were depressed villages, with the Negroes increasingly excluded from the former. The once orderly rows of houses and tiny churches in Birchtown had given way, especially after a mass Negro exodus for West Africa in 1792,[35] to roofless buildings, a single church, and holes in the ground that served as shelters against the winter.[36]

The Negro settlements elsewhere had started with hopes less high, and they fell less far. None prospered, but until the second decade of the nineteenth century none seems to have encountered the economic privations and the hardening of the social arteries so clearly evident in Shelburne County. Perhaps the very success of Shelburne in its first months, which encouraged a sense of independence from Halifax, contributed to the decline in interracial harmony. For elsewhere control from Halifax was more clearly and consistently demonstrated from the outset, and the colonial governors, John Parr and John Wentworth, had tried to smooth the way for free Negroes. Perhaps, too, and ironically, the presence in Shelburne County of four intelligent Negro spokesmen—Colonel Stephen Blucke, a mulatto schoolmaster who led the Black Pioneers, Moses Wilkinson and Boston King, Methodist preachers, and David George, a "Very Loud" Baptist minister [37]—sped the decline, for by 1791 each had created a clique which was suspicious of the others. The division between free Birchtown Negroes and slave Shelburne Negroes led the former to assume they were superior to the latter, and the fact that there was only one concentration of free Negro settlement in the county gave discontented white laborers an obvious and highly accessible focus for their frustrations.

Racial relations were better in Annapolis County at first, and there

34. Port Roseway Associates, Minute Books of Proceedings: petition of Overseers of the Poor to the Magistrate, Feb. 3, 1789.

35. See Chapter 3, below, pp. 61–78.

36. *Shelburne Nova-Scotia Packet: And General Advertiser*, July 27, 1786; SPG Archives, Dr. Bray's Associates Minute Books, *3, 405:* July 6, 1807; J. R. Campbell, *A History of the County of Yarmouth, Nova Scotia* (Saint John, 1876), pp. 144–45; "Early Negroes and Slaves," *Journal of Education* (Halifax), 4th ser., *18* (1947), 225–26.

37. Harvey, *Diary of Simeon Perkins*, pp. 232, 320; Smith, "Loyalists at Shelburne," pp. 76–77, which notes that Blucke was well enough recognized as the leading Negro in Birchtown in 1788 to entertain Prince William Henry (later King William IV) at dinner.

were fewer quarrels between Negro factions. Of the 486 grants and warrants for grants of land eventually made to free Negroes in the colony, nearly half were in Annapolis County; there settled the majority of Black Pioneers, who commanded more respect from the whites than any other Negro group could expect to do. There were slaves as well—the muster roll of discharged officers, disbanded soldiers, and Loyalists for June 1784, shows 210 in the area—but they were dispersed more widely than in Shelburne County. They as well as the free Negro settlers moved more quickly into villages away from the major towns, to Wilmont, Granville, Bear River, Sissiboo (later Weymouth), Saint Mary's Bay, and elsewhere. The relatively light concentration of Negroes at Annapolis was balanced by a concentration at Digby and at nearby George Brindley Town, where an early muster roll in May 1784 showed 139 servants. To the north, in King's County, there were 107 servants at Cornwallis, Horton, Parrsborough Strand, and a little later at Pine and Gibson Woods near Kentville. No one community became the focus of both white and slave Negro animosity, as Birchtown did; and there were no incidents of mob violence in the Annapolis Valley.[38]

Still, settlement did not go well anywhere in Nova Scotia, and misunderstandings over the nature and size of the promised grants of land rather than their segregation lay at the root of much of the Negroes' discontent, especially outside Shelburne County. In general, the government of Nova Scotia and, later, of New Brunswick offered a hundred acres of land to every head of a family, with an additional fifty acres for each member of that family, whether adult or child. A married couple with three children —the average free Negro family—might therefore expect to be granted three hundred acres of land. An alternative arrangement offered a town lot of one acre and fifty acres of farmland nearby. Several Negroes apparently were promised more land than this by officers who had no authority in the province; and in fact they received much less, as we have seen.

The situation was especially confusing to the Negroes of the Annapolis Valley. When seventy-four Loyalist Negroes applied for land near Digby in 1785 they received only their town lots, and when ninety-five more Negroes arrived the following year, they received no land at all. At Saint

38. A. W. Savary, *Supplement to the History of the County of Annapolis* (Toronto, 1913), pp. 106–32, in which the muster rolls appear; Arthur Wentworth Hamilton Eaton, *The History of King's County, Nova Scotia, Heart of the Acadian Land* (Salem, Mass., 1910), pp. 144–45, 233–36; Isaiah W. Wilson, *A Geography and History of the County of Digby, Nova Scotia* (Halifax, 1900), pp. 51, 91; Elizabeth R. Coward, *Bridgetown, Nova Scotia: Its History to 1900* (Kentville, 1955), p. 30; PANS, Harriet C. Hart, "History of the County of Guysborough," (unpubl. MS, Windsor, N.S., n.d.), pp. 67, 173, 208–10, 268–70.

John a hundred families were offered full allotments, only to find their land so far from the town lots—nearly eighteen miles—as to make one or the other untenable. Among those who arrived at Annapolis were two former sergeants in the Black Pioneers, Thomas Peters and Murphy Still. Peters had been a slave in North Carolina until he took refuge with the British troops there; he had then served with them, twice being wounded. Although illiterate he was ambitious and intelligent. On behalf of several of the Negroes of Digby, he and Still petitioned Governor Parr in August 1784, asking for an immediate grant of their lands. Parr responded by giving each of the petitioners twenty acres, together with one-acre lots in George Brindley Town, with the two sergeants to receive an additional ten acres. But Peters left for Saint John, where he hoped to get work as a millwright, before Parr's orders could be carried out.[39]

Although in both Annapolis and Shelburne counties some whites did conspire to gain possession of the Negroes' property, on the whole inefficiency and circumstance, not design, led to these retarded and stunted land grants. Indeed, many white settlers faced the same circumstances, for more Loyalists, white and black, arrived than the government had anticipated, and there were not enough trained surveyors to lay out the land promptly. Many settlers came late in the season, and surveys for them were hampered by the encroaching winter. Ironically, it was the Society for the Propagation of the Gospel, which otherwise attempted to help the Negroes by supporting interracial schools, that delayed the grants beyond the first year.

Governor Parr was not to blame. He had instructed the Deputy Surveyor, Thomas Millidge, to place the blacks in an "advantageous Situation," and Millidge had tried to do so. After laying out the twenty acres each for Peters's petitioners, Millidge was informed by the Surveyor-General, Charles Morris, that he had used some of the public reserves for Digby, especially glebe and school land. The Society for the Propagation of the Gospel was pressing for the return of all glebe land throughout the province; but Morris did not wish to see the Negroes suffer for Millidge's error, and he advised that he should try to assign glebe and school lots elsewhere to avoid a fresh survey. Millidge also wrote that he hoped the Negroes might be permitted to remain; and in time, and with modest adjustment, they took up their town lots. In 1788 the Surveyor-General laid

39. PANS, *359,* "Old Township and Loyalist Settlements, 1759," no. 65: Peters and Still to Parr, Aug. 21, 1784; *96,* no. 57: Leonard to John Greben, Oct. 29, 1778; PANS, Charles Morris Letterbooks, 1783–89, and Land Papers; CO217/63: Peters (signed with his mark) encl. in Henry Dundas to Parr, Aug. 6, 1791; NBM, A31: "His Majesty's Battalion of Provincial Chasseurs . . . ," pp. 29–31; Ira M. Sutherland, "Clements Township—Its History and Its People, 1783–1870" (M.A. thesis, Acadia Univ., 1957), pp. 58–63.

out additional land for other free Negroes, especially on the Bear River near Clements, where he was able to use properties that had been abanonded by white settlers who had returned to the United States. The following year he put a road through to the "Ethiopian bretherin," and 8,100 acres passed to 149 Loyalist Negroes and to twenty-three Black Pioneers. One hundred and thirty of these Negroes were given fifty acres each, as promised, and their schoolmaster and spokesman, Joseph Leonard, who had waited four years, received twice that. But several failed to take up the land, and rather than see the lots remain unimproved, Parr determined to grant them to the poor of either race in the community.[40]

Much of this the Negroes did not understand. They only knew that they had waited up to five years to be given the land promised to them; that during the winters they had been refused supplies unless they worked on the roads, a ruling seldom exacted against equally fractious whites; that somehow the land first laid out for them had, in part, been spirited away to be used by the whites of Digby; and that if they left their land, it did not remain theirs, open to them should they decide to return, but reverted to the colony. Some, such as Joseph Leonard, understood enough to know that the government was being bumblingly fair with them; most, led by the peripatetic Peters, who had returned, remained suspicious of the whites and fearful for their land. Some, after all, had received none.

Across the Bay of Fundy from Digby there were other black settlers. In 1784 New Brunswick became a separate colony. In the meantime, Black Pioneers had begun to arrive, formed three companies, and moved onto fifty-acre lots along the Nerepis River, at Milkish, and at Oroquaco. A muster at Saint John, then called Parrtown, showed 441 servants, mostly slave Negroes, that year. James Mayes, a Loyalist from New York, brought slaves to the Otnabog, while others were taken to Westfield, Carleton, Loch Lomond (back of Parrtown), and St. Andrews. Small groups of settlers with slaves spread out to Woodstock, well up the Saint John River, to Hopewell on the Petitcodiac, to Gagetown and Hampstead, and around Fort Beasejour. In the 1820s a slave was taken to Grand Manan Island as well.[41]

40. CO217/63: Richard Bulkeley to Dundas, March 19, 1792, with copy of "Enquiry into the Complaint of Thomas Peters a Black Man," 1791, with extracts or copies from Morris to Millidge, July 26, 1785, and Feb. 4, 1789; of Millidge to Morris, May 18, 1789; of Thomas Williams to Edward Brudenell, Dec. 11, 1784; of Solomon Hamilton and Leonard to Parr, n.d.; and of Millidge to Parr, March n.d., 1785, and reply, April 9, 1785. See also PANS, *419*, no. 3: Alexander Howe to Bulkeley, Oct. 28, 1791; and Christopher H. Fyfe, "Thomas Peters: History and Legend," *Sierra Leone Studies*, n.s., *1* (1953), 4–13.

41. W[illiam] O. Raymond, "The Negro in New Brunswick," *Neith, 1* (1903), 27–33; NBM, Misc. Collection, F53: John Coffin to A. Flewelling, and Jonathan Sher-

To Fredericton, well up the wide intervals of the Saint John River, came a number of distinguished Virginia and Maryland Loyalists who hoped to preserve slavery and the manner of life based upon it. Beverley Robinson, son of a speaker of the House of Burgesses of Virginia and a member of the first Council in New Brunswick, had many fewer slaves than the three hundred with which local legend credits him, but he was well provided for. Stair Agnew, Jacob Ellegood, and two Loyalists from New Jersey—Isaac Allen, a former judge of the New Jersey supreme court who at first settled in Nova Scotia, and the Reverend Jonathan Odell, who became the new colony's provincial secretary—all owned slaves in substantial numbers. Agnew, a Virginian, was particularly vocal in his pro-slavery arguments.

On the whole the Negroes' conditions were not as good in New Brunswick as in Nova Scotia, although for a period of time a shortage of labor meant high wages for the free Negroes. In Nova Scotia the colonial governors between 1782 and 1808, Parr and John Wentworth, sympathized with the Negroes' plight, while the ruling oligarchy at Fredericton was less interested. By 1800 Nova Scotia had moved against slavery as an institution by judicial means, when legal opinion in New Brunswick was still poised on indecision. Not surprisingly, when in 1791 they were offered an opportunity to sail for Africa, 222 Negroes from Fredericton, Saint John, and the river valleys responded positively.[42]

Only on Isle St. Jean—which in 1799 became Prince Edward Island—was slavery genuinely benign, and the number of slaves in the colony was very small. The concession granted by France to the Count de St. Pierre in 1719 included the right to hold slaves on the island, but there is no record of any Negroes there until the coming of the Loyalists. The first muster of disbanded officers, soldiers, and Loyalists, in June 1784, showed sixteen Negro servants. Later in the year other Loyalists moved on to

wood to same, June 1, 3, 1798; "Muster roll of a detachment of the Blk. Pioners for 61 days"; diary of Colonel Henry Nase, typescript MS; and James Mayes Papers: Land Grants and Petitions, family chart; Woodstock, N.B., Public Library: petitions of Richard Carankspoon and R. C. Wheeler; *Saint John Royal Gazette and New Brunswick Advertiser*, Aug. 20, 1799; James Hannay, *History of New Brunswick* (S⸱ ⸱nt John, 1909), *1*, 344–45; Grace H. Mowat, *The Diverting History of a Loyalist Town* (St. Andrews, N.B., 1932), pp. 23, 76; L. K. Ingersoll, Grand Manan Historical Society, to author, Aug. 16, 1965. On Raymond family interests in Africans, see PANS, Mrs. Andrew Lee, "A Memoir of the First Nova Scotian who went as a missionary to Foreign Lands," unpublished typescript.

42. *Fredericton New Brunswick Royal Gazette*, July 10, 1816; *Halifax Royal Gazette*, Sept. 7, 1790, March 18, April 1, 8, 15, 1802; NBM, Scrap Book Cb.: "Negroes—In the Maritimes"; New Brunswick Legislative Library, Fredericton: file of clippings from *Saint John Telegraph Journal*, 1937, no. 86; W. Stewart MacNutt, *New Brunswick, A History: 1784–1867* (Toronto, 1963), pp. 82–84.

Bedeque Bay. Among them was William Schurman, from New York, who purchased eleven thousand acres of land and in time became one of the colony's leading merchants and general traders. Schurman owned two slaves, brought them up in the Presbyterian church, remembered them in his will, and freed one to go to the United States. At Little York, Colonel Joseph Robinson from North Carolina settled with a number of Negro servants, all in fact slaves; one of them, who lived to be a hundred and five, was treated with special kindness for having rescued the colonel's wife and children from drowning. The Lieutenant-Governor, Edmund Fanning, a former judge of the supreme court of North Carolina, owned two slaves, and to one he gave both liberty and a farm. Other slaves were brought in from Rhode Island and Massachusetts to Summerside, Prince Town, and Charlottetown, the capital. Not more than five or six slaves appear to have been sold, and most seem to have been baptized and permitted formal marriage.[43]

Slavery received its only legal recognition on the island because of these baptisms. Fearing that Christian slaves might consider themselves free, or that white Christians might so construe baptism, the legislature passed an act in 1781 declaring that baptism of slaves would not exempt them from bondage. Although some casuists argued that slavery had no legal foundation in Prince Edward Island, members of the General Assembly recognized that, while it did not derive its foundation from this act, the act recognized that such a foundation existed; and in 1825, admitting that "Slavery is sanctioned and permitted within this Island" although "entirely in variance with the laws of England, and the Freedom of the Country," the Assembly repealed the act, with the clear intention of abolishing slavery. By this time few slaves can have remained in any case, for most of the Negroes now lived in shacks in Charlottetown, where they worked as occasional laborers, chimney sweeps, puntsmen, and market gardeners.[44]

There is no way to know how many of the several thousand Negroes in the Maritime provinces were slave and how many were free. The tendency to use the terms *servant* and *slave* interchangeably reflected a growing sensitivity to slavery as a moral and economic issue; it also has led to much

43. Ada Macleod, "Some Loyalists of Prince Edward Island," *Dalhousie Review, 10* (1930), 320; Smith, "Slave in Canada," 68–71, quoting bills of sale; Hallam, "Slavery," p. 7. The memorandum book referred to in Smith (p. 70) and the *Charlottetown Weekly Examiner* (Feb. 11, 1881) cannot be found in the Prince Edward Island Archives or in the Charlottetown Public Library.

44. *The Acts of the General Assembly of Prince Edward Island . . . 1773 . . . 1834* (Charlottetown, 1834), pp. 76, 372; Alexander Bannerman Warburton, *A History of Prince Edward Island* (Saint John, 1923), pp. 197, 368; William Renwick Riddell, "The Baptism of Slaves in Prince Edward Island," *JNH, 6* (1921), 307–09.

confusion. Most "servants" were slaves, but some were free Negro children who were bound out by their parents, and some were adults who entered white households as true servants after failure on their farms. While many baptismal records, wills, receipts, and advertisements for auctions, sales, and runaway slaves have survived, far more data would be needed to go beyond an informed guess. Popular and antiquarian literature relating to the Loyalists is filled with ill-judged estimates about the Negro population, and any exact conclusions relating to numbers are suspect. The data do provide a sufficiently diverse record, however, to make possible generalizations relating to the condition of the Negro during the period of British slavery.

White response to the new influx of Negroes at the end of the Revolutionary War changed the uniform and stable pattern of Negro slavery which the British in Quebec had inherited from the French nearly twenty-five years earlier into a variety of legal, economic, and social experiences. No longer were most of the slaves baptized as Roman Catholics, no longer did most work in houses as domestic servants, no longer were they owned chiefly by merchants and government officials, no longer were the majority of Negroes resident in towns and cities, and after 1793 a single code of laws no longer covered their legal position. Since Vermont, Massachusetts, Rhode Island, Pennsylvania, and within certain limits Connecticut, had abolished slavery by 1784, and it was prohibited in the Northwest Territory after 1787,[45] Negro slaves to the north had an additional sieve through which they could move, an extended area where, temporarily at least, they might seek out freedom. The nature of slavery in British North America thus changed in subtle but perceptible ways after 1783.

Perhaps most significant is the fact that the post-1783 Negroes brought a greater variety of useful skills to the frontier communities than the pre-revolutionary slaves ever provided. Several Negroes, slave and free, had trades, especially as millwrights, blacksmiths, sawyers, caulkers, and coopers. Others were printers: as early as 1766 William Brown, the founder of the *Quebec Gazette,* had wanted a Negro slave as his assistant, and ultimately he acquired three. John Neilson, his successor, William Moore, the printer of the *Quebec Herald,* and Fleury Mesplet, who began the first French newspaper in Montreal, kept slaves to help in their printing shops. Tavern-keepers used slaves as house servants, to make butter, and to wait on table. In Halifax domestics dressed in livery as door attendants, delivered notes, carried tiny boxes of charcoal to church or the

45. See William Renwick Riddell, "Additional Notes on Slavery," *JNH, 17* (1932), 368–73, and Arthur Zilversmit, *The First Emancipation: The Abolition of Slavery in the North* (Chicago, 1967).

theatre so that their mistresses' feet might be warm, and looked after the carriage horses. In Saint John, Negroes carved gates and fences, drove carriages, and a free man, Peter Thomson, kept a tavern there in 1797. In Birchtown, several Negroes went to sea.[46] In Upper Canada in 1799 Negroes built roads for the Loyalists, and at least one company had a black foreman. Two Negroes were contractors: Jack Mosee and William Willis undertook to open a road from Yonge Street, York, westward through "the Pinery"; and although at first the senior surveyor of the province found the road too narrow and improperly cleared, in time it was completed satisfactorily.[47] The skills the Loyalists' slaves possessed are best illustrated by those belonging to Sir John Wentworth of Halifax, after 1783 Surveyor-General of the King's Woods in North America. In February 1784, two weeks after having all of his slaves baptized, Wentworth sent nineteen of them to a kinsman in Surinam. One was a master sawyer, another a rough carpenter, a third an axeman, and three more were sawyers. Six women and four children accompanied the group, with two more adults to follow. None were field hands and but one male was a domestic.[48]

Increasingly Negroes apprenticed themselves to their former masters in order to gain training and yet have some guarantee of continued provisions. In areas where slavery was unpopular—around Pictou, in Nova Scotia, or in portions of Upper Canada—a slave might be freed upon agreeing to remain with the former owner as a paid servant. At Thurlow, in Upper Canada, as late as 1824 a mulatto boy was transferred to a new owner upon condition that he would "well instruct and use him" as an apprentice for ten years. In Nova Scotia a number of the Black Pioneers who were unable to scrabble a living from their bleak lands virtually became sharecroppers or tenant farmers for their white Loyalist neighbors.[49]

46. Dr. Bray's Associates Minute Books, *3:* Nov. 1, 1802; NBM, Thomson Family Papers: license to Peter Thomson, Oct. 1, 1797; *Halifax Acadian Recorder,* Jan. 25, 1919; Trudel, *L'esclavage,* pp. 107, 148, 320; Neilson, "Slavery in Old Canada," pp. 31–34. See also Francis Cleary, "Notes on the Early History of the County of Essex," and A. Philippe E. Panet, "The Labadie Family in the County of Essex, Ont.," Essex Hist. Soc., *Papers and Addresses, 1* (1913), 13 and 49, respectively.

47. OPA, Crown Land Papers, General Correspondence: agreement between Mosee, Willis, and Thomas Ridout, Feb. 2, 1799, and between Parker Mills and David William Smith, Surveyor-General, Jan. 13, 1799, and Reports, *3, 5;* Ontario Department of Lands and Forests, History Branch, Survey Records, Letters Received: W. Chewett, Senior Surveyor, to Smith, Feb. 11, June 22, 1799, pp. 396, 621.

48. PANS, *49,* 25–27.

49. See, for example, Lennox and Addington Historical Society Archives, Napanee, Ont.: assignment of mulatto Tom from Eli Keeler to William Bell, pp. 11, 654–58; "Copies of Original Documents from the Collection of the Society," Lennox and Addington Historical Society, *Papers and Records, 2* (1910), 41–42; *Fredericton*

Slaves appear to have changed hands somewhat more often among Loyalists than among the earlier French owners, possibly because for most of the period there was a buyer's market. Slave values dropped sharply in the Maritime Provinces between the late 1770s, when a young boy was worth £ 50 in Truro, and the late 1780s, when a man and a horse together were worth but £ 40 in the same community.[50] By the 1790s, £ 20 was a reasonable price for a man in Nova Scotia, and in New Brunswick prices appear to have been somewhat lower. Rewards offered for runaway slaves also declined from five guineas and twenty dollars in the 1770s to forty shillings and five to seven dollars in the 1790s.[51]

In the Canadas prices remained somewhat more stable under the British. During the French regime, levels had fluctuated widely: in 1743 Negro women sold for 800 livres and in 1749 one sold for 1,000 livres, while at the same time men cost 400 livres in 1748 and 500 livres in 1751. In 1757, a Negro boy in his prime brought 1,192 livres in two installments, but this was most unusual. If one assumes a livre to be worth 13.33 pence sterling, slaves in New France thus sold for less than £ 20 and for up to nearly £ 60. In Lower Canada in the 1790s slaves of similar ages sold for sums from £ 25 to £ 100, and once for £ 213, with £ 50 as a normal figure. In Upper Canada, on the other hand, prices generally were lower, and from 1800 on they fell steadily, to the last recorded sale in 1806. Slaves brought in across the international frontier cost a bit more, and in 1785, 1801, and as late as 1832 (illegally) sales were recorded of American slaves at values ranging from £ 43 to £ 60 each. Male slaves almost always were worth more than female, for they were more likely to be used in heavy or skilled work, while under the French, women had cost more since even the males were domestics, and women were more suited to the tasks demanded of them in the home.[52]

Royal Gazette, Feb. 28, 1786; George MacLaren, *The Pictou Book* (New Glasgow, N.S., 1954), p. 22.

50. George Patterson, *A History of the County of Pictou, Nova Scotia,* reprint ed. (Pictou, 1916), pp. 70–71; John Michael Murphy, *A Story of the Settlement of the Townships of Truro, Onslow, and Londonderry* [Truro, 1960], p. 120; Truro, N.S., Colchester Registry Office: Register Book, *1,* 468, Sept. 29, 1779; J. H. Meacham & Co., *Illustrated Historical Atlas of Pictou County Nova Scotia* (Philadelphia, 1879), p. 8.

51. *Halifax Journal,* Aug. 8, 22, 1799, Nov. 17, 1817; *York Upper Canada Gazette,* July 4, 11, Aug. 17, 1793, Jan. 18, 1797, Dec. 20, 1800; *Fredericton Royal Gazette,* May 16, 1786, Aug. 20, 1799; *Halifax Nova-Scotia Gazette,* Sept. 5, 1780; *Halifax Royal Gazette,* Sept. 7, 1790, July 3, 1792, Dec. 2, 1802; *Halifax Weekly Chronicle,* May 7, 1791, Feb. 8, 1794; *Quebec Gazette,* Dec. 14, 1789; *Niagara Upper Canada Guardian,* April 14, 1810; NBM, Scrap Book Cb. "Slavery."

52. For examples, see *Halifax Nova-Scotia Gazette,* March 21, 1775; *Halifax Royal Gazette,* June 24, July 1, 1800; *York Upper Canada Gazette,* Oct. 4, 11, 21, 28,

Where one may trace successive sales of the same slave, one finds that the price usually fell slightly. A mulatto girl, bought by Hector-Theophile Cramahé, English-born Lieutenant-Governor of Quebec, in 1778 for £ 50 Quebec money, was sold the following year to a captain in the navy, together with clothes and linen, for 45 livres, a loss of the clothes, linens, and something more than one livre. Sarah, a domestic, had cost her original owner £ 65, and in 1785 he was willing to sell for that or the equivalent in furs; he sold her for somewhat less, apparently, and later the same year Sarah was sold again for £ 36. In 1789 she was sold twice: for £ 36 and for £ 40.

But judgments about the gradual decline in slave values must be tempered by many considerations. Any close comparison between the price of slaves before 1763 and afterwards would be of small value, for conditions were quite different, the expectations held by French and British colonists, and by the Mother Countries, varied widely, and the source of supply for New France was limited. Comparisons between 1763 and after 1783 also are of little use, for the period is too short, the economy of all the colonies was disrupted too much by the war and subsequent dislocation of people and property, and to the west the danger of escape by slaves into Indian country was believed to be too great to give any consistency to prices. Even in times of relative stability, and between areas of like economic and social needs, comparisons are misleading, for at one time sturdy women who might mother a substantial number of slaves would be worth more than males, while at another a strong-armed boy of fifteen was of greater value than a man of thirty.

Of greatest importance in determining price was the fact that the obvious personal differences between slaves would be known intimately in small Loyalist communities with comparatively few owners. If Elizabeth Russell, the sister of the administrator of the goverment of Upper Canada, Peter Russell, knew that his slaves Pompadore and Milly were "adicted to pilfering and lying" and were "very indolent and dirty," so did most of the

---

1797, Dec. 20, 27, 1800, Feb. 22, 1806; *Saint John Royal Gazette*, April 11, 1786; Harold A. Innis, ed., *The Diary of Simeon Perkins, 1766–1780* (Toronto, 1948), pp. 143, 158, 164, for March 7, July 12, Aug. 29, 1777; New Brunswick Legislative Library: indenture, George Harding, July 8, 1797; PAC, Reynolds Family Papers, no. 48: bill of sale, Feb. 4, 1801; Norfolk Historical Society, Simcoe, Ont.: Thomas Cummings to Thomas Welch, Feb. 3, 1804; OPA: deed of sale, Henry Finkle to Joseph Allan, June 7, 1798; *BRH, 2* (1896), 186 and *33* (1927), 584; [Thomas Beamish Akins], "History of Halifax City," *Collections of the Nova Scotia Historical Society for the Years 1892–94* (1895), 8, 98; Smith, "Slave in Canada," pp. 13–16, 26, 54, 63–66; Riddell, "Slave in Nouvelle-France," pp. 323–24, 327–30; and E.-Z. Massicotte, "L'esclavage au Canada sous le regime anglais," *BRH, 24* (1918), 344–47. See Note on Currency, p. 60.

residents of York. Further, Pompadore was "a thief & every thing that is bad." Peter's slave Peggy was known to be troublesome and a corrupter of children, and when in 1806 Russell advertised her as a "tolerable Cook and washerwoman [who] perfectly understands making Soap and Candles," readers also knew that Peggy was so despised by Elizabeth that she was not permitted inside the Russell household.[53] At Windsor, in Nova Scotia, the slave of John Palmer, one Mintur, was famous throughout the district for his strength, and when sold he brought £ 100, while in Upper Canada a Negro employee of William Dummer Powell was equally famous for his tendency to run away and enlist in the army when drunk, forcing his master to buy his freedom.[54] If a slave at Trois Rivières, when thrown out of the house at one door for a violent temper, would "come in by another snapping her fingers" at her master, her idiosyncracies were well-known.[55] The market was not sufficiently extended to make it possible for slaves to be sold to purchasers ignorant of their character, health, and work habits.

On the whole, slaves appear to have been well treated, even though many were not domestics. Their small number eliminated the need for overseers, the brutalizing effects of slave breeding, and controls arising from fears of armed Negro rebellion. In the tiny communities news of mistreatment traveled quickly. Punishments were tempered by the law and by good sense: when a Negro woman hid stolen butter under her hat, her white owner was satisfied to see her writhe with embarrassment as the butter slowly melted down her face in an overheated room. In 1792 William Dummer Powell, as judge of the Court of Common Pleas of Upper Canada, sitting at L'Assomption (now Sandwich), sentenced a Negro to death for burglary; but in 1795, when a Negro boy of seventeen was convicted of the same offense and was sentenced to death by a jury, Powell appealed to the lieutenant-governor to show leniency because of the age of the offender and the undesirable effects of slavery upon his character. When William Jarvis, provincial secretary of Upper Canada, caught two of his slaves stealing gold and silver from his desk, they were tried in court with the full protection of the law rather than being summarily punished

53. Russell Papers: Peter Russell to Mathew Elliott, Sept. 19, and reply, Oct. 7, 1901; OPA, Joseph Willcocks Diary: Feb. 20, 1801; TPL, Elizabeth Russell Diary: Jan. 18, 27, Feb. 18, 1806; *Upper Canada Gazette,* Feb. 19, 22, 1806.

54. *Cornwall* (Ont.) *Daily Standard-Freeholder,* Dec. 8, 1949; Riddell, "Slave in Canada," p. 322, n. 13; Charles William Vernon, "The Deed of a Sale of a Slave Sold at Windsor, N.S., in 1799," *Acadiensis, 3* (1903), 253–54. In February, 1769, a Quebec tavern-keeper, Miles Prenties, advertized a child of nine months for sale, together with his mother; in June he advertized again, still giving the child's age as nine months, but prospective purchasers no doubt recognized that Prenties was being forgetful (*Quebec Gazette,* Feb. 23, June 15, 1769).

55. Philippe Aubert de Gaspé, *Les anciens canadiens* (Quebec, 1863), p. 292.

by their owner. One of the earliest murder trials in New Brunswick was of a Negro woman who killed her husband by thrusting a fork into his temple; she, too, was given the full benefit of the law and, when convicted, was branded rather than executed. During the War of 1812 refugee Negroes slaughtered unprotected cattle to sell the meat to the army, and although the death penalty was prescribed for the offense, none were executed. The ultimate sentence was given against one Jack York, convicted of the rape of one Ruth Stufflemine in 1800—and he escaped. In 1791 in Sydney, Cape Breton Island, a white man struck down a Negro who was trying to force his way into a public dance, and the killer was ostracized until, after a full trial, he was acquitted on the ground of self-defense.[56]

Incidents of genuinely harsh treatment were sufficiently uncommon to become focal points for local gossip and legend. Jupiter, a slave belonging to the Russells, was remembered for being trussed up in a storehouse for a day; near Bath, in Upper Canada, a tree to which a slave had been tied and beaten became a local landmark. At Annapolis a slave died from the effects of a whipping. In Windsor, Nova Scotia, a master killed his slave boy with a hammer, and in Truro an owner cut a hole in the lobe of a recaptured slave's ear and, after passing a knotted whiplash through the hole, dragged the slave to death. Neither master appears to have been punished although both were condemned by their communities. Matthew Elliott fixed a lashing ring to a tree in front of his house in Sandwich, apparently for psychological effect since few if any slaves appear to have been flogged upon it. One slave who was punished in this way belonged to William Brown, the printer, who in 1777 paid five shillings to have the public executioner whip his slave boy Joe in Quebec's market place.[57]

There is far more positive evidence of humane treatment. The slaves belonging to James Law, a trader at Fort Cumberland after 1761, were so well cared for, the phrase "as proud as Law's niggers" became a local

56. PAC, William Dummer Powell Papers, *1*, 606–08: Powell to Simcoe, n.d., 1795; PAC, Misc. Docs., *16*, pt. 2: Court of Common Pleas, March 18, 1788, July 19, 1793, Dec. 18, 1799, Sept. 22, 1800; NBM, Scrap Book, Cb. "Slavery," 1784, 1801; William Renwick Riddell, *La Rochefoucault-Liancourt's Travels in Canada*, whole no., *Thirteenth Report of the Bureau of Archives for the Province of Ontario, 1916* (Toronto, 1917), p. 154.

57. *Fredericton Gleaner*, June 1, 1926; *Windsor Daily Star*, July 30, 1948; Smith, "Slave in Canada," pp. 34, 48, 76–77; Riddell, "Slave in Canada," pp. 334–35; Neilson, "Slavery in Old Canada," p. 33; Jesse Edgar Middleton and Fred Landon, *The Province of Ontario—A History* (Toronto, 1927), *1*, 101; James Edmund Jones, *Pioneer Crimes and Punishments in Toronto and the Home District* (Toronto, 1924), pp. 11–12; Henry Scadding, *Toronto of Old: Collections and Recollections* (Toronto, 1878), p. 292; Silas Farmer, *The History of Detroit and Michigan or the Metropolis Illustrated . . .* (Detroit, 1884), p. 345.

proverb. Peter Russell paid a schoolmaster to teach the son of one of his slaves to read and write, and his account book shows that he provided well for his slaves; even to the notorious Peggy he gave an allowance of four shillings a week and paid her jail fees more than once.[58] Robert I. Dey Gray, Solicitor-General of Upper Canada, bought the freedom of the mulatto mother of one of his slaves in Albany for fifty dollars and brought her to live with his family; in his will he freed his woman servant and her children and left a trust fund of £ 1,200 for her while giving two hundred acres of land and £ 50 to her two sons. Isaac Bennett, in his will of 1803, provided that his two slave boys should be educated and set free. Frederick Devoue of Annapolis left his slave one hundred acres of land. The owner of the *St. John's Royal Gazette* in Newfoundland, by his will, gave his slave her freedom and provided that her children would become free at twenty-one. The slaves of Henry Denny Denson were attended by the family doctor and received gifts at Christmas. In 1790 Joseph Fairbanks of Halifax left his Negro domestic five pounds annually for life, and Edward Barron of Cumberland County, Nova Scotia, awarded two cows, six ewes, and freedom to his slave. Joshua F. de St. Croix of Granville bound his sons to pay his servant £ 10 yearly for life, while Stephen Reed of Amherst required his heirs to care for all of his slaves, freed by his will. When Henry Lewis, a slave belonging to William Jarvis, wrote to his master that he wished to purchase his freedom, he added that he had lived as well in Jarvis's house as a man could wish; Jarvis agreed to the sale.[59] In 1793 Peter Thomson, then a slave belonging to Charles McPherson of Saint John, purchased his freedom for £ 30, and when he died in debt from his tavern five years later, McPherson was one of two guarantors for those debts.[60] There are only two records of husband and wife being separated for sale, and but one instance of a young child being sold apart from his parents.

58. Russell Papers: account book, Sept. 4, 11, Oct. 16, 17, Nov. 2, 19, Dec. 17, 1803, Jan. 20, Feb. 26, July 10, Nov. 6, 14, 21, 1804; Russell to Elliott, Sept. 19, 1801, and replies, Oct. 7, 1801, Jan. 2, 1802.

59. Ibid.: Russell to William Cooper, April 28, 1799; TPL: bill from Cooper to Russell, Oct. 28, 1799; Elizabeth Russell Diary, Jan. 6, 1808; TPL, William Jarvis Papers, Misc., B55: Lewis to Jarvis, May 3, 1798; PAC, Misc. Docs., *21*, no. 1; PANS, F. W. Harris, "The Negro Population of the County of Annapolis," unpubl. paper (1920), pp. 7–10; J. F. Pringle, *Lunenburgh or the Old Eastern District* . . . (Cornwall, Ont., 1890), pp. 318–25; Smith, "Slave in Canada," pp. 16, 48–49, 64, 66–67, 84–85, 88–89; Neilson, "Slavery in Old Canada," p. 35; Riddell, "Slave in Canada," pp. 322–33, n. 13; Duncanson, *Falmouth*, p. 33; Margaret Janet Hart, *Janet Fisher Archibald* . . . (Victoria, B.C., 1934), pp. 79–82; Joseph R. Smallwood, ed., *The Book of Newfoundland* (St. John, 1937), 2, 235–36.

60. Thomson Family Papers: certificate, March 27, 1793, and warrant, June 10, 1820.

If owners appear to have used their slaves well, they used them nonetheless, for the slaves continued to die young, as parish records show, and to yearn for freedom, as advertisements for runaways demonstrate. Most wills treated them purely as property, together with furniture, cattle, and land. If the Reverend James Scovil, rector of Kingston, New Brunswick, provided in his will of 1804 that his slave boys, then twelve and nine, should be freed when they were twenty-six, he knew that the courts of the province had begun to move against slavery. If Jarvis agreed to sell Lewis his freedom, he was not unmindful of the fact that Lewis was writing from the comparative safety of Schenectady, New York, to which he had fled, and that a promise of repayment was better than recriminations and no money.[61] If Russell treated his slaves with kindness, he also appears to have tried to make one, even after giving him his freedom, stand as a proxy purchaser of land for him in order to widen the Russell holdings.[62] In Nova Scotia many slave-owners gave freedom shortly before the government's food rations were to end, for they felt that slaves of advanced age could not do enough work to justify their keep, and more than one such freed Negro had to ask his master to take him back. As one wise old man remarked to his owner when offered his freedom, "Master, you eated me when I was meat, and now you must pick me when I'm bone." [63]

The consolations of religion continued to help ease the burdens of being meat and bone. Most of the Loyalist Negroes, if communicants of any church, were Baptists, Methodists, or Anglicans, and missionaries of all three groups worked among them. A few Negroes were Presbyterians and Roman Catholics when they arrived, and the Anglicans and Catholics won a small number of converts. The Negroes preferred to follow black preachers, nearly all of whom were from the dissenting groups, however. Although slaves had attended Presbyterian and Anglican churches often before the Loyalists arrived, not until this mass migration directed attention to their spiritual needs did even the dissenting groups actively begin to proselytize among Negroes. The Anglican Church also welcomed them at first. In 1794 the vestrymen of Christ's Church, Fredericton, resolved that a wall seat in the North Gallery of the church should be allotted to "servants & people of colour," noting no distinction between the races while

61. PAC, "Individuals," *6:* Richard Norton Wilkinson, will, April 28, 1804; PAC, Misc. Docs., *30,* no. 2: will of Burger Huycke, n.d. 1787; Osgoode Hall, Toronto, Surrogate Court, Register A, pp. 3–12, 25–28: wills of Neil McLean, Oct. 2, 1795, Henry Ford, June 2, 1796 (probate), John Lawrence, March 29, 1798; Séguin, "L'esclavage dans la presqu'ile," p. 93; NBM, Extracts of King's County Wills, pp. 3, 24: n.d., 1804 and March 8, 1809.

62. The record on this point is not clear. See TPL, Minutes of Town Meetings [York], and Lists of Inhabitants: 1801, [p. 13].

63. Quoted in Smith, "Slave in Canada," p. 89.

clearly implying that most blacks were under servitude. In 1815, however, the vestrymen decided that a partition should be put across the seat to separate white from black, presumably because by then the majority of Negroes no longer were slaves or servants.[64]

The owners now came from all religions too. In the Midland district of Upper Canada, Methodists and Presbyterians kept slaves, and between 1791 and 1805 the register of the tiny church at Bath showed five baptisms. On the Bay of Quinté an Episcopal minister owned four slaves, and at Truro in Nova Scotia the Presbyterian pastor owned two, as did the minister at Onslow. The register for the Parish of Fredericton shows seven Negro baptisms in 1816–17, while the parish registers of baptism, marriage, and burial for Saint Paul's Church in Halifax contain several references to slave and free Negroes. In 1781 the Reverend John Breynton there wrote that he had baptized forty Negroes. Traveling missionaries from the Society for the Propagation of the Gospel performed baptismal and marriage rites throughout the Maritimes, charging Negroes half the usual fee for the service. In Lower Canada, Roman Catholic baptisms continued, and in Tracadie, Nova Scotia, a school was established in 1788 with SPG money, partially to offset the fact that Negroes were leaning toward the Catholicism of their French-speaking neighbors, a tendency that grew early in the next century.[65]

The Quakers of Nova Scotia alone among religious sects refused to hold slaves, although Thomas Dorland, a Quaker in Upper Canada, owned several. Those Friends who settled at Beaver Harbour, between the rivers Saint John and Passamaquoddy, signed an agreement before leaving New York late in 1783 that no slave master would be admitted, but this anti-slavery community failed after it was swept by fire in 1790. At Shelburne, Granville, Digby, and Saint John, Quakers tried to aid the indigent Negroes in their midst, and for five years Friends in Britain sent salt, clothing, and other provisions to the "Poor Blacks." [66]

64. Christ's Church rectory office, Vestry Minutes, Oct. 3, 1794, Jan. 31, 1815.

65. Christ's Church, Fredericton, rectory office: Register of baptisms in the Parish of Fredericton in the County of York, 1816–62: pp. 2–4, 8, 125–26; NBM, A-90: Gagetown Baptismal Register; Rawlyk, "Guysborough," p. 30; SPG microfilms, reel A-184: George Pidgeon to William Morice, July 22, 1800, Sept. 3, 1804, and Journal, *29*, 65, 229; Reginald V. Harris, *The Church of Saint Paul in Halifax, Nova Scotia: 1749–1949* (Toronto, 1949), pp. 63–65, 92, 185; A. H. Young, ed., *The Parish Register of Kingston Upper Canada 1785–1811* (Kingston, Ont., 1921), pp. 154–55, 157–60; *Montreal La Presse,* Jan. 11, 1947; "A Register of Baptisms for the Township of Fredericksburgh," OHS, *Papers and Records, 1* (1899), 36, 39, 43, 53; "Rev. John Langhorn's Records, 1787–1813—Burials," p. 63; "Marriage Register of Stephen Conger, J. P. Hollowell," p. 111.

66. Friends' House, London, Letters to and from Philadelphia: *1*, 301–02, Nov. 20, 1788, June 10, 1789; NBM, Pennfield Record Book; Nathaniel Banks, *The*

The more effective religious leadership came from some of the Negro divines, who not only preached the gospel and attempted to heal the sick but who were social activists as well. The most energetic of these leaders was the fiery Negro Baptist of Shelburne, David George.[67] A Virginian-born former slave who had escaped to live with the Creek Indians, George had found himself in the God of the Baptists and had learned to read. He was among the Negroes who were transported as free from Charleston. At first he preached to interracial groups in Shelburne; and although several whites and Stephen Blucke's Anglican blacks suggested that he should confine himself and his sermons—which were both loud and religiously obnoxious to the Anglicans—to the forest, he built a house on nearby land lent him by a white he had known in Savannah. Governor Parr gave him a quarter of an acre, and on this he and four Baptist converts opened their first church.

At first George was far less concerned for his race than for his faith. However, when he attempted to baptize one William Holmes, a white man who wished to become a Baptist, Holmes's sister resisted violently, and whether from racial or religious animosities, a body of disbanded and unemployed soldiers descended upon George's house in Shelburne, tipped it over, and attempted to burn his church. Beaten severely and driven into the nearby swamp, George slipped back to Shelburne, found his family, and took them away to Birchtown. There he ran afoul of Blucke again, and in a few weeks he was forced to return to Shelburne, where he found his former church had become a tavern. Turning to itinerant preaching, he addressed mixed congregations in Saint John, Fredericton, Horton, and Liverpool; and he nearly lost both legs when caught in a late spring snow-storm. Although he won many converts, by 1791 he seems to have concluded that he should speak for his race as well as for his religion, and he was among those who organized immigrants to go to West Africa when the opportunity was offered.

Life of the Rev. Freeborn Garrettson . . . , 5th ed. (New York [1840?]), p. 161; Donna Gallant, "Early Settlers in South-Western New Brunswick" (B.A. honors thesis, Mount Allison Univ., 1959), p. 56; Smith, "Slave in Canada," pp. 26–28; Wesley James Vesey, "Freeborn Garrettson: Apostle to Nova Scotia," *Methodist History, 1* (1963), 27–30.

67. On George, see "An Account of the Life of Mr. David George, from Sierra Leone in Africa; Given by Himself in a Conversation with Brother [John] Rippon of London, and Brother [Samuel] Pearce of Birmingham," *The Baptist Annual Register* . . . *for 1792* . . . (London), pp. 473–84; Anthony Kirk-Greene, "David George: The Nova Scotian Experience," *Sierra Leone Studies,* n.s., no. 14 (1960), pp. 93–120; and Ingraham E. Bill, *Fifty Years with the Baptist Ministers and Churches of the Maritime Provinces of Canada* (Saint John, 1880), pp. 19–26, which often is in error. A search of the Rippon Papers (BM, Add. MSS 25,386–89) revealed no further material.

Leadership for Negro Baptists thereupon temporarily passed to an Englishman, John Burton, and his wife. Burton opened a small church in Halifax in 1795 and ministered to a largely Negro congregation. In time his influence became so pervasive, the government informally left the management of the Halifax Negroes to him. But in 1809 the Nova Scotian Baptist Association adopted a resolution demanding an end to fellowshipping with all churches who admitted the unbaptized to "occasional communion," a decision directed against the antinomian Newlight group. In doing so, most Baptists opted out of the missionary movement, temporarily leaving the mission field—outside Guysborough—to the Anglicans and the increasingly liberal Wesleyan Methodists.[68]

The Negro Methodists also were divided. Approximately forty Negroes at Birchtown adhered to Lady Huntingdon's Connexion. The Countess of Huntingdon's followers were Calvinist Methodists who, upon the break between the Wesleys and George Whitefield, followed the latter. In 1785 the Countess's chaplain ordained a Negro, John Marrant, who went to Nova Scotia to work among the blacks. His autobiography, written in London in the year of his ordination, won immediate attention and ran to nineteen editions, including three published in Halifax. In it he told of a remarkable conversion after wandering in the wilderness without food or drink for, by his estimate, 55.5 miles over five days. Marrant aroused opposition from the leading Wesleyan minister in Shelburne, Freeborn Garrettson, and in 1787 Garrettson was able to inform John Wesley that most of the Negroes had given up Marrant's aberration. Those who did not joined the migration to Africa.[69]

Wesleyan Methodists took deeper root. John Wesley expressed particular interest in Birchtown and promised that the settlers there would "never want books while I live." The first Wesleyan missionary in the province, William Black, preached to two hundred free Negroes there in 1784 and won sixty souls to his Christ. He gave instruction to segregated classes of whites and slave Negroes at Shelburne in April, and in the two towns he recorded 180 Negro communicants. The next year he preached in Digby, where there were sixty-six Negro members of the Wesleyan chapel, and in 1786 he organized an interracial society at George Brindley Town

68. Bill, *Fifty Years,* pp. 65, 176; H. H. Walsh, *The Christian Church in Canada* (Toronto, 1956), p. 123.

69. Marrant, *A Narrative of the Lord's Wonderful Dealing with John Marrant, a Black, (Now Going to Preach the Gospel in Nova-Scotia) Born in New-York, in North-America* (London, 1785). Halifax editions were published under an altered title in 1812, 1813, and 1815. See also J. B. Elliott, *The Lady Huntingdon's Connexion in Sierra Leone* (London, 1851), pp. 14–15, and Banks, *Freeborn Garrettson,* pp. 152, 158.

with seventy-eight members. The two Negro Methodist preachers at Birchtown, Boston King,[70] an erstwhile shipwright, and Moses Wilkinson, who was nearly blind and could not walk, continued to command followings of their own.

Early in 1791 there were well over two hundred Negro Wesleyans in the larger Nova Scotian towns; but later that year nearly all, including King—who had gone to Preston—and Wilkinson, joined the exodus to Africa, and thereafter the Methodists took less interest in the Negroes. In his subsequent reports from Halifax, Black found no occasion to mention them. At Annapolis Royal and Saint John in 1804, and at Liverpool in 1806, itinerant Wesleyan preachers expressed concern for the few Negroes on their circuits, while activity was reduced for the time to an occasional visit, a few free Bibles, and a new winter quilt presented each year to one Scipio O'Connor and his wife by white Sunday School girls at Guysborough.[71]

The most persistent religious group, and the one with the best early record of genuine aid to the Negroes, was the Church of England through the instrumentality of a small philanthropic organization, The Associates of the Late Dr. Bray. A founder of the Society for the Propagation of Christian Knowledge and of the Society for the Propagation of the Gospel in Foreign Parts, Dr. Thomas Bray had devoted his life to the church, to the care of the poor, and to the reformation of prostitutes. Having lived in Maryland for some time, he wished to help the colonies as well. Shortly before his death he entered into an association with a few friends to resettle debtors in America, to establish parochial libraries in Britain, and "for Instructing the Negroes in the British Plantations in the Christian Religion." For these purposes he left £ 960, and from this small principal the Associates were able to provide books for several communities and to aid Negro schools in Nova Scotia, the Bahamas, and Pennsylvania.[72] For

70. On King see "Memoirs of the Life of Boston King, a Black Preacher," *Arminian Magazine, 21* (1798), 105–10, 157–61, 209–13, 262–65; *Toronto Globe,* June 3, 1911; *Shelburne Coast Guard,* Nov. 6, 1952; and Phyllis R. Blakeley, "Boston King: A Negro Loyalist who Sought Refuge in Nova Scotia," *Dalhousie Review, 48* (1968), 347–56.

71. Methodist Missionary Society, London, Muniment Room: North America, box 1, file 1A, reports from Black, Aug. 26, Oct. 10, from William Bennett, Nov. 16, 1804, and from William Sutcliffe, April 17, 1806; Matthew Richey, *A Memoir of the Late Reverend William Black, Wesleyan Minister* (Halifax, 1839), pp. 128–29, which is contradictory; John MacLean, *William Black: The Apostle of Methodism in the Maritime Provinces of Canada* (Halifax, 1907), pp. 28–29; T. Watson Smith, *History of the Methodist Church . . . of Eastern British America . . .* (Halifax, 1877), *1,* 143–44, 250–53.

72. H. P. Thompson, *Thomas Bray* (London, 1954), p. 97.

nearly a hundred and twenty-five years Dr. Bray's Associates supported Negro education in Nova Scotia and solicited from the SPG small sums to supplement their aid.

The Associates took the initiative in July 1784, writing to the Reverend John Breynton at St. Paul's in Halifax to ask him whether there was a Negro school there and, if not, whether one would serve a good purpose. Replying that he had "ever entertained a compassion for that unhappy part of the human species," Breynton conferred with Parr and suggested that the Associates open a school at Digby similar to one he had just begun in Halifax. This was done, and the Associates then offered to help establish a school at Birchtown under Colonel Blucke. The following year the Associates helped Joseph Leonard open a school in George Brindley Town.

The Negro schools were small, scattered, and few in number. The Associates limited themselves to providing a few books and a stipend of £ 9 for the teachers from April until October—the normal term—calculated with respect to the number of pupils, which was to be a minimum of thirty at each school. The catechism was to be taught, although enrollment was not limited to Anglicans. Slave children as well as free attended, and ages ranged from four to nineteen. Progress was glacially slow, for often teachers could not be found and when they could they either resigned at an imagined slight, incurred the displeasure of the government—which also aided the schools—or seemed doctrinally unsound; for if a teacher embraced "strange religious tenets," his pay was withheld. The Negroes were expected to provide buildings for the schools, and they were slow to do so: in November 1787, the blacks of Preston had drawn together enough timber for a building and had twenty pupils ready to attend, but although the Associates agreed to support the school many months passed before it was ready.[73]

Nonetheless, much good came from these schools. Although most teachers originally were white, they were replaced in time by Negroes, giving rise to new sources of leadership within the isolated black communities. Slave and free Negro children met in the same classroom, while their parents often had little contact. On occasion white pupils were admitted, slowing tendencies toward segregation. If instruction relied purely upon rote work, memories at least were disciplined, and not a few Negroes learned to read, write, do simple sums, and to sew; a company of Negro militia, all one hundred and twenty members having received some educa-

73. Dr. Bray's Associates, Canadian Papers, chest 4, box 12: Breynton to Associates, Nov. 15, 1784; Dr. Bray's Associates Minute Books, *3:* July 1, 1784, Feb. 2, July 11, 1785, March 26, June 4, 1787, June 5, July 3, 1788 (for Brunton read Breynton); *Abstract of the Proceedings of the Associates* ([London], n.d.), pp. 29–35; reports of J. W. Weeks, Oct. 10, Nov. 24, 1787, Viets, May 16, 1788, and Blucke, Dec. 22, 1787.

tion at the school in Digby, was formed in 1811. In keeping with the times, women teachers were paid half stipends, but the schools did offer one of the few opportunities for employment of Negro women. And by taking primary responsibility for the Negro schools at Birchtown, Brindley Town, Halifax, and Preston, the Associates eased the burden of the Society for the Propagation of the Gospel itself, which consequently was able to appoint teachers to the Negroes at Tracadie and elsewhere.[74]

On the whole the Negroes did not support the schools well. Groups would petition for a school, but once facilities were available—rudimentary as they were—they were dilatory about sending their children. In 1797 a school opened at Fredericton, and in 1798 the Halifax school, which had closed in 1791, opened again; the former was abandoned in 1800 because only twelve children were attending. As Reverend George Pidgeon reported at the time, the Negroes were "exceedingly importunate until they obtain[ed] the object of their wishes," but afterwards they were equally as "negligent and indifferent." In 1803 Roger Viets, a scholarly Yale graduate, known as the protector of the Digby Negroes, wrote with disappointment that, for him, the old question about equality had been answered: "the Africans in Digby have exactly the same Privileges as the white subjects, and as constant schooling, and yet have not made one Quarter of the Proficiency." They were, he added in disgust, always losing their books.[75]

But Reverend Viets's test was hardly a fair one, for the Negroes of the Maritime Provinces continued to live in poverty, near-peonage, and ignorance despite the sporadic if sincere attention of missionary societies and the Nova Scotian government. The white Loyalists, after all, could come to terms with their new environment quickly enough, for they were certain of their position in the world—and certain of the world too. They owned property, many were well-educated, most had commitments and goals attested to by their decision to carve out a new life in a raw colony. The Negroes were slaves, or had been less than a decade before. They were ignorant, unprepared for the new environment and unable to cope with it; for they had neither resources of position nor reservoirs of skill through which they might batter their environment about until it assumed a shape at least recognizable, if not comfortable, to them. Many had been field

74. SPG Journals, *29:* reports of Feb. 3, Sept. 25, 29, March 25, 1805; Dr. Bray's Associates Minute Books, *4:* Dec. 1, 1808, Feb. 5, Nov. 5, 1812; Dr. Bray's Associates Account Books (variously called Cash Books and General Account Books): March 7, 1796, Dec. 23, 1800, Feb. 7, April 26, 1801; Rawlyk, "Guysborough," p. 30.

75. Dr. Bray's Associates Minute Books, *3:* Dec. 3, 1789, Feb. 4, 1790, Sept. 1, 1791, Aug. 7, 1797, Feb. 5, 1798, Jan. 7, 1801, May 2, June 6, 1803, Feb. 6, 1804, Feb. 3, 1806, Nov. 2, 1807; *4:* July 6, 1809, March 7, 1811; Canadian Papers, chest 4, box 12: Pigeon [*sic*] to Associates, Feb. 15, 1800; Sabine, *Loyalists, 2,* 388–89.

hands, accustomed to close direction, little responsibility, a single crop, and a benign climate. When on arrival they first saw snow on the capes of Nova Scotia, some thought that it was sugar. Many believed in spirits and others drank them. One slave remarked, "I can't read, I can only meditate"; [76] many devoted their energies exclusively to meditation with their Lord until they were too exhausted to come to terms with His soil. Negroes at Birchtown and Shelburne were subject to social pressures because of their race and to attack by displaced white laborers; those at Digby and Annapolis lost months while waiting for their lands to be surveyed for them; those at Tracadie, Preston, and later Hammond's Plains were given unusually unproductive land. They did not prosper, they were not faithful in school attendance, often they failed to bring their land into production—and most remained illiterate; indeed, they lost more than their school books. As Viets implied, they were inferior—not for inherent, biological reasons, but for accidental, historical ones.

Because the Negroes recognized their own inferiority—and the fact that it would continue if they remained in Nova Scotia—the most ambitious, the most disgruntled, and perhaps the most easily swayed, determined in 1791 to follow an unlikely white Pied Piper across the sea to the coasts of Africa.

76. Henry Nase, *Westfield* (Saint John, n.d.), p. 76; Clara Dennis, *Down in Nova Scotia* (Toronto, 1934), pp. 342–43, 358.

Note on Currency

Sale prices were stated in livres, Quebec pounds, Halifax pounds, Halifax dollars, American dollars, Spanish dollars, and pounds sterling. The livre preceded the franc as a French unit; six livres equalled a crown. General James Murray estimated in 1762 that a livre was worth two shillings (Shortt and Doughty, eds., *Constitutional History of Canada, 1,* 47–81), but William Renwick Riddell convincingly contests this in "Slave in Nouvelle-France," page 318, note 5, and calculates the livre at 13⅓ pence. Two hundred Spanish dollars equalled £50 Quebec money, and both Quebec and Halifax pounds were about nine-tenths the value of pounds sterling (Riddell, p. 324, n. 19). My calculations are based on some fifty sales, all values converted to pounds sterling.

3. "Back to Africa," 1791–1801

For nearly three hundred years North American Negroes have talked of returning to Africa, their ancestral homeland. Not until late in the eighteenth century were there any concerted efforts to make such a movement possible, and by then "back to Africa" was as much a catch phrase as a potential reality, for many of the Negroes were speaking of a continent they had never seen. Serious discussion of Negro resettlement in Africa was begun not by blacks but by whites who through colonization societies wished to remove the Negroes, this "unnatural importation," before they could become economically and socially dangerous. By the 1830s some Negroes also spoke of transatlantic migration, playing briefly upon white and Negro emotions and seldom grappling with realities. Negroes in Canada were to share, although to a lesser extent, in all of the futile "back to Africa" movements of the nineteenth and twentieth centuries.

But twice, substantial numbers of Negroes from British North America did "return" to Africa—both times from Nova Scotia and both times to Sierra Leone. In each case the Negroes in Nova Scotia were brief sojourners there and had not put down roots: the migration of 1791–92 followed eight years after the arrival in the province of the majority of its participants, and the movement of 1800 followed four years after its body of Jamaican Maroons were brought into the colony. In both cases "back to Africa" was something more than rhetoric: from one-third to one-half of the adult Negroes who left for Sierra Leone in 1792 had been born in Africa. In both cases white men organized and paid for the ventures, in response to clearly stated Negro desires to be taken elsewhere than Nova Scotia.

The most significant of these movements began in Britain. Since the Revolution and Lord Mansfield's decision in 1772, thousands of free black men had been accumulating in British ports. Granville Sharp, the man responsible for bringing Somerset before Mansfield, persuaded the government to provide Liberated Africans, as they were called, with the beginnings of a new life in West Africa. A colony of free black men, grateful to Britain for succor, strategically placed, and effectively and economically controlled by themselves or by a company rather than by the Crown, would have great value. The only alternative site for resettlement of those Negroes already in English ports was Nova Scotia, which was increasingly thought to be "unfit and improper for the said Blacks." [1]

The first group of settlers, 411 in all (including nearly seventy white women of uncertain, or all too certain, reputation), sailed from England for the Province of Freedom in 1787. They negotiated with a local worthy, King Tom, for land, elected one of their number governor, and died by the score when the rains came. Next year Sharp sent new supplies, and the colony was formally established. In 1789 King Jimmy (or Jemmy), the successor to Tom, burned Granville Town, the chief center, to the ground and the settlers scattered into the inhospitable countryside. An infusion of new blood was needed or there would be no free Negro colony in West Africa. [2]

In the year of the initial settlement, 1787, a young Englishman who had decided to dedicate his life to abolishing the slave trade, Thomas Clarkson, began a diligent study of the causes, conditions, and supporters of slavery and its commerce. Clarkson, not Sharp nor William Wilberforce nor Sir Thomas Fowell Buxton nor any of those of greater fame to come, was the true father of abolitionism in Britain. He lived until 1842, by then a high priest of antislavery throughout the world, known intimately in the United States, British America, and France, and revered as a creator of African freedom. A pre-Victorian, Clarkson was one of those men who could write, it seemed, without pause and without end. His books and pamphlets numbered well over a hundred at his death—all piously framed, minutely detailed, irrefutably logical. He could write so much, simply because his mind, his art, and his convictions were one: he wrote of what he believed, and he believed with all of the firmness of the devout Christian. No groping for the precise word, no hesitation over the moral overtones of a phrase, no worry about a nuance imprecisely perceived, no concern with whether a source were genuine or merely useful to his argument slowed his pen. Essentially a grievance collector, his mind was a catalogue of injustices committed against the Negro, and Clarkson's *Essay on the Slavery and Commerce of the Human Species, Particularly the African* (London, 1786), which had won him a prize at the University of Cambridge, evolved into a basic handbook of the antislavery movement. [3]

1. R. R. Kuczynski, *Demographic Survey of the British Colonial Empire, 1, West Africa* (Cumberledge, Eng. 1947), p. 41.

2. The fullest and best history of the founding of Sierra Leone is Christopher H. Fyfe, *A History of Sierra Leone* (London, 1962), which contains a thorough bibliography.

3. The standard biography of *Thomas Clarkson, The Friend of Slaves* (London, 1936), by Earl Leslie Griggs, is inadequate, and there is a major need for a new one. I have examined the Clarkson Papers in the BM (Add. MSS 41,262AB-64); the New-York Historical Society in New York City; the Huntington Library, San Marino,

The Sierra Leone Company was formed in 1791 with Clarkson, Sharp, and Wilberforce, the antislavery group's parliamentary spokesman, among the directors, and with a London banker of considerable skill, Henry Thornton, as chairman. The Company's officers in London were to administer the floundering Colony, frame its laws, and promote its trade. Thornton pointed out that, although a few of the original settlers might be brought back to Granville Town, new men were needed. Clarkson, with his knowledge of worldwide slavery, thought of Nova Scotia.[4]

Conveniently, Thomas Peters, the former leader of the Black Pioneers in the Annapolis Valley, arrived in England in July bearing a petition on behalf of himself and one hundred and two Nova Scotian and one hundred New Brunswick Negro families. Addressed to W. W. Grenville, the former Secretary of State, the document stated that the Negroes had either not been given the lands promised them or had lost those lands unfairly. Peters was authorized "to procure . . . some establishment where [they] may attain a competent settlement for themselves and be enabled by their industrious exertions to become useful subjects to His Majesty." Some wished to remain in North America, while others, he thought, would be prepared to move to Africa.[5] From Granville Sharp, Peters learned of Sierra Leone's need for Negro settlers, and without specifically proposing to go there,[6] he submitted his memorial through Sharp to the Company.

Thornton forwarded the petition to the new Secretary of State for the Home Department, Henry Dundas (later Lord Melville), who wrote to Parr on August 6, ordering him to inquire into the complaints enumerated by Peters. If the statements were found to be true, Parr was to locate land for the Pioneers "in a situation so advantageous, as may make them some atonement for the injury they have suffered by [this] unaccountable delay." Dundas suggested that Sierra Leone might be an asylum for those who remained unhappy, while others might wish to enter His Majesty's service

Calif.; the libraries of Atlanta, Duke, and Howard universities; the Central Library and the East Suffolk and Ipswich Record Office, both in Ipswich; and Wilberforce House, Kingston upon Hull.

4. Huntington Library, Clarkson Papers, box 1: "My own report, relating to Sierra Leone and its future prospects read by me to the directors of that company soon after its Incorporation by Parliament" [ca. 1792]; Clarkson Papers, 41,263: to Wilberforce, n.d. [ca. 1815], pp. 155–82, a memorandum on the foundation of the colony written in reply to an attack by Robert Thorpe.

5. CO217/63: Peters [signed with his mark], encl. in Dundas to Parr, Aug. 6, 1791. The petition is printed in full in Christopher H. Fyfe, ed., *Sierra Leone Inheritance* (London, 1964), pp. 118–19.

6. Sierra Leone Archives, Fourah Bay College, Freetown: John Clarkson, draft diary, Aug. 6, 1791, makes it clear that Peters was ready to be moved from Nova Scotia but that he did not nominate Sierra Leone. The directors of the Company considered that he did, however.

in the West Indies. Parr was to send an officer through the colony to elicit reactions to these alternatives. Thornton was given a copy of the draft of this letter, and he suggested that the same message might be sent to Lieutenant-Governor Thomas Carleton in New Brunswick; but the Secretary of State declined to write further before hearing from Parr.[7]

Parr replied promptly and with some heat that Peters' complaints were misrepresentations. Indeed, he insisted, "having considered the Degraded situation in which these people are beheld in general, by His Majesty's Subjects of a different Colour, I have at all times peculiarly attended to their Settlements." He reluctantly ordered an investigation of the distribution of lots, protesting that "these People were put on Lands, and in a situation, then much envied."[8]

Peters, in the meantime, had talked with Sir Henry Clinton, whom he found ready to remember the men who had served under him, and had decided that no genuine redress of grievance would be found in Nova Scotia. Peters thereupon returned to enlist Negroes to go with him to Sierra Leone. Since he had come to England despite Parr's opposition, he could not expect cheerful cooperation with his efforts, and he avoided the capital and the seaward side of the province entirely, concentrating his recruiting at Annapolis, Digby, and Saint John, where he already was well known to the Pioneers.

Clearly the Company needed to send someone to work with Peters, someone who had the confidence of the directors and who might win the confidence of the lieutenant-governors. Thornton had difficulty in finding anyone to go, and Thomas Clarkson's younger brother John, who was working closely with Wilberforce in gathering information on the slave trade, volunteered. He sailed from Gravesend on the *Ark* on August 19, 1791, and after a long delay at Portland Roads caused by adverse winds, he arrived in Halifax on October 7.

Lieutenant John Clarkson[9] was one of those men whom twentieth-century psychologists would unhesitatingly term neurotic and eighteenth-century clerics would have deemed God-struck. Born at Wisbeach (as then spelled), Cambridgeshire, April 4, 1764, he was twenty-seven years old when he sailed out in the *Ark*. He had served in the Royal Navy since he

7. CO217/63: Dundas to Parr, Aug. 6, 1791. A copy, with a penciled notation identifying Peters as "a Black who served with the King's Troops during the late war," is in CO217/72. The draft Clarkson received was dated Aug. 3—CO267/9: Thornton to Evan Nepean, Aug. 3, 1791, and reply, Aug. 4.

8. CO217/63: Parr to Dundas, Sept. 27, 1791.

9. There is no biography of John Clarkson. Thomas Clarkson wrote a "Memoir of the Late John Clarkson, Esq.," for *The Herald of Peace*, n.s., 6 (1828), 428–32. A fuller version appears as "Biographical Notes on John Clarkson and the Clarkson Family," in the Clarkson Papers, Huntington Library.

was eleven, usually in the West Indies, and on seven different ships he had been much under fire. Clarkson was so disturbed by the bloodshed he saw during a boarding action against a French frigate, that he became an outspoken advocate of universal peace and resigned his commission. His particular passion was order, and all about him was disorder. Disingenuous and self-deluding attempts to assert his will, the only surely ordered thing he could find, were natural to him. His journal [10] shows that he was the sort of man who tries to give meaning to his life by keeping lists—lists of all of the books he intended to read, lists of the places he wished to visit before he died, lists of the skills he wanted to acquire. One can imagine John Clarkson writing little reminders to himself, once he was married, to kiss his wife more often and to speak more kindly to the children.

As Clarkson sailed from Gravesend, he carried with him both specific injunctions and general advice. His brother had provided much of the former—"In the Rivers in Africa take care of the Allegators [*sic*] and on the land of the Snakes"—but Wilberforce had also written to his friend, having concluded that he was "a young man of very great merit & a thousand good qualities including discretion." Addressing Clarkson as "My dear Adm[iral]," [11] Wilberforce set out several rules to be followed while in Nova Scotia. Most of these ("Don't talk about the abolition of the Slave Trade, except where you are sure of your company", keep out of local politics) were to insure that Clarkson did indeed act with the discretion credited to him. Wilberforce anticipated that Clarkson might be charged with spreading discontent among the Negroes and advised him to circulate an advertisement immediately upon arrival to stop false rumors about the Company's intentions. Most of the advice reminded Clarkson

10. Clarkson kept a detailed and revealing journal, from which the following account of his work in Nova Scotia is taken, and to which only supplementary references will be given. The extant sources, all of which were examined, consist of: (a) The first volume (of two) of the original draft diary, for August 6 to November 23, 1791, in the Sierra Leone Archives. (b) One copy, through March 18, 1792, at Howard University, Washington, D.C. (c) A second copy, the best, in PANS. (d) A third copy in the New-York Historical Society. (e) One copy of the second draft volume, covering March 19 to August 4, 1792, also in the New-York Historical Society. (f) A second copy of volume 2 was owned by Mr. Cecil Harmsworth King; I wish to thank Mr. King for giving me access to it, in his office at the *London Daily Mirror*. This copy has now gone to the University of Illinois. (g) Apparently a copy of volume 3, as well as the draft from which it was taken, covering August to December, 1792, have not survived, but Clarkson's Letterbook, beginning with July 17, 1792, is in the Sierra Leone Archives. Portions of Clarkson's journal have been published: in Ernest G. Ingham, *Sierra Leone after a Hundred Years* (London, 1894), pp. 18–167, from March 1792 to September 1793, and in [J. de Hart, ed.], "Diary of Lieutenant Clarkson, R.N.," *Sierra Leone Studies, 8* (1927), 1–114, from August 5 to November 26, 1792.

11. Clarkson Papers: Thomas to John, Aug. 28, 1791.

to be as harmless as a dove, while some showed him how to be as subtle as a serpent: "lead the Governors as soon as you can into incurring some expenses on account of the Expedition" so that, should they later hesitate, they could be reminded that "what may have been already spent will be so much thrown away." These Governors, Wilberforce saw, were the key to a successful mission, and Clarkson was urged to be as vague with them as possible, not to allude to the ill-usage the blacks had received, and to avoid them until it was necessary to enlist their support for the final transfer to West Africa. Initially, Wilberforce had also enclosed letters of introduction to the Governors, but thinking better of this he destroyed them, leaving the "Admiral" to obtain official confidence through "a kind of general Discretionary power to act for yourself." With this last exercise in indiscretion, the man who urged upon Clarkson "the utmost temper and prudence" provided the volatile agent with an excuse for exceeding the Company's instructions.

The Company expected opposition. For the Governors to agree to any plan for mass migration without at least a show of hesitation would be an admission of their own failure to meet the Negro problem at its source. Popular protests were also anticipated in those quarters where cheap black labor was used, or where Negroes virtually had become tenant farmers. Wilberforce expected that the Negroes' creditors would provide the chief stumbling block, however, and provision was made for Clarkson to pay off all legitimate debts for the settlers, the money to be treated as a loan to the debtor which would be recovered over the years in Sierra Leone. Advance information of this intention was not to be circulated in the colonies, for there would be Negroes who opted for Sierra Leone merely to escape from debt, and the amount of the monies owed would grow in the account books of the creditors. As Wilberforce concluded, Clarkson should, "by hesitating, draw in your opponents to rest all their opposition . . . on this one ground, and then by [your] coming forward and cutting it from under them, every difficulty will be at an end." [12]

When Clarkson arrived at Halifax, he went directly to Government House, where he learned that Parr had published part of Dundas's letter in the *Gazette* and that Peters had preceded him to New Brunswick. He contacted Laurence Hartshorne, a local hardware merchant and quondam Quaker whom the Company had appointed to help Clarkson engage tonnage, calculated at two tons for each adult and three quarters of that for each child. Together they distributed a broadside which announced that the Company would take to its colony any free blacks who were able to show the two agents character references worthy, in their judgment, to en-

12. Clarkson Papers: Wilberforce to Clarkson, Aug. 9 (incorrectly endorsed 8), 1791; HO42/19: Wilberforce to Nepean, Aug. 6, 1791.

title them to "Certificates of Approbation." Every adult male with such a certificate would, upon arriving in Sierra Leone, receive twenty acres of land "upon such terms, and subject to such charges and obligations, with a view to the general prosperity of the Company, as shall hereafter be settled by the Company," a clause that Clarkson did not explain. Ten acres would be allotted for wives and five acres for each child. The Company, its servants, and those who inhabited its areas could neither own nor traffic in slaves.[13]

Clarkson began circumspectly enough, but his resolve to deal "discretely and prudently" with both government and Negroes did not last. He was appalled by what he saw as he made his way along the Nova Scotian coast—especially so at Preston, where the Negroes were in a "deplorable situation," and at Birchtown, still tense, decaying, and divided. Even the free Negroes, he thought, were subject to a form of slavery, and not one in ten had received a full allotment of land. Stephen Blucke, who opposed Clarkson's plan as an "infatuation," and those whites who attended his public meetings to protest against the possible loss of the more able Negroes, merely quickened his growing conviction that the Negro had no place in Nova Scotia at all. For a man of peace, counterproposals to enlist all able-bodied free Negro men in the military for service in the West Indies, circulated at his own hotel within four days of his arrival, were especially painful. And the respectful attention and growing affection shown him by the Negroes played upon his emotions and his ego. The Company had enjoined him to encourage only those Negroes who showed distinct dissatisfaction with their life in Nova Scotia, and to leave all "to [their] own choice," but Clarkson was unable to contain himself.[14]

At Birchtown Clarkson turned from his uncomfortably neutral rôle to become a propagandist for a cause. On the outward voyage he had promised in his journal "not to sport with the [Negroes'] destiny," and later he declared that he did nothing "not authorized by the Spirit of my Instructions," instructions he interpreted disingenuously. The Company had stated quite clearly that each settler would be expected to pay one shilling a year as quitrent, and the directors expected to meet most of the colony's housekeeping expenses from this source. But at Birchtown, where nearly four hundred Negroes were waiting to hear him, Clarkson read out the Company's statement, and when asked to explain the "Terms, Charges, and Obligations," which were "afterwards to be settled by the Directors," he

13. PANS, 419, "Refugee Negroes, 1790–1734 [sic]," no. 1, broadside, Aug. 2, 1791; Clarkson Papers: J. P. Williams to John Clarkson, Aug. 12, and Matthew Clarkson to same, Nov. 5, 1791. A typical list of certificates of character are in these papers under Dec. 31, 1791.
14. CO217/72: Blucke's memorandum, copy, Nov. n.d., 1791.

promised that neither rent nor tax was involved. Further, finding that rumors were circulating to the effect that all of the settlers who had gone out at Sharp's behest in 1787 had been murdered, that the Company would renege on its promises to grant land, and that a rent would be charged, Clarkson sweepingly denied them all. Perhaps he thought it unimportant that he misrepresented the Company on so small a matter as a quitrent or over so insignificant a sum, or perhaps he expected the Company would change its policy. But he did lie to his prospective settlers, and the question of that insignificant sum was to be the chief cause of a rebellion in Sierra Leone in 1800 when they discovered that, as they thought, the Company had broken faith with them.[15]

If Clarkson were to succeed, he needed at least the neutrality of the lieutenant-governors; and it was the discovery that he lacked this, indeed that he might actively be opposed by Parr, that probably was most instrumental in his unconscious decision to become a propagandist for the migration scheme. On his second day in Halifax, Clarkson had dined again at Government House, on this occasion with a large party. The governor, as Clarkson confided to his journal, had seized upon the report of King Jimmy's activities in Sierra Leone, received that very day in fuller detail than previously known in Halifax, for "starting difficulties." Clarkson, by his own admission, scarcely used prudence: he cut Parr short and read him a lecture on duty. "The conversation dropped by the Governor's pushing about the bottle." [16]

During the following month, as Clarkson and Hartshorne made their rounds, a curious development in an already strained relationship with the governor came to light. On November 27, writing to Wilberforce, Clarkson asserted that to his "certain knowledge" Parr had received a letter in the same mail that had brought Dundas's original dispatch "desiring [that the governor] do all in his power to retard [our business]." Clarkson wrote in his private journal that the letter which undermined his work, and which presumably accounted for Parr's perceptibly stiffening resistance, was from "E.N.," but he chose not to tell Wilberforce this, although he asked him to rectify the "abominable" situation if he could.[17]

Who was "E.N."? The answer is easy enough,[18] but the reasons why he should have written such a letter remain obscure: "E.N." was Evan

15. BM, Clarkson Papers: printed statement signed by John Clarkson, Oct. 29, 1791.

16. Quoted in Sir Adams George Archibald, "Story of Deportation of Negroes from Nova Scotia to Sierra Leone," *Collections of the Nova Scotia Historical Society,* 7 (1891), 137–38.

17. Ibid., p. 138. The letter from "E. N." was dated August 8 (CO217/63: Parr to Dundas, Oct. 17, 1791).

18. Archibald, "Deportation of Negroes," p. 139, makes an incorrect guess.

(later Sir Evan) Nepean, the Permanent Under-Secretary of State
Dundas's department. It was he, in fact, who had provided Thornton a
thus Wilberforce with the draft of the original order to Parr, and he often
wrote on Dundas's behalf as well as in his own capacity.[19]

Dundas was an awesomely overworked man. As Home Secretary he
was responsible for local administration, Irish affairs, and the colonies,
and until 1794 for war operations as well. He also acted as President of
the Board of Control for India. Because the younger Pitt, in whose ministry
he served, trusted him, Dundas advised informally on foreign affairs too.
All of these areas of his work were presenting numerous problems in the
1790s. His mind was elsewhere than in Nova Scotia throughout 1791, for
he was preoccupied with enforcing in Scotland, the seat of his power, the
Corn Bill of that year, and in the days after July 15, with serious rioting
that had broken out in Birmingham. He had, in any case, been in the office
less than two months when presented with Peters' bill of particulars, and
he must have felt compelled to rely heavily upon Nepean, who had been
the under-secretary since the office had been created in 1782.

Clarkson assumed that "E.N." spoke officially, and he felt that Dundas
had betrayed the Company. But this is not at all clear. Had Nepean's
countermanding letter unambiguously spoken for Dundas, Parr presumably
could have taken even more vigorous steps than he did to block Clarkson.
Rather, it seems reasonable to assume that Nepean had written for himself,
perhaps intimating that Dundas had not meant his original dispatch—so
readily granted Thornton and possibly intended primarily for its effect in
London—to be taken literally. Parr's behavior throughout was that of a
man who had been given discretion, but not express orders, to be unco-
operative. And as Parr's reluctance took on more tangible qualities, Clarkson's devotion to his duty became more tangible.

Parr also had begun an inquiry into Peters' original complaints. He directed two local officials, Alexander Howe, a Justice of the Court of Common Pleas, and Job Bennett Clarke, a Justice of Peace for the County of
Hants, to investigate; and on November 16 they met with Peters at Annapolis and asked him to produce evidence on his petition. He recited the
sorry tale of Thomas Millidge's survey and Parr's alleged orders that the
land should be taken back from the Negroes, but the commissioners had
no difficulty showing that Millidge, Parr, and Charles Morris had acted
honorably. Unable to deal with the legal issues involved, Peters fell back
upon his own case alone, protesting that when he arrived in Annapolis he
had received only sixty-one days' provisions although an additional eighty

19. On Nepean, see *Dictionary of National Biography* (hereafter cited as *DNB*),
14, 222–23, by "J.K.L." [John Knox Laughton], and his obituary in *The Gentleman's
Magazine, 132* (1822), 373–74.

days' had been promised him. He was then forced to admit that he had left for Saint John in the late summer of 1785 rather than do the road work that was expected of all before they received their rations, and the commissioners cited the official correspondence to contend that, had Peters remained, he might have received a lot double that of all other settlers save two. As a coup de grâce, Howe produced testimony from Joseph Leonard in which he declared himself quite satisfied with the survey (although Leonard ultimately chose to go to Sierra Leone). In all, the investigation could hardly have harmed Peters more or have strengthened Parr at a more opportune moment.[20]

This report was sent to Dundas on the 19th; Clarkson protested his betrayal on the 27th; and all that saved him in his mission was that Parr had died on the 25th. Richard Bulkeley, Provincial Secretary and a senior member of the Council, became the administrator of the colony. He was far more helpful—possibly because in the first days of taking up the reins he was preoccupied with other problems, possibly because his amour propre was not touched by the exodus of blacks since he had not been responsible for their initial settlement and satisfaction, and possibly because he agreed with Clarkson's purpose. Then, too, a mass Negro exodus paid for by a distant company offered many opportunities for private enrichment, for much money would have to exchange hands before Clarkson could hope to get away. Bulkeley's attitude supports the probability that Nepean's letter had been unofficial, oblique, and not binding upon Parr's successor if he chose to ignore it. In any case, Bulkeley cooperated fully, and Clarkson was able to move forward with speed.

Parr had, in fact, left machinery which Clarkson could operate, for the Governor reluctantly had appointed boarding agents in the major ports. Alexander Howe, who had worked with Negroes in the West Indies, was to remain in Annapolis County; Michael Wallace, a member of the Legislative Assembly, was appointed for Halifax; and Major Stephen Skinner was assigned Shelburne. Skinner, who opposed the migration, was of limited help, and Howe was primarily interested in a "liberal stipend," but they all did their jobs, and Wallace was especially effective.[21]

Clarkson, with the help of Wallace and Hartshorne, brushed aside remaining obstacles. Blucke, who predicted the "utter annihilation" of the migrants, had asked Parr to grant him and each of his followers purchase money for a cow and two sheep as the price of their loyalty. A local worthy

20. CO217/63: Bulkeley to Dundas, March 19, 1792, with copy of "Enquiry into the Complaint of Thomas Peters a Black Man"; SPG Archives, Dr. Bray's Associates Minute Books: *3,* July 5, 1792, July 1, 1805, *4,* Nov. 2, 1809.

21. CO218/27: Bulkeley to Dundas, Nov. 29, 1791, and reply, Jan. 15, 1792; PANS, *419:* Wallace to Bulkeley, Nov. 25, 1791, Feb. 6, 1792, and reply, same date.

now promised to give those blacks who remained behind two years' provisions, and Skinner told the Negroes that if the full force of the law were brought to bear on their behalf, they could yet find a satisfying life in the colony. In the Halifax papers one Philanthropos warned that the settlers' rights and privileges had not been explained fully enough, while a soldier from the Black Carolina Corps took over the Halifax playhouse to argue in favor of a military life. Bernard Michael Houseal, SPG missionary to Halifax and later to Lunenburg, recalling how a former missionary to Sierra Leone had written of his misery and the blacks' illness, tried to get a copy of the damaging letter to circulate, but since he was a slave-owner his opposition no doubt seemed less than convincing.[22]

None could counter the influence of the Negroes' own religious leaders, all of whom had fallen into line behind Clarkson and his assistants. David George helped organize the Birchtown Negroes into companies; Moses Wilkinson and, at Preston, Boston King, proselytized for the venture; and all of the remaining adherents of Countess Huntingdon's Connexion, now led by Anthony Elliott and Cato Perkins—the latter ultimately to play a leading rôle in Sierra Leone—joined up. Even Parr's gross underestimate of the number of Negroes who would leave (he originally had guessed at thirty families), which meant that he had chartered pathetically inadequate tonnage, was partially offset by Hartshorne's frantic pursuit of all available ships; for, shortly before Parr's death, Hartshorne had seen that the migration would run to at least five hundred and had persuaded Parr to authorize twelve hundred tons of shipping and to arrange for medical care. Clarkson took up an additional eight hundred tons when he reached Halifax.[23]

Deciding that the entire group of Negroes should sail as a single fleet, Clarkson wrote to Peters to bring forward his Saint John, Fredericton, and Annapolis blacks to rendezvous at Halifax, while he looked to the Preston, Shelburne, and Birchtown contingents. The Birchtown group was the largest: there were five hundred and eighteen officially enrolled, and another twenty-six came overland. Clarkson kept a record of the original body,

22. CO217/63: Skinner to Parr, n.d., with copy of petition from Blucke; SPG Archives, West Africa, file 46: Patrick Fraser to William Morice, Sept. 15, 1787; and 1: Houseal to Morice, Nov. 21, 1791. C. F. Pascoe, *Two Hundred Years of the S.P.G.: An Historical Account of the Society for Propagation of the Gospel in Foreign Parts, 1701–1900* (London, 1901), p. 862, gives the spelling "Howseal" and his date of death as 1799, but the *Halifax Royal Gazette* for June 24, 1800, shows him alive and selling his Negro girl. Clarkson refers to the Philanthropus article; an examination of the Halifax newspapers has not produced it, but the PANS' file is broken.

23. Ibid., Oct. 25, Nov. 22, 1791; Clarkson Papers, 41,262B: "Remarks [in] Halifax," pp. 1–8, 12, 15–18, 21–23; Charles Bruce Fergusson, ed., *The Diary of Simeon Perkins, 1790–1796* (Toronto, 1961), pp. 130–31; Mitchell Library, Sydney, N.S.W., Thomas Haweis diary: *1*, June 29, 1794.

and they may be taken as representative. There were 151 men, 148 women, and 220 children.[24] The majority of adults were in their forties, and a few were eighty. Fifty-five of the Negroes had been born in Virginia; fifty-one were African-born, including one John Kizell, the son of a Sherbro chief and the only one who knew Sierra Leone well. Families were not large: David George, with six children, had more than most. The men had trades of sorts; virtually all were Baptists, Wesleyan Methodists, or Huntingdonites. As families the Negroes had held from ten to forty acres—George excepted—which they were selling at less than the land was worth. Surprisingly few were in debt. They were proud and insular, and they wished to be kept together both on board ship and in Sierra Leone, although they were willing to be settled near the Preston blacks, who were Clarkson's favorites.[25]

Even Clarkson's estimate was proving wrong, for by early December almost a thousand Negroes had gathered near Halifax, and although he and they champed, eager to leave, neither shipping nor provisions were ready. No one had any idea how many of the Negroes ultimately would embark, for some might decide against the adventure at the last moment, and more were coming in daily. The departure already was so delayed, additional clothing against a midwinter crossing of the Atlantic would be needed, and the ever-helpful Bulkeley supplied it before Clarkson asked. Ship captains were reluctant to make the voyage, for they would have to return across the Atlantic empty at the worst time of year, and they and their crews would be away for over six months in an unpopular cause. Here Wallace took the initiative and asked Bulkeley for authority to pay a set sum per vessel for a completed voyage rather than by the number of people carried, as first arranged, for captains were uncertain of how much they might expect to realize from their work. Slowly he and Hartshorne, with Bulkeley's assistance, assembled the needed tonnage, while several of the blacks now camping about Halifax fell ill and fourteen women moved into advanced stages of pregnancy. The emigrants spent Christmas day huddled about fires on the frozen hillsides, watching the fluttering white wings of an overdue snowfall and making dinner from fresh beef, a gift from Bulkeley. On Boxing Day Clarkson triumphantly hoisted his pennant on *Lucretia*, the flagship, and on January 7 Bulkeley transferred authority over the vessels to Clarkson.[26]

At last, the Halifax Custom House listed four ships, nine brigs, and two

24. These figures, as elsewhere in the Clarkson materials, do not balance.

25. CO217/63: "List of Blacks in Birch Town who gave in their names for Sierra Leone, Nov. 1791"; BM, Clarkson Papers: Theophilus Chamberlain to Hartshorne, Dec. 26, 1791.

26. The preceding paragraphs are a summary of PANS, Clarkson Journal, *1:* 98–148, in particular, together with PANS, *419:* Wallace to Bulkeley, n.d., Dec. 1, 5, 17, Bulkeley to James Marden, issuer of stores, Dec. 8, Clarkson and Hartshorne to

schooners as "outwards" for "Serra-Leona" on January 10. Waiting upon a favorable wind, they stood to until the fifteenth, taking on additional food and clothing. On the sixteenth they struck into deep water, a flotilla of fifteen vessels, 1,990 tons in all, with over 1,190 passengers.[27] Clarkson had returned to shore on the eleventh to pay £ 46 on the debts of eight of his passengers—half of which was on behalf of Peters—and to take leave of Hartshorne, who had worked untiringly and without recompense.

Clarkson maintained strict discipline over the emigrants both at Halifax and on the voyage, and it was he and not Peters or George who took command throughout. Repeatedly, Clarkson told his charges "to consider how much the character of Black People would depend upon their conduct," reminding them—as their leaders, black and white, always have reminded them—that each was a hostage to his race. Throughout the long wait on shore, under difficult circumstances, there was no public disorder at all, and during the six weeks of confinement on board overcrowded vessels, no one challenged Clarksons' authority.[28] Later, in Sierra Leone, Peters was to test the lieutenant's leadership—indeed, when writing from the Bay of Fundy he had reported solely to Hartshorne, ignoring Clarkson's presence—only to be utterly discredited for stealing from a corpse.[29]

But by now Clarkson seems to have crossed that line beyond which will,

---

Bulkeley, and Clarkson to Bulkeley, both Dec. 30—all 1791, and reply, Jan. 2, 1792; and BM, Clarkson Papers: Clarkson and Hartshorne to Bulkeley, Dec. 13, and reply, Dec. 14, 1791, and Negroes of Birchtown, Dec. 20, and of Halifax, Dec. 23, 1791, to Clarkson.

27. There is some confusion as to how many blacks gathered near Halifax and how many ultimately left with Clarkson. Most estimates hold that between 1,200 and 1,500 Negroes arrived to undertake the journey; since the actual number that went was between 1,190 and 1,196, remarkably few withdrew at the last moment. PANS, Clarkson's Journal, *1,* 353–54, lists 1,190 as his official count of emigrants; but the Sierra Leone Company, in *Substance of the report delivered by the Court of Directors . . . to the General Court of Proprietors . . . 1794* (London, 1794), pp. 4–10, refers to 1,196, with 65 deaths en route and 1,131 safe arrivals. Of the total, perhaps four hundred were children (PANS, 409, no. 18: bill of fare, n.d.; Clarkson Journal, *1,* April 11, 1793). Calculating the tonnage in relation to the passenger list does not help, for Clarkson had to abandon the Company's figures, and in any case his journal and the *Halifax Royal Gazette* (Jan. 10, 1792) disagree. Discrepancies remain, for we are told in different accounts that fourteen advanced pregnancies were taken on board the vessels, that either three or fourteen babies were born on the voyage, and that all infants born on the voyage survived. The *Royal Gazette,* May 29, 1792, refers to seventy deaths. BM, Clarkson Papers: Clarkson to F. Patterson, July 31, 1792, and the report of the Sierra Leone Company refer to sixteen vessels, but here the Halifax customs-house records may be presumed accurate.

28. PANS, *309,* no. 17: Draft, commission to Clarkson, Jan. 7, 1792; PANS, *19,* no. 2: scroll; PANS, Clarkson Journal, *1,* 290–368; *Halifax Royal Gazette,* Nov. 15, 1791, Jan. 10, 17, 1792; BM, Clarkson Papers: Bulkeley to Clarkson, Jan. 7, 1792.

29. BM, Clarkson Papers: Peters to Hartshorne, Oct. 10, 1791; Fyfe, "Thomas Peters," pp. 7–9.

not reason, drives men on. Exhausted, he had to be carried aboard the *Lucretia* when he returned from shore the last time; with compassion, he had insisted that most of the sick Negroes should be on board his own vessel, and from their presence, a cold caught while superintending the final boarding, or his own nervous and physical state, he fell deeply ill and took to bed. After six days the captain found him in his cabin, "rolling from side to side . . . covered with blood and water and very much bruised." He remained below until February 18, when he was brought on deck on a mattress. Four days later the *Lucretia's* captain, having caught fever from Clarkson, died. Not until within a week's sail of Cape Sierra Leone was Clarkson well enough to order all old clothing thrown overboard and new shirts distributed. In the meantime he suffered the death of his personal servant and began to lose his memory and to have fainting spells. By now he had accepted the unquestioning trust placed upon him by the Negroes, and he was dangerously close to thinking himself their saviour, praying that he might personally make atonement for the guilt of his passengers. At the end of the voyage he asserted that he could "do with [the Negroes] as he please[d] by lifting up his finger." The danger to both Clarkson and the settlers was that this was so.[30]

Seven of the vessels preceded his, the first arriving at Kru Bay on February 28; from the *Lucretia* Clarkson sighted land on March 6. Still too weak to walk, he hoped to throw his burdens and his body upon the Governor, who was to receive the fleet, and upon the Company's surveyor, who was to have lots ready for the immigrants. But now Clarkson learned that there was no Governor, for the man chosen, Henry Dalrymple, had defected and was soon to found a rival colony at Bulama—where Benjamin Marston, who had befriended the Blacks at Birchtown, had gone, shortly to die of fever. Wilberforce and Thornton had written to Clarkson at Sierra Leone on December 28 urging him to take up the newly created post of Superintendent. His brother also had written to counsel acceptance, for the position promised prestige, money, and an opportunity further to strike at the slave trade. John Clarkson was alone with his responsibilities.[31]

Seldom can there have been so many responsibilities to bear. The official surveyor had disdained to clear the bush and chose instead to play

30. A[nna] M[arie] Falconbridge, *Narrative of Two Voyages to the River Sierra Leone, during the years 1791–2–3* . . . , 2nd ed. (London, 1802), pp. 138–39; Dennis, *Down in Nova Scotia*, pp. 363–64; Clarkson's prayer, *Sierra Leone Studies*, n.s., no. 1 (1953), pp. 11–13, and with different punctuation, Ingham, *Sierra Leone*, pp. 164–66; BM, Clarkson Papers: Surgeon's register of medical cases.

31. BM, Clarkson Papers: Wilberforce and Thornton to Clarkson, both Dec. 28, and Thornton to Clarkson, Dec. 20, 1791, May 3, July 23, Sept. 14, 1792, and Thomas to John, Jan. 7, May 3, July 17, 1792; Raymond, "Founding of Shelburne," pp. 275–76.

soldier with the sixteen miserable men under his command. As Superintendent, Clarkson had no real authority over the Company's employees, who had arrived shortly before, or over the Council, of which he was but one of eight members. The councillors ordered needless and contradictory supplies without telling him. Consignments were landed without anyone to receive them, only to wash away or to be broken into by the soldiers. The salt fish the Negroes were given four days a week was as likely to be spoiled as not; the turnips were usually so. The wrong materials were sent, equipment for growing cotton arriving before foodstuffs or building supplies; molasses casks leaked, flour was shipped in rotting sacks, and the storehouse laboriously built by the Nova Scotians soon could be nosed from well away, as it stank of rotting cheese and rancid butter. The ship-carried fever continued to rage on shore; over forty more Negroes died within the first weeks, and nearly a hundred in all succumbed after the onset of the rains. The drunken Company surgeon limited himself to administering emetics and bloodletting; the doctors died; the storekeepers died; starving Bulama settlers descended upon the colony; a gunner shot his arm off and died; high winds destroyed the temporary huts; Peters died in June. By then, seven hundred of Freetown's twelve hundred inhabitants were ill and six or seven settlers were dying each day. White sailors insulted the blacks, and Clarkson had a Nova Scotian flog three whites before the assembled residents of the colony. Clarkson urged patience and prayer, and the preachers, especially George, counselled resignation and more prayer. By September the Nova Scotians were on the verge of rebellion, and only Clarkson's presence and persuasion held them in check.[32]

At last the Company responded to Clarkson's entreaties, which had become hysterical and incoherent, and gave him the full powers of Governor. Although the Nova Scotians could not see it then, the worst of times passed with midyear, through Clarkson's strengthened position and through the arrival of more responsible officials. In November the first land was allotted—not the promised twenty acres, indeed but a fifth of that, and often no more fertile than the land left behind in Nova Scotia—but nonetheless land presumed to be entirely the Nova Scotians' own. For Clarkson had continued to dissemble about the quitrent. Ultimately his charges were to discover that he had all too literally followed Thornton's advice, given in another context, to "connive and temporize" if necessary in order to achieve his good ends, and they rose in rebellion against the Company as a result of its efforts to collect the rents.[33]

32. CO267/9: Peters [signed with his mark] to Dundas, n.d. [ca. April, 1792]; Fyfe, "Thomas Peters," pp. 8–11, and *History of Sierra Leone,* pp. 36–48.

33. Clarkson Papers, 41,263: "History of the Colony of Sierra Leone," fragment, in Thomas Clarkson's hand, n.d., with 1813 watermark, and 41,262A: John Clark-

For Clarkson this did not matter. In December 1792, he left for England, and the Colony passed into the hands of the young, dour, immensely stable Zachary Macaulay. At home Clarkson remained active in the Society for the Promotion of Permanent and Universal Peace; after being abruptly dismissed from all connection with the Sierra Leone Company in April 1793, he married and devoted himself energetically to Whig politics, Church of England ritual, banking in East Anglia, and fathering ten children. By 1812 he stopped subscribing funds in support of Sierra Leone.[34] In 1828, sixty-four years old, he died.

The subsequent history of the Negro settlers in West Africa is not part of the story of the blacks in Canada. But certain reactions of the Nova Scotians to their early years in Sierra Leone tell us something of what they had learned from their North American experience. Wilberforce had advised Clarkson that "all Blacks instead of being called Blacks or Negroes, [should] by universal consent amongst you [be] called Africans, as a more respectable way of speaking of them." The new settlers did not think of themselves as Africans, however; they were simply "The Nova Scotians." They thought the earlier liberated Africans, as well as the native groups, were inferior to them, and they held themselves aloof from other North American Negroes who came later. Into the twentieth century the Nova Scotians remained an identifiable group, and until the 1870s they provided much of the energy, leadership, and knowledge of Western skills needed in the young and disastrously mismanaged colony.[35]

The Nova Scotian experience also had confirmed the settlers in their religions. Their preachers had come out with them, each with a following, and they created in Sierra Leone an enclave of eighteenth-century Christianity within a Moslem and pagan land. As their churches multiplied, they recalled often apocryphal tales of the early Nova Scotian ministers; of

---

son to Thornton (not signed, incorrectly endorsed from "Mr. Gilbert"), April 18, 1792; Sierra Leone Company, *Substance of the Report Delevered by the Court of Directors . . . to the General Court of Proprietors . . . 1794* (London, 1794), pp. 13–18, 50–52, 63–67.

34. *Sixth Report of the Directors of the African Institution . . . 1812* (London, 1812), not paginated.

35. Consult Arthur T. Porter, *Creoledom: A Study of the Development of Freetown Society* (London, 1963). The Nova Scotians and Liberated Africans combined in 1960 to protest against Britain's decision to give Sierra Leone independence, for they had expected that Freetown would "be the home of . . . settlers for ever in close alliance with Britain in the same way as Bermuda and the Channel Islands." See Denison House, London, Anti-Slavery Society Office, Sierra Leone file B18: J. E. Williams, Secretary, Settlers' Descendants' Union Youth Section, to Harold MacMillan, carbon, March 22, 1960; Ahmed Alhadi, *The Re-emancipation of the Colony of Sierra Leone* (Freetown [1956]), pp. 5–6; *Bo* (S.L.) *Advance,* March 6, *Freetown African Vanguard,* March 16, and *Renascent African,* March 18, 1960.

George, who introduced baptism to Africa; of Marrant, Wilkinson, Kizell, and King; and of Cato Perkins, Anthony Elliott, Prince Stober, Joseph Jewett, John Ellis, William Ash, Luke Jordon, and other divines who had been on the emigrant ships. Those few Freetown Creoles who today are willing to discuss their vaguely held conceptions of life in Nova Scotia think most often of two facets of that life: the cold and the godly; for they are convinced that surely no Negroes could now remain in so bleak and forlorn a land, and they are warmed toward it by their thoughts of how their present forms of worship were acquired there. Nova Scotia is not remembered plain in Sierra Leone, but it is remembered nonetheless.[36]

White Nova Scotian memories of the migration also grew blurred. The Sierra Leone Company, in the person of Clarkson, was seen as an instigator of trouble where none had existed. Outsiders had broken down a basically stable situation and had taken away at least five hundred good citizens, "honest, sober and industrious," leaving the poor, the thieves, and the unskilled. Nova Scotians were unwilling to admit that the Negroes had migrated because they considered they had been given, belatedly, inferior land by a people who thought them inferior. In his pocket notebook John Clarkson had summarized the reasons mentioned to him by the Negroes for wishing to quit Nova Scotia. There were three: the whites seldom paid fairly for the work done, often declaring the established pay to have been lower for Negroes than for whites once a task had been completed; some Negroes never had received land; and those who did had not been confirmed in it. In his journal he added a fourth reason: most of those who signed on said they did so for their children, "whom they wished . . . to see established upon a better foundation." [37]

Neither Clarkson nor the Negroes mentioned the climate as a reason for leaving, but the whites seized upon it to explain why otherwise happy settlers did not stay. Bulkeley concluded that the climate of Africa was the chief attraction, and by 1823 Thomas Clarkson himself implied that this was so. Throughout the century, popular opinion came to agree that a process of natural selection, beyond the control of white Nova Scotians, had given rise to the migration. Sir Adams George Archibald, a former Lieutenant-Governor, and the only man who had attempted to tell their story—in 1885 to the Nova Scotia Historical Society—saw the Negroes in this light. Black men, he concluded, spoke with "true . . . pomposity," showed no ambition, liked "an idle and lazy life," and had "no aim . . .

36. In August 1964, the writer interviewed five members of the Settlers' Descendants' Union in Freetown and attempted to contact many others, without success. These generalizations may therefore be based upon a highly unrepresentative sampling.

37. BM, Clarkson Papers: "Remarks [in] Halifax," pp. 8–9.

for anything beyond mere animal existence"; those who had been left behind were "the idle, the drunken and the dishonest." [38]

But Nova Scotia's problems with Negroes, and Negro problems with Nova Scotia, had not ended when Clarkson's fifteen ships dropped below the horizon. Almost before Dundas could authorize payment of the £ 13,592 spent to transport one body of blacks to Sierra Leone,[39] there was another waiting to go. The real significance of John Clarkson's mission had not been read: hundreds of Negroes had left the New World rather than remain in the face of what they regarded as an almost total lack of opportunity. Now the British permitted Nova Scotia to be used as a dumping ground for Negroes who might well have been placed elsewhere, and in 1796 a band of non-Christian, warlike Jamaican Maroons began a life of exile in the colony. They too, in time, followed the *Lucretia* down that horizon.

The Maroons were descendants of Negro slaves (and perhaps of Arawak women) who had escaped from the Spanish before the British conquest of Jamaica. To the late eighteenth century they were what the Turks, the Maori, and the Punjabis were for later times: almost legendary warriors, feared and respected for their courage and their cruelty. The Spanish taught the Maroons to fight the British as invaders, and for a century they remained hidden away in the island's interior, making sporadic raids upon white settlements. The original group was reinforced by many who escaped from British slavery; this influx also came to be known as *Maroons,* a term of no certain origin which may have meant "dwellers on mountain tops," "runaways," or "stray dogs," depending upon the book one reads.[40] The

38. CO217/63: Bulkeley to Dundas, Feb. 3, 1792; PSHS, Simon Gratz Autograph Collection: Samuel Hopkins to Levi Hart, July 29, 1793; Thomas Clarkson, *Thoughts on the Necessity of Improving the Condition of the Slaves in the British Colonies . . .* , 2nd ed. (London, 1823), p. 15; *Halifax Royal Gazette,* Jan. 17, May 29, July 3, 1792; *Halifax Acadian Recorder,* Feb. 7, 1818; *The Tourist: A Literary and Anti-Slavery Journal, 1* (1833), 236; David Allison, *History of Nova Scotia* (Halifax, 1916), *1,* 599–600; Edwin Crowell, *A History of Barrington Township and Vicinity, Shelburne County, Nova Scotia, 1604–1870* (Yarmouth, N.S., [1923?]), pp. 224–25; Archibald, "Deportation of Negroes," pp. 139–40, 148, 152–53.

39. CO217/63: Dundas to Bulkeley, Jan. 15, Bulkeley to Dundas, Feb. 6, March 20, and Thornton to Dundas, April 11, encl. Harthshorne to Thornton, Feb. 9, all 1792.

40. Sir Alan Burns, *History of the British West Indies* (London, 1954), p. 50, n. 4, cites the majority view: that "Maroon" is from French *marron,* a corruption of Spanish *cimarron, cima* being a mountaintop. Fyfe, *History of Sierra Leone,* p. 79, accepts "runaway slave." Duncan Campbell, *Nova Scotia, In Its Historical, Mercantile and Industrial Relations* (Montreal, 1873), p. 198, prefers "hog hunter," as does C. H. Cecil, "The Maroons in Canada," *The Canada-West Indies Magazine, 24* (1935), 23–25.

Maroons maintained their separate identity throughout the eighteenth century; in 1665, again in 1730–39, and once more in 1795 there were outbreaks of sufficient magnitude to be referred to as Maroon Wars.

The last Maroon War began in July 1795. Britain was again at war with France, and by July most regular soldiers had been transferred to other areas of the Caribbean. The last regiment on the island was dispatched for Hispaniola on the 29th, but in the face of possible rebellion among the Maroons it was intercepted early in August and brought back to Montego Bay. Lord Balcarres, the newly arrived Governor, proclaimed martial law and ordered the Trelawny Town Maroons, who were at the center of the renewed violence, to surrender themselves to these troops. Few did so, and on the day scheduled for their surrender they burned their village, successfully attacked the Governor's militia, and took refuge amidst the hanging mountains of the Cockpit Country. By the end of September they had inflicted a second serious loss on the local military, and the Jamaican legislature sent to Cuba for large hunting dogs to seek out and destroy the blacks in their stronghold.

Before the dogs arrived, Major-General George Walpole, who was in charge of the campaign against the Maroons, succeeded in limiting their food and water supply and appeared, if given time, to be on a victorious course. In December, forty Spanish chasseurs and 104 savage Cuban dogs landed at Montego Bay; the Maroons already had offered a truce, and news of this vicious weapon to be used against them confirmed them in their decision to surrender; on the twenty-first the Council of War gave them ten days in which to do so. At the end of this period fewer than two dozen Maroons surrendered, but Walpole took no action against them throughout January, and four hundred came forward during the month. Upon Balcarres's orders Walpole then advanced against the Maroons, holding the dogs in reserve, for both Governor and General knew that their use would lead to censure in England. By March, Walpole had crushed the revolt.[41]

The Jamaican legislature advised Balcarres that those Maroons in revolt

41. An unemotional summary of the Maroon War appears in Burns, *British West Indies*, pp. 445–48, 553–55. The chief accounts of the war are George Wilson Bridges, *The Annals of Jamaica* (London, 1828), 2, 219–40; R. C. Dallas, *The History of the Maroons*, 2 vols. (London, 1803); [A. W. C. L. Crawford], Lord Lindsay, *Lives of the Lindsays; or, a Memoir of the House of Crawford and Balcarres*, 2nd ed. (London, 1858), 3, 1–146, containing much of the correspondence of Alexander, Earl of Balcarres; and Bryan Edwards, *The History, Civil and Commercial, of the British Colonies in the West Indies* (Philadelphia, 1806), 1, 337–94, virtually an official Jamaican justification for governmental policy. The most recent examinations are A. E. Furness, "The Maroon War of 1795," *Jamaican Historical Review, 5* (1965), 30–49; and Carey Robinson, *The Fighting Maroons of Jamaica* ([London], 1969), pp. 79–154, which are not always in agreement. See especially pp. 45 and 123, respectively.

who had not capitulated within the original ten-day period should be deported. Walpole disagreed with this decision, for he had accepted surrenders throughout January on his secretly given promise that the Maroons would be allowed to remain on their land, and the Governor had privately agreed that he might take surrenders until the fourteenth in any case. Both Walpole and the Maroons felt betrayed by Balcarres and the narrowly legalistic vote of the legislature; the General could show his anger by refusing to accept that body's offer of 500 guineas for the purchase of a sword of honor, but the 556 Trelawny Maroons who were marched aboard transports in June 1796, to be removed, could only reflect that they were, after all, Thursday's children.[42]

Balcarres's way to stop a leak was to sink the ship. He wanted the Maroons out of Jamaica, and at once, and he chose not to wait to learn from London where he might send the Maroons with permanent settlement in mind. Although Sierra Leone and the Bahamas were suggested to him, he chose British North America instead. On June 3 Balcarres wrote to the new Lieutenant-Governor of Nova Scotia, Sir John Wentworth, that he was sending the Maroons to Halifax in three transports, with provisions to follow. He asked neither Wentworth's permission nor his advice, and since he had decided six weeks earlier on this course of action, he clearly meant to present the Nova Scotian Governor with a fait accompli. Balcarres also wrote to Prince Edward, the Duke of Kent, then Commander-in-Chief in Nova Scotia, that the Maroons might serve the military there, and the Jamaican legislature voted a sum of £ 25,000 for transport, provisions, and the purchase of land in the Canadas, New Brunswick, or Nova Scotia. Two white commissioners accompanied the Maroons to oversee their settlement—a not unusual arrangement, for since 1739 superintendents had resided among the Maroons to attend to their interests and to keep them under control. "I have saved the island," wrote Balcarres.[43]

42. CO217/69; Walpole to Balcarres, Dec. 24, 1795; WO1/92: Balcarres to Dundas, n.d. [Jan. 30], March 26, April 17, 1796. Only the Maroons from Trelawney Town were sent to Nova Scotia, while those of the other four Maroon settlements, many of whom had been loyal to the British, remained in Jamaica. Furness, "Maroon War," p. 47, gives the figure that sailed as "Over 560."

43. CO217/67: Balcarres to Wentworth, June 3, and Wentworth to Duke of Portland, the Home Secretary, July 23, 25, Aug. 13, William Scott to Portland, Sept. 8, Milligan and Mitchell to Portland and to Lords Commissioners of the Admiralty, both Sept. 27, all 1796; CO217/71: Balcarres to Edward, June 3, and Portland to Edward, Oct. 5, 1796; CO217/68: Robert Sewell to John King, April 19, 1797, and n.d., with extract of Walpole to Balcarres, Dec. 24, 1795; WO1/92: Balcarres to Dundas, April 20, Oct. 1, 1796. Later, the representatives of Jamaica argued that they had never intended for the Maroons to be put ashore at Halifax, which is nonsense. Duplicates and additional Balcarres letters, which do not change the narrative here, were examined among the Crawford Muniments in the John Rylands Library, Manchester.

The Maroons reached Halifax on July 21 and 23. Dozens of small craft converged upon the lead ship, and from one appeared Prince Edward to provide a welcome to the city; he found the Maroons "a smartly dressed body of men," and he told their superintendents to put them to work on the citadel then being reconstructed on the hill back of the port. Chafing from a long sea voyage and inactivity, the Maroons offered to work without pay, but they were given the usual wage, which was ninepence a day, and they labored as a unit to construct one of the fortress's bastions.[44]

The Maroons' initial reception contrasted favorably with that of the earlier Negroes. The weather was warm and they could live in temporary wooden barracks and tents that were set up for them near the citadel, their labor was needed, they could earn money from the outset, and since their legend had preceded them, they had the respect that a frontier and sea-going community naturally gives to brave men. Although the Maroons were not Christians, they received early and sensible attention from the Society for the Propagation of the Gospel, which through Wentworth appointed Benjamin Gerrish Gray their chaplain and teacher. Later, when sixty Maroons were converted and moved to Boydville in order to be apart from their unregenerate brothers, the government provided a liberal sum for a church and chaplain.[45]

Governor Wentworth thought he was the key to successful Maroon resettlement, and he welcomed them. A man who seems to have been genuinely free of racial bias, Wentworth felt that he understood "the Negro mentality." There were several Negroes in his Royal Nova Scotia Regiment, when he visited Digby he was attended by a company of the free black militia trained there, and apparently he took a Negro mistress, since his own charming wife was much in the arms of others. He was aware of the labor needs that lay ahead, and he hoped to have the Maroons help build a canal between Halifax and the Shubenacadie River and also to form a corps of Maroon and Indian riflemen. Wentworth liked to collect as many

---

44. *Halifax Journal,* July 21, *Halifax Weekly Chronicle,* July 23, and *Halifax Royal Gazette,* July 26, 1796; Arthur P. Silver, "The Maroons in Nova Scotia," in George U. Hay, ed., *Canadian History Readings* (Saint John, 1900), *1,* 183–89; Beamish Murdoch, *A History of Nova-Scotia, or Acadie* (Halifax, 1867), *3,* 147–65. There is a persistent legend in Halifax that one of the bastions of the present Citadel was built by the Maroons (see William H. Borrett, *East Coast Port and Other Tales Told Under the Old Town Clock* [Halifax, 1944], p. 33), but the works on which they labored were demolished (Harry Piers, *The Evolution of the Halifax Fortress, 1749–1928* [Halifax, 1947], p. 42, n. 6).

45. CO217/67: Wentworth to Portland, Sept. 20, 1796; CO217/69: John Oxley to Wentworth, June 16, 1798; Charles William Vernon, *Bicentenary Sketches and Early Days of the Church in Nova Scotia* (Halifax, 1910), pp. 226–28; Charles Walter Bayer, *Christ Church, Dartmouth, Nova Scotia, 1817 to 1959* ([Dartmouth, 1960]), pp. 15–16.

merit badges as life would allow, and he may have hoped to show that he could create racial harmony where his predecessor had failed; clearly he was intrigued by the color, the gaiety, and the energy that the Maroons brought to the colony. He helped the Maroon commissioners find three thousand acres to buy near Preston, with town lots in Dartmouth, and he promised to obtain an additional eighteen thousand acres later.[46]

Wanting to restore the Maroons' self-confidence, which he fancied their defeat had cost them, he appointed captains and majors among them. Officers' uniforms, ordered by Wentworth, included handsome coats and vests, cocked hats, scarlet cloth, and gold lace. White metal buttons on the vests, and a device—unlikely ears of maize and an olive branch held by an even less likely alligator—were designed for them. As a consequence, Wentworth thought, the Maroons "are exceedingly attached to me." Nor had they lost any of their self-respect, for they quickly let the local Negroes know that they despised all who had ever been slaves of the British.[47]

The two men appointed by the Jamaican Assembly to accompany the Maroons were not entirely pleased with the Governor's reception, however. William Dawes Quarrell, the first commissioner, was a level-headed and experienced man who understood the Maroons well; later he was to become a member of the Council in Jamaica. He wanted to see the Maroons broken up and dispersed throughout Nova Scotia, so that they might be absorbed quickly and at low cost; Wentworth was determined that they should be settled together. Alexander Ochterlony, the second commissioner, was less stable than Quarrell; and as he had been the first to go to Cuba to buy the hunting dogs (although it was Quarrell, in fact, who had ulti-

46. On Wentworth see *DNB, 20,* 1169–71; *Dictionary of American Biography* (hereafter, *DAB*), *19,* 656–67; Clifford K. Shipton, *Sibley's Harvard Graduates,* vol. *13, 1751–1755* (Boston, 1965), pp. 650–81; Lawrence Shaw Mayo, *John Wentworth, Governor of New Hampshire, 1767–1775* (Cambridge, Mass., 1921), and John Wentworth, *The Wentworth Genealogy: English and American* (Boston, 1878), pp. 536–48. There are two novels about Wentworth: Shirley Barker, *The Last Gentleman* (New York, 1960) and Thomas H. Raddall, *The Governor's Lady* (Garden City, N.Y., 1960).

47. CO217/67: Wentworth to Portland, July 25, Aug. 13, Sept. 21, 24, Oct. 8, 29, and replies Sept. 7, Oct. 6; memorandum of articles needed from England for Maroons, and Edward to Portland, Aug. 15, all 1796; CO217/68: Wentworth to Portland, April 21, 1797; Sheffield Central Library Archives, Earl Fitzwilliam Papers: Wentworth to Fitzwilliam, Sept. 25, 1796; *Extracts and Copies of* Letters *from Sir John Wentworth, Lieutenant Governor of Nova Scotia, to his Grace the Duke of Portland; respecting the Settlement of the* Maroons *in that Province* (London, 1797): July 23, 25, Sept. 20, Dec. 21, 1796; Will R. Bird, *This is Nova Scotia,* 3rd ed. (Toronto, 1955), pp. 193–95; Mrs. [Mary Jane] William Lawson, *History of the Townships of Dartmouth, Preston and Lawrencetown* (Halifax, 1893), pp. 163–65; *The Monthly Review,* n.s., *21* (1796), 414–21; *The European Magazine and London Review, 44* (1803), 36–41.

mately done so), not all of the Maroons trusted him. He wanted to settle the group in some tropical area, where he might be their colonel, and he pushed Sierra Leone, the Cape of Good Hope, or Santo Domingo upon the Maroons' leaders. Wentworth was determined that the Maroons should remain in the province. With each man bent upon his own path, a clash was inevitable.[48]

The center of Maroon activity was a spacious summer home built in 1792 by Francis Green, the Sheriff of Halifax, now renamed Maroon Hall, where the two commissioners set up residence. When Quarrell moved out in December, upon discovering that Ochterlony was working against permanent settlement, the hall became a "huge barrack of mountaineer banditti out of employment," a "fountain of Wantonness," a center of cockfighting and prostitution. Ochterlony took five or six of the most attractive Maroon girls to his bed, keeping what the surveyor for the Maroons, Theophilus Chamberlain, called "a seraglio for his friends." When one Maroon cut his own throat while fighting with his wife, the commissioner declared that despair over living in Nova Scotia was the cause. The province was "the Devils own Country, a Hell of a Country, a Country fit only for the Devil to remain in." In the meantime, Wentworth was admiring the copybook ability of five boys who were taught in the Maroon school nearby. "Good manners always procure us respect," they wrote, over and over again.[49]

By midwinter the Governor was receiving complaints from Haligonians against the Maroons. They listened to the various ministers of religion who moved among them "with contumely." They persisted in holding to plural wives, and to their burial customs, which seemed bizarre and unhealthy. They were given to swaggering about in their military garb, arrogant, rude, heathenish, and superstitious. The hard summer of labor now turned into a long winter of discontent: the Maroons protested that they could not grow yams, bananas, cocoa, or pepper, as they had expected to do, and they refused to work. When a few planted potatoes, other Maroons attacked them, apparently at Ochterlony's urging, concerned as he was that such signs of cooperation would root them to Nova Scotia. The winter proved to be particularly severe, with the snow standing seven feet deep. In the spring, which was the latest since 1749, Wentworth saw that his task would be far

48. CO217/67: Portland to Wentworth, Dec. 14, 1796; CO217/69: Gray to Wentworth, June 18, 1798; Bryan Edwards, *An Historical Survey of the Island of Santo Domingo together with an Account of the Maroon Negroes in the Island of Jamaica* . . . (London, 1801), pp. 355–56.

49. CO217/69: Chamberlain to Wentworth, June 20, 1798; CO217/70: Wentworth to King, Aug. 18, 1799; John Patrick Martin, *The Story of Dartmouth* (Dartmouth, 1957), pp. 99–100; Lawson, *History of Dartmouth,* p. 177.

more difficult than he had anticipated, and he asked the Maroons to give Nova Scotia a trial for at least one more year.[50]

For everyone, the second year was more difficult than the first. Wentworth confessed to the Duke of Portland, Dundas's successor in the Home Office, that the Maroons' "early life of hunting, predatory undisciplined war, and gratifications" had not prepared them for a Nova Scotian winter. Their dislike for shoes and stockings led to frostbite: "I do not find that any one has lost more than a joint of a Toe, or finger, and but a few of these." Shortly thereafter, he hinted that it might be best if the Maroons did not remain. Expenses had been more than anyone had expected, the Duke of Portland was insisting that Jamaica must meet the Maroons' costs, and he refused to send them to the Cape of Good Hope.

Jamaica failed to meet the new expenses, as they mounted well beyond all original estimates. In May, Balcarres warned Quarrell that the Jamaican House of Assembly would provide assistance only through July and would then limit subsequent expenditures to £ 10 per person. Wentworth wrote the Duke of Portland that this was insufficient, but the Duke did little more than to tell Wentworth that he had right on his side and that he, a new governor of a colony of considerably less importance than Jamaica, should personally see to it that Jamaica met its obligations.[51]

In July, the Maroons lost their two superintendents. Wentworth discharged Ochterlony early in the month for having retarded the progress of the Maroons in unspecified ways, and although he wished Quarrell to remain, he too resigned on the twenty-second, largely because of his opposition to the segregated pattern of settlement as a single community that Wentworth was intent upon. In June, Quarrell had asked Theophilus Chamberlain, who was in charge of the government's commissariat for the Maroons at Preston, to take up Ochterlony's duties, and in six days Chamberlain had the Maroons back in the field with the terse command, "No Work no Yam." [52]

Wentworth named Alexander Howe to be Ochterlony's replacement. Some thought Howe was expert in dealing with black men, and he did

50. CO217/68: Wentworth to James, May 28, and Oxley to Wentworth, May 31, 1797; CO217/69: Gray to Wentworth, June 18, 1798; Thomas Chandler Haliburton, *An Historical and Statistical Account of Nova-Scotia* . . . (Halifax, 1829), 2, 282, 287–89.

51. CO217/68: Wentworth to Portland, April 21, May 7, 17, June 2, Quarrell to Howe, Aug. 8, and reply, Aug. 9, encl. in Wentworth to Portland, Aug. 12, 1797, with bills of exchange.

52. Ibid.: Montague James to Walpole, April 23, 1797; CO217/69: Chamberlain to Wentworth, June 20, 1798; PANS, Chamberlain file. Ochterlony took temporary employment with Dr. Bray's Associates: SPG Archives, Associates' Account Books, April 26, 1801.

wish to see Negroes remain in Nova Scotia, as his initial opposition to John Clarkson had shown; but he had demonstrated little talent for working with Negroes and had made it reasonably clear that he saw them as a reservoir of cheap labor. The Maroons resented the loss of Ochterlony and Quarrell; they resented Howe's appointment even more.

The seasons brought no relief. Howe was unable to get lands laid out because of incessant rain. The cabbages the Maroons planted froze, and when Wentworth sent for half a ton of yams so that they might prove to themselves that they would not grow, the experiment merely added to their despair. Howe forced them to work at very low wages, making bricks, digging cellars, carrying stones, hoeing potatoes, making hay, or "any thing I direct them to do." He required that each Maroon who wished to go to Halifax must come to him for a pass. Nineteen Maroons died; pleurisy was common; Wentworth continued to be cheerful about lost toes. The only hopeful note was a mild autumn and a private agreement between the Maroons' Colonel Montague James and Wentworth that the Governor would forward petitions for removal on to Britain in exchange for the Maroons' giving the colony another winter—an agreement which Wentworth privately acknowledged would have to be patched together again, since he had no hope of success short of another two years.

By spring Wentworth and James had quarrelled, and circumstance was taking the matter out of the Governor's hands. He·had expected to be given time to demonstrate that Negroes could live "at their ease with their families on their *own lands"* in Nova Scotia, as a separate but equal yeomanry, but James, Walpole, and Balcarres defeated him. Many whites in Nova Scotia hoped to see Wentworth brought low, for as Surveyor-General of the King's Woods he had prevented speculation in land, and as a genuinely humane governor he had extended aid to penurious Indians as well as to the Maroons. Those who were not included in the gay social life he and his Lady, Frances, brought to the capital, or who were excluded from his patronage, encouraged the Maroons to complain of "unfelt distresses," for they were one more means by which Wentworth might be attacked. He not only had done his sum wrong, he had done the wrong sum: the majority of white settlers in Nova Scotia did not want him to find a solution to the Maroon problem at all; they wanted the Maroons removed.[53]

The Maroons and their voice in the Imperial Parliament, General Wal-

53. CO217/68: Wentworth to Portland, July 10, Aug. 12, Nov. 4, Portland to Wentworth, June [12], Sept. 11, and Oxley's report on health of Maroons, Nov. 1, all 1797; PANS, *419:* Wentworth to Assembly, June 29, 1797; Northamptonshire Record Office, Delapre Abbey, Northampton, Earl Fitzwilliam Papers, Box 53: Wentworth to Fitzwilliam, March 9, 1798.

pole, worked to the same end. In October, 1796, Walpole's friend Charles James Fox had asked the House of Commons whether the Jamaican government had not broken faith with the Maroons, and from that point forward, he, Walpole, and William Wilberforce had kept the Maroon issue alive in Parliament. When Bryan Edwards, member from Grampound (and later a historian of the Maroon War), defended the planters in their reliance upon the letter of the law, Fox replied that Jamaica had "too strictly kept" its engagement with the Maroons, a judgment difficult to contest.[54] In April, 1797, Colonel James petitioned Walpole to save his people from their "miserable situation," and at Walpole's request he sent two Maroons to England to apprise him of their needs. James also broke his promise to Wentworth to hold silent until spring, for on the very August day he made that promise he wrote to the Duke of Portland, and he did so again in the late autumn. In the spring of 1798, Walpole forwarded to Portland copies of letters he had received by "unusual channels," all of which contradicted Wentworth's optimistic reports: the Maroons were perishing from cold and hunger, they were ill-clothed and despised, and they were desperate to be taken elsewhere.[55]

The Duke of Portland turned upon Wentworth sharply. He ordered him to limit himself strictly to the functions of his office and not to interfere with the agents of Jamaica, and he refused to approve the new bills Wentworth had drawn for the Maroons. He also transmitted an unsigned letter that charged Wentworth with setting up a "Maroon Establishment" of Howe and twenty-four white (and one Maroon) functionaries, through whom he intended to plunder the island of Jamaica (already having spent £ 14,000 in the last twelve months, most of it needlessly). This letter, which appears to have been written by Quarrell, also charged that Wentworth's frequent reports on regular church attendance omitted to say that such faithfulness was stimulated by giving a bottle of rum to every group of four Maroons who came to services. There had not been one Christian marriage or burial, except at Boydville, and all hope of improving the

---

54. *The Senator: or, Parliamentary Chronicle* . . . [hereafter, *The Senator*] (London, 1796), *16*, 103–08. Edwards told Wilberforce that the Maroons were cannibals and would eat any missionary sent to them, even in Nova Scotia, a charge so ridiculous he did not attempt to repeat it in his book. See "The Maroons of Jamaica," *Atlantic Monthly, 5* (1860), 222.

55. CO217/68: James to Walpole, April [23], 1797; CO217/69: Walpole to Portland, July n.d., Thomas Meanwell to Walpole, James to Walpole, and James's petition, all April 23, Quarrell to Walpole, June 4, Andrew Smith to his brother, June 3, and James et al. to Portland, Nov. 4, all 1797 and all encl. in Portland to Wentworth March 8, 1798; Portland to Walpole, March 21, 28, 1798, latter encl. James's petition of Aug. 12, 1797; Walpole to Portland, March 23, encl. James's petition, n.d., and April 6, 1798, encl. James to Walpole, April 23, 1797.

morals of the Maroons had been frustrated by keeping them together as a body rather than dispersing them among Christian whites.[56]

Portland's asperity arose, at least in part, from the fire he found himself under in Parliament. General Walpole, who had won election to the House of Commons from Derby the year before, was a vocal member of the Opposition and a close friend of George Tierney, member from Southwark, the acting leader of the Opposition on the occasion of Charles James Fox's absence from the House. Walpole further earned the Prime Minister's dislike when, in May of 1798, Tierney challenged the younger Pitt to a duel and the General acted as second. In the House it was Tierney who, whenever Walpole spoke of the Maroons, seconded the motion, the speech, or the sentiment. Although Walpole invariably spoke with too much warmth and revealed more than once that his concern was more for his honor than for his Maroons, Tierney was consistently dangerous to Pitt's friend, Wentworth.

Determined to get all of the Maroons' complaints into the record, Walpole read out Colonel James's petition of August 1797 and moved to have an earlier June petition laid before the House. Dundas replied that no such paper as the June petition existed, to which Walpole replied with heavy sarcasm that he personally had given Portland the original and, in any case, that he retained a copy of it; Dundas added that if the document were addressed to the General rather than to His Majesty's ministers, it was not in fact a petition at all.[57] When Walpole asked to have the petition of April 1797 laid before the House, the Government replied that this document had been lost. The General read the covering letter he had written when forwarding the petition, whereupon Pitt pointed out that there was no proof that the alleged petition was authentic, even if it were to be found. Walpole then moved that the House should debate whether or not the negotiations he had held with the Maroons had been honored properly. The removal of the Maroons from the heat of the tropics to the arctic winds of Nova Scotia had been an act of gross inhumanity, he concluded.[58]

56. CO217/69: Portland to Wentworth, April 4, June 7, July 1, Wentworth to Portland, April 24, Oxley's returns of Maroons, March 1, April 1, all 1798; CO217/72: Portland to Wentworth, draft, March n.d., 1798.

57. This petition has not been found.

58. *The Parliamentary Register; or, History of the Proceedings and Debates of the House of Lords and Commons* . . . [hereafter, *Debrett's Parliamentary Register*] (London, 1798), *5*, 297, 307, 333, 407–09; *6*, 84–95, 231–32, 447. Three of Walpole's speeches also appear, in slightly different form, in William Woodfall, *An Impartial Report of the Debates that Occur in the Two Houses of Parliament* . . . [hereafter, *Woodfall's Parliamentary Reports*] (London, 1798), *2*, 65–66, 159, 430–37. The motion also appears in *The Senator* (London, 1798), *20*, 940–47. See [Bryan Edwards], *The Proceedings of the Governor and Assembly of Jamaica, in Regard to the Maroon Negroes* . . . (London, 1796), p. 27, which although pro-Jamaican,

Dundas was ready. Walpole's motion was tantamount to hauling the entire Jamaican Assembly before the House of Commons to answer to a charge which was purely of Jamaica's internal concern, he said. Correspondence already laid before the House was sufficient to answer the Government's critics, for Dundas trusted Wentworth completely. (Portland was awaiting the Governor's reply to the anonymous correspondent's charges against him, and made no comment.) Jamaica had been liberal in its aid to the Maroons, for nearly £ 50,000 had been spent for their welfare.[59] The Secretary of War then read an extract from one of Walpole's letters to Balcarres which revealed that the General had wished to settle the Maroons near Spanish Town, in the lowlands, where liquor might be used to break their spirit. (He did not read—since he did not have—another letter that would have revealed it was Walpole who first thought of using the Cuban dogs in Jamaica.) Did the General think his plan more humane than the obvious care Wentworth had lavished on the Maroons? Thereafter an embarrassed Walpole limited himself to requests for documents that would verify Jamaica's expenditure of the sum Dundas reported, and his motion failed by a vote of five to thirty-four.[60]

Wentworth's account of his activities, and what we must take to be Quarrell's own report to the Duke of Portland, disagree utterly. From the evidence, one may conclude that while the Governor's facts are not to be disputed, his relationship to those facts was not reported with candor. Certainly he was turning the presence of the Maroons to his own benefit, for he and Howe used them as body servants in a colony where such help was notably scarce; and the Governor may well have thought of his band of fierce warriors, fanatically loyal (as he thought) to himself, as a sturdy defense against more local dangers than the French. Wentworth had no love for Jamaica and would not have hesitated to plunder that colony's treasury. If he could help himself, his colony, and the Maroons at the expense of Jamaica and its representatives, then why not?

The Governor could not let the anonymous attack go unanswered, and on June 23 he dispatched a full plea of defense, together with testimonials

provides support for Walpole's position. The Wentworth-Portland correspondence was printed in *Papers relative to the Settling of the Maroons in His Majesty's Province of Nova Scotia* (London, 1798).

59. Dundas's sum seems reasonably correct, although lower figures have been suggested: £ 41,000 (Lawson, *History of Dartmouth*, p. 167); £ 46,000 (Haliburton, *Account of Nova-Scotia, 3,* 291); and £ 47,000 (John McGregory, *British America* [Edinburgh, 1832], *2,* 205).

60. *Debrett's Parliamentary Register, 6,* 84–95, 451–52; *Woodfall's Parliamentary Reports, 2,* 201, 726; *The Senator* (1800), *23,* 998, 1694. *Woodfall's, 2,* 437, and *The Senator, 20,* 947, give the vote as 5–34; *Debrett's, 6,* 95, cites a vote of 5–35. See also Furness, "Maroon War," p. 41.

from Howe, Chamberlain, Gray, and others. In every case, he insisted, save for a minor error over a marriage, he had been scrupulously correct; rather than wishing to see expenses mount, he held them in check by quieting all talk of transporting the Maroons elsewhere. The financial problems arose from Jamaica's failure to meet its obligations, and a humane man could not do otherwise than draw bills if the Maroons were to be fed. Ochterlony had been the cause of the Maroons' discontent: he had forced those who received wages to divide them with those who did not, removing all incentive; he had slurred Wentworth to the Maroons, and he had assured them that if they refused to work the government would be compelled to remove them to Africa; he had insisted that the Maroons should receive equal pay, leading to demands among white Nova Scotians that the Maroons be sent away. Wentworth had employed Maroons as servants at Government House and had paid them the same rate as English servants only to combat prejudice.

Two of the accompanying testimonials are convincing. One charge in the anonymous letter had been that Wentworth and Howe were lining their pockets with rebates after paying four times the necessary price for flour. Lawrence Hartshorne was one of the two suppliers, and having served to the complete satisfaction of such diverse personalities as Parr, Clarkson, and George earlier, he spoke to this point with some authority. He submitted a certificate from the Clerk of the Peace demonstrating that, in fact, he had furnished flour well under the price set by the Court of Sessions. And John Oxley, whom Lord Balcarres himself had appointed surgeon to the Maroons, submitted an unqualified statement of support for the Governor. Nor did he back Quarrell in his contention that the Maroons should have been dispersed throughout the colony, for this would have broken down family ties, removed the Negroes from their one market, Halifax, and taken those who had received land around Boydville away from their only basis for stability. In any case, Wentworth had brought the more refractory Maroons down from Preston to Bedford Basin in the spring, so there now were three settlements, and any further fragmentation would be foolish.[61]

But Wentworth's affection for the Maroons was sorely tried by Montague James and the Preston group, who threatened to kill cattle for food. The Governor dispatched armed soldiers to rattle sabers at them, scattered the five ringleaders of the settlement and their families to remote towns

61. CO217/69: Portland to Wentworth, Nov. 9, and Wentworth to Portland, June 23, encl. Oxley, June 16; Gray, June 18, Chamberlain, Hartshorne, and John Tremain, June 20, Howe, James Moody, June 23, all to Wentworth; and Wentworth to King, June 26, all 1798. CO217/70: Wentworth, "Statement of Facts respecting the Settling of Maroons in Nova Scotia . . . ," May 29, 1799.

throughout the province, and gave further encouragement to the settlers in Boydville, where James Palmer was organizing a small band of hard-working, Christian converts into a model of Wentworth's hopes. All of the Maroons would yet be self-sufficient, Wentworth predicted, if provisions could be continued at least until the autumn of 1800.[62]

Portland accepted Wentworth's explanations, but he and the Governor realized that neither of them could be Ezekiel nor the Maroons their valley of dry bones. While the Duke wrote warmly that Sir John was "incapable of concealing, as he is of knowingly misrepresenting, any fact, which it is his duty to make me acquainted with," he nonetheless encouraged Jamaica to send out an agent to take charge of the Maroons' finances. And while he refused to receive any more Maroon petitions in his official capacity— even one so engagingly phrased as that of January, which protested that they could never "thrive where the Pine Apple does not"—he nonetheless asked Wentworth to answer each of their complaints, and those of Quarrell who no longer was writing anonymously, as they were raised. The Secretary of State wanted to keep these complaints from becoming the subject of further attention in the House of Commons, and the best means of doing so might be to bow to the Maroons' request and send them either to Africa or, as they now suggested, to Australia.[63]

How Sierra Leone again came to mind is not entirely clear. While the Maroons were being boarded at Montego Bay for Halifax, that African colony had been considered briefly and then put aside. Early in January 1799, Henry Thornton sent a new petition from the Maroons to Portland, and he may have received it from Walpole via Wilberforce. Certainly the initiative came from Nova Scotia; equally certainly it did not come from Wentworth, who was genuinely surprised when he learned in May that negotiations for the transfer of the Maroons already were well advanced.[64]

Throughout February and March Portland and Thornton worked out a plan for the transfer. In March Lawrence Hartshorne, who was in London, prepared a paper about the Maroons for the Sierra Leone Company, apparently without telling Wentworth. Misinformed that the removal of

62. CO217/70: Wentworth to Portland, April 13, May 5, encl. Palmer et al. to Wentworth, May 5, 1799.

63. CO217/69: Portland to Wentworth, July 31, 1798; CO217/70: Thornton to Portland, and reply, Jan. 4, 1799, encl. Wentworth to Portland, Nov. 17, 1798.

64. CO217/70: Maroon petition, n.d., encl. in Thornton to Portland, Jan. 5; Portland to Wentworth, Jan. 17, reply, May 5, 1799; *Halifax Evening Mail*, Aug. 5, 1924; Fyfe, *History of Sierra Leone*, p. 80; Douglas Brymner, "The Jamaica Maroons —How They Came to Nova Scotia—How They Left it," *Proceedings and Transactions of the RSC* [hereafter, RSC, *Proceedings and Transactions*], sec. 2 (1895), p. 90. Haliburton, *Account of Nova-Scotia, 3,* 291, wrongly credits Wentworth with thinking of Sierra Leone first.

the Nova Scotians in 1792 had cost £ 30,000, and estimating that the Maroons might be resettled for little more than a third of that, while if they remained in North America they might well cost £ 10,000 annually to maintain, Portland scented a bargain. He offered to pay for transportation and settlement, as well as the costs of education for the Maroons, if the Company would accept and administer them. In May the acting Governor of the colony, John Gray, tentatively selected a site for them on an offshore island where they could live off the land reasonably soon after arrival, and he requested provisions for only four months.[65]

Wentworth complained to Portland on May 30 that news had arrived of these negotiations with the Sierra Leone Company and that the Maroons, convinced they were soon to be removed, refused to work at all. Even the Boydville group now wished to go to Africa, although by separate vessel, to be settled away from the Preston blacks. "Nor will they believe I heard nothing of it," the Governor plaintively wrote, in effect asking the Duke to tell him of his plans. On the same day Portland dispatched a bristling note, charging Wentworth with continuing to disregard all requests for vouchers on the Maroons' expenses and warning that until they were submitted, Wentworth personally would be held responsible for every bill.

By secret letter on June 10, Portland at last told Sir John Wentworth of his plans: Walpole and the Preston Maroons had won. Pleading heavy expenses and the passage of time without clear evidence of successful assimilation of the Maroons to Nova Scotia, Portland revealed that the *Asia* would arrive in October to carry them to Africa. Clothing and provisions would be purchased in England and shipped out on the *Asia,* so that expenses could be controlled from London, and the Governor's sole duty was to get the Maroons ready to embark, with their agricultural implements, and to sell their land and houses as advantageously as possible after they left. Portland charged Wentworth with the impossible task of withholding knowledge of the plan from the Maroons until the last minute, for this was knowledge they already had. John Gray also wrote to Wentworth, warned that the Maroons must understand that they would receive no provisions after the first months in Sierra Leone, and suggested that since much trouble had developed with the Nova Scotians over alleged

65. CO217/70: Portland to Wentworth, Jan. 17, 20, Thornton to Portland, Feb. 23, Thornton to King, March 11, 19, Portland to the Company, March 5, resolutions of the Company, Feb. 23, March 8, all 1799, and unsigned memorandum, ca. Feb., 1799; CO267/10: Portland to Company, draft, March n.d., Gray to Portland, May 6, June 10, Thornton to King, July 20, Council to Directors, May 8, June 10, and Gray to Council, May 13, all 1799; CO270/4: Sierra Leone Council, Minutes, Sept. 30, Oct. 28, Dec. 10, 1799; Claude George, *The Rise of British West Africa . . .* (London, 1904), pp. 462–68. Ultimately the transfer and attendant expenses were to cost the British government over £ 60,000.

promises made to them, before embarking each Maroon should be given a paper setting forth the Company's terms, the papers to be read to them before witnesses.[66]

Portland noted that the wishes of the Maroons were not to be considered; not one Maroon was to be permitted to remain in Nova Scotia. If the Boydville group was afraid to travel on the same vessel as the Preston Maroons, measures could be taken to see to it that no one carried a weapon aboard ship. Thus warned, Wentworth set out to account for every Maroon. Two families had gone to Windsor, on the far side of the province, to work for William Cottman Tonge, a member of the Assembly, and they too were ordered back, possibly because Wentworth detested the man. "Neither Mr. Tonge, nor the Maroons . . . shall be suffered to frustrate my instructions to send them *all* to Africa," Wentworth wrote, although he privately hoped that Palmer's Boydville blacks might nonetheless refuse to go, and while in public he said nothing against the Duke of Portland, in private he felt otherwise: Lady Wentworth wrote to her close friend in England, Lady Fitzwilliam, that the Duke "has conducted himself with great duplicity." [67]

The *Asia* sailed with Portland's orders and the Company's terms,[68] in the second week of October—much too late to get the Maroons away before winter unless captain and crew were unusually efficient and fortunate. They were neither. The vessel sailed into the St. Lawrence River first, where it was commandeered for military work at Quebec, and when it was released, a portion of its crew deserted and the ship ran aground. Freed of earth, it was held fast by ice. In early December Wentworth learned that the Maroons were to be kept in Nova Scotia throughout the winter at the colony's expense. Portland's insistence on speed had merely led to more antagonism between whites and blacks in Nova Scotia, since all had expected to be rid of the problem long before Christmas.

Wentworth had not learned his lesson. He tried to charter another vessel, although he had been instructed to do nothing, and after organizing the Maroons so that they might embark on six hours' notice, he purchased a quantity of brandy and tobacco for the voyage. Portland replied in a

66. CO270/4: Wentworth to Portland, May 30, replies, May 30, June 10, Sept. 7, 1799.

67. Ibid.: depositions of Moody, July 2, and Wallace, July 15, and Wentworth to Portland, Aug. 17, and to King, Aug. 18, and Portland to Wentworth, Oct. 8, 9, 1799; CO217/71: deposition of Barclay, May 25, and Fraser to Wentworth, May 31, 1799; Earl Fitzwilliam Papers, box 57: Lady Wentworth to Lady Fitzwilliam, Aug. 3, 1800. *Antigonish* (N.S.) *Casket,* July 8, 1943, and Thomas J. Brown, *Place-Names of the Province of Nova Scotia* (n.p., 1922), p. 19, state that Maroons remained at Tracadie and Preston, respectively; but the first is definitely mistaken and the second probably so.

68. CO267/10: Thornton to Portland, Oct. 5, 1799.

scorching letter that Wentworth's unwarranted deviations from instructions were intolerable, that the brandy and tobacco would have to be sold at once, and that he was to keep his hands off all Maroon affairs thereafter. Eventually Portland suspended Wentworth's salary and refused to release it until he had accounted for all expenditures. Thornton wrote that the cost of hiring another vessel was prohibitive, and in any case no land was ready in Sierra Leone for the Maroons, since all was in turmoil over an expected French attack. In February, Portland drafted a note to the Company advising that another ship was being sent out later in the month and to expect the Maroons in May, but this dispatch apparently was not sent, and assuredly no such vessel appeared off Halifax during the winter. In the meantime, the *Asia's* Captain, George Ross, had traveled overland to Halifax and was living in Maroon Hall in order to become acquainted with his future passengers.[69]

The *Asia* arrived on the last day of May, and by June 6 Wentworth had the Maroons ready to embark. When the Agent of Transports on board the *Asia* found that he needed fourteen new crew members, he foolishly sent to England for them rather than hiring men in Halifax, much to Portland's displeasure. Not until August 3, then, one year late, did the Maroons depart. Several clandestinely sold their tools and four deserted to escape going. In a less-than-clear statement typical of Wentworth's later dispatches, the Governor reported that the *Asia* had taken aboard "Five hundred and fifty one persons in good health except those who are ill." The Agent, with the help of Chamberlain and Seth Coleman, Jamaica's agent, took the usual inventory of personal possessions as the Negroes boarded.[70]

The Maroons were by no means as badly off in terms of material possessions as the Nova Scotians, who had voluntarily preceded them. Major John Jarrett, his wife, and one of his daughters, for example, owned two coats, four vests, one pair of trousers, six shirts, four pairs of stockings, three pairs of shoes, two hats, twenty-four handkerchiefs, three walking sticks, sixteen gowns, fifteen petticoats, ten shifts, two women's hats, an apron, two towels, a tablecloth, a box of trinkets, twenty-one blankets, and miscellaneous bedding. There were three other Jarrett children, all presum-

69. CO217/73: Wentworth to King, Dec. 3, 21, 1799, Jan. 20, 1800, Wentworth to Portland, Dec. 21, 1799, and reply, draft, Jan. n.d., 1800; CO217/74: Thornton to King, Feb. 12, and Portland to Thornton, draft, Feb. 13, 1800; CO217/75: Office for Auditing Public Accounts to Lords Commissioners of H.M. Treasury, Oct. 21, 1801; PANS, "Negroes: Duplicate Accounts of the Final Settlement of the Jamaica Maroons in N.S., 1798–1804."

70. CO217/75: Wentworth to Portland, June 10, encl. Wentworth to the Lieut.-Sheriff, June 6, and reply, June 7, and Portland to Wentworth, draft, July n.d., all 1800.

ably provided for in much the same way. Such entries are typical. Of the 550 Maroons recorded on the return (one seems to have escaped the census), there were 151 men, 177 women, and 222 children.[71]

The Maroons refused to sign the terms proposed by Ross but acceded to them verbally. At the last minute they offered to send five hundred slaves back to Nova Scotia from West Africa to replace their lost labor; no one was listening. The *Asia* then sailed, manned by a party of forty-five soldiers to make up a full crew and to keep the Maroons in order. Again acting against instructions, but firm in his conviction that the Negroes deserved better rations than the very meager fare provided by the Company, Wentworth added tea, sugar, wine, and molasses to the provisions; and since no one had thought to mention medicines, he also supplied them.[72]

The crossing was a poor ending to life in Nova Scotia. At least twenty-five Maroons died and one committed suicide; one baby was born, Ross quelled a near mutiny, and the steward in charge of provisions proved to be a thief. In mid-voyage one of the Maroons' officers, Montague Johnston, complained that they were not receiving their full supplies and asked to superintend the weights. The transport agent admitted that he often substituted grog for rum, and his steward, a Nova Scotian Negro of Loyalist descent, confessed that the Maroons also had been defrauded of a portion of their bread ration. The supply of beef ran out because the same steward had sold some before leaving Halifax. Johnston was granted his wish.[73]

The *Asia* anchored off Sierra Leone on September 30, and Ross and the Maroon officers went ashore. The news that greeted them was no less surprising than the welcome Clarkson had received eight years before: the colony was in a state of insurrection and the Maroons were needed immediately to suppress the rebellion. The Nova Scotian settlers had successfully resisted the levying of quitrents and had enlarged their list of grievances into a general attack upon the Sierra Leone Company. Four days before the *Asia* arrived, a majority of the Nova Scotians, especially from Cato Perkins's congregation, had risen in anger and pillaged the houses of the loyal. Johnston consented to lead a Maroon attack on these rioters, and in a few days the rebellion was over. Granville Town became theirs, and the Company granted the Maroons a thousand acres; within the month nearly all were living ashore. A very few were to find their way back to Jamaica years later.[74]

71. CO217/75: Wentworth to Portland, encl. certificates and return, Aug. 6, 7, 1800.

72. Ibid.: Wentworth to Gray, Aug. 5, to Portland, Aug. 6, and reply, draft, Oct. n.d., 1800; Brymner, "Jamaica Maroons," p. 90.

73. Fourah Bay College Library, Sierra Leone Room, Freetown: Diaries of George Ross. The first of five volumes begins in mid-voyage.

74. CO2/1: Charles Stevenson to John Sullivan, March 10, 1804; Fyfe, *History*

Wentworth had been a genuine friend to the Maroons in Nova Scotia. He had risked much on their behalf, for Portland was a powerful man, a necessary reinforcement to Pitt during his first administration. Wentworth had no wish to attract the enmity of the Portland Whigs, for he was too wise in the ways of political machination to misconceive his own relatively flimsy basis of power. Yet he persisted in the face of Portland, the Preston Maroons, and many in the white Nova Scotian community, to champion what he thought was the Maroons' cause. In the final analysis he was wrong, for his paternalistic insistence upon attending to the Maroons' needs over their own leaders' wishes to escape this "Nova Scarcity" was ill-calculated to placate so vigorous a body. Wentworth had been a more earthy, more practical Clarkson, and for the blacks it was unfortunate that they encountered in so brief a span two men so resolutely convinced that they knew what was best for them in all situations.

For the most part, the Loyalist Negroes were sons of the North American climate; many were trained to the rudiments of individualized agriculture, and if they had been given good land quickly might well have succeeded in Nova Scotia. The Maroons were of a different breed. They understood the tropics and longed for the warmth and the soil familiar to them. Nor was there anything voluntary about their presence in Nova Scotia. The Loyalist blacks had found their leaders among their preachers, sincere and honest men who gave little thought to other than spiritual needs until Clarkson arrived. The Maroons more consistently followed their own elected officers, men of a rigidly negative cast who opposed all efforts to set them on a path other than that for which they already had suffered.

But if one must choose between the courses, surely that of the Maroons' own leaders was to be preferred, for through such leadership they retained their inner sense of dignity, their pride as a group, their cohesion and force. Certainly the third major influx of Negroes into Nova Scotia, the Refugee Blacks, were to demonstrate a notable lack of precisely these qualities. If Wentworth's efforts had in the course of time led the Maroons into the degradation that became the lot of the Refugees, he too might well have opposed his own plans.

By the time the Refugee Negroes arrived, fresh from a life of slavery in the United States, conditions had changed for most black men in British North America. While there still were slaves, public opinion had turned fully against slavery. In the year of the Maroons' departure, Nova Scotia moved against the institution; and in the decade between 1793 and 1803 an indigenous Canadian abolitionist movement won its major victories.

---

of Sierra Leone, pp. 85–86; Joseph J. Williams, "The Maroons of Jamaica," Boston College Graduate School *Anthropological Series, 3* (1938), 389–90. Thomas Wentworth Higginson, *Travellers and Outlaws: Episodes in American History* (Boston, 1889), pp. 116–49, contains a useful chapter on the Maroons.

4. The Attack on Slavery in British North America, 1793–1833

The first province to take action against slavery, and the only one to legislate against it, was Upper Canada. The Lieutenant-Governor, John Graves Simcoe, a Loyalist, led the attack. He had already condemned slavery during a brief tenure in the House of Commons as member for St. Mawe's, Cornwall, in 1790, and before he arrived in Upper Canada to take up his office, he wrote privately that both Christianity and the British constitution were opposed to the practice. He would not, he promised, give his assent to any law that "discriminates by dishonest policy between the natives of Africa, America or Europe." As an administrator, Simcoe could be petulant and a dissembler, but he gave no one cause to doubt his constancy and sincerity in opposing slavery and discrimination. While he wished to encourage immigration under the Imperial Act of 1790, he saw that unless modified its effect would strengthen slavery, and he spoke of issuing a proclamation freeing all slaves. While Simcoe welcomed black settlers who had begun to arrive in 1791, he refused to allow them to take up land together in segregated communities.[1]

Simcoe did not have long to wait, for in March 1793 he was able to throw the legality of slavery into question, while directing attention to the dangers the practice held for the new province. At the first meeting of the Executive Council on March 21, Simcoe, Chief Justice William Osgoode, and Peter Russell, owner of many slaves, heard one Peter Martin, a Negro employed by Colonel John Butler, superintendent of Indian affairs, tell how a Negro girl, Chloe Cooley—who belonged to a resident of Queenston, William Vrooman—had been bound and, despite violent resistance on her part, spirited across the Niagara River to be sold to Americans. An eyewitness added that many other people intended to sell their Negroes as

---

1. See William Renwick Riddell, "The Slave in Upper Canada," *JNH*, 4 (1919), 372–86, which also appears in *The Journal of the American Institute of Criminal Law and Criminology*, 14 (1923), 249–78; OHS, *Papers and Records*, 14 (1927), 63; and "Canadian Letters: Descriptive of a Tour Through the Province of Lower and Upper Canada in the Course of the Years 1792 and '93," *The Canadian Antiquarian, and Numismatic Journal*, ser. 3, 9 (1912), 67, 161–62. Smith ("Slave in Canada," pp. 43–48, 90–122), discusses slavery in its decline, but often erroneously, confusing names and dates.

well. The Council resolved that the Attorney-General, John White, should prosecute Vrooman for disturbing the peace.[2]

Osgoode and Russell knew that the owner was fully within his rights, for they already had consulted the Attorney-General on the matter, and the Council's resolution can have had no other purpose than to focus public attention on the possibility of mass sales of slaves across the frontier. White, who had practiced law in Jamaica, understood the slave code, and he pointed out that Vrooman had broken the peace no more than if he had sold a cow. Nor could anything be done about future sales under the present law.

Given an excuse for action, Simcoe moved to a frontal assault. On his instructions, White introduced to the House of Assembly a bill for the gradual abolition of slavery. The Attorney-General guided the bill through the lower house against, as he wrote, "much opposition but little argument." [3] This opposition came from merchants who recently had bought slaves from Indians at low prices in anticipation of substantial resale profits, and from a bloc of farmers who, although agreeing that slavery should be curtailed, wanted to be free to import new slaves for two years. Of sixteen members of the Assembly, at least six owned slaves, and in the Legislative Council Russell, Richard Cartwright, and James Bâby were slave-masters. White was skillful and Simcoe was persistent, however, and within two weeks the bill received unanimous passage.[4]

Upper Canada's act to abolish slavery freed not one slave. Its title, an act "to prevent the further introduction of slaves," reflected the compromise from which it was framed: Simcoe, Osgoode, and White wished to end slavery, while the owners wanted their present title in slave property confirmed. In truth, the bill, which was given the royal assent on July 9, might not have been legal had anyone chosen to challenge it, for it ran directly contrary to the Imperial Act of 1790; however, in these years before the

2. Ernest Alexander Cruikshank, ed., *The Correspondence of Lieut. Governor John Graves Simcoe, with Allied Documents relating to His Administration of the Government of Upper Canada* [hereafter cited as *Simcoe Correspondence*] (Toronto, 1923), *1*, 304.

3. William Renwick Riddell, *The Life of John Graves Simcoe, First Lieutenant-Governor of the Province of Upper Canada, 1792–96* (Toronto, 1926), p. 201, quoting White's diary for March 14.

4. Cruikshank, *Simcoe Correspondence*, 2 (1924), 53–54: Simcoe to Dundas, Sept. 16, 1793. A search in the papers of David William Smith, a slaveholding member of the Assembly, and of Peter Russell, both in TPL, and of John Graves Simcoe, in OPA, has provided no information on the debate or the vote. That Smith owned slaves is shown by OPA, Crown Land Letters: William Dickson to Smith, Nov. 8, 1797. On other owners, see Casey, "Midland District," p. 18; Smith, "Slave in Canada," p. 40; and C. C. James, "The First Legislators of Upper Canada," RSC, *Proceedings and Transactions, 8,* sec. 2 (1902), 104.

Colonial Laws Validity Act, no one contested Upper Canada's power to limit slavery within its own borders, and by the time the Imperial Parliament clarified the status of contradictory colonial enactments, slavery was illegal throughout the Empire.

The act violated no existing public property, and as part of the compromise it discouraged manumission. Any master who freed his slave was to provide security that the former slave would not become a public charge. No one was to be enslaved for any reason thereafter, while those who were lawfully slaves in 1793 would continue as such until death. All children born after the act was passed would become free at twenty-five years of age; until they were free, masters were to provide "proper nourishment and cloathing" for them. Any children born to these slaves before they reached twenty-five would be free at birth. No indenture could be entered into for a period longer than nine years. No slaves could be imported, either from the United States or from other British colonies.[5]

The clause providing for gradual abolition was unpopular among slaveowners, however, despite the protection it gave them in holding their property. Attorney-General White was unseated in the next election, largely because of his rôle in championing the legislation; and the wife of the Provincial Secretary, William Jarvis, wrote to her father in London that Simcoe had "by a piece of chicanery freed all the Negroes," an untruth compounded, and suggested that he had also "rendered himself unpopular." Consequently, shortly after Simcoe left Upper Canada, a group of owners attempted to restore the slave trade. In 1798 a Virginia Loyalist, Christopher Robinson, member for Addington and Ontario, introduced a bill into the House of Assembly to permit immigrants to bring Negro slaves with them, reaffirming the Imperial Act of 1790, and the House passed Robinson's bill by a vote of eight to four. Largely through the efforts of two republican-minded members, Richard Cartwright and Robert Hamilton, the upper chamber bottled up Robinson's bill until the end of the session. In the absence of Simcoe and White, the chief opposition to slavery came from the Solicitor-General, Robert Isaac Dey Gray, member from Stormont and himself a slave-owner, who was able to block any further attempts to alter Simcoe's work.[6]

    5. PAC, Misc. Docs., *16*, pt. 2: Act of July 9, 1793; Alexander Fraser, ed., *Sixth Report of the Bureau of Archives for the Province of Ontario, 1909*, pp. 33, 35–36, 38, 41–43; and idem, *Seventh Report . . . 1910* (both Toronto, 1911), pp. 25–26, 32–33.

    6. TPL, William Jarvis Family Papers: Hannah Jarvis to Samuel Peters, Sept. 25, 1793; PAC, Misc. Docs., *21*: Gray to Katharine Valentine, Feb. 16, 1804; Fraser, *Seventh Report*, pp. 67–70; William Renwick Riddell, *Upper Canada Sketches: Incidents in the Early Times of the Province* (Toronto, 1922), pp. 57–59; Riddell, *The Legal Profession in Upper Canada in Its Early Periods* (Toronto,

With no prospect of increase from new imports, slavery declined steadily in Upper Canada after 1793. The bill did not prevent selling slaves across the international frontier, however, despite Simcoe's wish, and many owners must have hedged their losses by disposing of slaves in New York, at least until 1799, when purchase was made illegal there. Nor could the province police remote settlements: apparently John Thomas of Brant brought slaves in from Tennessee as late as 1809, contrary to the law, and in 1795 some Oswegatchie Indians carried away Negro slaves far beyond the reach of the magistrate. Nonetheless the bill had the desired effect, for it made slavery untenable over time and it encouraged slaves to escape into the free areas of the Northwest Territory, Vermont, and New York. By 1807 slave-owners in the Western District of Upper Canada had suffered such losses to Detroit, in the territory of Michigan, where the Negroes formed into a militia, that ten of the owners petitioned the Lieutenant-Governor, Francis Gore, to stop "the Evil, . . . the Facility of Escape to the American States," which thus deprived British subjects of their property. Although Britain made representations to the United States, little could be done, since extradition arrangements had lapsed, and Gore does not appear to have been energetic in pursuing the matter.[7]

Outside Upper Canada slavery was not abolished, but by 1800 the courts had placed effective limitations on its expansion. This was particularly true of Nova Scotia and Lower Canada, in which legislative action would have been more difficult to achieve. At Newark (later, Niagara) both houses were small, intimate affairs, and in the first two sessions there was no Opposition as such; the fifty-member lower and the fifteen-member upper houses in Quebec were more unwieldy and already grouping into political factions. Although the Lower Canadian House of Assembly entertained a bill to abolish slavery three months before the Upper Canadians did, nothing came of it: on February 26, 1793, the member for Cornwallis, Pierre-Louis Panet, introduced such a bill; after its second reading, however, it was tabled and heard of no more.[8]

1916), pp. 155–56; Riddell, *Life of Simcoe*, p. 427; Riddell, "Slave in Canada," pp. 322–24, n. 13, and p. 385, n. 20.

7. TPL, Jarvis Papers: John Pearson to Jarvis, April 16, and J. Walton to Jarvis, May 7, 1798; Charles and James C. Thomas, "Reminiscences of the First Settlers in the County of Brant," OHS, *Papers and Records, 12* (1914), 67; Cruikshank, *Simcoe Correspondence, 4* (1930), 61, 154: Col. McKee to Joseph Chew, Aug. 11, and Lord Dorchester to Simcoe, Dec. 3, 1795; PAC, Upper Canada Land Petitions, Book A, *1:* Elisha Anderson, affidavit, April 14, 1796; FO5/52: "Memorial of the Slave Owners in the Western District of said Province," Feb. 9, encl. in Gore to David M. Erskine, April 24, 1807; PAC, Upper Canada Sundries, *6:* Erskine to Gore, May 26, 1807; [M. A. Leeson], *History of Macomb County, Michigan* . . . (Chicago, 1882), pp. 103–06.

8. *Quebec Gazette*, April 25, 1793; Viger and Lafontaine, "L'esclavage en

But other means for stunting the growth of slavery were at hand: the press and the courts. Already William Brown, proprietor of the *Quebec Gazette,* and his nephew and successor, John Neilson, erstwhile slave-owners both, had begun to attack slavery. Brown appears to have held no slaves after 1789, and Neilson seems to have sold his by 1793; from 1790 on the *Gazette* printed antislavery poetry, English- and French-language versions of slave-ship atrocity stories, and related material well calculated to decrease support for slavery.[9] Upper Canada, on the other hand, had no newspapers until 1793.

Since the lieutenant-governors of Lower Canada took no interest in slavery, the initiative fell to the courts, and especially to the Chief Justice of the Court of King's Bench in Montreal, James (later Sir James) Monk. Massachusetts-born, but not a Loyalist, having been taken to Halifax in the year of its founding, Monk had been trained in the law in Nova Scotia and in 1774 called to the English bar. Starting in 1794 he was Chief Justice in Montreal and a member of the Legislative and Executive Councils. In 1798 he released two Negro slaves, Charlotte and Jude, who had been brought before him in separate actions. In the latter case he gave the opinion that while magistrates were empowered to commit slaves, apprentices, and servants to houses of correction for punishment, the relevant statute—framed in 1562 for rather different conditions—did not authorize committals to jails or prisons, and there were no houses of correction in Lower Canada. Having found a legal technicality to effect the release of the slave, Monk nonetheless went on, in an obiter dictum, to say that slavery did not exist in the province and to warn owners that he would apply this interpretation of the law to all subsequent cases.

Thrown on the defensive, the slave-owners of Montreal responded on April 1, 1799, with a lengthy petition presented to the House of Assembly by Joseph Papineau and John Black, members from Montreal and Quebec respectively. The petitioners attempted to meet both Monk's specific and general arguments. For the owners, Papineau moved that the province should establish houses of correction so that slaves could not be freed on technicalities. More important, they held that in Lower Canada slavery was fully sustained by the law, referring to Raudot's ordinance of 1709, the Imperial Act of 1790, and—mistakenly—to an Imperial Act of 1732. This act had provided for the sale of Negro slaves, among other possessions, for debts against estates, and it had applied to the whole of the then

---

Canada," pp. 27–28; *Journals of the House of Assembly,* pp. 179, 255, 315, 541; L. M. Lemoine, "Slavery at Quebec," *The Canadian Antiquarian, and Numismatic Journal,* 4 (1876), 159–60; *BRH,* 2 (1876), 136.

9. *Gazette,* Dec. 16, 1790, June 21, 1792, Oct. 17, Dec. 12, 1793; Trudel, *L'esclavage au Canada français,* pp. 175, 215–16.

British colonies in North America. Unfortunately from the memorialists' point of view, this act had been repealed with respect to slave property in 1797, and it never had applied to Indian slaves. Papineau's petitioners cannot have been too hopeful of success, in any case, for they ended by asking that the Assembly either protect them in their property or pass a law abolishing slavery entirely; for their slaves were restive and potentially dangerous when held under conditions of uncertainty.[10]

The petition gave rise to a bill, modeled upon that passed in Upper Canada, which would have recognized and regulated slavery, limited its life, and prohibited slave imports. Introduced in April 1800, by James Cuthbert, member for Warwick, the bill was read twice, tabled, and not taken up again. Cuthbert brought in similar bills in 1801 and in 1803, but they too failed of passage.[11] Those who wished to see slavery abolished entirely, and those who opposed any limitations upon slavery at all, allowed the bills to fall between them, and the generality of the rural members of the legislature were unlikely to aid their Montreal and Quebec compatriots in retaining property that increased the social distance between town and country. All did agree on the need for houses of correction, although when a bill establishing such institutions was passed in 1799, any attempt to require that slaves should be committed to them was unsuccessful. As Monk himself had pointed out, under the act of 1562 they could be so committed, and the owners' cause thus fell to a hostile court which would not make use of the law.

Monk, now reinforced on the Court of King's Bench by Pierre-Louis Panet and Pierre-Amable DeBonne, both of whom were opponents of slavery when seated in the Assembly, confirmed this view in February 1800, in the case of Robin alias Robert, a black. Robin, a slave claimed by one James Fraser, had fled from Fraser's farm in March 1799 to live with a Montreal tavern-keeper. Upon Fraser's request, Robin was committed to the new house of correction in Montreal, from which he was brought before the court on a writ of habeas corpus. Panet, and a New York Loyalist, Isaac Ogden, heard the case. The Chief Justice was either a very bad jurist or a very determined man, and there is no evidence of the former. Clearly, he felt that the law was what the judges said it was, for he turned the petitioners' own document against them, discharging Robin on the ground that the Imperial Act of 1797, which had revoked the slave clause within the act of 1732, had abolished all legislation relating to

10. Viger and Lafontaine, pp. 29–33; *Journals of the House of Assembly, 1799,* pp. 122–29. In *Le Pantheon canadien* (Montreal, 1858), p. 211, François Bibaud discusses Papineau's effort but mistakenly dates the petition 1797.

11. *Journals of the House of Assembly: 1800,* pp. 159, 219, 223, 227, 243, 269; *1801,* pp. 54, 72, 234, 290; *1803,* pp. 160, 188, 208–10. "Tabled" is used here in the present North American rather than the British sense.

slavery in the province. This opinion was utterly mistaken but no less effective for that, and the result of Monk's disingenuous decision was to throw the burden of proof of ownership upon the master and, in the face of hostile courts, to render slavery virtually untenable in Lower Canada.[12]

Although the lower house did not take action either for or against slavery, in 1829 the Executive Council, by indirection, recognized the effects of Monk's decision. Early in the year one Paul Vallard helped a mulatto slave to escape from his master in Illinois and flee to Lower Canada. On behalf of the owner, the American Secretary of State formally requested Sir James Kempt, the administrator of Lower Canada, to surrender Vallard to American authorities for theft. Kempt turned to his council, which informed him that fugitives might be given up only when the crime with which they were charged in the United States was a crime in Canada as well: "The state of slavery is not recognized by the Law of Canada. . . . Every Slave therefore who comes into the Province is immediately free whether he has been brought in by violence or has entered it of his own accord." Vallard was not surrendered, and while the advice of the Executive Council did not have the weight of law, slavery thereafter was treated as if it were illegal in Lower Canada.[13]

The pattern of progress was similar in Nova Scotia, where two successive Chief Justices dedicated themselves to "wearing out" slavery by waging a judicial war of attrition upon slave-owners. Both justices, Thomas (later Sir Thomas) Andrew Strange from 1791 to 1796 and Sampson Salter Blowers from 1797 to 1833, avoided any direct decisions as to the legality of slavery, for they well knew that it was legal, despite a pious declaration in the House of Assembly in 1787 to the effect that slavery did not exist in the colony and ought not to be mentioned. Strange, Blowers, and a Gaelic-speaking minister, Reverend Dr. James MacGregor, between them capitalized on public indifference and hostility to slavery to stifle it by the turn of the century.

MacGregor, a youthful Anti-Burgher Presbyterian, who arrived at

12. PAC, Misc. Docs. *16*, no. 121: *Dominus Rex* vs. *Robin alias Robert,* Court of King's Bench, February term, 1800, and printed in Viger and Lafontaine, pp. 56–63; Riddell, "Slave in Canada," succinctly summarizes the case, pp. 311–13. The Imperial Act of 1732 is discussed by Auguste Gosselin, in "La Declaration de 1732," RSC, *Proceedings and Transactions, 6,* sec. 1 (1900), 23–52. Various accounts refer to an alleged decision by Chief Justice Osgoode of Montreal in 1803, in which he declared slavery inconsistent with the laws of Lower Canada and gave freedom to all. But Osgoode had left for England in 1801. Arthur R. M. Lower, in *Canadians in the Making: A Social History of Canada* (Toronto, 1958), p. 164, refers to a compromise measure to abolish slavery in 1804.

13. The original record is in PAC; it is quoted verbatim in William Renwick Riddell, "An International Complication between Illinois and Canada arising Out of Slavery," *Journal of The Illinois State Historical Society, 25* (1932), 125–26.

Pictou from Scotland in 1786 or 1787, soon condemned the neighboring presbytery of Truro. Its minister, Daniel Cock, made the mistake of being ponderous, elderly, the owner of two slaves, and in error on eight points of church doctrine. MacGregor declared that he would "rather burn at the stake than keep communion" with a man so evil. Cock already had been attacked as a slave-owner by an itinerant American Baptist preacher, but as a Scot and a Presbyterian, MacGregor would be heard where others were not.[14]

The exchange that followed was a remarkable one, for although the arguments produced on both sides were hardly new to North America, for that time and that place the attack on and the defense of slavery contained in the resulting public letters were unusual. In 1788 MacGregor published his views in an open *Letter to a Clergyman Urging him to set free a Black Girl he held in Slavery,*[15] which he had printed in quantity, apparently in Halifax. The *Letter* was filled with personal abuse, but it contained an excellent summary of all of the religious arguments that could be mounted against slave-holding. Anticipating the chief defenses as he supposed Reverend Cock would make them, MacGregor systematically strove to demolish each: that black men were creatures of the devil, as shown by their color, was scarcely true, he argued, for white men only thought the devil black as an opposite to themselves; in Africa black men thought him white. In truth, God made men black by design, to protect them from the sun. Further, "the devil being a spirit can have no colour, and it is merely by a figure of speech we call him black." As to the argument that slaves were better off captive than free, MacGregor replied by asking why, if this were so, did Cock not become a slave as well? That Negroes were slavish was true, but this arose from circumstance, not from natural causes, and Negroes would show themselves "as noble and free and high spirited as ourselves" if given their liberty. Although the Bible showed that the Jews were slaves, MacGregor wrote, one people's forfeit of liberty did not apply to another's, and if Moses made laws permitting slavery, there was no evidence that he approved it. While ancient man had not progressed sufficiently to see the evil in slavery, surely modern, enlightened eighteenth-

14. NBM, Ward Chipman Papers: Blowers to Chipman, Dec. 22, 1799; Riddell, "Slave in Canada," pp. 368–69; Greaves, "Negro in Canada," p. 19; Stanley E. Archibald, "Early Pioneer Farming Advancement in Nova Scotia," Colchester Historical Society, *Proceedings, Reports, and Program Summaries, 1954–1957* ([Truro], n.d.), pp. 56–57.

15. There are three known copies of the eleven-page pamphlet: at Dalhousie University and the Legislative Library of Nova Scotia, in Halifax, and in the Saint John Free Library. MacGregor's grandson, George Patterson, reprinted all but the last few sentences of it in his *A Few Remains of the Rev. James MacGregor, D.D.* (Philadelphia, 1859), pp. 167–88.

century man could do so. In an all-embracing and somewhat irrelevant peroration, MacGregor denounced all "Protestants, Presbyterian ministers, who of all others, should keep farthest off from [Babylon]," who were to be "found publicly committing fornication with the Great Whore, drinking themselves drunk, and stupefying their consciences with their filthy wine [of Catholicism]! But blessed be God, though hand join in hand, the Negroes shall be free."

Heady brew now but small beer then, perhaps, for MacGregor's followers were accustomed to the harsh language of religious controversy, and the Presbyterian divine saw Cock's slave-holding errors within a doctrinal context. The members of the Truro Presbytery indignantly denounced this tirade, as did those at Colchester, and since Cock declined to reply, Reverend David Smith of Londonderry did so for him in two public letters. His argument was a familiar one, as MacGregor's attack also had moved along well-worn paths: in a dozen places the Bible upheld slavery, Negroes were like children who needed parental guidance, emancipation would do them untold injury, they would lead idle and abandoned lives and be tempted into crime. Further, Smith wrote, MacGregor was not sincere in his protestations since he too had purchased a slave, albeit to grant her freedom, for paying for freedom if it were one's natural right was as "heinous a crime" as keeping a slave; the entire controversy was a cloak under which MacGregor meant to incite "a spirit of faction and party" over matters not directly related to "the faith and practice of the church." [16]

Almost upon arrival in Pictou, MacGregor had purchased the freedom of a slave girl from her owner, Matthew Harris, undertaking to pay £ 50 over three years, giving up three-quarters of his first year's income to the purpose. When Smith charged him with owning a slave, he was not yet the legal owner. MacGregor also persuaded Harris to give a mulatto his freedom, and he bought the indenture on a Negro woman for another £ 10. The slave girl married George Mingo, a Black Pioneer, and they became respected members of MacGregor's congregation, while the mulatto married a Swiss woman and moved to the United States. Cock's slave thereafter was called Deal MacGregor, since the young pastor had spoken of her as "his sister," although in spite of MacGregor's efforts she remained with Cock until he died in 1805.[17] But by his purchases and his pamphlet

16. This account of the controversy is drawn from admittedly biased sources—the works of George Patterson, especially *A History of the County of Pictou, Nova Scotia* (Pictou, 1916), written in 1877, pp. 70–71, 97, and *Memoir of the Rev. James MacGregor, D.D.* (Philadelphia, 1859), pp. 112, 150–58, 516. Local histories support Patterson's account, but they too are based upon it and MacGregor's pamphlet. Cock cannot speak in his own defense, for all of his papers were destroyed by fire in 1796: see Thomas Miller, *Historical and Genealogical Record of the First Settlers of Colchester County . . .* (Halifax, 1873), pp. 147–51.

17. An inconsistent account appears in Smith, "Slave in Canada," pp. 57–58.

MacGregor had focused attention on slavery far more sharply than had been done in any of the other colonies, and until his death in 1830 he continued to speak out for Negro equality in the Pictou area.

Whether Strange and Blowers were party to this controversy, there is no way to know. But the Chief Justice and the Attorney-General (as Blowers was from 1785 until he succeeded Strange) were determined to make slavery as difficult to maintain as possible. They were insistent on iron-clad proof of ownership, and if such could not be produced, verdicts were returned for the slaves. Strange, who had studied with Lord Mansfield soon after the Somerset decision, intimated that owners could be prosecuted for sending Negroes outside the province against their will, although he wisely cited no statute; and on one occasion he discharged a slave at Annapolis because, even though the plaintiff proved that he had purchased her legally in New York, Blowers held that there was no proof the original owner was entitled to sell her. Under such constant judicial pressure, slave-masters were increasingly prepared to transmute slavery for life into a contractual relationship for a specified number of years, and the terminology "a black man living with" slowly replaced "a slave owned by" in local records. The latest known public sale of a Negro in Nova Scotia occurred in 1807; and well before Blowers retired from the bench or MacGregor from the pulpit, slavery was all but extinguished in the province.

Strange and Blowers shared the common law's respect for property and for the sanctity of contracts, and they were unwilling to go as far as Monk had done and declare all slaves free. They talked about the matter often, and as Blowers wrote in 1799, they decided to move slowly in order not "to throw so much property as it is called into the air at once." [18] That both were opposed to slavery, however, they made clear in every relevant case that came before them.

The single most important of these cases was that of the Negro Jack, who ran away from his owner, James DeLancey of Annapolis, and took up employment with one William Woodin in Halifax. DeLancey asked his lawyer, Thomas Ritchie, to obtain Jack's wages in lieu of the slave himself, which Woodin refused to give. In 1801 the court awarded DeLancey £ 70, but Woodin's counsel, Attorney-General Richard J. Uniacke, himself a former slave-owner, appealed on the ground that Negroes no longer could be slaves. The highest court agreed to entertain this motion the following term. In the interim DeLancey asked the former Attorney-General of Prince Edward Island, Joseph Aplin, who was living in Annapolis County, to prepare an ex parte opinion to be submitted to lawyers in England.

18. Blowers to Chipman, Dec. 22, 1799, as printed in I. Allen Jack, "The Loyalists and Slavery in New Brunswick," RSC, *Transactions, 4,* sec. 2 (1898), 149–50. Unfortunately, Blowers destroyed all of his papers: John Doull, *Sketches of Attorney Generals of Nova Scotia, 1750–1926* (Halifax, 1964), p. 21.

Aplin's statement, and the accompanying opinions of the British lawyers, form the most extensive legal defense of slavery ever offered in British North America.[19]

Not Aplin, nor his English experts, nor Ritchie, to whom Aplin gave his brief, were able to stand against Blowers. Quite correctly, Aplin pointed out that although slavery had not been established in Nova Scotia by specific enactment, neither had it been authorized in Virginia or Antigua, where it was unquestionably legal. Citing the reference to Negro slaves in the inn-keepers act of 1762, he won the full approval of his English consultants, among them the Attorney-General of England. But apparently Aplin was criticized for turning outside the province for opinions on slavery, and he wrote to Blowers to explain that DeLancey had paid him to prepare the brief and therefore was free to publish it; for himself, Aplin said, he would refrain from printing it in the *Royal Gazette* so close to the time of the hearing, even though he would be unable to prevent its publication after the hearing was over. Aplin sent a copy of the document to Blowers and disassociated himself from it.[20] Late in 1802 Aplin's material was published in New Brunswick as a pamphlet outside Blowers' jurisdiction, and it appears to have been without effect.[21] Thus forewarned, the Chief Justice bypassed Aplin's statement entirel,, for it was not only unofficial but irrelevant to the charge against Woodin, which now was one of trespass. In 1803 the case was dismissed, and although DeLancey was able to offer documentary evidence of his purchase of Jack, the court did not order that he be returned to his master. DeLancey's death the next year effectively ended efforts to return Jack to slavery, and thereafter no one carried a case for recovery of a slave to the highest court.

The only concerted attempt by Nova Scotia's slave-owners to reassert their property rights was an apologetic effort in December of 1807. Twenty-seven Loyalists from Annapolis County, who between them held eighty-four slaves, petitioned the Assembly through John Warwick, the member for Digby, to bring some order into the chaos created by the judicial decisions. "Your petitioners are far from pretending to advocate Slavery as a System," they confessed, but "owing to certain doubts now entertained by The King's Courts of Law in this Province, such property is rendered wholly untenable by your petitioners whose Negro Servants are daily leaving their service and setting your petitioners at defiance." The owners

19. The best account of this case appears in Smith, "Slave in Canada," pp. 105–11, although he transcribes Alpin's brief inaccurately and is confusing about dates.

20. NBM, Odell MSS: draft, Alpin to Blowers, n.d. [Sept. 1801?].

21. Aplin's pamphlet appeared as *Opinions of Several Gentlemen of the Law on the Subject of Negro Servitude in the Province of Nova Scotia* (Saint John, 1802). The original draft is in Odell MSS: Oct. 20, 1801.

thought that perhaps "the peculiar circumstances of this Province, or perhaps the true interests of Humanity," might require abolition of slavery; they wished the Assembly either to regulate slaves so that property would be secure, or to sacrifice that property for the public good, paying just compensation. That the British government knew slavery was still legal in Nova Scotia had been shown four months earlier when the Governor-in-Chief of Canada, Sir James Henry Craig, was instructed to provide a census of the province that included the "free and unfree, and slaves." [22]

The provincial legislature met neither of the Annapolis petitioners' alternatives. The petition was accepted by a vote of seventeen to nine, and on the same day Thomas Ritchie, now member for Annapolis, introduced a bill to regulate slavery. It failed to move past its second reading, and after suffering a number of amendments, was dropped. Less than three years later an S.P.G. missionary in the Annapolis Valley reported that all Negroes were free, "as our provincial laws provide." [23]

In the provinces of New Brunswick, Prince Edward Island, and Cape Breton (separate until 1820), slavery was not limited by either legislative or judicial means. Only in New Brunswick had it taken any firm hold. There slavery continued to be observed well into the new century, and an advertisement for a runaway slave appeared in the *Royal Gazette* as late as July 10, 1816. On but one occasion was an effort made to condemn slavery to the same wasting death it had met in Lower Canada and Nova Scotia, and once again, if now by indirection, Justices Strange and Blowers were involved.

The first Chief Justice of New Brunswick, George Duncan Ludlow, had come to the province from New York in 1783–84 and, in the words of an opponent, had been "very strenuous in support of the masters' right as being founded on immemorial usage and custom in all parts of America ever since its discovery." Blackstone on custom would not have agreed with this usage, but Ludlow had recent history on his side: by the time of the Revolution, the legal presumption in many, although not all, colonies was that a Negro was a slave unless he held papers of manumission. Servants usually emphasized their sense of distinction by refusing to sit at table with blacks. Ludlow also argued that since all colonial acts were referred to the Crown, ample opportunity had been afforded to His Majesty's legal

22. PANS, "Petition of Slave Proprietors in Annapolis County 1807," Dec. 3, submitted Jan. 9, 1808; PAC, transcripts of Letters Patent, Commissions and Instructions: to Craig, Aug. 29, 1807.

23. *Journal and Proceedings of The House of Assembly: 1807*, Jan. 9, 11, 12, 1808, pp. 155–57, 159; and *1808*, Dec. 3, 8, 15, pp. 272, 281, 295; W. A. Calnak and A. W. Savary, *History of the County of Annapolis . . .* (Toronto, 1897), p. 284; Haliburton, *Account of Nova-Scotia, 2,* 280–81; SPG Archives, Dr. Bray's Associates Minute Books: *4,* March 7, 1811, 73.

advisers to apply Lord Mansfield's decision in the colonies had they wished to do so. Only in referring to a "Common Law of the Colonies" did Ludlow press too far, although here, too, he presumably was drawing upon his inadequate knowledge of the idea of "custom," not on a divergent body of legal opinion.

Not until 1800 did the opponents of slavery in New Brunswick have an opportunity to test Ludlow's reasoning. In February a writ of habeas corpus, issued by Judge Isaac Allen, brought before the court a slave woman, Nancy Morton, claimed by a Loyalist from Maryland, Caleb Jones, as his property. She had been sent to New Brunswick in 1785 and apparently was purchased by the Virginia Loyalist, Stair Agnew, for £ 40 in 1791. Agnew had given her to Jones to keep, perhaps without transferring title, but full documentation on two previous sales was available. Now at issue was more than the freedom of a single Negro, for Ward Chipman, the Solicitor-General, decided to challenge the legality of slavery in the province as his friend Blowers was doing in Nova Scotia.

New Brunswick's finest legal talent assembled in Fredericton. On the bench were Allen, himself a slave-owner, Chief Justice Ludlow, and Puisne Justices Joshua Upham, whose wife owned six or more slaves, and John Saunders. Upham had lost one of his own slaves shortly before, under an execution for murder. Five lawyers defended the master: Jonathan Bliss, the Attorney-General; John Murray Bliss, subsequently Solicitor-General and Upham's son-in-law; Thomas Wetmore, later to be Attorney-General; William Botsford, later Solicitor-General; and Charles J. Peters. As counsel to the slave there were two unpaid representatives, Chipman and Samuel Denny Street, a hot-headed lawyer who attempted to strike John Murray Bliss during the proceedings. All were Loyalists; Upham, both Blisses, and Chipman came from Massachusetts and, except for John Murray Bliss, were graduates of Harvard College; Ludlow and Wetmore, who had matriculated at King's College, were from New York; Botsford, a graduate of Yale College, had come from Connecticut; Saunders was a Virginian by birth, and Allen had been judge in New Jersey. Blowers was the unseen presence, for Chipman turned to him for advice, and the Nova Scotian Chief Justice had been a member of the same Harvard graduating class, that of 1763, as Upham and Bliss.

Chipman prepared a brief that ran to eighty pages of foolscap, and he alone searched every available source. While working up the case he wrote to Blowers for help with "the broad question" of slavery, added that he was "a volunteer for the rights of human nature," and confided that the court was divided, with Ludlow upholding slavery and Allen opposed to it. Blowers responded immediately with a set of notes, and he repeated Strange's advice that a formal adjudication on the legality of slavery was best avoided in favor of a series of flanking movements. Chipman based his own brief upon a narrow range of legal texts and collections of statutes, especially the laws of New York, Massachusetts, and Virginia—the only ones available to him in Fredericton. He maintained that "the custom of tolerating slavery" was not binding in New Brunswick and had not been so in Nova Scotia before the new colony was severed from it in 1784. Public opinion was against slavery in both provinces; neither supreme court had upheld slavery; and there was no act of the Nova Scotian Assembly that recognized slavery. The silence of the laws held against slavery in either colony.

Chipman knew that this was not true but his purpose was to defend Nancy Morton, not to prepare an accurate disquisition on history. When he wrote to Blowers afterwards, he remarked upon his relief that the counsel for the master had not stumbled upon the Nova Scotian act of 1762 for the regulation of servants and slaves. "In searching your laws . . . I found this clause, but carefully avoided mentioning it." [24]

But Chipman's carefully prepared argument was not rewarded, for the court divided. Ludlow and Upham found for Jones while Allen and Saunders wished to free Nancy Morton; no judgment was entered, and she was sold for a period of fifteen years. Agnew, angered by Allen, challenged him to a duel, which Allen refused; Street's attack on Bliss resulted in a duel and an indictment of both duelists; Chipman threatened Jones with an action for false imprisonment; and Allen, freeing his slaves at the conclusion of the proceedings, entered into correspondence with Wilberforce. [25]

The following year, writing in the *Saint John Royal Gazette*,[26] one of the judges upheld the legality of slavery on the basis of the Imperial Act of 1790, but in doing so he also recognized a common complaint among the early Loyalists. Those who had arrived in the first three or four years of Loyalist settlement felt at a disadvantage to the "late Loyalists," who did not come until after 1790, for they presumed that the act protected the

24. NBM holds the original of this brief; it is printed in full in Jack, "Loyalists and Slavery in New Brunswick," pp. 155–84. Nothing further was found in the Ward Chipman Papers, PANS, which cover only 1784–91. See also *Journals, General Joseph Gubbins*, as Colonel inspecting militia units in New Brunswick, 1811, 1813, pp. 9, 15 respectively (held by Miss Di Gubbins, Bowne End, Bucks.).

25. *Saint John Royal Gazette, and New-Brunswick Advertiser*, Feb. 12, 18, 1800; NBM, Scrap Book no. 13, p. 49; Patricia A. Ryder, "Ward Chipman Sr.: An Early New Brunswick Judge," *University of New Brunswick Law Journal*, 12 (1959), 74. The duel is discussed in David Russell Jack, "An Affair of Honor," *Acadiensis*, 5 (1905), 173–77; several accounts confuse the participants and the challenger.

26. July 28, 1801. The *Gazette* for 1784–1800 contained several offers of rewards for fugitives, but very few thereafter.

latter without securing slave property to the former. This, the correspondent noted, was not the case: by permitting newcomers to sell their slaves after a year had passed, the act recognized that slaves were property, and no distinction was made as to owners. Slavery therefore continued in New Brunswick, although as elsewhere—if more slowly—owners began to pay wages to their slaves and to free them on the basis of an indenture.

The heroes of abolition in British North America were its judges, men who by judicial legislation moved against an institution that still retained sufficient public support in Nova Scotia, New Brunswick, and Lower Canada, to prevent popularly elected assemblies from abolishing slavery themselves. Here, too, as in French Canada, those who have examined the means by which slavery was limited in the provinces have encouraged the growth of local myths. The most common of these is that judges from New York tended to support slavery and those from Massachusetts to oppose it, with the attendant suggestion that because of parallel resemblances between the institutions of New Brunswick and New York, and of Nova Scotia and Massachusetts, Nova Scotia led the way in judicial abolition.[27] But in truth each judge seems to have been doing his duty as he saw it with little reference to his pre-Loyalist background, and an examination of the birthplaces, education, and previous places of residence of the several lawyers who participated in the key trials by which slavery was set in course of extinction reveals no pattern of significance. Slavery was brought down in the British provinces by men who were doing the jobs they were appointed to do: to defend a slave-owner and to find all arguments for him, or to attack an owner and to find all arguments against him.

While slavery remained legal in all British North American colonies until 1834, the combination of legislative and judicial action had so severely limited its growth, applicability, and confidence as virtually to end the practice by the 1820s throughout the provinces. The last known private advertisements for slaves appeared in Halifax in 1820, in Quebec in 1821; occasional wills of a later date attest to slaves as property, and local legends throughout eastern and central Canada credit various Negroes with having been the "last slave" to die.[28] There could have been considerably more slaves in 1834 than legend suggests, however: in Upper Canada

27. Smith, "Slave in Canada," p. 102.

28. Clipping, "A. D." (probably Arthur Doughty), May 5, and Douglas Brymner, May 15, 1886, in MS "Slavery in Canada," no. 50, Chateau de Ramezay, Montreal; Riddell, "Slave in Canada," p. 373; Smith, pp. 95, 116; Neilson, "Slavery in Old Canada," p. 41 n.; James Cleland Hamilton, "Slavery in Canada," *Transactions of the Canadian Institute, 1* (1889–90), 106. The act provided that children not yet six years old might be bound out by a special magistrate until their twenty-first birthday, but no one appears to have invoked this section in British North America.

a girl of ten in 1793 would have been fifty-one years old, and any children born to her after 1809, when she was twenty-six, could still have been slaves under the law. Without the Imperial Act of 1833, or further colonial legislation, Canada could have harbored a residue of slaves into the 1850s or later. But because of the courts, the number of Negroes held in slavery even in the 1830s must have been negligible.

Slavery was abolished throughout the British colonies by an Act of the Imperial Parliament,[29] passed on August 28, 1833, to take effect on August 1 of the next year. All slaves above the age of six became apprenticed laborers to their owners; the period of apprenticeship was not to extend in any case beyond six years, when former owners would have no further claim to the Negroes. Children not yet six years old might be bound out by a special magistrate until their twenty-first birthday. Owners would be compensated, and £ 20,000 was set aside for this purpose. The act provided for commissioners who would apportion the sum into nineteen shares, one each to be assigned to sixteen colonies in the Caribbean (British Honduras, although not yet a colony, was treated as such for the act), Bermuda, the Cape of Good Hope, and Mauritius. Significantly, no share was provided for British North America, nor were the provinces mentioned at any time in the act, showing clearly that, for purposes of emancipation, the British government did not consider slavery to exist in those provinces. There is no record of any slaves passing into apprenticeships, or of children being bound out, in the North American colonies, although a handful of slaves and their children would have qualified. The Imperial Act freed nearly eight hundred thousand slaves; probably fewer than half a hundred of these were within British North America, to which the act was applied even though without specific designation. When John Baker, a Quebec-born mulatto, and one of the slaves freed by the will of Robert Isaac Dey Gray in 1804, died in Cornwall, Ontario, in 1871, the last person to have lived as a slave in British North America was gone from the scene.[30]

If this death provides a formal punctuation to the history of slavery in Canada, the operative full stop had been given to that story by Simcoe, Monk, Strange, Blowers, and Chipman between 1793 and 1808, after which no one spoke in public defense of slavery. And when the government of Jamaica proclaimed full freedom from all apprenticeships two years ahead of schedule, on July 9, 1838, the Negroes of Toronto met to celebrate the final emancipation of their race within the British Empire. Each

---

29. PRO 30/6/71, fols. 913–39.

30. Baker's story is told in James Cleland Hamilton, "The African in Canada," *Proceedings of the American Association for the Advancement of Science, 33* (1890), 366–68.

July since, first at Toronto and London, and latterly at Windsor, Ontario's Negroes have continued to meet in memory of Emancipation Day.[31]

Why did slavery not survive in British North America? Why was slavery impracticable although not illegal before 1834? The reasons are clear enough, and they do not differ markedly from the causes of the decline of slavery in New France. Even before the Loyalist migrations, public opinion had not supported slavery as either necessary or moral; and if public opinion had not yet condemned slavery, indifference to the economic and moral issues it raised characterized British North Americans by the 1780s. Many English-speaking Canadians disliked slavery because of its association with the Americans. For all, slavery stood in marked contrast to the expressed attitude of the English (and after 1778 of the Scottish) courts. While many Loyalists owned slaves, the majority came from the New England and upper Middle Atlantic states which had abolished slavery or were in the course of doing so by the 1790s. The English-speaking settlers thought slavery morally wrong; the French-speaking residents—increasingly conservative, orthodox, given to challenging institutions which did not pay—thought slavery economically unsound. Neither Loyalists, secure in knowing who and what they were, nor French Canadians needed slavery to create barriers between races, for there were more subtle barriers available to them. In short, no one needed slavery, and while many would tolerate it, they were not prepared to resist an active group of opponents, especially when those opponents were commanding figures in the government or the courts.

Yet, why was slavery thought not to be needed? Largely for negative reasons. Many believed that Negroes—virtually the only slaves by the turn of the century—were useless in a northern climate. Most owners saw that relatively small slave-labor gangs of fifteen or fewer men were unlikely to be any more effective in the long run than fifteen indentured servants, also black. The hardships of carving out a new life in British North America gave prestige to manual work more quickly than in the United States, and no one group was set aside as hewers of wood when all had to hew. The majority of slaves brought by the Loyalists were domestics, living intimately with the family, further softening barriers and eliminating social distances. Having a slave to help at one's town house in August was fine; having six hungry mouths to feed when food was in short supply in the winter was quite another matter. Slave-owning was identified with wealth in any case, and in frontier societies popular assemblies were little interested in preserving an artificial gap between classes. The depreciation in slave values also contributed to a general desire to be rid of slave property

31. *Toronto Church,* Aug. 3, 1838; *Chatham Journal,* Aug. 28, 1841.

which, in a northern climate, was expensive to feed and clothe, as paralyzing winter of 1789 in particular showed.

Most important was the simple fact that an owner's hold on a slave physically chancy and legally uncertain. The frontier continued to act as a sieve; as more American states abolished slavery, the area of freedom to the south increased; and in the Maritimes escape to the sea always was a possibility. The necessity to defend sales in court, to offer more than ordinarily clear titles, to pursue runaways in the face of public indifference, and to become involved in fruitless petitionings was distracting, frustrating, and costly. In 1793, when two female slaves were purchased in Florida for resale in Nova Scotia, the transaction was legal, profitable and simple; when a Loyalist arrived a decade later with slaves he had accepted in North Carolina as payment on a debt, he found that they could not be sold. When Colonel DeLancey died in 1804, he owned six slaves worth but £ 133— one of them mad, without value, a burden upon the estate.[32] To the south Negro slavery was an economic institution, in the provinces it was merely a convenience; and when no longer convenient, slavery was discarded. Fortuate indeed was Canada to have set in motion in 1793, the year of Eli Whitney's invention of the cotton gin and the passage of the first Fugitive Slave Act, the extinction of slavery within its borders.

But if slavery had ended in British North America, the Negro was still there, and after 1815 in increasing numbers. For a third time Nova Scotia became the chosen land for a body of displaced Negro refugees. And in the coming of the Refugee Negroes following the War of 1812 lay the real beginnings of racism in Canada.

32. Smith, "Slave in Canada," pp. 26, 115.

5. The Refugee Negroes

"I have felt my color in my pride and I should have suffered often the pain of being skinned alive could it make me white." [1] So spoke a late nineteenth-century descendant of the Refugee Negroes, as they were called, who were brought to Nova Scotia between 1813 and 1816. Unlike the Black Pioneers who were proud in their sense of Loyalism, and the Maroons who were crude but vigorous in their military unity, the Refugee Negroes were a disorganized, pathetic, and intimidated body who seemed unable to recover from their previous condition of servitude, their sudden voyage up the Atlantic to Nova Scotian shores, and their persistent lack of leaders. They unwittingly fanned the sparks of a more conscious, more organized, white racism than Nova Scotia had known, just as the last vestiges of slavery were passing. These new arrivals clasped their freedom to them, willed themselves to do well, did not want to leave their new found land—and yet failed utterly.

The Refugee Negroes were among the jetsam of the War of 1812. Several hundred slaves sought refuge behind British lines during the war, as they had done in the Revolution. Nor were British marines and sailors above forcing slaves to leave against their wishes.[2] On April 2, and again on April 7, 1814, the commander of the British fleet on the Atlantic Coast, Vice-Admiral Sir Alexander Cochrane, issued proclamations that promised all residents of the United States who came to one of His Majesty's ships or military posts a choice of military service or of free transportation to a British possession in North America or the West Indies, where they would "meet with all due encouragement" as Free Settlers.[3] The proclamations served a good end badly. Cochrane did not mention slaves by name, and he had no authority to bind other colonies to encourage settlers once they arrived. Ugly rumors that these escaped slaves were resold into captivity in the West Indies were carefully investigated and proved false; but in time,

1. Quoted in PANS, Lenore DeWolf Rathbun, "First Freed Slaves at Five Mile Plains and Vicinity," p. 37, typescript MS written in Halifax in 1950, from interviews with great-grandchildren of Negro settlers and diaries of the author's parents and grandparents.
2. PANS, *112:* Dalhousie to Bathurst, Dec. 29, 1816.
3. The original proclamation appears in William R. Manning, ed., *Diplomatic Correspondence of the United States–Canadian Relations, 1784–1860* (Washington, 1940), *1,* 647–52, and the second in WO1/141, pt. 1.

by international arbitration, the Emperor of Russia was to find that Cochrane had acted wrongly and that Britain owed the United States $1,204,960 for 3,601 slaves thus carried away from Maryland, Virginia, North Carolina, Louisiana, and Georgia. The majority of these, twenty-four hundred, came from the first two states, and the bulk of those, in turn—nearly two thousand—were taken to Nova Scotia.[4]

But Cochrane's proclamation was meant to deal with a situation that already existed, not with one he created by virtue of it. Already a large number of Negroes had found their way to the British lines, and in September 1813, 124 of these were taken to Halifax without Cochrane letting the government there know that they were coming.[5] The Lieutenant-Governor of Nova Scotia, Sir John Coape Sherbrooke, confronted with a fait accompli resembling that the Jamaican Legislature had presented to Wentworth, unhappily administered an oath of allegiance to the Refugees and ordered them to the interior of the province to search for employment. "I have no doubt," he reported to the Colonial Secretary, Lord Bathurst, "but that they will be able to maintain themselves comfortably by their Labour." Foreseeing that others would come, he asked whether or not the Home Government would provide clothing and rations for them. Bathurst responded by sending out a thousand pairs of worsted stockings.[6]

4. PRO, Admiralty 1/508: Cochrane to Pultney Malcolm, Feb. 17, 1814, to James Monroe, March 8, and to John Wilson Crocker, Feb. 26, March 13, 1815; and 1/509: Cochrane to Crocker, March 13, June 7, and Thomas Spalding to Edward Griffith, May 22, and reply May 23—all 1815. The accuracy of the list of 3,601 slaves is to be doubted if all of it was compiled as badly as that portion pertaining to Nova Scotia. Among the supporting documents to the arbitration was a copy of a rations list for Refugees victualed at Halifax between April 1815 and October 1818, which was treated as "a return of American refugee negroes who have been received" in the province; the two are not, of course, the same thing. See John Bassett Moore, *History and Digest of the International Arbitrations to which the United States has been a Party* (Washington, 1898), *1,* 387–89.

5. Admiralty 1/507, pt. 4: Cochrane's report, countersigned "I approve," Sept. 28, 1814; PANS, *420:* "Manuscript Documents, Province of Nova Scotia. Refugee Negroes, 1813 to 1816," nos. 1–8, showing arrivals on seven vessels. My tabulation of the lists differs from Charles Bruce Fergusson, ed., *A Documentary Study of the Establishment of the Negroes in Nova Scotia between the War of 1812 and the Winning of Responsible Government,* PANS pub. no. 8 (Halifax, 1948), p. 11, n. 32, which gives 133 as the total. Fergusson brings together twenty-nine of the most important documents on the Refugee settlers from PANS; he precedes them with a lengthy historical commentary, in which he cites many other sources in PANS. I have checked each of these documents independently, but except for occasional, minor, and debatable differences with respect to punctuation and capitalization, Fergusson's quotations are accurate, and since his book is more readily available, I cite it rather than the original documents. Copies of several of the COdocuments cited below also may be found in PANS, although with a different numbering.

6. *Halifax Acadian Recorder,* Sept. 18, 1813; WO1/142: J. Barker, Deputy Store-

As expected, many more Refugees arrived following Cochrane's proclamation. In May, June, and July 1814, the first authorized settlers reached Halifax; in September came "a *few* hundred Negroes (dead and alive)"; [7] in October, as Sherbrooke complained to Cochrane, a ship discharged its passengers, who "conducted themselves in a most disorderly manner," [8] without informing him. In 1815 nine hundred more Refugees came, from Amelia Island via Bermuda to Halifax and Annapolis Royal. The British government shipped out quantities of clothing in anticipation of their needs: three thousand pairs of shoes, five hundred Dutch caps, hundreds of yards of linen and brown serge, a thousand jackets, trousers, and waistcoats, two thousand cotton shirts, and two thousand more worsted stockings. These took twelve months to arrive, however, as they were misdirected to Bermuda, and the Refugees went without them for their first winter. At Sherbrooke's request, the Assembly voted a sum of money to meet the immediate needs of the Refugees, while it warned him that the interests of the province were not being served by bringing in "a separate and marked class of people, unfitted by Nature to this Climate, or to an association with the rest of His Majesty's Colonists." [9] Sherbrooke promised to send the Assembly's address to Bathurst, only to receive a letter from Cochrane forecasting the arrival of two thousand more Refugees. The Governor suggested that this "unexpected importation . . . for which I was totally unprepared, may . . . involve me in some difficulty" but since doubtless the Refugees already were on their way from Bermuda, he would deal with them as best he could. Nearly five hundred arrived shortly afterwards.[10]

Although the influx was larger than Sherbrooke or the Assembly had expected, both attempted to deal with it sensibly and fairly, if not always efficiently. Halifax was accustomed to taking whatever the good of the Empire demanded of it, to "lying out in the wet" and serving; and it was ready to do so again, although the Assembly protested against the discrimination involved in their being required to help emigrants "whose Character,

keeper-General, to Robert Arbuthnot, Dec. 1, 1814; CO217/92: Sherbrooke to Bathurst, Oct. 18, 1813.

7. Fergusson, *Documentary Study,* pp. 11 ff., quoting *Halifax Acadian Recorder,* Sept. 3, 1814; *Recorder,* April 1, 29, May 13, 1815, Aug. 24, 1816.

8. Quoted in Fergusson, p. 14.

9. CO217/95: Invoice, Nov. 24, Barker to George Harrison, Nov. 25, Dec. 8, 1814; PAC transcripts, Treasury Letters, *13:* S. R. Lushington to H. Goulburn, Oct. 28, 1815, and *14:* Harrison to same, July 10, 1816: PANS, *305:* Petition to Sherbrooke, April 1, 1815; *Journal and Proceedings of the House of Assembly,* [hereafter, *House of Assembly Journal, 1815*] (Halifax), pp. 107–08.

10. *House of Assembly Journal, 1815,* pp. 32–33, 45, 104; *1816,* p. 198 [83]; CO217/96: Sherbrooke to Bathurst, April 6, Oct. 16, 1815; Fergusson, *Documentary Study,* p. 12.

Principles, and Habits are not previously ascertained," steps that were normally taken with those who did not arrive as the displaced byproducts of a war. Bathurst replied in July, pointing out that as the war had ended, the problem would take care of itself. He thought the Council was unduly alarmed about the effect the Refugees would have on the labor market, for surely a frontier settlement would absorb as many workers as it could get, and with the opening of coal mines, which the Assembly anticipated shortly, the Negroes would find "new sources of occupation." In November he admitted that it had been contrary to his intention that so many Negroes from the southern United States were sent to Nova Scotia, and he urged Sherbrooke to forward all Refugees who would go to Trinidad, while approving the Lieutenant-Governor's plans to grant them land if they wished to stay.[11]

For the first few months, the Refugees were administered from a series of ad hoc decisions. In September 1814, a few were admitted to the poorhouse in Halifax, and in October the Commissioners of the Poor told Sherbrooke that the Negroes were in dire need. He ordered the remainder of those who required medical assistance or who could not work into the poorhouse. There they were given rations, males receiving the allowance usually allocated to the wives of soldiers. To prevent fraud in the victualling, Sherbrooke required a well-controlled issue of stores and a weekly return, signed by two of the commissioners.[12]

By March seventy-four of the black inmates of the poorhouse had died. Smallpox in particular was a constant problem. In October 1814, Seth Coleman, a Quaker who had befriended the Maroons and those Refugees taken to Dartmouth, warned that disease was spreading dangerously. Sherbrooke gave vaccine to Coleman, who was self-taught in the handling of simple medicines, and told him to inoculate all of the poor, white or black, in Dartmouth and Preston. Coleman, moving among the Refugees as quickly as he could, treated as many as forty on a Sunday, when the Negroes visited one another, and "5 to 8 per week day." In four months he reported that "a total stop" had been put to the disease on his side of the harbor: 285 Negroes, 79 whites, and 59 Indians had been vaccinated. Nonetheless, the danger of an epidemic remained, for smallpox had broken out on Melville Island, where new arrivals initially were kept, and the buildings there had not been fully fumigated.[13]

11. CO218/29: Bathurst to Sherbrooke, June 13, Nov. 10, 1815; *House of Assembly Journal, 1815,* pp. 107–08; PANS, *88:* Bathurst to Sherbrooke, May 10, 1815; *214:* Council Minutes, July 26, 1815, quoted in Fergusson, p. 22.

12. Fergusson, pp. 14–16; *House of Assembly Journal, 1815,* pp. 30, 91, 113.

13. Fergusson, pp. 15–17; *Halifax Acadian Recorder,* April 1, May 13, 1815; *House of Assembly Journal, 1816,* pp. 138, 152–53, 160; PANS, *419:* report of health officers on brig *Ceres,* Aug. 23, 1816.

At first the Assemblymen appear to have thought that no further arrangements were needed to deal with the new arrivals. As Sherbrooke suggested, the Refugees were to disperse into the low hills back of Halifax. Concentrating Negroes together, as Wentworth had done, had not proved successful, and in any case, single blocs of coastal land sufficient to provide for all in one place no longer existed. As many settlers did, they would receive provisions for two years, until they could bring in their first crops, together with seeds and simple agricultural implements. Forest cover would provide them with the materials for building houses and with firewood, and in the winter they could work as woodsmen. This was done with those Refugees who were landed in 1814 and early in 1815.

But Bathurst suggested as early as October 1814, that the Refugees might be put in the hands of the Collector of Customs, who had machinery at his disposal for dealing with prizes of war and forfeiture to the Crown. In April 1815, Sherbrooke turned to an Order-in-Council of 1808 which carried into effect the Act for the Abolition of the Slave Trade passed the year before. This had given the chief customs officer primary responsibility for settling recaptives.[14] The Council approved Bathurst's proposal, provided that it could review expenses every three months and that tight controls would continue to be applied to provisions.[15]

On the whole this system worked well. The Collector of Customs, T. N. Jeffery, took over Melville Island, in the North West Arm; the island had been used for American prisoners of war between 1812 and 1814, and the Negroes were to receive approximately the same ration and the same room as had the prisoners.[16] A merchant from Halifax, Lewis de Molitor, contracted to supply the provisions: for each male over the age of twelve, a pound of bread, a pound of potatoes (or a gill of pease), half a pound of beef, half a pound of Indian meal, a third of an ounce of salt, and a quart of spruce beer on four days of each week, with a pound of Indian meal, half a pound of potatoes (or pease), half a pound of pork, an ounce of coffee, a quart of spruce beer, a pint of molasses, and the same salt ration on three days in each week. All females over twelve received two-thirds of this. The sick had rice gruel, tea, sago, and arrowroot added to their diet, with the other foods in reduced portions; the beef and vegetables were made into soup and issued at messes. Although the contract did not call for it, sugar also was given from time to time. In all, the

14. CO217/96: copy, Viscount Castlereagh to Sir George Prevost, April 10, 1808, encl. in Sherbrooke to Bathurst, April 6, 1815.

15. Fergusson, pp. 22–23.

16. LC, John Mitchell Papers, 1810–99. Mitchell was agent for the Exchange of American Prisoners of War in Halifax. The bulk of these four volumes of manuscripts shows that the Refugees received the same rations as the whites. One of the prisoners, as well, was a Negro (*Toronto Globe*, Jan. 13, 1875).

arrangement was not ungenerous, and none of the Refugees appears to have complained.[17]

The government also opened a hospital within the Melville Island prison, and a surgeon vaccinated over five hundred Refugees during the summer of 1815. By May the population of the island rose to six hundred, more than the facilities were meant to accomodate, but no one was kept on the island for long, and in June the total was nearly halved. The numbers continued to drop as arrivals slackened and the Negroes were moved onto the land more quickly, and by the end of the year there were fifty-nine Refugees within the old prison. During this time 107 Refugees died on the island. By May, 1816, when there were thirty-nine Refugees left, together with ten in the Black Hospital, Sherbrooke—who was leaving for a new post in Quebec the following month—ordered that all save those who were ill should be taken to Preston; the sick were removed to the hospital of the Halifax poorhouse, where the government continued to support them, and in June the island depot was closed down.[18]

The Melville Island establishment had been an expensive operation. Jeffery received one guinea for each Refugee registered with him. De-Molitor was reimbursed ninepence for each ration issued to those Negroes who were in health and, until October 1815, a shilling and seven pence for each ration given in the hospital; and he was paid one shilling daily per Negro in good health and two shillings daily for each who was ill. To these costs were to be added those for vaccines, coffins, and the wages of a part-time medical attendant—who was paid three shillings and ten pence daily—a clerk, who received £ 200 (later halved), and a steward, who was paid seven and six daily. For the first three months alone, Jeffery submitted bills for £ 2,036.[19] The accounts were approved by a committee of the Council, and there is no hint of fraud involved, but the cost nonetheless was high and those concerned were generously rewarded. Not surprisingly, Bathurst suggested that no charges should be made for surveying

17. Fergusson, p. 24. Abstracts and full returns of daily victualings, accounts, receipts to suppliers, tenders, articles of agreement, and the Council's reports, appear in PANS, *420*, nos. 13–74, 78–85, 88–92, 94–125. The reference to sugar is in no. 79, William Best to Henry H. Cogswell, Nov. 9, 1815.

18. CO217/98: Sherbrooke to Bathurst, June 5, 1815; Fergusson, pp. 25–27.

19. The records are inconsistent. Figures for Melville Island do not coincide: DeMolitor's first bill implies that there were 450 Refugees, or that several missed rations from time to time; the surgeon's reports show five hundred vaccinations, but many apparently were not inoculated; the figures on rations suggest 320 adults at a time when Jeffery's allowance was for 727 Refugees of all ages. The government's agreement with DeMolitor was to supply Refugees from May 1, but his accounts show that he began doing so on April 27. When DeMolitor lost the account for supplying rations in hospital, he was given an extra penny on each regular ration a bit later. These documents fill PANS, *320*.

resettlement land, and in the new year he told Sherbrooke's successor, the Earl of Dalhousie, who arrived in October 1816, to cut expenses drastically.[20]

Under Sherbrooke, some of the Negroes made a start in what he regarded as the right direction. He, like Wentworth before him, felt that he understood Negroes and that he was close to them; he disagreed with his predecessor on two points, however: although he thought highly of the black militia at Digby and of the color-bearer of the 104th Regiment, who was a Negro, when it marched overland to Quebec in the winter of 1813–14, he felt that the Refugees, at least, were an unmilitary people whose future in Nova Scotia lay in becoming small, independent farmers as quickly as possible. Further, as Halifax was crowded with black children who, because of high wages paid during the war, had streamed into the city to take servants' jobs, he thought that relative dispersal was to be preferred to concentrated, all-Negro settlements. This would mean that the Refugees might be absorbed into the province socially, becoming a black yeomanry rather than casual laborers. He and Blowers, who employed Refugees himself in order to help, thought that families had to be kept together; the latter, as President of the Council, recommended that Dalhousie should withhold rations from heads of families who were absent from musters, for too many fathers were leaving their wives and children to come to Halifax in search of employment. Dalhousie agreed with the basic principle Sherbrooke had laid down.[21]

Still the system did not work, for neither the Nova Scotian legislature nor the British government was prepared to provide the long-range support or the careful planning necessary for the resettlement of a group of displaced persons so inadequately equipped to meet their own needs. Dalhousie found the entire system in a state of confusion when he arrived. Many Negroes were wandering about claiming relief, and he suspected a number were not entitled to it. In Sherbrooke's absence the Adminstrator, Major-General George S. Smyth, had not kept the accounts properly, and the Negroes had fallen into "a state of starvation," having been left in "the most deplorable" condition. The new Governor thought that the Refugees would need supervision and provisions for at least another year, and he leaned toward renewing the arrangement with the Collector of Customs. But in December, the Council responded by advising that only those Refugees sent by Admiral Cochrane from April 1815 on, should be eligible for help—a curious conclusion since Cochrane had issued his

20. CO218/29: Bathurst to Dalhousie, Jan. 17, 1817.

21. SPG Archives, Dr. Bray's Associates Minute Books, *4:* Nov. 5, 1812, Feb. 10, 1814; PANS, *419:* order for rations, May 16, 1816; *421:* Blowers to Dalhousie, Nov. 29, 1816; *Saint John Telegraph,* May 27, 1884.

proclamation a year before that; even discounting those Negroes who arrived in September of 1813, admittedly not under the terms of his orders, several hundred came in 1814 who certainly were. Further, the Council added, any blacks who had no fixed place of residence or who were receiving wages should not be permitted rations. The effect of this foolish decision was to encourage many who had taken work to leave it, since the province proposed to guarantee rations until June 1, 1817.[22]

Nor did the plan to place the Refugees on the land succeed. The Surveyor-General, Charles Morris, was too optimistic about the work habits of the Refugees, and they, in turn, were displeased with the fact that they did not receive outright grants; for most held land on tickets of location or licences of occupation. The plots were too small in any case, and the soil was sterile; most lots were of ten acres, even though Morris later estimated that no family, however industrious, could live on less than a hundred acres and have a proper fuel supply. He hoped that the Refugees might support themselves by furnishing vegetables, berries, poultry, and fish to the Halifax market. None of the Refugees was able to raise chickens; they proved to be poor fishermen, even though the province gave them fishnets; and their crops of potatoes, turnips, and cabbages failed so persistently that most were forced to fall back on berry-picking and other casual labor.

For the first year at Preston, Morris designed an ambitious plan for the Refugees. He proposed that Chamberlain, the Deputy Surveyor, organize the first fifty men on the land into work gangs; they could build two houses with stone chimneys each day, he thought, and in six weeks five hundred people could be accommodated. Later arrivals would clear land around the houses, and all could plant crops in the spring; thus, in a single season, the community would take root. With Chamberlain in charge of issuing provisions and withholding them from those who did not work, the Negro men, more comfortable with gang labor techniques, thus put up 144 huts and houses on the 208 lots Morris and Chamberlain laid out for them.[23]

But the high hopes of early spring were misguided. The ground remained

22. CO217/98: Lushington to Goulburn, July 10, 11, and Jeffery to Dalhousie, May 26, encl. in Dalhousie to Bathurst, Dec. 2, and Minutes of Council, Dec. 4, encl. in Dalhousie to Bathurst, Dec. 29, all 1816; Fergusson, p. 29. The Assembly's worry over the Refugees increased when news arrived of a Negro uprising in Jamaica in 1816 (CO218/29: Bathurst to Sherbrooke, July 4, 1816).

23. Fergusson, pp. 40–41, 45; PANS, *421:* "Report of Lands cleared by the People of Colour in the Settlement of Preston," May 10, 1861, printed in Appendix in Fergusson; PANS, *419:* Chamberlain to Morris, Jan. 4, 1816, and drafts of Morris's proposals, nos. 72, 73, n.d.; *119:* plans for Preston, 1816, 1822, 1827, 1835–36, nos. 20–29, 32, 35, two of which (nos. 28, 29) are printed in Fergusson, as appendixes 26, 27.

frozen until June, and little planting was possible for the following season. The huts, built too hurriedly of green materials, warped and split. Almost all were without floors or cellars, and if potatoes did not freeze in the ground, they froze in storage. No one taught the Refugees how to conserve fuel, and their common land soon was denuded as they burned its wood into charcoal. The men were able to clear little more than a quarter to an acre of land per family. In midwinter Jeffery's muster revealed far more Refugees in need than Dalhousie had expected. He placed Richard Inglis of the Commissariat Department in charge of provisions, moved the supplies into rented stores, and cut the cost of rations from ten to five pence each. Nonetheless, bills continued to mount: for food, seeds, tools, for rent, for wages, for surveying, for ferrying Inglis and his horse back and forth from Halifax to Dartmouth. During a single winter Chamberlain passed out thirty-six tons of biscuits, ten tons of rice, twenty-four tons of beef, and eight tons of pork. At the end of all this effort nothing had changed.[24]

Dalhousie concluded that his efforts were not going to succeed. "Permit me to state plainly," he wrote to the Colonial Office, "that little hope can be entertained of settling these people so as to provide for their families and wants, they must be supported for many years. Slaves by habit & education, no longer working under the dread of the lash, their idea of freedom is Idleness and they are altogether incapable of Industry." He wished that they might be restored to their masters in the United States or be sent to Sierra Leone: "either of these plans I believe would be agreeable to the greater part of them; but to the West Indies they will not go." [25]

The provincial Council agreed. On April 30, 1817, it advised that the Refugees should be reminded that all rations would cease on the first of June. On May 15 all single men were to be given two weeks' supplies and told to find work; any who wanted to return to the United States were to be taken there. In the meantime, those who had cleared land would receive seed potatoes and tools once more, for crops had failed and tools had a way of disappearing. Enquiries were to be made to see whether any Negroes would go to Trinidad.[26] Dalhousie approved, added that the aged and infirm should also be granted rations, and appealed to Bathurst to

24. CO217/98: Sherbrooke to Bathurst, April 20, Jeffery to Sherbrooke, May 26, encl. in Dalhousie to Bathurst, Dec. 2, 1816; CO218/29: Bathurst to Sherbrooke, Feb. 5, 1816; PANS, *419:* Samuel Head to Morris, Feb. 1, 1816; *421:* documents on charges, and Dalhousie to Blowers, Nov. 15, 1816; John Patrick Martin, *The Story of Dartmouth,* p. 125, citing the account books of John Skerry, ferryman.

25. CO217/98: to Bathurst, Dec. 29, 1816, and quoted in Fergusson, p. 30.

26. PANS, *414,* 109–12: Minutes of Council, April 30, 1817, and quoted in Fergusson, p. 31.

provide assistance for yet one more year, or until the crops planted in the spring of 1817 might be harvested. He reduced the costly establishment to a single man, Inglis, who was paid ten shillings a day and provided with an allowance for a horse, rations, lodgings, and fuel.[27]

Reluctantly Bathurst agreed to Dalhousie's entreaties and sustained the issue of rations until the next year. In October 1818 Inglis gave out the last of the rations, but by March of 1819 the Refugees again were near starvation. The House of Assembly refused to grant more, and Dalhousie continued to dole out Indian meal and pork a month at a time, hoping that the Colonial Office would approve. He cut back even this meager diet, and he warned that "the habits of [the Refugees'] life and constitutional laziness will continue & these miserable creatures will for years be a burden upon the Government."[28]

Like Shakespeare's medlar tree, the time was rotten, not ripe, for someone to insist upon a Draconian solution once again: to transport—by persuasion if possible, by force if necessary—all the Refugees to Africa or to the West Indies. Neither Sherbrooke nor Dalhousie had found any enthusiasm among the Negroes for such a move, for they all professed to fear that this was a scheme to return them to slavery; but in May 1817, the Governor wrote that some would go to Tobago or Trinidad. The moment was lost. A penny-pinching Treasury forced Bathurst to temporize, insisting that any removal had to be approached slowly, through negotiations for chartered merchant ships; and even had another Clarkson appeared who, in his enthusiasm, could have convinced all of the Refugees of the benefits of such a move, the delay would have allowed time for their old fears to return.[29]

Acting upon direct invitation from Trinidad in 1820, Sir James Kempt, now Lieutenant-Governor of Nova Scotia, did find ninety-five Refugees, nearly all from Beech Hill, who were willing to be moved. On January 6, 1821, this tiny band sailed from Halifax aboard the schooner *William,* with Richard Inglis in charge throughout the voyage, at an ultimate cost of nearly £ 487 sterling. They were well-received, being placed together on land in north Naparima; they also were illiterate and had no means to pass news back to the majority in Nova Scotia. When Kempt ordered a transport, which had discharged its passengers in Halifax, to take as many more

27. CO217/99: Dalhousie to Bathurst, Jan. 3, 23, May 16, June 14, 1817.

28. Ibid., June 10, 1819; CO218/29: replies, Oct. 30, 1817, July 10, 1819. In 1845 the Bishop of Nova Scotia wrote the same: the Africans would "be a perpetual burthen to this community" (Dr. Bray's Associates Minute Books, *6,* Nov. 18).

29. CO218/29: Bathurst to Dalhousie, Jan. 17, Feb. 24, March 12, June 14, 1817; CO217/99: Dalhousie to Bathurst, May 16, 1817.

Refugees to Trinidad as wished to go, not one could be found, for they read the silence of their brethren as proof that they had been enslaved there.[30]

Periodically thereafter, the Council entertained visions of removing the Refugee blacks to the West Indies, although nothing further was done. In 1825 the Assembly thought to prime the pump by sending "a few of the more intelligent" to Trinidad to see the good life there; none would go. In 1836 the lieutenant-governor sent agents to the Refugees at Preston and Hammond's Plains to discuss a move to Trindad or Demerara. The Negroes listened and, from "a foolish and indefinite fear of again being brought into bondage," refused to leave. The very few who had begun to do relatively well at farming had no reason to move; the rest were unwilling to move without them. Some of the men, one agent thought, would have gone, but the women would not, and many felt "some jealousy lest such as remain should possess the improvements of all that might leave." In 1839 Trinidad dispatched a representative to ask Negroes to come as laborers, and he too was rebuffed, at which point the tenuous link forged between Nova Scotia and Trinidad in 1821 snapped.[31]

What had gone wrong with the Refugee resettlement in Nova Scotia? Why was the result of this miserable story so depressing to all? Many conditions worked to assure that the Refugees' opportunity to begin life anew was limited. They differed from the Negroes who had preceded them; most came from Maryland and Virginia, and thus were products of an area and a time of considerable softening in the rigors of the slavery system. Virtually none were trained to any particular skills, unlike the slaves who accompanied the Loyalists; most had been field hands who lacked the indoor slaves' incidental knowledge of domestic chores and who had not learned how to live side by side with white men. Originally from the South, they suffered more than the northern Loyalist Negroes from their sudden injection into a new climate. Not having been permitted their own plots of land, they knew little of independent agriculture. Their ignorance, according to a white missionary who had ministered to Loyalist and Maroon

30. CO296/5: Bathurst to Sir Ralph Woodford, June 14, 1821; PANS, *422:* nos. 20–30, 53; PAC, Treasury Letters, *19:* Harrison to Navy, June 9, July 4, 1821; Fergusson, pp. 36–37. See also K. O. Laurence, "The Settlement of Free Negroes in Trinidad before Emancipation," *Caribbean Quarterly,* 9, nos. 1/2, 26–52.

31. *House of Assembly Journal, 1836,* 1014–15, 1020; PANS, "Negroes: Papers relating to Negro Refugees, 1815–1818" [*sic*]: Archibald Gray to Thomas W. James, May 11, 1836; PANS, *422:* nos. 51–54; Fergusson, pp. 34–37, 46–47, and App. 16: Sir Colin Campbell to Glenelg, Aug. 25, 1837. For an accurate, if fictional, treatment of Refugee life to this date, see the play "Coming Here to Stay: The Negroes in Nova Scotia," by David A. Giffen, presented in Nova Scotia in 1967. I wish to thank Mr. Giffen for sending me a typescript copy.

Negroes earlier, was profoundly greater. And to many of the leading whites, this ignorance was deepened by the fact that virtually all of the Refugees were Baptists, trapped in "the Labyrinths of Error & Enthusiasm," [32] while most of their predecessors originally had been Anglicans and Wesleyans.

The Refugee Negroes had arrived at the worst of times. Cheap white labor was plentiful: sixteen thousand immigrants had come during the dozen years previous, and sixty thousand more were to pour into the province in the next twenty-five years. In 1816 disbanded soldiers and out-of-work fishermen from Newfoundland cluttered the Halifax labor market. Further, the early winters which confronted the Refugees were unparalleled in their severity. In 1815, "the Year of the Mice," entire fields were destroyed. Mice could cut down an acre of late-sown grain in three days; they burrowed into the ground to eat the potatoes; as winter came they went into the water and died, "forming a ridge like seaweed along the edge of the sea," [33] and codfish were caught with the bodies of mice in their maws. The Negroes were found to subsist "on what [whites] should think literally nothing." [34] This devastation was followed by "the Year without a Summer," for the frost lay hard in the woods in June and later that month the snow fell to a depth of ten inches. In any case, the land given to the Refugees was poorer than most, for the best already had been taken up.[35]

Understandably, the Refugees proved unable to help themselves. No leader emerged quickly to be their Blucke, Leonard, Peters, or James. So recently escaped from slavery, they at first assumed that freedom involved no responsibilities. Their rations of spruce beer were curtailed, for they could not be bothered to fetch water for it. In the winter of 1815 they must

32. SPG Archives, Journals: T. H. C. Parsons to Arthur Hamilton, Oct. 29, and to Bishop Robert Stanser, Dec. 5, 1821; Dr. Bray's Associates Minute Books, *4*, May 1, 1818.

33. George MacLaren, *The Pictou Book* (New Glasgow, 1954), p. 211.

34. Coleman to William Sabatier, March 23, 1816, quoted in Fergusson, p. 19.

35. At the time the owners of the land to which the Refugees were sent maintained that their's was good soil, but this seems untrue. A manuscript map of Nova Scotian soils, made in 1940, shows that the Negroes were placed in areas of stony land with shallow topsoil over bedrock (Directive Committee on Regional Planning, Nova Scotia, Yale University Library Map Room); and many sources—both contemporary and recent—refer to the rocky nature of the Preston, Porter's Lake, and Dartmouth farms. On other areas see, for example, Sutherland, "Clements Township," pp. 65–66; Nicholson, "New Glasgow Region," p. 49; and "A New Map of Nova Scotia, Newfoundland, etc. from the latest authorities" (John Cary, 1811, London), Morse Collection, Yale University Library. James F. W. Johnston, *Notes on North America, Agricultural, Economical, and Social* (London, 1851), *1*, 137–39, comments on the poor igneous and metamorphic country behind the Negroes' settlement on Loch Lomond, in New Brunswick.

have suffered from the cold because they stole blankets from each other. They did not build their schools, even when subsidized teachers were provided, because of petty disagreements over building sites, and other schools were suspended because teachers and pupils quarrelled. The Refugees lost the favor of the Anglican Bishop because they had "no notion of gratitude"; and one of their white teachers turned on them when they suggested that it was "a great favour" conferred upon him to attend his school. By 1824, although repeatedly given grants of seed for corn and potatoes, they had fallen into petty thievery and begging from door to door in Halifax. Their troubles were real, had they cared to pick them up, but they preferred to let them lie on other men's doorsteps.[36] Lawrence Hartshorne, still a friend of the Negro, finally lost patience, and in 1817 he wrote that they "consider themselves an oppressed and degraded people by White People, consequently not bound by any moral obligation to be honest and faithfull to their Masters or employers . . . individually there are some clever fellows amongst them . . . but a large proportion I am bold to say, never will [succeed] in such a Climate as this." [37] He concluded that they too should be sent to Sierra Leone.

By no means were the whites without fault. One of the Refugees' white schoolteachers, James Fortune, took a Negro mistress; another, together with her daughters, had Negro children deliver notes inviting army officers to sleep with them when school was out (as a result, some of the Negroes were given to "lascivious" ideas). Land claims were abused and manipulated for the private profit of presumed white benefactors. Often the Negroes were reviled and persecuted by a minority of the white settlers, as "a burden," "bad subjects," "a tax on charity," "anything but the pride of Nova Scotia," "neither prosperous nor useful"—this last the judgment of a text used throughout the Nova Scotian schools in the 1840s and illcalculated to remove the growing prejudice against Negroes. As late as 1826 a Negro woman was publicly whipped in Shelburne. Blacks were the butt of local jokes: boys blocked up their chimneys, were they fortunate enough to have any, or slipped plugs of chewing tobacco into their kettles. One of their supporters, Seth Coleman, warned that they had "many Lurking Enemies," and Theophilus Chamberlain, who had befriended both Clarkson and the Maroons, wrote of "the squibs that ignorance or ill nature and contempt has induced some silly Body to through [*sic*] out against

36. PANS, *420:* Coleman to Richard Tremain, March 5, and Best to Cogswell, Nov. 9, Dec. 7, 9, 1815; CO217/92: Sherbrooke to Lord Bathurst, Oct. 22, 1813.
37. Dr. Bray's Associates Minute Books: *4,* Nov. 7, 1817; BM, Clarkson Papers, 41, 263: Hartshorne to Robert Banley, March 8, Nov. 2, 1821; **Minute Books:** *5,* July 2, 1824, Nov. 11, 1831; *6,* Dec. 2, 1836.

them." A visitor in 1861 found anti-Negro prejudice in Nova Scotia as strong as in the northern United States. The Refugees, it seemed, had come to the province "to be free, to be frozen, and to starve." [38]

Finally the Refugee Negroes failed to develop because they became wards of the state and were to remain so. They were not alone in receiving aid, for the province helped many Irish and Scots immigrants at the same time, but for reasons partially if not primarily within their control, the Negroes did not pass, as the other settlers did, out of this early stage of tutelage. In the mid-1830s, Thomas Chandler Haliburton's fictional Sam Slick saw that, "We have two kinds of slaves, the niggers and the white slaves. All European labourers and blacks, who came out to us, do our hard bodily work, while we direct it to a profitable end." But in that end the Negro alone among these new groups of settlers could conclude, with Henry David Thoreau, that "I have not got much to say about Canada, not having seen much; what I got by going to Canada was a cold." [39]

The subsequent history of the Refugee Negroes, although briefly told, is important to our story. Not only are the majority of present-day Nova Scotian Negroes their descendants, but they remained an identifiable group late into the nineteenth century. Their presence provided a focus for growing anti-Negro sentiment, and they in turn were a cause for further division among the Negroes themselves.

Resettlement on more fertile lands, well away from Halifax, struck the Assembly as a possible solution to their and the Negroes' dilemma, but the blacks agreed to move only if nearly half of them were placed on the same location. In 1838 the Lieutenant-Governor, Sir Colin Campbell, thought such a wholesale replanting would cost £ 600, and he turned to the Colonial Secretary, Robert Grant, Lord Glenelg, who despite his Clapha-

38. Dr. Bray's Associates Minute Books, *4:* Nov. 13, 1823; *Halifax Acadian Recorder,* April 21, Aug. 25, 1823; Calvin L. Hatheway, *The History of New Brunswick, from its First Settlement* . . . (Fredericton, 1846), pp. 34–35; "A Nova-Scotian" [Charles Boidman Owen], *An Epitome of the History, Statistics, etc. of Nova-Scotia* . . . (Halifax, 1842), p. 70; Sir James E. Alexander, *L'Acadie; or, Seven Years' Explorations in British America* (London, 1849), *2,* 130; PANS, *419:* Coleman to Sherbrooke, April 16, and Chamberlain to Morris, Jan. 4, 1816, the latter quoted in Fergusson, pp. 29, 41; Hugo Reid, *Sketches in North America; with some account of Congress and of the Slavery Question* (London, 1861), pp. 290–92; Fred T. Congdon, "Movement of the United Empire Loyalists from the United States to Canada," The United Empire Loyalists' Association of Canada, *Annual Transactions, 1904 to 1913* (Brampton, Ont., 1914), pp. 138–39.

39. [Haliburton], *The Clockmaker; or, The Sayings and Doings of Samuel Slick, of Slickville* (Halifax, 1836), p. 30; Thoreau, *A Yankee in Canada, with Anti-Slavery and Reform Papers* (Boston, 1866).

mite credentials refused to help, maintaining that aid for such a purpose would set a bad precedent and that the idea that the Negroes should necessarily be landed proprietors rather than hired laborers was, in any case, a "mistaken & mischievous notion." Furthermore, the surveyor-general thought that the Negroes "would be received with no very friendly feeling by the white population" at their proposed destination, in Pictou County. The next year Joseph Howe, member for Halifax County and later to be Prime Minister of Nova Scotia, made a suggestion similar to Campbell's. While the British government finally agreed to make Crown Lands conditionally available, neither administration was willing to meet the costs of resettlement.[40]

Removal, then, was not a possible solution; neither was the continued stop-gap of a provincial dole. Perhaps a grant of £ 2,000 or more might have been of some genuine assistance, but the Assembly could not see a dark cloud without thinking of its silver lining: each year from 1821 it handed out £ 100 in relief funds, with the hope that the next year would be the last. At first the money was given to the poorhouse to use rather than have the Refugees know that it came from a government which had so sternly announced that no more would be forthcoming, a subterfuge soon abandoned. Between 1828 and 1832 Lady Sarah Maitland, the Lieutenant-Governor's wife, made the Refugees in Halifax the object of her charity, and by 1833 the annual relief vote was broadened to include Negroes who had not been among the Refugees. Public funds were tight, and the legislature was caught between the fact that this body of paupers would starve without the tiny annual subsidy and the growing fear that a sum so small would do no more than assure another pinching year. Some members felt that support for the Negro poor was a local rather than a provincial matter, and in 1846 they narrowly failed to block the annual grant. From 1845 to 1848 and 1850 to 1851 the potato crop failed and the hay crop died. In 1851 the Assembly tried a direct gift of money, ranging from two shillings and sixpence to twelve and six per person; in 1854 the grant was £ 300, and still no end in sight. Throughout, the Refugees made fleeting and pathetic attempts to bring in crops sufficient to sustain them for a full winter, only to be in distress by late March of each year, and for over four decades the province continued to give them aid.[41]

The Assembly did consider other measures. A member proposed es-

40. Fergusson, pp. 108–09; PANS, *77:* Glenelg to Campbell, Jan. 8, 1839; *House of Assembly Journal, 1838,* App. 32: John Spry Morris to Rupert D. George, Aug. 1, 1837.

41. For examples, see *House of Assembly Journal* for each year from 1823 to 1858; PANS, "Negroes": accounts of expenditures, Feb. 20, 1852, and list of recipients of seed potatoes, 1857; Dr. Bray's Associates Minute Books: *5,* Feb. 4, 1831; *7,* May 16, 1848, April 16, 1850.

tablishing a knitting factory for Negro women; small grants were given from time to time to help with Negro schools and chapels; and, most important, when the more ambitious Refugees began to point out that they had exhausted the wood cover on their land, they were given fresh lots ranging from ten to a hundred and fifty acres, with an expectation of wiser use of the timber cover in future. In 1828 Lieutenant-Governor Kempt ordered a survey of all holdings so that he might confirm land grants, but after surveying fifty lots and finding the expense higher than expected, the surveyor-general stopped. Having no money to buy new land, having no clear title to the land they occupied and thus unable to sell it, the Negroes were "tied to the land without being able to live upon it," as a hundred of them said when petitioning the Assembly in 1841. In May 1842, the Council responded at last—twenty-seven years after the Refugees had been placed on the soil—and granted the Preston Refugees outright ownership over eighteen hundred acres of land. Many must have sold almost immediately and left, for in the next census in 1851, the population of Preston had fallen to its lowest.[42]

The province also took one negative step: the Assembly sought to bar entry to other freed slaves who might repeat the Refugees' pattern. Some Nova Scotians feared that, when the Imperial act to abolish slavery took full effect in August 1834, the colony would be inundated by liberated Negroes. Accordingly, on April 16, 1834, the Assembly passed "An Act to prevent the Clandestine Landing of Liberated Slaves . . . from Vessels arriving in the Province." A constable was stationed in the harbor to forestall any vessel from discharging "Slaves, liberated Slaves, Felons or Convicts"; the master of any ship landing such would be fined £ 15 per Negro; if he refused to enter into a bond upon arrival, he could be fined £ 100. Those whom the master thought would be good citizens could come ashore, on pain of forfeiting his bond if any became a public charge within the year. In 1836 the Assembly attempted to renew this act, only to have the Imperial government disallow it on the ground that it was discriminatory, opposing the purposes of the emancipation bill of 1833 by placing disabilities upon a people now entitled to the same rights as any of His Majesty's subjects.[43]

42. Dr. Bray's Associates Minute Books, *5,* June 4, 1824, June 1, 1827; PANS, *419:* Chamberlain in re Moses Seineor [*sic*], n.d.; *422:* report, March 19, 1821, petition, Aug. 18, 1826; PANS, "Negroes": miscellaneous bills and accounts, 1818, 1850, 1856; PANS, Land Papers: Peter Johnson et al. to Kempt, Dec. 10, 1827; PANS, "Crown Land Papers—Peninsula, Halifax County, 1840–1871," pp. 408–09; Fergusson, pp. 45–46, 50, 110–11, 114–15; *House of Assembly Journal, 1836,* p. 936.

43. *House of Assembly Journal, 1834,* pp. 580, 590–91, 625, 631, 664–65, 675, 679, 1702; *The Statutes at Large, passed in the Several General Assemblies . . . of Nova-Scotia* (Halifax), *3,* 342–44.

But all was not entirely bleak. While Preston declined, the Refugee settlement at Hammond's Plains grew, slowly and painfully, toward a kind of stability. Placed on the land late in 1815, the settlers there had a slightly more favorable location, for they were near the main road to the interior and their timber cover was more varied. While they too received only ten acres at first, the settlement was smaller, escheated land was granted to them more quickly, and there were more competitive white settlers nearby. Nonetheless, Hammond's Plains also fell into the vicious circle of crop failure, annual grant from the Assembly, and sickness from malnutrition. In the winter of 1826–27 fever raged through the settlement, taking twenty-one lives, until Dr. John C. Carter, the Staff Apothecary to the army, waded through snowdrifts to bring tea, biscuits, and medicines to the sufferers. In 1834 the Assembly confirmed six hundred acres of land to thirty of the Refugees, and slowly their hamlet took on form, growing from its disease-ridden low of 440 in 1827 to overtake Preston by 1851. In the 1850s an SPG missionary, William Taylor, moved in amongst the Refugees and taught them how to build secure houses and how to plow their land. A few of the Negro men married white women, and slowly the community began to be assimilated into the more comfortable and prosperous world of Halifax County. Until 1941 Hammond's Plains would remain, marginally, the largest chiefly Negro town in Nova Scotia.[44]

Elsewhere Refugees also moved toward the interior. Along Bedford Basin their settlement became known as Africville. Others made their way furthur, to Liverpool, Truro, Shubenacadie, and Tracadie. A small group reached Cape Breton Island where, near Whycocomagh, a few would learn Gaelic and be the progenitors of Rudyard Kiplings' silent black cook who, in *Captains Courageous,* "called himself MacDonald and swore in Gaelic." For the first time, Negroes lived throughout Nova Scotia, and also for the first time they were broken into clearly identifiable groups. Yet while they were dispersed, they continued to cluster in a few counties, unassimilated and unwanted.[45]

A number of the Refugees settled in New Brunswick as well. In April 1815, mindful of Admiral Cochrane's warning that two thousand Negroes were on their way to Halifax, Sherbrooke had asked the President of New Brunswick whether he could help absorb some of the blacks. The

44. PANS: *422:* John Starr to George, and report, both Jan. 16, and Carter to Dr. Baxter, n.d., all 1827; *448:* "Census for the County of Halifax," 1838; Fergusson, pp. 51–54, 93–94, and App. 13, p. 100: Land Grant, Oct. 20, 1834; Dr. Bray's Associates Minute Books, *7:* Nov. 20, 1855, Nov. 20, 1856.

45. Dr. Bray's Associates Minute Books, *4,* March 1, 1822; Dr. Bray's Associates Letter Books: C. B. Dalton to John Inglis, July 8, 1839; Kipling, *"Captains Courageous": A Story of the Grand Banks* (uniform edition, London, 1925), pp. 48, 248.

Council had replied that, provided someone else paid for transport, the colony would accept up to five hundred Refugee settlers. Sherbrooke had then directed the *Regulus,* lying off Halifax with 269 Refugees on board, to proceed directly to Saint John without landing in Nova Scotia. Apparently the vessel did land, however, for when it reached New Brunswick late in May 371 Refugees disembarked.[46] Ward Chipman the elder then sought out a suitable location for the Refugees, and he visited Loch Lomond, in back of Saint John, to see whether the settlers there—who included Loyalist Negroes—would accept them. He suggested that each family should be placed on twenty acres of land, to be confirmed on evidence of improvements after three years. In November 1816, the new Provincial Secretary, William Franklin Odell, was asked to assign the land, and despite his father Jonathan's firm conviction that Negroes were inherently inferior, "designed to be subservient to others . . . *slaves by nature,"* the younger Odell did so. In January, one of the Refugees, William Flood, prepared a petition on behalf of himself and forty of the Negroes asking for "aid . . . in any shape" to enable them to take up this land in the spring, since they had exhausted all of the preceding summer's crop. The Refugees remained in Saint John until the summer of 1817, when they moved to Willow Grove, near the Loyalist blacks on Loch Lomond.[47]

The new undertaking at Loch Lomond never prospered. A Saint John sailmaker, Robert Roy, tried to help the Black Settlement, as it was called; otherwise the white community appears to have ignored it, and soon the Refugees were reduced to selling birch brooms in Saint John. The young people drifted into the city, and the adults became stable boys or servants in a nearby hotel. New Brunswick gave significantly less aid to the Refugees than Nova Scotia had done, although in the 1820s the Lieutenant-Governor, Sir Howard Douglas, granted them ninety-nine year leases to their lands. The only white man willing to live amongst them opened an Anglican school in 1825, only to close it after a Baptist preacher from Maine was warmly received at the lake on three occasions during the following year.

46. CO217/96: Smyth to Sherbrooke, April 13, Sherbrooke to Bathurst, May 6, 1815; NBM, Scrap Book, no. 13; clipping from *Saint John Globe,* n.d. The *Saint John Daily Telegraph,* Feb. 12, 1875, gives the number of Refugees as 318, while James Hannay, *The History of New Brunswick* (Saint John, 1909), *1,* 344–45, says "about four hundred." MacNutt (*New Brunswick,* p. 163) accepts 371.

47. NBM, Hazen Collection, *4:* Chipman to Hailles, Oct. 23, 1816; NBM, Odell Estate MSS: unsigned letter to Odell, apparently from Chipman, Nov. 2, 1816, and portion of MS, beginning with p. 7, unsigned but apparently in the hand of Jonathan Odell; Patricia A. Ryder, "Ward Chipman, United Empire Loyalist" (M.A. thesis, Univ. of New Brunswick, 1958), p. 99; PAC, Lawrence Collection, Ward Chipman Papers, *10:* Flood's petition, Jan. 26, 1817; *Journal of the House of Assembly of the Province of New-Brunswick* . . . (Fredericton, 1817), p. 15.

The white community viewed Loch Lomond as a source of trouble. In 1824 the Negroes—Refugee and Loyalist—collectively were charged with breaking the peace; in 1830 one of their number, Shadrach Nut, and several Negro women were attacked and nearly beaten to death; and in 1847 twenty-four Negroes were tried for riot and assault after setting fire to the house of one Plato Loopee and attacking his family as they fled. Two years later, during a severe spring storm, the blacks were "a cause of great trouble and expense" to Saint John, the Alms House Commissioners having to provide them with a quantity of Indian meal.[48]

Other Negro settlers fanned out into the province. A quantity of blacks from the Royal West Indies Rangers, originally destined for Halifax, were put down on the Saint John–St. Andrews road in 1819; a number of freed slaves from Virginia took up the north side of Otnabog Lake, and in 1830 the province granted them land. While many of the Refugees remained in Saint John, others went to Fredericton, where they lived near the Indians of Kingsclear.[49]

Refugee blacks also mixed with Loyalist Negroes at Elm Hill, near the mouth of the Otnabog. Founded by freed slaves from New York, probably in 1806, Elm Hill arose from an unwanted marshland where nearby forest cover provided an ample supply of firewood and, in the winter, an opportunity for useful employment as lumbermen. Leadership, provided at first by two Loyalist Negroes, Posania Hopewell and Joseph McIntyre, and later by a Refugee preacher, Emanuel Neiles, was effective, and the settlement grew to over two hundred.[50]

While the Refugee Negroes were not accepted by the general population as equals, there were white men who were prepared to assist them. Individual acts of private philanthropy were numerous, and a desire to help the Negroes overcome their illiteracy or to save their souls—essentially the motives that carried missionaries into Africa during the same century—

48. SPG, *Report of the Society for the Year 1825* . . . (London, 1826), pp. 105–07; Bill, *Baptist Ministers and Churches of the Maritime Provinces,* p. 577; *Saint John Globe,* Aug. 13, 1847; NBM, Scrap Book Cb. no. 13: Clarence Ward.

49. Registry Office for York County, Fredericton: *1,* 215; MacNutt, *New Brunswick,* p. 163; William Francis Ganong, "A Monograph on the Origins of Settlements in the Province of New Brunswick," RSC, *Transactions, 10,* sec. 2 (1904), 157, 179.

50. In the *Saint John Telegraph-Journal* of Oct. 11, 1948, Ian Sclanders reported that Sir Guy Carleton granted land to the Negroes so that "they got a valley of their own." This is mistaken, for Sir Guy (then Lord Dorchester) had retired to England in 1796. The lieutenant-governor was his brother Thomas, but as he left for England in 1803—although retaining his office—the actual grant must have been made by the administrator. Sclanders (Oct. 11, 1937) also wrote that the Negroes purchased their land for fifty cents an acre, which is almost certainly incorrect. In any event, granted land is not to be confused with purchased land. See also Jessie I. Lawson and Jean MacC. Sweet, *This is New Brunswick* (Toronto, 1951), p. 52.

was present in the Maritimes too. The Refugees even more than the Black Pioneers or the Maroons were viewed as proper objects for both public and private charity, but both forms of assistance more often than not presupposed some material gain as well.

Theophilus Chamberlain, a genuine friend of the Negro for thirty years, did not fail to gain from that friendship something more tangible than the Refugees' respect. In 1792 he had offered to survey land without charge for those Negroes Clarkson left behind in Halifax, and he had been a provisioner to the Maroons. He advised the Surveyor-General, Charles Morris, on where to place the Refugees, and he gave willingly of his time and energy in surveying frontages for them. He also surrendered some of his property in exchange for land in the interior of the province. Nonetheless, when Morris settled upon Preston as the town site for a portion of the Refugee blacks—chiefly because there was a large bloc of escheated land there which originally had been granted to disbanded soldiers following the Revolutionary War—Chamberlain, together with Michael Wallace, one of the certifiers of the expenditures on behalf of the Refugees, were found to be the owners of an essential acreage, formerly given to the Maroons, in the midst of the projected settlement. Chamberlain had paid less than £ 150 for three hundred acres of the Maroons' land; he now sold this land to the province for £ 500. Wallace, who had improved his property considerably, received the same sum.[51]

But on the whole private philanthropy was sincere enough. One Rufus Fairbanks of Porter's Lake helped six families whose children had "scarcely a Dud to cover them," although he did receive compensation from the province later. John Rule and John Bazelgette leased land to Refugees for an annual quitrent of a shilling, provided the occupants put up log houses and cleared an acre annually, and neither reclaimed his property until five years after the Negroes had failed to meet even these simple conditions. Reverend William Cochran conveyed twenty acres of good land near Windsor for a shilling an acre, and when the residents failed to improve upon it adequately, he purchased it back—as he need not have done—at four times the amount he was paid for it. Lawrence Hartshorne offered thirty acres of land to each of five families in fee simple at Parrsboro, and to ten families at Addington, and he promised to give a cow to each family as soon as it had enough land cultivated to cut hay sufficient for keeping her through a winter. Individual acts of charity—the schoolmaster

51. PANS, *419:* nos. 127, 128, accounts of sales of Maroon property by auction; nos. 121–23, abstracts of vouchers for cash paid on account of Maroons; no. 79, description of relinquished lands; and no. 100, warrant to Wallace; Fergusson, pp. 68–70: Morris to Sherbrooke, Sept. 6, and Chamberlain to Morris, Nov. 11, 1815; PANS, Chamberlain File.

who sold his own food supplies at below cost, the Quaker who distributed medicines without charge, the merchant who gave away axes, the whites who took up a collection so that the Negroes of Digby might build a school—showed clearly enough that some had no desire to exploit the Negro. And since the age held that God and Knowledge were the twin paths to salvation and security, emphasis was placed on supporting churches and schools for the Refugees, and hardly at all upon political solutions to what were conceived of as problems to be met with "Christian Resignation." [52]

The Refugees therefore never became a political force, although on occasion they were wooed by contending parties. Disorganized and uneducated, they took little political initiative; religious and temperate to a fault, they seldom thought of politics as a path to material well-being, giving their cherished votes to whomever promised them the most. Until 1918 the franchise in Nova Scotia was open only to male British subjects by birth or naturalization who (except between 1854 and 1863) held property. Unlike the Loyalist Negroes, many of the Refugees were not British by birth, and there was some question whether the oath of allegiance administered to them upon their arrival had fully naturalized them. The Refugees did not gain unqualified freeholds until the 1830s, and while holders of tickets of location could vote, they were not encouraged to believe this. Assured in 1836 by Joseph Howe that they might vote, many nonetheless did not, and in 1841 they complained that they could not exercise their vote "without being at every Election questioned, browbeaten and sworn." In the general election of 1847 both parties sought out their attention, the Tories canvassing on a house to house basis, offering bread, cheese, and liquor to gain a hearing, and sending hay to those Negroes who pledged their support. This was unusual, however, and Howe pointed out quite correctly that it had been he and the Liberals who had confirmed their grants of land, making them proprietors instead of tenants of the Crown, had brought them into jury service for the first time in 1845, and had first assured them of their right to vote. Speaking in May to the Preston Negroes, then led by Sampson Carter, Howe charged the Tories with "original sin" toward the blacks, told them that the Liberals would never give them special grants on the premise that they were an inferior people, and handsomely swept into office in August with Refugee approval. Such moments were unusual, however; and although enfranchised, the Refugees

52. Dr. Bray's Associates Minute Books: *4,* Dec. 7, 1821; *5,* Nov. 14, 1828. PANS, *419:* memo, Dec. 23, 1824, and deeds, Fairbanks, Oct. 24, 1815, Cochran, Jan. 29, 1816; *420:* Fairbanks' certificate, Oct. 30, and Hartshorne to George, April 14, 1815; *421:* Fairbanks to Cogswell, March 4, 1816; *422:* Bazelgette to Rule, April 25, 1823; Fergusson, pp. 17, 19, 21, 55.

did not participate actively in politics themselves, with the single exception of a Negro who unsuccessfully contested a ward election in Saint John in 1820.[53]

Nor were the Negroes in any position to help themselves through education. The Nova Scotian public school act of 1811 provided for government aid to communities once a schoolhouse was built, a schoolmaster appointed, and £ 50 raised by local subscription, and no Refugee settlement was able to meet these conditions. The Assembly authorized two Negro schools through the Army Fund in 1816, but neither was opened, and until the 1860s the province limited itself to small grants to Negro schools in Halifax, Bridgetown, and Hammond's Plains, and to a fruitless discussion of the need for a Negro normal school. In 1832 the Assembly amended the law so that any district having fifteen or more scholars, and otherwise unable to maintain a school, might receive a grant up to £ 70, with an additional £ 5 for books, and four years later the Board of School Commissioners was given the authority to use a portion of those funds to open schools for Negroes, whether a common school existed or not.[54] These two changes had the effect of putting schools legally but not actually within the reach of black initiative and of segregating black from white children.

Christian missionaries tried to fill the gap between black and white. The Society for the Propagation of the Gospel opened schools at Preston and at Hammond's Plains in 1818 and 1820 (the latter closed in 1834) and continued to support Loyalist schools in Tracadie, Yarmouth, Digby, and after 1833, in Sackville. The Associates of Dr. Bray reopened their black school in Halifax in 1824, with Refugee and Loyalist Negroes both attending, took over the SPG school in Preston in 1827, and aided four schools elsewhere.[55] In 1843 the Colonial Church Society also began to support a Sunday school in Preston. A public subscription in Halifax raised £ 300 for an African School in the capital, and in 1836 it opened with over fifty (of nearly three hundred eligible) children attending, only to burn to the ground eight months later. The Bishop of Nova Scotia, John Inglis, worked

53. Fergusson, p. 66 and App. 21, p. 115: William Dair, et al. to Lord Falkland, recd. Feb. 23, 1841; Raymond, "Negro in New Brunswick," p. 34; *Halifax Nova Scotian,* May 10, 17, 24, Aug. 9, 1847.

54. Fergusson, p. 60.

55. Ibid., pp. 60–64, 117–18; SPG Journals: T. A. Grantham to Inglis, July 1, 1827; SPG Papers, C/CAN/NS: E. W. Morris, reports, n.d., 1844, April 19, 1848, Feb. 18, 1850; Dr. Bray's Associates Minute Books, 5: March 7, 1828, June 5, Nov. 13, 1829, Nov. 14, 1834; William Moorsom, *Letters from Nova Scotia* (London, 1830), p. 141; Charles William Vernon, *The Story of Christ Church, Dartmouth* (Halifax, 1917), pp. 53–54; Colonial Church Society, *Eighth Annual Report* (London, 1844), pp. 26–27; *Ninth* (1845), p. 32; *Tenth* (1846), p. 29; *Eleventh* (1847), p. 22.

assiduously to collect new funds, writing to the legislature, the SPG, Dr. Bray's Associates, and the Society for Promoting Christian Knowledge, and from each he received a small gift, sufficient to cover the costs of a simpler structure, opened late in 1840.[56]

The African School was a genuine force for good, and when in 1844 the Assembly struck the institution from the annual grants list, several of the legislators visited it and came away sufficiently impressed to restore the subsidy. From 1836 until 1854 the schoolmaster was Daniel Gallagher, an able teacher who, despite being blind in one eye, won the approbation of Negroes, Assembly, and churchmen alike by teaching—in addition to reading, writing, sums and the catechism—geography, navigation, palm-weaving, and the Bible, while his wife taught knitting and other domestic arts. The legislature memorialized Gallagher for his career, spanning forty years as a teacher, and when he retired Bray's Associates discovered that he had paid for the furniture, maps, and fuel for the building from his own meager salary. The African School fell into almost immediate decline thereafter, however, for the Negroes wanted full control over its affairs, and the Archdeacon, Robert Willis, opposed the Refugees, finding them "unsteady & unsatisfactory." [57]

Dr. Bray's Associates were unable to continue to support schools in all of the Refugee communities. In 1858 the Associates suffered heavy losses through the failure of their bankers, and they reduced their aid to small sums while urging the Nova Scotian Assembly to provide more money. In 1860, by drawing upon funded property in England and ground rents from an estate in Philadelphia, the Associates were able to aid six schools; but the latter source was cut off in the next year with the outbreak of the American Civil War, and the Inglis' Boys School, as the African School in Halifax was now called, closed down. Plans to assist a school that the Negroes of Port La Tour had established in 1840 and to keep the African Girls' School in Halifax open failed when all remittances from the United States ceased; and the Associates turned to exhorting the people of Halifax, who since the 1850s had been enjoying an unprecedented prosperity during what later generations would call Nova Scotia's Golden Age, to take up "this good cause." The Associates did continue to dole out small sums to other schools, however, and after the Civil War, when the Philadelphia

56. *Report of the Society for Promoting Christian Knowledge for 1837* . . . (London, 1837), pp. 73–74: Inglis's appeal, Nov. 15, 1836. Society for Promoting Christian Knowledge, Archives, London: Money Grants Voted Book, 1840–1923, p. 245, shows a grant to the church school in Hammond's Plains as well.

57. Fergusson, p. 62, and App. 15, pp. 104–05: petition, Willis, Feb. 4, 1836; Dr. Bray's Associates Minute Books: 5, Feb. 1839, June 7, 1842; 6, April 23, July 16, 1844, Nov. 18, 1845; 7, July 20, 1847, March 18, 1851, March 15, Nov. 15, 1853, July 18, Nov. 28, 1854, Nov. 20, 1855.

rents once again were available, to three new ones. The boys' and girls' African Schools reopened in Halifax, and in 1873 the province took responsibility for them.

In the same year the Associates reviewed their support for Negro schools in Nova Scotia. Plagued with a constant drift toward the Baptist faith among the parents, with masters who padded school attendance records, with the refusal of white teachers to board and lodge in Negro homes (even Bishop John Inglis thought that sending "a well educated but ill-behavored" white man to teach Negroes was a penance), with buildings that leaked, and with Negro "unsteadiness" in support, and declining itself as a philanthropic body, Dr. Bray's Associates slowly withdrew from the province thereafter, reducing gifts to a token in 1886. Until 1904, however, this faraway arm of the SPG continued to send £ 25 each year to the school in Hammond's Plains.[58]

The Society for the Propagation of the Gospel opened Madras System schools for Africans in Saint John, Fredericton, and St. Andrews, in New Brunswick; and Dr. Bray's Associates introduced the system at Digby. In Fredericton the townspeople subscribed £ 60, and the legislature granted £ 100, so that Negroes might have a school of their own, and the new lieutenant-governor, George S. Smyth, took a special interest in the school in Saint John until his death in 1813. But throughout the Maritimes, the schools remained poor, unsystematic, and undependable, and the cycle of ignorance continued: in time most of the teachers in the black schools were products of the African School in Halifax, itself poorly equipped if sometimes well-staffed, and as the Bishop of Nova Scotia wrote in 1856, the whites "in general care so little for [the Negroes], that assistance cannot be obtained." [59]

58. Dr. Bray's Associates Minute Books: *4,* May 1, 1818, June 1, 1821; *6,* July 5, 1839, April 20, 1841, April 5, 1842; *7,* June 21, Nov. 14, 1853, April 17, Nov. 20, Dec. 10, 1855, July 15, Oct. 21, 1856, Oct. 20, 1857, April 20, July 20, 1858; *Report for the Year 1859 of the Institution Established by the Late Rev. Dr. Bray and his Associates* . . . (London, 1860), p. 10, and thereafter—with title slightly altered—for 1860–62, 1864–66, 1868, 1871–74, 1878, 1886, 1889–90, 1895–96, 1899–1910; SPG, *Report of the Society for the Year 1824* . . . (London, 1825), pp. 65–66; *Report for 1827,* pp. 110, 132.

59. SPG Journals: census of parish of Fredericton, Oct. 1824, reports of George Millar, St. Andrews, June 22, 1824, Dec. 1, 1826, and of John Inglis, Nov. 10, 1818, April 23, 1832, with *notitia scholastica,* April–June 1825, and ecclesiastical returns; C/Can/NB: Frederick Coster box; NBM, Calendar of Church MSS, *1,* 31, 37; *The Sixth Report of "The Governor and Trustees of the Madras School in New-Brunswick* . . ." (Saint John, 1825), p. 4; *The Eighth Report* (1827), pp. 3–6, 11; Dr. Bray's Associates Minute Books: *4,* Dec. 7, 1821; *5,* Dec. 7, 1827; *7,* July 15, 1856. See also City of Southampton Archives, George S. Smyth Papers: Thomas Bonner to Smyth, Sept. 28, 1821; *Fourth Annual Report of the . . . Madras School . . . in New Brunswick* (Saint John, 1823), passim.

In any case, as the Bishop noted, most of the Negroes and virtually all of the Refugees were dissenters, and the more prosperous settlers, largely Anglican and Presbyterian, were none too eager to help Baptists and Wesleyans of any hue. The greater portion of the Bishop's effort among black men went into Bermuda which, until 1839, was in the Diocese of Nova Scotia. In 1841, the provincial Assembly granted the Negro Methodists of Liverpool £ 25 toward the cost of building a chapel, but this was rare. Most of the Refugees had been Baptists before they came; in 1821 the Loyalist Negroes of Tracadie—Roman Catholic as well as Anglican—and in the 1840s those in Digby, were similarly led astray, as the SPG missionaries reported. Although Anglican missionary Archibald Gray visited Hammond's Plains twice a month, it remained staunchly Baptist as well; in 1877 Fundy, in 1880 Weymouth, and in 1884 Joggin fell to the Baptists.[60]

The reactions of William Nisbett, appointed Anglican catechist at Preston in 1825, were representative. Nisbett soon lost patience with his charges, writing that they were universally superstitious, mad, ridiculous, and given to "monstrous absurdities, that they believe, and substitute in the place of Religion." He was utterly opposed to their insistence on "experiencing God"; and those, such as one William Redman, who twice told him of seeing a person before him on a cross whom he stabbed with a knife, drawing out blood and water, confounded him. Nisbett damned the Refugees for being "indolent to an extreme, insensible to kindness, dishonest and untrue, so that notwithstanding all their pretenses to what they call spiritual experience, they lie in a deplorable state of moral degradation." In exasperation, he left in 1829 for Bermuda to work with the Society for the Conversion of the Negroes. The Bishop shared his feelings: "The blacks are a peculiar people," he wrote, "altogether a miserable set." [61]

The leaders of these black Baptists were the white John Burton, who was still active, Duncan Dunbar, a white who from 1817 until 1826

60. Dr. Bray's Associates Minute Books: *4,* Nov. 6, 1818; *5,* March 7, 1828, Dec. 6, 1842; *7,* July 15, 1856; *Report for the Year 1877 of the Institution Established by the Late Dr. Bray & His Associates* . . . (London, 1878), p. 9, and for 1880–82, 1884; *House of Assembly Journal, 1841,* pp. 88, 167, 182; SPG Papers, C series: reports of Roger Viets, May 1, 1824, Joseph Clarke, April 10, 1829, Gray, March 25, 1834, Feb. 9, 1836, Feb. 21, 1840, Jan. 9, 1844, Jan. 5, 1845, Jan. 15, 1858; George Edward Levy, *With the Pioneer Baptists in Nova Scotia: A Sketch of the Life of David Nutter* (Wolfville, N.S., 1929), pp. 49–50.

61. SPG Journal, *38:* Inglis's reports, Jan. 19, 1827, April 11, 1828, later encl. Nisbett's report, Dec. 31, 1826; *40,* Inglis's report, April 11, 1829; *43,* Edward Wix's report, June 9, 1832; Dr. Bray's Associates Minute Books, *7:* May 16, 1854, Nov. 20, 1855; Rathbun, "Five Mile Plains," pp. 61–62. Blood must be seen in a vision before anyone can be baptized in the Preston Baptist Church today.

preached to the Negroes of New Brunswick, and Richard Preston, a Negro not himself a Refugee. Burton had healed the rift between his congregation and the white Baptists, and in 1822 his followers were admitted to the provincial association of Baptist churches. Soon after Preston arrived. His mother had been among the Refugees, and upon his escape from Virginia he sought her out in Nova Scotia, finding her in the town that bore his name. Burton taught him at first, and in 1831 Preston was sent to London to solicit aid for a church. There he was ordained and heard Wilberforce, Clarkson, and Buxton speak. Preston took charge of Burton's old congregation upon his return to Halifax in 1832, organized an abolitionist society to open up contacts with like-minded Negroes in Boston, became a friend of Joseph Howe, the editor of the *Novascotian,* and founded churches in Hammond's Plains, Annapolis, Salmon River, Bear River, Digby, and Weymouth. In 1854 Preston summoned representatives from twelve of the African churches, as they were called, to Granville Mountain for the first of several conferences meant to promote harmony within the faith, and from this meeting came the African Baptist Association of Nova Scotia.[62]

Preston contributed strongly to the developing isolation of the Refugees from the rest of the Negro community. He had less success among Negroes of Loyalist descent, and six of their churches remained outside his Association. Many Loyalist Negroes preferred going to "white" churches, usually in twos or threes to avoid public censure, and they moved amidst the generality of the community more readily. By reminding the Refugees that they had found their religion "in the forests, behind the stone walls, in the cane brakes, in the cotton fields, and in the rice swamps," Preston helped them to maintain a sense of their historical identity while cutting them off from those Negroes who had turned their back upon their southern origins. Still, Preston gave the Refugee Negroes something more than Christian resignation and religious enthusiasm to sustain them; for through his ability to organize and direct his fellow blacks, he created a viable and lasting church organization, and he stressed interracial cooperation to the point that, upon his death in 1861, a white man succeeded him.[63]

Other settlers poured their energies into religious enthusiasm, suffered extreme privations, were placed on sterile land, and were the objects of private and public philanthropy, without sinking into quasi-serfdom as the

62. Pearleen Oliver, *A Brief History of the Colored Baptists of Nova Scotia, 1782–1953* (Halifax, 1953), pp. 22–27, 30; Jeremiah Chaplin, *Duncan Dunbar: The Record of an Earnest Ministry* . . . , 4th ed. (New York, 1878), pp. 26–27, 29, 120–27; P. E. MacKerrow, *A Brief History of the Coloured Baptists of Nova Scotia, and their First Organization as Churches, A.D., 1832* . . . (Halifax, 1895), pp. 15–31.

63. MacKerrow, *Coloured Baptists,* p. 17.

Refugees did. The primary differences lay in the facts that the Refugees were, as John Inglis wrote, "very ignorant"; that the color of their skin marked them out for special censure, especially from their Irish and Acadian neighbors; and, most important of all, that white settlers whose crops failed repeatedly could move westward into New Brunswick or southward into the United States, to try again under other conditions. The Refugees—holding their land initially on tickets of occupation rather than by direct ownership—often were tied to Halifax County, and by the time they were in a position to sell their pitiful properties, most had lost the will to do so.

Nonetheless, the primary responsibility for the developing pattern of semisegregated all-Refugee communities lay with the Negroes themselves, for the province had offered to resettle them in smaller groups elsewhere. They preferred to work at the odd jobs for which they felt prepared in order to stay near the capital—selling brooms, berries, rum, and Christmas wreaths, working as general laborers and stable boys—rather than to persist in the staple trades of Nova Scotia: farming, fishing, and lumbering. In 1837 Lord Glenelg, the Colonial Secretary, had concluded that the fruitfulness of the soil was not the Refugees' central problem: "If the want & privations from which they have so long suffered have not furnished sufficient inducement to active and industrious habits, I should fear that the mere occupation of rich Land would fail of that effect." [64] In 1847 a well-informed observer reported that master workmen objected to taking Negroes for training since "white and coloured boys, in the same shop would quarrel so frequently, that the trouble would exceed any advantage that might arise from such apprentices." One boy was taken on by a painter, while the rest remained trapped by their unwillingness and inability to work together on their poor soil, by depressing cycles of short-term employment (aggravated by a trade depression in 1849), and by discriminatory white barriers against gaining any specialized skills. Although rebuffed time and again by the whites when they attempted to find permanent work, the Refugees did not look elsewhere.

Nor did the Refugees wish to cooperate with the Loyalist Negroes or with those who did not share their Baptist faith. Even within their own communities, they did not learn to work together for themselves. In January 1827, when Archdeacon Willis visited Hammond's Plains to investigate the fever raging there, he found a naked, freezing man, clothed only in a jacket, whose legs were so diseased the flesh was dropping away. He had wished to be taken to the poorhouse, but he had no money, and no one among his fellow-Refugee neighbors would move him without pay. [65]

64. Fergusson, App. 17, p. 108: Glenelg to Campbell, Oct. 25, 1837.
65. PANS, *422:* Inglis to Kempt, Jan. 15, 1827; Dr. Bray's Associates Minute Books, *7:* July 20, 1847, April 16, 1850.

The Loyalist Negroes did not offer the hand of friendship either, for except in New Brunswick and perhaps in Tracadie, the arrival of the Refugees hurt them, and they knew it. The Loyalist blacks were proud of being identified with the early settlement of the colony. Some had carved out small if adequate competencies for themselves near Guysborough, Shelburne, Digby, and Annapolis Royal, and they did not wish to be associated with the newcomers. All of the Refugees had been slaves; many of the Loyalists, especially those of Black Pioneer descent, had been free men, and they were not entirely above the popular assumptions about the stigmata of slavery. Their religions initially were different, their attitudes were different—and yet their skins were the same. When a body of unruly white immigrants followed upon a relatively adjusted contingent of their tribal kin after two generations, no identification necessarily was formed in the public mind; unruly Scots in 1820 did not damn quiet Scots who had come in 1780. However, the white population of Nova Scotia tended to think of all black men as one.

By the end of the nineteenth century the white community confused the descendants of slaves, Loyalists, Maroons, and Refugees with each other, as the Negroes themselves did, seeing the Negro as a monolithic group not given to the same wide divergences as the white man. Many Negroes knew otherwise, and little Negro unity developed. At first no common front was offered against discrimination, for none was wanted. By the mid-century, as improved communication, their religion, their poverty, and white discrimination began to bring the various Negro groups together, it was too late to break down the patterns of prejudice they encountered. In the end the whites were right: all Negroes, within a narrowing range of expression, became one; for they remained poor, they remained badly educated, and above all they remained that which they could not alter, black. These conditions applied throughout British North America, and most of all to another group of refugee Negroes—the fugitive slaves making their way into the two Canadas.[66]

66. Properly, *Refugees* refers only to those Negroes in the Maritime Provinces who came as a result of the War of 1812. The word was also applied to fugitive slaves who fled to Upper and Lower Canada, however; and after 1850 *refugee* and *fugitive* were synonymous in local usage in Canada West. In the chapters that follow the contemporary labels are used, with the distinction between the two groups preserved by upper- and lower-case designations.

6. The Coming of the Fugitive Slave, 1815–1861

" 'Where's Canala? I didn't see it—' cried the four-year-old, as if it were a herd of cows or a pair of horses that we had flown by on the road and called his attention to the sight too late, so that he was always desperately looking back. // 'All that land on the other side of the river. That's all Canada.' " [1] So it seemed at first to the fugitive slaves, the next and ultimately the predominate group of Negroes to arrive in the British colonies, for initially they thought the whole of British North America would be a haven of refuge, not from slavery alone but from prejudice as well. In the four decades prior to the passage of the Fugitive Slave Act in 1850, Negroes from the United States struck out indiscriminately for the Canadian border, with the thought that, once on the other side, an equality of treatment would be theirs.

Such was not always the case. As in the northern American states, residents of the colonies responded in varying ways to the arrival of black men and women, most of them indigent, many of them fugitives. Conditioned by previous experiences with Negroes, as in the Maritime Provinces, or by little or no experience at all, as in the frontier settlements of Upper Canada, British North Americans displayed no uniform patterns of prejudice. Some Negroes were treated well, and some ill; some Negroes were thought to be assets to their communities and others, liabilities; a few Negroes found the promised land they had sought, and most found at least a place where they could stand upright as free men. But if there were few emergent geographical patterns of white responses, there were quite clear drifts of public opinion on "the Negro question."

On the whole the Negroes who came to British North America on their own, without the assistance of the British government, were well received into the 1830s. By the end of that decade, voices of protest could be heard in various quarters of white Canada against an unchecked Negro immigration, and in the 1840s and 1850s the Negro found himself distinctly unwelcome in many areas of the provinces. Several conditions governed the speed and the nature of these shifts in opinion.

Five developments in particular may be singled out for primary examination. First, by the late 1820s Negroes were arriving in substantial numbers; and when in 1830 a body of free blacks from Cincinnati, Ohio—a free state—founded a collective Negro community in Upper Canada, the

1. Paul Goodman, *Our Visit to Niagara* (New York, 1960), p. 34.

spectre of a black swarming began to be taken seriously by many Canadians. Prejudice rose as the number of Negroes rose; earlier Negro arrivals anticipated this and hoped to forestall discrimination by slowing the threatening flood to a trickle. The result was a division in Negro ranks, exacerbated by sectarian controversies, that helped confirm the whites in their belief that the Negroes were incapable of self-leadership and cooperative action.

Second, by the 1830s Negroes in the United States were showing every sign of having decided not to leave North America. Their spokesmen, through the so-called National Convention movement, declared opposition to Negro colonization in Sierra Leone, Haiti, Jamaica, or Trinidad, while speaking favorably of the Canadas. White Canadians wished to see the Negro free, and if the Negro so wished it, resettled; but if resettlement were to be carried out on a massive scale in British North America itself, they were less certain of their liberal sentiments.

Third, and paradoxically, many of the Negro arrivals were showing a distressing ambivalence toward their adopted country. They asserted their loyalty and their love for the Crown, and many served in the armed forces, voted, and acquired property. Yet, when given an opportunity, many returned to the United States. They seemed to some white Canadians to be too transient to help the frontier community for long, except as a temporary reservoir of cheap labor; they showed too many signs of an exile mentality. To other whites they seemed all too permanent, all too determined to think in terms of decades and generations of life within British North America rather than of a return, once the great reckoning came, to the United States.

Fourth, British North Americans became aware of the moral and legal problems that might well be involved in harboring fugitive, or self-stolen, property. Extradition of such alleged criminals became a major issue between Britain, the United States, and the provinces. More than the passive acceptance of the derelict and pitiful was called for; positive acts of succor, as well as positive stands on complex international problems, were needed.

Further, after 1840 many Negroes showed every sign of organizing themselves for a long seige within their northern stronghold, as the aims of the newly founded British-American Institute were to confirm. Amidst Canadian church groups, therefore, the moral problems of aiding Negroes who were of a different faith—or even of the same faith—became increasingly apparent, promoting the growth of all-Negro religious bodies. These bodies were given to beliefs and practices that often separated their adherents from the dominant Anglican, Presbyterian, and Roman Catholic churches.

From the prevailing clusters of ideas arose yet other conditions that the Negroes themselves could not hope to control. If the Negro was needed as labor for a frontier community, he was less needed when that community had passed to a more mature stage. If welcome to fell trees, to lay roads, to cut ties, and to introduce tobacco culture in the 1820s and 1830s, the Negro was needed less in the 1840s, when the Irish—willing to work at equally menial and physically demanding tasks and less likely to raise difficult social questions—began to arrive in large numbers. The decline of cheap lands and the consequent drift of the Negro to the towns also contributed to changing attitudes, for in the city the black man was more visible, and his presumed peculiarities more starkly revealed. Further, in the background lay many unassimilated fragments of thought about race itself, the cultural baggage of earlier centuries, which might be applied differentially from place to place by varying groups of whites. By 1850, both Canada West and Nova Scotia, the two major centers of Negro settlement, had established separate schools so that they might preserve the assumption of equality of opportunity while slowing cultural assimilation.[2] It is to this long and complex period between the War of 1812 and the enactment of the Fugitive Slave Act, to these several facets of the developing Negro-white relationship in Canada, overlapping as they do into the 1850s and later, that we must now turn.

When the early fugitive Negro arrived in Upper Canada, he generally stopped quite near the border. Without funds, he could not move deeply into the interior; as an exile, he wished to remain close to the frontier for an eventual return; if a farmer, as most were, he preferred those near regions which seemed less dramatically different to the soils that he knew best. Small knots of Negroes settled at Welland and St. Catharines, back from the Niagara River; at Colchester, Windsor, and Amherstburg, opposite Detroit; near London, Chatham, and Dresden, in the center of the long peninsula of fertile lands that dipped south against Lake Erie almost to the latitude of New York City; and more slowly in Toronto, Oro, and in the Queen's Bush. Later arrivals were naturally attracted to places where Negroes had already established themselves. The fugitive Negro sought out his own kind increasingly as time passed, scorning the descendants of the Loyalist and slave Negroes in the Canadas, who themselves preferred to remain apart from the new arrivals.

Amherstburg, adjacent to Fort Malden, was the most important of these early settlements, and in the 1820s fugitive slaves helped make it the center of a modest but flourishing Canadian tobacco culture. Introduced by a

2. Jean R. Burnet, "Ethnic Groups in Upper Canada" (M.A. thesis, Univ. of Toronto, 1943), pp. 32, 57–58, 122.

Virginia white and by Kentucky and Virginia Negroes in 1819, tobacco was ready for export to Montreal in 1821, where it commanded a good price. In 1824 a visiting English farmer observed that Negroes were arriving at Amherstburg weekly to work in the tobacco fields. In six years the export of tobacco rose from virtually nothing to nearly six hundred hogsheads each year, and yields up to two thousand pounds per acre were possible. But by 1827 the local tobacco market was glutted, the quality of the leaf had dropped, and the price fell by half. Thereafter, whites tended to take over growing as well as marketing.[3]

There were nearly six hundred Negroes living in Amherstburg and in the back concessions of Colchester by 1827. In the latter community they were not well received and acquired a reputation for "being thievish and otherwise immoral." The two groups of Negroes were separated by twelve miles of marsh, and only slowly did they begin to work together. In Colchester their leader, Reverend R. Rolph, a Baptist of "contemplative cast," was unable to prompt his people to exert themselves, and the village remained "a wretched settlement" for some time, in contrast to another riverfront town, Sandwich, which also attracted Negroes, especially after a race riot in Detroit in 1833 sent many hurrying across the river.[4] The assessment rolls for 1849 and the raw census data for 1851 show that Negroes in these three towns were not yet uniformly segregated. They lived together in blocs of forty or less, with many whites interspersed, and in terms of residence many were well integrated into these communities. On the whole they seem to have been accepted, until the Irish began settling near Amherstburg in the late 1840s.[5]

3. Ontario Dept. of Lands and Forests, Thomas Smith Papers: no. 37, 1803; John Howison, *Sketches of Upper Canada* . . . (Edinburgh, 1821), p. 201; Joseph Pickering, *Inquiries of An Emigrant; being the Narrative of an English Farmer from the Year 1824 to 1830* . . . , 4th ed. (London, 1832), pp. 96–97; *The Imperial Magazine; or, Compendium of Religious, Moral & Philosophical Knowledge, 10* (1828), 774; Audrey Saunders Miller, ed., *The Journals of Mary O'Brien, 1828–1838* (Toronto, 1968), p. 75; Fred Coyne Hamil, *The Valley of the Lower Thames, 1640 to 1850* (Toronto, 1951), pp. 123–26, 145. See *The Canadian Cigar & Tobacco Journal, 48–62* (1942–56), passim, for articles on the origins of the industry; and *Traité sur la culture du tabac canadien* [n.p., 1882?], passim.

4. SPG Papers: G. Archbold, report, June 15, 1829; James Logan, *Notes of a Journey through Canada, The United States of America, and the West Indies* (Edinburgh, 1838), p. 70; "A Member of the Brethren's Church," *The History of the Moravian Mission among the Indians of North America* . . . (London, 1838), pp. 310–11 n.; Amelia M. Murray, *Letters from the United States, Cuba and Canada* (New York, 1856), p. 117.

5. Fort Malden National Historic Park Museum (hereafter Fort Malden): assessment rolls for the township of Colchester, 1844, 1845, 1847, 1848, 1849; PAC, Census of Canada, raw data as reported on census books, for Township of Sandwich, 1851 (3 vols.; Amherstburg missing).

On the eastern end of the peninsula Negroes also found ready employment and relative acceptance at first. By 1827 there was an international
community of Negroes along the Niagara frontier, and the final emancipation of all slaves in New York in that year was celebrated on both sides of
the border. During the 1830s and 1840s many of the waiters in the hotels
near Niagara Falls were Negroes, receiving the same wages under the
same conditions of work as whites, and several were guides leading tourist
descents under the falls. Travellers to the area agreed that Negroes could
have steady employment and access to land as fertile as any settlers occupied.[6]

By the 1840s black settlers might also be found much further afield. In
1827 there were enough Negroes at Chatham to justify support from Dr.
Bray's Associates; still, eleven years later an international traveller,
Frederick Marryat, found them living there in "a sad dirty hole," and when
cholera struck, the first to die was a black man. From 1825 on there were
Negroes at Fairport (which in 1854 became Dresden), and in 1832 they
were in sufficient force near Hamilton to name their own settlement
Colborne, in honor of the lieutenant-governor. Another traveller remarked
upon seeing blacks at Brantford in 1830 and at Guelph and Waterloo in
1833. In 1846 white residents of Brantford asked that the Negroes there—
fifteen families—be sent away into Queen's Bush, and one of their number,
William Jackson, urged removal into the area, although the Surveyor-
General pointed out that the land on which he settled was part of the
Clergy Reserves and could not be given to him. Eventually a black community grew near the Conestogo River midway between Waterloo and
Guelph. Other travellers reported seeing Negro farms as far north and
east as Penetanguishene, Collingwood, Owen Sound, and Barrie.[7]

6. LC, Margaret Hall (Mrs. Basil Hall) MSS, 4,138, Add. 1: Mrs. Hall to "my
dearest Jane," July 4 (finished July 15, 1827); F. S. Abdy, *Journal of a Residence
and Tour in the United States of North America, from April, 1833, to October, 1834*
(London, 1835), *1*, 300–01, 312; Western Reserve University Library, Elizur Wright
Letters: Wright to son, Elizur, Jr., June 3, 1837; Friends' House, London: Journal
of John Candler and Wife, S.22, July 7, 1850; Columbia University Library, William
J. Wilgus Papers, *3:* "Some Account of a Trip to the Falls of Niagara performed in
the Month of May, 1836 by Thomas S. Woodcock," pp. 21–22; William Chambers,
Things as They are in America (Philadelphia, 1854), pp. 103, 107; [Isabella S.
Trotter], *First Impressions of the New World* (Boston, 1859), p. 54; John C. Geikie,
George Stanley: or, Life in the Woods . . . (London, 1864), pp. 377–78; and William H. G. Kingston, *Western Wanderings; or, A Pleasure Tour in the Canadas* (London, 1856), *1*, 313–14.
7. SPG, *Report of the Society for the Year 1827* . . . (London, 1828), p. 168,
and *for the Year 1828*, p. 155; Adam Fergusson, *Practical Notes, made during a
Tour in Canada, and a Portion of The United States, in* M.DCCCXXXI, 2nd ed. (Edinburgh, 1834), pp. 122–23, 127; J. J. Hawkins, "Early Days in Brantford," Brant

Perhaps the most distant Negro farmers were at Oro, on the western shore of Lake Simcoe. As the Penetanguishene Road was extended northwards, free Negroes who labored on it began to open up farms along the western fringe of the lake; and from 1819, led by George A. Darkman, they settled near some Highland Scots to whom they often hired themselves out as field hands. In 1830 the government ordered a survey on behalf of the Negro settlers, who were illegal squatters. Some eleven hundred acres were set out for them, with an additional nine hundred acres in the following six years, and perhaps a hundred and fifty Negroes—organized by one John Little, a black, and by a white preacher, A. Raymond, and his wife—occupied the lots. Relations between white and black farmers were good, and German settlers, in particular, were helpful, giving the Negroes seed on credit. Some even spoke of sending a Negro member to Parliament. But Oro failed to grow; Raymond left, and in 1847 his replacement, Reverend R. S. W. Sorrick, a fugitive slave, abandoned the area to seek out the more favorable climate of Hamilton, taking the majority of the settlers with him. The few who remained at Oro built a church and, under James Thompson, struggled on into the second and third generation through the 1860s, when Oro virtually ceased to exist as a Negro community.[8]

Historical Society, *Papers . . . 1908–1911*, p. 47; Sydney Jackman, ed., *A Diary in America, with Remarks on Its Institutions, by Frederick Marryat* (New York, 1962), pp. 165, 170; Joseph Edward Sanderson, *The First Century of Methodism in Canada* (Toronto, 1908), *1*, 265; *Midland Free Press*, March 31, 1954; Elsie McLeod Jury, *The Establishment at Penetanguishene, Bastion of the North, 1814–1856* (London, Ont., 1959), p. 33; Hamil, *Valley of the Lower Thames*, p. 173; Elizabeth Spencer, "Descriptions of London and Its Environs, 1793–1847," *Western Ontario History Nuggets*, no. 31 (1964), p. 29; Syracuse University Library, Gerrit Smith Miller Papers: C. Corwin to Smith, July 8, 1854; Etobicoke Historical Society, *Bulletin*, no. 12 (July 1961), p. 3; OPA, location ticket for James Long, 1829, and Robinson Papers, list of Negroes resident in Toronto, July 25, 1840; Oxford Historical Society, Woodstock, Ont.: partial list of Negro settlers to 1854; Hiram Walker Historical Museum, Windsor, Ont.: list of Negroes, and map of Negro settlements as of 1850.

8. W. E. O'Brien, "Early Days in Oro," Simcoe County Pioneer and Historical Society, *Pioneer Papers*, no. 1 (1908), pp. 22–27; Barrie Public Library, Fred Grant Collection: *52*, 254–56; Miller, *Journals of Mary O'Brien*, p. 95; J. Herbert Cranston, *Huronia, Cradle of Ontario's History* (Barrie, Ont., 1949), p. 23; Andrew F. Hunter, *A History of Simcoe County* (Barrie, Ont., 1909), *2*, 143–45; William Loe Smith, *The Pioneers of Old Ontario* (Toronto, 1923), pp. 306–07; Thomas Rolph, *A Descriptive and Statistical Account of Canada: Showing Its Great Adaptation for British Emigration . . .* , 2nd ed. (London, 1841), pp. 184–85; PAC, Upper Canada Land Petitions, no. 395: June 13, 14, 1836; OPA, land declarations, Oro, 1836; OPA, Mrs. Edward George O'Brien, journal: March 7, 1830; Simcoe County Surrogate Court Office, Barrie: will of Darkman; Garrit Smith Papers: Silas Hawley to Smith, March 1, 1841; Adelaide Leitch, *The Visible Past: Pictorial History of Simcoe County* (Toronto, 1967), p. 96. A frequently erroneous account of "The Negro Settlement of Oro" by E. C. Drury may be consulted in typescript in the Orillia Public Library.

If Negroes in Amherstburg, along the Niagara frontier, and at Oro enjoyed a degree of equality in the initial years of settlement, most observers reported that the degree diminished as time passed. Into the early 1840s, white servants were hard to find and the Negroes continued to do well; by the end of the decade conditions were changing rapidly for them. Sentiments such as those expressed by Mary Warren Breckenridge of Clarke Township for the period before the War of 1812—that " 'One great misery of life . . . was the unpleasantness of being obliged to sit at table with one's servants, a black one sometimes being amongst them' "—were rare enough at first.[9] But in the late 1830s many of the churches were restricting Negroes to a back gallery, called the "Nigger Heaven," and increasingly the blacks were viewed "with no small disfavour," as "unwelcome intruders." In 1835 the magistrates of the Western District of Upper Canada protested the removal of troops from Amherstburg, for they did not wish to be defenseless against "the very numerous and troublesome black population . . . who are almost daily violating the laws," and in 1840 the Lieutenant-Governor, Sir George Arthur, himself friendly to the fugitives, expressed his fear that further immigration would lead to grave racial problems.[10]

Casual segregation patterns began to emerge. In 1848—a year when fugitive arrivals fell off temporarily—a visitor saw that most Negroes lived apart in the "least valuable corners of the towns," and Henry Highland Garnet, a radical abolitionist from New York, thought "color phobia" as serious in the Canadas as in the United States. The Negro was, according to a spate of observers, "despised and deserted," "little better than a nuisance," "scarcely useful," unable to find white wives (except, on occasion, among the Irish), "as a class, . . . not at all a desirable population," to be "shunned and kept at a distance"—the object of growing prejudice. By 1855 William Davies of Toronto would complain that he met "Free Niggers . . . at every step," and the foundress of the Ursuline Community at Chatham, who had befriended Negroes, would confess that Canadians were tired of them. When in 1853 the Elora debating society chose as its

9. Sir Richard H. Bonnycastle, *The Canadas in 1841* (London, 1841), *1*, 173–74; Russell Lant Carpenter, ed., *Memoires of the Life and Work of Philip Pearsall Carpenter* . . . (London, 1880), pp. 179–80; Catherine F. Lefroy, "Recollections of Mary Warren Breckenridge of Clarke Township," OHS, *Papers and Records, 3* (1901), 110–13.

10. *The African Repository and Colonial Journal, 6* (March 1830), 27–29; "Two Brothers," *The United States and Canada, as Seen by Two Brothers in 1858 & 1861* (London, 1862), p. 107; Isaac Fidler, *Observations on Professions, Literature, Manners, and Emigration, in the United States and Canada, made during a Residence there in 1832* (London, 1833), pp. 381–82; Hamil, *Valley of the Lower Thames*, pp. 313–14; James R. Brown, *Views of Canada and the Colonists* (Edinburgh, 1851), pp. 62–63, 289.

subject the question, "Whether have the Indian or the Negro suffered most from the aggression of the white man?", all assembled agreed that Negroes were thieves. When informally segregated schools were given the authority of law in 1850 and when, in 1853, the property holders of Chatham asked the government to block all further Negro immigration, the growing hostility was clear.[11]

This reaction to fugitives was tempered by an ambivalent anti-Americanism. To accept the runaway slave was one way to demonstrate the superiority of British liberties and to strike at the Republic, economically as well as morally. Further, Canadians thought, Americans were less likely to wish to annex the provinces, for Northern abolitionists wanted to see the refugees under British protection and southerners had no desire to add more free territory to the nation. In fact, however, the abolitionists often favored annexation; and since the Negroes were Americans, as well as exiles, some observers feared that they might prove disloyal to their adopted refuge in a time of conflict with the United States.

But the fugitives were consistently true to the British government, demonstrating their loyalty, as they thought, by supporting the status quo in both local and provincial elections. Before the rebellion of 1837–38, William Lyon Mackenzie, its Upper Canadian leader, noted that Negro settlers were "opposed to every species of reform in the civil institutions of the colony," that they were "extravagantly loyal," and that they were prepared to "uphold all the abuses of government and support those who profit by them." In July 1837, an American abolitionist, James G. Birney, visited Toronto and wrote to Lewis Tappan, one of the founders of the American National Anti-Slavery Society, that the fugitives favored conservative rule. A conservative Member of Parliament reported that "there are not in his Majesty's dominions a more loyal, honest, industrious, temperate, and independent class of citizens than the colored people of Upper Canada." Until the 1850s Negroes rallied to support conservative candidates in the southwestern part of the province, and in 1843 the Mayor of Toronto would permit a circus to enter his city only if there were no

11. "A Southern Lady," *Letters on the Condition of the African Race in the United States* (Philadelphia, 1852), p. 8; Garnet, *The Past and the Present Condition, and the Destiny of the Colored Race* (Troy, N.Y., 1848), pp. 25–29; Chambers, *Things as They are in America*, pp. 27–28; John Shaw, *A Ramble through the United States, Canada, and the West Indies* (London, 1856), p. 49; "W. M. G.," "A Sabbath among the Runaway Negroes at Niagara," *Excelsior: Helps to Progress in Religion, Science, and Literature*, 5 (1856), 40–41, 43; "Canadian Colonization," *The Freewill Baptist Quarterly*, 1 (1853), 403–06, 408, 413; William S. Fox, ed., *Letters of William Davies, Toronto, 1854–1861* (Toronto, 1945), p. 45; *Canadian Baptist Magazine*, 4, (1841), 191; Rhodes House, Oxford Univ., Anti-Slavery Papers: Hiram Wilson to John Scoble, n.d. [ca. 1842]; "Impressions of Canada West in the 1850s," *Western Ontario Historical Notes*, 17 (1961), 8. On the schools, see Chapter 12.

Negro songs sung, "to save the feelings of the gentlemen of colour" who so strongly supported his administration. In Nova Scotia the three hundred members of the Charitable African Society of Halifax resisted the introduction of responsible government in 1846, and when a group of Montreal businessmen issued an Annexation Manifesto in October 1849, calling for union with the United States, Negroes throughout the Canadas were quick to denounce it, fearing that the Washington government would extend slavery to the provinces.[12]

Negroes served in the militia in the provinces, and they were neither segregated nor denied modest promotions. They were enrolled in the Kent Militia in 1793, and deserters from the black militia of Detroit were employed at Fort Malden in 1807. Upon the declaration of war in 1812, a Negro, Richard Pierpont, who had served with Butler's Rangers, proposed to raise a company of blacks along the Niagara frontier; and this was done, although under the command of a white man, Captain Robert Runchey. The Negroes were tried in battle at Queenston in October, and twenty-seven members of the Black Corps, as it was called, were among those who attempted to repulse an American attack on Fort George in May of the following year, retiring under heavy fire. The company saw service at Burlington Heights, Stoney Creek, and Fort Mississauga, until late in 1813, when Lieutenant James Robertson, possibly a Negro, took command. Thereafter the group was used as a labor corps, although individual Negroes served with other regiments. In Nova Scotia, Negroes continued to drill at Digby, the men of Preston were issued a motley array of captured American uniforms during the war, and in 1821 Halifax County authorized the creation of a new corps of black pioneers. As late as 1875 Negroes were collecting pensions for service in the War of 1812, and in 1902 Toronto planted a monument to the "Regiments Colored Corps and Indians," traditionally the site for an annual ceremony by Negro veterans of Canada's wars.[13]

12. [Elizur Wright], "Fourth Annual Report of the American Anti-Slavery Society," *The Quarterly Anti-Slavery Magazine*, 2 (1837), 350–51; Mackenzie, *Sketches of Canada and the United States* (London, 1833), p. 291; Dwight L. Dumond, ed., *Letters of James Gillespie Birney, 1831–1857* (New York, 1938), *1*, 395–96: Birney to Tappan, July 14; *St. Catharines British American Journal*, Jan. 1, 1835; *Chatham Journal*, Sept. 4, 1841; TPL, Robert Baldwin Papers: Adam Wilson to Baldwin, July 12, 1843; OPA, Toronto City Council Papers: petitions, July 20, 1840, Oct. 14, 1841, March 9, 1842, April 21, 1848; *Halifax Novascotian*, Jan. 21, 1841, July 31, Aug. 10, 1846 (formerly, *Nova Scotian*).

13. Fort Malden, Farney Papers, p. 401; Hamil, *Valley of the Lower Thames*, p. 78, n. 1; PAC, Pierpont's petition, July 21, 1821; Ernest Green, "Upper Canada's Black Defenders," OHS, *Papers and Records*, 27 (1931), 366–70; Ernest Alexander Cruikshank, ed., *The Documentary History of the Campaign upon the Niagara Frontier in the Year 1813* (Welland, Ont., 1896), *2*, 73, 331; and . . . *in the Year*

Negroes played a larger rôle during the Rebellion. When Mackenzie plunged Upper Canada into revolt in December 1837, nearly a thousand Negroes volunteered for service within the month. "The Natural hatred of the coloured people to the Americans would be a guarantee for their fidelity" wrote one observer, although Sir Francis Bond Head, the Lieutenant-Governor whose ham-fisted activities had brought on the crisis, emphasized loyalty to the Crown rather than fear of enslavement in his handsome acknowledgment of the Negroes' quick response.[14]

The performance of the Negro units was a mixed one. Conflicting and overlapping orders lessened the effectiveness of the three companies of colored troops, as initially led by Captains Robert Runchey, Jr., and James H. Sears, both white. Runchey absconded to the United States with his company's pay in August of 1838; but Sears and Major Ogden Creighton, a retired British army officer who took command of all colored companies on the Niagara frontier in May, finally employed their men to guard American prisoners, patrol the canals, and protect the Detroit and Niagara borders against filibusterers. Negroes were on duty opposite Navy Island when the *Caroline* incident took place, and the Second Essex Company of Coloured Volunteers manned Fort Malden from Christmas Day, 1837, until May, and helped to capture the schooner *Anne*. Elsewhere they guarded bridges and public buildings. By the end of the rebellion, five Negro companies were authorized, although none was recruited to full strength—despite the efforts of Creighton, who befriended Negroes outside the service and employed them at his residence. Once the crisis had passed, the companies were depleted by desertions. In October 1838, the Adjutant General asked for two new Negro companies; but neither saw battle, and in 1840 the men were put to work clearing roads.[15]

Black volunteers remained in uniform for some years after the rebellion,

1814 (Welland, Ont., 1908), *1,* 29, 51, 71; A. J. Kerry and W. A. McDill, *The History of The Corps of Royal Engineers, 1* (Ottawa, 1962), 17–18; L. Homfray Irving, *Canadian Military Institute: Officers of the British Forces in Canada during the War of 1812–15* (Welland, Ont., 1908), pp. 40, 76; Bird, *This is Nova Scotia,* p. 196.

14. State Papers, Upper Canada, *31:* Stephen J. Miller to R. B. Sullivan, April 7, 1838; Fred Landon, "Canadian Negroes and the Rebellion of 1837," *JNH, 7* (1922), 377–79. Head's statement appeared in the *Upper Canada Gazette,* March 6, and the *Sandwich Western Herald,* April 3, 1838; its wording is changed slightly in his book, *A Narrative* (London, 1839), p. 392.

15. Farney Papers: pay list, Captain John Calwell's company, Dec. 29, 1837; OPA, petition of William Taylor, June 18, 1840; *Sandwich Western Herald,* Jan. 3, Feb. 10, 17, Dec. 13, 1838; *Chatham Journal,* Jan. 22, April 23, Aug. 6, 1842; PAC, C 801, p. 442: account for volunteer force, and C 612, p. 1: order of Richard Bullock, Oct. 31, 1838; *The Toronto Almanac and Royal Calendar of Upper Canada for the Year 1839* (Toronto, 1839): "The Militia Register," p. 75; Green, "Black Defenders," pp. 373–77, 380–86.

and while their work was valuable, they also elicited considerable dislike. The least educated of the Negroes had joined the service—in 1839, four of 135 privates were literate [16]—and they were ill-equipped to rise in the ranks; only one other Negro, William Allen, became an officer. Disputes over pay, the usual petty thievery associated with any army billet, and incidents between troops and civilians in Chatham, Chippawa, Hamilton, and St. Catharines added to the whites' growing annoyance. Although the Negroes had been hailed a few years earlier by Head, the residents of Chatham and Hamilton rejoiced at their removal in 1842–43, ascribing to them "a great deal of mischief, [and] rioting." [17]

Transferred to the Welland Canal to keep order between two feuding factions of Irish workmen, the Negroes were involved in frequent clashes which, although not racial in origin, left racial memories. When construction had advanced to the point that water could be let into the channel, many laborers were discharged, leading to further riots. Two constables were beaten with shovels and axes at Aqueduct (later Welland), and the Colored Corps was called in to make arrests. The Negroes warded off an attack upon customs officers who were trying to stop smuggling, and in 1849 the corps rescued a constable from a mob. Four days later a clash between Orangemen and Irish canallers, in which two men were killed and perhaps seven were injured, was put down by the corps. The Irish, who disliked both red coats and black men, found the combination intolerable, and a canal mob set upon an unarmed detachment of off-duty Negro soldiers at Aqueduct. Shortly before the waterway opened for navigation in June 1850, the last Colored Corps disbanded.[18]

Thereafter, Negro troops were used sparingly. Despite the Governor-General's suggestion, an independent Negro rifle company failed to materialize in 1850. During the Crimean War a number of public-spirited Canadians offered to raise black regiments for the British Army, but the British officials suspected that their object was to get on the half-pay list as officers when the units were disbanded; a counter-proposal that Negroes be sent out on garrison duty to the West Indies or Bermuda also failed. Throughout the Civil War many Canadian Negroes served in the Northern army—largely for Massachusetts, New York, and Michigan regiments—and Northern recruiting agents and crimps were active among the Negro

16. PAC, C 1049: May 1839, pay list and acquittance roll for the "coloured corps," signed with marks.

17. *Montreal Gazette,* Oct. 13, 1840; *Hamilton Argus,* Aug. 29, 1842; *Chatham Journal,* April 29, 1843; TPL: Arthur to Lord Sydenham, Oct. 22, 1840; Morleigh, pseud., *Life in the West: Back-Wood Leaves and Prairie Flowers* . . . (London, 1842), pp. 228–91; FO115/354, p. 92; FO115/357, p. 93; FO115/372, p. 94.

18. WO1/552: Sir Charles T. Metcalfe to Lord Stanley, June 20, 1843; *Montreal Witness,* May 13, 1850; Green, "Black Defenders," pp. 387–89.

settlements. In St. Catharines Negroes formed a drill unit in 1862, which was not used, and several Negroes volunteered during the Fenian scares of 1865–66 and 1871. Separate Negro corps were not enrolled in Canada West after 1850, however, for public opinion was against it.[19]

Negroes also served usefully in the other provinces. A company was raised in Canada East in 1846. In New Brunswick Negroes regularly were taken into the York County Militia, and two became captains. A proposed separate Coloured Company was unable to find sufficient volunteers, and in 1846 regimental orders enrolled the Negroes in the county militia once again, though requiring them to parade in the rear of their units. Not until 1868 was the designation "African" removed from the registers, but except when marching, Negroes appear not to have been segregated in the province.[20]

Prior to 1830, Negro movement into Upper Canada was largely without organization and in small bands. It was, in a sense, self-selective; for only the most determined, and therefore perhaps the most skillful, cunning, and best educated reached Canadian soil. The majority of fugitives who fled to the provinces were probably from the upper South, and most stayed for a period of time in one of the free Northern states; for until the passage of the Fugitive Slave Act in 1850 there was no immediate spur to continue the northward journey. Many therefore had made at least a partial adjustment to a free soil economy and to a northern climate. And because they could stop their flight short of the Canadian border and find a degree of freedom, to continue to British territory was an act of conscious choice, in part a positive decision rather than a negative impulse arising from fear, as it would become after 1850. Thus, one may assume that the nature of the pre-1830 Negro migrants was somewhat different from those who came after slavery became a pronounced sectional issue; and further, that the nature of that migration changed again after 1850, when the motivations for movement were seen in yet a different light.

These generalizations can be carried too far. Negroes feared the slave-

19. CO42/598: Alexander Macdonald to Sir Edmund Head, encl. in Head to Sir William Molesworth, Aug. 15, 1855; *New York National Anti-Slavery Standard*, Oct. 31, 1850; *St. Catharines Constitution*, Jan. 9, 1862; *Detroit Tribune*, March 22, 1914; *The Crisis*, 20 (1920), 286; Columbia Univ. Lib., L. S. Alexander Gumby Collection: Frederick Douglass file.

20. PAC, Sorel and Royalists, Misc. Papers: Thomas Stephens to William Henry, Oct. 7, 1846; *An Almanack, for the Year of Our Lord 1830* . . . (Saint John, 1830), not paginated, showing African members of Saint John City Militia and York County Militia; *1833*, showing promotions in latter; NBM, Order Book, 5th Battalion of York County Militia: June 24, 1839, Sept. 1, 1846; *McMillan's New Brunswick Almanac and Register . . . 1868* . . . (Saint John, 1868), unpaginated militia list. See also pp. 278–79.

catcher before 1850: as early as 1828 two hundred fugitives in Upper Canada petitioned the lieutenant-governor, Sir Peregrine Maitland, for land so that they might live together, not only because they preferred it for social reasons but because they wished to reduce the danger of being kidnapped and carried back to the South.[21] Nor was life in the free Northern states genuinely free for the Negro. Already education was separate and unequal in many areas; frequently Negroes could not testify except in cases involving other Negroes; often Negro property owners could not settle their estates upon their families. After 1830 new immigrants to the United States, crowding into cities, displaced free black laborers. Negroes could not ascend the ladder of success as other ethnic groups did. Each new arrival was expected temporarily to take his place at the bottom of that ladder, but if his skin were white, he could hope that in time economic opportunity would move him upward; not so for the black man, always shoved back down the ladder by each successive wave of Europeans. Nonetheless, until roughly 1830 the Negroes in the North did not find discrimination backed by a sufficiently wide range of legal institutions across a sufficiently wide extent of territory to think collectively in terms of seeking self-exile.[22]

Those who did think of leaving the United States were given a number of choices. The American Colonization Society, organized in 1817, hoped to transport thousands of Negroes to the West African coast. By 1830 the Society had settled only 1,420 Negroes in Liberia; most abolitionists, realizing that more root-and-branch remedies were needed at home, turned against the African colonizationists, as Negro groups had done from the beginning. They, in turn, advocated resettlement in Haiti, South America, Trinidad, Jamaica, the Far West, the Missouri River Valley, and British North America. Each destination produced its entrepreneurs, more often self-seeking than philanthropic, and each proposed goal also gave rise to its black opponents. The majority of the Negro leadership agreed that "repatriation" was neither feasible nor moral; the Negroes of the United States had become North Americans and should remain so. Almost before the American Colonization Society had announced its plans, such spokesmen as Richard Allen, founder in Philadelphia in 1794 of the Bethel Chapel, the Mother Church of the African Methodist Episcopalians, and James Forten, wealthy leader of the Philadelphia Negro community, spoke out against the Society; in 1827 Allen declared himself in favor of emigration only if the goal were the Canadas. While the Colonization Society ap-

21. William Renwick Riddell, ed., "A Petition," *JNH, 15* (1930), 115–16: Ancaster, U.C., June 18.

22. The condition of the free soil Negro is described in Leon F. Litwack, *North of Slavery: The Negro in the Free States, 1790–1860* (Chicago, 1961).

proved of British North America as one haven, it felt results there would be limited and precarious.[23] Nonetheless, to most Negroes the problematical choice and the practical one did not coincide. They could remain slaves or they could flee; if they fled, they could go to the Northern states, to the Far West, or to the Canadas. There were no other real alternatives.

The immediate impetus to the first organized attempt on the part of free Negroes to resettle themselves in the Canadas arose from the city of Cincinnati's decision in 1829 to enforce the state of Ohio's Black Code. The Ohio River towns, like those along the lower Wabash in Indiana and throughout Little Egypt in southern Illinois, shared many social characteristics with the Southern states. Although Ohio had abolished slavery in 1802, state laws passed in 1804 and 1807 required the Negro to furnish a certificate of freedom issued by a court, without which he could not be employed. Any Negro entering the state after 1807 had to provide a bond of $500 within twenty days of his arrival, as a surety of his good behavior. These regulations had fallen into disuse; but early in 1829, with the number of Negroes in Cincinnati having risen to nearly three thousand, and in the face of increasingly vocal Southern protests, the city announced that the laws would be enforced and that Negroes would be declared ineligible for militia service, denied the right to carry arms, and withdrawn from jury service. In 1830–31 these restrictions were applied, and the city authorities gave the Negroes sixty days in which to register and to bond themselves. In mass meeting the blacks of Cincinnati decided to send two of their number, Israel Lewis and Thomas Cresap, to see whether Upper Canada would provide a haven; in the meantime, they were refused a thirty-day extension on the time limit. A white mob stalked the Negro section of the city for three days. Rioting followed.[24]

The nominal President of the Negro colonization group, James C. Brown, wrote to the newly appointed Lieutenant-Governor of Upper Canada, Sir John Colborne (later Lord Seaton), to ask whether Negro settlers would be welcome. Lewis and Cresap (and possibly one Stephen Dutton) delivered the query personally. Legend holds that Colborne replied, "Tell the Republicans on your side of the line that we do not know men by their color. If you come to us, you will be entitled to all the

23. John Hope Franklin, *From Slavery to Freedom: A History of American Negroes,* 3rd ed. (New York, 1967), pp. 234–38; "Colonization in Canada and Hayti, compared with Colonization in Liberia," *The African Repository and Colonial Journal, 8* (1832), 225–39; Fred Landon, "Negro Colonization Schemes in Upper Canada before 1860," RSC, *Proceedings and Transactions, 23,* sec. 2 (1929), pp. 73–80.

24. See Richard C. Wade, "The Negro in Cincinnati, 1800–1830," *JNH, 39* (1954), 43–57; and Herbert Aptheker, ed., *A Documentary History of the People of the United States* (New York, 1951), pp. 102–03.

privileges of the rest of his Majesty's subjects." [25] Certainly he received them favorably.

The Negro agents then approached the Canada Land Company which, from 1823, was disposing of a million acres of land running back from the shores of Lake Huron. The company agreed to sell four thousand acres to the Cincinnati settlers for $6,000, to be paid by November 1830; the original colonists might resell the land to later arrivals in order to gain capital for purchasing yet another tract, with a view to obtaining the whole of a township. But the Negro negotiators had, in fact, no funds, and when those who awaited them in Ohio turned to the state legislature for help, they received none. Further, the mayor of Cincinnati, worried over the prospective loss of a valuable labor force, now asked them to delay their plans so that he might find ways of having the newly enforced laws repealed. At this juncture the Quakers of Ohio and Indiana provided a solution, purchasing the land themselves through their agent, Frederick Stover. The Quakers could raise money for only eight hundred acres, well below the original contract made with the company, which responded with reluctance to sell land directly to Negro settlers in the future.

The resulting settlement was as poorly managed as poorly launched. A few Negroes arrived as early as October 1829, to settle near Lucan, the chosen site, well in advance of the final negotiations. The prospect of restored racial harmony in Cincinnati cut the migration to well under a third of the anticipated three thousand, and not more than half of these dispersed into Upper Canada. Even then, most did not go to the new colony, and it was reinforced by other Negroes from elsewhere in Ohio and a few from Boston, who heard of it through the pages of Benjamin Lundy's sporadically issued abolitionist newspaper, *The Genius of Universal Emancipation,* or who saw it on a map of Upper Canada hurriedly prepared by a Baltimore Negro, Hezekiah Grice, to guide prospective migrants.[26] At no time did the tiny Negro community of Wilberforce, as the struggling settlement was named, rise above a population of two hundred, with perhaps eight hundred more in the general Lucan-Biddulph area.[27]

25. Minor changes are rung upon this statement, depending upon the secondary account consulted. This version is drawn from the nearly contemporary source, [Harriet Martineau], *The Martyr Age of the United States of America* (Boston, 1839), p. 6.

26. The map is advertized in the *Genius;* I have been unable to locate a copy of the original.

27. The origins of the Wilberforce settlement are examined by Fred Landon in three articles: "The History of the Wilberforce Refugee Colony in Middlesex County," London and Middlesex Historical Society, *Transactions, 9* (1918), 30–44; "Wilberforce, an Experiment in the Colonization of Freed Negroes in Upper Can-

Nonetheless Wilberforce was important. Its presence worried white settlers, and especially so when the initial reports of success were much inflated, for they saw it as the first of perhaps many planned Negro communities.[28] To others, its very lack of genuine plan seemed to support the prejudice that Negroes were incapable of planning. Its failure by 1836, after a period of internecine strife, may well have made other Negro groups doubly hesitant, for no more so-called utopian settlements were attempted for nearly ten years. Yet, good did come from the effort as well. The threat of going to Wilberforce was a safety valve for the Negroes of Cincinnati and won for them minor but real concessions. A highly favorable statement, whatever its exact wording, had been elicited from the governor of the province. The Highland Scots, English, and Tipperary Irish neighbors had not been unfriendly.[29] The idea that the Negro should be trained to enjoy freedom, when it came, and that through pooling resources and cooperative activity he might prosper, was given currency. While the talk of other havens in Africa and the West Indies was not stilled, the alternatives were made clear. And a visit in 1832 by Lundy, the Quaker abolitionist, led to considerable publicity for resettlement in general and for Upper Canada in particular.

Lundy, one of the earliest and most persistent antislavery advocates and the man responsible for enlisting William Lloyd Garrison to the cause of abolitionism, was particularly interested in the problem of colonization. He visited Haiti twice and Texas three times (also sending James C. Brown there), as well as journeying to Upper Canada to investigate the life led by the fugitive slaves. Lundy printed a diary of his trip in his newspaper during the spring of 1832, and his conclusion that "No place perhaps in the northern or north-western part of America presents a stronger and

ada," *RSC, Proceedings and Transactions,* 3rd ser., vol. 31 (1937), sec. 2, pp. 69–78; and "Fugitive Slaves in Ontario: A Digest of Two Papers . . . ," The Historical Society of Northwestern Ohio, *Quarterly Bulletin,* 8 (1936), [1–6]; and most usefully by William H. and Jane H. Pease, in *Black Utopia: Negro Communal Experiments in America* (Madison, Wisc., 1963), pp. 46–62, 172–75. See also Landon, "Agriculture among the Negro Refugees in Upper Canada," *JNH,* 21 (1936), 304–12. These accounts are contradictory on population and acreage. Brown's story is told in Benjamin Drew, *A North-Side View of Slavery; The Refugee: or the Narrative of Fugitive Slaves in Canada . . .* (Boston, 1855), pp. 239–48.

28. *North American Review,* 76 (1832), 128–31. Typically, Thomas Nye, a Montreal lawyer, recorded in his journal in 1837 that the "Africans . . . [are] said to be 10,000 at Wilberforce" alone, a patently ridiculous statement (New-York Historical Society, New York, Misc. MSS: journal, p. 17, Dec. 12). See also Rush R. Sloane, "The Underground Railroad of the Firelands," *The Firelands Pioneer,* n.s., 5 (1888), 32, 35–36, 46.

29. Jennie Raycraft Lewis, *Birr and Beyond* (London, Ont., 1958), p. 19; Lewis, *The Luck of Lucan* ([Lucan, Ont.], 1967), p. 11.

richer soil" helped to allay some fears about the little-known northern land. His trip was undertaken in mid-winter, however, and he was not able to examine the ground closely because of a heavy snowfall. Basing his conclusions upon the nature of the timber cover he observed, he pronounced the land good, added that the winter was not harsh, and confirmed that Negroes were *"free and equal."* The settlers had cut a road for the Canada Company, receiving credit for the work against the purchase of additional acres of land, and they already had a hundred head of cattle and swine, a few horses and oxen, and "a good substantial sawmill." In time land values would rise, nearby London would "become a place of wealth and importance," and Wilberforce would thrive.[30]

But it did not thrive. As soon as the Cincinnati settlers had reached Wilberforce, they had reorganized themselves, with administration vested in a Free Colonization Board. The chairman was Austin Steward, who had recently arrived from Rochester, New York, and he provided the colony's principal guidance until leaving in disgust in 1837. Brown remained on, Cresap and Dutton dropped from sight, and Lewis was appointed, together with two Negro Baptist preachers, Benjamin and Nathaniel Paul, as agents for the settlement, to travel throughout the provinces and the Northern states soliciting funds. Almost immediately these spokesmen fell to quarreling with each other, and the grandiose scheme collapsed.

The key to success or failure lay with Steward and the Pauls. It was Israel Lewis who persuaded Steward to leave a successful grocery business in Rochester to settle at Wilberforce, and it was Lewis who negotiated the original sale of land. But Steward, who saw in Wilberforce an opportunity to show himself as a natural leader, and possibly even to win election to the Upper Canadian Parliament, quickly replaced the man who had brought him to the colony; indeed, it was on Steward's suggestion that it was given its name. Frustrated and angry, Lewis quarrelled with Brown and threatened him with a gun; and according to Steward, admittedly a prejudiced witness, he introduced a mistress into the puritanical settlement, failed to render adequate financial returns, and burned the subscription books. In 1831 Lewis was dismissed from office, and he responded by bringing suit for defamation of character; apparently his appointment was renewed, however, for he soon left on a new mission to the United States. He turned to begging for funds, which embarrassed many Negroes,

30. Lundy's journal ran in the *Genius* from March to May; the articles are reprinted by Fred Landon, ed., "The Diary of Benjamin Lundy Written during His Journey through Upper Canada, January, 1832," OHS, *Papers and Records, 19* (1922), 110–33. Landon has also written "Benjamin Lundy, Abolitionist," *Dalhousie Review,* 7 (1927), 189–97; and "A Pioneer Abolitionist in Upper Canada," *Ontario History,* 52 (1960), 77–83. See also Amherstburg Public Library, Boyle Collection: Lundy's autograph, probably on the occasion of his visit to Amherstburg.

especially those outside the community who would not benefit from what he received, and he then refused to give up the $700 thus collected. He defaulted on a note held upon him by Steward, against whom he made charges of theft, forcing the case to court in 1833.[31]

Friends of the Wilberforce experiment deplored this washing of dirty linen in public. Lyman A. Spaulding, a New York abolitionist leader, wrote early in 1832 to caution Steward and Brown "to keep perfectly quiet" about Lewis: "you must agree among yourselves, not suffering any difference of opinion to become public," for nothing was to be gained by sordid publicity. But sordid publicity will out: in the spring a meeting of the inhabitants directed the Board of Managers to dismiss Lewis again, replacing him with Reverend James Sharpe of nearby London, and Lewis returned home, according to Steward, declaring that he would cut the managers' throats. On Christmas day, 1832, the board issued a public warning against Lewis and this was reprinted throughout the abolitionist press. Arthur Tappan, who had just organized the New York City Anti-Slavery Society, issued his own public notice, revealing that Lewis had collected nearly $1,500 under false pretenses, and in March 1833, a public meeting in Wilberforce resolved that Lewis's conduct was "ridiculous in the highest degree. . . ."[32]

The cleavage was widened when Lewis successfully exploited other dissensions within the colony to bring Benjamin Paul to his side. Declaring that the majority in Wilberforce was dissatisfied, Lewis organized a Wilberforce Colonization Company, with himself as President and Agent, so that he could not be discharged, and Paul and others authorized him to sell certificates of stock for a manual labor academy within the colony. The public may have confused academy with colony, for Lewis's Wilberforce Colonization and High School Company of Upper Canada, as it was re-

---

31. Much of the record, such as it is, is hostile to Lewis, for it is drawn from Steward, *Twenty-Two Years a Slave, and Forty a Freeman: Embracing a Correspondence of Several Years, while President of Wilberforce Colony, London, Canada West* (Rochester, N.Y., 1859); and from the statements of Lewis and Steward reprinted from the *Liberator* in Carter G. Woodson, ed., *The Mind of the Negro as Reflected in Letters written during the Crisis, 1800–1860* (Washington, D.C., 1926), pp. 179–91. But Steward was by no means honest in all that he said—compare pp. 180–81, for September 1831, with pp. 184–85, written in March 1833, although referring to May 1831. Pease and Pease, *Black Utopia*, pp. 48, 53–57, have not entirely succeeded in avoiding Steward's inconsistencies. See also Howard W. Coles, *The Cradle of Freedom: A History of the Negro in Rochester, Western New York and Canada* (Rochester, N.Y., 1941), *1*, 41–77, and the Peases' introduction to the reprint edition of Steward's book in Robin W. Winks, ed., *Four Fugitive Slave Narratives* (Reading, Mass., 1969).

32. Woodson, *Mind of the Negro*, p. 625: Spalding to Steward, et al., Feb. 4, and pp. 189–90: to Lisbon Wine, et al., March 12, 1833.

styled, was successfully soliciting funds in New York in 1834. Lewis returned to Wilberforce once more in 1839, remarked upon the poor condition of the schoolhouse, built earlier with Quaker aid, and ordered the roof taken off, promising to put another on. He then disappeared, leaving the colony with a roofless school (never replaced) and a heavy burden of debt, since those who had given him money were demanding restitution. He finally died in poverty in Montreal.[33]

The settlers at Wilberforce made the proper and, under the circumstances, courageous decision to repay all those who had given money to Israel Lewis. Nathaniel Paul had gone to England in the fall of 1831, before the break with Lewis, to find funds for a manual training institute at Wilberforce. This school had not been part of the founders' original intention, although they had agreed to incorporate it into the community. Arthur Tappan had purchased land in New Haven, Connecticut, for a Negro seminary, only to have the community's white residents hold a protest meeting, following which the city officials condemned the project. Someone, probably Tappan, who already had given $1,000 to the scheme, suggested putting the school at Wilberforce, and Paul was charged with the responsibility of finding the necessary additional funds for this "gem of the purest lustre, which the United States has proudly dashed away." [34] Thus he was in England, armed with a letter of introduction from Lieutenant-Governor Colborne. Logically, he might be given the additional task of finding the restitution money.[35]

If Lewis was a felon, Paul was a fool. He spent four years in Britain, lecturing feverishly to raise money. But when Lewis pre-empted the manual labor school as his own, and won Paul's stay-at-home brother, Benjamin, to his side, Paul did nothing. Without security, Nathaniel lent William Lloyd Garrison, who was in England in 1833, £ 40 for his return journey to America, and Garrison refused to repay Arthur Tappan, against whom Paul was drawing his expenses, arguing that all had been spent in a common antislavery cause; later Garrison denied receiving the money at all. Another lawsuit followed, which embarrassed the Canadian colony and

33. Woodson, pp. 181–83, 626–27: Lewis to the Public, n.d., and to Garrison, Feb. 11, 1833, and Steward to J. Budd, June n.d., 1833; Pease and Pease, pp. 51, 57–58. In 1840 the legislature declined to act on Lewis's petition to incorporate yet another school (*House of Assembly Journal,* 5th sess., 13th Parl., Jan. 20, 21, and App., *1,* pt. 2).

34. C[harles] Stuart, *Remarks on the Colony of Liberia, and the American Colonization Society: With some Account of the Settlement of Coloured People, at Wilberforce, Upper Canada* (London, 1832), p. 11.

35. "Wilberforce Settlement, in Upper Canada," *The Baptist Magazine for 1832, 24* (1832), 158–60; *The Liberator,* June 22, 1833; Pease and Pease, pp. 58–60; Woodson, pp. 628–29: Paul to Steward, Dec. n.d., 1833.

angered Tappan. Further, Paul had no head for figures, spending the money he collected on good causes for which he could not account. When nearly four years had passed, Steward began to fear that Paul was another Lewis, and he sent out one Henry Nell to England to bring him back. Nell persuaded Paul to return to Wilberforce to give an accounting— and then Nell himself dropped from sight into England with the money Steward had given him, leaving a wife and children behind in Upper Canada.[36]

Paul did return, with a white wife, and he submitted a full account on his mission. During his years in Britain he had collected over $8,000 for Wilberforce. Over the same years his expenses had been $7,000. Further, his salary was $50 a month. Wilberforce thus owed him nearly $1,600! With this report he left the settlement, returning to Albany, to die a pauper in 1839.[37]

Wilberforce, too, died a pauper. White settlers petitioned against further sales to Negroes. The Canada Land Company was unwilling to take more financial risks or to antagonize prospective white purchasers. An agent for the company thought that "the greater number [of Negroes] were people of bad character, idle and dissolute"; the company would buy the land back and pay the Negroes for their improvements so that the colony might be broken up. Benjamin Paul died in 1836; Steward, virtually penniless, returned to Rochester early in 1837; Lundy, who had continued to speak on behalf of the settlement, died in 1839; Brown resettled in Toronto. By 1840 the population had dropped to a hundred. Before the end of Wilberforce's first decade, it no longer existed in an organized sense, although a few of the Negro settlers stayed on. In the 1850s their number fell to fifty; in 1872 the last of the original officers, Peter Butler, who had been the much put upon Treasurer, died; and in 1878 only four of the original founders or their families remained near the Ausable River site. As the editor of the *Montreal Witness* wrote, " 'where is the Wilberforce settlement?' and echo answers where?" [38]

36. Woodson, pp. 662–63: Garrison to Steward, June n.d., 1856; Walter M. Merrill, *Against Wind and Tide: A Biography of Wm. Lloyd Garrison* (Cambridge, Mass., 1963), pp. 72, 343 n. 20; LC, Tappan Family Papers: Garrison to Lewis Tappan, Dec. 17, 1835, Feb. 29, 1836; Steward, *Twenty-Two Years a Slave*, pp. 311–42; Paul, *Reply to Mr. Joseph Phillips' Enquiry* . . . ([London, 1832]), passim.

37. Woodson, pp. 637–38: Steward to W. C. [*sic*, for Henry] Nell, Dec. n.d., 1835; Knill [Nell] to John Scoble, n.d., in *The Emancipator*, Sept. 15, 1836, cited in Pease and Pease, p. 175, n. 23; *The Liberator*, June 22, Nov. 23, 1833.

38. PAC, M.G. 19, B 31: Reminiscences of Two Negroes at Lucan [1919]; Patrick Shirreff, *A Tour through North America* . . . (Edinburgh, 1835), p. 178; Jennie Raycraft Lewis, *Sure An' This is Biddulph* ([Biddulph, Ont.], 1964 [i.e. 1966]), pp. 15–20; *London* (Ont.) *Free Press*, April 10, Aug. 9, 1943, Aug. 19, 1961; Fred Landon Collection: letter, n.d., on Bowzer [Butler] family; *Witness*, July 19, 1854.

The failure to resolve internal disputes, the expense of endless lawsuits, and the blackened reputation of all the leaders had reduced the potentially promising settlement to a status considerably inferior to less formally organized Negro communities. The idea of an all-Negro self-help experiment had suffered a major setback, and especially so since observers agreed that the fifty-acre allotments were fertile and well-timbered, the location for markets was good, and the bulk of the settlers were temperate and religious. No defense could be made, as in Nova Scotia, on the grounds of tardy grants, sterile soil, or a warlike nature. The Wilberforce Negroes were in no way above the mass of indigent Irish settlers who were arriving at the same time, and contrasts between poor whites and the philanthropically aided Negro farms were not to the Negroes' credit. Indeed, once the settlement was abandoned, it was the Irish settlers themselves who moved onto the farm lots and successfully brought them into production.[39]

While Wilberforce was running away into the sand, the Negroes of the free states were continuing to debate the virtues of colonization. When Hezekiah Grice, James Forten, and other Negro leaders had met in convention in Philadelphia in 1830, they scorned "foreign emigration" but did not view the Canadas as falling under this general condemnation, urging the American Colonization Society to turn its attention to Upper Canada in particular. A succession of near-annual conventions followed. Austin Steward first heard of Wilberforce at the Philadelphia conference, of which he was a vice-president, before Israel Lewis had contacted him, and a few participants there had been among those who went to Wilberforce. In 1833 the third convention appointed a committee to look into the general question of Canadian settlement, and in 1834 the delegates pronounced such emigration acceptable. A discussion of the alternate sites for resettlement was a yearly ritual thereafter, and basic positions changed very little. Convening in Toronto in 1851, shortly after the Fugitive Slave Act took effect, the delegates resolved to encourage Negroes in their efforts to reach the Canadas, and at Rochester in 1853 they condemned all emigration from the hemisphere. They also considered "intertropical" New World sites; and during a confused meeting in Cleveland a group calling itself the National Emigration Convention of Colored People sheared away from the larger movement in order to investigate such areas for settlement, while rejecting the Canadas from fear that soon they would be annexed by the United States.[40]

39. [Justine O'Danski], *Middlesex County* ([London, Ont., 1964]), pp. 13–14.

40. See John W. Cromwell, "The Early Negro Convention Movement," The American Negro Academy, *Occasional Papers*, no. 9 (1904), pp. 1–23; Bella Gross, *Clarion Call: The History and Development of the Negro People's Convention Move-

The most consistent alternate choice lay in the Caribbean, and Haiti in particular. The grand old man of British abolitionism, Thomas Clarkson, had blessed Haiti as early as 1819 while consistently opposing other sites, and its President had encouraged North American Negroes to come in 1824. In 1854 the Emigration Convention determined to investigate three possibilities, the Niger Valley, Central America, and Haiti. Grice, who initially had favored emigration solely to Upper Canada, had gone to Haiti in 1832 and had not returned. Divided, the emigrationists who favored following him asked a former New Haven Negro preacher, James Theodore Holly, who had moved to Canada West, to open negotiations with the republic.[41]

Holly visited Port-au-Prince in 1855, and to the Chatham convention the following year he presented an account of his negotiations. He had gained nothing more than a promise from Haiti's dictator, Faustin Souloque, to "welcome all . . . emigrants," although Holly tried to create the impression that Faustin positively sought Negro settlers and would "offer the most liberal inducements"; he had told the Haitians that his Emigration Society could send ten thousand colonists in seven years. The delegates rightly remained suspicious of such grand schemes, however, and Holly's efforts bore little fruit, although he continued to advertise Haiti and to solicit support in Canada West. But in 1859, when a revolution installed Fabre Geffrard as the new President, Haiti asked James Redpath, a young Scots journalist who had worked with Negroes and to whom the Chatham convention had turned in 1856 for further information on the tiny nation, to act as a general emigration agent in British North America and the free states.[42]

Redpath was one of those not uncommon creatures of the mid-century, an entrepreneur of the self who explosively spent his considerable talents

ment in the United States (New York, 1947); and James Walter Fisher, "Proposals for Negro Colonization of the Western Hemisphere, 1850–1867" (M.A. thesis, Howard Univ., 1937). The Philadelphia meeting is discussed in detail in "The First Colored Convention," *The Anglo-African Magazine, 1* (1859), 305–10.

41. PSHS, Robert Vaux Papers: Thomas Clarkson to Vaux, March 8, 1819; Thomas Hodgkin Papers, privately held by Thomas Hodgkin, Ilmington, Warwickshire: Thomas Clarkson to Hodgkin, June 2, 1840; and Letterbook G: Hodgkin to Henry Highland Garnet, Aug. 29, 1860; *Windsor* (C.W.) *Voice of the Fugitive*, Feb. 17, 1851; *Montreal Gazette,* July 1, 1850, Feb. 11, 1853; Tinsley Lee Spraggins, "Negro Colonization on the Eve of the Civil War," *The Negro Educational Review*, 9 (1958), 65–77; Louis R. Mehlinger, "The Attitude of the Free Negro toward African Colonization," *JNH, 1* (1916), 276–301.

42. Compare Holly to Frank P. Blair, Jan. 30, and J. M. Whitfield to Blair, Feb. 1, 1858, in Woodson, pp. 499, 501; Holly's "Thoughts on Hayti," *The Anglo-African Magazine, 1* (1859–60), 185 ff.; and Charles F. Horner, *The Life of James Redpath and the Development of the Modern Lyceum* (New York, 1926), pp. 109–10.

and even greater energies in whatever directions the moment might take him. He responded to Geffrard's invitation with a burst of activity: travelling to Haiti, he persuaded the legislature to pass a homestead bill which would give every family that arrived five *carreaux* (just over sixteen acres) of land; he opened an Haytian Bureau of Emigration in Boston; he launched a newspaper, the *Palm and Pine;* and he wrote and published *A Guide to Hayti* in which he observed of the whites there that "Exemplary conduct on their part enables them to overcome the social disadvantage attached to their unfortunate colour," [43] an intentional parody of the pious remarks about Negroes passed in guides to British North America. Early in 1861 he offered free passage to St. Marc and allotments from the public domain, and in May 111 Negroes, including some from Canada West, sailed from New Haven for Haiti with Holly.

Resettlement in Haiti did not prove attractive to most British North American Negroes. The outbreak of the Civil War in the previous month raised too many questions about the future. While Redpath's agent in Canada West, John Brown, Jr., the son of the martyr of Harper's Ferry, initially wrote that a large number of Negroes from Buxton, Chatham, Dresden, and Rondeau had "the Haytian fever," Isaac C. Carey and Alexander Tate, who replaced him when he joined the army, were less sanguine. William Wells Brown, a Negro writer, travelled in Nova Scotia and the Canadas on behalf of the scheme; and although he reported that fifteen hundred Negroes had attended four of his meetings, he thought not more than fifty would emigrate. Carey wrote from his Windsor office that the members of the Chatham Cotton Growing Association, a wishful group of southern fugitives, would go, and Redpath persuaded the Haitian government to help Canadian Negroes by offering free passage from the interior to New York or Boston. All was to no purpose; Tate and Redpath fell out, army recruiting agents offered more attractive lures, the more successful Negroes were tied by their realty, and the initial reports coming back from the first body of settlers were unfavorable. Further, Canadian whites engaged a black agent, William P. Newman, to tell the Negroes that Redpath meant to sell them into slavery and that they would be forced to become idolators—that is, Roman Catholics—in Haiti. Newman hoped to divert settlers to Protestant Jamaica, from which he was also taking a fee. [44]

43. (Boston, 1860), p. 194.

44. LC, Papers of F. W. Pickens and M. L. Bondam, *2:* Redpath to Pickens, Jan. 31, 1861; LC, West Indies Collection, *2,* Redpath Papers, "Report of James Redpath, General Agent of Emigration to Hayti, to the Honorable M. Plésance, Secretary of State of [*sic*] Exterior Relations of the Republic of Hayti": Brown, Jr., to Redpath, March 25, Redpath to Plésance, March 31, April 17, May 6, 27, June 8, 10, 24, July 15, Aug. 11, 17, 19, 20, and Redpath to Auguste Elie, July 20, Aug. 22, 27—all

Redpath proved to be no less a visionary than Holly, writing in August 1861, that ten thousand settlers soon would be ready to leave. In September he reduced the figure to two hundred. An Emigration Club in Toronto, with sixty-one members, agreed to go, and similar clubs were formed in Hamilton and St. Catharines. Redpath then suggested that the whole of Buxton might go to L'Archais, if Geffrard would appoint an American agent to superintend the project on the scene, and he guaranteed there would be one hundred thousand emigrants in five years if Haiti would eliminate the abuses in its government and provide the floundering St. Marc settlers with better land. After all this expansion, contraction: in October the mountain was seen to be a molehill, and 113 settlers, including the white wives of a few Negroes among the May group—largely from Puce River, Little River, Buxton, and Toronto—sailed for St. Marc. The next month Redpath lectured Haiti on its criminal neglect of the newcomers and declared that bad reports had killed interest throughout the provinces; in December he confessed that he was going to send any other emigrants to Jamaica, where his former opponent, Newman, was ready to receive them properly.[45]

The flirtation with Haiti was not quite over, however. Although the Haitian government closed its Boston office, it continued to encourage agricultural settlement. The American consul in Haiti wrote that Christian Negroes would dislike the place, for the "great 'bestial' sin of the world, excess of indulgence in sexual intercourse," was too common. "Men who give all their strength to women," he thought, "can have little for any thing else." An abortive coup, rumors that the Federal government would annex the island state if victorious in the Civil War, and growing tension between a black majority and the mulatto leadership, made Haiti singularly unattractive in Canadian circles, and no Negroes from British North America appear to have participated in the Ile à Vache fiasco which followed, nor in the Chinqui project in Central America, although Isaac Carey volunteered to help. In time, most of the emigrants from Canada West returned to North America.[46]

1861; William Edward Farrison, *William Wells Brown, Author & Reformer* (Chicago, 1969), pp. 342–45, 348–49.

45. Redpath Papers: Redpath to Plésance, Aug. 11, Sept. 7, Oct. 5, 13, 20, 21, Nov. 22, 1861.

46. FO35/38: Spenser St. John to Lord John Russell, May 27, 1863; NA, Foreign Affairs, Consular Dispatches, Aux Cayes, *3:* B. E. Sanford to William H. Seward, March 19, April 30, 1862; NA, Interior Department Records, Slave Trade and Negro Colonization, *4:* Cary to A. U. White [*sic,* for Whiting], April 24, 1862. Passengers for Isle à Vache were carried by Henry Sweetland of St. John's, Newfoundland (contract, March 3, 1863), but the list of 424 who sailed shows that none were from British provinces (oath, Charles K. Tuckerman, April 12, 1863, and list, n.d.).

Nor would British North American Negroes go to the dependent West Indies. Just as the efforts in Nova Scotia in the 1830s and 1840s had met with rebuffs, attempts in Canada West in the 1840s and 1850s were equally scorned. In 1841 a protégé of Anglican Bishop John Strachan, Peter Gallego, went to Jamaica on behalf of some Ancaster Negroes; but when he returned in 1844 to publish a proselytizing pamphlet, no one would follow him.[47] The year before, Thomas Rolph,[48] a leading spokesman in the Canadas for Britain's North American Colonial Committee, agreed to recruit black emigrants in Canada West for the government of Trinidad and to go with them as their "surgeon and protector." With the tacit support of Lieutenant-Governor Arthur, he met with the Negroes of Colchester, Sandwich, and Amherstburg to discuss growing evidence of anti-Negro feeling. Neither then nor again in 1843 did Rolph win any converts.[49]

Such attempts were unlikely to succeed, for the Imperial administration was opposed to them. When Trinidad's agent had sought out colonists in Nova Scotia in 1841, the Governor-General, Lord Sydenham, wrote to the Colonial Secretary, Lord John Russell, asking him to discourage any further transfers. In 1845 the Colonial Land and Emigration Commissioners

47. OPA, Bishop John Strachan Papers: Strachan to A. M. Campbell, April 28, 1840; SPG, *Report for the Year 1840* . . . , pp. lxv–lxvi; *Chatham Journal,* Aug. 21, 1841, June 1, 1844; *Utica* (N.Y.) *The Friend of Man,* July 6, 1841. The pamphlet has not been found.

48. The activities of Rolph and Gallego are reviewed in John K. A. Farrell, "Schemes for the Transplanting of Refugee American Negroes from Upper Canada in the 1840's," *Ontario History, 52* (1960), 245–49, but the account is garbled, and it unfortunately confuses Thomas with John Rolph. On the former, see W. S. Shepperson, *British Emigration to North America: Projects and Opinions in the Early Victorian Period* (Minneapolis, Minn., 1957), pp. 40–46.

49. Thomas Rolph, *A Brief Account, together with Observations, Made during a Visit to the West Indies* . . . (Dundas, U.C., 1836), p. 178; *Hansard's Parliamentary Debates,* 3rd ser., vol. 77 (Feb. 13, 1845); Rhodes House, Anti-Slavery Papers: Wilson to Scoble, Oct. 24, 1842; *The Friend of Man,* March 7, 1838; *Montreal Gazette,* Dec. 24, 1840; *Norfolk* (U.C.) *Observer,* Dec. 5, 1840; Rolph, *Emigration and Colonization: Embodying the Results of a Mission to Great Britain and Ireland, during the Years, 1839, 1840, 1841, and 1842* . . . (London, 1844), pp. 309–20. Rolph apparently was something of a charlatan: he claimed to be a member of the Royal College of Surgeons when he arrived in Upper Canada, and W. Stewart Wallace accepted this and other statements (Wallace, *The Macmillan Dictionary of Canadian Biography,* 3rd ed. [Toronto, 1963], p. 645). But he was not a member of the College (W. R. LeFanu, Librarian of the College, to author, Aug. 8, 1966). When he returned to England, he said he had been an army surgeon in Toronto, although his name is not on the roll of the Army Medical Service. Rather, he attended members of the local militia (see William Canniff, *The Medical Profession in Upper Canada 1783–1850* . . . [Toronto, 1894], pp. 603–05). Rolph died in 1858, unbalanced by a charge of neglect in a midwifery case.

reported that no one had left the Canadas for the West Indies and that all such proposals should be discontinued. While a later governor, Sir Edmund Head, was willing to entertain an emigration proposal in 1859, nothing further was done beyond the occasional visit of an informal agent, or the passage of resolutions in Jamaica, Trinidad, and British Guiana urging North American blacks to move to the Caribbean.[50]

The African flirtation was even less productive. Martin R. Delany, a Negro doctor who after a close association with abolitionist Frederick Douglass on *The North Star* had moved to Chatham in 1856, was the chief advocate of resettlement in West Africa. An early Afro-American nationalist, Delany thought integration of the races neither likely nor desirable. Accordingly, in 1858 he organized the Niger Valley Exploring Party, which consisted of himself; Amos Aray, a Chatham doctor, as secretary; James W. Purnell, a Chatham merchant, as a commercial reporter; an official artist; and a naturalist. Although told to promote "the political and other interests of the Colored Inhabitants of North America, particularly the United States and Canada," they also were instructed to limit their activities to gathering scientific information and not to encourage emigration to Africa. Thus slowed by conflicts within the sponsoring board, Delany set out on his own early in 1859. Unknown to him the party's naturalist, Robert Campbell of Philadelphia, issued a circular in London promising that, if their report were favorable, a number of Negroes in the Canadas and the free states who wished to grow cotton would be prepared to emigrate.[51]

Delany and Campbell both signed a treaty with the Alake of Abeokuta on December 27, 1859, which provided that North American Negroes would settle on any unoccupied land "in common with the Egba people." [52]

50. PAC, G 20, *1:* H. MacLeod to Arthur, March 22, 1841; G 12, *56:* Sydenham to Russell, April 23, encl. E. de St.-Remy, "Secretary of the Colored Population of Upper Canada," to Sydenham, April 5, 1841; Anti-Slavery Papers: Memorials and Petitions, Rolph to Scoble, Feb. 8, 1843, pp. 194–200; *Report of the Public Archives [of Canada], for the Year 1937* (Ottawa, 1938), pp. 703, 725–26; *New York National Anti-Slavery Standard,* Oct. 9, 1851; *Fifth General Report of the Colonial Lands and Emigration Commissioners, 1845* (London, 1845), p. 21; *Nineteenth General Report . . . , 1859,* pp. 52–53; *Anti-Slavery Reporter,* n.s., 8 (1860), 113–14; William G. Sewell, *The Ordeal of Free Labor in the British West Indies* (New York, 1861), p. 308.

51. "W. M. C.," "Martin Robinson Delany," *Journal of the National Medical Association,* 44 (1952), 232–38; A. H. M. Kirk-Greene, "America in the Niger Valley: A Colonization Centenary," *Phylon,* 23 (1962), 225–39; *Chatham Planet,* Oct. 12, 1858; Redpath Papers: Redpath to G. R. Haywood, April 10, 1861. It is interesting to note that Harold Cruse, in his corrosive and, I believe, correct analysis of *The Crisis of the Negro Intellectual* (New York, 1967), p. 6 n., also places Delany in this light.

52. Delany, *Official Report of the Niger Valley Exploring Party* (New York,

Anglican missionary pressure led to the repudiation of the agreement after the two agents left for England. Delany also tried to persuade the African Aid Society in Britain, which sought to encourage emigration from British North America to the West Indies, Liberia, or Natal, to include the Niger. He then returned to Canada West to present his report to his sponsors. But the Civil War, with its attendant naval blockade, dislocation of sea routes, and distortion of the cotton market, destroyed Delany's plans, and he left the province to join the Northern army. The following year a Pan-Negro spokesman, Edward W. Blyden, toured Nova Scotia urging blacks to emigrate to Liberia, also without success.[53]

One reason such recruiters were not successful was that, for the most part, fugitive slaves felt safe under the British flag. Even so, on occasion this safety was questioned. In the 1830s and 1840s, as American requests for extradition of Negroes tested the British North American haven, abolitionists were able to draw attention to the steadily mounting number of blacks in the Canadas.

The first formal request for extradition of a fugitive slave had been declined by the Administrator of Lower Canada, Sir James Kempt, who had just arrived from Nova Scotia. In 1829 one Paul Vallard had aided a slave to escape from his master in Illinois, bringing him to Montreal. The American government formally asked for the surrender of both men. Kempt turned to his Executive Council for an opinion, and he was advised that a fugitive should be given up only if his offense would have made him liable to arrest by the laws of Canada. Clearly this was not the case, and extradition was refused.[54]

Still, persistent rumors that Negroes were being spirited back into the northern states undermined morale in the black settlements. Often enough these rumors appeared to have some substance, as when in 1830 a fugitive

---

1861); Robert Campbell, *A Pilgrimage to My Motherland: An Account of a Journey among the Egbas and Yorubas of Central Africa, in 1859–60* (New York, 1861). The latter contains the text of the treaty, pp. 143–45; the English edition of the former omits several pages. Richard F. Burton, in his classic *Abeokuta and the Cameroons Mountains: An Exploration* (London, 1863), *1*, 94–98, heaped scorn on Campbell, the "Africo-Canadians," and the treaty, which was "sublime in its impudence" (p. 268).

53. Hollis T. Lynch, *Edward Wilmot Blyden: Pan-Negro Patriot, 1822–1912* (London, 1967), p. 33.

54. Riddell, "An International Complication between Illinois and Canada arising out of Slavery," pp. 123–26. Earlier, in 1819, the United States had asked whether fugitive slaves could be followed in pursuit into Canada and had been given a negative reply (*Report on Canadian Archives, 1897* [Ottawa, 1898], p. 100: Hillier to Goulburn, Sept. 24).

was nearly captured from the home of Charles Bâby, his benefactor in Sandwich, and was rescued in the face of an attack upon both men, or in 1836, when a professional slave-hunter carried off two fugitives from St. Catherines. The relevant laws needed clarification; and the Negroes wished greater protection, especially as they rose in number after 1834, buoyed upward to the Canadas in the new knowledge that slavery was illegal throughout the British Empire. By 1840 there were said to be nearly twelve thousand fugitives in the two Canadas, and some of them viewed the dangers of kidnapping and extradition as very real.[55]

Mistakenly so, because the British and Canadian governments already had moved to protect the fugitives. In 1833 Upper Canada passed an act to provide for the capture and extradition of "Fugitive Offenders from Foreign Countries," and added that the Governor-in-Council was free not to deliver up a person if he deemed it inexpedient to do so.[56] This permissive clause left judgment on the merits of each case to the Governor, and ordinarily he could be counted on to exercise compassion toward a fugitive slave whose only crime was self-theft, a patent impossibility where slavery did not exist.

Later that year the Canadian government refused to extradite two fugitives from Kentucky, Thornton Blackburn and his wife. Arrested in Detroit, the woman had escaped to Upper Canada in disguise, while a mob rescued the husband, wounding a sheriff. Lieutenant-Governor Colborne was opposed to slavery, as was the most powerful member of his council, John Strachan, then Archdeacon of York; and no one was surprised when Colborne replied to Michigan's request negatively, invoking a technicality in order to do so. The following year a request for a fugitive slave from Virginia was refused on similar grounds.[57]

In two subsequent cases, the Canadian haven again held firm. In 1837 one Solomon Mosely, or Moseby, who had escaped from Kentucky by stealing a horse, was arrested and placed in Niagara's jail. The Negroes of the area, led by Herbert Holmes, a mulatto teacher, encircled the building by day and night to prevent Mosely's transfer. When a deputy sheriff,

---

55. *Chatham Journal*, Dec. 23, 1843; *Amherstburg Echo*, Sept. 7, 1888, April 14, 1949; William Lewis Bâby, *Souvenirs of the Past* (Windsor, Ont., 1896), pp. 132–40; PAC, State Papers, Upper Canada, C 247–65; British and Foreign Anti-Slavery Society, *Third Annual Report* (London, 1842), p. 164.

56. *Statutes, of His Majesty's Province of Upper Canada* . . . (York, [1833]), pp. 37–38.

57. June Baber Woodson, "A Century with the Negroes of Detroit, 1830–1930," *The AME Church Review*, 68 (1953), 38–49; PAC, State Papers, Upper Canada, *61*, 31–48, 137–63; PAC, R.G. 1, E 1, *54:* Minutes, Sept. 6, 1834; Riddell, "Slave in Canada," pp. 343–47.

with a military guard, led the fugitive out shackled to a wagon, the Negroes seized the reins, the sheriff ordered the guards to fire, and a riot ensued. Holmes was killed, as was another man—possibly bayoneted in anger rather than in self-defense—and Mosely escaped. Over twenty Negroes were arrested. In the inquest that followed, the sheriff and guards were cleared of blame, but the Negroes were released. Mosely was allowed to return to Niagara at a later date.[58]

Almost immediately after the riot at Niagara, the Canadian government was faced with a well-prepared request for the extradition of another Kentucky fugitive, Jesse Happy, who also had escaped by stealing a horse. Public opinion had run high over the Mosely affair, with many supporting the police officers in the performance of their duty, "unhappy as it may have been." Lieutenant-Governor Sir Francis Bond Head found himself under pressure from two directions. A careful investigation of Jesse Happy followed, while public opinion swung increasingly behind the fugitive, as it was learned that his offense was over four years old, and that he had left the horse on the American side of the border and had written his former master to tell him where he might find it. As Head observed, while even the clothes and manacles of a slave were the property of his master, "surely a slave breaking *out* of his master's house is not guilty of the burglary which a thief would commit who should force the same locks and bolts in order to break *in!*" The Chief Justice, John (later Sir John) Beverley Robinson, who had drawn up the act of 1833, and who was the son of the Virginia Loyalist and former slaveowner, Christopher Robinson, thought that theft was clear enough and asked whether a white would not be surrendered under like circumstances. He thought it undesirable to encourage Negroes in their view of Canada as a place of safety. The Executive Council, noting the passage of time and observing that to give up the fugitive was, in effect, to subject him to a double penalty—one for the crime upon which the surrender took place and the other his return to slavery even if acquitted—suggested that the matter be submitted to London for advice.

The Colonial Secretary, Lord Glenelg, the Claphamite, and the Foreign Secretary, Viscount Palmerston, agreed that the time had come to decide upon a policy. Glenelg's view was that each case should be examined on its merits, and that Happy had not taken the horse with theft in mind.

58. Riddell, "Slave in Canada," pp. 347–50; PAC, State Papers, Upper Canada *40*, 217–32; Janet Carnochan, "A Slave Rescue in Niagara Sixty Years Ago," *Niagara Historical Society,* paper no. 2 (1897), pp. 8–17; Anna Brownell Jameson, *Winter Studies and Summer Rambles in Canada* (New York, 1839), *1*, 246–50; *The Friend of Man,* Oct. 11, Nov. 22, 1837.

The Law Officers of the Crown—among whom was the Attorney General, John Campbell, biographer of Lord Mansfield and in all probability the actual author of the famous words so often ascribed to Mansfield—also advised that the fugitive should not be surrendered, for there should be evidence of a criminal act which "would warrant the apprehension of the accused Party, if the alleged offence had been committed in Canada." This appeared to provide a sweeping defense of fugitive slaves; for since slavery did not exist in Canada the crime of escape could not exist there, and the use of the horse in Happy's case had been to effect escape and not for theft. Further, in future requests for extradition all evidence had to be taken in Canada, so that if it proved false, charges of perjury could be brought. Glenelg happily adopted this opinion as a general instruction for lieutenant-governors in British North America, and Jesse Happy was set free.[59]

The British and American governments soon realized the need for a treaty to cover extradition, for numerous instances had arisen of white criminals using the frontier for refuge. The Americans hoped to see the treaty include fugitive slaves; the British were determined that it would not. Canadian abolitionists were particularly sensitive to this danger, since most cases would arise upon their soil. Three Negroes, including Peter Gallego, asked Thomas Rolph to send a petition to Queen Victoria through Lord Durham—recently arrived as Governor to inquire into the causes of the late rebellion—asking that fugitive slaves receive special protection under any forthcoming treaty. The petition was lost or ignored; Rolph wrote to Lord John Russell, deplored Durham's "criminal negligance," and argued that extradition should be "placed beyond the control of caprice or expedience." The Negroes then suggested that no black claimed as a fugitive should ever be surrendered and that they should be tried for any alleged crime within Upper Canada.

Rolph's letters had some effect. Palmerston took the Negroes' fears seriously and concluded that neither robbery nor horse-stealing should be extraditable, lest they be used as pretexts for recapturing fugitive slaves. Russell agreed, while replying to Rolph that no special provisions should be made in the treaty for Negroes, since "it would not be lawful to deliver up a fugitive slave in any circumstances in which a white man would not also be delivered up." Nor could trial by jury be given for offenses charged

---

59. CO42/439: Head to Glenelg, Oct. 8, 1837, with enclosures; CO42/456: W. Fox Strangeways to James Stephen, Feb. 28, 1838; FO5/390: Fox, draft, in re Robert Cooper, May 3, 1843; PAC, State Papers, Upper Canada, *35*, 205–37; J. Mackenzie Leask, "Jesse Happy, A Fugitive Slave from Kentucky," *Ontario History, 54* (1962), 87–92; Fred Landon, "The Fugitive Slave in Canada," *The University Magazine, 18* (1919), 270–79.

with having been committed under foreign jurisdiction. A strict interpretation of the decision of the Law Officers in 1838 would be sufficient to protect the fugitive slaves.[60]

While this was true enough, the atmosphere in which these rather academic decisions were made was changed dramatically in 1841 by the Nelson Hacket (or Hackett) case.[61] Valet and butler to a wealthy Arkansan, Hacket stole a beaver overcoat and a racing mare from his owner, as well as a gold watch and a saddle from two other parties, and fled to Canada West. His master caught up with him in Chatham, Hacket was placed in jail, and the Acting Governor of Michigan demanded his surrender. The Governor General, Sir Charles Bagot, refused on the ground that the request should come from the state of original jurisdiction; and so in November of 1841 an impeccably formal document arrived from Arkansas. The Colonial Secretary, Lord Stanley, had expressly told Bagot to give his attention to restoring good relations with the Republic. Bagot also recognized that Hacket had committed a crime, by stealing a watch and saddle that were not necessary to his escape. Unwilling to see the Canadas become "an asylum for the worst characters provided only that they had been slaves before arriving here," [62] the Governor General ordered the fugitive's surrender. During the night of February 8, 1842, Hacket was rowed across the Detroit River. For the first time, criminal extradition had brought a fugitive slave back from Canada West.

Public opinion in Canada West, abolitionists in the United States, and the Colonial Office all expressed dismay. In conjunction with the *Creole* case, which involved a related problem in the Bahamas—news of which had reached London only a fortnight before Bagot's dispatch—the British saw a pressing need for a treaty of extradition. Since Lord Ashburton already was preparing for general discussions with the American Secretary of State, Daniel Webster, with a view to a treaty which would deal with several outstanding issues, this too could be heaped upon his plate.

The treaty that emerged was a good one even though neither abolition-

60. CO42/462: Rolph to Russell, Aug. 23, with encls., Sept. 24, Oct. 29, Nov. 3, Dec. 10, and replies, May 17, Sept. 20, 1839. FO5/346: Stephen to J. Backhouse, Dec. 30, 1839; *Sandwich* (U.C.) *Western Herald*, Aug. 14, 1838; *The Friend of Man*, Feb. 28, 1838; *Anti-Slavery Report, 1* (1840), 207.

61. See Alexander Lovell Murray, "The Extradition of Fugitive Slaves from Canada: A Re-evaluation," *CHR, 43* (1962), 298–314, which corrects Roman J. Zorn, "Criminal Extradition Menaces the Canadian Haven for Fugitive Slaves, 1841–1861," *CHR, 38* (1957), 284–94; and Zorn, "An Arkansas Fugitive Slave Incident and Its International Repercussions, *Arkansas Historical Quarterly, 16* (1957), 193–40. Documentation on this and related cases appears in *JNH, 12* (1927), 226–27, 232, 235, 240, 279, 286, 303, 453. See also *Anti-Slavery Reporter, 2* (Sept. 1, 1842), 1–2.

62. CO42/488: Bagot to Stanley, Jan. 20, 1842; FO115/79: Aberdeen to Russell, March 3, 1842, with encls.; *Montreal Gazette*, Aug. 6, 1842.

ists nor fugitives thought it so. Desertion, mutiny, and revolt on board ship were not included among extraditable offenses. While robbery was, the British reasoned that the principles applied by the Canadian courts would still hold, in that self-theft—including the theft of a horse in order to effect escape—would not be considered offenses under Canadian law. In its tenth article the treaty thus gave full effect to the Canadian act of 1833, making the pragmatic, protective British approach bi- rather than uni-lateral. Senator Thomas Hart Benton of Missouri saw the weakness in the treaty from the point of view of the slave states, complaining that the British provinces were lands "where abolitionism is the policy of the government, the voice of the law, and the spirit of the people," while the British abolitionist Charles Stuart thought the tenth article a "pledge . . . that we will be slavecatchers." [63]

Before leaving the United States, Ashburton met with members of the American and Foreign Anti-Slavery Society, at their request, to allay such fears. He also sent a memorandum to Sir Robert Peel which showed that he was alert to the dangers involved.[64] Thomas Clarkson examined the article carefully and saw that the future would turn upon interpretations of the meaning of robbery, the only offense on which fugitive slaves were likely to be chargable; for he reasoned that, since most were illiterate, forgery would not apply—apparently not realizing that fugitives often forged their passes—nor would arson or piracy. Although the treaty took away the discretionary power, making it mandatory that a fugitive be surrendered if found guilty of a crime as defined by Canadian law, protection arose from the provisions that full proof of identity—"seeing so many black people are alike"—would be required, and that the accused would be able to testify in his own behalf. Clarkson nonetheless concluded that fugitive slaves should be totally exempt from the operation of the treaty; and the British and Foreign Anti-Slavery Society, embracing this view, never departed from it.[65]

While natural, such fears were not warranted. Palmerston, Russell, and Ashburton, as well as other highly placed British officials, had no intention of allowing the treaty to operate against the fugitives. While the con-

63. [Benton], *Thirty Years View* . . . (New York, 1856), *2*, 447; Murray, "Extradition of Fugitive Slaves," pp. 309–10; *Montreal Gazette*, Dec. 21, 1842, Oct. 10, 14, 1850; Anti-Slavery Papers: Minute Books, Sept. 30, 1842, and Clarkson to Sir Charles T. Metcalfe, Dec. 7, 1843.

64. BM, Peel Papers, *320*, Add. MSS 40,500: Ashburton to Peel, Jan. 20, 1842.

65. University College, University of London, Lord Brougham Papers: Clarkson to Brougham, Oct. 24, 1842, March 16, July 1, 1843; *National Anti-Slavery Standard*, Jan. 30, 1851; Anti-Slavery Papers: Minute Book of the British and Foreign Anti-Slavery Society, Oct. 28, Nov. 25, 1842, Feb. 24, Aug. 25, 1843; *Anti-Slavery Reporter*, *4* (1843), iii; *Toronto Globe*, Aug. 10, 1850.

tinued agitation of the abolitionists no doubt helped keep them and their Canadian counterparts alert to the danger within the treaty, they needed no prodding. Lord Stanley assured the House of Commons that the fugitive's motives always would be examined in determining whether the treaty would apply; further, courts not magistrates would determine whether a case had been made for extradition, and it was understood that petty theft (as in the stealing of the clothes off one's back) was not robbery. All depositions relating to an extradition case were to be sent to London for review, a decision the newly arrived Governor General, Sir Charles Metcalfe, had already anticipated. With these assurances, the treaty was passed, and was ratified in August 1843. Six years later the Canadian government enacted a new extradition law of its own.

No fugitive slave was ever surrendered to the United States under this law or the Webster-Ashburton Treaty. The principles enunciated by the Law Officers in 1838 continued to prevail even under the added pressures of the Fugitive Slave Act of 1850. In 1856 a Negro, Daniel Drayton, tried to sell goods stolen in New York to a Toronto auctioneer, was arrested, and finally released because the charge was that of stealing from a shop, which although a felony, was not so under the treaty—an interpretation not then applied to white men. Twice when local magistrates improperly gave up fugitives contrary to the treaty the government punished the officials responsible. In 1856 one Archy Lanton, who had stolen two horses, was left in the care of his American pursuers by a careless constable and was kidnapped; the Attorney-General removed the two responsible magistrates from office. When in 1858 a Negro who was charged with receiving stolen goods was taken prisoner by two Hamilton policemen and given to American authorities, both were held for assault and imprisonment, and when a jury could not agree in the face of a judge determined to convict, they pled guilty. Significantly, not one of these three Negroes was a fugitive slave, so the Webster-Ashburton Treaty had the effect of helping free Negroes as well.[66]

The last case of a fugitive slave to come before the Canadian courts put to the test the application of the two most damaging charges under the

66. Edward Thompson, *The Life of Charles, Lord Metcalfe* (London, 1937), p. 397; CO42/605: Head to Louis Labouchere, Nov. 21, 1856; *Toronto Globe,* Dec. 10, 1858, Jan. 17, 1859; *Provincial Statutes of Canada . . .* (Quebec, 1849), pp. 144–46; Alexander Lovell Murray, "Canada and the Anglo-American Anti-Slavery Movement: A Study in International Philanthropy" (Ph.D. diss., Univ. of Pennsylvania, 1960), pp. 532–36. Extradition is discussed in detail on pp. 117–201 of this excellent monograph. The Lanton (or Lorton) case was especially complex, however, for theft in Canada West was also involved. See Allan Perkin, ed., *North into Freedom: The Autobiography of John Malvin, Free Negro, 1795–1880* (Cleveland, Ohio, 1966), pp. 75–78; and *Voice of the Fugitive,* Aug. 27, Sept. 10, 24, 1851.

treaty: murder, and assault with intent to commit murder. In 1853 one Jack Burton killed Seneca T. P. Diggs, a white neighbor of his Missouri master, when Diggs and four of his slaves attempted to seize Burton while he was visiting his wife on a nearby plantation. Escaping to Canada West, Burton met Laura S. Haviland, an American missionary working among the fugitives of Windsor. Having taken the name of John Anderson, the fugitive persuaded her to write a letter for him to his father-in-law, using a return address in Michigan as protection. When a white southerner arrived, seeking Anderson, she warned him; he fled to Chatham and dropped from sight. In the autumn of 1860 Anderson, now calling himself William Jones, was found working near Brantford, and there a local magistrate, learning from an angry Negro that Anderson was wanted for a crime in Missouri, put him in jail.[67]

Released, then rearrested on a warrant sworn out in Detroit, Anderson was charged with murder and brought before Chief Justice Robinson on the Court of Queen's Bench. The decision, given in mid-December in a courtroom packed with spectators and armed police, was for extradition. A mob outside was dispersed only when Anderson's counsel told them to leave, and four days later at a mass meeting in Toronto with the mayor presiding, the influential leader of the Irish community, Thomas D'Arcy McGee, condemned the decision, as did the thunderous voice of the Reform press, the *Toronto Globe*. Anderson's counsel, Samuel B. Freeman, led an able appeal to the Court of Common Pleas, and on February 16, 1861, with Civil War looming in the neighboring republic, Anderson walked away a free man, acquitted on a technicality arising from a defective warrant that had omitted four words from the treaty itself. Thus, article ten proved equal to its task: the defense of fugitive slaves against whatever crime they might have committed if it was done as a necessary part of the act of escaping.

Public reaction to the Anderson case was intense. In the interim between the first decision and the hearing of the appeal, almost no issue of the *Anti-Slavery Reporter*, organ of the British and Foreign Anti-Slavery Society, was without a full account of growing popular opposition to a surrender.[68] The Canadian press reported daily on the clamor, comparing

67. Riddell, "Slave in Canada," pp. 355–57; Fred Landon, "The Anderson Fugitive Case," *JNH*, 7 (1922), 233–42; *London* (Ont.) *Free Press*, Feb. 11, 1928; C. W. Robinson, *Life of Sir John Beverley Robinson, Bart., C.B., D.C.L., Chief-Justice of Upper Canada* (Edinburgh, 1904), pp. 326–27; Frank Yeigh, "Famous Canadian Trials, VIII—Anderson, The Fugitive Slave," *Canadian Magazine*, 45 (1915), 397–401.

68. *Anti-Slavery Reporter*, 9 (1861), 22, 31–32, 34–36, 42, 45, 54, 57, 60, 65, 85, 90, 106, 109, 133, 164, 215; also *Toronto Globe*, Nov. 14, 28, 30, Dec. 3, 12, 20, 1860, Jan. 7, 8, 19, 23, Feb. 16, 1861.

Anderson to Garibaldi, to a ravished Negro maid seeking to escape from her abductor, and to the manly symbol of all Africa. Some newspapers, and the British society, suggested—quite erroneously—that Britain had promised never to give up any fugitive under any pretext whatsoever. The American press followed the case closely, and Gerrit Smith, a leading New York abolitionist, twice visited Canada West to address meetings on behalf of Anderson. The Anti-Slavery Society of Canada sponsored rallies and resolutions, and at a mass meeting in Hamilton only two men in an audience of over seven hundred would defend the principle that treaties must be adhered to, whatever the consequences. No incident of the decade so focused Canadian attention upon the problem of the fugitive slave.[69]

The various extradition cases served the purpose of making many Canadians aware of their growing involvement in the antislavery struggle to the south. When the first case had arisen, and Thornton Blackburn and his wife were not extradited, there had been no Anti-Slavery Society of Canada. There had been less than ten thousand Negroes in the Canadas; now over sixty thousand were claimed for the provinces. There had been but a single, failing, Negro settlement at Wilberforce; now there were clusters of Negroes in villages of their own throughout the southwestern portion of Canada West. The issue of extradition had brought publicity to the Canadian haven; and as that haven proved time and again—despite fugitive and abolitionist worries—to be secure, more and more fugitives from slavery followed the North Star of which they later would speak with such affection.

That the affection was not wholly misplaced may be seen in the British reaction to the Anderson affair. Unable to interfere while the fugitive's fate still lay before the Canadian courts, Governor General Sir Edmund Head nonetheless had prepared a lengthy dispatch for the Colonial Office strongly hinting that he might refuse to turn Anderson over to American authorities, even though so grave a step would involve a possible breach of treaty obligations. The Colonial Office, in turn, sent Head instructions not to surrender Anderson, whatever the decision, until the Law Officers might render an opinion, and in March—after the fugitive's release—the opinion was given: that the Canadian government need not give Anderson up.[70] Safe, had he known it, by the pragmatic application of British law, Anderson was the symptom rather than the cause of a profound change in the Negro's position in British North America.

69. An excellent treatment of the press appears in Murray, "Canada and the Anglo-American Anti-Slavery Movement," pp. 539–75.

70. HO45/7232: Head to Duke of Newcastle, Jan. 15, with encl., Frederic Rogers to H. Waddington, Jan. 17, Feb. 23, both with encls., and opinion of the Law Officers, March 20, encl. in John Greenwood to Waddington, April 1, all 1861; Anti-Slavery Papers: Thomas Henry to Louis Alexis Chamerovzow, Dec. 20, 1860, Feb. 4, 11, 16, 1861.

That change was a slow one. One by one the alternatives to colonization within the New World had proved unattractive to the vast majority of Negroes during the three decades before the Civil War. Resettlement continued to prove difficult, and the Wilberforce fiasco had delayed other organized attempts to found Negro self-help agricultural communities in Canada West. But the growing Negro Convention movement, the discussions of colonization elsewhere, and the obvious and increasing pressures upon the fugitive slaves in the free northern states made other Negro communal experiments on Canadian soil inevitable. A second attempt began in 1842.

7. The Canadian Canaan, 1842–1870

Perhaps the most significant of the attempts to plant a Negro colony in Canada West was one initiated in 1842 under the promising name of Dawn. This institution, formally called The British-American Institute, was more representative of both the successes and the failures of such communal experiments than was the forlorn effort at Wilberforce; it also gained far greater fame, partially because of the close association with it of Josiah Henson, a Negro firmly believed by many to be Harriet Beecher Stowe's Uncle Tom—in real life saved from death. The popular identification of Dawn and Henson as synonymous was unfortunate, but they were irrevocably linked in the public mind and have remained so in history.

Dawn represented an attempt to adjust to the presumed realities of a white America. Many Negroes believed in the middle-class success ethic that lay behind one of the United States's chief messages to the world: hard work, clean living, education, and an eye for the main chance would bring a man, unless flawed by character or caught by bad luck, to the top. The Negro, however, was so flawed, in terms of the hard truths of a white-dominated world, and many realized that the demise of slavery alone (which surely was coming) was not enough to give the Negro his place in the line inexorably marching toward success. Manual labor institutes, practical training, the fundamentals of a bookish education, and some understanding of how a capitalist economy actually worked, were essential. A brief respite from the world was needed so that the Negro might be his own master. A firm belief in education, and the instant status it gave, lay behind the many assumed titles, the Doctors, Professors, and Reverends who sprang so quickly from black soil. In a communal society, the Negro could train himself to use freedom, could come to follow the mores, reflect the virtues, and accept the ethics of the dominant white society. In short, the values of the Negro community experiments were normative ones; the Negroes accepted the free world as it was, or as they saw it to be, and they did not intend to retreat from it permanently or to reform it, slavery aside. Rather than turning their backs upon white society, they sought a temporary refuge in which to prepare themselves for a full place in that society.

If the conditions of a frontier society had shaped America, the Negroes would create their own frontier. Many knew they could not hope to do this, for some cherished cultural values of their own—although these were few and largely unremarked upon in a prenegritude era—and others recognized that distinctions based on skin color rather than place of origin, language, accent or religion would be infinitely slow to pass. These realists, too, often sought out all-Negro communities, less as places of preparation than as mutual benefit societies that would bury them and, perhaps, care for their families afterwards. Dawn was representative of both strands of thought, with the activist, preparatory strand dominant.

Dawn began in Ohio. In 1834 the Board of Trustees of the Lane Seminary in Cincinnati told students and faculty that they were not to organize antislavery activities, and among the Lane Rebels, as they were called, who left for the more liberal atmosphere of Oberlin College, was Hiram Wilson. In the fall of 1836, with $25 given to him by Charles Grandison Finney, Wilson went to Upper Canada to see for himself how the fugitives were faring; and in the spring he returned to attend the annual meeting of the American Anti-Slavery Society as a delegate from the province. With the help of the Society and five Oberlin students, he began what he hoped would be a series of schools within the growing black communities—schools not restricted to Negroes—and late in 1837 he addressed a newly formed Upper Canada Anti-Slavery Society about the merits of educating fugitives. He also borrowed heavily, and although by the fall of 1839 his work in Amherstburg was well known in Northern abolitionist circles, he confessed to the Peterboro antislavery leader, Gerrit Smith, that he was trusting in the Lord to pay a debt of $10,000. In 1840 the American Anti-Slavery Society commended him to the "liberal patronage of every true-hearted abolitionist," and the next year Smith and others organized a Rochester-based committee to help channel money, Bibles, and clothing to the several schools—ultimately fifteen in all—begun by or inspired through Wilson's work.[1]

1. The previous paragraphs draw upon LC, Papers of the American Anti-Slavery Society: minutes of Dec. 4, 1833, Oct. 23, 1839, Jan, 15, 1840; *The Emancipator,* Dec. 22, 1836; *Toronto Constitution,* Nov. 16, 1837; *The Friend of Man,* Jan. 17, Feb. 14, May 9, June 28, 1838; *The Anti-Slavery Standard,* July 8, 1841; *The Liberator,* April 10, 1846; American Anti-Slavery Society, *Fourth Annual Report* (New York, 1837), p. 19; BPL, Amos A. Phelps Papers, *10:* Wilson to Phelps, Aug. 19, 1839; BPL, Weston Papers: Maria F. Rice to Maria W. Chapman, Oct. 23, 1839; BPL, William Lloyd Garrison Papers, *9:* Wilson to John A. Collins, Aug. 17, 1840; Historical Records Survey, *Calendar of the Gerrit Smith Papers in the Syracuse University Library: General Correspondance* (Albany, N.Y. [1941]), *2,* 108, 129, 255: John Roberts, Aug. 8, 1837, Wilson, Dec. 18, 1839, and Ray Potter, Jan. 25, 1846, to Smith; PAC, C 1, *803:* Wilson to Sydenham, June 18, 25, 1841; PAC, G 20, *310:* Rice to Metcalfe, July 3, 24, 1844; and Clayton S. Ellsworth, "Oberlin and the Anti-Slavery Movement Up to the Civil War" (Ph.D. diss., Cornell Univ., 1930), pp. 47–48, 168.

Wilson attracted the attention of a Quaker philanthropist in Skaneateles, New York, James Cannings Fuller, who wished to help fugitives without violating his principle that Americans must not interfere in Canadian matters. Schools that were controlled from the United States were therefore not agreeable to him; but missions firmly rooted in Canadian soil, although run according to Wilson's principles, were acceptable.[2] Fuller accordingly raised much of the initial money for The British-American Institute, a school for the "Education Mental Moral and physical of the Colored inhabitants of Canada not excluding white persons and Indians." [3] He sought money on a tour of England, contacted Gerrit Smith, and agreed to serve on the new school's board. In November, after briefly considering Owen Sound, the sponsors purchased two hundred acres of land near Chatham, Canada West, for $800. Thirteen months later they opened the doors of a manual labor school to its first twelve students. The trustees were three white men—Fuller; Reverend John Roaf, a Congregational minister from Toronto who was active in anti-slavery work there; and Frederick Stover of Norwich, Canada West, who had been associated with Wilberforce—and three Negroes: Peter Smith, George Johnson, and James C. Brown, who had left Toronto.

Around the Institute grew the community, and since the whites considered that the town was in charge of the school—as, in fact, it was not—Dawn itself stood or fell on the school. The Institute came to own perhaps three hundred acres of land on a bend of the river Sydenham; the Negro settlers owned another fifteen hundred, on which they raised tobacco, wheat, corn, and oats. In time, the population rose to five hundred or more, and the community was served by its own saw- and gristmills, a brickyard, and a rope walk. Lumbering proved modestly rewarding, and in 1850 a cargo of black walnut wood was sold in Boston. In all, the Negro settlers increased the value of their land by a dollar an acre in five years.

The man most responsible for Dawn's initial fame was Josiah Henson, one of the few Negro leaders in Canada West who at first won nearly universal approval—both for his own activities and, later, for being taken for Mrs. Stowe's Uncle Tom. Henson and Uncle Tom are so intertwined, in fiction if not in fact, and they were so mutually identified by sympathetic whites in the Canadas and in Britain, that the story of one cannot be told

2. For Fuller's attitude on noninterference, see PSHS, Simon Gratz Autograph Collection: Fuller to Seward, Dec. 31, 1837, Feb. 29, 1840; and *Calendar of the Gerrit Smith Papers, 2,* 181: Fuller to Smith, Oct. 15, 1841.

3. Quoted in Pease and Pease, *Black Utopia,* p. 64, from the Kent County Registry Office, Chatham; Dawn is discussed on pp. 63–84. See also OPA, R.G. *1,* Records of the Crown Lands Department: Watson to R. B. Sullivan, March 29, 1841.

without the other, nor can either be separated from the ŀ
British-American Institute. In many ways Henson's saga
of the problem of the intelligent fugitive slave of the time
left free to be himself, to assimilate if he wished into the mɑ.
Canadian life, for he became the focus of abolitionist attention, a tooı ᴠ.
used in a propaganda campaign which was not above much juggling with
the facts, however proper the ultimate goals may have been.

Henson was born near Port Tobacco in Charles County, Maryland,
on June 15, 1789. He passed through the hands of three owners, became
a Christian in his eighteenth year, and was maimed for life when one
of his master's enemies beat him with a stake, breaking his arm and
possibly both of his shoulder blades. At twenty-two Henson married, and
during the next forty years he would father twelve children, eight of whom
survived. Recognizing that, on the whole, he was owned by a fair man, he
worked hard to ingratiate himself, toiling and inducing others to toil "many
an extra hour, in order to show my master what an excellent day's work
had been accomplished, and to win a kind word or a benevolent deed from
his callous heart." [5] His sense of loyalty was so strong that he personally
conducted eighteen of his owner's slaves to Kentucky, passing by the
Ohio shores yet resisting the temptation to run away. He remained in
Kentucky for three years, became a preacher in the Methodist Episcopal
Church, and was made an unofficial overseer, trusted with considerable
freedom of movement. He then returned to his owner in Maryland, preaching in Ohio on the way and thus collecting $275, a horse, and some clothes,
with which he hoped to purchase his freedom. The owner agreed to sell
for $450, and by disposing of horse and clothes, Henson raised $350 and
signed a note for the rest. When he returned to Kentucky, he learned that
his owner now claimed that the sale price was $1,000, and the slave was
unable to disprove this. Henson still did not flee, however, although the
Ohio River was nearby.

Henson's decision to escape arose from what he regarded as moral
mistreatment in New Orleans. Asked to accompany his owner's nephew
south, he realized that despite denials he was to be sold, and on the journey
he took up an axe to kill his sleeping companions—only to realize that as
a Christian he could not. He was saved from being sold, and parted from

4. *The Life of Josiah Henson, formerly a Slave, Now an Inhabitant of Canada:
Narrated by Himself* (Boston, 1849). This first edition is rare: known copies are in
the BM, BPL, Yale University Library, and Uncle Tom's Cabin and Museum, Dresden, Ont. No doubt there are others, but since a reprint edition, issued by the
Museum in 1965, is more readily available, page references are to it. The original
handwritten manuscript of the autobiography is in the BPL.

5. *Ibid.*, p. 8.

the wife he had left in Kentucky, only because his companion fell seriously ill while in Louisiana and asked Henson to take him back to his home. Henson did so, but he resolved that the decision to sell him, together with his owner's "attempt to kidnap me again, after having pocketed three-fourths of my market value, absolved me from any obligation . . . to pay him any more, or to continue in a position which exposed me to his machinations." [6] He decided to flee to Canada.

His escape showed foresight and considerable courage. By a ruse he drew out his son, who normally passed the night in the proprietor's house, and choosing a time when because of the routine of the plantation they would not be missed for three days, he crossed the Ohio River to the Indiana shore. He carried his two smallest children on his back in a large knapsack; two others walked, as did his wife. On October 28, 1830, about six weeks after they began, the Hensons gratefully threw themselves on Canadian soil, Josiah executing "sundry antics which excited the astonishment of those who were looking on." [7]

Henson adjusted quickly to a life of freedom. On his second attempt he found employment. Home was an old shack from which he expelled pigs but in which, for the first time, his family could enjoy privacy and "some of the comforts of life, while the necessaries of food and fuel were abundant." He worked for both shares and wages, purchased some livestock, resumed preaching, and saw his boy Tom given two quarters' of schooling at the expense of his employer. Josiah had an excellent memory, and for some time he was able to give the impression that he could read the Bible by memorizing the passages he heard; but one day his son asked, "Why, father, can't you read?", and Josiah, a man of great and stubborn pride, confessed that he could not. The twelve-year-old lad then set out to teach him how, and in time Josiah learned "to read a little." [8] Soon after, he took employment with one Benjamin Riseley, who allowed him to call prayer meetings in his home.

At one of these meetings a small group of Negroes decided to invest their earnings collectively in land. "It was precisely the Yankee spirit which I wished to instil into my fellow slaves, if possible," Henson later wrote,[9] and in the fall of 1834 he set out to find a suitable area for them. He rented cleared lots near Colchester, where he and his followers learned to raise tobacco and wheat. According to Henson, he learned that the grantee had not complied with some of the conditions for his allotment, however, and he wrote to the lieutenant-governor, who advised the

6. *Life of Josiah Henson*, pp. 44–45.
7. Ibid., p. 55.
8. Ibid., pp. 59–61.
9. Ibid., p. 63.

Negroes to apply to the legislature for relief. Upon doing so they found themselves freed from rent, although now subject to the usual improvement clauses. They had meant to leave the site quickly, but given this boon they remained for seven years.

Henson was now devoting most of his thought to the problem of how fugitives like himself might best adjust to Upper Canada. As he saw,

> The mere delight the slave took in his freedom, rendered him, at first, contented with a lot far inferior to that which he might have attained. Then his ignorance led him to make unprofitable bargains, and he would often hire wild land on short terms, and bind himself to clear a certain number of acres; and by the time they were cleared and fitted for cultivation his lease was out, and his landlord would come in, and raise a splendid crop on the new land.

Also, the Negroes often raised only tobacco, tempted by the high price it brought, but this created a glut on an already depressed market, and the Negroes who had not diversified with wheat were driven to the wall. To correct this, Henson "set seriously about the business of lecturing upon the subject of crops, wages, and profits." [10]

While in Colchester, Henson met Hiram Wilson, and from 1836 on the two worked together. When Fuller returned from England with funds to establish his manual labor institute, it was Henson and Wilson who called a convention in June 1838, to determine how and where the money might best be spent. As Henson knew, Negroes increasingly were excluded from the public schools of the province, and upon his urging the delegates decided to found The British-American Institute. In 1842 Henson moved to Dawn, having established contact with a group of Boston Unitarians who supplied him with modest funds. "We look to the school, and the possession of landed property by individuals, as two great means of elevation of our oppressed and degraded race," he later wrote in his autobiography.[11]

This autobiography was first published by Arthur D. Phelps in Boston early in 1849. Hoping to earn some small income for The British-American Institute, Henson spoke of his experiences to Samuel A. Eliot, a former mayor of Boston who was well known for his moderate antislavery views. Eliot not only was the ghost-writer for *The Life of Josiah Henson, formerly a Slave, Now an Inhabitant of Canada,* but he paid for its printing.[12] In

10. *Life of Josiah Henson,* pp. 65–66; *Boston Recorder,* Jan. 7, 1818.

11. MHS, George Ellis Papers: Henson to Ellis, March 16, 1846; *Life of Josiah Henson,* p. 70; Lawson Memorial Library, Univ. of Western Ontario, London: Henson's deed of property.

12. MHS, Amos A. Lawrence Papers: Lawrence to Nathan Hale, Nov. 7, 1850, and to Samuel Morley, Nov. 30, 1852. On Eliot, see C[laude] M. F[uess], "Samuel Atkins Eliot," *DAB, 6* (1931), 81–82, which incorrectly dates Henson's book 1843.

style, pace, and proportion the account reflects the straightforward, un-embellished simplicity of Henson's life. Clearly, he was an unusual man, alert and intelligent. Equally clearly, he emerged as a natural leader to other Negroes, for he understood figures where they did not, and he was imaginative and independent in his approach to immediate problems. The narrative also showed that Henson was vain behind his facade of humility—proud, possessive, and prone to seek out quick approbation rather than long-range solutions. He needed to lead, and often led well, but he rather enjoyed manipulating the lives of others, if always for what he conceived to be their benefit. He seemed immensely stable, given neither to recriminations nor to a paralyzing fatalism, and in the main he was an effective spokesman for the Negro, despite his deeply felt need to please. If Dawn succeeded, much would be due Henson; otherwise, he was un-likely to win recognition outside a limited circle.

But three years after the publication of Henson's *Life,* there appeared a book which was to enlarge this circle immeasurably. In 1851 a Wash-ington weekly paper, *The National Era,* began the serial publication of a long story written by Harriet Beecher Stowe, the wife of a professor at Bowdoin College in Maine. Originally to have carried the subtitle, "The Man that Was a Thing," Mrs. Stowe's narrative, renamed "Uncle Tom's Cabin; or, Life Among the Lowly," ran in the *Era* from June 1851 until April 1852. Uncle Tom quickly built up a following, and ten days before the last installment appeared, the whole story was issued in two volumes, to be sold for a dollar. The novel swept the Northern states, Britain—where in London alone twenty different pirated editions were published within the year—and the Continent.[13]

In British North America as well everyone seemed to be reading about Uncle Tom.[14] A Montreal monthly periodical, *The Maple Leaf,* serialized the book with an abridged conclusion from July 1852 until the following June. The *Toronto Globe,* edited by an ardent abolitionist, George Brown, printed extracts and the famous fifth chapter in its entirety. Within weeks

13. The best examination of the impact of *Uncle Tom's Cabin* on England is Frank J. Klingberg, "Harriet Beecher Stowe and Social Reform in England," *AHR, 43* (1938), 542–52, while Edith E. Lucas, *La littérature anti-esclavagiste au dix-neuvième siècle: étude sur Madame Beecher Stowe et son influence en France* (Paris, 1930), and Grace Edith Maclean, " 'Uncle Tom's Cabin' in Germany," *Americana Germanica,* n.s., *10* (1910), whole no. (New York), are adequate. The Montreal edition was taken from the first Paris printing of *La Case de l'Oncle Tom.* The se-quence of publishing in England, from which the Canadian sequence may be deduced, is described in William Talbot, "Uncle Tom's Cabin: First English Editions," *The American Book Collector, 3* (1933), 292.

14. See Fred Landon, "When *Uncle Tom's Cabin* Came to Canada," *OH, 44* (1952), 1–5.

there were separate Toronto and Montreal editions based upon the Boston printing.[15] In St. Thomas townspeople widely viewed a diorama illustrative of Mrs. Stowe's more poignant scenes, in Toronto strolling players dramatized the novel in the streets, and the London Mechanics' Institute library doubled its order for copies. In Montreal *Case du Père Tom* was an immediate success, and Wilfrid Laurier, one day to be Canada's Prime Minister and then a boy of ten, borrowed a copy from a college friend and annoyed his landlady by burning his lamp through the night in order to finish it. Hundreds of young boys who, less than ten years later, would enter the Northern armies, devoured the one-volume edition.[16] Only in Nova Scotia and Prince Edward Island did Mrs. Stowe receive a mixed press: in a lengthy review in *The Provincial,* a new Halifax monthly, an anonymous critic observed that *Uncle Tom's Cabin* had been discussed by everyone and that it justly condemned slavery, adding, however, that its author either had overdrawn her case or that Negroes in Nova Scotia were unusually inferior. "The insufferable arrogance and uncleanly habits of Colonial negroes make it almost impossible for us to hold association with them"; "We are unwilling even to occupy the same conveyance, and disdain to sit at the same table"; "we have no hesitation in pronouncing them far inferior in morality, intelligence, and cleanliness, to the very lowest among the white population." The *Charlottetown Islander* also cautioned against romances which described exceptional cases rather than the rule.[17]

The hold *Uncle Tom's Cabin* took on the public imagination was secure

15. *The Maple Leaf, 1* (1852), 3–13, and variously through 177–84, and vol. 2 (1853); *Globe,* April 24, 27, 1853; *Montreal Gazette,* April 3, 17, 1852. Landon, "When *Uncle Tom's Cabin* Came to Canada," and other authors refer to a Halifax edition in the same year. I have examined a mint copy of this edition, held by the Yale University Library, and while the title page lists Halifax as the place of publication, I believe that Halifax, England, rather than Nova Scotia, is meant. The price is given as one shilling, but from 1858 the decimal system was used in Canada, and the Halifax merchants had taken up dollars and cents long before. The publishers, Milner and Sowerby, are unknown to the PANS (Miss Phyllis Blakeley to author, Oct. 7, 1966). The Yale copy is incribed as a gift to Elizabeth Ann Langridge, and no such family name occurs in any Nova Scotian genealogies. The County Records of the West Riding of Yorkshire confirm that a registration for a printing press was issued in Halifax to William Milner in 1836.

16. London Public Library, London, Ont., Minute Book, London Mechanics' Institute, 1851: Aug. 9, 1852; Eleanor Shaw, "A History of the London Public Library," typescript (London Public Library, 1941), p. 15; *Toronto Weekly North American,* Feb. 2, 1852; *St. Thomas Weekly Dispatch,* June 21, 1853; Oberlin College, Misc. Corres.: Wilson to Hamilton Hill, May 24, 1853; John I. Cooper, *The Story of Three Hundred Years* ([Montreal, 1942]), p. 80.

17. "Literature of Slavery," *The Provincial, 2* (1853), 3–8; *Islander,* Nov. 28, 1856; *New Glasgow* (N.S.) *Eastern Chronicle,* June 10, 1868.

and long-lasting—certainly longer in British North America than in the United States. In 1932 a report on reading habits among Canadian secondary school students showed that *Tom* still was the most popular American book there, and into the 1950s sales in Toronto, in particular, continued briskly.[18] In its several dramatized forms *Tom* became a perennial favorite for travelling troupes, and with the addition of bloodhounds to pursue Eliza across the ice floes, "Tom shows" played to appreciative audiences throughout English-speaking Canada. A touring group carried Tom and related minstrelsy into New Brunswick and Nova Scotia in the 1860s and 1870s; a surfeit of Eva, Eliza, Topsy, and St. Clair drove Abbey's Double Mammoth Uncle Tom's Cabin Company to turn the simple adaptation first presented by Halifax-born George Howard in Troy, New York, in September 1852, into an extravaganza, with two uniformed, segregated, black and white brass bands, which together with the South Carolina Jubilee Singers and Plantation Troubadors, marched through the streets of smalltown Ontario.[19] By the 1880s rural communities might be exposed to Tommers five or six times in the decade. Ironically, similar groups performed to segregated audiences in Dresden, Ontario, in 1919 and 1923 (a mile from Josiah Henson's grave), and into the 1920s the almost lunatic jollity, the cringing piety, and the blackface distortions of the shows continued to attract crowds in the Maritimes.[20]

The explosive, and utterly unexpected, effect of her work may have frightened Mrs. Stowe. Assuredly, the virulence of the Southern attack upon her novel disturbed her. Even friendly reviewers doubted her book's veracity: *The Times* found Tom too pure to be believable and thought that Mrs. Stowe's "honest zeal" had outrun her discretion.[21] She had

18. Arthur A. Hauck, *Some Educational Factors affecting the Relations between Canada and the United States* (Easton, Pa., 1932), p. 22; Albert R. Hassard, " 'Uncle Tom's Cabin' Recalled," *Onward, 41* (1931), 2; *Toronto Globe & Mail,* Dec. 2, 1952.

19. Carl Wittke, *Tambo and Bones: A History of the American Minstrel Stage* (Durham, N.C., 1930), pp. 98–103, 110, 222; J. Frank Davis, "Tom Shows," *Scribner's Magazine, 67* (1925), 350; Donald A. Smith, *At The Forks of the Grand: 20 Historical Essays on Paris, Ontario* (Paris, n.d.), pp. 182–84; Phyllis R. Blakeley, *Glimpses of Halifax, 1867–1900,* PANS pub. no. 9 (Halifax, 1949), pp. 77–78; F. Lauriston Bullard, "Uncle Tom on the Stage," *Lincoln Herald, 48* (1946), 19.

20. W. A. Hewitt, *Down the Stretch: Recollections of a Pioneer Sportsman and Journalist* (Toronto, 1958), p. 114; TPL, Thomas H. Scott Collection: "Behind the Footlights," MSS Autobiography; TPL, Baldwin Room: broadsides, playbills, and clippings relating to the Negro theatre in Canada; New York Library for the Performing Arts, Lincoln Center: Saint John programme, April 29, 30, May 1, 1920; Uncle Tom's Cabin Museum; playbills; Harvard College Library, Theatre Collection: playbills for LaRue's Minstrels, The Harmonears (Halifax), and Sam Sharpley's Minstrels (Quebec); *Toronto Globe,* Oct. 15, 1861; *Brantford Review,* Nov. 4, 1880.

21. Sept. 3, 1852.

claimed to be a close student of the slave states; and having lived in Cincinnati at the time of the Lane revolt, she was, in fact, tolerably well informed. But she saw that the novel could not stand alone, undefended, and she therefore sallied forth to her own defense, vigorously, massively— but not forthrightly.

Accordingly, she constructed *A Key to Uncle Tom's Cabin: Presenting the Original Facts and Documents upon which the Story is Founded . . .* , which was published in Boston in 1853. The title was less than honest; for the documentation she brought together in the *Key,* while amply supporting much that she had put in her novel, had not been in her possession at the time Uncle Tom was created; quite simply the *Key* was a post hoc attempt to buttress a thesis already expressed. Not unnaturally, she made the best case for herself in assembling her materials, and in an opening chapter she made clear her belief that to have injected documentation into the novel would have been to clog its narrative flow. In this she undoubtedly was correct, although her rather self-conscious theory of the relationship of reality to fiction was an afterthought.

To collect material for her *Key,* Mrs. Stowe consulted various books while in Boston. She leaned most heavily on Theodore Dwight Weld's horrific compilation of atrocity stories, *American Slavery as It Is: Testimony of a Thousand Witnesses,* published in 1839; and she also used Henson's *Life,* from which she quoted at some length (with slight inaccuracies), identifying him as "pastor of the missionary settlement at Dawn, in Canada." She also wanted to send someone to the Canadas to enquire into the condition of the fugitives but appears not to have done so. Once she related Henson to one of the figures in her novel, George Harris; and once she found in Henson's narrative an "instance parallel" to Tom's Christian dedication. Later she credited most of *Uncle Tom* to Weld's book, which she said she had kept in her workbasket by day and under her pillow at night.[22]

At no time during the early years of her success, or of Henson's small fame arising from his narrative of 1849, did Mrs. Stowe identify Henson with Uncle Tom. To the contrary, she found as many "striking parallels" to her novel in the narrative of Solomon Northrop as in Henson's. She never referred to having met Henson, and in the *Key* she cited his memoirs but no conversation. On one occasion she said that the death scene of Uncle Tom was the first she wrote, while living in Brunswick (in which case, no relationship to Henson was likely); and on another occasion she

22. *Key,* pp. 19, 26, 174; BPL, Weston Papers: E[liza] Wigham to [Mary A. Estlin], April 28, 1853. *The Anglo-American Magazine, 3* (1853), 212–15, published in Toronto, while not liking the *Key,* felt that it provided all necessary proof that the novel was accurate.

said that this scene was written after she had composed the death of Little Eva, in Andover, Massachusetts. In 1878, apparently feeling that contradiction had gone too far, she said that once she had written letters for a former slave woman, who had become a servant in her own family, to a slave husband who remained in Kentucky, and that it was this "faithful slave" who was "a pattern of Uncle Tom." In the same essay she admitted that it was after her account began to appear in *The National Era* that she went to Boston to reinforce "her *répertoire* of facts" by consulting, among other books, those by Weld and Henson, particulars from which were "inwoven with the story." [23] Again, the sequence is not clear, and Mrs. Stowe seemed incapable of clarifying it; but nothing said publicly by the author of *Uncle Tom* gave real substance to any contention that Josiah Henson and Uncle Tom were one and the same.

Nonetheless, they became so in the public mind, and some evidence was offered for this contention. Writing in 1911, Charles and Lyman Stowe, her son and grandson, said that she had met Henson in Boston in January of 1850, at the home of her brother, Lyman Beecher.[24] In the 1878, or fourth, revised edition of his life, Henson asserted that he had met her in Andover where he told her the story of his life, and indeed in 1876, in a private letter, Mrs. Stowe said that Henson had visited her there.[25] Upon this basis, Henson was able to imply, and others who chose to use him for their own purposes were able to assert, that he and Tom were the same man, that Tom yet lived, and that Eliza, Eva, and George were drawn from Henson's family and friends.

None of these alleged facts will bear close scrutiny. Mrs. Stowe did not move to Andover until 1852, so if Henson visited her there, it was after she had completed all but a chapter or two of her novel. Henson was in Boston twice in 1850, both on occasions after the Fugitive Slave Law was passed in September; and in any case, Mrs. Stowe was in Cincinnati, not Boston, in January, coming on to the latter in May.[26] The first edition of his narrative, as published in 1849, appeared early in the year while Mrs. Stowe was still in Cincinnati, and when she began writing furiously in February of 1851, she apparently mentioned neither Henson nor his book to anyone, although she normally shared her ideas freely with her

23. Introduction to 1878 edition, reprinted as *Old South Leaflets*, no. 82 (Boston, n.d.), pp. 1, 5–6; and Florine Thayer McCray, *The Life-Work of the Author of Uncle Tom's Cabin* (New York, 1889), p. 72.

24. Charles Edward and Lyman Beecher Stowe, "How Mrs. Stowe Wrote 'Uncle Tom's Cabin,' " *McClure's Magazine, 36* (1911), 613–14.

25. On the alleged Andover meeting, see Charles Nichols, "The Origins of Uncle Tom's Cabin," *Phylon, 19* (1958), 328–34.

26. Lawrence Papers: Lawrence to Garrison, Feb. 16, 1851; and Charles Edward Stowe, *Life of Harriet Beecher Stowe* (Boston, 1890), pp. 130–31.

husband. Had she communed with Henson before his book was written, as he later implied, surely he would have mentioned it in an early edition of his own *Life,* for he was not slow to acquire fame by dropping names; and if he had talked with Mrs. Stowe while she was writing her book, she need not have journeyed to Boston to "re-enforce" her facts by reading his account. If Eva, Eliza, or George had any place in Henson's life, would he not have mentioned that place before 1878—at least in his 1858 edition, published well after they were household names? [27] Clearly, although he later hinted otherwise, he was not the "slave husband" to whom Mrs. Stowe wrote letters on behalf of her servant, for Josiah's wife was with him in Kentucky. Presumably, she did not meet him, as he also suggested, while in Kentucky; for he was a slave in Daviess County, well removed from the Mason and Garrard county homes she visited.

Mrs. Stowe and Henson did reinforce each other, however, and she wrote an introduction to the second or 1858 edition of his book, in which he carried his story to 1852. Even at this date—when association with Mrs. Stowe would have brought a cachet to Henson's account—he made no mention of any meeting; nor did she in her introduction, which was bland and noncommittal. Moreover, the introduction was retained unaltered in Henson's 1878 edition, in which he claimed to have met her in Andover; but either she met Henson there after *Uncle Tom's Cabin* was written or both unaccountably had forgotten their venue.

Under the impact of abolitionist need, Henson's desire to please led to numerous changes in successive editions of his memoirs.[28] Perhaps spokesmen need be neither honest nor consistent but merely convincing, and Henson was at least this—and no one had occasion to compare the various editions of his narrative. Such a comparison is revealing of his ability to weave his presence into almost any event that would provide a moral or add to his stature. He could exaggerate, transmuting the mundane into the dramatic—his broken shoulders became more crippled with each edition [29]—and he could move with the times, as he did when he excised the more obsequious passages from the original version of his

27. The 1858 edition was apparently rewritten by Samuel A. Eliot. The previous year Eliot, who had served in the House of Representatives in 1850–51, and who refused to become an abolitionist although he continued to oppose slavery, had retired to Cambridge (his investments having gone sour) to live in genteel poverty.

28. For a detailed examination of the various later editions, and an extension of the present argument, see my introduction to the 1969 reprint edition of Henson's 1881 autobiography as one of Winks, *Four Fugitive Slave Narratives* (Reading, Mass.).

29. His manumission papers, which he ultimately regained, refer only to his having stiff arms from an injury to the elbows. See Alvin McCurdy Collection: Brice Selby, March 9, 1829, copy.

life for later editions, struck entirely a passing reference to being arrested for debt, or added a chapter in 1851 on his exploits in returning to the South to help other fugitives to escape, a phase of his activities he had unaccountably forgotten in 1849.[30] He incorporated a pious refusal to participate in the Nat Turner rebellion into a later edition, although the rebellion actually took place after he had reached Canada West. He claimed that he personally had written his books, although in 1849 he had recorded that he learned to read "a little" and one of his abolitionist supporters noted that he could "barely write and cannot read."[31] In a post-Civil War edition of the autobiography he said he was a Captain in the Second Essex Company of Colored Volunteers, which he was not. Although his first wife died and he remarried, there was no second wife in the 1858 edition of his book. Perhaps the most important, and also the more subtle, of the changes lay in the title of the book itself. The new account was *Truth Stranger than Fiction: Father Henson's Story of His Own Life.* Thus he (or more properly, Eliot for him) invoked the spirit of Lord Byron, widely known to be the center of one of Mrs. Stowe's spiritual obsessions, for Byron had written in 1823 that "truth is always strange,/ Stranger than fiction." Throughout, he and his editors were consistent in seeing that his life was a great moral lesson, that original phraseology was embellished and twisted to make a homiletic statement clearer, and that his readers fed upon the thought of his acceptance by Queen Victoria, Lord John Russell, or President Rutherford B. Hayes. Still, Henson was true to his own lights, and he did resist becoming Uncle Tom at first, although in the end he succumbed to the pressures of financial need, the desire for prestige, and a fading memory.

It was not Henson who first or most persistently insisted that he was the original of Uncle Tom, and since he wrote none of the lives himself, one must find his ghostwriters as culpable as he in building the legend. In public lectures long after the Civil War, Henson repeatedly was introduced as Uncle Tom, but initially he appears to have been careful not to make the claim explicit himself:

30. See pp. 7, 67 from the 1849 (reprint) edition, for suppressed sentences; and the 1858 edition, pp. 150–64, for an added chapter in which Henson says that he delivered one hundred and eighteen slaves to freedom.

31. See Lawrence Papers: Lawrence to Hale, Nov. 7, 1850, and Jessie L. Beattie, *Black Moses, The Real Uncle Tom* (Montreal, 1957), p. 85. This unfortunate biography confuses more than it helps, for it mixes the several editions of Henson's narrative indiscriminately, accepts all that he says at face value, assumes that the 1849 account was not edited (p. ix) and later wrongly names an editor (p. 172), and at several points misreads or manufactures evidence and conversation. That Henson could write more than "a little" in fact, is shown by his letter of March 16, 1846, to George Ellis, Boston Unitarian, in the Lawrence Papers.

It has been spread abroad that " 'Uncle Tom' is coming," and that is what has brought you here. Now allow me to say that my name is not Tom, and never was Tom, and that I do not want to have any other name inserted in the newspapers for me than my own. My name is Josiah Henson, always was, and always will be. I never change my colours. (Loud laughter.) . . . You have read and heard some persons say that " 'Uncle Tom' was dead, and how can he be here? It is an imposition that is being practised on us." . . . Very well, I do not blame you for saying that. . . . A great many have come to me in this country and asked me if I was not dead. (Laughter.) Says I, "Dead?" Says he, "Yes, I heard you were dead, and read you were." "Well," says I; "I heard so too, but I never believed it yet." (Laughter.) "I thought in all probability I would have found it out as soon as anybody else."

Thus did Henson skirt the edges of truth, adding that all should realize that Mrs. Stowe was writing a novel, and concluding—with a deft change of subject—that if the audience would refer to chapters 34 through 57 of the *Key to Uncle Tom's Cabin,* "I think you will there see me." [32] The *Key* ran to only forty-nine chapters.

Others were less clever at avoiding the central question, or chose not to. In 1851 there appeared a slightly altered London and Edinburgh edition of Henson's narrative, together with a preface by Thomas Binney, Minister of the Weigh-House Chapel in London, where Henson made one of his most effective appeals for money. This edition was an abolitionist handbook as the 1849 version had not been, for it included an appendix on runaways in the Canadas, on specific fugitive slave cases, and an appeal for £ 2,000. The edition of 1858, printed in Boston, with Mrs. Stowe's rather flat preface replacing Binney's more impassioned one, followed. A "revised and enlarged" London edition was next, in 1877; it retained Mrs. Stowe's preface, added an introduction by George Sturge and Samuel Morley, English abolitionists, and carried a title page specifying that Henson was Uncle Tom.

The editions from 1877 were, in fact, almost entirely the work of John Lobb, youthful managing editor of London's weekly *Christian Age.* Lobb had been a religious journalist who knew how to attract an audience: when he took over the faltering *Age* in 1872, its circulation was five thousand, and in four years he raised the figure to eighty thousand. Morley and Sturge asked him to help solicit money for Henson, still in need of assistance at debt ridden Dawn, and in seven months Lobb attracted

32. *Dumfries and Galloway Standard,* April 25, 1877. I should like to thank the Ewart Public Library in Dumfries for supplying a photostat of the original report.

£ 3,000.[33] Together with Henson, he went to Windsor Castle to be received by Queen Victoria, who asked all of her domestic staff to come to meet "the real Uncle Tom." Adding an index and drawing from Henson the promise that Lobb's would be the "only authorized edition" of his life, the editor soon had sales moving up to ninety-six thousand. In 1877 Lobb also wrote—without Henson's assistance but drawing from his book—*The Young People's Illustrated Edition of "Uncle Tom's" Story of His Life,* which contained a preface by the Earl of Shaftesbury and "Uncle Tom's Address to the Young People of Great Britain," which Henson almost certainly did not dictate. Again, nowhere was Henson made to say specifically that he was Uncle Tom, although Lobb—outside conveniently manipulated quotation marks—did so for him. Lobb's narratives sold a quarter of a million copies and became a Sunday School favorite; but Henson seems to have received very little money from the enterprise and his estate certainly received none.[34]

Lobb thereupon left the *Christian Age* and set himself up as a publisher. After Henson's death he advertised the book as dealing with "Legree, who maimed Josiah Henson for Life," and with "Eva, who was saved from Drowning by Josiah Henson, &c.," [35] and he declared that the narrative had been translated into twelve languages.[36] At the turn of the century Lobb turned to spiritualism; he communed with seven hundred dead over three years, including Shakespeare, Lincoln, Gladstone, Shaftesbury—and Henson; for the restless Josiah, still insinuating himself into events, was "a frequent visitor at the seances." [37]

For Mrs. Stowe, Henson would stay no more dead than he did for Lobb, and she continued to be contradictory and evasive. In 1876, while Henson was on a lecture tour in Britain, the Reverend William H. Tilley, Rector of the Cronyn Memorial Church in London, Ontario, sought con-

---

33. On Lobb, see his edition of *Talks with the Dead: Illustrated with Spirit Photographs* (London, 1906), pp. xv–xx. The Royal Archives, Round Tower, Windsor Castle: Journal of Queen Victoria, confirms that she received Henson, his second wife, and Lobb, on March 5, 1877; and in her entry of March 4, she refers to reading the book. Henson claimed to have dined with Lord John Russell, and with the Archbishop of Canterbury. The official register in Lambeth Palace Library, London, does not include Henson's name—although this is not conclusive evidence that the visit did not take place, of course.

34. Fred Landon Collection: Jean Tallach and Landon exchange, July 7, 9, 15, 1935; LC, Carter G. Woodson Collection of Negro Papers, 5: sketch of Henson by Julia [sic] Tallach McKinley; Jean Tallach, "The Story of Rev. Josiah Henson," Kent Hist. Soc., *Papers and Records, 7* (1951), 43–53.

35. Lobb, *Talks with the Dead,* p. [118], advertisement (which was dropped from the 1907 edition of this book).

36. Of the alleged editions in translation, only four have been found.

37. Lobb, *Talks with the Dead,* p. 32.

firmation of Henson as Tom, possibly because of a brief association of Bishop Benjamin Cronyn with Henson earlier. Mrs. Stowe's reply of May 15 was made public, but it was seldom quoted in full, and time and again her letter was cited to prove that she had admitted the relationship. In fact, she was as unclear as usual, avoiding any direct identification:

> I take pleasure in indorsing, with all my heart, that noble man, Josiah Henson, who I believe to be worthy of all the aid and help which any good man may be disposed to give. It is also true that a sketch of his life . . . furnished me many of the finest conceptions and incidents of "Uncle Tom's" character—in particular the scene where he refused to free himself by the murder of a brutal master. . . . He once visited me in Andover, and personal intercourse confirmed the high esteem I had for him.

She did not say when the visit took place; but as we have seen, had the meeting been in Andover, it could not have been before she wrote her novel.[38] Nonetheless, in a special introduction to an 1881 London, Ontario edition of Henson's *Life,* Lobb asserted that Mrs. Stowe had "quite settle[d] the point," quoting a barely relevant extract from *The Times* in which she did nothing of the kind. Plagued by further inquiries, Mrs. Stowe wrote to the editor of the *Indianapolis News* in 1882 that Uncle Tom was "not the biography of any one man." She died in 1896 having left the incubus of Josiah still firmly upon Tom's back.[39]

But of what relation is Uncle Tom to the story of the Canadian Negro? [40] Precisely this: as Canadians came increasingly to assign Tom's rôle to Henson, as the myths of the North Star, the Underground Railroad, and the fugitives' haven "under the lion's paw" grew in the post-Civil War years, when these myths no longer could be tested, Canadians came increasingly to congratulate themselves upon their lack of prejudice and to contrast themselves favorably with the immoral and once slave-ridden United States. The true contrast was favorable enough, indeed; but that the greatest, the best-known, the most pious black fugitive of all time should have sought out Canadian soil for his resurrection bred a growing Canadian self-satisfaction with racial conditions above the forty-ninth parallel. If Uncle Tom came to Canada, could conditions need improving?

38. See *London* (Ont.) *Free Press,* Aug. 20, 1932, and *Windsor* (Ont.) *Daily Record,* June 18, 1877, on the Stowe-Tilley exchange.

39. Lobb, *Autobiography of the Rev. Josiah Henson,* 1881 edition, p. 13; *Indianapolis News,* July 27.

40. Nothing said here is meant to detract from the significance of *Uncle Tom's Cabin* itself, a work of creative if sentimental imagination emboldened by contact with an ugly reality. It stands as a considerable work of art, quite apart from any question of its sources.

No year has passed since the late 1860s without a stream of self-congratulatory Canadian newspaper accounts, editorials, and memoirs appearing in April or September of each year—on the anniversaries of the outbreak of the Civil War or of the passage of the Fugitive Slave Act—in which Henson has not been cited as sufficient and sole evidence to prove that Canadians shared none of the American racial virus, that in this one area, at least, the pressures of continentalism had been successfully resisted.[41] That Henson himself allegedly wrote that "in Canada, black children are despised"; that many Canadian Negroes had considered Henson self-serving and sly; that to Negroes "Uncle Tom" was becoming a pejorative term—all were ignored in the recurring annual flush of pride in the presence of "the real Uncle Tom's grave" on Canadian soil.[42]

In the end Henson too embraced the legend. In the year before his death he lectured in the Park Street Baptist Church in Hamilton; he was ninety-three and past caring, and for the first time he categorically assured his listeners that he was Uncle Tom, exhibited a picture Queen Victoria had given to him, and rambled on for two and a half hours, until he was led from the platform. In May 1883, when Josiah died, fifty wagons followed his hearse to the graveside, a Negro band from Chatham played, nine Negro preachers prayed, and his body was frozen in ice.[43]

Over the years, the link between Uncle Tom and Josiah Henson grew stronger, and whether thrust upon him by Mrs. Stowe's need or grasped by his own showmanship, to the general public the identification was complete. His cabin and grave became tourist attractions, and Dresden, the center of Ontario's most openly practiced color bar, advertised itself as the Home of Uncle Tom. The grave became the scene of Negro Masonic pilgrimages.

---

41. For examples of the forms the annual eulogies take, see the following, which are representative of dozens more: *Montreal Family Herald and Weekly Star,* Sept. 19, 1928; *Toronto Globe,* Jan. 19, 1935; *Montreal Star,* June 9, 1937; *Detroit Times,* May 1, 1958; Tannis Lee, "Uncle Tom's Cabin," *Imperial Oil Company Review, 13* (1952), 4–6; *Hamilton Review,* July 18, 1952; *The Canadian Woodman* (Oct. 1952), p. 2; *The Sentinel* (Dec. 1957), pp. 6–7; and Winifred Kincade, *The Torth: Ontario Monuments to Great Names* (Regina, Ont. [1962]), pp. 153–57.

42. Four scholars have previously questioned the association between Henson and Uncle Tom. In 1946 J. Winton Coleman, Jr., in "Mrs. Stowe, Kentucky, and Uncle Tom's Cabin," *Lincoln Herald, 48,* 6, presented a better case for Lewis Clarke, who escaped in 1841 and who did talk with Mrs. Stowe. In 1937 Fred Landon challenged the myth (*Montreal Star,* June 22), and in a 1947 review he noted that Henson "made little practical contribution to the welfare of his people" (*CHR, 28,* 440). William H. and Jane H. Pease, in "Uncle Tom and Clayton: Facts, Fiction, and Mystery," *OH, 50* (1958), 62, 68, found Henson "shrewdly devious" and a "mystery."

43. *Hamilton Times,* Jan. 13, 1882. On Victoria's picture, see New York Public Library, Schomburg Collection, abolition materials: no. 137, Henson MS.

Henson's house—for years used as a chicken coop—was opened as a museum in 1948, and the cemetery of The British-American Institute was restored by the Ontario Historic Sites Board, which gave the considerable force of its approval to the Henson saga by placing a plaque near the old home to honor the man "whose early life provided much of the material for . . . 'Uncle Tom's Cabin'." [44]

Henson thus became the best known of all Negro Canadians,[45] his narratives the most frequently used sources, his life the archetypical fugitive experience. Yet the problems his much-altered autobiography raise are as important as any they solve; indeed, because of the many changes he and others made, the events with which Henson more appropriately may be identified—the arrival of fugitive slaves, and the rise and decline of the Negro community movement in Canada—were rendered more than ordinarily unclear. In *Tales of Unrest* Joseph Conrad wrote that "The sustained invention of a really telling lie demands a talent which I do not possess"; Henson might well have said the same, for his history of the Dawn settlement was accurate enough to be accepted but is not accurate enough to trust. Perhaps most of the problems Henson left for us are no more important than the question of how badly, and in precisely what way, he was injured by his master; perhaps he did little more than Sir John Wentworth had done in his search for life's merit badges. But as the narrative of the quintessential Canadian Negro and the man most responsible for Dawn itself, his account—both as source and as a historical event that gave rise to a cluster of ideas about the position of the Negro in Canadian society—is important to the broader and more significant story of how a relatively well-conceived experiment could so signally fail.

Three men must be accorded primary responsibility for that failure: Henson, Hiram Wilson, and John Scoble. Unclear aims, poor management,

44. *Toronto Star,* June 28, 1930; *Toronto Globe,* July 5, 1930, April 28, 1946; *London* (Ont.) *Free Press,* Jan. 14, 1947; *Huron Church News* (Oct. 1959), pp. 8–9. On Henson's Masonic connections, see Fred Landon Collection: Alvin McCurdy to Landon, Feb. 26, 1950, and exchanges between Landon and Charles Fey. Efforts to interest the National Urban League of the United States, or the Association for the Study of Negro Life and History, in restoring the cemetery failed. See "Letters about 'Uncle Tom,'" *The Negro History Bulletin, 24* (1960), 64–65.

45. Even so, Henson has been unfortunate in his biographers. The only acceptable statement on Henson is B[enjamin] B[rawley], "Josiah Henson," *DAB, 8,* 564–65, together with an obituary in the *New York Daily Tribune,* May 6, 1883. The biographies, chief of which is Brion Gysin, *To Master—A Long Good Night: The Story of Uncle Tom, A Historical Narrative* (New York, 1946), are discussed in my *Four Fugitive Slave Narratives.* Most recently, see Gilbert Osofsky, ed., *Puttin' On Ole Massa* (New York, 1969), which refers to Henson in relation to fugitive slave accounts.

religious sectarianism, and black factionalism held Dawn back from the beginning; and the personalities and abilities of the men most charged with its success piled white alienation upon Negro disenchantment. Even Henson's charitable Boston Unitarians, always ready to put the best face upon his actions, found him "not very judicious" and, upon providing him with funds for his first English trip, warned him to be "square as a brick" in all matters.

This Henson was not. When he brought some polished boards to Boston to sell, as the first products of Dawn's sawmill, he accepted payment for them from Amos Lawrence and his friends without crediting the sale against the original loan extended by the same group; and he failed to answer repeated requests from them for a promised note acknowledging his continued indebtedness. At London's Crystal Palace Exhibition, to which he carried more black walnut boards, he took credit for this product of Dawn's industry, although the boards he displayed had been cut and polished by another Negro who had arrived recently from Oberlin, William P. Newman. Henson promised at least one religious group to accept no aid from members of any other faith and then promptly did so; and in London he apparently spoke in favor of emigration to the West Indies despite his denials when he returned to Canada West. During the Civil War he was not above inducing members of the Negro settlement to enlist in the Northern armies, contrary to the laws of the province; and for "safe-keeping" he retained the bounty money paid to the enlistees, which led to his arrest for violating the foreign enlistment laws and to ugly rumors that not all of the bounties reached their destinations.[46]

Still, Henson was a man of courage, energy, and imagination. In 1858, in reply to Charles L. Remond's militant suggestion that Southern slaves should resort to insurrection, he could rise before the Convention of Colored Citizens of Massachusetts, to cry out—over the opposition of the convention as a whole—that "As he didn't want to see three or four thousand men hung before their time, he should oppose any such action, head, neck and shoulders." He was a man who could help sell property on which Dawn's gristmill stood and then, in the middle of the night, dismantle the mill and rebuild it elsewhere. William King, leader of the only relatively successful communal experiment among Negroes in Canada, would write many years later that "Henson was more than a match for

46. MHS, Amasa Walker Papers: Wilson to Walker, Jan. 15, 1848; MHS, Edward Everett Papers: Wilson et al. to Everett, July 3, 1843; Lawrence Papers: Lawrence to Henson, Feb. 6, 1849; Oberlin College, Misc. Corres.: Wilson to Hamilton Hill, April 25, 1843, Jan. 6, 1849; Rhodes House, Anti-Slavery Papers, C 23/26: Wilson to Scoble, Feb. 24, 1852; *African Repository and Colonial Journal, 27* (1851), passim; *Salem* (Ohio) *Anti-Slavery Bugle,* Oct. 4, 1851; *The Liberator,* March 1, 1850, Oct. 10, Aug. 13, 1858.

anyone that ever tried to curb his authority, or to call him to an account. . . . We got the money, said Henson, with directions to spend it according to the best of our Judgment. We have spent it according to our Judgment, and that is an end to the matter." Complex, devious, and ever watchful, Henson was not a man to be bested; but neither was he the person to provide stable leadership for an "oppressed and denationalized people." [47]

Nor was Hiram Wilson such a leader. An able organizer when on his own, he worked badly as a member of a team, and he too was careless of finances, devious in his approaches to possible contributors to the cause, and given to self-praise. He was able to come down squarely on both sides of the burning questions of the day—claiming to oppose the system of "begging ministers" who went from house to house soliciting funds while doing much the same himself; able to write to William Lloyd Garrison in tones of praise while taking an anti-Garrisonian stand with others; and willing to court Edmund Quincy, an editor of *The Liberator* in Garrison's absence who considered Henson "a time-serving sycophant," while continuing to support Henson at Dawn. He also could engage in a sustained feud with other missionaries, most notably Reverend Isaac Rice—an encounter that revealed the character and preoccupations of both men.

Rice was a strange, distant, and often pathetic figure who found himself in competition with Wilson for the tiny supply of money, food, clothing, and books which friends of the fugitives sent to "the great gate of Freedom" at Amherstburg and Windsor. Having given up a comfortable Presbyterian church in Ohio in 1838, from which he arrived on the Detroit frontier as destitute himself as his future charges would be, Rice had written to a variety of antislavery groups in the United States for support. It was Rice who first realized that freight charges and duties on the gift parcels would prove to be greater than their worth; and it was he who first wrote to the Governor General to ask, unsuccessfully, for remission of the duties—a boon never formally granted, but one which was allowed in practice by customs officials along the frontier from 1844, after Wilson added his voice to the request.

Rice was unsystematic, unbusinesslike, an "amalgamationist," and a Garrisonian. Wilson knew that the minister—tattered, ill, with hollow eyes and rotting teeth, and often reflecting the intense religious introspection

47. Lawrence Papers: Eliot Lawrence, H. Ingersoll Bowditch, May 31, 1849, April 12, 1850 agreements; Lawrence to Scoble, March 30, 1851, May 7, and reply, June 25, 1853; Lawrence to Samuel Morley, Nov. 30, 1852; [Eliot] to Lawrence, Dec. 21, 1852, May 5, 1843; Lawrence to Abbott Lawrence, March 7, n.d., and to Roaf, June 20, 1853; MHS, Edmund Quincy Papers: Quincy to Elizabeth Neall Gay, Nov. 2, 1851; Fred Landon Collection: King to James Cleland Hamilton [spring, 1889], and Anne Straith Jamieson to Landon, July 1, 1931.

which led him to move from the American Missionary Association to the Free Will Baptists—was not welcome in many homes in Canada West. Rice held himself apart; built a receiving and sick room onto his shack on a back street in the Negro section of Amherstburg; often refused to reply to the frequent questionnaires that arrived from antislavery societies in Britain and the United States, asking about the condition of the fugitives and whether money was needed; and was short when he did reply (money was always needed, Rice would retort). Cholera, madness, and poverty engulfed him, and he and other teachers were tired of "talking themselves down to the grave for want of books" while abolitionists debated whether to supply materials published by one tract society as opposed to another. In short, Rice was maddeningly tactless and inconsistent, for his disregard for religious labels was contrary to his own religious enthusiasms, and his willingness to accept help from any source contradicted his extremist views on slavery.

Wilson enjoyed being unctuous and was good at it, and he probably felt that Rice was hurting the larger cause in much the same way as Henson did. When Rice broke with his wife, Wilson—who was loyal to his marriage until his wife's death—was scandalized; when Rice chose to be baptized by Negroes rather than by white Baptists, and then failed to choose Wilson's friend, Anthony Binga, the elder of Amherstburg's black Baptists, Wilson was angry. When Rice chartered a steamer and took sixty Negroes with him to Chatham (presumably paying for the trip from mission funds) in order that he might be baptized in the muddy Thames, Wilson broke with him completely. He passed along rumors that Rice had taken an adulterer into his home and was permitting drunkenness *"and other* abominations" (by which he meant free love) in the mission station; whereupon Rice counterattacked, charging Wilson with a calculated plot to destroy confidence in his work, revealing that unnamed Americans had offered a band of blacks $4,000 to displace him, and organizing a new relief board with himself as Secretary and one Nelson Brown as President, and with the alleged adulterer, Wilson Jones, in a responsible position. This board appointed two "beseeching agents," established committees of information in Colchester, Anderdon, and Sandwich—which Wilson regarded as his preserve—and added fuel to the growing controversy over the "begging system." This feud ended only when Rice abandoned the field in 1853, leaving British North America in a cloud of debt.[48]

48. The record on Wilson and, in particular, on Rice is not clear. The following account is based upon *Amherstburg Quarterly Mission Journal, 1* (1852), Aug. 25, Sept. 13, Oct. 1, 3, 12, 17, 23, 29, Dec. 1, 16; Fisk University, Nashville, American Missionary Association (hereafter AMA) Archives: Rice to Tappan, July 14, 1848,

Wilson drew a larger feud to Dawn itself, however. He visited England during the World Anti-Slavery Convention of 1843, touring provincial towns to raise funds; and the British and Foreign Anti-Slavery Society supported him in this work. In 1840–41, as the British anti-slavery movement had fragmented along lines analogous to the American movement, this Society had become identified with an anti-Garrisonian stance; and through its *Anti-Slavery Reporter* it attacked those it regarded as extremists, women who wished to participate in the movement on a basis of equality with men, and those British societies—in Bristol, Leeds, Manchester, Edinburgh, Glasgow, and Dublin—which seceded in order to remain true to Garrisonian principles. Wilson thus became identified as an anti-Garrisonian despite his efforts to keep his fences mended, a position he shared with Henson, but one which many residents at Dawn appear to have opposed.[49]

This opposition was led by a Negro Baptist preacher, William P. Newman, the same Newman who was in charge of the sawmill at Dawn, and the man who later would advocate emigration to Jamaica.[50] Newman had arrived early in 1845, and he soon became Secretary of The British-American Institute's Executive Committee. After an examination of the records, he asked Henson to return from one of his eastern trips to discuss some missing funds. Henson and Wilson defended themselves in a public meeting, and the Executive Committee refused to chastise Henson, although he

---

Wilson to George Whipple, July 4, 1850, Tappan to Whipple, Jan. 24, 1848, March 29, 1852, David Hotchkiss to Whipple, Dec. 14, 1850, Feb. 28, 1852; *Oberlin Evangelist:* 6 (1844), 5, 172–73, 187; 7 (1845), 39, 70, 78–79, 143, 179–80, 191; 8 (1846), 86; *10* (1848), 167; *14* (1852), 123; *15* (1853), 29; *Voice of the Fugitive,* 1851–52, passim; *North Star,* Sept. 27, 1843; *The Liberator,* March 1, 1850; LC, Tappan Papers, 4: Tappan to Rice, April 8, 1843; PAC, G 20, *410:* Rice to Metcalfe, July 3, 24, 1844; Weston Papers: Lewis Hayden to Maria W. Chapman, May 14, 1846; Windsor Registry Office: list of property holders, Marble Village, Anderdon, 1856; Levi Coffin, *Reminiscences,* 2nd ed. (Cincinnati, 1880), pp. 249–50; Harvard University, Houghton Library, Charles Sumner Papers, Autographs, *3:* Wilson, Oct. 22, 1850; MHS: Thomas Wentworth Higginson Papers: Frederick W. Sanborn to Higginson, June 4, 1859.

49. On the split within the British antislavery movement and its reflections in the United States, see Howard R. Temperley, "The British and Foreign Anti-Slavery Society, 1839–1868" (Ph.D. diss., Yale Univ., 1960); C. Duncan Rice, "The Anti-Slavery Mission of George Thompson to the United States, 1834–1835," *Journal of American Studies,* 2 (1968), 13–31; Alma Lutz, *Crusade for Freedom: Women of the Antislavery Movement* (Boston, 1968); and Gilbert Hobbs Barnes, *The Anti-Slavery Impulse, 1830–1844* (Washington, 1933).

50. Beattie, *Black Moses,* pp. 174, 200; J. F. Johnson, *Proceedings of the General Anti-Slavery Convention, Called by the Committee of the British and Foreign Anti-Slavery Society, and held in London . . . 1843* (London, [1843]), p. 287; Murray, "Anglo-American Anti-Slavery Movement," p. xxiii.

did not account for the funds he had collected. Newman then charged that the good Uncle Tom had threatened to cut his throat, and he resigned to return to Ohio. The following year, at a Negro convention in Drummonds-ville, Newman's chief complaint was sustained. Henson suffered close questioning and the delegates appointed a committee—which they had no authority to do—to audit the Institute's books, on the grounds that Dawn belonged to "the People of Colour in Canada generally."

From Ohio Newman kept up the attack on Dawn's leadership. He suggested that Negroes disliked Wilson—producing a rebuttal from the Third Annual Conference of the True Wesleyan Connexion of Canada, a black organization conveniently chaired by Henson. Newman thereupon turned to Frederick Douglass's *North Star* to denounce Henson and Wilson. For whatever reason, Wilson resigned from Dawn, declaiming his desire to "suffer, if need be [rather] than to make a noise about my humble ser-vices"; and in 1849 he opened a new haven for fugitives in St. Catharines, from which vantage point he and his second wife carried on a running battle with Rice and Newman.

Dawn was now openly compromised in its leadership. Money had ceased to flow in from Britain, partially because of the famine in Ireland, and Canadians were reluctant to give support to a colony so obviously strife-ridden. Fuller had died, and Tappan—who was now listening to Rice—would no longer channel funds from the United States. The best hope lay in new sponsorship. Two of the trustees gave public notice that they would not be responsible for the Institute's debts, and the trustees put Henson in charge of the sawmill and some forested land with instruc-tions to use both so that Dawn's indebtedness might be paid off within four years. They then placed the school and the remainder of the land under the American Baptist Free Mission Society.[51]

Newman opposed this move and the Free Mission Society; and when he left for Britain in 1850—ostensibly to raise funds—the Mission Society's members believed that he hoped to bring back sufficient money from the British and Foreign Anti-Slavery Society to take over the Institute once again. Since the Mission Society took a Garrisonian line, such an event was to be deplored. Nominally, the Baptist's leader at Dawn was Reverend Samuel H. Davis, but Newman now returned as a Baptist missionary, and

51. Univ. of Michigan, William L. Clements Library, James G. Birney Papers: Wilson to Birney, Sept. 3, 1845; Anti-Slavery Papers, C23/34: Wilson to Scoble, Aug. 6, 1845, Roaf to Scoble, Dec. 31, 1851; Oberlin College, Misc. Corres.: Wilson to Hill, Jan. 6, 1839, June 12, 1845; *Gerrit Smith Calendar, 2,* 139: Scoble to Smith, Oct. 30, 1852; *Voice of the Fugitive,* Dec. 16, 1852; *Anti-Slavery Reporter,* n.s., 7 (1852), 1–4; *Report of the Convention of the Coloured Population, Held at Drum-mondsville, Aug., 1847* (Toronto, 1847), passim; John Scoble, *Uncle Tom's Cabin Almanac or Abolition Momento* (London, 1853), passim.

in Henson's absence he called a meeting in Chatham at which those present passed a number of resolutions—duly published in Garrison's *Liberator*—against Henson's mission. When Henson reached London, he found handbills that had preceded him denouncing him as an "imposter" and an investigating committee of the BFA-SS ready to insist that all monies he collected should pass through an agent appointed by the Society: the Secretary, John Scoble. The American Baptists sent Reverend Edward Mathews scurrying to London as a one-man truth squad, to make known the resolutions brought forth by Newman's meeting, and Mathews widely circulated a pamphlet allegedly containing these statements. The BFA-SS's committee asked both Mathews and Henson to appear before it; and when questioned, the former admitted that the Chatham meeting was not made up of Negroes from Dawn and, more damagingly, that he had forged the most condemnatory resolution himself for insertion in his pamphlet. The British society thereupon decided to support Henson and to send Scoble to Dawn to investigate conditions there prior to deciding how best to help the maligned colony.

The result of Henson's visit, and the conniving of Newman and Mathews, was to bring Scoble to Canada West as resident superintendent of Dawn and to intensify the quarrel with the more extreme abolitionists. In the fall of 1851 Scoble visited the community and called a public meeting, at which John Roaf presided. Mathews accused Scoble of trying to take the Institute away from the American Baptists to serve the British society's own purposes; and Mary Estlin, the Garrisonian who led the Bristol and Clifton Ladies' Anti-Slavery Society, detected a plot by Henson and Lewis Tappan to enthrone the moderate views of the anti-Garrisonians at Dawn. Samuel J. May, Jr., a colleague of Garrison's, wrote to Sydney Howard Gay, editor of the *National Anti-Slavery Standard,* that Scoble was a crafty villain who would not be worth £ 120 on a Richmond auction block, and he promised to supply documents to support Mathews' contentions— documents which he later had to say Garrison had lost. In the meantime, Scoble returned to London to report, decided to move to Canada West, and late in 1852 came to Dawn once again, now backed by warm testimonials from the BFA-SS. With Henson's help, Scoble gained the support of some of the Institute's trustees, including Roaf, ousted the Baptist Free Mission group, ordered Newman out of Dawn, and placed the school under the same management as the settlement once again.[52]

52. BPL, Garrison Papers, *16:* Wilson to Garrison, April 6, 1846; BPL, Weston Papers: Frances H. Drake to Maria W. Chapman, Oct. 31, 1843; [Emma Michell] to [same], Aug. 30, 1852; John B. Estlin to [Caroline] Weston, Dec. 29, 1851, March 20, and to Chapman, April 3, 1852; Mathews to [Mary A.] Estlin, April 30, 1852; same to [Caroline Weston], May 16, 1857; BPL, Samuel May, Jr. Papers: May to John B.

Scoble enjoyed a short honeymoon. The *Globe,* British and American newspapers, and even some of the local conservative press—which had opposed Dawn earlier—praised him, and Henson worked closely with him. Scoble would remain at Dawn for over fifteen years, well beyond the effective life of the community itself.

For Scoble plunged Dawn into even greater and more far-reaching controversies. He inherited the old ones: several of the trustees refused to recognize his authority, the *Liberator* continued its attacks, and the local and black-owned *Provincial Freeman,* committed to Garrisonianism, amalgamation, and the Free Mission group, remained unconverted. Scoble also created new controversies: taking to himself the best house, one well-separated from the black residents, and (according to Henson) the best livestock and equipment as well, Scoble dabbled in scientific farming. Aloof, cantankerous, and in an habitual stance of anger, he alienated members of the Canadian Anti-Slavery Society in Toronto, allowed the "begging system" to continue, and sold timber for his own profit. Rumor had it that Scoble had refused to have his portrait painted while seated next to a Negro at the Anti-Slavery Convention of 1840 in London, and whether this report was true or not—as it apparently was [53]—Scoble quickly showed himself to be a white liberal of the most paternalistic sort, who could not tolerate sharing responsibility with black men. By 1854 those who had opposed Henson refocused their attention on Scoble, and four times before 1861 he would be publicly censured for mismanagement, charged with "ignorance of the usages of this country, . . . pomp and pride of deportment, and . . . [a] petulant and over-bearing spirit." When Scoble at last rose to defend himself, he launched a scurrilous attack against all blacks in such terms as to confirm the widely circulated rumors.[54]

After 1854, therefore, Dawn descended into a quagmire of quarrels so intense as to obscure once again the entire idea of a self-contained Negro community. One of the trustees, James C. Brown, called a public meeting

---

Estlin, May 2, 1848; Columbia Univ., Sydney Howard Gay Papers: Tappan to Gay, Nov. 3, 1851, May to Gay, March 28, April 24 [1853]; *The Liberator,* July 2, 1852; *Minutes and Proceedings of the General Convention, for the Improvement of the Colored Inhabitants of Canada, Held by Adjournments in Amherstburgh, C.W., June 16th and 17th, 1853* (Windsor, 1853), pp. 2–19; Pease and Pease, *Black Utopia,* p. 178, n. 27.

53. Tom Taylor, ed., *Life of Benjamin Robert Haydon, Historical Painter . . .* (London, 1853), *3,* 143–44. The painting hangs in the National Portrait Gallery, London. It shows Scoble seated next to Henry Beckford, an emancipated slave from Jamaica. See BM, Clarkson Papers, Add. MSS 41267A: Benjamin Robert Haydon to Clarkson, July 11, 1840, 214–15; and Willard Bissell Pope, ed., *The Diary of Benjamin Robert Haydon, 4* (Cambridge, Mass., 1963), 644.

54. For these and subsequent developments, with accompanying documentation omitted here, see Murray, "Anglo-American Anti-Slavery Movement," pp. 88–97, 458–76.

in August 1855, from which came a court case directed against Scoble. He, in turn, was defeated in an effort to obtain provincial incorporation of the Institute, ostensibly in order to upgrade the school associated with it but actually to gain the force of provincial approval for a Declaration of Trust—the document under which he had assumed his rôle with the permission of but a portion of the original trustees at Dawn. The *Provincial Freeman,* which had hounded Henson under the editorship of Mary Ann Shadd (or Shad), a black Quaker-educated former school teacher,[55] passed to the editorship of William P. Newman in 1855 and moved to Chatham, where it redoubled its efforts. When Scoble wrote to the new Secretary of his old organization, Louis Alexis Chamerovzow, he found that the British and Foreign Anti-Slavery Society now refused to countenance any other schemes for resettling fugitives. Scoble sued Henson—still the figurehead for Dawn—for payment on a personal loan (leading Henson to strike all reference to Scoble from post-1858 editions of his autobiography);[56] and in 1861 Scoble undertook a suit in chancery against Henson over eighty acres of land, a suit he was unwise enough to win.[57] The Scoble-Henson rift was irreparable, both reputations were beyond recovery among their respective clienteles, and Dawn was a shambles.

The rest of the sorry story of Dawn need not be recited in any detail. Henson, Wilson, and Scoble had led badly. Newman, Shadd, Brown, and the Garrisonians had mounted repeated attacks which would have required men of unusual ability, tact, and honesty to meet. Scoble angered local whites as well by plunging into politics in 1857, and when he ran—without success—for the Legislative Council in 1859 and in 1861, he lay himself open to the charge of using Negro votes to gain his end just when white fears about such bloc voting were at their height. He accused the Baptist Free Mission members of theft, alienating Baptist support throughout the province, while Henson already had alienated most Congregationalists. In 1868, in the midst of new scandals, Scoble severed his connection with the depleted Dawn although Henson remained; and the Institute closed, selling its land, the proceedings being used four years later to endow the Wilberforce Educational Institute for black and white children in Chatham.

The immediate significance of Dawn, apart from the mythical qualities attaching themselves to the figure of Uncle Tom, lay in its ignominious

55. The record on Mary Ann Shadd is unclear, and the only sketch of her contains several errors or contradictions of other evidence: the essay by S. C. Evans in Hallie Q. Brown, ed., *Homespun Heroines and Other Women of Distinction* (Xenia, Ohio, 1926), pp. 92–96.

56. Henson last mentioned Scoble on pages 183, 185, of his 1858 edition.

57. The question of the court cases is extremely confused: see Lauriston, *Romantic Kent,* pp. 234–38; Murray, "Anglo-American Anti-Slavery Movement," pp. 474–75; and Pease and Pease, "Uncle Tom and Clayton," p. 67.

and public failure. The Secretary of the Canadian Anti-Slavery Society, Thomas Henning, was driven to conclude that "a few escaped slaves" could not be expected to take "wild land in a remote and unsettled part of the country" and turn it into a community with all the Burkean nuance property-holding implied. Benjamin Drew, who visited Dawn in 1854, and who was predisposed toward finding success, piety, and an attractive family life amongst the fugitives he interviewed, confessed that Scoble's settlement left "an unfavorable and melancholy impression." Turning his argument, in part, upon Dawn, Samuel Gridley Howe would conclude in 1864—after visiting Canada West on behalf of the Freedmen's Enquiry Commission—that self-segregated communities were unwise since they prolonged dependence: "Taken as a whole, the colonists have cost to somebody a great deal of money, and a great deal of effort; and they have not succeeded so well as many who have been thrown entirely upon their own resources." Certainly Dawn's failure deepened the white distrust of the fugitives in their midst and added to the burden of prejudice that all Negroes in Canada West had to bear.[58] William Wells Brown, himself a fugitive slave and admittedly—as an immigration agent for Haiti and the victim of an earlier slander by Scoble—a biased observer, passed harsh but sound judgment upon Dawn: "No place in the Western Province has excited more interest, or received a greater share of substantial aid, than this Association, and no place has proved itself less deserving." [59]

In truth, one enterprise was less deserving—The Refugee Home Society.[60] This body ultimately arose from a Negro convention held in Windsor in 1846. Isaac Rice and a black Methodist preacher, T. Willis, organized the gathering with support from Lewis Tappan, Hamilton Hill (a friend of Hiram Wilson's at Oberlin College), and philanthropists in Detroit. The convention selected a large tract of land north of Amherstburg, some of it already held by Negroes, which might be purchased for $1.50 an acre,

58. Anti-Slavery Papers, C32/38A: Henning to Chamerovzow, Jan. 17, April 19, 1856; *Anti-Slavery Reporter*, n.s., *4* (1856), 110–13, 124–38; Pease and Pease, *Black Utopia*, pp. 80–81, 178–79; Drew, *North-Side View of Slavery*, p. 312; Samuel Gridley Howe (actually written in large measure by James McKaye), *The Refugees from Slavery in Canada West: Report to the Freedmen's Inquiry Commission* (Boston, 1864), pp. 69–70; William Wemyss Anderson and John Scoble, *Canada and Jamaica: Two Addresses* (New York, 1851), p. 16; Farrison, *William Wells Brown*, p. 347. A general search of Howe papers in a variety of depositories revealed no personal manuscript material relating to his visits to Canada.
59. *Pine and Palm*, Oct. 19, 1861.
60. The Refugee Home Society is discussed in Pease and Pease, *Black Utopia*, pp. 109–22, 183–84, and Murray, "Anglo-American Anti-Slavery Movement," pp. 406–57. I have independently examined most of the evidence they cite, and here will give only documentation for direct quotations or for material not contained in these treatments.

and launched the Sandwich Mission. By 1851 Willis, acting for the Mission, had purchased two thousand acres and had reserved land for a church and school. An elective board of overseers was to assist a board of trustees, appointed by the white backers from Michigan; liquor was forbidden within the Mission, and no one was to bring court action against a settler without first submitting his dispute to the trustees for arbitration, so that community disputes might not be aired in public.

But the new dream did not flourish either. The scheme grew grandiose: in November of 1850 a new convention, meeting at Sandwich, proposed the purchase of thirty thousand additional acres for resale in order to make the community self-perpetuating, with two-thirds of the income from such sales to be invested in more land. The leadership was weak and distracted: Josiah Henson was President, Rice was ill, and Wilson was warning his friend Hill off the enterprise. In any event, the Sandwich project was swallowed up in a larger one in 1852.

The genesis of the new organization, to be called The Refugee Home Society, is not entirely clear. A body of that name was formed in Michigan in 1851, largely from the backers of the earlier proposal. At the same time, the Sandwich convention group took a new title, the Fugitives' Union Society. The two bodies united in 1852 under the former rubric. Authority now fell to Detroit, and a Congregational minister, Reverend H. D. Kitchell. The local American Missionary Association agent in Amherstburg, David Hotchkiss (who privately despised blacks), and Negroes Henry and Mary Bibb,[61] were given local leadership. The Society elected three different sets of officers within two years; when a much-delayed constitution appeared, it proposed the purchase of fifty-thousand additional acres of land, each family to receive twenty-five acres; and farmland was to be accompanied with town lots. Within three years the Society purchased some two thousand acres and resold half, and one hundred and fifty Negroes moved onto the land, although not always contiguously, thus destroying any semblance of a true community. In 1858 one of the Detroit members, Horace Hallock, the Society's Treasurer,[62] would sell it an additional two hundred and ninety acres along the Puce River, where other blacks already had settled.[63]

61. On Bibb, see Fred Landon, "Henry Bibb, A Colonizer," *JNH*, 5 (1920), 437–47, and *Narrative of the Life and Adventures of Henry Bibb, an American Slave, Written by Himself* . . . , 3rd ed. (New York, 1849).

62. This is the person Dwight Lowell Dumond calls Harvard Hallock in his *Antislavery: The Crusade for Freedom in America* (Norton Library ed., New York, 1966), p. 410, n. 20. This work contains a chapter on the Fugitives in Canada West (pp. 335–42), based on relatively little original research. With respect to British North America, at least, the volume is marred by minor errors, misconceptions, and simplistic readings, and therefore is not cited elsewhere here.

63. Windsor Registry Office: plan for lot 7, Refugee's [*sic*] Home Society, 1853, list

The Society was destroyed by factionalism. In 1854 many Negroes were angered by an increase in surveying charges—for a survey which they understood already had been made—and by a reduction of the period for improving their land. James Theodore Holly, who had spoken on behalf of the Society, now gave his support to Haitian colonization. Mary Ann Shadd reported in the *Provincial Freeman,* in which she opposed all such communal experiments because that retarded the goal of integration, that the settlers would never receive deeds to the land, and rumors suggested that the price soon would be raised. Only refugees were accepted, eliminating those free Negroes who brought some capital with them; and as residents understandably failed to meet their payments, the Society unwisely brought suit against them, ignoring its own provisions for arbitration. When the settlers won, the Society's shaky finances were thrown into chaos. At the same time Mary Shadd's open hostility toward Henry Bibb—now the editor of a competing Negro paper, the *Voice of the Fugitive,* designated the official organ of the Society—as well as equally vocal opposition from the American Baptist Free Mission Society, just ousted from Dawn, opened the way for the public scandals the original trustees had tried to avoid. Although the white press—and especially the *Kent Advertiser* and *Planet,* of Chatham, the *Windsor Herald,* the *Toronto Leader,* and the *Hamilton Spectator,* all consistently anti-Negro—did not pillory the settlement, as it had Wilberforce and Dawn, the two feuding Negro newspapers would now reveal all.

The nature of the dissonance among the Negro voices in Canada West became most apparent in this dispute over The Refugee Home Society. Two issues were at the center of the controversy. All of the Negro communitarian experiments were based upon white philanthropy and, in order to sustain them, upon sending into the provinces, the United States, and abroad agents who would solicit funds and gather up old clothing. Few could do so with dignity, and most resorted to simple begging at church and antislavery society meetings and from house to house. Mary Ann Shadd, Samuel Ringgold Ward—briefly the nominal editor of the *Provincial Freeman*—Peter Payntz, President of Windsor's new Anti-Slavery Society, and others of their thinking resented the implication that the fugitive slave could not make his own way. Ward opposed "exclusive settlements" and Negro churches, arguing that the "population must of necessity become more or less mixed" so that whites might come to know "enlightened progressive coloured people." Miss Shadd, who had

of burials, list of lots sold by Hallock; *Amherstburg Quarterly Mission Journal, 1* (1852): Aug. 25, Oct. 17, 20, 23, Dec. 8; Birney Papers: Rice, et al., to Birney, July 16, 1846; *Report of the Refugees' Home Society, Held at Farmington, Mich. 29 Jan. 1852 . . . and . . . in Detroit, Michigan, Aug 25, 1852 . . .* (Windsor, 1852); *Anti-Slavery Reporter,* n.s., *6* (1851), 201–02.

broken with all institutional religions because she felt churches were segregationist, resented any evidence of dependency upon whites, denounced begging in all its forms as "materially compromising our manhood, by representing us as objects of charity," and attacked The Refugee Home Society in particular since its trustees were white, its financial base lay in Michigan, its local Negro spokesman, Bibb, was a mulatto, and a white man, Reverend Charles C. Foote, was its principal almoner and agent.[64]

The Shadd faction was quite correct in its assessment of the Home Society's begging system: numerous abuses could arise. The Society's agents took a twenty percent commission on the money they begged, and Foote allowed himself twenty-five percent; the land obtained with the remaining money was not given outright to the Negro settlers, each receiving five acres free only on the condition of purchasing twenty more. The price was no lower, and in some cases higher, than the government price for comparable land. On this evidence, Mary Shadd charged all of the agents with malfeasance. Bibb, she concluded, was the tool of Detroit whites who were mulcting the fugitives, men deliberately chosen from the more ignorant levels of the refugees so that they would ask no questions.

They did ask questions, however; and in the welter of accusation and counteraccusation that followed, the truth cannot be recaptured. A Windsor-based white, Alexander McArthur, wrote to the nondenominational American Missionary Association to defend the Shadd faction in its view that Bibb and his second wife, whom he claimed the fugitives did not trust, were to blame for the Society's slow progress; but McArthur's testimony was suspect, since Hiram Wilson—who was Bibb's friend—had persuaded the AMA not to appoint McArthur as an agent. McArthur remained to become the local representative of the Missionary Society of the Illinois Conference of the Methodist Church. Bibb, in turn, revealed that Miss Shadd, who was running a small school in Windsor, had been accepting money for this purpose from the American Missionary Association, despite her own public position against cooperation with formal groups and white men, and the Association thereupon cut her off. While Bibb turned against begging, it was too late to change the Home Society, for he died in August of 1854, placing Reverend Foote—who had been

64. Ward, *Autobiography of a Fugitive Negro: His Anti-Slavery Labours in the United States, Canada & England* (London, 1855), pp. 126–43, 163, 205, 218, 227–28; *Canadian Free Press*, Sept. 9, 1852; Drew, *North-Side View of Slavery*, pp. 323–28; *The Liberator*, Nov. 5, 1852; AMA Archives: McArthur to Whipple, July 2 (with clipping), Dec. 22, and Mary Shadd to Whipple, Dec. 28, 1852. On Ward, see F[red] L[andon], "Samuel Ringgold Ward," *DAB*, 19 (1936), 440; and Vincent Harding's foreword to the 1970 Ebony Classics edition (Chicago), pp. v–ix.

warring upon Isaac Rice until the latter's retirement from the scene—
in the ascendancy. Foote sought out more funds from the American Missionary Association, with which he opened schools for fugitives at Puce
and Little rivers and in Chatham. Thereafter the activities—although not
the land—of the Home Society were merged with those of the AMA.
In the meantime, white residents of Windsor blocked an attempt by Bibb's
formal successor, the head of the Colored Vigilance Committee of Detroit,
George de Baptiste (also a mulatto, and caterer to Detroit's exclusive
Boat Club), to purchase town lots for the settlers. In 1861 some sixty
families were living on land acquired through the Society, but the Civil
War marked an end to this: the Little and Puce river groups migrated to
Geffrard's Haiti in October, Foote returned to Michigan, and the AMA
withdrew its support. In its annual report for 1860, the Society admitted
that all was not well—an understatement, since this ill-conceived and
badly run effort to aid Negro settlers failed as ignominiously as its predecessors.[65]

At the same time The Refugee Home Society was finding that some
clouds have no silver linings, a fourth and, as it would prove, last effort
to found an organized Negro communal experiment was begun near
Chatham by a vigorous Presbyterian, William King. This settlement, which
King named after the reigning Governor General, Lord Elgin, would
demonstrate that with proper leadership, some good luck, a persistent
willingness to dodge obstacles, including those of one's own creation, and
hard work, an all-black village could achieve a substantial degree of
stability. For if Elgin, and King's coterminous Buxton Mission, were not
the "perfect success" that their founder judged them to be, they nonetheless erased some of the bad image left by Wilberforce, Dawn, and The
Refugee Home Society.[66]

65. *The Liberator,* Oct. 15, 1853; *Frederick Douglass' Paper,* May 20, 1853, Aug.
11, Nov. 17, 1854, Jan. 26, 1855; *Anti-Slavery Reporter,* n.s., 9 (1861), 18–19; C. M.
Burton, *The City of Detroit, Michigan, 1701–1922* (Detroit, 1922), *1,* 478–83; Burton
Hist. Coll., Scrap Book 5, p. 163.
66. Of all the communal Negro settlements in Canada West, Elgin is the best
known, and its story has been told on several occasions. The account in Pease and
Pease, *Black Utopia,* pp. 84–108, 179–83, is nearly impeccable, and I have followed
it, together with the *Third, Fourth, Sixth* through *Eighth,* and *Tenth and Eleventh
Annual Reports of the Elgin Association* (issued annually in Toronto, the year following the report's date). The Peases' documentation is full and readers are directed
to it, the notes that follow here being limited, for the most part, to sources they do
not cite or to references for data they do not use. Other secondary accounts include
J. Cleland Hamilton, "The African in Canada: The Rev. William King and the
Elgin Association," *Knox College Monthly, 12* (1889), 30–37, which was the first
semischolarly article on Buxton; W. N. Sexsmith, "Some Notes on the Buxton Settle-

Born in County Londonderry, Ireland, in 1812, King had both a sound classical and a wide practical education. He had attended the University of Glasgow, had been rector of a select academy in Louisiana—where he had married the daughter of a local plantation owner and had purchased slaves as house servants—and had then become superintendent of the preparatory division of a college. When he returned to Scotland to study theology at Edinburgh, he worked in one of the city's worst slums, as what another generation would call a welfare officer. He suffered much adversity—his son, his wife, and his daughter all died—and he turned to missionary work for the Free Presbyterian Church, going to Canada West in 1846.[67]

Having inherited his wife's property, King now decided to free his slaves, fourteen in number, and to bring them to Canada as the nucleus for a colony. He had felt unhappy because of his ownership of human property, even though his church did not view slave-holding in itself as sinful, and so he asked the Toronto Synod for permission to return to Louisiana to settle his affairs, having to confess, as he had not before, that he owned Negroes. The synod asked for and received his resignation; but, upon his return to the province in 1848 with fifteen blacks (one infant purchased on the way), all now free men, he was accepted back into the Toronto Presbytery.

King was an exceptionally able leader, much the best of the several attracted to the cause of the fugitive slave in the Canadas. By education and experience he could balance the practical with the bookish; by moral position he could urge freedom for all without a blind and fractious condemnation of those who were not prepared to take the abolitionist path. He wanted to educate the refugees both "for time, [and] for eternity." Above all, he was a man of detail who left little to chance, to friends, agents, or even—in the secular range of his activities—to God. He also recognized, as many men of good will do not, the fatal tendency of the kind-hearted to expect others to shoulder part of their burden, and he did

---

ment, Raleigh Township, Kent County," Kent Hist. Soc., *Papers and Addresses* (1919), pp. 40–44; Fred Landon, "The Buxton Settlement in Canada," *JNH, 3* (1918), 360–67; and S. H. Howard, "Ontario's Forgotten Colony," *The Imperial Life-Guard, 29* (1946), 17–21.

67. On King's life, there is his manuscript autobiography in the King Papers, PAC, together with broadsides, affidavits, his first wife's will, and notes on speeches; the notes of Rev. W. R. Gregg, in the Fred Landon Collection, London, Ont.; William H. and Jane H. Pease, "William King: From Master to Servant," *Rensselaer Review of Graduate Studies, 16* (1959), 3–10; Annie Straith Jamieson, *William King: Friend and Champion of Slaves* (Toronto, 1925); and Victor Ullman, *Look to the North Star: A Life of William King* (Boston, 1969). The last, while journalistic and uncritical in use of sources, is based on extensive research in Louisiana, Britain, and Canada.

not allow himself or his enterprise to become utterly dependent upon a sponsoring body. His independence led to criticism, for he retained four of his emancipated slaves as house servants at Elgin; and he built for himself and his second wife, whom he married in 1853, a large, comfortable house with a southern piazza on a double allotment of land. This was not an effort, as some maliciously claimed, to live the life of the southern planter without the attendant guilt, but rather a conviction that as the patriarch of what must be a model community, he should maintain some distance between himself and those he would teach.

Elgin differed in three important respects from previous Negro settlements. A stock company, legally incorporated within Canada West, was to raise the capital for the purchase of land and to act as the legal agent for the community. Both Dawn and Wilberforce unwisely had rejected this approach, while King's creation placed a board of twenty-four well-known and financially meticulous businessmen in control of the financial arrangements for Elgin, with Judge Skeffington Connor as their President. Secondly, the stock company would not be self-perpetuating, as was the organization upon which The Refugee Home Society was based, for it would be dissolved when sufficient land had been purchased and occupied. Thirdly, although in his initial petition to the Governor General, King had included "an industrial school" among his plans, and at least twice again he would suggest that one be opened, he nonetheless put such a school—with its tendency to perpetuate the Negro in semi-skilled trades— low on his priorities, reasoning that the skills of the artisan could be acquired through practical work in the blacksmithy, carpentry, cobblers' shop, and grist- and sawmills that he would open. School time, he thought, was best reserved for creating a body of literate settlers who could exercise their rights as citizens. For King also was insistent that the fugitives within his colony should become British subjects, both to assure the local populace that they intended to stay and in order to cut down at least marginally on transiency. To prevent local squabbles from being aired in public, he provided for an all-Negro community arbitration court.

Urged on by Reverend Robert Burns, a leading antislavery advocate,[68] the Toronto Synod approved King's idea, appointed him missionary to the fugitive slaves, created a committee to publicize the project and to solicit funds, and agreed to open a mission within the settlement. The stock company, called the Elgin Association, was organized in June of 1849, and in the following year, received its incorporation by the province, the Governor General—upon whom King had called in person with James

68. On Burns, see R. F. Burns, ed., *Life and Times of the Rev. R. Burns, D.D., F.A.S., F.R.S.E., Toronto* (Toronto, 1872), pp. 188–92, 279–83.

Redpath, a leading Montreal merchant—giving his blessing. By 1854 the association had purchased nearly nine thousand acres of land at $2.50 an acre, much of it forested in oak so that the timber cleared from home sites might later be sold at profit. A pot and pearlash factory, run by a skilled technician brought in from Ohio; a sawmill, financed by a special Buffalo and Toronto Stock Company led by Wilson R. Abbott; and a shingle factory, were under construction.

Elgin thus showed many signs of having been carefully planned, as the numerous local and foreign visitors to it remarked during the 1850s. King chose a site through which a military road had been cut and near which, in time, the railroad—to which he hoped to sell cord wood—might pass. Through one of the stockholders, Charles Berczy, the postmaster of Toronto, he gained a post office for Elgin (which the other Negro communities had lacked), thereby providing communication, a position of responsibility to be held by a black settler, and official inclusion in the provincial gazeteers. He established minimum standards for all houses: none could be smaller than 18 feet by 24 feet by 12 feet and all were to stand 33 feet away from the road and have land cleared 64 feet from the roadway; a drainage ditch two feet deep was to run across the front of each property, all were to have a garden in front enclosed by a picket fence, and prizes would be given each year for the best kept house and grounds. Each family was to take up fifty acres. Not all of the houses conformed to the standards at first, but by 1854 seventy-four did so and eight surpassed the model. There was also a brick, two-story hotel and a general store; and at the settlement's center stood the mission, a school, post office, and King's home.[69]

That King recognized the divisive effects of religious controversy is shown by his willingness to have other groups build their own churches. His church, organized within the context of the settlement, was the Buxton Mission, sponsored by the Toronto Presbytery and supported by gifts from local churches and by a substantial philanthropist, James Thompson. But land was made available for Methodists and Baptists as well, hopefully in order to exclude itinerant black preachers sent out by the begging groups. King preferred to solicit funds himself; and in American, Irish, and British tours he collected money, books, and pledges. The Upper Canada Bible Society founded a branch at Elgin in 1861, trainee students from Knox College came to work at the Mission, and King acquired a library larger than any between London and Windsor. Although in time

69. OPA, Land Dept. Records: J. H. Price to P. W. McMullin, Dec. 14, 1848; PAC, Map Room, "Plan of the Elgin Settlement in the Township of Raleigh, County of Kent, Canada West."

there were more Baptists and Methodists than Presbyterians at Elgin, King turned none—even Roman Catholics, of whom he strongly disapproved [70] —away so long as all settlers could continue to furnish certificates of good moral character.[71]

King also saw the need to pursue the problems of civil rights in a systematic way. Three of the 126 stockholders, Adolphus Judah (together with J. G. Joseph, one of the two Jews who were major share-holders), Wilson Abbott, Toronto's most successful Negro businessman, and one David Hollin, formed a subcommittee to find means of securing the settlers in the full exercise of their rights. From Malcolm Cameron, a member of the ministry of Sir Francis Hincks, they received a public promise that they would not be kept from purchasing land, attending the common schools, or exercising all privileges of citizenship. The question had been put because from the outset Elgin became the focus for a serious attack against all Negro settlers.[72]

The attack was serious because it was politically as well as racially motivated.[73] On March 8, 1849, well before King had purchased any land in the province, the Western District Council sent a petition to the Legislative Assembly opposing as "highly deleterious to the morals and social condition" of the area any black settlement. In June the Presbyterian Synod in Toronto received a similar petition, signed by 377 inhabitants of Raleigh, asking that body not to introduce a "Colony of . . . Vicious Blacks" into the midst of "an old, Well Settled Township" to which "Moral, Industrious, and Intelligent" white residents had given "Years of Toil." Chatham's sheriff called a public meeting in August to consider

70. King Papers: undated talk [ca. 1859].

71. Drew, *North-Side View of Slavery,* pp. 291–98; *Anti-Slavery Reporter,* n.s., 8 (1860), 294; Anti-Slavery Papers: Minute Book of the British and Foreign Anti-Slavery Society, Jan. 6, 1860; University College, London, Brougham Papers: King to Brougham, July 12, 1860.

72. OPA, Robinson Papers, "List of Coloured Persons . . . ," p. 66; *National Anti-Slavery Standard,* Feb. 21, 1850; *Montreal Witness,* July 18, 1851, July 19, 1854, Jan. 18, 1860; Joseph J. E. Williams, *Principles of American Slavery . . .* (Hamilton, 1858), pp. 10, 16–18, 26. The Cameron exchange appears in William Renwick Riddell, ed., "Records Illustrating the Condition of Refugees from Slavery in Upper Canada before 1860," *JNH, 13* (1928), 201–03.

73. See William H. and Jane H. Pease, "Opposition to the Founding of the Elgin Settlement," *CHR, 38* (1957), 202–18, which provides full documentation. I have found John K. A. Farrell, "The History of the Negro Community in Chatham, Ontario, 1787–1865" (Ph.D. diss., Univ. d'Ottawa, 1955), unreliable. Farrell has prepared a useful bibliography, however, in his catalog to the Negro History Exhibit held at the University of Windsor in 1965, *The Ontario Negro: An Outline of Negro History and Development* (Windsor, 1965).

how to prevent Negroes from purchasing land, and the chairman of the group, George Young, warned that property values would fall. Although King was present at the meeting, an unruly crowd resolved that, while Negroes should enjoy all political and moral privileges, they should enjoy these privileges elsewhere; that a vigilance committee should be appointed to ferret out any plans to import more blacks into the area and to prepare further petitions; and that the people of the United States should accept the burden of their own sins: "Let the slaves of the United States be free, but let it be in their own country." [74]

The voice behind these resolutions was that of an English-born renegade Tory, tinner, and real estate speculator, Edwin Larwill, member of the Western District Council. He provided a Baedeker of prejudice, listing the many reasons why Negroes should not come to Canada West: they were poor stock and would crowd out the better European settlers; they might bring on war with the United States; as objects of dislike, they could only be unhappy; they were hoping to intermarry with whites; philanthropically financed communities such as Elgin gave Negro immigrants undue advantages over settlers coming from elsewhere; if Negroes would only work hard enough, they would need no communal colonies; public opinion was against the blacks, and so too was God, who meant the races to be separate; since Negroes could not govern themselves they were not fit to live in a democratic society; property values would fall; the crime rate would increase; race riots would result; and the climate was unsuitable. He only failed to mention witchcraft.

During the next months Larwill gathered support for his views. Some members of the Chatham meeting, moved by King's presence, prepared an address in favor of the Elgin Association, only to have the document stolen. At Larwill's urging the Raleigh Town Council adopted an anti-Negro petition, to which he apparently added a section that the council had not voted, before he transmitted the tampered manuscript to Governor General Elgin. As amended, the petition suggested that a poll tax should be levied against American-born Negroes, that the vote, public schools, and jury service should be denied them, and that all Negroes should be forced to post bonds for good behavior as under the black codes of Ohio. Elgin was unmoved, and two weeks after this doctored petition reached Quebec, the Association purchased its first land with his active support.[75]

74. Burton Hist. Coll.: broadside, "A Public Meeting being Held in Chatham . . . ," Aug. 18, 1849; *Amherstburg Courier*, Oct. 27, 1849; *Journals of the Legislative Assembly* (1849), p. 138; (1850), pp. 37, 77, 127. A petition was also received from Colchester: (1850), pp. 69, 108, 220.

75. *Journals of the Legislative Assembly* (1851), pp. 82, 101; *Journal of the Legislative Council* (1850), pp. 50, 78, 187, 192–93, 195, 214; Pease and Pease, *Black*

King proved himself a courageous and intelligent leader who knew how to use Negro votes as a bloc to protect Elgin's interests, as Larwill had predicted he would do. The qualified Elgin settlers—the law required that rural electors own or rent real property of a yearly value of $20—cast their ballots as King told them to, and they provided the margin of Larwill's defeat in the next election, putting the antislavery editor of the *Toronto Globe,* George Brown, in his place as a Councillor. In 1853 their three hundred votes helped elect King's good friend, Archibald McKellar, a Chatham lawyer, to the legislature. Larwill ran again in 1854 and won, if briefly; for his tactics and speech were so like those of many southern American senators as to be an embarrassment to Canadians. To the Assembly he proposed a provincial poll tax on Negroes, asked for restrictions on abolitionist groups, and demanded that the Elgin settlement's finances should be investigated—and could find no one to second his motion. As Larwill mixed racist harangues with placatory appeals to the United States in order to win a more favorable reciprocal trade treaty, then under negotiation, those who were not disturbed by the one were offended by the other. McKellar displaced Larwill in 1857, again by a margin attributable to the Negro vote. Still, since Larwill now became the Kent County registrar, he was in a position to influence the number of black voters.

Black votes also contributed to the defeat of Colonel John Prince, a lawyer, although he had first risen to office partially on the basis of Negro support. During the so-called battle of Windsor in 1838, when a body of American filibusters killed a Canadian black who refused to join forces with them, Prince had summarily executed those responsible. Many Negroes had credited Prince, wrongly, with having meant to avenge the death of a black brother. Thereafter Prince, a Conservative, had spoken favorably of black settlers, and he allowed them to use his Sandwich estate for their annual picnics in celebration of West Indian emancipation. Still, Prince had done nothing for the Negroes in the legislature, and they were beginning to defect from him before Larwill began his campaign. Prince's public change of policy coincided with Larwill's downfall and also with the government's dismissal of the two Windsor magistrates— one a personal friend of Prince—who had surrendered an American Negro to Detroit contrary to established procedures. Prince now denounced Negroes as "animals" fit only for slavery, declared that the majority were criminals, wished all black settlers far away on Manitoulin Island, and concluded with another original thought: "They might as well try to

Utopia, pp. 104–07; Robert Stuart Woods, *Harrison Hall and Its Association, or a History of the Municipal, Judicial and Educational Interests of the Western Peninsula* (Chatham, 1896), pp. 136–37; Hamil, *Valley of the Lower Thames,* pp. 321–22.

change the spots of the leopard as to make the black a good citizen." [76]
The Colonel cast himself against McKellar in 1861, to lose by the margin
of Elgin's voters—since with foresight McKellar had accompanied King
to Britain the year before to help him raise funds.

King, Larwill, and Prince had thus brought about a complete reversal
in the Negroes' political preferences. Until 1848 Alexander Mackenzie's
earlier complaint that they invariably voted for the conservative party was
correct, and they would continue doing so in the Maritime Provinces. But
as King's influence spread outside Elgin, bloc voting in favor of those
candidates who promised to do the most for the Negro settlers became
commonplace. On the whole the votes now sent to Clear Grit, or reform,
candidates such as Brown and McKellar.

With the coming of the Civil War and the decline in the Negro population, Elgin's vote was less important. McKellar remained a friend of the
black man until he retired from public office in 1879. Others—notably
Arthur Rankin, representative from Essex County; Sir Allan McNab, who
represented Hamilton from 1841 until 1857, and the Western District
in the Upper House from 1860 until his death two years later; Isaac Buchanan, who was consistent in his aid to Negroes in the Hamilton area;
and even John Scoble, who at last won a seat in the assembly in 1863—
also spoke out on behalf of black constituents. Nonetheless, except for
Abraham D. Shadd, Mary Ann's father, who took a seat on the Raleigh
Town Council in 1859, no Negro won an elective office in Canada West
before the war. King predicted a black man would never be elected to
Parliament with the support of white voters—a prediction that held true
until 1968. With the end of the war, and the passing of the all-Negro
communities, the Negro votes—and the black settlers as targets for political invective—lost their importance.

The Civil War also marked the passing of all efforts, in the words of
Isaac Rice, to establish "a Canadian Canaan." The fugitives had not found
all that they had hoped to find in British North America, for as King remarked in 1860, they were unable to "roll back the prejudice against
them." Wilberforce had ended in disaster; although Dawn and The Refugee
Home Society struggled on into the Civil War years, they long since had
forfeited all respect among the more thoughtful blacks; even Elgin, despite
weathering its time of troubles well, was in decline, and when over seventy
of its residents (including two of King's servants) went off to fight in the
war, a corner was turned, for few came back. When a smallpox epidemic
forced Elgin's schools to close, many of the settlers thought the time had
come to return to the South, there to form a self-sufficient cotton-producing

76. Hamil, pp. 236–37; *Toronto Globe*, June 20, 1857; Daniel G. Hill, "Negroes in
Toronto," *OH*, 55 (1963), 89–90; Morrison, *Garden Gateway*, pp. 68–75.

colony. King, rebuffed by David Livingstone in his personal desire to send black missionaries to Africa, was willing to consider such a new venture, and he went to Washington to consult the British Ambassador, the American Secretary of State, William H. Seward, and the head of the Freedmen's Bureau, Major O. O. Howard.

King's visit to Washington brought Samuel Gridley Howe north in 1863 to survey the condition of the fugitive slaves for the Freedmen's Enquiry Commission. Howard had suggested that the Negroes should remain in Canada West until military force no longer was needed to pacify the South, but he assumed that in time they would wish to return to the states from which they had fled. Howe's report, actually written by a member of the traveling commission, James McKaye, upon the basis of interviews conducted by Howe, Robert Dale Owen, and the Secretary of the Commission, J. M. W. Yerrington, appeared to confirm this view.[77] While commenting favorably upon the Buxton Mission, the report condemned the "spirit of caste" that arose from all-Negro settlements and concluded that Canadian prejudice and the northern climate would drive the fugitives back to the United States. During the next months many of Elgin's settlers, with King's disappointed permission, sold their property—at first to local Negroes, as their nonalienation clauses required, and especially to the Shadd family, and then to whites—in order to move to the South.

The Elgin Association issued its last annual report for 1873. When the records were closed the following year, a portion of the refunded loan was paid at a reduced rate, while some stockholders cancelled their shares as a gift to Elgin. All who asked for payment in full received it, however. The Presbyterians rented out the manse, using the income to keep King on salary until his retirement in 1880. At that time the synod invested $3,000 on his behalf, the interest from which would be his pension. In 1887, King's second wife died, and he spent his declining years in Chatham, looked after by a niece and speaking occasionally at Presbyterian meetings. King died in January 1895; his last freed slave followed him three years later.[78]

But King, like Henson, remained alive to at least some Canadians; and once more it was Harriet Beecher Stowe who provided him with a second identity. In 1858 she published in Boston a two-volume novel, *Dred, A Tale of the Great Swamp,* in which she introduced a new hero, Edward

77. Samuel Gridley Howe, *Refugees from Slavery,* pp. iv, 102.

78. Brougham Papers: King to Brougham, July 12, 1860; *Anti-Slavery Reporter,* n.s., *9* (1861), 280; Chatham-Kent Museum, Chatham: "Buxton (North) Session Book," Jan. 19, 1863, entries for 1864, 1867, 1873–75, 1880, passim; *The Acts and Proceedings of the Twenty-First General Assembly of the Presbyterian Church in Canada* (Toronto, 1895), p. 1; Jamieson, *William King,* pp. 176–205. For an obituary, see *Boston Herald,* Jan. 7, 1895.

Clayton, a white who lived on a tidy little exile farm in the Canadian wilderness. In order to forestall a repetition of the charges brought against *Uncle Tom's Cabin,* she provided insistent documentation, telling her readers that what she said of Clayton's village was "all true of the Elgin settlement, founded by Mr. King." [79] Her identification of Clayton with King was an explicit one, and King accepted it. *Tom* had been an exciting book, and for all its moralizing it may still be read with pleasure; *Dred* clearly was a chore for its author to write as it is for us to read. In fiction as in life, less eager for publicity than Josiah Henson had been, William King gained little fame as the prototype of Edward Clayton. Henson would be remembered and King would not.

Still, in comparison with previous Negro communitarian efforts, the success of William King's Elgin was marked. Three hundred families were put onto the land, nearly five thousand acres were brought under cultivation, eight hundred head of livestock were, in the early 1860s, providing meat and produce, and a Negro-owned chewing-tobacco factory in Hamilton was thriving upon Elgin-grown leaf. Most of the settlers became citizens, voted in local elections, and some served as constables or postmasters.[80] The principle of self-help, according to Benjamin Drew when he visited in 1855, had created men of "a manly, independent air and manner." Elgin's temperance hotel was noted as one of the best in the district, even though the provincial Sons of Temperance barred Negro members; several of the settlers were singled out as unusually skilled artisans; there was little drunkenness or petty theft, and in an age of lower-class incontinence but four illegitimate children were born within the colony. Elgin had provided an instrument by which anti-Negro politicians had been drawn out and beaten back. The Elgin schools—the first opened in 1850, enhanced by two tax-supported district schools during the decade—were recognized as superior to the nearby public institutions; and whites had turned to Elgin for their children's education, providing a salutary if brief period of interracial education. No serious scandal ever touched the colony, and King was tricked by dishonest agents only once, and then after the Civil War, when he was aged. By 1860, blacks trained at the mission were employed in schools throughout the area, although black teachers for white pupils disappeared when most sought out better opportunities in the United States. From Elgin came a judge of the circuit court of Mississippi,

79. See Pease and Pease, "Uncle Tom and Clayton," pp. 68–73.
80. The figure of three hundred families is drawn from King to Hamilton, Nov. 23, 1889, in the Fred Landon Collection, and that on acreage from *A Sketch of the Buxton Mission and Elgin Settlement, Raleigh, Canada West* (Birmingham [Mich.], [1866?]), Reverend Gregg's personal copy in the OPA. See also King's testimony in Howe, *Refugees from Slavery,* pp. 107–10.

a member of the American House of Representatives, and a United States Senator, James T. Rapier of Alabama.[81]

Elgin was not an unqualified success; and Howe, Ward, and Mary Shadd may have been correct in their premise that such black utopias merely postponed the day of integration rather than hastening it. Both Howe and Thomas Henning feared that King's dominance led to continued dependency in subtle ways. Most men of liberal persuasion were not yet thinking of amalgamation of the races, and the strain of paternalism in King, while akin to that in Scoble, was at least unmarred by arrogance or the patronizing assumption that his charges would remain children for all time. There were failures that were experienced in common with the white community nearby: short crops in 1854, 1858, and 1859; weevils and grain rust; and the retarding effect of the panic of 1857, which made money tight. There were failures common to organized settlements: some of the land proved to be swampy; the potash factory burned in 1859; and when the Association's stock first matured, in 1864, it was not repaid, leading to a law suit and the necessity of refunding. King may have been mistaken in his insistence that anyone who came to the colony must furnish a certificate of character; for while this contributed to stability and a higher moral tone, it limited Elgin to those fugitives least in need, since there were many who had been in the province long enough to have won friends in the white community who could vouch for them. Perhaps an all-Negro community had not proved itself viable on the strength of Elgin's relative success, but King's experiment clearly did demonstrate to the whites of Canada West that Negroes could work hard, and together, in the face of social and economic adversity. The verdict on Elgin, and a proper one for the product of a Scotsman's dream, must remain that of a Scottish court—case not proven.

The Canadian Canaans—Wilberforce, Dawn, The Refugee Home Society, and Elgin—had been rooted in religious beliefs as well as in nineteenth-century notions of self-help. All cities set upon a hill were not literally conceived, however; and several church bodies and missionary organizations preferred to help individual fugitive slaves rather than enter into the far more complex world of quasi-secular community development. These organizations contributed to the refugees' welfare, to white aware-

81. Howe, pp. 102–04, 109–10; *Anti-Slavery Bugle*, Oct. 4, 1851; Pease and Pease, *Black Utopia*, pp. 107, 182, n. 38. On Rapier, see Eugene Pieter Romayn Feldman, *Black Power in Old Alabama: The Life and Stirring Times of James T. Rapier, Afro-American Congressman from Alabama, 1839–1883* ([Chicago], 1968). The John H. Rapier Papers at Howard University contain twenty-six letters which deal with the movement to, and life in, Canada.

ness of the black arrivals, and to that consciousness of caste—or sectarianism—which Howe condemned.

The churches of Canada were not in agreement on how to deal with the fugitives or with the problem of slavery. Some were segregationist, as Mary Shadd implied all were; and yet even she bridled when an English missionary claimed that Canadians were fully as prejudiced as Americans. Certainly much of the financial support for the cause of abolition came—in the Canadas as in Britain, and to a lesser extent in the Maritime Provinces as well—from church-based societies. Yet, ecumenical Christian agreement on the issue of slavery was not forthcoming.

Even though the most vocal supporters of the antislavery cause in Canada West were ministers, dissension between them and their denominations limited the effectiveness of those who wanted to help the fugitives. Some churches strongly opposed the begging ministers while others encouraged them; some accused North American Christianity as a whole of harboring slavery while others singled out particular groups for bitter attacks. Whether a Canadian church might continue to fellowship—as the term then had it—with a congregation of the same denomination even in the free soil North was the subject of heated debate, since many of the Northern churches in turn fellowshipped with their counterparts in the slave states.[82]

In Canada, Baptists were the first to speak out against slavery, beginning in the late 1830s. In February of 1841 the Ottawa Baptist Association passed resolutions approving the American Baptist Anti-Slavery Convention and refusing communion to any slave-owner. Three other regular Baptist associations, the Niagara, Haldimand, and Western eventually followed; but since each association was autonomous in such matters, the Baptist Church as a whole took no clear stand, and one association, the Grand Ligne, retained ties with proslavery elements in the American South. The Negro Baptist congregations severed their ties with tainted American Baptist conventions, and from 1848 a few churches, designated Union Baptists, fellowshipped only with antislavery churches in the United States —the Free Will and Free Mission groups—although largely for doctrinal reasons.[83]

82. See Alexander L. Murray, "American Slavery as a Disruptive Factor in Canadian-American Church Relations," unpublished paper read at the CHA meetings, Montreal, 1961. Murray's thesis—that the issue of slavery disrupted cross-border Protestant church relations—was challenged by William H. Pease in an unpublished commentary following the address. Pease suggested that doctrinal issues and politico-economic problems led to the break in North American fellowshipping patterns, a conclusion with which I agree while following the main outlines of Murray's argument. I wish to thank both for giving me copies of their papers.

83. *Canadian Baptist Magazine, 1* (1838), 205; *4* (1841), 239, 243; *Canadian*

Indeed, doctrine and finance appear to have played as large a rôle in determining whether Canadian churches would sever their ties with American churches as the slave question did. The Presbyterians, in particular, were placed under strain on all three counts; and since they were a large and influential body in Canada West, their soul searchings—as well as the work of their antislavery ministers—attracted the most attention. The Synod of the Free Presbyterian Church of Canada was connected with the Free Church in Scotland. The latter group, after a major disruption in Scottish Presbyterian circles, sent a deputation to the United States in 1844 to solicit funds; Southern churches gave nearly £ 3,000. Two members of the American Anti-Slavery Society, together with Frederick Douglass and George Thompson, the "English William Lloyd Garrison," and Garrison himself thereupon launched a campaign against the Free Church with the cry, "Send Back the Money." [84] The once-Garrisonian president of the Anti-Slavery Society of Canada, Michael Willis, from his new chair of theology at Knox College, Toronto, worked to prevent a similar rift in Canada West; but as a leader of the Toronto Presbytery he also sought to persuade the Synod of the Free Presbyterian Church of Canada to condemn slavery along with all American churches that did not do so. The Free Church Synod accepted the first demand readily and, over some opposition, the second; when both resolutions were forwarded to the Moderator of the American church, with a letter from the Canadian Moderator, the Reverend Dr. Robert Burns, the American Old School Presbyterians refused to accept them.

Here, too, more than the question of slavery was dividing the groups, however, for the Canadian Old School General Assembly also had refused to take up the slavery question. The Americans severed connections with those who followed Willis and Burns, and thereafter the Canadian Presbyterians passed a resolution each year denouncing slavery and any churches that harbored it. In 1851 the Synod of the Presbyterian Church of Canada, in response to American suggestions that Canadians were not entitled to opinions on slavery, adopted a resolution written by Willis to the effect

Evangelist, 3 (1853), 58–59; *The* [Toronto] *Gospel Tribune and Christian Communicant, 3* (1856), *56;* American Antiquarian Society, Worcester, Mass., Stephen and Abby K. Foster Papers: Carrie to Abby Foster, Jan. 14, 1851; *Anti-Slavery Missions* [of the American Baptist Free Mission Society] (Boston, n.d.), passim; Anti-Slavery Society of Canada, *Second Annual Report* (Toronto, 1854), pp. 10–11; Alexander F. Kemp, *Digest of the Minutes of the Synod of the Presbyterian Church of Canada* . . . (Montreal, 1861), pp. 349–55. On the Grand Ligne, see Walter N. Wyeth, *Henrietta Fuller and the Grand Ligne Mission: A Memorial* (Philadelphia, 1898), pp. 95, 111.

84. See George Shepperson, "The Free Church and American Slavery," *The Scottish Historical Review, 30* (1951), 126–43.

that slaveholding was "inhuman, unjust, and . . . dishonouring" of all Christians.[85]

It was a Free Church Scot, John James Edmonstoune Linton, who gave the next escalation to the slavery controversy in the Canadian churches. Linton, originally an agent of the Canada Company, author of emigration handbooks, and a schoolteacher in Stratford, had arrived from Perthshire in 1833. In the summer of 1854 he turned his full attention to an attack upon the American Tract Society. This organization supplied religious literature to Canadian churches through the Upper Canada Tract Society; Thomas Henning, in an anonymous editorial for the *Toronto Globe,* already had pointed out that the Society not only refused to supply antislavery materials but removed from its books all references to slavery. Although Linton sought to expose other groups, arguing that the Methodist Episcopal Church's *Canada Sunday School Advocate* was merely a reprint of its New York equivalent, he was primarily concerned with cleansing his own church. He compiled lists of books that had been expunged by the American Tract Society, wrote many letters to local newspapers, in New York as well as at home, and took out advertisements in the *Globe* to make his views known. In an astringent pamphlet, Linton attacked the American Sunday School Union and the American Board of Commissioners for Foreign Missions; and he sent out a thousand copies of the Unanimous Remonstrance of the Fourth Congregational Church of Hartford, Connecticut, which was an exceptional denunciation of the American Tract Society. Linton then demanded that all churches in the Canadas should stop handling, and all bookstores cease to sell, the publications of the American societies. Henning issued a pamphlet of his own, accusing the Presbyterians, Methodists, and Baptists of "dilly-dally" over fellowshipping. Linton wrote for the *Provincial Freeman* until its demise and also added to his repertoire his own "newspapers"—*Voice of the Bondsman* and *The Challenge,* a pamphlet issued in twenty-four numbers from 1854 until 1860 in Stratford and, latterly, Toronto—which, while primarily concerned with temperance, also flayed the churches over their passivity on the issue of slavery.[86]

85. *Montreal Witness,* Feb. 1, 1847; Gratz Autograph Coll.: Willis to Burns, May 5, 1842; James Grant Wilson and John Fiske, eds., *Appleton's Cyclopaedia of American Biography,* 6 (New York, 1899), 539; Murray, "Slavery as a Disruptive Factor," pp. 4–5.

86. Murray, pp. 7–9; [Linton], *Slavery Question: Report of the New York General Association, 26th August, 1855* (Stratford [1855]), pp. 1–7; Henning and Linton, *Slavery in the Churches, Religious Societies, etc.: A Review* (Toronto, 1856), pp. 4–8, 21–39; *Windsor Herald,* June 6, 1856; *Toronto Globe,* May 29, Sept. 25, 1857, June 4, Nov. 23, 1858; Linton, *A Prohibitory Liquor Law for Upper Canada, being a Bill for an Act to Prohibit the Sale by Retail, &c., with Remarks . . .* (Toronto,

The campaign mounted by Linton and Henning had little effect, for Linton went too far. Lewis Tappan, to whom Linton sent his circulars, supplied him with information at first, especially censoring the American Tract Society. "The same course of reasoning adopted in justification of [expurgated texts]," he wrote, "would justify the circulation of a mutilated Bible. If a portion of the country addicted to Sabbath breaking will not endure the 4th Comd. why should it not be left out; if another portion is given to lasciviousness why not leave out the 7th commandment & so on. . . . A mutilated Gospel is not the Gospel." Soon Tappan was sorry that he had given Linton his unguarded support, however, for the Stratford polemicist showered him with letters, with requests for more lists of mutilated tracts, and with gratuitous advice on infidelity. At last the beleaguered New Yorker replied plainly, "Had I leisure it would give me much pleasure to be your constant correspondent. I admire your zeal, your intrepidity, . . . and your determination to enlighten the good people of Canada. . . . But I am somewhat advanced in life, . . . and you must depend upon some younger men to collect the information you want. If I answer promptly all your communications I would neglect other matters of importance." Even John Dougall, a Montreal publisher and philanthropist who aided both The Refuge Home Society and Elgin, broke with Linton completely over the tracts, which he continued to sell. Linton then turned his attentions to the sympathetic minister of Hartford's Fourth Congregational Church, William W. Patton. The end result was that the Upper Canada Tract Society decided, in 1856, to distribute American tracts through its own agents, rather than American colporteurs; an Anglican weekly newspaper, *Echo,* accepted Linton's strictures against American tracts; and most Canadian Presbyterians—who had been taking publications from the Old School Presbyterian Board in Philadelphia—turned to Scotland for their literature.[87]

Linton attacked other denominations, but with even less success. The Congregational Union of Canada condemned slavery in 1846 and in its meeting of 1853 asked that aid be extended to fugitives. However, it too was a decentralized religious body in which each group made its own decisions about whether to continue to use American tracts, and for this reason its newspaper, the *Independent,* sought to remain neutral. Unitarians and Anglicans also were unshaken; but since the first took their lead from

---

1860), whole no. 24 of *Challenge;* Vera Ernst McNichol, *Reveries of a Pioneer: Mornington* (Kitchener, Ont., [1966]), p. 187.

87. Lewis Tappan Papers, Letterbooks, *9:* Tappan to Linton, Dec. 17, 1854, May 5, 21, 1855; Journals, *14:* Jan. 6, 13, Feb. 26, April 14, 1855. On Tappan, see Bertram Wyatt-Brown, *Lewis Tappan and the Evangelical War against Slavery* (Cleveland, Ohio, 1969).

antislavery New England and the second from antislavery old England, neither lent moral support as a body to slaveholders (although one Anglican periodical, *Church,* was not opposed to slavery). Quakers alone escaped Linton's wrath, for they were active in the Canadas, as in the United States, in aiding fugitive slaves, and maintained at least one school for them through their Negro and Aborigine Education Fund.[88]

Only the Wesleyan Methodists were badly exposed on the issue of slavery, and Linton did not neglect them. While members of the Methodist New Connexion were consistent in their stand against slavery from 1852— as were those of the Primitive Methodist and Methodist Episcopal denominations—the largest body, the Wesleyan Methodists, originally required Negroes to take communion separately, and from 1844 fellowshipped with the Methodist Episcopal Church (North) which, because of its border state members, remained silent on slavery. In 1855 Linton sent his evidence against the American church to the annual Canadian Wesleyan conference, without effect, and when the *Christian Guardian*—the chief Methodist paper—argued that the Methodist Episcopal Church in the North was quite different from that in the South, Henning accused the Canadians of following the expedient path. But here, too, the Canadians were acting as the British did, for the practice of transatlantic Methodists was to ignore slavery as best they could. Nor did the Methodist Missionary Society, primarily interested in Christianizing the Indians of British North America, concern itself with fugitive slaves, despite the quiet efforts of James Richardson, editor of the *Christian Guardian* and, after 1858, Bishop in Toronto.[89]

The fellowshipping controversy also reached interdenominational groups, of course, and those most directly effected were the Young Men's Christian Associations in the Canadas. The YMCAs had joined with the Americans in 1854; the next year the Toronto association withdrew because the enlarged group would not adopt a resolution to include bond as well as free. In 1856, when the confederation held its annual conference

88. S. A. Zielinski, *The Story of the Farnham Meeting, a Quaker Meeting in Allen's Corner* . . . (Fulford, P.Q., 1961), pp. 50–52. The Quakers' Negro and Aborigines' Fund, created in 1845, provided modest sums to aid black schooling in Canada West. See *Negro and Aborigines' Fund Report,* 1850 (London [1851]), p. [1]; *1853* (London, 1854), p. 3; *1854 and 1855* (London, 1855), p. [4].

89. William H. E. Elgee, *The Social Teachings of the Canadian Churches: Protestant, the Early Period, before 1850* (Toronto, 1964), pp. 173–75; Fred Landon, *Western Ontario and the American Frontier* (New Haven, Conn., 1941), p. 199; Thomas Webster, *Life of Rev. James Richardson, a Bishop of the Methodist Episcopal Church in Canada* (Toronto, 1876), pp. 185–89, 197. A search of the Minutes and Correspondence of the Methodist Missionary Society in the London Archives for this period revealed no mention of the Negro with respect to the Society's British North American mission.

in Montreal, the host association asked that slavery be put on the agenda, and when it was not, resigned. The YMCAs in Kingston and Halifax also broke with the American body, the latter to rejoin in 1862; but not until 1867 would the rift be healed in the Canadas.[90]

Of far greater importance was another interdenominational body, the American Missionary Association. The first such organization in the United States to support work among the fugitive slaves in Canada West, the AMA left no doubts about where it stood on slavery; but it was American, not Canadian, and its presence was resented as a foreign intrusion in the provinces. Further, while not rent by indecision over slavery, it was divided by petty quarrels which contributed to the factionalism that helped to engulf the Negro utopias.

Established on a nonsectarian basis in 1846, although most of its agents were Congregationalist, and with several abolitionists among its officers, the AMA began by sending money into the province, providing $833 by 1848 to aid Hiram Wilson, Isaac Rice, and indirectly Fidelia Coburn, a wealthy young lady from Maine who opened a school for fugitives in Queen's Bush. In that year nine missionaries based in Canada West, including Wilson and King, met with her to discuss how they might attract systematic support from an evangelical church. Shortly thereafter the AMA received applications from some of them and, in October, agreed to help support Rice, Reverend John S. Brooks, and his wife (the former Miss Coburn), at Mount Hope, near Wellington, by acting as a clearing house for any funds donated specifically for their use. Thus began a program in the province that would last for sixteen years.[91]

The total impact of the Canada Mission, as it was called, was relatively slight. During those sixteen years some $9,000 would be channeled into the province, together with many boxes of books and clothing. While receipts for the Mission at first exceeded expenditures, by 1851 the situation was reversed, and with ten missionaries in the field, the AMA thought it best to cut back. After 1855 in particular the Association itself began to decline. The white Canadian response to the AMA cannot be said to

90. *Canadian Evangelist, 3* (1853), 58–59; *Montreal Gazette,* April 15, 1939; Murray, "American Slavery as a Disruptive Factor," p. 7.

91. AMA, *Second Annual Report, 1848* (all reports published in New York in the year of the report), pp. 16–17, 28, quoted in Clifton H. Johnson, "The American Missionary Association, 1846–1861: A Study of Christian Abolitionism" (Ph.D. diss., Univ. of North Carolina, 1958); *Anti-Slavery Reporter,* n.s., *37* (1849), 6; *American Missionary, 2* (1847), 8; *3* (1848), 94–95; *4* (1849), 6; American and Foreign Anti-Slavery Society, *Annual Report* (New York, 1846), pp. 33, 77–79. I have drawn upon Johnson's excellent dissertation for the summary that follows. See also Fred Landon, "The Work of the American Missionary Association among the Negro Refugees in Canada West, 1848–1864," OHS, *Papers and Records, 21* (1924), 1–8, which contains some errors.

have been favorable: there was but one life member of the Association i Canada West in 1859 when there were 1,187 in Massachusetts. Nor di most blacks respond to the white missionaries, and from 1853 in particular, the efforts of the whites to denigrate the many black begging preachers, even though echoed by the *Provincial Freeman,* further alienated the Association's agents from their clientele.[92]

The work of these agents can be quickly told. The Brookses were joined at the Mount Hope Mission by Mary Teall, an able white teacher financed by a Baptist church in Albany. After an arsonist burned down their school in 1849, the Brookses resigned their commissions and left for Sierra Leone, giving their property (valued at $2,000) to the AMA. Miss Teall was reinforced by her sister Susan, although the interracial school, renamed Mt. Pleasant, declined rapidly as Negroes left in the face of white refusal to sell them land. Rice, "a man of piety but eccentric," severed his relationship, and David Hotchkiss and his wife, Wesleyan Methodists, took over his old mission in Amherstburg. In 1851 Hiram Wilson opened an AMA school in St. Catharines, with his second wife. In 1852 Reverend Elias Kirkland and his wife (also Wesleyan Methodists), after nine years at Dawn together with Theodosia Lyon, began to teach in New Canaan, only to ask to be relieved the following year because of Negro preference for black preachers. This school, also interracial, continued under Miss Lyon, a morbid woman who, believing that freedom was a temporal condition of no worth if not accompanied by salvation, rejoiced in the deaths of any children who showed the "evidence of a change of heart" needed to assure their being carried "right home to heaven."

Such piety did not save the situation, however. In 1853 the Tealls left Canada West for Jamaica. The Association cut its ties with Wilson and suspended the school at Windsor run by Mary Ann Shadd. When a proposed missionary was condemned in the *Provincial Freeman* for being white, the AMA admitted the Canada Mission was "a hard . . . uninviting field." Only Hotchkiss, despising both Negroes and himself, carried on: in 1857 an incendiary burned his church to the ground, and two months later the house into which he moved his services also was put to the torch, leading him to transfer his mission to the Refugee Home colony at Puce River, whereupon his wife died. In the meantime a Negro, Reverend L. C. Chambers, took up an appointment to Chatham, only to move to Ingersoll within the year. Thereafter, Hotchkiss remained the sole AMA worker in the province until his resignation in 1862 because of the emigration of most of his Puce and Little River congregations to Haiti.

92. AMA, *Fourth Annual Report,* 1850, pp. 14, 27–30; *Fifth,* 1851, pp. 32–35; *Sixth,* 1852, pp. 31–34; *Seventh,* 1853, pp. 49–50; *Eighth,* 1854, p. 48; *Tenth,* 1856, pp. 43–44; *Eleventh,* 1857, pp. 36–37; *Twelfth,* 1858, p. 32; *Thirteenth,* 1859, p. 33; *Fourteenth,* 1860, pp. 10, 29–30; *Sixteenth,* 1862, pp. 26–27.

At the same time the Association again began to support Mary Ann Shadd —now married to George F. Cary—in running the school in Chatham, until he too left for Washington late in 1864.

The American Missionary Association proved that educated whites were no more able to achieve harmony and stability than were ignorant black fugitives. The Canada Mission lacked any systematic plan, as shown by the frequent shifts from school to school and by the changing list of teachers. A combination of religious rivalry, moral rigidity, and subtle racism only partially concealed by the paternalism of Hotchkiss and others, crippled the operation from the outset. The hostility of the Negroes was open, and yet the AMA appointed only two black missionaries—Chalmers and Shadd —and once suspended the latter because she was not evangelical, having been brought up as a Roman Catholic before her conversion to African Methodism. The Association cut off the New Canaan school when the pious Miss Lyon married against the wishes of the local population, and dismissed Wilson for having openly encouraged begging and for writing bleak reports of the life of the refugees when the AMA wished to emphasize its successes in order to attract more funds.[93]

The question of whether or not to support begging continued to separate the missionaries and the Negroes. In a number of public meetings between 1849 and 1860, many militant blacks under the persuasion of the Shadd-Ward arguments adopted resolutions against any "begging system." In September 1854, in Amherstburg, several anti-Rice Negroes formed a True Band Society to attack begging, to set up a black-administered emergency fund, and to arbitrate disputes so that the local press could not broadcast them to the world. Within two years there were fourteen True Bands in Canada West, enrolling members from both sexes, collecting modest dues, and providing relief; and the parent body, now in Malden, claimed six hundred members. As the organization grew, it undertook to convince Negroes of the need for regular school attendance, to prevent additional fragmentation within black church ranks, and to persuade fugitives to disperse throughout the province, in order both to hasten integration and to allay prejudice by decreasing concentration in any one area. In Toronto a parallel body also founded in 1854, the Provincial Union Association, with Thomas F. Carey and Wilson R. Abbott as its leaders,[94] worked for the same goals.

93. AMA, *Third Annual Report,* 1849, pp. 21–23; *Fourth,* pp. 27–30; *Eighth,* p. 48, *Ninth,* p. 46; *Tenth,* p. 44; *The Provincial Freeman,* June 24, 1854; Johnson, "Christian Abolitionism," pp. 234, 268, 273, 288, 291 (n. 23), 321, 344–55; *Report of the Committee on the Negro and Aborigines' Fund . . . 1856* (London, 1856), p. 2.

94. Drew, *North-Side View of Slavery,* pp. 236–37; William H. Siebert, *The Underground Railroad from Slavery to Freedom* (New York, 1898), pp. 230–31.

Many Negroes saw no harm in the begging system, especially during the initial years of adjustment, and they countered the True Bands by pointing out that seeking alms was a common Christian practice. Two of the True Bands, in London and Chatham, actually endorsed begging; and unscrupulous itinerants—many not themselves fugitives—formed small groups of three or four men, took the name of a society, appointed one of their number an agent, and divided the proceeds solicited from a gullible but increasingly cynical public. The American Missionary Society remained fence-bound, approving of begging while insisting that clothing and money should be distributed only to new arrivals and school children, an unrealistic stand that led to much dissension. In Amherstburg, David Hotchkiss exposed one self-styled agent who sold the clothing he collected in the Northern states through a number of Windsor merchants; and when Hotchkiss's well was poisoned, he was convinced that "imposter preachers" were responsible. Rumor whispered that Negroes had burned the AMA school at Mount Hope in retaliation for the Brookses' refusal to surrender their clothing packages. One begging society, the Union Mission Board, sent at least four agents to the United States who returned nothing to the fugitives; a second, the Amherstburg Missionary and African Enterprise Society, existed only in the minds of its collectors; and another, led by Reverend William Mitchell in Toronto, gained notoriety for using old and fraudulent credentials and for keeping no records. Unfortunately for the opponents of the begging system, their champion, Samuel Ringgold Ward—having accepted an appointment from the Anti-Slavery Society of Canada to collect money in Britain while on a lecture tour—also fell from grace, being charged with swindling a London tradesman; he did not return to the province, taking up residence in Jamaica on fifty acres of land given to him by a British Quaker philanthropist, John Candler, in 1855, to die there in ca. 1866. Thus did the beggars, mounted, run their horse to death. As these mendicant years placed added strains upon black-white relations in the Canadas, a bewildered public, knowing not whose almoners to believe, believed none.[95]

The missionary arm of the Anglican faith, the Colonial Church and School Society, proved to be no less confusing. Originally founded as the Newfoundland School Society in 1823, and taking on the larger title after amalgamation with the Colonial Church Society in 1851, this organization

95. *Toronto Globe*, Dec. 23, 1859, Dec. 27, 1861; *Voice of the Fugitive*, March 11, May 26, 1852; *Oberlin Evangelist*, *14* (1852), 115, 123; AMA, *Fifth Annual Report*, pp. 34–35; *Gerrit Smith Calendar*, 2: Whipple to Smith, Jan. 29, 1850; "Coloured Imposters," *Anti-Slavery Reporter*, n.s., *12* (1864), 111–12; Johnson, "Christian Abolitionism," pp. 347–49. Ward had been an effective opponent of slavery, however, as shown by Benjamin Quarles in *Black Abolitionists* (New York, 1969), pp. 133, 138.

supported a short-lived but initially quite effective school in London, with Reverend M. M. Dillon, a former army officer who had served in the West Indies and the Canadas, in charge. Dillon had sold his commission, taken Holy Orders, and gone to Antigua and Dominica as a missionary, to return to England in 1852 because of ill health, whereupon he asked for appointment to a "cold colony." At this time Mrs. Alexander Kinnaird, wife to an Anglican philanthropist, acting upon a suggestion from Samuel Ringgold Ward, who was then in London, was seeking to establish a Mission to the Free Colored Population in Canada, with herself as president of the body and with the West London Branch of the Society as sponsor. Dillon drew himself to her attention during the Society's 1853 annual meeting, and in June of 1854 it commissioned him its agent to found a school in Canada West.[96]

As teachers, Dillon took with him to North America a layman, R. M. Ballantine, who was a graduate of a training college in Jamaica, and two West Indian girls, Mary Anne and Sarah Titré. After a brief survey of the fugitive slave settlements and of Montreal, where a missionary from the Society had been appointed to the poor, Dillon selected London as the site for his school—partially because the Rector of St. Paul's Church, Benjamin Cronyn, offered him classroom space and partially because the Negroes of Toronto opposed him, detecting some duplicity in his approach to race. As he wrote to the Negroes, he favored integration: "We come to you not as a separate class to whom we have a peculiar and special mission, but we come to you in common with your white brethren, desiring to set aside all distinctions . . . [and] affectionately invite you into our schools on equal terms with your white bretheren." Yet he also spoke of sending black missionaries to Africa, and he praised the separate settlements. Governor General Elgin and his successor gave the enterprise their blessing, and it flourished. Within eight weeks classes were transferred to a schoolhouse. The white children of the troops stationed in nearby barracks attended as well, the first to accept instruction from Negro teachers. An additional £ 200 was raised in London to support the school in its sudden growth, which according to Dillon reached an enrolment of four

96. For additional but occasionally erroneous detail, see J. I. Cooper, "The Mission to the Fugitive Slaves at London," *Ontario History, 46* (1954), 133–39. Cooper gives Dillon's name as "Martin M." while the records read "Marmaduke Martin." The story may be unraveled from *The Provincial Freeman,* March 25, 1854; West London Branch of the Colonial Church and School Society, *Occasional Paper,* no. 4 (1855), pp. 3–11, 15; and PAC, *Minutes of the Colonial and Continental Church Society* (the name taken in 1861) (microfilm): A-23, nos. 5012–21, 5070, 5260, 5297, 6312, 6344, 6361, 6387, 6397, 6489, 6505, 6515, 6532, 6568, 6610, 6617, 6677, 6686, 6740, 6754, 6767, 6807; A-24, nos. 62, 66, 72, 89, 100, 106, 111, 117, 125, 132, 139, 142–43, 148, 159, 182, 186; A-324, *17th Annual Report,* pp. 16, 20, 41; A-325; July 12, 1855.

hundred; the parishoners of St. Paul's welcomed Negroes to church services, encouraging them to come forward in their turn, rather than in a group at the end of the service, to take communion; and a local corresponding committee was organized for the parent society. As applications reached 960 in 1855, Dillon took over the artillery barracks for additional teaching space.

Yet even this noble effort soon declined, and for familiar reasons. The Society refused to wage war against slavery in the United States, dismissing all "abstract questions" as irrelevant to the pressing problem of aiding fugitives in the province. Two new teachers were added to the Fugitive Slave Mission, as it was now called, but one—John Hurst—did not share Dillon's apparent openness, finding the "real negro . . . very ignorant." Money supplied through Missionary Working Parties in Britain remained in short supply. The education given did not appeal to all of the fugitives, and while the Society was pleased to learn that the boys at the school were the equal of any in the province in their knowledge of Genesis, there were many refugees who desired a more practical curriculum. The black population of London more than doubled during the mission's first two years, straining its resources; and as a general depression moved over the province, Dillon was forced to appeal for funds outside the Society's own channels.

The strength of such a mission was as fragile as the health and minds of its leaders, and both began to fail. In the long winter of 1855–56, the Titré sisters fell ill, one "spitting blood," and they returned to Dominica; Dillon collapsed, and during his depression attacked the Secretary of the Colonial Church and School Society for misrepresenting him through garbled reports. The Society discovered that he had exaggerated attendance figures, and Negroes found that he talked quite differently to the whites than to them. Hurst and Dillon quarrelled, and the latter lashed out at the *Provincial Freeman* for wanting amalgamation of the races, a charge that disillusioned those Negroes who thought that Dillon also had wanted this. He then alienated Cronyn and his corresponding committee by saying that the latter had caught the former out in an unscrupulous land deal, a patent lie which he withdrew too late to appease Cronyn. By May 1856, the situation—darkened by Dillon's resort to sexual innuendo—had so deteriorated that the Anglican Bishop of Toronto set up a committee (actually at Dillon's request) to investigate his conduct. When the committee failed to clear his name, Dillon and Ballantine resigned in the summer of 1856, the former fleeing to Philadelphia.[97]

The Colonial Church and School Society continued to support a school

97. OPA, Strachan Papers: John Strachen to Dillon, June 6, 1856, and letterbooks, April n.d., 1857.

in London and expanded until it had eleven workers in the field. Under Hurst and Williams, more Negroes were admitted, for Dillon had observed an informal quota which kept the black enrolment at slightly below half the total. As larger numbers of Negroes moved in, the white pupils moved out. The teachers resorted to a monitorial system to keep attendance high, despite local objections; Ballantine returned, Hurst received a salutary lesson from two Negroes who suggested that white men might better spend their time removing prejudice from themselves rather than with black men who "would do very well" if left alone; and William P. Newman, then at Dawn, and a former opponent of Dillon's school, invited Hurst to open a mission there. The Society chose nearby Dresden instead, thus avoiding the feud among Henson, Scoble, and Newman, as well as any confrontation with the Baptist Free Mission Society. Thereafter, less emphasis was placed on the school in London. In 1858 a South Carolina Negro with missionary experience in Liberia, Reverend T. A. Pinckney, came to act as a traveling agent and teacher in Chatham, an appointment which displeased Hurst and Williams, since Pinckney was a Methodist, and Williams, in particular, was now primarily concerned with forestalling baptisms to other faiths. In 1859 the Society was further damaged by one of its Negro clergymen, who undertook a begging tour of Canada East without permission; and in that year the school in London closed, the Society putting a good face upon the decision by stating (as was true) that separate classrooms were unnecessary since the public schools accepted Negro pupils.

The Civil War brought most of these declining efforts to a halt. In 1861 the Chatham and a new Hamilton school closed, for Negroes had lost interest, many returning to the United States, others seeking out public classrooms, and the rest turning their backs upon white-administered missionary bodies. From time to time teachers were sent on circuits from the Society's offices in Toronto and London, and schools were fitfully revived throughout western Canada. Indeed, efforts continued on a small scale and under a new name—the Mission to the Coloured Population in Canada—until 1883, and nine missionaries were kept in the field, although largely in non-Negro areas. Nonetheless, the brief rôle played by the Colonial Church and School Society in helping the fugitive slaves to discover their Canadian Canaan was virtually at an end by 1866.[98]

The American Baptist Free Mission Society had passed along this route

98. *Minutes of the Colonial and Continental Church Society:* A–24, nos. 195, 199, 211, 218, 237–41, 251, 256–63, 290, 307, 321, 325, 396, 411, 422, 427, 566, 586, 682; A-25, nos. 53, 299, 345, 349, 358, 360, 364, 372, 374, 427, 459, 483, 496, 511, 534, 567, 605; A-325: Nov. 6, 1856, and *Annual Report,* 1862, pp. 67, 70; A-326: Sept. 30, 1862; A-632: 1872, p. 49; A-634: 1880, pp. 32–50; A-635: 1882, p. 28, 1883, p. 33; Mission to Fugitive Slaves in Canada: being a Branch of the Operations of the Colonial Church and School Society, *Report for the Year 1857–8* (London,

before. This body included both white and black churches after 1848, when the Amherstburg Association of black Baptists became an auxilliary of the larger organization. Although the Association cut this tie in 1851, a new Negro Baptist Association formed in 1850 and, taking the name of the Canadian Anti-Slavery Baptists, filled the same position. The Free Mission Society briefly administered Dawn and supported Reverend Newman as he did battle against anti-Garrisonians, sent itinerant agents into Canada West, financed two spinsters who opened schools in Chatham and Hamilton, and in 1859 sent Mary Teall back to Queen's Bush for a brief visit. Feuds with Hiram Wilson and over Dawn would vitiate the Society's good work, however, and it soon retired from the scene. Nonetheless, it alone may have provided what many Negroes most wanted—a sense of separate black identity, through its willingness to accept a parallel and non-integrated religious body which unhesitatingly condemned slavery. From the presence, and in part from the work, defective as it was, of the American Baptist Free Mission Society would emerge, following the Civil War, self-conscious, separatist, and institutionally proud Negro Baptist associations which, together with African Methodist and British Methodist Episcopal churches, would provide the core for Canada's all-Negro religious denominations.[99]

What had the Negro settlements, the missionary societies, and the churches accomplished? Much and little—fugitive slaves had been cared for across more than a decade, and some had acquired a stake in Canadian society, land, a sense of belonging, and the courage to show pride. Canada had acquired a substantial if passing Negro population, an opportunity to show itself above prejudice—which it missed—and a chance to give reality to its insistence upon institutional equality—which it grasped. When the fugitives returned to the United States at the end of the Civil War, Canadians congratulated themselves on succor well given and on a growing problem well avoided. Few white British North Americans thought that the Negroes left for reasons other than the climate or a desire to return to their places of birth. Few remarked upon the fact that black residents of Hamilton—a city which saw a population increase of fifty percent between 1851 and 1861, and a rise in the number of laborers by 250 percent—remained clustered in ghettoes, admittedly of their own making, or that all were in the lower six percent of the city's earning capacity. Canadians did not reflect upon the number who fled to the United States because Canaan had not kept its promise. Although many Negroes remained be-

---

1858), pp. 2, 7–17, 21; PAC, G 20, Governor-General's Secretary, *59:* Dillon to Lord Bury, Jan. 10, 1856, with encls.

99. Murray, "Anglo-American Anti-Slavery Movement," pp. 67–68. The society's journal appears not to have survived.

hind, they somehow were not thought to be Canadian Negroes, for one always anticipated that they too would follow their brethren to the United States.

But not all Negroes had come to Canada hoping to find a Canaan. Some had come in blind terror, propelled rather than drawn, to escape more than punishment. Most had been poorly organized, and many never benefited from the work of the white organizations. As Linton had seen, others would turn to secular bodies that wished to make no claim upon their souls. Canaan, after all, was prominent in the Aprocrypha, not a source always to be trusted; while the Underground Railroad, the Anti-Slavery Society of Canada, and the bitten bullets of a John Brown were real enough, to be drawn upon within the secular world of a shared North American experience, a continental abolitionism. It is to these facets of the fugitive's story that we now turn.

8. A Continental Abolitionism?

The Underground Railroad plays a dual rôle in the story of the continental movement to abolish slavery. It was unquestionably the highly effective means by which a number—an exaggerated and indefinite number—of fugitive slaves reached British North America. It was the cause of a legend that would make it possible for Canadians to reinforce their self-congratulatory attitudes toward their position on the Negro, and to strengthen those self-congratulatory assumptions into the twentieth century. The latter rôle was more demonstrable than the former.

To say that the Underground Railroad was enlarged by legend is not to say that it did not exist. Clearly, there was a loose network of abolitionists, perhaps predominantly Quaker, who communicated with one another in order to make known various places of refuge where fugitive slaves might go during their journey from the slave states to the free border cities of the north and to the British provinces. Thousands of fugitive slaves were helped in this manner, being passed on from hand to hand, fed, clothed, and hidden, and on occasion given transport or money for the purchase of tickets. In some areas—especially southern Illinois, Indiana, and Ohio— the so-called Underground Railroad agents worked clandestinely, living amidst proslavery or anti-Negro neighbors. But in many other areas further to the north the Railroad was seldom underground, being well known to local newspapers and law officers alike—as in Syracuse, Detroit, and Toledo. That the Railroad did help many fugitive slaves reach Canada West in particular, yet that its importance was much exaggerated, is now well demonstrated.[1] Both aspects of this legend are central to an understanding of the position of the Negro in the Canadas during the decade before, and the several decades after, the Civil War.

Canadian legend today claims that at least sixty thousand *fugitive* slaves were resident in Canada West in 1860. Contemporary estimates ranged from fifteen to seventy-five thousand, with many whites accepting figures closer to the latter. If this were so, the black population of Canada West in the 1850s was around 4 percent of the total, since the 1861 census

1. See, in particular, Larry Gara: "Propaganda Uses of the Underground Railway," *Mid-America,* n.s., 23 (1952), 155–71; and idem, "The Underground Railway: Legend or Reality?", *Proceedings of the American Philosophical Society, 105* (1961), 334–39.

for the province showed 1,396,000. That the Negro population did increase precipitously in the southwestern part of the province also is clear, a condition that helps to explain the rapidly rising anti-Negro sentiment in that portion of Canada West as well as the tendency to overestimate Negro numbers. If so many fugitive slaves did find refuge in the single province, two other conclusions follow: the great majority returned to the United States at the end of the Civil War, since the Negro population in 1871 was undeniably but a fraction of sixty thousand; and the Canadians could rightly take credit for harboring—and for at least a decade and a half giving aid to—a quite substantial body of refugees from the political and social conflicts of the Republic.

Yet, both the estimates of the Negro population, and the conclusions relating to fugitive slaves that flow from these estimates, must be tempered by a number of observations:

1. While contemporary accounts often suggested that sixty thousand or more fugitive slaves were present in Canada West, in fact at least both Canada West and Canada East were meant—as one may see when the estimates are read in context; and on occasion all of British North America was indicated. Thus, the sixty thousand should be read against a total population of over three million. In fact, the black segment of the population probably gained only a percentage point in the 1850s, since there was massive white immigration during the decade.

2. While the estimates implied that they referred to fugitive slaves only, again when read in context nearly all show that they applied to the total black population. The figures often were given out in ignorance of the presence of many free Negroes from the northern states and of free Canadian Negroes who traced themselves back to the American Revolution. One may ask, What is said of the British North American attitude toward Negroes when all were assumed to be fugitives? [2]

3. In any event, the estimates utterly ignore the official censuses of the governments of the Canadas. The census for Canada West in 1851 showed a total of 4,669 Negroes, while official estimates suggested 8,000; the census for 1861 showed 11,223; and other official figures raised the total to 13,566. The 1861 census, in particular, was thought at the time and has proven since to be quite inaccurate. [3]

2. Siebert, *Underground Railroad*, p. 219; Booker T. Washington, *The Story of the Negro: The Rise of the Race from Slavery* (New York, 1909), 2, 240. Contemporary authority for the estimate of a total of sixty thousand Negroes in the Canadas appears in "W. M. G." "A Sabbath among the Runaway Negroes at Niagara," *Excelsior*, 5 (1856), 41. Typical exaggerations include the estimate of Thomas Nye, mentioned in chapter 6, note 28, above.

3. See M. C. Urquhart and K. A. H. Buckley, eds., *Historical Statistics of Canada* (Cambridge, 1965), pp. 1–4, for an analysis of the inaccuracy of the early census

4. Further, no accurate figures can be given either for the number of fugitive slaves in the whole of the British North American provinces, or for the total number of Negroes. Many attempted to pass for white when in the Canadas, many were not enumerated, and census takers might reasonably have confused fugitive American with free American blacks, since the former often claimed the status of the latter, especially because of their misplaced fear of extradition.

5. Samuel Ringgold Ward, a fugitive slave himself, wrote in his autobiography in 1855 that reaching Canada was a most difficult task, and that *"but few* comparatively can come." This would seem a logical conclusion, for the Canadas were far away and little known to the fugitives, and many were told that the colonies were uninhabitable for black men. One must assume that the majority of the total number of fugitive slaves did not reach the Canadian provinces and remained in the free northern states.[4]

6. This being so, how many might have reached the Canadas? Official reports suggested that the slave states lost perhaps a thousand runaway slaves a year. Assuming this to be so for the period 1830 to 1860, even had every single fugitive reached Canada safely, the total would have been only 30,000.[5] As it was, many died en route, disappeared and could not be accounted for, returned to the South to escape another time and be counted again (for one man escaping twice is two escapes, although he is still but one man when on Canadian soil), or remained in the North.

7. Thus, contemporary accounts tended to refer to fugitives as "passing through" Syracuse, Albany, or Cleveland "on the way to Canada." All of these were assumed to have reached the Canadas. But many—perhaps the majority—stopped short of the Canadian border; and many were counted more than once, "passing through" Albany and, at a later date, "passing through" Syracuse, Rochester, or Buffalo. No doubt, there were many, like William Wells Brown, who set out for Canada West and, finding ice on Lake Erie had curtailed steamer traffic, simply stayed in Ohio.[6]

returns. The census of 1851 is believed to have underenumerated the province's total population by a hundred thousand. Both it and that of 1861 undercounted children.

4. Ward, *Autobiography,* p. 158; Gara, *The Liberty Line: The Legend of the Underground Railroad* (Lexington, Ky., 1961), pp. 37–40, 67, 111, 145, 149, 161, 185–90. Gara has drawn upon the Siebert Papers in the Ohio State Historical Society and Harvard's Houghton Library; I have examined both collections and accept his conclusions.

5. However, in 1855 a Southern judge guessed that the slave states had lost "upwards of 60,000 slaves" (Kenneth M. Stampp, *The Peculiar Institution: Slavery in the Ante-Bellum South* [New York, 1964], p. 118).

6. See William Edward Farrison, "A Flight Across Ohio: The Escape of William Wells Brown from Slavery," *The Ohio State Archaeological and Historical Quarterly,* 61 (1952), 272–82, and Brown's *Narrative . . .* (Boston, 1847). A typical entry

8. Related to this terminological guesswork was the tendency for abolitionists, in letters, newspaper accounts, and their autobiographies, to rejoice at having put a fugitive "on the stage for Canada." This phrase could be invoked in Cincinnati—where it meant nothing, since no stage ran from southern Ohio to Canada—as well as in Buffalo, where it had genuine meaning. To count a fugitive who boarded a stage in Cincinnati, or even Oberlin, as being safely in Canada is similar to assuming that a Hungarian refugee who was seen leaving Budapest in 1957 arrived safely in Vienna.

9. The abolitionist press quoted each other at length, usually but not always with credit, and with repetitious figures—all of which served to create the impression that refugees were reaching Canada West in waves. *The Voice of the Fugitive* would report that forty Negroes had arrived in Amherstburg; six weeks later the same item would be reprinted in another abolitionist journal in New York or Ohio. The forty fugitives one read of in June were the same forty that one had read of in April.[7]

10. The free Negro population in the northern states, and the total Negro population in British North America—fugitive and free—showed an excess of females. Most fugitives were males. One might conclude that the majority in either population therefore consisted of nonfugitives.

11. Many southerners, who had some reason to wish to exaggerate their losses, did not think the Canadas harbored large numbers of fugitive slaves. The *New Orleans Commercial Bulletin* suggested in 1859 that fifteen hundred slaves had escaped each year for fifty years. This figure applied to the entire South and was said to represent an outer limit of the possible; even so, this would have accounted for but seventy-five thousand fugitives, the upper figure sometimes given for Canada West alone. When the *Baltimore Sun* said, in 1856, that all living fugitives were worth thirty million dollars, it also suggested that the average value was nearly $9,000, a patent untruth.[8]

12. The abolitionists, who might also have wished to exaggerate their successes, were less sanguine. In 1861 the American Anti-Slavery Society estimated that the total number of slaves who had escaped was well below seventy-five thousand. Most were thought to be in the North.[9]

---

would tell how "a female, Patsey Williams, of Kentucky, on her way to Canada, passed through Rochester Thursday" (*Stratford* [C. W.] *Beacon,* May 31, 1861).

7. And the "six covered wagons filled with Negroes" hailed by the *Owen Sound Comet* on May 18, 1852, were the same covered wagons earlier praised by the Detroit press.

8. Gara, *Liberty Line,* p. 153, quoting *Baltimore Sun* of March 13. The *St. Catharines Journal* estimated in 1857 that "1,500 to 2,000 slaves" were brought to Canada annually, predicted an end to slavery in the South, and that there would be no blacks in Canada by 1900. See The St. Catharines and Lincoln Historical Society, *St. Catharines A to Z by Junius 1856* ([St. Catharines, 1967]), p. [70].

9. Ibid., pp. 38–40.

13. The fugitives who did reach the British provinces were by no means entirely happy. A number returned to the northern states, through which they had passed while seeking out the North Star, further reducing the total in the Canadas. At the beginning of the Civil War, more returned.

14. After the Fugitive Slave Bill was passed, abolitionists on the border, such as Henry Bibb, Isaac Rice, and Hiram Wilson, reported that fugitives were arriving at the rate of thirty a day. This seems a substantial figure, and indeed it was when so many descended upon the strained resources of Rice or Wilson. Yet were this so, the post-1850 fugitive black population of Canada West alone (setting aside those who returned to the North or died in the province) would have been 110,000 in 1860, a clear absurdity. At the height of the fugitive influx, the total Negro population of Amherstburg—the single most important entry point for refugees—was at most eight hundred; and during the eighteen months of initial panic after passage of the bill, even the *Toronto Globe* set the figure at no higher than three thousand.[10]

15. On occasion free Negroes from the northern states moved into the Canadas and pretended to be fugitives in order to attract the sympathy of Canadian abolitionists or to benefit from the fugitive slave hostels. In 1854, for example, a free black barber from New Hampshire twice raised money to reach Canada by claiming that his master was pursuing him. Many of the begging preachers appear to have been free men.[11]

16. One of the most publicized of the Underground Railroad depots was that run by the fugitive J. W. Loguen in Syracuse. His activities were not secret, and once in a free state a fugitive could learn of Loguen and his work. Yet in nearly nine years in Syracuse, Loguen—whose account is exaggerated on other matters—saw but fifteen hundred fugitive slaves, not all of whom moved on to the Canadas.[12]

17. Studies of Negro songs and folk tales in Canada show relatively few references to fugitives. More important, recent investigations of southern slave songs show that Canaan, the Promised Land, and the New Jerusalem were equated most often with Africa and seldom with Canada. In the South, those slaves who contemplated other lands did not appear to have had the British provinces uppermost in their minds.[13]

10. *Anti-Slavery Reporter*, n.s., *4* (1856), 135; *Toronto Globe*, June 10, 1852; *Montreal Gazette*, Oct. 4, 1860. See W. H. Withrow, "The Underground Railway," RSC, *Proceedings and Transactions*, sec. 2, *8* (1902), 73; Fred Landon, "Canada's Part in Freeing the Slave," OHS, *Papers and Records, 17* (1919), 74–84; and Landon, "The Negro Migration to Canada after the Passing of the Fugitive Slave Act," *JNH, 5* (1920), 22–36.

11. Siebert, *Underground Railroad*, p. 249.

12. Loguen, *The Rev. J. W. Loguen, as a Slave and as a Freeman: A Narrative of Real Life* (Syracuse, N.Y., 1859), p. 444.

13. Helen Creighton, "Folklore of Lunenburg County, Nova Scotia," National

18. This is not surprising, for the slaves were kept in ignorance of British North America, and most of them were probably not, at the moment of their escape, thinking of taking refuge under the lion's paw. Slaveholders emphasized the harshness of the northern climate, denied their slaves maps or the education that would enable them to read them, and suggested that all Canadians spoke French, worshipped idols, and executed black men upon arrival. Lewis Clarke, in memoirs published in 1845, said that he had been told that Canadians would skin his head, eat his children, poke out their eyes, and wear their hair as coat collars. Even so astute a Negro as Frederick Douglass thought that Canada was where "the wild goose and the swan repaired at the end of winter" and not "the home of man." [14]

19. These estimates, confusions, and exaggerations were added to by the publications of contemporary observers. In 1860, Reverend William M. Mitchell published in London an influential book on *The Under-Ground Railroad*. A free Negro who had been a slave driver, Mitchell lived in Toronto after 1855 as an agent for the American Baptist Free Mission Society. He claimed that the railroad had been operating for a quarter of a century and that "nearly two thousand" fugitives reached "Canada" each year. This would have meant a total fugitive population of fifty thousand; and allowing for deaths his estimate was forty-five thousand. This figure, then, is well below many of the estimates, and yet it is given by a man who had every reason to enlarge it, since he used his book as a medium by which he solicited funds for his church and school in Canada West; many of the communitarian settlers condemned him as "a pious fraud." [15] Later it was suggested that in 1860 alone five hundred Negroes "from Canada" went into the slave states to rescue others, a figure that surely confuses border crossings into the North for business, social, and religious purposes with antislavery journeys. Even so industrious and courageous a person as Harriet Tubman made not more than nineteen (and probably fifteen) such trips over eight years.[16]

Museum of Canada, *Bulletin No. 117* (Ottawa, 1950), pp. 86, 127; Creighton, "Songs from Nova Scotia," *Journal of the International Folk Music Council, 12* (1960), 84–85; W. J. Wintemberg, "Some Items of Negro-Canadian Folk-Lore," *The Journal of American Folk-Lore, 38* (1925), 621; Arthur Huff Fauset, "Folklore from the Half-Breeds in Nova Scotia," ibid., pp. 300–15; Fauset, ed., *Folklore from Nova Scotia* (New York, 1931), pp. vii–xiv.

14. *Narrative of the Sufferings of Lewis Clarke, during a Captivity of More than Twenty-Five Years, Among the Algerines of Kentucky . . .* (Boston, 1845), pp. 39–40; Douglass, *Life and Times of Frederick Douglass* (Hartford, Conn., 1884), pp. 198–99.

15. Mitchell, *The Under-Ground Railroad*, pp. 3–5, 71, 113.

16. Herbert Aptheker gives this figure in *The Negro in the Abolitionist Movement* (New York, 1941), p. 16, perhaps drawing it from Benjamin Brawley, *A Short History of the American Negro*, 2nd rev. ed. (New York, 1927), p. 78.

Another of the chief accounts of the Underground Railroad was by William Still, a free Negro who from 1847 was on the staff of the Pennsylvania Society for Promoting the Abolition of Slavery. Philadelphia was a prime entrepôt for fugitive slaves, and many visited Still at his home; during fourteen years of active work on behalf of escaping slaves, including a visit to Canada West in 1855, he kept detailed records from which, in 1872, he published his *Record of Facts*. Subsequent students of the Railroad drew heavily upon this massive volume of 780 finely printed pages, twice revised and extended, of narratives and letters.[17] Yet a close reading of Still's work, together with an examination of his manuscripts, does not support the notion that great streams of fugitives reached British North America through the medium of "the Road." Still gives evidence on 892 fugitives in his volume—although there appear to be more, some are repetitions—and he provides names for most. Of these, he gives evidence clearly showing that 112 reached the Canadas, and he asserts on nine other occasions, without evidence, that fugitives did so; the rest are left departing from Philadelphia with "their faces set Canada-wards." From the names provided by Still, one may identify five more who reached Canada West, unknown to him. No doubt there were others, for many fugitives changed their names—if not always radically, as when John Atkinson became John Atkins—and a number, not alone on Still's evidence, could have passed for white after arriving in the provinces. Nonetheless, the figures that one may project as safely having reached British North America via Philadelphia are not, despite Still's frequent usage of Canada as a presumptive goal, very large.[18]

20. Subsequent scholarship added to the figures. Many volumes repeated the estimates. Some, such as Homer Uri Johnson's *From Dixie to Canada: Romances and Realities of the Underground Railroad*, published in 1894,[19] are presented as factual, when they were in truth a pastiche of tales. Other works, such as the highly influential treatment by Wilbur H. Siebert, *The Underground Railroad from Slavery to Freedom*— the first genuinely scholarly study of the fugitive slaves' escape routes, published in 1898—further fed the legend. Siebert (whose position at his

17. Still, *The Underground Rail Road: A Record of Facts, Authentic Narratives, Letters, &c* . . . (Philadelphia); Siebert, *Underground Railroad*, p. 234, n. 1; Drew, *North-Side View of Slavery*, p. 43. I have examined the Letter Book of William Still, and the Journal of the Pennsylvania Anti-Slavery Society Underground Railroad in the PSHS, and they add little to Still's published account.

18. A number of Still's letters have been reprinted in Carter G. Woodson, ed., "Letters Largely Personal and Private," *JNH, 11* (1926), 104–75. See also Larry Gara, "William Still and the Underground Railroad," *Pennsylvania History, 28* (1961), 33–44; and C. Lightfoot Roman, *The Underground Railroad* (Valleyfield, P.Q., [1933]), passim.

19. (Orwell, Ohio), vol. 1 (no further volumes published); 2nd ed., 1896.

university was in European rather than American history) worked from published materials, a lengthy questionnaire he sent to aging antislavery advocates, and from conversations with former fugitives. He did not verify the published accounts—many of them repetitive, taken from each other— against manuscript sources, and he accepted the answers to his question- naire at face value. His descriptions and references—to "taking an agency" for the Railroad, or "employees of the U.G.R.R."—tended to suggest a greater degree of organization than existed.[20] Even so careful a scholar as western Ontario's Fred Landon, the foremost student of the Negro settle- ments in Canada West, was content to accept from Siebert and elsewhere the estimates of sixty thousand fugitives, did not distinguish carefully between fugitive and free Negroes, and reported that after 1850 "the early trickle which had become a stream turned for a time into a torrent." Siebert's work, Landon concluded, was "authoritative." [21]

That Siebert's Underground Railroad existed is quite true. Many brave and selfless men labored for it in behalf of the fugitive slaves. Thousands of fugitives did find refuge in Canada West. And one should not denigrate the estimates contemporary to 1860 without putting something in their place. This is difficult, for the censuses were inaccurate, the fugitives often stayed in the Canadas only a few weeks, and no figures are available with consistency from school, tax, or voting records, since some but not all provide an indication of color. On the basis of my own research, the best I can offer—in addition to the statement in the Appendix—is that by 1860 the black population of Canada West alone may have reached forty thousand, three-quarters of whom had been or were fugitive slaves or their children, and therefore beneficiaries of the Underground Railroad.

But the legend outgrew the reality in Canada, as legends invariably do without the correctives of time, logic, or scholarship. And the legend fed the twentieth-century assumption that nearly all black men in Canada

20. Siebert wrote many articles on the underground railroad, as well as his mas- sive book, cited previously, *The Underground Railroad from Slavery to Freedom* (see pp. 29, 70–72, 76, 151). He confuses the date of his interviews, however (compare p. 194 n. 1, and p. 249 n. 4). The uncritical acceptance of his book is shown in the Siebert Papers in the Houghton Library, vol. 45 of which contains letters and reviews (including Canadian ones) on its publication. See, for example, the *Montreal Star*, Jan. 28, 1899.

21. Landon, "Canada and the Underground Railroad," Kingston Historical Society, *Reports and Proceedings* (1923), p. 17, and "The Underground Railway along the Detroit River," *Michigan History, 39* (1955), 63–68. The chief volumes that build upon Siebert are: Hildegarde Hoyt Swift, *The Railroad to Freedom* (New York, 1932); Henrietta Buckmaster [Henkle], *Let My People Go: The Story of the Under- ground Railroad* (New York, 1941); and William Breyfogle, *Make Free: The Story of the Underground Railroad* (Philadelphia, 1958).

today are descendants of fugitive slaves, the slave condition, poverty, and America—inheritors of the disgrace of both caste and mark. In 1956 when a journalist, J. C. Furnas, asked acquaintances to guess at the total number of fugitive slaves, the average reply set the figure at 270,000; some answered a million.[22] Is it little wonder, then, that one heritage of the fugitive slave period, for Canadians, is an easy assumption of Negro uniformity? The legend of the Underground Railroad and its aftermath has united all Canadian Negroes into a single group in the eyes of white Canadians, reinforcing those prejudices which grow from the notion that an ethnic group must be viewed as a single social unit. To Canadians, Negroes were a monolith, both because of their color and because of their presumed origins as fugitive slaves—origins probably shared by no more than half the Negro population of Canada today.

British North Americans who read the literature of the Underground Railroad, the fugitive slaves, and the abolitionists in general also were reinforced in their consciousness of moral purity. Some few accounts—by Drew, Henson, Ward, Israel Campbell, and Austin Steward in particular [23] —remarked upon the incidence of prejudice in the Canadas and compared Canada West to the northern states; but the great mass of fugitive narratives were unstinting in their praise of the Canadian haven and found no occasion to mention the quasi-segregated pattern of life developing there, the numerous demeaning incidents that the fugitives encountered, or the morass of conflicting claims made upon the confused fugitive by missionary groups, communal settlements, and school societies. In the thirty most widely known fugitive slave accounts published between 1836 and 1859, British North America is mentioned in all but four; of these twenty-six accounts, few can be said to provide anything like a realistic picture of conditions in Canada West.[24]

The structure of these fugitive slave narratives tended to be similar. Often the fugitive was said to have "much white blood" flowing in his veins, was forced to watch drunken masters down great quantities of whiskey (for the books also preached temperance), and had to listen to foul language ("d—n, b———s, and b———h") from which religion was a solace taken despite the master's disapproval. During the flight one was usually helped by Quakers, met a band of Indians, and kissed the earth of Canada. Much was written off as "substantially, if not literally, true," as Loguen remarked. For the white reader, interest focused upon the exciting

22. Furnas, *Goodbye to Uncle Tom* (New York, [1956]), p. 239.

23. Henson, Ward, Steward, and Drew have been cited previously. Campbell's account, an unusually able one, was *Bond and Free: or, Yearnings for Freedom* . . . (Philadelphia, 1861); see especially pp. 199, 203–39, 251–64, 291–97.

24. See those titles discussed in Nelson, "Negro in Literature," pp. 60–67.

moment of escape from the master and the long journey northward to freedom; a secondary interest lay in accounts of life on the plantation, culminating in a series of brutalities which precipitated the decision to flee. Little space was given to the post-escape life of the fugitive, in part because the narratives often were written soon after the fugitive had arrived in the North or in Canada, and in larger part because the later aspects of the story held less intrinsic interest. Even Benjamin Drew, in his *A North-Side View of Slavery*—published in Boston in 1856 by John P. Jewett, the enterprising publisher of *Uncle Tom's Cabin*—gave most of his space to accounts of how the fugitives escaped, despite his announced intention to provide a record of "the history and condition of the colored population of Upper Canada."

Representative accounts were those by J. W. Loguen, Moses Roper, and Laura Haviland, and those on Harriet Tubman. Loguen was born in Tennessee, the natural son of a white man and a slave mother. His flight to freedom, in 1834–35, was a daring undertaking; during his five years in Canada West he learned to read, took a two-hundred-acre farm (which he lost because of a partner's bad judgment), and spoke of acquiring British citizenship. He turned to teaching school in Utica, New York; became an elder in the African Methodist Episcopal Zion Church (and in 1868, a bishop); and was for some years a teacher and minister in Syracuse, where he was one of the prime movers in the "Jerry rescue," leading to his taking temporary refuge with Hiram Wilson in Canada. He died in 1872. Loguen's autobiography, which is contradictory and unclear on dates and sequences, became an important primary source for historians. Although Loguen stated that there was no Underground Railroad at the time of his flight, the *Dictionary of American Biography* later would note how his escape revealed that "preliminary surveys" had been made for the underground system and that "a few lines already ran . . . as unerringly as railroads run through the large towns and cities." [25] On the other hand Roper, whose narrative sold widely in England, went on to London. Later he became famous in British North America through a lecture tour.[26]

It was in Sarah Bradford's biography of Harriet Tubman in 1869 that several of the songs allegedly sung as the fugitives crossed the Suspension

25. See *Loguen, as a Slave and as a Freeman,* which despite its date (1859) contains letters for 1860; W[illiam] H. A[llison], "Jermain W. Loguen," *DAB, 11* (1943), 368–69; James Egert Allen, *The Negro in New York* (New York, 1964), pp. 74–75; and Rhodes House, Oxford, Anti-Slavery Papers: Wilson to Scoble, Feb. 24, 1852. The Syracuse Public Library's copy of Loguen's book contains a note indicating that he was sixty-three when he died, which suggests that he was born in 1810 (the *DAB* says 1813); the *New York Tribune* for Oct. 1, 1872, contains an obituary.

26. Roper's account was *A Narrative of the Adventures and Escapes of Moses Roper, from American Slavary,* 3rd ed. (London, 1839).

Bridge at the Niagara frontier were first recorded. The most famous words betrayed abolitionist and non-Negro origins, however, even as printed in the Bradford account:

> I'm now embarked for yonder shore,
>> Where a man's *a man* by law.
> De iron horse will bear me o'er,
>> To 'shake de lion's paw';
> Oh, righteous Father, wilt thou not pity me,
> And help me on to Canada, where all de slaves are free.
> Oh I heard Queen Victoria say,
>> That if we would forsake,
> Our native land of slavery,
>> And come across de lake,
> Dat she was standing on de shore,
>> Wid arms extended wide,
> To give us all a peaceful home,
>> Beyond de rolling tide.

To this Bradford added, "No doubt the simple creatures . . . expected to cross a wide lake instead of a rapid river, and to see Queen Victoria with her crown upon her head, waiting with arms extended wide, to fold them all in her embrace." [27]

Laura Haviland, a white Canadian-born Quaker "Superintendent of the Underground," also was the subject of much postemancipation writing in Canada. Her narrative, *A Woman's Life Work,* although rambling, unclear, and filled with fictitious dialogue, unquestionably shows that she aided several fugitives to escape, knew Hiram Wilson and Isaac Rice, and was to the Detroit frontier what Harriet Tubman was to the Niagara. In addition to her active part in the Anderson extradition case, Laura Haviland taught school and, hoping to avoid denominational strife, opened a Christian Union Church in the Puce River area in 1852–53 with the support of Henry Bibb and two Detroit philanthropists. She suffered all the publicized rigors of the Canadian climate, frequently awakening "with snow sifting on her face, and not infrequently [finding] the snow half an inch or more deep on her bed upon rising in the morning." [28] The point at

27. Sarah Bradford, *Harriet Tubman: The Moses of Her People,* 2nd ed. (New York, 1886); Smith College, Sophia Smith Collection: Martha Coffin Wright to Lucretia Coffin Mott, n.d. [1860]; Earl Conrad, *Harriet Tubman* (Washington, 1943), passim. Conrad suggests there were fifteen trips, Bradford mentions nineteen. The author visited the Harriet Tubman Memorial Home, near Auburn, New York, but found no useful memorabilia.

28. See Mildred E. Danforth, *A Quaker Pioneer: Laura Haviland, Superintendent of the Underground* (New York, 1961), passim (the quotation is from p. 122);

issue, of course, is not whether Loguen, Roper, Tubman, Haviland, or others who left moving memoirs—Lewis Clarke, William Wells Brown, William Harrison—were honest, for on the whole they were, but that their narratives were not always used honestly by those who generalized from them, adapted them to their own purposes, reprinted out-of-context extracts in the *Anti-Slavery Reporter,* or judged the generality of fugitive life in British North America upon the basis of them.

What of those fugitives who did reach British North America? White residents frequently referred to how black they were, and there is some evidence that these fugitives were, on the whole, blacker than the norm. The majority—68 of 86 fugitives on whom Benjamin Drew gave such data—came from the border states, where owners prized blackness in their slaves because they could not go to free states and pass as whites. Most refugees were Methodists or Baptists, if they professed any religion at all. Very few were from cities. A number were free men. Of 114 refugees upon whom Drew commented, twelve were born free and kidnapped into slavery or fled from fear of being kidnapped. Five were passing as white. Ages ranged widely, with many being middle-aged (or, as Isaac Rice defined the term, over thirty-three) and many much younger. Nearly all were destitute, coming as one said "like terrapins, [with] all we had on our backs." A number arrived heavily armed.[29] Their abhorrence of slavery was genuine, and on several occasions Negroes attempted to abduct slaves of southerners who were foolish enough to bring them into the provinces.[30]

The post-1850 fugitives entered Canada West by a greater variety of routes than the earlier refugees, and outside the Utopian colonies they were more widely dispersed. From Ogdensburg and Cape Vincent, in New York, they crossed the lower St. Lawrence, and from Port Ontario, Oswego, Rochester, and Lewiston they set out across Lake Ontario,

Augustus Diamond, *Levi Coffin: The Friend of the Slave* (London, 1915), p. 37; Haviland, *A Woman's Life Work* (Grand Rapids, Mich., 1881), passim; and "Text of Rev. Wm. Harrison's Sermon at Baptist Church, Amherstburg, Oct. 10/43," unpubl. MS held by Alvin McCurdy, Amherstburg.

29. Drew, *North-Side View of Slavery,* p. 133; *National Anti-Slavery Standard,* March 6, 13, May 5, Oct. 10, 17, 24, 31, Nov. 21, 1850, Feb. 6, May 22, 1851; *New York Weekly Tribune,* Oct. 5, 26, 1850.

30. On attempted abduction, see as examples, TPL, scrapbook of extracts from diary of Mrs. Amelia Harris: Sept. 30, 1859; *The Honorable Elijah Leonard: A Memoir* (London, Ont., n.d.), pp. 47–48; *Toronto Globe,* Oct. 8, 1858, Sept. 9, 1859; Orlo Miller, *Gargoyles & Gentlemen: A History of St. Paul's Cathedral, London, Ontario* (London, Ont., 1966), pp. 92–94; and Robert Sellar's quasi-fictional *True Makers of Canada: The Narrative of Gordon Sellar, who Emigrated to Canada in 1825* (Huntington, Que., 1915), pp. 100–03, 116–22.

usually for Kingston, Cobourg, or Toronto. They made their way over the lakes on steamers, in smaller craft, and in one instance by floating across on a wooden gate—to land at Point Pelee, the ports of Burwell, Rowan, Talbot, and Stanley, at Long Point and Fort Erie, and elsewhere. The steamer *Arrow,* moving between Sandusky and Detroit under its noted Captain J. W. Keith, transported a large number of fugitives; and small vessels under Robert Wilson put in with "grain" which had been sent out from an Ashtabula warehouse for human cargo. Toronto, Brantford, Oakville, Collingwood, London, and the village of Shrewsbury, saw sharp rises in their black populations as a result of such traffic. Others went among the French near Windsor but, finding them "distant," moved away from the Detroit frontier, several establishing a short-lived all-Negro town, New Kentucky, in 1860. In 1851 the *Voice of the Fugitive* said that twenty-five hundred Negroes were at work on the railroad, and Ingersoll attracted a number once the line was open to Windsor because wood for the railway engines was cut and stored there. Some few went to the oil field near Petrolia, at Oil Springs.[31]

Just how sharp the rise was in specific communities cannot be said. In 1852 Isaac Rice thought there were between one and two thousand Negroes in Hamilton, while there were "not far from one hundred" in Brantford and between two and three hundred in London. He set the black population of Chatham at fifteen hundred,· and on the Detroit frontier at four thousand. Two years later Drew found a thousand Negroes in Toronto, mostly in the northwest section of the city, which then had a population of forty-seven thousand. He thought there were forty Negroes in Galt, two hundred in Windsor, five hundred in Amherstburg (of a total population of two thousand), nearly the same in Colchester (of fifteen hundred population), and two thousand in or near Chatham of a total population of six thousand. Dr. Howe found seven hundred Negroes in St. Catharines, although the census had reported 472, and in Hamilton he found five hundred where the census had enumerated only 62—unlikely, given the large numbers reported for nearly a decade earlier. The census

31. *Montreal Gazette,* Aug. 10, 1853; Drew, p. 300; *London* (Ont.) *Free Press,* June 21, 1926, June 30, 1956; *Oakville* (Ont.) *Weekly Sun,* Sept. 7, 1960; Siebert, *Underground Railroad,* pp. 83, 148–49; O. K. Watson, "Along the Talbot Road," *Kentiana* (n.p., 1939), p. 67; O. K. Watson, "Early History of Shrewsbury," Kent Historical Society, *Papers and Addresses,* 6 (1924), 83–84; Lauriston, "Negro Colonies," p. 96; John Nettleton, "Reminiscences, 1857–1870," Huron Institute, *Papers and Records,* 2 (1914), 13–15; Fred Landon, "Over Lake Erie to Freedom," *Northwest Ohio Historical Quarterly,* 17 (1945), 132–38; Landon, "Fugitive Slaves in London Ontario before 1860," London and Middlesex Historical Society, *Transactions, 10* (1919), 37; Landon, "The Fugitive Slave Law and the Detroit River Frontier, 1850–61," *Detroit Historical Society Bulletin,* 7 (1950), 5–9.

reported 510 Negroes in Toronto, while Dr. Howe found 934. The proper numbers were not known and cannot now be recovered, but it is clear that while the Negroes were not so numerous as subsequent myth-making and contemporary abolitionist propaganda would lead one to believe, they nonetheless were substantial, and on occasion—in Chatham, for example—comprised as much as a third of the population.[32]

Conditions for the fugitives were, as before 1800, mixed. Some adjusted readily and soon enjoyed relative prosperity. John W. Lindsey, who could pass for white, was worth $10,000 or more, as were Aaron Siddles and Henry Blue of Chatham. John Little and his wife—who moved into Queen's Bush—came to have over one hundred acres under good cultivation, could lend a friend $2,000, and owned a horse and carriage. In London, A. B. Jones, who had arrived penniless, soon owned several properties, one worth $4,000; and his brother, Alfred T., ran a prosperous pharmacy. Some fugitives became brakemen on the Great Western Railroad, which paid well, while others helped clear new lands around Colchester. Apprentices earned $2.50 a week, and waiters, especially around Niagara and in Toronto, received wages of $12.00 a month.

Still, lodgings might cost $15.00 a month and earnings were seldom sufficient to replace clothing left behind, to pay for the journey to Canada of wives and children who had remained in the South, or to pay doctor's bills. Most fugitives, badly dressed for the Canadian winters,' arriving "like frogs in Egypt," were consumptive: one Toronto woman lost ten children from tuberculosis.[33] Thomas F. Page, a young man from the upper South, reported "I do not like Canada, or the Provinces. I have been to St. John, N.B., Lower Province, or Lower Canada, also St. Catharines, C.W., and all around the Canada side, and I do not like it at all. The people seem to be so queer." The more frequent sentiment probably lay closer to that expressed by John H. Hill, a skilled carpenter and an officer in a company of Negro rifle guards, who wrote to William Still, "I wants you to let the whole United States know we are satisfied here because I have seen more Pleasure since I came here than I saw in the U.S. the 24 years that I served my master." "It is true," he added the following year, "that I have to work very hard for comfort but I would not exchange

32. *Amherstburg Quarterly Mission Journal, 1,* Sept. 25, 28, Oct. 12, 1852; Drew, pp. 94–95, 118–19, 136, 147–48, 234–35, 321, 348–49; Siebert, pp. 220–21; Howe, *Refugees from Slavery,* pp. 15–16. In 1843 Hiram Wilson had put the Negro population of Canada West at sixteen thousand (BPL, Samuel J. May, Jr. Papers, *1:* circular, Sept. 30).

33. *London Free Press,* June 12, 1954; M. Murray, "Stories of the Underground Railroad," *The Methodist Magazine and Review, 48* (1898), 221–22; Mitchell, *Under-Ground Railroad,* pp. 158–67; Siebert, pp. 205, 223; Drew, pp. 149–53, 198–233, 250, 270–73; Still, *Underground Rail Road,* pp. 2, 51, 77, 152, 319, 324, 490, 598.

with ten thousand slave that are equel [*sic*] with their masters. I am Happy, Happy." "Those that will work," remarked another, "do well—those that will not—not; it is the same here as everywhere. It is the best poor man's country that I know of." [34]

Until the economic panic of 1857, this judgment was a fair one. Jerry of the famous rescue became a barrel-maker in Kingston, and the equally famous Shadrach opened a restaurant in Montreal. In Toronto one Lemon John prospered by peddling his special ice creams about the streets, and in Saint John the city's ice trade was the monopoly of a Negro, Robert Whetsel. Joseph Mink became wealthy by managing a line of stages running from Toronto. In Colchester, Nathan S. Powell survived by manufacturing and selling Powell's Indian Tonic. In Bronte a refugee opened the first blacksmith shop; in Otterville a fugitive ran the only saloon. Still others made rope, worked as fishermen, in the brickyards and slaughterhouses, in livery stables, and as carpenters. Many women were servants, as they had been in the South, or opened dress-making or wig shops. In Hamilton, Negroes were in charge of the dead cart during the 1850s—a fact that cuts two ways—and New Brunswick had a black hangman who was regarded as standing apart from humanity, as had been the executioner of Quebec, Mathew Leveille of Martinique, in the previous century. Many Negroes, it was said, were "well dressed, quite clean and interesting," and owned houses that were "patterns of neatness." [35]

Indeed, the desire of most fugitives, once they had looked about and had overcome the initial period of adjustment, was to acquire a house and land. Most of the whites shared this goal, representative as it was of the middle-class values to which the fugitives often attached themselves. One, John Long, had owned land in the area that became Toronto in the 1830s,

34. Still, p. 333, Oct. 6, on Page; pp. 194, 197, Hill to Still, n.d. [late 1853], and Sept. 14, 1854; Robert Jones to Still, Aug. 9, 1856, p. 272; and pp. 250–54; Drew, p. 172.

35. Fort Malden "Fugitive Slave File"; *New York Tribune,* Oct. 24, 1857; *London Free Press,* July 5, 1924, April 30, 1932; *Toronto Star,* Aug. 11, 1943; NBM, "Whetsel Family" file; *The Life of Rev. James Thompson, The World's Wonder* (Richmond, Va., 1885), pp. 13–23; Eber M. Pettit, *Sketches in the History of the Underground Railroad . . .* (Fredonia, N.Y., 1879), p. 53; Nina Moore Tiffany, "Stories of the Fugitive Slaves, II: Shadrach," *The New England Magazine,* n.s., 2 (1890), 283; Blodwen Davies, *Storied York: Toronto Old and New* (Toronto, 1931), p. 68; Marjorie Freeman Campbell, *A Mountain and a City: The Story of Hamilton* (Toronto, 1966), p. 113; Lloyd A. Macham, *A History of Moncton Town and City, 1855–1965* (Moncton, N.B., 1965), p. 67; A. Carle Smith, *The Mosaic Province of New Brunswick* (Saint John, 1965), p. 93; André Lachance, *Le Bourreau au Canada sous le régime français* (Quebec, 1966), pp. 79–81; *Colonial Church and School Society Report for 1856–7* (PAC microfilm): A-325, p. 55, Nov. 1, 1856.

and a number had acquired property in the Niagara district before 1850 and without benefit of communitarian practices. By 1853, one investigator estimated, 276 Negroes in London owned real estate valued at $13,504—an average higher than for whites in the city.

In 1862 Dr. Howe found that one in eleven of Malden's Negroes paid taxes on property, while one in thirteen in Chatham were so taxed. (In both cases, one in every three or four whites owned ratable property.) But in Windsor one in five blacks, and only one in seven whites, were rate-payers. In this case, however, the average assessment on white-owned property was $18.76, while on black it was $4.18; in Chatham the figures had been $10.63 and $4.98 respectively.[36] And prejudice operated to keep even those Negroes who could afford better properties from moving else-where.

Few fugitives attempted to deny that they encountered substantial prejudice. In the 1850s city directories began to designate those residences and businesses owned by Negroes. Blacks were expelled from camp meet-ings, and those churchmen who—like Cronym in London—wished to help educate the fugitive, now argued that separate schools were needed because of white opposition. Dresden was called "Nigger Hole" by those who had opposed the Dawn settlement; racial jokes increased in the press; Negroes who, a decade or two earlier, had been able to employ whites to work for them no longer could do so. Throughout British North America blacks were thought, by some, to be responsible for "all the outrageous crimes, and two thirds of the minor ones"; chicken coops and laundry lines were said to require special protection where black men were about; and their women were blamed for an alleged rise in prostitution. Hotels in Hamilton, Windsor, Chatham, and London refused blacks admission, and they could not purchase cabin-class tickets on the Chatham steamer. The *Montreal Gazette,* turning back to the Nova Scotian experience, suggested that the fugitives should be sent to Sierra Leone. Beginning in 1855, auctioneers at the sale of building lots in the Windsor area refused to take bids from any Negroes, the city's *Herald* remarking that an owner had the right to "preserve his property from deterioration." Negroes should wish to stay with their own people, and if they did not they were welcome to leave. To oppose intermarriage and social mixing was not to be pro-slavery. So long as blacks remained in Canada West, the *Herald* warned, they would "ever have to contend with their superiors," and thus one

36. Edwin C. Giullet, *Toronto from Trading Post to Great City* (Toronto, 1934), p. 310; [Archibald Bremner], *City of London Ontario, Canada: The Pioneer Period and the London of To-day* (London, 1897), pp. 60–61; Howe, pp. 61–62; Siebert, p. 232.

helped them by refusing to sell them land. Canada West had become, according to Samuel Ringgold Ward, writing in what John Scoble called his "belligerent spirit," "beneath and behind Yankee feeling" in its color-phobia.[37]

The widely held Canadian view that there was a disproportionate number of Negroes in prison, jails, or the insane asylum was current well before 1850—and it cannot be supported. In 1851 the provincial institution for the insane in Canada West had only one Negro among 220 patients. The *Reports of Penitentiary Inspectors* tended to emphasize the "high percentage" of Negroes behind bars, while noting that fugitives educated only to slavery naturally were more prone to petty crime. Nor are the percentages particularly high: in fact, of the 3,223 persons who enjoyed Toronto's jail in 1859, 117 were black. Of 1,057 women committed in 1856, only eight were black; and of the Kingston penitentiary's 125 prisoners, eight also were Negroes. But each Negro offense received major publicity: when blacks burned down the barns of three of their opponents; when a Negro stabbed a colleague in a raffle, another murdered an Indian, and two beat a white to death—all in 1852; when one Negro killed another over noise in a Negro church in 1853; and when two black men murdered a mail carrier in 1859 and were hanged. Throughout these years the begging preachers and agents continued to be much in the news over their suits, assaults, and petty thefts.[38] Public opinion considered that fugitives were too often not punished for minor crimes out of sympathy for their condition: "it was found," according to the *Montreal Gazette* as early as 1842, "to be a sufficient reason to be an Indian or

37. *Windsor Herald*, Oct. 20, Nov. 3, 1855; *Montreal Gazette*, April 18, Sept. 16, 1851; *Sarnia Observer*, Nov. 25, 1859; *Hamilton Canadian Illustrated News*, 1 (1862), 8, 44, (1863), 131; Chambers, *Things as They are in America*, pp. 27–28; Delany, *Niger Valley Exploring Party*, p. 71; Ward, *Autobiography*, pp. 144–46, 202; Lauriston, *Romantic Kent*, p. 383; Edith C. Firth, ed., *The Town of York, 1815–1834: A Further Collection of Documents of Early Toronto* (Toronto, 1966), pp. 333–34.

38. See, for example, *Windsor Herald*, Jan. 4, 1856; *London* (C.W.) *Times*, May 4, 1849; *Toronto News of the Week*, Aug, 28, Nov. 6, Dec. 24, 1852, March 12, 1853; *The Friend of Man*, Aug. 30, 1837; *Brantford Expositor*, July 31, Aug. 6, 1852; the Inspector's Reports in the Appendixes to the *Journal of the House of Assembly of Upper Canada*, 1837–38, and the *Journals of the Legislative Assembly of the Province of Canada*, 1841–43, 1860; Linton, *Liquor Law*, p. 24; and James Silk Buckingham, *Canada, Nova Scotia, New Brunswick, and the Other British Provinces in North America, with a Plan of National Colonization* (London, n.d.), p. 67. Of 5,346 people committed to Toronto jail in 1857, only 78 were Negroes (W. G. Brownlow and Abram Pryne, *Ought American Slavery to be Perpetuated?* . . . [Philadelphia, 1858], pp. 237-38).

Negro to escape the gallows, no matter what crime they may have committed." [39] In short, the record was broken even before it was played.

This rising tide of prejudice, remarked upon by nearly all of the white
members of Canadian antislavery organizations and many of the refugees
themselves, was ascribed by most to four groups of people. All singled
out the American-born settlers—or those who had acquired "Yankee
ways"—who moved into the Niagara peninsula and, in greater numbers,
into the extreme southwest corner of the province. Most had occasion to
include Irish settlers as a source of anti-Negro sentiment. Others suggested
that former planters from the West Indies and their children—having lost
their patrimony and now displaced from what they considered to have been
a leading position in Imperial society—were enemies of the black man.
Finally, nearly everyone had an amorphous body of villains to blame,
those "lower orders" of whatever ethnic or national origin (including but
not limited to the Irish settlers) with whom the Negroes competed for
work and with whose women black men allegedly were able to make
their way. To prove any of these contentions would be impossible; of
the fugitive at the time no proof was asked. They were, many perceived,
what James G. Birney—twice the Liberty Party's presidential candidate—
had predicted they would be: "an *inferior class*" in the "bleak and hyper-
borean regions." [40]

Why this should have been so may not be answered clearly. Certainly
imported prejudices played a rôle. Certainly the pressures created by a
growing awareness of mass Negro arrivals, to compete for labor and
allegedly to add to the crime rate, contributed. The persistence of self-
conscious Negro associations, of separate communities, of improvement
societies such as the Sons of Uriah or the Negro Order of Odd Fellows,
and of all-Negro churches, were both a symptom of prejudice and a con-
tributor to it. Unquestionably the flow of fugitives changed in character
after 1850 as a result of the Fugitive Slave Act, that desperate compromise
by which nationalist American statesmen attempted yet again to hold the
union together. The new fugitives were not only more numerous but
poorer, more ready to take fright, armed and suspicious. Among British
North Americans there was a growing awareness of the many moral
ambiguities thrust upon them by the fugitives and their problems. This
awareness helped to induce that confusion which has always been present

39. [D. N. Haskell], *The Boston Committee in Canada: A Series of Eight Letters
reprinted from the Boston* Atlas (Boston, 1851), p. 19; *Anti-Slavery Reporter,* n.s.,
4 (1856), 134, 166, 229–30; *The Provincial Freeman,* July 4, 1857.
40. Quoted in William H. and Jane H. Pease, eds., *The Antislavery Argument*
(Indianapolis, Ind., 1965), p. 46.

when Canadians have had to deal with issues not of their own making but arising mostly from the unfortunate circumstance of sharing a continent with a giant neighbor where confusion and moral ambiguity were magnified, more passionate, and seemingly endemic.

In short, and as we have seen, British North Americans shared the patterns of prejudice found in the North, although these patterns appeared in colors muted by distance from the central scene of action. So, too, were these patterns varied even within Canada West, and economic realities again provided the conditions that led to those differences. Systematic prejudice—in the schools, in the churches, in the sale of property—was mild in the eastern part of the southwestern peninsula, in Hamilton, and north into Toronto, while it was relatively stringent in the western part. One explanation for this observable difference—noted at the time and clear from the evidence now—is that Hamilton and Toronto were prosperous, especially after 1854 and even after 1857 despite the slump, and that the building trades were in need of much semiskilled labor, so that Irish and Negro alike could find jobs; while at the frontier on the west, opposite Detroit, the economy was not able to absorb the new arrivals. Prejudice, always individual, was also a matter of the moment, the place, and the market, however, for discrimination was widely practiced in St. Catharines, despite this geographical generalization.

But if many of the cherished beliefs of Canadians—then and since—about the haven they provided fugitives from federal marshals are myths, or at least exaggerated, a countervailing fact also remains indisputably true: in British North America, the Negro remained equal in the eyes of the law—after the abolition of slavery, and setting aside the growing tendency toward segregated education, a most damaging exception to be dealt with in a later chapter. Although challenged in 1851, Negro jurors and jury foremen served in Toronto and elsewhere, and Negroes gave evidence with full legal protection. They generally were taxed as the white man was, were punished in no harsher a manner than any other criminals, and cast their votes openly and with impunity. British consuls looked after the black Canadian's interests when he was abroad with the same care that any British subject might expect, and even American consuls in the British provinces treated Negro Canadians with the respect that was their due.[41] If social and economic realities did not conform to legislative and

41. *Anti-Slavery Reporter,* June 21, 1843, and n.s., *4* (1856), 230; *Voice of the Fugitive,* July 2, 1851; *Toronto Globe,* Oct. 8, 1859; *Ottawa Citizen,* May 3, 1867; PRO, BTI/479: Francis Waring, consul, Norfolk, Va., to J. T. Briggs, Oct. 25, and encls., in re New Brunswick Negro Antonio Nicholas; NA, Foreign Service Post Records, C.D., Halifax: cases of destitute Negro seamen (e.g., no. 6, R. W. Fraser

legal forms, those forms at least limited the ways in which prejudice might make itself felt.

Still, the hierarchy of the unequal will have its way. In British North America, as in the United States, the Kingdom of Individuals would be long in coming. Even those who felt most committed in that cause, members of the Anti-Slavery Society of Canada and others who worked with the abolitionists to cleanse North America of that which George Brown accepted as a continental rather than merely American stain, were limited in their effectiveness by that sense of paternalism which may so easily shade into a racism no less hurtful for its presumptive benevolence; for such paternalism reveals the quiet arrogance of those who feel that they have all to give to an underprivileged group and nothing to learn from it. Can one condone wholly—or condemn entirely—the blind, well-meaning certitude of that missionary-teacher who, reporting to the Colonial Church and School Society in 1856 of her Negro charges, concluded that "The worse they are, the more need there is for British Christians to instruct, enlighten and reform them"? [42]

The major thrust in the Canadian contribution to worldwide abolitionism came not from the British mission boards, the self-segregated, self-help communities, the begging ministers, or the isolated Negroes of the Maritime Provinces. These groups were interested in helping those blacks who were citizens in British North America and in easing the adjustment of the fugitives. Certainly individual members of some of the communities helped to flay slavery through the press or hoped to weaken it by journeys south of the border to guide fugitives toward freedom. Certainly, too, many reasoned that any aid given to fugitives in British North America made the provinces additionally attractive, and that by creating a magnet for runaway slaves, they were helping to sap the strength of the institution. But as collective bodies they did not attack slavery directly. Abolitionism in British North America was expressed through attempts to subdue prejudice within the provinces and efforts to lend vocal and moral support, and limited financial aid, to the more exposed but also far more effective abolitionist groups in the United States. [43]

The first major Canadian antislavery society was created to combat the growing evidence of organized, group prejudice in Canada West. Three

to William L. Marcy, Nov. 8, 1853; and no. 7, Dec. 14, 1854); Murray, "Anglo-American Anti-Slavery Movement," pp. 324–27.

42. A-325, *Report for 1856–7*, p. 60: Nov. 1.

43. A longer version of the material that follows appears in Robin W. Winks, "'A Sacred Animosity': Abolitionism in Canada," in Martin Duberman, ed., *The Anti-Slavery Vanguard: New Essays on the Abolitionists* (Princeton, N.J., 1965), pp. 301–42.

events in and after 1850 in particular—the Larwill election campaign, a public petition relating to segregated schools, and the passage of the Fugitive Slave Bill—made such a society imperative in the minds of those who had followed the color question in the United States with growing apprehension. There was a ready-made group of Negro sympathizers in the white Canadians who had contributed to the support of Wilberforce, Dawn, and Elgin.[44]

Foremost among Canada's abolitionists was George Brown, the powerful editor of the province's most important newspaper, the *Toronto Globe.* Brown had shown an interest in the condition of the Negro in Canada from the journal's inception in 1844. He, his brother Gordon, his father Peter, and his sister Isabella formed the nucleus of an antislavery society in Toronto; and Isabella's husband, Thomas Henning, was the first secretary of the Canadian Anti-Slavery Society as well as a member of the *Globe*'s editorial staff until 1854.[45] Far more restrained than Garrison's *Liberator* and far more forthright than the lesser abolition sheets, the *Globe* provided the antislavery group with a forum for the "sacred animosity" its owners held toward slavery.[46] In his paper Brown attacked Henry Clay, the Fugitive Slave Law, Larwill, Prince, and separate schools with equal force, for—as he wrote—Canadians had the "duty of preserving the honour of the continent" against slavery.[47]

The Toronto-based group were able to ground their work on previously established channels of communication. In 1827 Samuel Cornish and a Quebec-educated Jamaican, John Browne Russwurm, editors of *Freedom's Journal,* which they published in New York for two years, had sent agents into Canada to solicit support. Negroes in Windsor had established a short-lived antislavery society there, and Upper Canadians, led by John Roaf, a Congregational minister, had attended a temperance convention in Saratoga Springs, New York, in 1837, making contact with many American abolitionists.[48] As a result, Reverend Ephraim Evans, a Wesleyan Meth-

44. On the Negro issue in politics, see Winks, "Abolitionism in Canada," pp. 317–18, n. 28.

45. J. M. S. Careless, *Brown of the Globe, 1: The Voice of Upper Canada, 1818–1859* (Toronto, 1959), pp. 102–03; Syracuse Univ., Gerrit Smith Miller Papers: Henning to Smith, Feb. 2, 13, 1861, Oct. 12, 1863; Columbia Univ., Gay Papers: Henning to Gay, May 27, 1852, Feb. 18, 1854, April 11, 1855.

46. A phrase drawn from the *Toronto Globe's* notice, on June 8, 1860, of Charles Sumner's speech before the Senate, "The Barbarism of Slavery." See *The Works of Charles Sumner* (Boston, 1874), *5,* 124.

47. See, for example, editorials of Feb. 7, March 19, May 28, Aug. 10, Sept. 19, Oct. 5, Nov. 9, 1850; Feb. 22, March 6, 27, April 3, 12, 18, May 10, 13, June 20, Sept. 18, 25, Nov. 27, Dec. 18, 1851; and March 24, 1852.

48. Aptheker, *Abolitionist Movement,* p. 33; Washington, *Story of the Negro, 2,* 292–93; M. A. Garland, "Some Frontier and American Influences in Upper Canada

odist and editor of the *Christian Guardian,* formed an Upper Canada Anti-Slavery Society in Toronto late that year. It grew to claim 106 members but did not last out the decade. Still, abolitionist leaders in the United States were coming to know the Canadian scene reasonably well. Garrison (whose father had been a Canadian) lectured in the province, as did Gerrit Smith and Elihu Burritt, the latter for the New England Anti-Slavery Tract Society at first; and Arthur and Lewis Tappan had been in business briefly in Montreal. Scoble's initial efforts at Dawn, Henson's willingness to exploit his association with Uncle Tom, and correspondence by the Reverend Michael Willis and Montreal's John Dougall with the Tappans, Smith, and others, made the establishment of a formal Canadian society virtually inevitable. Roaf and Willis attended an antislavery meeting in New York in 1846, and the Canadians saw that their advocacy of freedom for the Negroes should be "unlimited by national boundaries, [and] unfettered by civil or ecclesiastical domination." They wished "the immediate and universal abandonment" of slavery. By this they meant "gradual emancipation immediately begun." [49]

The passage of the Fugitive Slave Act was the catalyst that led to the formation of an enlarged and more durable antislavery society. In 1850 a meeting was held "on behalf of slaves" coming to Canada West, in the Mechanics' Institute in Toronto, and during the year the Browns worked through the *Globe* to create additional interest. In 1851, in particular, Torontonians were given frequent opportunities for public debate. Between February and May, the *Globe* editorially chastised its journalistic opposition for being soft on slavery, while under the collective name "Common Sense" a substantial group publicly protested Canadian support for the antislavery movement in the United States. Frederick Douglass delivered a heated oration in St. Lawrence Hall, and Paola Brown, a remarkably large-lunged young woman, who had been a member of the black colony at Woolwich in 1832, shouted to audiences throughout Canada West: "Slave-holders, I call God, I call Angels, I call Men, to witness, that your destruction is at hand, and will be speedily consumated, unless you repent." [50] In September

prior to 1837," London and Middlesex Historical Society, *Transactions, 13* (1929), 26–27.

49. *Annual Report of the American and Foreign Anti-Slavery Society* (New York), 1877, p. 32; 1848, p. [3]; 1850, p. 154; 1851, pp. 15, 101, 110–12, 114; 1852, pp. 15, 26; 1853, pp. 173–77, 191; *Fourth Annual Report of the American Anti-Slavery Society* (New York, 1837), pp. 34–35, 140.

50. *Toronto Globe,* Aug. 10, 1850, March 6, 18, 1851; *Montreal Witness,* Feb. 15, 1853; *Charlottetown Islander,* March 4, 1853, Sept. 12, 1856; *London Free Press,* Dec. 2, 1933; Brown, *Address intended to be Delivered in the City Hall, Hamilton, February 7, 1851, on the Subject of Slavery* (Hamilton, 1851), p. 49; Jesse E. Middleton, *The Municipality of Toronto: A History* (Toronto, 1923), *1,* 247; Fred Landon, "The Anti-Slavery Society of Canada," *JNH, 4* (1919), 33–40.

a North American Colored Convention met in Toronto. The fifty delegates approved killing pursuers in self-defense and asked Henry Bibb, the Negro journalist from Windsor, and T. F. Fisher and J. D. Tinsley of Toronto, to prepare an appeal to Negro residents in Canada West to found an agricultural league similar to the struggling land societies. By July 1852, a constitution had been adopted for "The American Continental and West Indian League," which was to promote settlement throughout the New World, and Bibb was organizing an auxiliary unit in Windsor.[51] Acting independently, Garrison wrote to a Toronto friend, Mrs. Caroline H. Dall, and asked her to organize a supplementary relief fund for fugitives there, which she did. Also in 1851 Harriet Tubman moved to St. Catharines to begin seven years of Canadian residence, during which time she guided fugitives into the province. This was the year of Larwill's campaign on racist lines in Chatham and of the first Negro petition against the rising separate schools.[52] Clearly, something larger, more dedicated to principle, better organized, than these individual actions was needed to deal with the growing ferment.

The Anti-Slavery Society of Canada fulfilled this need. It was organized "to aid in the extinction of Slavery all over the world" by any lawful and practical means. On February 26, 1851, a public meeting at Toronto's city hall, with the mayor in the chair, launched the new organization with a view to ending "the common guilt of the civilized and Christian world." A committee was appointed to correspond with antislavery societies in the United States and Britain, and a constitution and bylaws were prepared. The new society elected Dr. Willis, the Principal of Knox College, as President, Thomas Henning as Secretary, and Andrew Hamilton as Treasurer. Fourteen local Vice-Presidents were named to the Executive Committee, including three Negroes, A. Beckford Jones, Henry Bibb, and Wilson R. Abbott. George Brown, John Roaf, and Samuel Ringgold Ward were included on the Committee, and Charles Stuart was the Corresponding Secretary. Henning was instructed to get advice from John Scoble, then Secretary of the British and Foreign Anti-Slavery Society, Lewis Tappan, as Secretary of the American and Foreign Anti-Slavery Society, and Sydney Howard Gay of the American Anti-Slavery Society.[53]

51. The original title of the group was to have been the Canadian Foedus Agricultural Union. See *Voice of the Fugitive,* May 21, Aug. 27, Sept. 18, Oct. 22, Dec. 17, 1851, and July 1, 1852.
52. Houghton Library, Siebert Papers, *1:* Mrs. Caroline H. Dull, Aug. 25, 1889; Smith College Library, W. L. Garrison II Collection: funeral address on occasion of death of Lewis Hayden, April 11, 1889; Conrad, *Harriet Tubman,* pp. 45-72, 115–18; Bradford, *Harriet Tubman,* pp. 39–53.
53. Anti-Slavery Society of Canada, *First Annual Report* (Toronto, 1852), pp. 9–12, 24.

The new President, Michael Willis, was a Scot who had come to Canada in the 1840s. In 1847 he became Professor of Theology in Knox College, Toronto, where he was the voice of the local Free Church Presbyterian community. From an early interest in the poor he had moved on to slavery, and he had gained a local reputation as a debater of much skill on the subject. Known for his energy and his "earnest and nervous style" of speech, Willis was ideally suited for his position. He had the efficient support of his wife, Agnes, who handled much of his correspondence, organized sewing groups among the fugitive women, and was treasurer to the Toronto Ladies' Association for the Relief of Destitute Colored Fugitives which, from 1853, corresponded with a like group in London. Willis lost no time in contacting Sydney Gay to let him know of his own group's purposes, and as a result Willis was one of the speakers at the Eleventh Annual Meeting of the American Society in May of 1851. At the meeting he became a friend of Gerrit Smith and remained so until his death.[54]

Secretary Henning had been an early abolitionist, but since in 1836 he had joined Linton in publicly charging the churches with harboring slavery he was not welcome in all professedly antislavery homes. He proved an indefatigable correspondent—as was his wife for the ladies' auxiliary— and he maintained contacts with American abolitionist friends, such as Gerrit Smith, well into the 1870s. (It was Henning who would deliver the writ of habeas corpus by which the fugitive Anderson went free in 1861.) Immediately after the Canadian society was established Henning wrote to Scoble, Tappan, and Gay, and he and the society subscribed to all of the antislavery organs they could, often reprinting material from them in the *Globe*. The society clearly hoped to avoid being entangled in the many divisive arguments that had so damaged the antislavery cause elsewhere, for as Henning wrote to Gay in 1852, his group wanted to cooperate with all societies. But although Henning's carefully worded letters helped the Canadian society avoid clear commitment to issues it considered tangential, his strong views on several issues that ultimately proved crucial to the abolitionist movement were to bring him directly into the arena of controversy.[55]

54. See obituary notices on Willis in *Toronto Weekly Globe,* Aug. 29, 1879, and *Acts and Proceedings of the Sixth General Assembly of the Presbyterian Church in Canada* (Toronto, 1880), p. 59. See also *Montreal Witness,* Nov. 23, 30, 1846; *Toronto Globe,* Nov. 27, 1851; Still, pp. 127-28, 318; Drew, p. 238; *Ladies' Society to Aid Fugitives from Slavery* (London, 1855); and Willis, *Death Made Tributary to the Glory of God* . . . (Toronto, 1869), pp. 25–35.

55. Gay Papers: Henning to Gay, April 29, 1853; Gerrit Smith Papers: Henning to Smith, Dec. 7, 1874; *Barrie* (C.W.) *Northern Advance,* March 25, 1853; Rhodes House, Anti-Slavery Papers, C32/46: Henning, deposition.

In the first year the society limited itself to playing Lady Blessington, gathering information, and seeking to define its position. The Ladies' Association provided a hundred fugitives with money and clothes. The Anti-Slavery Society went on record as having no confidence in the American Colonization Society or any plans to transport Negroes to the West Indies and so advised the Governor General when he inquired, adding that the members of the society rejoiced in Canada's ability to shelter fugitives. The society operated a small adult evening school to train fugitives in agricultural pursuits, endorsed Dawn and the Refugee Home Society, surveyed the Negro population of Canada West, fed refugees, sponsored speakers—including John Cordner, Francis Parkman's brother-in-law; Elihu Burritt; Frances Ellen Watkins (after 1860, Harper), a free Negro orator who won distinction in New England; and H. Ford Douglass, new editor of the *Provincial Freeman*—issued a "Statement in Regard to the Colored Population of Canada," fought extradition, and held annual soirées to raise funds. The women's auxiliary helped to obtain fourteen thousand signatures in British North America for the Stafford House Address, a remonstrance directed by 563,000 women of Britain to the ladies of America.

Most dramatically, the society directed attention to itself and to the issue of slavery when, in April of 1851, Henning was able to persuade Frederick Douglass, Samuel J. May, Jr., and George Thompson to speak from the same platform. Thompson was Britain's chief Garrisonian and the prime impetus behind Edinburgh's Society for the Abolition of Slavery, and he had won the notoriety of being condemned by Andrew Jackson, a distinction many Canadians cherished. Addressing a crowd of two thousand men and women, Thompson reminded Torontonians that the slave was God's child and thus their brother. May was more explicit in his call for Canadian help. "I ask you, members of another nation, to assist in overthrowing one of the institutions of my country." [56]

By the second year Willis was able to tell Scoble that the society wished to act upon May's call, moving on from an emphasis on relief to a more direct expression of abolitionist sentiment, and he sent Samuel Ringgold

56. Anti-Slavery Papers, C23/26: Willis to Scoble, Feb. 12, 1852; ibid., E2/8, Minute Book: March 5, 1852, Oct. 3, 1856; Anti-Slavery Society of Canada, *First Annual Report*, pp. v–vi, 12–18, 22–24; *Barrie Northern Advance*, March 26, 1852; Still, pp. 755–61; *Voice of the Fugitive*, Oct. 21, 1851; Gerrit Smith Papers: Joshua Leavitt to Smith, May 4, Dougall to Smith, May 6, June 29, 1840; Donald Savage, ed., *Life and Labors of the Rev. Wm. McClure, for More than Forty Years a Minister of the Methodist New Connexion* (Toronto, 1872), pp. 202–03; Univ. of Rochester, William Henry Seward Papers: Willis and Henning to Seward, Feb. 28, and draft reply, March 9, 1863; Julia Griffiths, ed., *Autographs for Freedom* (Auburn, N.Y., 1854), pp. 187–89.

Ward throughout the province on a speaking tour. Henning helped to organize branches of the parent body in Grey County, Hamilton, Windsor, and Kingston, to which Ward was to speak; and in London Reverend William McClure, an Irish New Connection Methodist who had the support of a local man of means, John Fraser, founded a branch with A. B. Jones, the Negro pharmacist, two physicians, and Congregational and Presbyterian ministers on the board. John Dougall, editor of the *Witness* in Montreal, was a one-man corresponding society for that city; and in St. Catharines an independent Refugee Slaves' Friends Society, helped by the Mayor, Elias Adams, and the local member for Parliament, William Hamilton Merritt, cooperated closely in the work of sending fugitives on to Toronto. In 1855 the parent society was ready, therefore, to hire its first full-time agent, an American, Reverend J. B. Smith, who opened an office in Toronto (only to close it two years later). Henning wrote articles for British antislavery journals while Willis attended the 1858 meeting of the British and Foreign Anti-Slavery Society in London. The Canadian society's annual reports were sent to interested parties including, in 1863, the American Secretary of State; and Willis and Henning were Corresponding Members of the American and Foreign Anti-Slavery Society, the former addressing that body at its 1851 annual meeting.[57]

The Toronto society was of importance within the province but it had little impact elsewhere. It seldom had enough money, or enough followers, or enough direct contact with the daily routine of the antislavery crusade, to have any real influence outside Canada West. Indeed, Canadian abolitionists in general seemed cut off from the mainstream, as they were; and except for Henning and Roaf, who corresponded extensively, most were content to await what might come to them to do, the exhortations of Thompson and May notwithstanding. Ultimately the society suffered from the same divisive influences that operated in Britain, the United States and among the fugitives themselves—religious dissension, "the woman question," and unreliable agents—compounded by growing anti-Americanism and increased attention to unrelated local political problems. Money often was given only for specific purposes, as when the Governor General earmarked his £ 10 for relief; and even George Brown, whose *Globe* offices printed the annual reports, expected to be paid for those services. Most important, however, was the fact that the abolitionist movement in Canada could gather little strength from the chief political preoccupations of the leaders of society, for it was not related organically to a political party as it was in the United States. If local by-elections on occasion involved "the Negro question," provincial elections never did;

57. The Kingston society seems to have been inactive, for not once from 1851 to 1860 does the *Kingston Daily Whig* appear to have mentioned it.

and no major Canadian political party ever championed the Negro, then or since.[58]

The society did what it could from its shaky base. The aged Thomas Clarkson was added to the Executive Committee, as was William McClure.[59] A resolution in praise of *Uncle Tom's Cabin* was passed, fifteen hundred copies of the first annual report were distributed, and Willis, Henning, and Ward traveled for the society in Britain. Nonetheless, in 1855 the group was nearly inactive, and by 1857 it had retreated to its initial position of being a fugitive slave relief organization and an opponent of "colour-phobia" in the Canadas. The society could, in truth, do little more; in any event, it did far more than the Abolition Society of Halifax, an auxiliary of the American and Foreign society which contented itself with interracial picnics, or the antislavery caucus of Charlottetown, Prince Edward Island, which met but once, in 1853.[60]

There were other means of supporting the cause of abolition of course. One could prepare antislavery addresses quite independently of the

58. *Toronto Globe,* April 3, 5, 12, 19, 1851, Dec. 18, 1852, Jan. 4, March 22, 28, 1853; Anti-Slavery Society of Canada, *Sixth Annual Report* (Toronto, 1857), pp. [3], 6–11; Anti-Slavery Papers, C6/86: Dougall to J. H. Tredgold, April 4, 1840; Merle Curti, ed., *The Learned Blacksmith: The Letters and Journals of Elihu Burritt* (New York, 1937). See also Peter Tobis, *Elihu Burritt* (Hamden, Conn., 1968); Murray, "Anglo-American Anti-Slavery Movement," pp. 231, n. 51, 271–73; *The Colonial Protestant; and Journal of Literature and Science, 1* (1848); *The Provincial Freeman,* May 16, 1859; and *Anti-Slavery Bugle,* Oct. 4, 1851. Frances Harper's Toronto speech became famous by being included in Lydia Maria Child's *Freedmen's Book* (Boston, 1865), a compilation of excerpts meant for reading aloud to the postwar freedmen (pp. 243–44). Even George Brown momentarily wavered during the war, when he feared a federal invasion of the Canadas in retaliation for the anti-Northern sentiment expressed in his newspaper. His brother Gordon held the *Globe* to a staunch antislavery line even then, and it was Gordon, not George, who received a gold watch from the pro-Northern American community in Toronto at the end of the war. See Fred Landon, "The Canadian Anti-Slavery Group," *The University Magazine, 17* (1918), 546. Ironically, George Brown would be assassinated by a discharged employee smarting under the taunt, among others, of being partially Negro and hiding the fact. See A. R. Hassard, *Famous Canadian Trials* (Toronto, 1924), pp. 158–72; E. C. Kyte, ed., *Old Toronto* (Toronto, 1954), pp. 195–201; and J. M. S. Careless, *Brown of the Globe, 2: Statesman of Confederation, 1860–1880* (Toronto, 1963), pp. 366–72, without reference to the Negro issue.

59. BPL, Garrison Papers, *36:* McClure to R. D. Webb, Oct. 23, Dec. 3, 1868; Anti-Slavery Society of Canada, *Second Annual Report* (Toronto, 1853), p. iii. For an obituary of McClure, see *Minutes of the Forty-third Annual Conference of the Methodist New Connexion Church of Canada held at Owen Sound, Ontario . . .* (London, Ont., 1871), pp. 10–11.

60. Anti-Slavery Society of Canada, *Second Annual Report,* pp. vi, 7–12, 19–28; Gay Papers: Henning to Gay, April 11, 1855; Gerrit Smith Papers: Henning to Smith, Jan. 9, 22, Feb. 2, 13, 16, 1861, Aug. 11, 1862, Oct. 12, 1863; *Toronto Globe,* Jan. 1, 1864; *Charlottetown Islander,* March 18, 1853.

societies: in Nova Scotia Reverend William Sommerville, a Reformed Presbyterian from Cornwallis, attacked slavery repeatedly; and in Canada East two ministers, J. M. Cramp and W. Taylor, used their journal, *The Colonial Protestant,* to present mild antislavery protests. One could contribute to mission aid societies. One could, when the Civil War broke out, enlist in the Union army and fight against the slaveholders, as some eighteen thousand British North Americans did.[61]

One outspoken abolitionist who appears not to have been active in any of the Canadian societies was Alexander Milton Ross. A Corresponding Member of both the British and Foreign Anti-Slavery Society, and the Anti-Slavery Society of France, Ross was not at all hesitant about interfering in the affairs of another country. He had moved to the United States as a youth, and, after a talk with Gerrit Smith in 1855, when he was twenty-three, he decided upon an active career of running fugitives from the deep South to Canada. Ross made at least five trips to the southern states, posing as a bird-watcher; and in five years he was instrumental to the escape of thirty-one or more blacks, sixteen of whom met with him in an emotional reunion in London after the war. John Greenleaf Whittier dedicated one of his poems to Ross, a Falstaffian figure who thought well enough of himself to write two volumes of autobiography replete with derring-do. Ross was equally taken up with other reforms than abolition, however, and for all of the energy he expended, his accomplishments seem disproportionately small. An ardent vegetarian, he worked on a plan to make man into a grass-eater to give Canada "mastery in war," since "an army in the field could live largely on grass" in the summertime, while "General Winter" would end all troop movements for the remainder of the year. He offered his services as a doctor to Benito Juarez, although he did not go; and he led the antivaccination cause in Canada, edited an ornithological journal, and wrote on butterflies, moths, and wild flowers. If he portrayed himself as larger than life, he did remain consistent, unlike many fellow whites, in his commitment to the Negro, continuing to work for their acceptance in Canadian society into the 1870s before turning his attention to the problems of the Indian.[62]

61. Sommerville, *Southern Slavery not Founded on Scripture Warrant: A Lecture* (Saint John, N.B. 1864); OPA, Canniff Family Papers: package 13, MSS speech and article by William Canniff; University of Toronto Library, John Charlton Papers: MS autobiography, pp. 137–38; Fred Landon, "Abolitionist Interest in Upper Canada," *Ontario History, 44* (1952), 165–72; Robin W. Winks, "The Creation of a Myth: 'Canadian' Enlistments in the Northern Armies during the American Civil War," *CHR, 39* (1958), 24–40.

62. On Ross, see Houghton Library, Ralph Waldo Emerson Papers: Ross to Emerson, Dec. 26, 1864, Aug. 12, 1875, Jan. 13, 19, 1878, March 11, and Dec. n.d., 1879; Anti-Slavery Papers, C66/121: Ross to Charles H. Allen, Jan. 27,

One might also support one of the many British and American, or few Canadian, newspapers that espoused the Negro's cause. Brown's *Globe* and Dougall's *Witness* seldom missed an opportunity to attack slavery, and others ran occasional editorials against the institution while still suggesting that blacks were not overly welcome (Edward John Barker's *Kingston Daily British Whig* may have been typical in this respect in printing only seven antislavery notices in eleven years).[63] There were the specifically antislavery newspapers to read as well. Bibb's *Voice of the Fugitive,* which he issued from his Windsor office from 1851 to 1853; its competitor, Shadd's *Provincial Freeman,* published in Toronto and after 1855 in Chatham; Linton's Stratford sheet, *The Voice of the Bondsman,* which he distributed free until his health failed; and *The True Royalist and Weekly Intelligencer,* launched in Windsor in 1860 by Reverend A. R. Green, which did not last out the next year.

These newspapers are symptomatic of the many problems that prevented any single antislavery endeavor in British North America from being an unqualified success: they were quarrelsome, vindictive, naïve, and frequently unintelligent. *The True Royalist*—founded as the organ of the British Methodist Episcopal Church of British North America, with Green as a self-proclaimed bishop, in opposition to an older Negro church, the British Methodist Episcopal Church in Canada—served only a schismatic purpose. Henry Bibb and Mary Shadd refused to cooperate to further the Negro cause and used their presses to attack each other. Ultimately an incredible variety of sensitivities, distractions, foolish quarrels, prideful hurts, and personal ambitio·ns held the antislavery groups back far more than in the United States, where manifestations of the same petty spirit were overridden by men and forces of much greater power.[64]

The chief supporters of the antislavery cause in Canada West were ministers, and dissension between them also crippled the Society: Willis,

---

April 29, 1886; LC, Edith Rossiter Bevan Autograph Collection, *3:* Ross to Rossiter [?], Feb. 1, 1878; Cornell Univ., College Papers: Ross to Burt Green Wilder, March 24, 1877; Ross's books, *Recollections and Experiences of an Abolitionist: From 1855 to 1865* (Toronto, 1872) and *Memoirs of a Reformer* (*1832–1892*) (Toronto, 1893); Fred Landon, "A Daring Canadian Abolitionist," *Michigan History Magazine, 5* (1921), 364–73; and "Reflections," *Saturday Night, 32* (1919), 2.

63. See Richard H. Grover, "Dr. E. J. Barker's Attitude towards Slavery as Expressed in the Kingston Daily British Whig January 1, 1849—December 20, 1860" (unpubl. research paper, Queen's Univ., 1966), based on all issues except for 1856. I should like to thank the author for sending me a copy of his paper.

64. Thomas Clarkson's wife offered a lock of her husband's hair for sale at an antislavery fair, and the lock eventually found its way to Canada West, whence she received at least four letters demanding that she attest to its authenticity. Henning ultimately broke with Scoble because the latter failed to send a (deserved) letter of thanks for lodgings.

Henning, and Brown held the organization together, and all were Presby-terians. Where a denomination was not shared, often doctrinal differences were added to others. At the 1857 annual meeting of the Canadian Anti-Slavery Society, Reverend Robert Dick, with support from Henning, brought to the floor Linton's explosive allegation of proslavery collabora-tion on the part of several religious bodies; and the *Globe* and a Toronto paper, *The Church,* squared off against each other over the question of whether slavery was a proper subject for religious controversy.

Linton's and Henning's attacks on fellowshipping were tinged with a more generalized anti-Americanism which further limited the effectiveness of the abolition movement in Canada. Dislike for the United States as a whole often found its most effective expression in denunciations of slavery and of the Federal government, and even northern travelers in the prov-inces were referred to by otherwise non-Garrisonian Canadians as slave-holders. John Charlton, a young abolitionist, noted that prejudice against the United States was so strong around Simcoe that American maps were not allowed in classrooms. While Canadians considered themselves well informed on American matters, there were those who could ask whether Buffalo was in the state of New Orleans. From its founding in 1846 Dougall's *Montreal Witness,* a "weekly review and family newspaper," attacked the United States and slavery as being synonomous. In the first volume alone, no fewer than twenty articles, poems, and editorials were devoted to antislavery. A typical piece related how a young slave girl was hanged in New Orleans for striking her mistress, remarked that the reli-gious press of the North had been silent on the incident, and concluded that the affair was "a hideous offshoot of American Republicanism and American Christianity." The highly emotional description, representative of this form of popular Victorian pornography, told in detail how the victim, "a young and beautiful girl," had been ravished by her master, her infant torn from her arms, and had died on the gallows, "the rope tighten-ing around her delicate neck . . . [while she was] swinging there alive for nearly half an hour—a spectacle for fiends, in the shape of humanity." The story was not compromised for its readers by its assumption that New Orleans was in Mississippi or that the editor of the *Witness* apparently could see "beneath that dark skin a *white* soul wrung by mortal agony." [65]

The Canadian abolitionist movement, like the American, was in fact several movements which from time to time seemed to confuse lesser issues with greater. In 1832 William Lloyd Garrison had published a pamphlet,

65. Charlton Papers, MS autobiography, p. 167; *Montreal Witness,* Jan. 5, May 18, July 6, 20, 27, Aug. 3, 10, Sept. 21, Oct. 12, Nov. 16, Dec. 12, 21, 1846 (the quotations are from June 8, p. 190, and June 22, p. 206, italics added), and March 24, 1852; *Barrie Northern Advance,* Oct. 9, 1850.

Thoughts on African Colonization, in which he denounced for what they were plans to remove the Negro to Africa, Haiti, or the British West Indies —plans which accepted the basic proslavery argument that the Negro was innately inferior. Five years later, in 1837, a schism within the ranks of the abolitionist movement began when a group of antislavery men from Andover Theological Seminary attacked Garrison's outspoken language, his willingness to give women a place on the lecture platform, and his denunciation of the apparent indifference of organized religion to slavery. In 1840 Garrison succeeded in having a woman elected to the business committee of the American Anti-Slavery Society; and several members, led by the society's president, Lewis Tappan, bolted the meeting to form the American and Foreign Anti-Slavery Society. Another schism issued from Garrison's decision, made clear in 1844, that the American Constitution was a protector of slavery and that if necessary the Union itself should be dissolved to achieve abolitionist ends.

These schisms were felt in British North America as well. The question of American disunion was not central to Canadian thought, although there were those who argued that a fragmented American Union would restore to Britain control of the balance of power in the Americas, a balance lost following the Clayton-Bulwer Treaty.[66] But the "women question" loomed large, as did concern for "good taste" in fighting slavery. The Canadian Anti-Slavery Society cooperated with women's organizations while including few women on its own programs, and Henning continued to correspond with Garrisonians and anti-Garrisonians alike. In the United States the "mute" and "moral suasionists," as Garrisonian Frances H. Drake wrote, divided their time between promoting migration to Canada and opposing those who wanted immediate abolition.[67] Because many of the northern antislavery spokesmen who toured British North America were opposed to Garrison's views, Canadians were well informed on the nature of the schisms.

Charles Stuart represented the problems these issues, compounded by distance and anti-Americanism, posed for Canadian abolitionists. Born in Jamaica, Captain Stuart had served in the East India Company and had lived in both England and the United States, where as one of Charles Grandison Finney's Holy Band he had helped bring Theodore Dwight Weld into the anti-slavery movement. He had resided in Amherstburg between 1817 and 1822, where he had helped Negroes to establish themselves on the land before he moved to Utica and then to England, there to work with Nathaniel Paul in opposition to all overseas colonization

66. Robin W. Winks, "A Nineteenth-Century Cold War," *The Dalhousie Review,* 39 (1960), 464–70.
67. BPL, Weston Papers, *19:* Drake to Maria Weston Chapman, Oct. 31, 1843.

schemes. In 1850 he again settled in Canada West, at Lora Bay, and became a member of the new Canadian Anti-Slavery Society. His attacks on the American government, to which he had once been friendly, were couched in the Garrisonian prose of immediatism: he emphasized "the deep filth of sin in which [the United States] is now proudly wallowing" and found that he could not "dutifully expose my wife and myself, to the outrages of of [sic] a power so ferocious, so hypocritical, and so base as [America's] present, de facto, government." The American people, he said, were "democratical-demagogical."

Stuart was torn by religious doubts which resolved themselves in religious dogmatism, and he wrote with "a confused medley of polemical theology, whining cant and complementary bombast" that soon wearied his correspondents.[68] When Weld became a Unitarian, Stuart stopped writing to him, convinced that they could not meet in the next world. He wrote incessantly to Gerrit Smith, sometimes about their common interest in the Negro but more often to persuade Smith that Christ was God. Stuart joined Tappan's antifeminist group, and he asserted that the idea that "whatever is morally right for a *man* to do is morally right for a *woman* to do" was an "insane innovation . . . [to be] vigorously resisted." He attacked the American and Foreign Anti-Slavery Society as "a woman's rights group"; opposition to women, he concluded, was in "the cause of liberty and love." [69] He forbade the use of any products of slave labor and would not permit sugar or cotton in his home—for which his wife, whom he held to a most rigorous religious orthodoxy, had to find substitutes. Stuart's opposition to slavery had once been effective, for he had helped the Amherstburg fugitives, had drawn Weld and others into the movement, had raised funds in England for Negro education at Wilberforce, and had represented Jamaica at the 1840 world antislavery convention in London. But when his help could have mattered most he was pursued by the Hound of Heaven while himself pursuing the hares of mid-Victorian masculinity. Unfortunately, Stuart was all too representative of many of the Canadian abolitionists who, neither more nor less human than their American

68. Fort Malden Museum, Amherstburg Deeds: indenture, Stuart and Herbert Palmer Cox, Jan. 12, 1826; Gerrit Smith Papers: Stuart to Smith, Jan. 8, Aug. 12, 1853, April 16, 1855, Sept. 26, 1857; Edward A. Talbot, *Five Years Residence in the Canadas* (London, 1824), *1*, vi; Charles Stuart, *Is Slavery Defensible from Scripture?* (Belfast, [1831]), passim.

69. BPL, Garrison Papers: *11*, circular, Stuart to R. Wardlow, n.d., 1841; *10*, Stuart to J. A. Collins, Nov. 4, 6, 7, 1840; *3*, circular, Stuart to the Friends of Religion and Humanity, Nov. 1, 1833; BPL, Phelps Family Papers, *21*: Stuart to Phelps, draft, June 11, 1841; Gerrit Smith Papers: Stuart to Smith, Feb. 21, March 9, 30, April 20, May 22; Sept. 28, 1861; PSHS, Gratz Collection: Stuart to Smith, April 26, May 13, 1837, Tappan to Smith, Aug. 25, 1838.

counterparts, became preoccupied with less important and unrelated issues. He continued to write innumerable tracts of no perceptible merit and, in his declining years, of little perceptible impact.[70]

But within the borders of British North America, the issues which preoccupied those of an activist persuasion were not less important. Since abolitionism was not related to any political party or movement in the provinces, even though more closely identified with the Clear Grit reformers in Canada West than with other groups, and since slavery—however international in its moral implications—was not practiced in the provinces themselves, other social needs must have seemed more urgent. The names of those who spoke out against slavery, as authors of letters to the local press, frequently do not appear on the membership or contribution rolls of the anti-slavery societies; and even figures like Brown, Linton, and Ross gave their greater energies to other crusades. At no time did membership in the Anti-Slavery Society of Canada exceed two hundred; and there were, perhaps, not over twenty individuals who might be identified as being at the core of Canadian abolitionism in the 1850s.

Finally, the Canadian antislavery movement also suffered from cupidity, false ambition, inefficiency, and dishonesty. In ten years several of the early heroes of the Canadian movement had lost their effectiveness through one or more of these human failings. Among those who fell from grace, as we have seen, were Henson, Ward, Wilson, and Scoble. When Wilson borrowed heavily, expecting the Lord "to find means of paying," antislavery philanthropists in the United States had to do so for Him. Henson's ineffectual attempts to meet his obligations, and Scoble's personal ambition and paternalistic manner, were damaging to the society indirectly, but Ward's alleged defection dealt it a particularly serious blow.[71]

Samuel Ringgold Ward was "the original nigger" according to Wendell Phillips; he was so black, the abolitionist maintained, that one could not

70. See Fred Landon, "Captain Charles Stuart, Abolitionist," *Western Ontario History Nuggets,* no. 24 (1956), pp. 1–19, reprinted on OHS, *Profiles of a Province: Studies in the History of Ontario* (Toronto, 1967), pp. 205–14; Barnes, *The Antislavery Impulse,* pp. 14, 213–14; John J. Bigsby, *The Shoe and Canoe, or Pictures of Travel in the Canadas . . .* (London, 1850), *1,* 263–66, which is often in error; and Stuart's polemical *The Emigrant's Guide to Upper Canada . . .* (London, 1820). Although Fred Landon says that Charles Stuart and Charles Stewart were the same man, and although Stuart was on occasion addressed as Stewart, there was an abolitionist of the latter spelling in Detroit. The two have been confused in some accounts.

71. Oscar Sherwin, *Prophet of Liberty: The Life and Times of Wendell Phillips* (New York, 1958), p. 212; Gay Papers: Henning to Gay, Oct. 25, 1851; Pease and Pease, *Black Utopia,* pp. 116–17; Anti-Slavery Papers, C23/33: Wilson to Scoble, June 12, 1844; C/32: Henning to Chamerovzow, Dec. 10, 1855, Jan. 17, 1845; *Toronto Globe,* May 2, 1857.

see Ward when he shut his eyes.[72] He was also an unusually vigorous and highly intelligent spokesman for a logic that the relatively mild Canadian abolitionists were unprepared to follow through to its conclusion. Ward was not a perfectionist, as Garrison was, and in 1853 he professed not to wish to give offense to those who opposed Garrison; but he was a man who understood that slavery and racism, while related, were different things— something that many saw, and like Scoble, chose to ignore. Ward wanted slavery ended. Right now! That was disquieting enough to those who wondered whether Canadians should interfere in the affairs of a powerful neighbor. More disturbing, he saw that many abolitionists might well wish to end slavery without any commitment to creating racial equality. He found this view abhorrent, and he often said so. Since he was a black man himself, and frequently more articulate than his listeners, he was not popular even among those who employed him; and the charges which ultimately branded him as dishonest arose in large measure because Scoble and Henning felt that Ward had hidden from them his true Garrisonian colors until the Canadian society—professedly neutral but not with respect to immediatism—had financed Ward's trip abroad.

The *Provincial Freeman,* once his newspaper, also felt betrayed by him, since he sent little if any of the $6,000 he collected in Britain back to Canada. At this juncture Ward's autobiography was published in London and received much praise in Britain, and Henning felt constrained to note it favorably lest he reveal the dissension in the Canadian society's ranks. Mary Shadd, angry that the Toronto officers had refused to sponsor a bazaar on behalf of her paper, and under the mistaken impression that they had done so for *Frederick Douglass' Paper,* brought Ward's disaffection into the open. Henning then revealed the subtle racism of which Ward had suspected him, and which he already had shown in anonymous articles for the *Anti-Slavery Reporter,* by writing a patronizing letter to the *Freeman* suggesting that the Shadd group would "gain the respect and confidence to which the colored man is . . . entitled . . . when he is worthy of them." The journal found this condescending, for Henning had meant, the *Freeman* said, that when the Negro would "behave properly, their superiors will consider the propriety of giving them their due." Thus did Henning forfeit the confidence of two fractious but hardheaded blacks, Ward and Shadd, and provide international advertisement for the inability of black and white to work together in Canada save as patron and client.[73]

72. *Anti-Slavery Reporter,* n.s., *4,* 136; *The Provincial Freeman,* June 3, 10, 24, 1854; Ward, *Autobiography,* pp. 66, 405; Anti-Slavery Papers, C23/61: Scoble to [Chamerovzow], April 7, 1853; C31/38A: Henning to same, Dec. 10, 1855, Jan. 17, 1856; Murray, "Anglo-American Anti-Slavery Movement," pp. 275–77.

73. Winks, "Abolitionism in Canada," p. 336, n. 59.

Perhaps the most famous meeting of abolitionists on Canadian soil, in retrospect, was that held by John Brown in Chatham in May of 1858.[74] Brown visited St. Catharines in April in company with J. W. Loguen, to learn whether he might enlist support from fugitive slaves in Canada West. He wrote to his son that he was "succeeding *to all appearance,*" and he paid Harriet Tubman what he took to be a supreme compliment, addressing her in the masculine gender and remarking that she was "the most of a *man* naturally; that *I ever met* with." She had hooked her "whole team" to his cause, although just what this cause was he did not say.[75]

Brown arrived in Chatham on April 29, and the following day sent out a call for "a very *quiet* convention" of the friends of freedom. Martin Delany later stated that Brown spoke only of a desire to establish a Subterranean Pass Way which would make Kansas rather than Canada the terminus of the Underground Railroad. Delany agreed to become "president" of an organization to further the SPW. No word had been mentioned of inspiring Negro revolt. Nor did Brown mention such a scheme to James Madison Bell, the Negro poet with whom he stayed while in Chatham.[76]

What transpired at the convention is not clear. Meeting in the First Baptist Church on May 8 and 10, giving out that they were organizing a Negro Masonic Lodge, twelve white and thirty-four black men—at first under the chairmanship of William C. Munroe, a Negro—apparently discussed guerrilla warfare against slaveholders. Delany, who cochaired the session, insisted that Harper's Ferry was never mentioned, but others— Israel Shadd of the *Provincial Freeman,* J. H. Kagi, who was named provisional secretary of war under the government Brown proposed to form and who had prepared the way for Brown in Chatham, Osborn P. Ander-

74. See John Cleland Hamilton, "John Brown in Canada," *Canadian Magazine, 6* (1894), 119–40; Fred Landon, "From Chatham to Harper's Ferry," ibid., *53* (1919), 441–48; Landon, "Canadian Negroes and the John Brown Raid," *JNH, 6* (1921), 174–82; and W. E. Burghardt DuBois, *John Brown* (Philadelphia, 1909), pp. 243–60.

75. Cornell Univ. Library, Autograph Collection: Brown to wife, April 6, [1858] (date originally written as 1858 and altered to 1856); Ohio State Historical Society: Brown to his son, April 8, 14, 1858; Fisk Univ. Library, Nashville, Tenn.: Brown to Day, April 16, 1858; Princeton Univ. Library: Brown to Frederick Douglass, June 22, 1858; Osborne P. Anderson, *Voice from Harper's Ferry . . .* (Boston, 1861), pp. 9–15; *Ingersoll* (C.W.) *Oxford Herald,* April 15, 1858.

76. Frank A. Rollin, *Life and Public Services of Martin R. Delany . . .* (Boston, 1868), pp. 83–95; Richard D. Webb, ed., *The Life and Letters of Capt. John Brown . . .* (London, 1861), pp. 99–106; Fred Landon Collection: transcripts, Brown to wife, May 1, 12, 25, 1858; *London Free Press,* March 15, 1941; B. W. Arnett, "Biographical Sketch of J. Madison Bell . . . ," *The Poetical Works of James Madison Bell,* 2nd ed. (Lansing, Mich., 1901), pp. 5–10.

son, who was to be a member of Brown's Congress, and Reverend Thomas M. Kinnaird of Toronto, a free Negro printer who may not have been present but who was privy to the proceedings—later suggested otherwise. A constitution was distributed at the end of the meeting, and Brown entrusted the printing of copies of it to a Negro printer in St. Catharines. Brown then wrote to his abolitionist friend in Massachusetts, Thomas Wentworth Higginson, that he would take no rash steps—three days after writing to another friend to ascertain whether an arms cache was in safe hands. On the 29th Brown left Chatham, to return later while aiding a number of fugitives in their escape from Missouri, but never to reconvene his convention or to call his provisional government into being.[77]

When Brown struck at Harper's Ferry, Virginia, on October 17, 1859, nearly eighteen months after the Chatham Convention, all of Canada West at once linked the two events. The Canadian press reported on the raid, capture, and ensuing trial, conviction, and execution in detail; and the more perceptive newspapers—such as the *Toronto Globe*—saw that the bells were down: if tension mounted further, civil war would follow. That Franklin B. Sanborn, George L. Stearns, and Samuel Gridley Howe, three members of the so-called Secret Six—northern abolitionists who helped finance John Brown's activities—fled to Canada as soon as they learned of the events at Harper's Ferry, seemed further to relate the raid itself to the province. Virginia's Governor Henry A. Wise drew the lesson plain: the "compact of fanaticism and intolerance" had sprung from British soil, and the "predatory war" of the abolitionists was being carried on from Canada itself. Had not John Brown, Jr., been seen with Loguen throughout Canada West, organizing branches of the League of Liberty? Had not Charles Stuart met with Brown at Gerrit Smith's home in February of 1858? Had not Anderson, who escaped from the fiasco at the Ferry, fled to Canada, as did Frederick Douglass? Was it not a Canadian Negro, Mary Ann Shadd, now Cary, who prepared Anderson's notes for publication? There was, Wise hinted, a "sectional organization" which originated in the Canadas, intent upon subverting the American way of life. Abolitionists, *De Bow's Review* concluded, were a "vile, sensuous, animal, brutal, infidel, superstitious Democracy of Canada and the Yankees." [78]

77. MHS, John Brown Papers: Brown to Higginson, May 14, 1858; Gratz Collection: Kagi to Brown, June 23, 1857; May Papers, *1:* Brown to family, Feb. 10, 1859; BPL, Higginson-Brown Collection: Franklin B. Sanborn to Higginson, June 4, 1859; Ohio Historical Society: Brown to E. A. Fobes [Forbes], May 11, 1858. The actual printing of the constitution took place in Hamilton (see *Hamilton Spectator,* June 14, 1958, and Yale Univ. Library copy of *Provisional Constitution and Ordinances for the People of the United States*).

78. LC, Franklin B. Sanborn Papers: Sanborn to Ralph Waldo Emerson, Aug. 3, 1857, Nov. 10, 1859, Jan. 26, Feb. 3, 1860; Concord Free Public Library, Concord,

Canadian reaction to the raid and its aftermath was, in fact, mixed. Some wrote to warn Wise of future plots. One John Smith of Quebec comforted the Governor by noting that "lower Canada dont go in for Niggers like the Upper Canada folks." The *Toronto Leader* and the conservative press in general railed against Brown's "insane raid" and warned that the South would tolerate little more. Even William King and Archibald McKeller thought Brown was a fanatic. But the execution of Brown turned Canadian attention from the raid to the slavocracy once again. King concluded that Brown's martyrdom was "one of the brightest pages" in America's history. On the eve of the execution a public meeting was held in Montreal to express sympathy for the Brown family, and a thousand attended—although when the collection was taken, the plate held only $65.86. Members of the legislature informally raised $400.00 for Brown's widow (which was not sent when the trial made public the nature of Brown's involvement in the Pottawatomie murders). Mrs. Brown did receive a collection taken up at a memorial service held in Toronto, at which Reverend Kinnaird delivered the funeral sermon.[79]

Then, and in the years to come, the fact that Brown may have plotted his raid—in general if not precise terms—in Chatham was to press the abolitionist stamp on Canada West more firmly than Canadian anti-slavery societies, mission aid to fugitive slaves, and antisouthern editorials in the *Globe* and *Witness* could ever do. Many Canadians had rejoiced at the thought, as Ward suggested, that slaveholders hated no country in the world so much as Canada. Canada West was the home of Uncle Tom, of the Chatham Convention, and of perhaps sixty thousand fugitive slaves. That any of these ingredients could be even partially mythical was scarcely to be conceived. That they would become any less legendary in the years to follow was not to be expected.

The significance for Canada of this international phase of abolitionism is, in any case, rather different than students of the antislavery movement

---

Mass., Sanborn Papers, 5: Sanborn to Theodore Parker, Oct. 22, 1859; Sanborn, *Recollections of Seventy Years* (Boston, 1909), *1,* 147; *London Free Press,* Nov. 3, 1859; PAC, George Brown Papers, 5: Oliver Mowat to Brown, Dec. 15, 1859; *Toronto Globe,* Dec. 22, 28, 1859; Hallie Brown, *Homespun Heroines,* pp. 95–96; Fred Landon, "Canadian Opinion of Southern Secession, 1860–61," *CHR, 1* (1920), 258.

79. LC, Brown Papers: Smith to Wise, Oct. 28, C. B. Wright to Wise, Dec. 5, 1859; PAC, King Papers: notes for a speech on Brown, Dec. 2, 1861; Anderson, *Harper's Ferry,* p. 55; *Chatham News,* March 25, 1941; *Montreal Witness,* Oct. 26, 1859; Fred Landon Collection: photostat of broadside by Harvey C. Jackson; *Toronto Globe,* Oct. 20, 21, Nov. 3, 18, 22, 23, 25, Dec. 2, 8, 9, 12, 14, 16, 23, 1859; *Berlin* (C.W.) [now Kitchener] *Berliner Journal,* May 3, 1860; Alexander M. Ross, "John Brown in Canada," *Canadian Magazine, 4* (1893), 392; Lauriston, "Negro Colonies," p. 97.

have been inclined to think. The chief importance credited to Canada has been twofold: as a haven for fugitive slaves Canada was said to be a stronghold of freedom for the Negro in an alien North American environment; and at the time of the Civil War, Canada was expected to provide pro-Northern moral support against the slavocracy. Both of these traditional interpretations of Canada's rôle in the antislavery crusade have been seriously overemphasized, and as a result the true significance of Canada's place in this phase of the long story of the Negro's quest for freedom has been mistaken.

Much of Canada's participation in the abolition movement resulted from geographical proximity rather than from ideological affinity. Negroes fled to Canada, as we have seen, for negative rather than positive reasons; and once there they encountered race and color prejudice not unlike they found in Massachusetts or Ohio. Free they were but equal they were not. Indeed, America's deferred commitment to equality was deferred continentally rather than nationally. Obviously British North America could not avoid an issue so likely to convulse the continent. But the surprise lies not in the extent of the Canadian involvement so much as in the general ineffectiveness of that involvement. While there were short-lived abolitionist societies in the provinces, such societies could be formed easily and without any necessary financial or political commitment: when the society of 1837 was founded in Toronto, there were 1,006 antislavery societies in the United States, 213 in Ohio alone, and 33 in Maine. Abolitionists in the United States were misled by their Canadian counterparts to assume that the provinces would stand behind the North when the Civil War came. As Samuel Gridley Howe wrote to Theodore Parker in 1860, "I look with the more interest upon Canada, because it seems to me she is to be the great and reliable ally of the Northern States. . . . When the lines are fairly drawn what an immense moral aid it will be to the North to have such a population as that of Canada . . . at her back!" [80] But when the lines were fairly drawn, British North Americans proved to be anti-Northern, opposed to a war fought to preserve the Union, in fact rather inclined to the Southern position once they saw that Lincoln was not, as he said, fighting to end slavery. The Civil War did not result in victory for the Canadian abolitionists, for they shared the general Canadian postwar fear that the Federal triumph had intensified the dangers of annexation by an avaricious republic bent on continentalism. The war did, however, promote Canadian unity and contribute to the creation of the Dominion of Canada in 1867.[81]

80. L. E. Richards, ed., *Letters and Journals of Samuel Gridley Howe* (Boston, 1906–09), 2, 447, March 25.

81. See Robin W. Winks, *Canada and the United States: The Civil War Years* (Baltimore, 1960).

Nor, ironically, did the Canadian abolitionist movement lead to any fundamental improvement in the condition of the Negroes in British North America, even though this was the most consistent goal of the Canadian Anti-Slavery Society. In the United States the movement helped to bring on a Civil War which added yet another dimension to the commonly shared Negro American story. Today the black American may, on the whole, assume himself to be the product of a common historical experience with slavery, war, and reconstruction; and as he wages his civil rights campaigns, he does so with at least some sense of historical continuity and of ethnic unity. But in Canada the Negro's position was different from the outset, and the Negro Canadian who emerged from the period of abolitionism and Civil War differed even more markedly than before the war from the Negro American.

After 1861 Canadians were to lose interest in the fugitive slaves, for the grander vistas of the Civil War—news of the battlefield, of possible British intervention, of the Emancipation Proclamation, and of the assassination of President Lincoln—would overpower the interest, never intense, in the Anti-Slavery Society, the missions to the refugees, and the communal experiments. With slavery torn from the South, Negroes no longer would need to flee, and those who already were living in British North America would wish to return to their homeland. Just as the American Missionary Association had closed down its petty operations in Canada West during the war, so too did most Canadians appear to close their pocketbooks, their schools, and their churches to the fugitives still in their midst. That fugitives might be seeking to escape from something other than slavery itself occurred to few; for most Canadians had accepted the body of myths which accompanied Eliza as she scurried across the ice flows that, miraculously, bound Kentucky and Canada together. Harriet Martineau, during her famous visit to the New World, was told that "the sublimest sight in North America is the leap of a slave from a boat to the Canadian shore," since that leap transformed the black "from a marketable chattel to a free man." [82] Perhaps theologians had not yet begun to speak of "a leap of faith," but it was precisely this kind of leap which those fugitives had made. And as with all too many leaps of faith, the gap between the known and certain, and the unknown and assumed, would prove to be as wide as the real Ohio.

82. Ward, p. 158.

9. West of the Rockies

While the larger dramas of the approaching Civil War were being played out in the Canadas, a number of Negroes moved to Victoria, on Vancouver Island, to found a black colony that survives to the present day. From 1858, when the first black settlers arrived,[1] until well into the twentieth century, when the transcontinental railroads began to give at least some Negroes a sense of a more widespread Canadian community, the Negro in the Far West remained cut off from many of the problems that would arise for his brethren to the east. The early story of the Negro in British Columbia thus stands apart from the larger Canadian record.

The first Negro settlers came from California, where they were the subject of much controversy and some abuse. In 1850 the state legislature began to restrict Negroes, first by disqualifying them from giving evidence against white men and then, in 1852, by entertaining legislation which would have permitted newly arriving slave-owners to retain their property despite the 1849 state constitution's prohibition of slavery. The Negroes of San Francisco, in particular, who owned taxable property estimated at five million dollars in value, felt under attack. In January 1858, in his inaugural address, the new governor decried abolitionist activities. In the same month one Archy Lee, a slave held by his owner despite California law, was arrested as a fugitive.[2] In February, the San Franciso Board of Education ordered that Negroes must attend special schools, and the state Supreme Court ruled that Lee's owner might keep him. On March 19 the legislature took up a bill to restrict the immigration of Negroes, an act which would have required all blacks in California to register.[3] The pattern of attack on the Negroes' position was ominously similar to the situation blacks faced in Cincinnati in 1839, and the local results were much the same.

1. The *Victoria Colonist,* June 15, 1861, says that two Negroes were members of "a *corps* of 'Invincibles'" who defended the colony prior to 1858. See B. A. McKelvie and Willard E. Ireland, "The Victoria Voltigeurs," *British Columbia Historical Quarterly* [hereafter, *BCHQ*], 20 (1956), 221–39.

2. For the background in California, see F. W. Howay, "The Negro Immigration into Vancouver Island in 1858," RSC, *Transactions* (1935), sec. 2, pp. 145–56; and Rudolph M. Lapp, "Negro Rights Activities in Gold Rush California," *The California Historical Society Quarterly,* 45 (1960), 3–20.

3. Carl I. Wheat, ed., " 'California's Bantam Cock': The Journals of Charles E. De Long, 1854–1863," in *California Historical Society Quarterly,* 9 (1930), 256, 281–82 n. 87; San Francisco Department of Public Schools, *Twelfth Annual Report of the Superintendent* . . . (1864), p. 31 .

The Negroes of San Francisco gathered in Zion Church on April 14 to consider emigration. They discussed Sonora and Vancouver Island; and on the third evening of the rally, Jeremiah Nagle, captain of a steamer that plied the run to Victoria, offered to answer questions about the British colony. Sixty-five Negroes, including Archy Lee, released that day under an order issued by the United States Commissioner, decided to make up an initial party of settlers. On April 20, thirty-five of them sailed in Nagle's ship, the *Commodore,* together with three delegates, one Mercier, Fortune Richard, and Wellington Debey Moses, who were to talk with the Governor of Vancouver Island.[4]

After an unpleasant voyage, the *Commodore* reached Victoria on April 25; and on a day that was warm and clear, and made "most beautiful" by blooming peach trees, four hundred and fifty whites bound for the gold strike on the Fraser River went ashore. The Negroes preferred land to gold, however. Their first act was to rent a room for an evening of prayer. The delegates called on the Governor, James Douglas, the next day, and he received them warmly. The Anglican minister and chaplain to the Hudson's Bay Company, Edward Cridge, invited them to his services, and the local authorities confirmed that Negroes would be accepted as settlers without legal discrimination. They could purchase land for a pound an acre—a relatively high price—one quarter to be paid in cash and the remainder in four years, the land to be untaxed until paid for. After nine months as landholders they could vote and serve as jurors, and they might become British subjects after seven years of residence.[5]

The delegates wrote to San Francisco that Victoria was "one of the garden spots of this world." Mercier returned to Zion Church, where three hundred and fifty people, white and Negro, met to hear him tell of the warmth shown by Douglas and Cridge, and of how Vancouver Island was a "place which has unfolded to us in our darkest hour, the prospect of a bright future." The following week the Negroes formed an emigration company; resolved not to create institutions for their own segregation, whether churches, schools, or clubs; and prepared for a general exodus. Fifteen more blacks reached Victoria on May 16, and thereafter, in numbers that were not counted but which may have reached four hundred families,

4. James William Pilton, "Early Negro Settlement in Victoria" (B.A. essay, Univ. of British Columbia, 1949), pp. 11–12. In *Some Reminiscences of Old Victoria* (Toronto, 1912), p. 215, Edgar Fawcett, the novelist, said that Mifflin Wistar Gibbs—not Mercier—was a delegate; but Pilton appears to be correct. Rudolph M. Lapp, in *Archy Lee: A California Fugitive Slave Case* (n.p., 1969), p. 62, is less certain that Lee went to Victoria.

5. Robert W. O'Brien, "Victoria's Negro Colonists—1858–1866," *Phylon, 3* (1942), 15–16.

California's Negroes joined the larger throng of emigrants pouring north.[6]

These Negroes were not fugitives. They were "actuated by no transitory excitement," as their resolutions made clear, for they were leaving the United States permanently. Most owned property that they were able to sell, although at a small loss, and therefore they could quickly acquire a stake in the new society. The first settlers, who purchased land in April— when the population of Victoria was only eight hundred—arrived ahead of the major flow of Americans, and their property appreciated rapidly as the city grew to seventeen thousand by July. One man paid $3,200 for a building in June and was collecting $500 monthly rental on half the structure by midyear. Within two years the Negroes owned potentially taxable properties valued (by their estimation) at £50,000.[7]

The Victoria Negroes were also literate and skilled, and these skills were in demand. Mifflin Wistar Gibbs, a mulatto born in Philadelphia in 1823, and his partner, Peter Lester, had been such successful clothing and shoe merchants in California that the San Francisco school board offered to exempt the latter's daughter from segregation. They opened a general merchant house that soon competed on favorable terms with the Hudson's Bay Company store. Joshua Howard, a self-styled lawyer, Samuel Ringo, who ran a popular restaurant, bakers, barbers, tailors, caulkers, and five men who held certificates to teach—such were the emigrants. Willis Bond, who had been a slave, was referred to by a Speaker of the House of Assembly as "one of the cleverest men white or black that I have ever met," and as an auctioneer, contractor, and landlord he enjoyed both acceptance and prosperity. In 1862 a traveler noted that the Negroes were "a far more steady, sober and thrifty set than the whites by whom they are so much despised"; and when a number applied for citizenship early in 1864, under a law passed the previous year, the records showed that virtually all could read.[8]

Victoria's establishment accepted the Negroes from the outset, thus setting the tone to which many British residents responded. Governor Douglas sympathized with the Negroes' condition in California; he knew

6. *San Francisco Daily Evening Bulletin*, May 7, 12, 1858, quoted in Howay, "Negro Immigration," pp. 155–56; Mifflin Wistar Gibbs, *Shadow and Light: An Autobiography* (Washington, 1902), pp. 61–63.

7. O'Brien, "Negro Colonists," pp. 16–17; *Victoria Times*, Feb. 25, 1911; *Victoria Daily Colonist*, Feb. 2, 1958.

8. Edward Mallandaine, ed., *First Victoria Directory: Comprising a General Directory of Citizens . . .* (Victoria, 1860), pp. 26, 30, 32-34, 36; C. P. Lyons, *Milestones on Vancouver Island* (n.p., 1958), p. 86; Pilton, "Early Negro Settlement," pp. 17–22; *Victoria Daily Colonist*, Oct. 8, 1961; Frederick P. Howard and George Barnett, comps., *The British Columbia and Victoria Guide and Directory for 1863 . . .* (Victoria, 1863), pp. 55, 63, 76; Richard C. Mayne, *Four Years in British Columbia and Vancouver Island . . .* (London, 1862), pp. 351–52.

that the island needed all the settlers it could get, and he may have hoped that the blacks would serve as police or help to fight Indians. His knowledge that his mother was either a West Indian mulatto or a Creole obviously increased his concern. Further, *The British Colonist,* under the editorship of Amor de Cosmos, was strongly pro-Negro, urging the white citizenry to recognize the "sobriety, honesty, industry, intelligence and enterprise" they would bring with them.[9]

Also important was the fact that Reverend Cridge was close to Douglas and that, as the commanding Anglican divine, he had the imprimatur of the Hudson's Bay Company, a power so great that some said "H.B.C." meant "Here Before Christ." When the black colonists arrived Cridge noted in his diary, "I feel this is a juncture of great importance & needs much wisdom & prayer on my part," for he realized that there would be whites who would refuse to worship with them, as there were. But in late May, when a copy of the *San Francisco Daily Evening Bulletin* reached him in which Cridge read of the Negroes' praise for his having made them feel like men, he put behind him any doubts raised by those whites who complained that "Ethiopians *perspired,"* their *"aromatic luxury"* getting in the way of pious thoughts. Until his death Cridge remained a firm defender of equal rights. He found the Negroes' "manner and conversation marked by as great propriety and accuracy as those of middle tradesmen in England," and that contrary to what he had read, they were "industrious, sober and religious, and . . . delighted with freedom." [10]

The Hudson's Bay Company was equally color-blind, for it had employed Negroes before. Stephen Bonga, an Indian-Negro, had become famous along the north shore of Lake Superior for his ability as a guide and trader, as had his father George, who had gone to school in Montreal. Earlier, travelers had observed two black men at Fort William in 1817, and another served the company as a middleman (canoe paddler) in 1818.[11] Other Negroes were in the Company's employ in 1794, 1795, and 1819.[12]

9. W. Kaye Lamb, "Some Notes on the Douglas Family," *BCHQ, 17* (1953), 42–43; Dorothy Bakey Smith, ed., "The Journal of Arthur Thomas Bushby, 1858–1859," ibid., *21* (1958), 171–72; *The British Colonist,* Feb. 5, 1859.

10. BCA, Cridge Diary: May 16, 18, 19, 23, 25, 1858; BCA, Cridge Correspondence: Cridge to Colonial and Continental Church Society, July 5, 1858; BCA, Cridge Record Book: J. J. Moore to Cridge, Sept. 4, 1858; *Victoria Gazette,* Aug. 24, 1858; Kinahan Cornwallis, *The New El Dorado: or, British Columbia* (London, 1858), pp. 259, 283–84; Alexander Begg, *History of British Columbia from its Earliest Discovery to the Present Time* (London, 1894), p. 285.

11. Kenneth W. Porter, "Negroes and the Fur Trade," *Minnesota History, 15* (1934), 421–33; Bertha Heilbron, "A Pioneer Artist on Lake Superior," ibid., *21* (1940), 152–53; Ross Cox, *Adventures on the Columbia River* (London, 1831), *2,* 333.

12. E. E. Rich, *The History of the Hudson's Bay Company, 1670–1870* (London,

The new Negro settlers also were fortunate in having Mifflin Wistar Gibbs as their chief spokesman.[13] As a general grocer and outfitter for prospectors, he was in a good position to speak to the prime interests of the settlers: how to get to the goldfields quickly and with the proper equipment. Born free, he carried none of the stigma of slavery; having read widely and worked for antislavery groups in Pennsylvania, he was both educated and well informed on the history of his race. Already a man of some wealth, he was able to settle in a fashionable part of Victoria and to hire an Indian manservant before any hint of prejudice arose. In 1861 he won public favor by helping to organize a Negro militia. An English barrister, David Babington Ring, tutored Gibbs in law, and in 1862 Gibbs unsuccessfully ran for the town council. In 1866 he was elected, giving the Negroes a voice in public affairs, especially when Gibbs became chairman of the city's finance committee. In 1867 he contracted to build a railroad from the Queen Charlotte coalmine to Skidgate Harbour, and he personally shipped the first cargo of anthracite over it. As another Speaker of the House, Dr. John Sebastian Helmcken, wrote, Gibbs was "a superior man and very gentlemanly." [14]

Finally, the Negroes were helped by the fact that some moved to the interior of the island or to the mainland, so that their numbers were not so obvious. A few went to the diggings where two were killed in shooting accidents. Three, hoping to make the strike that would enable them to buy freedom for their wives and children, went to Yale.[15] After trying farming, Moses moved to Quesnel and later to Barkerville, where he died in 1890. A moneylender and barber, he shaved clients as often as they wished for a monthly charge of $3.00; and his books show that he opened charge accounts, one Gentle Annie buying perfume, pomade, lace, and expensive underclothing from him by installments.[16] At Leechtown, near Sooke

---

1959), vol. 2, *1763–1870,* p. 381. The Hudson's Bay Company Archives, Beaver House, London, contain over fifty references to the blacks employed by the company. I should like to thank Miss Alice M. Johnson, archivist for the Company, and her staff, for seeking out the references and for allowing me to verify them.

13. Sue Bailey Thurman, *Pioneers of Negro Origin in California* (San Francisco, 1952), pp. 50–64; *Victoria Daily Colonist,* Feb. 9, 1958; *Montreal Star,* April 21, 1962.

14. Report of Sanitary Commission, Oct, 6, n.d. [1868?], and Report of Committee appointed to Memorialize H. E. the Governor to Grant certain Crown Lands situate within the City Limits to the Corporation for Municipal Purposes, draft, June 11, 1867—both signed by Gibbs—in my possession; *Victoria British Colonist,* July 22, 1859; *Victoria Colonist,* Aug. 31, 1907; *Victoria Daily Times,* May 23, 1862; *Montreal Star,* April 21, 1962; Gibbs, *Shadow and Light,* pp. 102, 110; BCA, Reminiscences of Helmcken (written in 1892), 5, 74–76.

15. Cridge Diary: May 25, 26, 1858; *Vancouver Province,* Oct. 1, 1935.

16. BCA, Wellington D. Moses Diaries and Account Books, 1869, 1873–83, 1885–89, passim; *Kamloops Sentinel,* May 21, 1929; Edward Mallandaine, ed., *The*

Harbour, a Negro found a gold nugget worth $75.00. In the Cariboo gold-
fields of the 1880s one Lowhee Jack, later to be murdered in Victoria, became a well-known figure; and in 1912 J. Burgon Bickersteth, a visiting
Anglican divine from England, found a Negro barber and once and future
preacher, as far afield as Tête Jaune Cache.[17]

But most of the Negroes remained in or returned to Victoria, to work
on farms, in the shops, or on the new wharf at Esquimalt—or to move
north to Saanich, Saltspring Island, and Nanaimo. In 1859 the government
allowed settlers to pre-empt land on the Saanich Peninsula; and Fielding
Spotts, a cooper who had been with the first group of emigrants, moved
into the area late that year. Charles Alexander, who had gone to the
Fraser River, returned to join the several Negro families then opting for
farmland. He helped organize an interracial Methodist Church, won election to the school board, and was active in the local temperance and
agricultural societies. Spotts also prospered, purchased a hundred acres of
good land, and was accepted by his white neighbors. Although his name
does not appear on the voters' list until 1874, he too was elected a school
trustee. His son, Fielding William, remained on the property until 1902,
when he moved to Vancouver.[18]

A substantial proportion of the pioneer property owners on Saltspring
Island were Negroes. Their leaders were Louis Stark and his wife Sylvia,
former slaves, who arrived with fifteen cows and took up a hundred acres
of land; Abraham Copeland, who had owned property in Indianapolis before emigrating first to Canada West and then to Victoria with the original
California group; and John Craven Jones, who held a teaching certificate
from Ohio. Making Ganges Harbour their base, the Negroes opened up
small farms, and one, Howard Estes, who had purchased his freedom, ran
goats.[19] Game, fish, and wild berries carried the settlers through the first

First Victoria Directory, Third Issue, and British Columbia Guide . . . (Victoria,
1869), p. 39.

17. Bruce Ramsey, *Ghost Towns of British Columbia* (Vancouver, 1963), p. 64;
M. Eugenie Perry, "A Visit to Leechtown, Vancouver Island's Deserted Mining
Camp," *United Empire Review, 19* (1928), 636; F. W. Lindsay, *Cariboo Yarns*
(Quesnel, B.C., 1962), p. 15; J. Burgon Bickersteth, *The Land of Open Doors:
Being Letters from Western Canada* (London, 1914), pp. 190–91.

18. BCA, South Saanich Public School Visitors' Journal, Nov. 5, 1877; BCA,
Augustus F. Pemberton Diary: April 29, May 1, 7, 12, 13, 19, 21, 22, 25, 1858;
[George H. Glover], *History of the United Church of Canada: North and South
Saanich Areas* (Sidney, B.C. [1956?]), pp. 3–5; Victor E. Virgin, *History of North
and South Saanich Pioneers and District* (Victoria, [1959]), pp. 32–33, 43–47, 56;
Saanich Peninsula and Gulf Island Review, Jan. 31, 1951, Jan. 2, 1952; *Saanich Star,*
Nov. 1, 1951; *Vancouver Daily Province,* Feb. 2, 1937.

19. Eric A. Roberts, *Salt Spring Saga* (Ganges, B.C., 1962), pp. 16–17, 32, 42,
65; [E. F. Wilson], *Salt Spring Island British Columbia* ([Victoria], 1895), pp. 19, 22;
Margaret Shaw Walter, *Early Days among the Gulf Islands of British Columbia,*

summer, that of 1859, but during the winter supplies ran low. The following year Cowichan Indians began to single out blacks—to whom they considered themselves superior—as targets for molestation; the colonists petitioned the government for protection, which was given.[20] In 1868 an Indian murdered two of the Negro settlers; and afterwards the Stark family moved close to Nanaimo, where Louis was killed by being pushed from a cliff, allegedly by an Indian. The family then returned to the island to live, Mrs. Stark dying there in 1944 at the age of 106.[21]

There was little racial antagonism on the tiny island. A Methodist missionary visited the Negroes regularly; a Bermudian, Henry Wilkinson Robinson, was elected municipal clerk; Copeland was elected to the school board; and Jones opened a school at Vesuvius in 1864, together with another Negro, Frederick D. Lester, and taught until 1869 or 1870 without pay, walking to reach other students at outlying settlements. Jones also persuaded the Negroes not to arm themselves in the face of Indian attacks, a decision that was instrumental to keeping peace on the island. In 1873 he was elected to the town council, and local administration has remained interracial to the present time.[22]

In Victoria the Negroes wished to contribute some service to the booming community, for Gibbs and others realized that they might best win widespread acceptance in this way. Several at first volunteered to join the fire brigade, but the white members refused their help. In August of 1859 the Negroes suggested to Douglas that they would form a military group, under the aegis of the Hudson's Bay Company; and with the Governor's encouragement they did so, refusing admission to white men except for one who was their bandmaster.[23] A drill sergeant from a vessel then in the harbor taught the Negroes small arms usage; they elected three officers, including one of their original delegates, Fortune Richard; and in April of

2nd. ed. ([Victoria], 1958), pp. 17, 62–67; *Vancouver Sunday Province,* Aug. 30, 1931; *Vancouver Daily Province,* Jan. 16, 1941, Aug. 6, 1963. Several accounts state that Jones was a university graduate, but clearly he was not. See BCA, F168/2: J. P. Booth et al. to P. Hankin, Oct. 26, 1869. Bea Hamilton, *Salt Spring Island* (Vancouver, 1969), pp. 10–25, contains useful new information.

20. BCA, f1000/1: Thomas H. Lineker to Douglas, July 9, 1860.

21. *Victoria British Colonist,* March 24, Dec. 21, 1868; BCA, Pioneers of the Colonies questionnaire, p. 90: Mrs. Sylvia Stark, March 1928; BCA: Stark to Joseph W. Trutch, Chief Commissioner of Lands and Works, Nov. 3, 1869, Dec. 22, 1870; A. F. Flucke, "Early Days on Saltspring Island," *BCHQ, 15* (1951), 173–74, 185, 188–89, 194–95.

22. BCA, Diaries of Reverend Ebenezer Robson: Feb. 21, Oct. 13, 1861; BCA, F168/2: Hankin to Booth, Jan. 27, 1870; Vancouver City Archives: W. D. Anderson to J. S. Matthews, n.d.; *Saanich Peninsula and Gulf Islands Review,* Nov. 15, 1944; *Victoria Colonist,* Jan. 16, 1873; personal interviews, June 1965, August 1969; *New York Times,* March 7, 1965.

23. BCA, F748/13: G. Heaton, Sheriff, to Douglas, Aug. 15, 1859.

1860 took the name of The Pioneer Rifles, remaining the only rifle corps on the island until the summer of 1861. Largely self-financed, the Negroes provided eighty percent of their operating costs from entrance fees and subscriptions, the remainder ultimately coming from the government. When the whites then organized a Vancouver Island Volunteer Rifle Corps, the Pioneers sent a deputation asking to be permitted to vote in the election of the lieutenant-colonel who would command the new unit, since they assumed they would be taken into it. To great applause the chairman of the organizing meeting ruled that Negroes could not participate.[24]

As a consequence, the separate Negro rifle unit continued until 1864, although it was no longer able to meet its costs. When Arthur Edward Kennedy, a former governor of The Gambia and Sierra Leone and an old army man, arrived to replace Douglas, the Negro troops were told that they could not bear arms during the official reception in his honor. Their captain, Richard H. Johnson, drafted an address that he presented to Kennedy as soon as he assumed office, expressing regret that Negroes were excluded from the ceremonies "on account of an anti-English prejudice against our color" and asking that "non-recognition of distinction in class, creed, color, or nationality" should continue.[25] The corps presented the statement while in uniform and bearing arms, contrary to instructions. The following day Kennedy unofficially reviewed them in ranks and advised them to disband, whereupon the corps marched to the Hudson's Bay Company to turn in their arms. Johnson then opened a temperance house and mission.[26]

Not all of the Pioneers gave up their arms, however, for in June of 1866 the Colonial Secretary belatedly wrote to the corps asking that they return twenty-five rifles, issued in conjunction with the initial plans for Governor Kennedy's reception two years earlier. Their lieutenant replied that he

24. BCA F218/1: Richard and William Brown, July 31, 1862, and Richard to W. A. G. Young, ca. Dec. 1861; *Victoria Colonist*, Jan. 9, 1862; F. A. Robertson, "The 5th B.C. Regiment C.G.A.," *The Khaki Call, 10* (1926), 3–6; Robertson, "5th (B.C.) Regiment Canadian Garrison Artillery and Early Defences of B.C. Coast: Historical Record" (typescript, 1925), owned by the 5th Heavy Anti-Aircraft Battery of the 5th Regiment, and on deposit at the BCA: *4*, 1–5; *5*, 1–2; J. S. Matthews, "'Men of Color' Formed British Columbia's First Volunteer Soldiers," *Museum Notes, 5* (1930), 62–65. BCA, ED/D348: Thomas Deasy to Matthews, Sept. 1, 1934, mistakenly suggests that the blacks were West Indians.

25. *Addresses presented to His Excellency A. E. Kennedy, C. B., on Assuming the Government of Vancouver Island* [Victoria, 1864], pp. 17–18.

26. BCA, F845/1–4: Johnson and E. A. Booth to Douglas, March 3, June 19, 1863; Johnson to Young, March 3, and to Henry Wakefield, Oct. 3, 1864; A. H. Mitchell, "B.C.'s First Soldiers were Black," *British Columbia Digest, 3* (1948), 52–55; *Vancouver Sun*, March 17, 1951.

did not consider the corp disbanded but merely inactive through lack of official support, and he threatened to make public correspondence that would show racism to be the cause of their decline. He did not do so, however, and the Negroes surrendered the symbols of their brief authority.[27]

The collapse of the Negro corps can probably not be ascribed primarily to prejudice, for once a military man had examined the colony's defensive needs, he could not have thought so small a group of partially trained and inadequately equipped riflemen sufficient. Northwards the Indians were continuing sporadic depredations against the settlers, and southwards rumors of a possible war between Britain and the Federal Government following the conclusion of the Civil War then raging pointed to the need for more and better measures. But anti-Negro feeling nonetheless was rising, just as a general hierarchical sense was beginning to be evident in the once rudely democratic colony. Thousands of American emigrants, including many southerners and settlers from the California the Negroes had fled, were bringing with them their assumptions about racial propriety and racial distance; and as the Americans began to acquire property, the Negro holdings became less important. Indeed, within three years after the first black settlers had arrived, discriminatory remarks began to appear in the Victoria press. By 1863 suggestions were turning into actions.

This racial erosion was first seen in the church. In June 1858, William F. Clarke, a Congregational minister in Waukesha, Wisconsin, accepted a commission from the English Congregational Union's missionary arm, The Colonial Missionary Society, to go to Vancouver Island to open a mission. A friend of John Roaf, Clarke was an abolitionist whose reputation traveled before him, and after his first service in Victoria a number of whites asked him whether he was planning to maintain an interracial church. Discovering the Victoria Negroes to be "superior to any body of coloured people with whom it has been my lot to meet," Clarke refused to set them apart to worship in a "negro corner." The Negroes knew that if they established a church of their own they would be segregated; although a Negro minister had come from San Francisco with them, they had attended Cridge's services rather than hold any of their own, and many now hoped to become permanent members of the Congregational Independency. In the face of growing criticism, Clarke continued to welcome them until the arrival of a second Congregational minister.[28]

27. BCA, F845/3: Wakefield to Lester, n.d., Lester et al. to Young, June 12, and Randel Ceasar [*sic* for Randall Caesar] to Young, June 13, 1866.

28. See P. H. Reid, "Segregation in British Columbia," The Committee on Archives of The United Church of Canada, *The Bulletin*, no. 16 (1963), pp. 4–15, which draws upon Clarke's correspondence and reports as published in *The Canadian Independent*

This minister, Matthew Macfie, established a competing service, contrary to the expectations of his sponsors, the Congregational Union; and he let it be known that Negroes would be separated. The Congregationalists in Canada West wrote in support of Clarke's position and affirmed their abhorrence of slavery, but in England the church was more worried about the problems that would arise from a divided mission. Early in 1860 the Victoria segregationists circulated a petition in which they posed the question, "shall white men or niggers rule in this Colony?"—a query answered by a resounding affirmation of white rule.[29] While not participating, Macfie ascribed the desire for segregated services to a need for more refined practices than Clarke proposed. In public meeting the Negroes resolved that "no man shall allow his family to go to Mr. Macfie's church, to be put in the niggers' corner." [30] In the meantime, the Colonial Missionary Society declined to express an opinion on the subject of a "negro corner." Since there was a black preacher in Victoria, the Committee felt Clarke was being obstinate, for he should minister first to the British and European settlers and not permit "the promiscuous attendance" of Negroes to divide the all-too-small number of Congregationalists.

Clarke's reply to the Committee was remarkably modern.[31] To express no opinion, he wrote, was to take "the side of the aggressor and transgressor," for the church labored "under a grevious mistake in supposing [it had] prudently abstained from all expression of opinion." There had been no racial issue until Macfie had raised one, and in taking up the "great commission" to preach to all, Clarke was following in the only Christian footsteps he knew. The charge given Clarke had been to preach to the colonists, a word that embraced all men. The Committee was weak in conviction, willing to tolerate that progeny of slavery, segregation. It had undermined Clarke, who had the growing support of his church members. He concluded, "You appear to think that Mr. Macfie, deeming his course 'conscientiously right,' was necessarily raised about all criticism and rebuke. But deeming a thing 'conscientiously right' does not make it so. Consciences may be warped. They may be misled. . . . It is possible to be *conscientiously wrong,* as well as 'conscientiously right.'" Clarke thereupon resigned to return to Canada West.

Magazine, 5 and *6* (1859–60). A confused account appears in Douglas Hill, *The Opening of the Canadian West: Where Strong Men Gathered* (New York, 1967), pp. 109–11.

29. Macfie, *Vancouver Island and British Columbia* (London, 1865), pp. 388–91; Frederick Ellsworth Walden, "The Social History of Victoria, British Columbia, 1858–1871" (M.A. thesis, Univ. of British Columbia, 1951), pp. 18, 22–23.

30. Quoted in Roland G. Wild, *Amor de Cosmos* (Toronto, 1958), p. 99.

31. BCA: Clarke to Thomas James, Secretary of the Colonial Missionary Society, March 30, 1860.

The Reverend Macfie's defense was equally modern. "Mr. Clarke flattered himself," he wrote to the Society, "that he could revolutionize public sentiment on this point [of separate seating], though deeply rooted for ages, and he made it *primary*. I argued the subject with him kindly, and suggested a change of policy to give the whites, who form the staple of the colony, a chance of hearing the Gospel." Macfie thought himself neutral: "I took no part in discussing whether the prejudice was well founded or not; I simply treated it as a matter with which we, as public teachers, had nothing to do. I held that we could not afford to offend people by introducing innovations." [32]

Too late, Clarke won his point. The officers of the Colonial Missionary Society in London discussed both sets of correspondence. Perhaps the placid inanity of Macfie's letter impressed them; perhaps Clarke's insistence on resigning moved them—certainly, that the chairman of the Congregational Union of Ontario and Quebec, the Reverend Henry Wilkes, already had asked them to reconsider their decision must have done so. They gave no reasons for a change of heart, but in October they resolved that the arrangements described by Macfie "must be immediately discontinued, and freedom of access secured to every part of the building to all persons, without distinction of colour." When Macfie complied, no Negroes came to his services, and after he was called back to Britain in 1864 to help raise funds, the Victoria mission closed, a failure Dr. Wilkes ascribed solely to the controversy over the "negro corner." [33]

During the same months that the Negroes lost the support of Reverend Clarke, they had to decide whether to offend the Governor and the Hudson's Bay Company or Amor de Cosmos and *The British Colonist*. Not unreasonably, one of their number, Jacob Francis, persuaded them to give their support wholly to the former. The issue arose over the election of January 1860. De Cosmos was a self-styled reformer who wrote as though half mad and acted as if he wished to play all a tragedian's emotive rôles simultaneously; born plain Bill Smith, he had chosen his romantic name in protest against mediocrity. He now denounced Douglas as a dictator, yet one who bowed to a "Family-Company-Compact" which encouraged "toadyism, consanguinity, and incompetency." Although a Nova Scotian, de Cosmos had worked as a photographer in the California goldfields, and the Negroes apparently regarded him as an American; for —oblivious of the initially pro-Negro content of his newspaper—they voted unanimously for Company men rather than for reformers. De Cosmos lost the attorney generalship by forty-six votes (while claiming

32. Quoted in Reid, "Segregation," pp. 14–15.

33. *The Canadian Independent Magazine*, 7 (1860), 181; John Wood, *Memoir of Henry Wilkes, D.D., Ll.D., His Life and Times* (Montreal, 1887), p. 66.

the margin was fifteen, a margin he credited to eight Negroes fraudulently encouraged to cast ballots on the strength of their oath of allegiance to the Crown).[34]

De Cosmos was bitterly angry. In an exceptionally long editorial on January 12, he (or his political editor, Charles Bedford Young) charged the Negroes with disloyalty, ignorance, cringing obeisance, and corruption. They would deeply regret the course they had pursued during the elections, he warned, for they had voted on promises, not performance. "They may try to flatter themselves into the belief that they were gaining a triumph over American prejudices . . . but . . . they have willfully sold themselves to the worst enemy of their country, arrayed themselves on the side of an oppressive monopoly, and aroused in British minds a feeling of bitterness which bodes no good for them in the future." The Negroes had followed no principles and had fallen before moral bribery: [35]

> by their own admission they would have voted for the devil, if he had made fair promises on the nigger question . . . all they want is fair *promises* of an indefinite amount of that myth called social equality—a bow and a hypocritical smile from a white Attorney General [George Hunter Cary], a mock auctioneer, or a government hireling. For these they are willing to sell themselves, their friends, and country. No wonder the world is so ready to believe that the colored race is unfit for freedom. . . . The truth is—and the sooner it is told the better,—the colored people do not know what are their equal rights, and are not satisfied when they have them. They always want a little more liberty than white men, and if they don't get it, they fancy themselves ill treated. . . . Who then, but themselves, are to blame for the prejudices existing against them?

"Will . . . Englishmen be slaves to slaves?" he asked, professing to reveal that these puppets now controlled the political balance of power in the colony.

Social as well as political arteries were hardening. In November 1860, the chief theater in Victoria distributed a broadside stating that henceforth Negroes would not be given access to the dress circle or to orchestra seats. Moses, Francis, and two of the officers of the Negro rifle corps, writing on behalf of two hundred and sixty petitioners, asked Governor Douglas for redress. A group of more impatient blacks attempted to take seats in the

34. *The British Colonist,* June 15, 1859; Walden, "Social History of Victoria," pp. 23–24; Wild, *Amor de Cosmos,* pp. 45–46, 97–103; James William Pilton, "Negro Settlements in British Columbia, 1858–1871" (M.A. thesis, Univ. of British Columbia, 1951), pp. 92–100.

35. *British Colonist,* Jan. 12, 1860.

parquette, and a riot ensued. De Cosmos used the occasion to warn that there would be repeat performances if the Negroes did not "by uniform good conduct and moderation, [trust] to a gradual change in public opinion." [36] He nonetheless continued to insist on equal rights for Negroes in British North America, and he hailed the decision of a local judge to set free a fugitive slave boy who had been taken off an American mail boat on which he had attempted to flee from Washington Territory. George Hunter Cary, the Attorney General for whom the Negroes had voted, successfully argued before the court that the fugitive was free as soon as he was brought ashore.[37]

Still, no firm color line was drawn, for there was no one in authority who wished to draw it. In 1861 Negroes who took seats in the dress circle of the principal theater had flour thrown upon them; but in 1862, upon learning that the Bank Exchange Saloon did not serve blacks, Jacob Francis was able to integrate it through the decision of the magistrate of the police court, Augustus F. Pemberton. A close friend of Cridge, Pemberton answered de Cosmos's perjorative query, "Shall a Black Man Drink at a White Man's Bar?", with a qualified yes: while he warned that a fine would be levied for a second offense, he also admitted that the proprietor could charge Negroes whatever he liked. Blacks were excluded from Queen Victoria's birthday ball and from the farewell banquet for Douglas in 1863; and in 1864 they found that they were not to be called for jury duty. When Victorians formed a literary institute, Negroes placed their names on the subscription list, and the list was closed. The local temperance society disbanded rather than admit blacks to membership. In 1864, when Negroes again were relegated to the balcony of the theaters, the new Governor expressed sympathy and did nothing.[38]

Among the Negroes there had been agreement on how best to meet such evidence of prejudice, as shown by their uniform decision not to open a church of their own and by their bloc voting in the election of 1860. But this most important remaining source of Negro strength, their sense of unity, was broken in 1863 when the House of Assembly considered a bill that would have denied a seat in the House to anyone not British born. The Negroes thought this was aimed at them for many had been natural-

36. *British Colonist,* Oct. 4, Nov. 6, 7, 10, 1860; BCA: Moses et al. to Douglas, n.d.

37. BCA, EB/F62: John R. Fleming, affidavit, Sept. 26, 1860; Robie L. Reid, "How One Slave became Free: An Episode of the Old Days in Victoria," *BCHQ, 6* (1942), 251–56.

38. BCA: Francis et al., petition to Kennedy and reply, both Oct. 5, 1864; Macfie, *Vancouver Island,* pp. 390–91; *British Colonist,* May 21, Sept. 28, 1861, June 26, 28, 1862, March 11, 1864, May 9, 1865, Jan. 10, 1866; *Victoria Daily Colonist,* Feb. 15, 1962; Pilton, "British Columbia," pp. 119, 192–95, 201. Also see dialect reports of "Dixie" [Isaac Dickson] in *Cariboo Sentinel,* June 12, supplement, and July 1, 1865.

ized, while the West Indians among them, conscious of their British birth, supported the bill—as did Selim Franklin, one of the candidates who had received full Negro approval three years earlier. The *Victoria Evening Express* hinted that American-born Negroes were angry because both Lester and Gibbs hoped to run for seats in the Assembly; and a Jamaican, J. Cathcart, advised all West Indians to stand behind Franklin, which they did, supplying the seven-vote margin of his victory—and the bill's—in January of 1864. Led by Lester and Willis Bond, with Gibbs not attending, the American group declared the Jamaicans (and three American blacks who had voted with them) traitors to Negro unity and called for a boycott of Cathcart's business. At the same time one of their white defenders, Cary, came under attack for champerty, and shortly afterwards a by-election further exacerbated relations. By 1866 the Negroes also had begun to believe that the courts, and especially Circuit Judge Matthew Baillie Begbie, disliked them.[39]

Gibbs remained the key to Negro unity, and he was trying to cover both sides of a very wide street. He continued to support Sir James Douglas and later Kennedy, but he remained close to de Cosmos as well, and on occasion he chose to call himself a West Indian. As a Negro, Gibbs leaned toward the protective arm of the establishment; as a businessman he moved increasingly toward the reformist position. By 1868, even though elected to the Victoria City Council, he was writing anonymously in a San Francisco newspaper in support of annexation to the United States, largely because he felt the colony would benefit economically; [40] and he supported union with the new Dominion of Canada for the same reason, as a founder of the Confederate League and the delegate from Saltspring Island to the Yale Convention to discuss confederation. Finding the government rotten and the colony stagnant, he decided to return to the United States in 1869,[41] eventually to become a judge in Little Rock and, in 1897, American Consul to Madagascar. In doing so, Gibbs

39. *British Colonist,* May 31, June 18, 21, 25, 1866; *Victoria Daily Colonist,* Feb. 16, 1958; Frederick W. Howay, *British Columbia: The Making of a Province* (Toronto, 1928), p. 158; Pilton, "British Columbia," pp. 101–10, 153–65; BCA, F142f/6: Begbie to Young, Sept. 20, 1863.

40. "Bell's Letter" appeared in *The Elevator,* a weekly interracial newspaper published by Philip A. Bell, on May 8, June 26, and July 31, 1868. See also Oct. 23, 1868. That Gibbs, rather than Bell, was the author may be deduced from the first of these.

41. In 1871, Edward Mallandaine, ed., *The First Victoria Directory, Fourth Issue, and British Columbia Guide . . .* (Victoria), p. 108, still listed Gibbs as a resident of Victoria, while several accounts, including the *National Cyclopaedia of American Biography, 10* (New York, 1909), 114, say that he left in 1868. However, Gibbs remained on the island until March 1869 (Gibbs to the Mayor, Nov. 18, 1868, March 13, 1869, letters in my possession), and he was on the tax roll until 1881.

merely followed many other American Negroes who had begun to return southwards after the Civil War in search of new economic opportunities. With their leader lost, and after further Negro removals to the mainland, Victoria fell under the conservative dominance of the West Indian group, and no black—save for a mulatto artist, Grafton T. Brown, who in 1885 visited the city with the support of the lieutenant-governor—would again rise to prominence in the century.[42]

Until the twentieth century the Negro population of British Columbia remained stable, while declining rapidly relative to the total population. Estimates on the number of Negroes who arrived at Victoria in 1858 vary from four hundred to nearly nine hundred, with perhaps the most reliable contemporary observer setting the figure at six hundred.[43] In 1872 the provincial census reported 462 Negroes, but a number of those on Vancouver Island appear to have been missed. A count taken the previous year showed 217 blacks on the island. In 1931 the province-wide census reported 533 Negroes; in 1951 there were 438; and in 1961, 1,012. Well over half of these lived in Vancouver, and the Negro population of Victoria had been reduced to a handful.[44]

On the whole, racial attitudes also were stabilized. There were few incidents because there were few Negroes. Discrimination was permitted no formal entry into the province, and in 1872 Negroes once again were placed on jury lists. More than half a century after the first Negroes arrived, the provincial press was no less vocal in defending their rights than the *Colonist* had been; and in 1924, when the Ku Klux Klan established a Klavern in Vancouver, the *Sun* opposed it effectively. As elsewhere in Canada, a color line in places of entertainment and in restaurants clearly was visible before World War I, but Negroes were not barred from the common schools, public office, or the churches, as they were in Ontario and Nova Scotia.

42. Yale University, Beinecke Rare Book and Manuscript Library: Confederate League, Declaration, Constitution, List of Officers, May 21, 1868; Begg, *British Columbia,* pp. 378–79; *Victoria Colonist,* Oct. 2, 1868, Nov. 28, 1882, May 24, June 26, 27, 29, July 5, 1883; *Victoria Daily Colonist,* Aug. 30, 1959. The BCA holds a folder of photographic reproductions of twenty-three of Brown's paintings, as well as three of the originals. (Brown may not have been a mulatto.)

43. Macfie put the Negro population at 400 (p. 388); writing in 1912, Fawcett set the figure at 800 (*Old Victoria,* p. 215), while O'Brien (p. 15) suggests 865. In 1923 one of the noncommissioned officers of the Negro rifle unit, Corporal S. J. Booth, told the City Archivist of Vancouver, J. S. Matthews, that the proper figure was 600 (*Victoria Daily Colonist,* Sept. 9).

44. *Lovell's Gazeteer of British North America* (Montreal, 1873), p. 47; R [sic] Edward Gosnell, *Year Book of British Columbia, 1903* (Victoria, 1904), p. 302; *Ninth Census of Canada, 1951, Population* (Ottawa, 1953), *1,* 32–1, p. 2; *1961 Census of Canada, Bulletin 1.2—5, Population: Ethnic Groups* (Ottawa, 1962), 38/17, 18.

If the time when the Negro was fully an equal—as he clearly had been in the heady spring months of 1858—had passed, on the whole he probably continued to enjoy a greater approximation to equality in British Columbia than anywhere else in Canada, whether running a cannery on the Fraser River, serving in the Saanich Indian Police, or on school boards and as aldermen and teachers. In 1890 one Charles Lucas of Vancouver wrote a lengthy public letter to his Negro friends in Ontario asking all Afro-Americans to come west. There, he said, "we may have equal chances with other races of making ourselves happy and will be free from the intimidation and murder, which is frequent in the South." British Columbia was a "far more promising field for colonization," again under discussion, than Mexico or Haiti. To the *Detroit Plaindealer,* a Negro paper, a correspondent wrote that the western province could "accomodate more than half of the eight million of oppressed Afro-Americans." Canada was not a country where "shot guns, rifles, [and] lynching" were permitted, and before Britain "would allow her loyal people to be treated like they are in the South she would bath [*sic*] Canada in blood." Most Negroes preferred to avoid such a blood bath, and while a few answered this call, to become farmers and wharf laborers, there was no increase in the province's black population until after World War II.[45]

Even from 1909 to 1914, when Negroes moved in small colonies onto the plains of Saskatchewan and Alberta, few entered British Columbia. In 1912 a Vancouver real estate broker advertized in *The Crisis,* the journal of the National Association for the Advancement of Colored People in the United States, for one hundred "respectable colored families" to purchase four hundred acres of cleared land near the city.[46] Apparently he had not thought to check with the Canadian immigration officials, since months before they had made it clear that Negroes were not wanted. But if there was trouble in paradise, it was minor, and it was to be viewed against the backdrop of a growing anti-Negro sentiment in Canada that was to reach its height between 1909 and 1930.

45. *London* (Ont.) *Dawn of Tomorrow,* Aug. 9, 1924; *Plaindealer,* Jan. 17, Feb. 7, 21, April 11, 1890; BCA: William Daniel Anderson to Matthews, Sept. 7, 10, 1934.
46. *The Crisis, 4,* 255.

10. To the Nadir, 1865–1930

The drama of the Civil War fascinated Canadians. The agony of secession helped to convince their leaders that they must shape a Confederation in which the distribution of powers was the reverse of the American model. The flow of some eighteen thousand British North American recruits into the Northern armies, and the subsequent inflation of that figure into a myth of over forty thousand Canadian enlistments in the cause of anti-slavery, fed the Canadian sense of moral superiority. Lincoln's insistence that the conflict was to preserve the union, not to free slaves, quickened anti-Americanism in the provinces to the point that the majority of newspapers, even when actively anti-Southern, refrained from any endorsement of the North. As one British abolitionist wrote from Montreal, were southerners fighting for independence and emancipation rather than for independence and slavery, many would prefer to support them. The presence of the martyred Lincoln's funeral train in Buffalo—where hundreds of Canadians crossed the Suspension Bridge to view the body—underscored the senseless violence unleashed by the war. In the midst of such drama, those Negroes who remained in the British provinces were virtually forgotten, and they would not be remembered again for over half a century.[1]

Even during the war, Canadian Negroes were reminded that their haven was a purely legal rather than functionally social one. In March of 1863 a major race riot broke out in Detroit, and visiting Canadian blacks from Windsor were attacked, whites pursuing them across the border; one Negro died. Armed Windsor Negroes were dissuaded from seeking vengeance in Detroit only when news reached them that a white mob stood ready to "exterminate" them. In 1864 black voters in Toronto protested against a city councillor who persisted in calling them "niggers." In the spring of the next year, when French-Canadians who had fought in the

1. BM, Austen Henry Layard Papers, Add. MSS 39,113: W. Williams to Layard, Jan. 20, 1865; *Canadian Illustrated News, 1* (1863), 86; *Toronto Globe,* Jan. 1, 1864; Pierre Savard, "La presse québecoise et la guerre de sécession," La société historique de Québec, *Cahiers d'histoire* no. 13, *Mosaïque québecoise* (Quebec, 1961), pp. 111–28; Winks, *Civil War Years,* pp. 206–43. The majority of the 2,632 foreign-born Negroes in Massachusetts in 1890 probably came from the Maritime Provinces (see Frederick John Brown, "Migration of Colored Population," *Publications of the American Statistical Association,* 6 [1898], 46–48).

Northern army were demobilized at Windsor, they celebrated their release by a raid upon a black church during Sunday evening service. The National Freedmen's Relief Association, despite strenuous solicitations in Toronto in 1864–65, received little clothing and less money. And Lincoln's Emancipation Proclamation, for which Canadians had waited in earnest of the North's abolitionist intentions, served only to deepen the blacks' misery. Many white Canadians—fearful that the proclamation, delayed until 1863, would foster a "general irruption" of Negroes into Canada West—renewed their efforts to exclude black children from the common schools, refused work to those few new refugees who did arrive, and encouraged those already present to return to the dis-United States. As an antislavery lecturer noted in Montreal, no one really contemplated "race mingling," however much an end to legal bondage might be sought.[2]

Not surprisingly then, Negroes began to drift away from the provinces to the Northern states, and after 1865, to the South. Relatively few left the Maritimes before the general "great exodus" from that region late in the century; but perhaps two-thirds of those in the Canadas, more recently arrived and often with family ties in their former homes, moved in reverse down the Underground Railroad—now openly and often still in poverty, yet not uncommonly with an education and the small proceeds from the sale of a plot of Canadian land. Others served in Negro regiments, recruited in Canada West by Osborn P. Anderson, Thomas F. Carey, or Josiah Henson. Seven hundred left Buxton alone. Of the seventeen Negroes admitted to the Mississippi bar between 1873 and 1894, three (including A. W. Shadd, Abraham's son) were from Canada West; as were Charles V. Roman, one of the founders of the National Medical Association; Elijah McCoy, a leading Negro inventor; and eleven of the "progressing and rising" Men of Mark, singled out in 1887 by Reverend William J. Simmons in his book of that title, as being among the leaders of black society in the United States.

That Canadians generally referred to the new migration and such losses as a "returning" or "going back" to the South, underscored the white assumption that blacks were unnatural to the northern landscape. And why not? Had not many fugitives said that they would return to the South if slavery were abolished? Did not Robert Dale Owen, who had accompanied Samuel Gridley Howe on his fact-finding tour in 1863, predict that all

2. *New York Daily Tribune,* March 9, 1863; *Toronto Globe,* Aug. 20, 1864; *Toronto Leader,* May 5, 1865; *Detroit Free Press,* March 7, 1873; *A Thrilling Narrative from the Lips of the Sufferers of the Late Detroit Riot, March 6, 1863 . . .* (Detroit, 1863), pp. 12–13, 20; Anti-Slavery Society, *Seventeenth Annual Report* (Hopkinton, Mass., 1863), p. 27; *The Freedmen's Advocate, 1* (1864), 30–31; H. L. Gordon, *A Lecture on the Harper's Ferry Tragedy* (Montreal, 1860), pp. 3–5.

would "go home" because of a "primal law . . . of thermal lines"? Had not William King himself concluded that "there will be one great black streak reaching from [Elgin] to the uttermost parts of the South" once the slaves were freed? [3]

Accordingly, the Canadian friends of the Negro turned their interests elsewhere: Ross to ornithology, Henning to his ill health, McClure to his memoirs, King to his preaching. A few voices continued to speak out: Malcolm Cameron, who helped to educate bright black boys in the law; Charles Stuart's widow, who for fifteen years sent small sums to Gerrit Smith in support of the Freedmen's Bureau; or John Hurst, the missionary for the Colonial and Continental Church Society who, until his resignation in 1873, continued to remind Englishmen that there still were black Canadians in distress. Isaac Rice, who was inclined to speak the truth too bluntly, told Gerrit Smith in 1869 that a $5.00 donation to the Amherstburg hostel simply would not do: the Civil War had killed all aid societies, and the blacks who remained in Canada were viewed as intruders by the whites and as exiles by themselves. But even Smith was listening no longer, having struck Rice and Amherstburg's Negroes from his list of worthy causes. When Sir George Williams, the founder of the Young Men's Christian Association movement, chose to contribute $100 to Negro aid at his Toronto convention in 1876, he designated it for Americans only, being unaware of a need in the city itself.[4]

Canadian blacks, once individuals to many whites, now became the stock figures they had been in Southern mythology. No longer addressed by their Christian names, they were hailed affectionately as Lemon John, Black Bill, Pop Eye, Old Shack, Susan's Bill, Taffy Mary, Big Charlie, Black Sam, or the "colored man with [the] white soul." The caricatures of

3. *Toronto Weekly Mail,* May 17, 1863; *Toronto Mail and Empire,* July 6, 1928; *Toronto Star,* Aug. 24, 1933; *Collingwood* (Ont.) *Enterprise-Bulletin,* Aug. 25, 1949; Owen, *The Wrong of Slavery, The Right of Emancipation and the Future of the African Race in the United States* (Philadelphia, 1864), pp. 210–11, Supplement, pp. 28, 43–45; Irving C. Mollison, "Negro Lawyers in Mississippi," *JNH, 15* (1930), 41, 46–47, [62]; ibid., *20* (1935), 116–17; Simmons, *Men of Mark: Eminent, Progressive and Rising* (Cleveland, Ohio, 1887), especially pp. 115, 133, 254, 600, 621, 863, 981, and 1013.

4. Syracuse Univ., Gerrit Smith Papers: Rebecca Stuart to Smith, Feb. 20, April 19, 21, June 1, 1865, Rice to Smith, Dec. 25, 1868, Jan. 10, 1869, Smith to Hiram Wilson, Oct. 7, 1873, Henning to Smith, Dec. 7, 1874; BPL, Garrison Papers, *36:* McClure to R. D. Webb, Oct. 23, Dec. 3, 1868; *Canadian Churchman,* Nov. 27, 1930; *London* (Ont.) *Free Press,* March 26, 1910; *Mission to the Coloured Population, Late Fugitive Slave Mission: being a Branch of the Operations of the Colonial and Continental Church Society* (London, 1866), pp. 3–4; ibid. (1869), pp. 5–11; James Cleland Hamilton, *Osgoode Hall: Reminiscences of the Bench and Bar* (Toronto, 1904), pp. 43–44.

blackface minstrelsy, of Snowball Livingston and the Honey Boy singers, replaced the vigorous independence of Samuel Ringgold Ward, William King, or even the now beloved scoundrel, Josiah Henson. When the Toronto Press Club staged a burlesque of *Uncle Tom's Cabin*—once so popular on the boards—as *Uncle Tom's Taxi-cabin,* the emotion and the meaning behind the original were forgotten. In 1901, when a black sensationalist, William H. H. Johnson, published in Vancouver an essay filled with bloodhounds, mutilations, attempted rape, incest, floggings, and sudden discoveries of long-lost sons—the whole a potpourri of the fieriest of abolitionist tracts—Canadians reminded themselves, quite properly, of the irrelevance of this tale to their experience. Canada had played an honorable rôle in the continental attack on slavery, had harbored fugitives from that condition, and had sent them home or seen them to their grave.[5]

But relevance is a matter of degree and lies within the conscience. News of black governments in the Reconstruction South was relevant, as were accounts of Negro attacks upon whites. The conservative *Montreal Gazette* often found occasion to state that, on the basis of the Reconstruction experience, "the niggers" were a lazy, debauched, improvident, and vicious lot. When the state government of Louisiana appeared to have fallen into Negro hands in 1868, the *Gazette* asked its readers to "imagine us in Canada, as the result of war, or annexation, or anything else, ruled by blacks." Nowhere, said the editorialist, may the two races "exist together as equals."[6] Certainly not in the new Dominion of Canada after 1867.

By the end of the century most of the original fugitives who had remained in Canada had died. In 1901 there were, by the census count— still inaccurate when enumerating blacks—only some 17,500 Negroes in the Dominion. Of these, however, 13,600 were not yet twenty-one. For the first time some Canadians became aware that their country might con-

5. SPG Papers, Missionary Reports, 1873: T. A. Goode, Dec. 20; *Toronto Christian Guardian,* March 25, 1903; Adam S. Green, *The Future of the Canadian Negro* (Truro, 1904), p. 9; Ella Hilborn, "The History of the Negro Population of Collingwood," Huron Institute, *Papers and Records, 1* (1909), 40–42; *Toronto Globe,* June 12, 19, 1909, May 6, 1911, Jan. 5, 1938; Agnes Dunbar Chamberlin, "The Colored Citizens of Toronto," Women's Canadian Historical Society of Toronto, *Transactions,* no. 8 (1911), pp. 11–12; *Hamilton Spectator,* April 29, 1916; *London Free Press,* Feb. 23, 1924; *Toronto Star,* Nov. 10, 1938, Oct. 23, 1940, March 24, Sept. 2, 1943; George Mullane, *Footprints Around and About Bedford Basin* ([Halifax], n.d.), pp. 34–36; Johnson, *The Horrors of Slavery,* passim; Mary Brehaut, Prince Edward Island Historical Society, to author, n.d. [1960]; Bremner, *City of London,* p. 60.

6. *Montreal Gazette:* July 17, 25, 29, Sept. 29, Oct. 19, 1868; July 2, 1869; Feb. 26, March 25, May 5, July 6, Dec. 17, 1870; Feb. 6, 21, Oct. 5, 9, 26, 1871; Jan. 6, Feb. 3, Oct. 12, 16, 1872; June 19, July 31, 1873; May 4, Aug. 13, 1874; April 22, Sept. 7, 1875; June 14, Nov. 4, 6, 1876; June 1, Nov. 13, 28, 1877.

tinue to be a home for a small but highly visible black minority, and that the Negro race could well increase. Earlier postures of acceptance shown by whites could now turn to gestures of rejection, for Canada was susceptible to the same pseudo-anthropology and pseudo-science that grew in western Europe, Britain, and the United States between 1870 and 1930. As the study of race was "scientifically" organized, as stereotypes of the Negro became more widely known in Canada, as the forces gathered under the rubrics of nationalism and racism began to have their effect, the Negro in Canada found himself sliding down an inclined plane from mere neglect to active dislike. The general movement of Americans—including black Americans—into the Canadian West, the outbreak of a war fought to make the world safe for democracy, the all too evident inability of the Negroes to unite behind a single leader, and a deluge of overt racist propaganda covertly present in much popular literature, had effects in the Dominion not unlike those in the United States. During the early decades of the present century evil moved with as much grace as virtue, and the Negro sank to his nadir in Canada.

Virtue and evil were often two sides of the same coin. On Saturdays the streets around the postoffice in Halifax were taken up with the Green Market, where country produce was sold by Acadians, Indians, and Preston Negroes (who controlled the low bush berry trade) in a hurly-burly, friendly atmosphere. In Saint John there were Negroes who preached to mixed congregations, a lawyer with a mixed practice, and—when Robert Walker founded a well-edited journal, *Neith,* in 1904—at least one black of some literary distinction. In 1885, when Robert Whetsel died in Saint John, there was genuine mourning marked by no racial bias, the *Daily Sun* noting in a substantial obituary that Whetsel was one of the city's "representative colored citizens" whose word was his bond. If Negroes seemed unsuccessful at coping with life's complexities, preferring to live together in kinship groupings upon which whites frowned and which appeared to decrease their competitive drive, they were different after all, "kind of funny," simple and unambitious. As a Toronto newspaper noted, Canadians wished to see the Negro "work out his own intellectual, moral, and economic salvation if he is to be saved." [7]

Saved from what? The prejudice was latent. Too many God-fearing Maritimers had read the Bible not to think the Negro inferior. "I am

7. NBM, clippings on marriages and deaths: C9, Whetsel; Charles H. Lugrin, *New Brunswick: (Canada) Its Resources, Progress and Advantages* ([Fredericton?], 1886), p. 185; *McAlpine's Saint John City Directory for 1874–75 . . .* (Saint John, 1874), p. 308; *for 1882–83,* p. 249; *The Week* (Toronto), 4 (1887), 433; *Saint John Freeman,* Dec. 4, 1897.

black but comely" sang the Song of Solomon's Shulamite maiden, and on this *but* hung centuries of beliefs from which the Canadian could no more escape than could devout Christian Southerners. The currency of common speech revealed the prejudice. As in portions of the United States, so too in Canada was it necessary to be "free, white, and twenty-one" to assert one's independence. If one were particularly noted for honesty, one was "a white man," and if one performed a noble act, it was "a white thing to do." Rudyard Kipling's Gunga Din, a native water bearer for the army, after all, "for all 'is dirty 'ide . . . was white, clear white, inside." In Ontario, "niggering" continued to be used as a verb in lumbering, Negroes were "sooties," and later "dinges" and "jigaboos," as in the United States. Men who were swarthy were "exceedingly sensitive" to any suggestion that they might be Negroes—ironically, precisely this charge appears to have helped derange George Bennett, the assassin of George Brown. Blacks, one popular advertisement informed its readers, lived next to nature and had perfect digestion and healthy teeth (an enviable condition whites might achieve only by recourse to Stuart's Dyspepsia Tablets). "It is a well known fact," reported one Ontario publication, "that every different race of people emits a different smell, it being an especial characteristic of the Negro." The *Windsor* (Nova Scotia) *Mail* found Negro "peculiarities . . . so abnormal that . . . he sinks to the level of the animal," being fond of gin and fried liver, of outlandish religion, witchcraft, sex, and song. In Vancouver in 1903, there were said to be one hundred and thirty-eight "dusky houchie kouchie girls" from the "jungles of Africa" who did "business by the gleams of a red torch" upon black skin. In 1898 the Canadian Wheelmen's Association singled out the Negro settlement near Loch Lomond, in New Brunswick, as a tourist attraction—"a romantic, as well as a somewhat tragic reminder of . . . slavery"—and by 1901 McDougall Street in Windsor, Ontario, "settled for a mile on each side by Negroes," was an equally romantic "historic" place.[8]

8. A "Canuck" [Michael G. Scherck], *Pen Pictures of Early Pioneer Life in Upper Canada* (Toronto, 1905), p. 49; J. B. London, *A Tour through Canada and the United States of America* . . . (Coventry, 1879), pp. 46–47; *Halifax Morning Chronicle*, Feb. 14, 1908; PANS, "Windsor Antiquities: Cuttings from Windsor Mail Newspaper, 1876," p. 5; W. J. Wintemberg, "Folk-Lore of Waterloo County, Ontario," National Museum of Canada, *Bulletin No. 116*, whole no. (Ottawa, 1950), p. 49; [R. T. Lowery], "The Street in Red," *Lowery's Claim*, no. 25 (1903), p. 2; [J. M. Barnes], *Maritime Provinces Road Book* (Saint John, 1898), p. 58; Margaret Claire Kilroy, "Local Historic Places in Essex County," Essex Historical Society, *Papers and Addresses, 1* (1913), 25; Ray Corry Bond, *Peninsula Village: A Story of Chippawa* (n.p., n.d.), p. 72; Walter S. Avis, et al., eds., *A Dictionary of Canadianisms on Historical Principles* (Toronto, 1967), p. 511. See also supra, p. 259, n. 58.

Another romantic reminder of slavery was the minstrel show. When Callender's Colored Minstrels filled every seat in Academy Hall in Halifax in 1884, when J. W. McAndrew, the Watermelon Man, Haverly's Mastodon Minstrels, A. G. Field's troup, or Jack Diamond the dancer toured Canada, they purported to speak for the Negro—on occasion with compassion and even affection, but usually with ridicule and low humor. From ca. 1880 until 1927 the Royal Military College in Kingston enjoyed its own burnt cork shows, for the actors were, of course, white men. Not until 1932 would a group of black actors tour Canada; Richard Huey of Louisiana produced *Porgy, In Abraham's Bosom,* and *Harlem.* But in 1965 the Smokey Mokes Minstrels, repeatedly referring to themselves as "niggers," were still playing to good houses in Nova Scotia, and until 1960 one all-white fraternal organization continued to appear in Ottawa's annual parade in blackface.[9]

Most Canadians may have assumed that real Negroes were no less amusing than these whites in blackface. As in the rural portions of the northern states, Negroes were subjects of fun. When Negroes met at Sandwich to celebrate emancipation each year, they were "laughable and ludicrous," and especially so when "dark doves cooed to their dusky mates" from the leafy coves of Sandwich Wood. The noted Canadian cartoonist John Wilson Bengough, of *Grip* fame, included among his repertoire the inevitable picture of a cowering Negro held up before a judge for chicken stealing; and Henri Julien, another turn-of-the-century caricaturist, won applause for his By-Town Coons—prominent Canadian politicians disguised as minstrelmen. As the city fathers of Toronto remarked in 1897, although a Negro had qualified for the city regimental band, he could hardly be given a place on it since he would look "like a black horse among a lot of white ones." A Chatham barber won local fame when he declined to cut a Negro's hair because he had no black soap. Many small Ontario towns could boast of their pet blacks, who would regale youngsters with tales of slavery down on the old plantation, sing Negro spirituals, and play the fiddle. In Hamilton "fun-loving boys" would gather outside the African church to hear the noises of worship; and when they removed the church steps, cried fire, and watched the bodies pile five deep as the frightened blacks poured from the building, the

9. *Halifax Morning Chronicle,* April 15, 1884; Fulton Stanley Knight, *This is Meaford, 1875–1956* . . . ([Meaford, Ont.], 1956), p. 21; *Memories . . . along the Border: Seventy Five Years of Our History, 1885–1960—A Story of the Village of Cartwright Manitoba* (Steinbach, Man., [1960]), p. 53; TPL, broadsides: "The Octaroon," Royal Lyceum, n.d.; Frederick W. Bond, *The Negro and the Drama* . . . (Washington, 1940), pp. 106–07; *Atlantic Advocate, 47* (1957), 6–7; *Fredericton Gleaner,* Oct. 22, 25, Nov. 3, 1965; Richard Arthur Preston, *Canada's RMC: A History of the Royal Military College* (Toronto, 1969), p. 203.

town historian found it amusing. In time those wooly-headed uncles, Remus and Tom, and the faithful mammies, Lize and Chloe, were part of the mythology that was the heritage of smalltown Canada as well as of rural midwestern America.[10]

This mythology was reinforced by what Canadians read. In Canadian short stories and novels, as in the minstrel shows, Negroes were frightened of horses, ghosts, little girls, dogs, and honest men. In Major John Richardson's classic, *The Canadian Brothers* (1840), the leading figure's Negro servant was noble, faithful, and simple to a fault. In *Battling Malone: The Pugiliste* (1925), Louis Hémon, the famed author of *Mariä Chapdelaine,* spoke of the "horrible American nigger" whose smell "rouses disgust and rage in so many white men." In the adventures of that dullest of all homespun philosophers, Thomas Chandler Haliburton's Sam Slick, the reader encountered extraordinary conceptions of "Negro lingo": "Oh my Gor! —only tink old Scippy see you once more! . . . Oh, Massa Sam, you no recollect Old Scip—Mass 'Siah's nigger boy? How's Massy Sy, and Missey Sy . . . ? De dear little lily, de sweet little booty, de little missy baby. Oh how I do lub em all." George de Boucherville, Hiram A. Cody, Augustus Bridle, and Eugène Seers gave central rôles to Negroes; and in his durable *Sunshine Sketches of a Little Town,* first published in 1912, humorist Stephen Leacock hinted at an outside world flashing past his Mariposa (Orillia), as a Pullman car brought visions of "cut glass and snow-white table linen, smiling negroes and millionaries with napkins at their chins." Helen Campbell Bannerman's *Story of Little Black Sambo,* first published in 1899, was a Canadian classic too, still selling well in its sixteenth printing in 1969.[11]

Those who were not listening to the old literature often were bowing

10. Bengough picture on wall of William Lyon Mackenzie House, Toronto; Julien, *Album* (Montreal, 1916), passim; Hamilton (Ont.) Public Library, G. C. Porter MS, "The Model Negro Community in Kent County" [ca. 1899], passim; Arthur W. H. Eaton, "Chapters in the History of Halifax, Nova Scotia," *Americana, 10* (1915), 835; *Detroit Free Press,* Aug. 2, 1867, Aug. 2, 3, 1873; *Saint Paul Western Appeal, 4* (1888), 1; ibid., *13* (1897), 1; *Detroit Plaindealer,* Dec. 20, 1899; Mabel Burkholder, *The Story of Hamilton,* 2nd ed. (Hamilton, 1939), pp. 144–46.

11. Richardson (Montreal), *1, 79*; Hémon (Paris), p. 178; *The Provincial, 1* (1852), 217–18; Rowland E. Robinson, *Out of Bondage and Other Stories* (Boston, 1905), pp. 1–47; W. B. Bezanson, *Stories of Acadia: Part Three* (Kentville, N.S., 1933), pp. 37–49; Elna Bengtsson, "The Language and Vocabulary of Sam Slick," *Upsala Canadian Studies, 5* (1956), 46–47; de Boucherville, *Une de perdue, deux de trouvées* (Montreal, 1874), *2,* 54–69; Cody, *The King's Arrow: A Tale of the United Empire Loyalists* (Toronto, 1921); Bridle, *Hanson, A Novel of Canadianization* (Toronto, 1924); Payzant, *People: A Story of the People of Nova Scotia,* pp. 173–97; Louis Dantin [Seers], *Enfances de Fanny* (Montreal, 1951); Leacock (London), pp. 6, 55. The first Canadian writer to deal with a Negro-related theme without prejudice was to be Morley Callaghan in *The Loved and the Lost,* in 1951.

before the new science. Both increasingly appeared in the same company, for Britain's romantic novelists of the nineteenth century were fond of racial theorizing. Sir Walter Scott saw conflict between Saxon and Norman in racial terms, and the Lady of the Lake pitted Saxon against Celt. Disraeli's Conigsby prattled on about race, as later did G. A. Henty, G. Manville Fenn, Charles Kingsley, Kipling, H. Rider Haggard and John Buchan. Metahistorians like Comte Arthur de Gobineau sought reasons for the fall of some societies and the rise of others, and concluded that—as man would fornicate—biological decline and mental mediocrity were the result of carelessness in the choice of partners. Pre-Darwinian anthropologists had emphasized conflict between geology and the Bible, and the multiple origin of races. Since such a doctrine carried a potential attack on orthodox Christianity, the theory of polygenesis appears to have been little discussed in Canada, where orthodoxy ran high and where one must remain firm in the fundamentals of the faith in the face of the Roman Catholic threat from Quebec; but when discussed, polygenesis admitted of the real possibility of an inherent hierarchy among human beings. Later in the century the popular mind would seize upon the simplifications of social Darwinism and, a little later, of Freudian psychology. The Victorian British, with their intolerance of public sexual looseness, projected the promiscuity they denied themselves upon others—and especially upon Negroes, about whom lascivious stories revolved. While these tales had always been present—in the *Thousand Nights and One Night,* in the accounts dredged up by Richard Burton, or in the pseudo-Aretino erotic plates, *La Puttana Errante*—the new quantifying sciences seemed to provide a rationale for them. Scientists set out to find whether the popular notion that the male Negro sex organ was larger than the white was true or not, to measure and to classify human beings in terms of pubic hair, polychesia, and cranial capacity. Canadians accepted the usual turn-of-the-century smorgasbörd of racial truths, half-truths, lies, and irrelevancies; and they selected their beliefs no less and no more intelligently than other northern peoples who did not have daily and intimate contact with substantial numbers of black men and women. On the whole, therefore, racial attitudes in Canada followed the continental norm above the Mason-Dixon line.

To this conventional wisdom Canadians could add one doctrine of their own: since Negroes could not stand so cold a climate, they should be barred for their own good. In fact, blacks had lived in the severe northern climate for two and a half centuries, and there are little if any appreciable racial differences in tolerances to cold.[12] Ironically, in 1909 a Negro,

12. See Walter R. Chivers, "Northward Migration and the Health of Negroes," *The Journal of Negro Education, 8* (1939), 34–43; and H. T. Hammel, "Terrestrial

Matthew A. Henson, who had been born in Maryland, was to be hailed as the codiscoverer of the North Pole with Admiral Robert E. Perry; and while the claim of discovery was disputed, no one questioned that Perry and Henson had survived the Arctic. Henson had hoped that his triumph would quiet contentions that Negroes were unsuited to the North; but if Canadians could ignore the presence of thousands of Negroes in Nova Scotia who had survived, they could ignore Henson as well.[13]

Between 1880 and 1930 even those scholars most charged with keeping the record straight—historians—buried the Negro under a sense of embarrassment over slavery, and from an apparent conviction that black history was not worth telling in its own right. During the decade of the 1880s French-Canadian historians began to explore the early years of French slavery in North America, only to have François-Xavier Garneau recast the past sufficiently to place most of the blame for what his generation regarded as an immoral institution directly upon the English; John Neilson, William Canniff, and Thomas W. Casey, in turn, found the French primarily responsible. Few, if any, antiquarians or historians of the time were interested in slavery or in the Negro, as such; and they consistently expressed their surprise at discovering, over and over again, that slavery had existed within Canadian territory. Sulte in Quebec, Smith in Nova Scotia, Scadding, Canniff, and Thomas Conant in Ontario—relying largely on the generalizations of Garneau, on the fragmentary records collected by Viger and Lafontaine, and on scant documents published from 1886 by the Dominion Archivist, Douglas Brymner—were content to conclude that the virus of slavery came from the south, that it was inherently unnatural to the northern landscape, that most blacks descended from slaves, and that the condition had such lasting effects on Negroes as to make them inferior.

These attitudes, held by men who thought themselves objective and scholarly, were fully in keeping with the fledgling social science of the day; and it is not surprising, therefore, that amateur historians and local antiquarians were even more patronizing of the Negro past. In 1884, when Jonas Howe, a New Brunswick manufacturer who helped found his province's historical society, addressed that group on slavery, he thought talented Negroes to be rare, and the fact that he had fought for the Confederacy during the Civil War was not entirely obscured. In the late

Animals in Cold: Recent Studies of Primitive Man," in John Field, ed., *Handbook of Physiology* (Washington, 1965), *4*, 413–33.

13. The best study of Henson is Floyd Miller, *Ahdoolo!—The Biography of Matthew A. Henson* (New York, 1963). Henson gave his own account in *A Negro Explorer at the North Pole* (New York, 1912). For an excellent obituary see *The Explorers Journal, 33* (1955), 28–31, 93. I would like to thank Mr. Herbert M. Frisby of Baltimore for sending me much Henson material not cited here.

1880s and early 1890s, when a Toronto attorney, J. Cleland Hamilton, wrote and rewrote his articles on "The African in Canada," he made no effort to hide his conviction that the Negro had no place in Canadian society. When Arthur P. Silver, a dry goods merchant in Halifax, wrote of the Negro in Nova Scotia, he had access to materials relating to Theophilus Chamberlain, whose grandson he was, but he had little good to say of the black men Chamberlain had helped. Even William Renwick Riddell—distinguished jurist, after 1906 member of Ontario's High Court of Justice, and an authority on the mosquito—who wrote careful treatises on the legal position of the slave in French and British North America, pitied the slave for classical notions associated with doctrines of natural liberty and thought the abolitionists "fiendish." The Faithful Native Bearer marched through the pages of Hamilton and Riddell with as steady a gait as in the novels of Henty or Haggard.[14]

By the twentieth century, then, a once vague mythology about what the Negro could and could not do had taken on a more exact form. Language, literature, the theater, science, and even history had informed generations of Canadians of the Negro's inability to adapt to the north, of his love of pleasure, of his sexual appetites, his unreliability, laziness, and odor. There were enough of these people in Canada without adding to the problem. Americans, who had a long experience with blacks, were moving to segregate the Negro. If Canadians did not wish to follow the Americans in giving segregation the force of law, or if Canadians did not want black ghettoes to develop in their cities as they were beginning to in the major American centers, they would be well-advised to block the problem at its source: the border.

Canadians had discussed the problem of undesirable immigrants before, and they had not agreed on what constituted an undesirable. While some said that any body of people who could not assimilate readily fell under this heading, assimilation is difficult to define, and it has been especially so for Canadians, who had reason to emphasize cultural plural-

14. For a representative treatise of the time, see J. R. MacCrimmon, "The Apology of Slavery" (M.A. thesis, McGill Univ., 1909). On Howe, see *Saint John Telegraph,* May 27, 1884, and NBM, Scrap Book 6, N; on Silver, see *Halifax Herald,* June 24, 1897, *Halifax Morning Chronicle,* Feb. 15, 1908, and PANS: C. St. C. Stayner, comp., "Etter Family Genealogy" (1953), p. 24. A typical article by Hamilton is "The African in Canada," *Knox College Monthly and Presbyterian Magazine, 12* (1889), which he frequently reprinted with minor revisions; see also William King to Hamilton, Aug. 19, Dec. 23, 1899, in the Fred Landon Collection. On Casey and J. Taylor Wood, see Lennox and Addington Historical Society, Napanee: William N. Ponton to Casey, Feb. 19, 1902, and *Evening Mail,* Oct. 20, 1900, respectively. On Riddell, consult *Journal of the American Institute of Criminal Law and Criminology, 4* (1913), 12 n., and *The Canadian Bar Review, 9* (1931), 573–74. The reference to abolitionists comes from *JNH, 5* (1920), 265.

ism. During the 1850s concerned Canadians had warned against the dangers posed by indigent black fugitives, and in 1899 the House of Commons debated placing restrictions on Galicians and Doukhobors. But until the twentieth century the majority of legislators were silent on the issue or supported Alexander Mackenzie who, as Liberal Prime Minister in 1878, advised that no British community should legislate against any class of people.[15]

A long period of public concern over the nature of the changes taking place in the Canadian population undermined Mackenzie's view. In 1843 an emigration agent in Kingston was convinced that "the man who is satisfied with a plentiful supply of the comforts and necessaries of life & the means of bringing up a family and afterwards educating them for professions or trades in which, with common industry they can scarcely fail of success, is almost sure to become a useful & happy Member of Society" in Canada. While this sentiment had not changed substantially by 1890, Canadians worried that non-British and western European people would not respond to all of the canons associated with the success ethic of Samuel Smiles or Horatio Alger. French Canadians wished to see the Slavs—"the scum of Europe"—slowed in their flow so that some of an alleged one hundred thousand French-speaking Americans who wished to come northwards might do so. Clifford (later Sir Clifford) Sifton, Minister of the Interior from 1896 to 1905, wanted "a stalwart peasant in a sheepskin coat"; while Agnes C. Laut, a respected popularizer of Canadian history, warned in 1915 of the "dangers within, not without" already posed by too many Jappy-Chappies, Chinks, and Little Brown Brothers who could not be assimilated. There were "dangers of dilution and contamination of national blood, national grit, national government, national ideas," she wrote; for self-seeking "Jews and Polacks and Galicians" would corrupt Canada. "Theoretically," she added, ". . . the colored man should be as clean and upright and free-and-equal and dependable as the white man; but . . . practically he isn't." As for intermarriage, "we do not propose poisoning the new young life of Canada."[16]

15. Canada, House of Commons, *Debates, 1878, 1,* 1209, March 18.

16. Columbia University Library, Toronto Emigration Office Manuscripts, 1835–92, *2:* A. B. Hawke to A. C. Buchanan, Dec. 7, 1843; Canada, House of Commons, *Sifton in Relation to His Times* (Toronto, 1931), p. 317; Laut, *The Canadian Commonwealth* (Chautauqua, N.Y., 1915), pp. 112, 116–22, 127–37, 138–39, 155; Laut, *Ah I My Brother's Keeper?* (Toronto, 1913), p. 39; Sunder Singh, "The Hindu in Canada," *The Journal of Race Development,* 7 (1917), 361–82; George Winter Mitchell, "Canada—Saviour of the Nordic Race," *The Canadian Magazine, 61* (1923), 138–40; House of Commons, *Debates, 1928, 2,* 319, Feb. 9. On the attitudes of two Canadian nationalists, Sir George R. Parkin and Colonel George Taylor Denison, see Carl Berger, *The Sense of Power: Studies in the Ideas of Canadian Imperialism, 1867–1914* (Toronto, 1970), pp. 162–63.

The target of much of the new century's exclusiveness was the Asian, and in particular the Indian—in Canada occasionally called a Sikh, although many were Hindu. In 1907 extensive rioting swept Vancouver, stirred by the presence of Chinese and Japanese laborers reputedly able to live off the smell of a greasy rag. In 1910 the number of Indians who might enter Canada was limited—although not by racial designation—by orders-in-council; and when the Supreme Court of British Columbia found the initial order invalid, special injunctions were applied for that province alone. In 1914 a Hindu from the Punjab sent the *Komagata Maru,* a Japanese vessel loaded with Indians, to Vancouver harbor to test the special order; and when immigration officers and police, with deportation writs in hand, attempted to board the ship to transfer its passengers to one bound for Hong Kong, the Indians resisted violently, only to be taken away under naval escort.

Between 1900 and 1920, when this Canadian racial awareness was at its height, a conjunction of circumstances worked to bring American Negroes to Canada's gates, and thus they caught some of the flak thrown up against the larger target. Black urbanization, begun during the Civil War, had been accelerating rapidly. A search for greater job opportunities, the desire to escape from an increasingly rigid Southern social structure, and pressures exerted by industry in World War I promoted mass movement toward the cities and the north. The exodus of Negroes from the South served in small measure to prod some of those who had gone before into Canada, the newcomers pushing the earlier arrivals onward. The Negro population of Cleveland multiplied fifty-six times, and that of Chicago sixty-three times, between 1870 and 1930. Although numbers remained comparatively small, as Detroit, Buffalo, and Boston grew in Negro population, Canadian near-border communities such as Windsor, Hamilton, and Saint John also grew. Sydney, Nova Scotia, also received a new, if small, flow of blacks in 1899, when three carloads of Alabamians were brought to work in the iron furnace there. When whites protested, the manager of the furnace assured them that local conditions required segregation of the Negroes in any case.

In the Middle West and across the plains states agricultural conditions were growing poor, and showed little prospect of early improvement. Virgin land was scarce, land prices and rents were rising, credit facilities were inadequate, and mechanization was cutting into the labor demand. Dakota land cost fifty dollars an acre in 1900, while comparable land across the border in Saskatchewan was selling for two dollars. Sensing the opportunity, the Canadian government had begun an intensive campaign to attract American farmers, from 1897 opening immigration agencies in over twenty-one American cities. Sifton stressed the healthful climate of western Canada, praised Americans as vigorous, resourceful, and law-abiding—in every sense desirable—and offered to welcome all who would come.

Six hundred thousand Americans responded. Since Sifton had mentioned no restrictions, and since the *Saint Paul Broadax,* a Negro newspaper, in 1901 ran articles in which the premier of Manitoba extended cordial invitations to all readers (articles that were reprinted without acknowledgment from the general press), the Negro American assumed that he was included. He was not.[17]

In Kansas and Oklahoma several thousand Americans lived in all-Negro towns where they had learned something of dry land farming as they imagined they would have to practice it in Canada, and where they already were settled into rigid patterns of segregation. Others, including a number who had left Buxton in the 1890s, lived in Nebraska. They were highly mobile—in 1920, 66.6 percent of Oklahoma's Negroes had been born elsewhere. They thought in terms of group movement rather than individual border crossings. They already had been exposed to emigrationist propaganda, beginning in the 1880s when a Tennessee Negro who had lived in Windsor, Ontario, for a time, Benjamin "Pap" Singleton, had tried to persuade Kansas blacks to colonize Canada, Cyprus, or Liberia. In 1902 one C. W. Brown, a janitor, organized a Vancouver chapter of the Colored National Emigration Association, basically a back-to-Africa group, which nonetheless brought added black attention to the Canadian West. And most Negroes shared the general mythology about Canada, the fugitive's haven.[18]

The attractions of Canada would have passed unnoticed had not the disadvantages of Oklahoma been made so plain. Until 1908 the area was the Indian Territory, administered by the federal government and less subject to discriminatory legislation than the adjacent states. With the coming of statehood also came a succession of restrictive acts, and in time Oklahoma would pass under the dominance of the Ku Klux Klan.

17. Karel Denis Bicha, "The Plains Farmer and the Prairie Province Frontier, 1897–1914," *Proceedings of the American Philosophical Society, 109* (1965), 398–440; *Broadax,* March 22, 30, April 13, May 10, 17, Aug. 13, 1901.

18. See Harold M. Rose, "The All-Negro Town: Its Evolution and Function," *Geographical Review, 55* (1965), 362–81; Mozell C. Hill, "Basic Racial Attitudes toward Whites in the Oklahoma All-Negro Community," *American Journal of Sociology, 49* (1944), 519–23; Walter L. Fleming, " 'Pap' Singleton, the Moses of the Colored Exodus," ibid., *15* (1909), 61–82; Van B. Shaw, "Nicodemus, Kansas: A Study in Isolation" (Ph.D. diss., Univ. of Missouri, 1951); *Voice of the People,* Sept. 1, 1902; *London Free Press,* Aug. 26, 1939; Kansas State Historical Society, Topeka: Singleton's Scrap Book, containing *Topeka Times,* Sept. 28, 1883, and *Topeka Commonwealth,* Aug. 21, 23, Oct. 21, 1883.

In 1910 the government organized Okfuskee County, where the Negro population ran over forty percent, in order to put all Negroes in one township; and in Okemah and Weleetka, the county's two largest communities, blacks were under heavy attack. The state denied Negroes the vote through a grandfather clause and literacy tests; the United States Circuit Court of Appeals failed to uphold Negro protests against new Jim Crow regulations on railroads; and in May 1911, whites hanged two Negroes from a railway bridge across the North Canadian River, just below the all-Negro town of Boley. From 1909 until 1911, Oklahoma's Negroes in particular had reason to seek refuge under the lion's paw.[19]

There had been Negroes in the Canadian West before, of course, and especially in British Columbia, but there had been very few on the plains. The Red River census of 1870 listed five Negroes; a black laborer lived near Killarney, Manitoba, in 1890; and the memory of a giant ex-slave, Daniel Williams, who had been hanged for murder at Fort Saskatchewan in 1880, inspired western mothers to frighten their children by telling them that "Nigger Dan" would get them if they did not behave. Henry Mills, who had worked at various whiskey posts in and near the short grass county, and his son David, who was an interpreter in the 1880s, had become local legends—as did one Nigger Molly, who called herself "the first white woman in the west," a classification the Indians would have accepted, since they called David Mills *Sixapekwan,* or "Black White Man." [20] From 1896 until his death in 1915—save for two brief periods— Alfred Shadd, a great grandson of Abraham Shadd, practiced medicine in Kinistino and Melfort, Saskatchewan, and encountered no prejudice. He experimented with breeding cattle, edited the *Melfort Journal,* and twice ran unsuccessfully for office as a Conservative. Most important of all had been John Ware, "the Negro Cowboy," who became a legend in his lifetime after arriving in 1882. One of the finest riders in Alberta's range history, Ware died in 1905 when his horse fell with him, and he was honored by having a mountain, a creek, and a coulee named after

19. See Asa Wallace Dagley, "The Negro of Oklahoma" (M.A. thesis, Univ. of Oklahoma, 1926); Mozell C. Hill, "The All-Negro Society in Oklahoma" (Ph.D. diss., Univ. of Chicago, 1946); Mozell C. Hill and Eugene S. Richards, "Demographic Trends of the Negro in Oklahoma," *The Southwestern Journal,* 2 (1946), 47–63; and Nathaniel Jason Washington, *Historical Development of the Negro in Oklahoma* (Tulsa, Okla., 1948).

20. F. W. Gershaw, *A Brief History of Southern Alberta, "The Short Grass Area"* (n.p., [1956]), pp. 51–52; C. M. MacInnes, *In the Shadow of the Rockies* (London, 1930), p. 99; Stephen William Wilk, *One Day's Journey* (Calgary, Alta., 1963), p. 152; Peter Freuchen, *The Legend of Daniel Williams* (New York, 1956), passim; Everett Sorgard, "Bill Jackson," *Coyote Flats Historical Review 1905–1965* (Lethbridge, Alta., 1967), p. 357; Hugh A. Dempsey, "Black White Man," *Alberta Historical Review,* 6 (1958), 7–11.

him—as Nigger John—and by having his log cabin moved to adorn a provincial park; in time a pseudo-folk song would be composed to his memory. But one or two such Negroes were a romantic curiosity; a hundred, especially in the atmosphere of the early twentieth century, were a "racial menace." [21]

The first bloc of Oklahoma Negroes arrived in Saskatchewan in October of 1909. They sought out isolation from white communities, proximity to railheads, and distance from the American border. Unwilling to move from the railroads that had brought them—unlike the whites who had begun to pre-empt good land at some distance from the tracks—the black settlers had to accept inferior allotments, since the richer farmland near the lines was already taken up. Two hundred Negroes spread out into Manitoba and as far east as the Thunder Bay area, and a few blacks from Chicago settled in Saskatoon. However, the great majority were among the founders of Maidstone and Wilkie, in Saskatchewan, and of Junkins, Breton, Clyde, and Amber Valley in Alberta; others would settle in Lloydminster, on the border between the two new provinces.[22]

The black settlers first took up land in the Eldon district, just north of Maidstone. Saskatoon lay one hundred and fifty railroad miles to the southeast. The leaders of the all-Negro Eldon community were Julius Caesar Lane, then fifty-nine, and Mattie Hayes, a slim and determined woman of sixty who had been born a slave in Georgia. She and her husband Joseph brought their ten sons and three daughters, and their grandchildren, from Tulsa and Muskogee, together with ten other families, and until her death in 1953 "Mammy" Hayes was the matriarch of Maidstone. (After World War I the younger colonists would move from the land to larger, nearby towns—Lloydminster, North Battleford, Saskatoon, and eventually to Edmonton and Regina—and by 1960 the Negro population of Maidstone and Eldon had dropped to less than forty.) [23]

21. Glenbow Foundation Archives, Calgary: Eleanor G. Luxton, "Interview with Nettie Ware—Vulcan, August 1956," typescript, pp. 1–6; Grant MacEwan, *John Ware's Cow Country* (Edmonton [1960]), passim; Stu Phillips, *Echoes of the Canadian Foothills,* Rodeo Records (1956): "Nigger John"; Ullman, *Look to the North Star,* pp. 204–05. I am grateful to John Ware's daughter, Nettie, of Kirkaldy, Alberta, for sending me newspaper cuttings relating to her father's life. On Shadd, see Timothy Ryan, *Voices of the Past: A History of Melfort and District* ([Melfort], 1965), pp. 46–48.

22. *Calgary Eye Opener,* July 11, 1902; *Chicago Defender,* July 17, Oct. 21, 1911, Nov. 16, Dec. 28, 1912. Canadian Department of the Interior, *Railway Map of the Dominion of Canada* ([Ottawa], 1914), sheets 4 and 5, compared with the 1909 edition of the same map, sheet 6, show the pattern of settlement. On Thunder Bay, see the reminiscences of J. P. Bertrand, sent to the author by Keith Dennis, President of The Thunder Bay Historical Society, Port Arthur, July 1961.

23. *Between the Rivers . . . Maidstone, Saskatchewan, 1905–1955* ([North Battle-

The government required all settlers to pay $10.00 for one hundred and sixty acres of land, to live on that land for six months in each year for three years, and during that time to clear a minimum of thirty acres, dig a well, build a house valued at $300, and erect fencing worth $200. The Eldon group did so with some success. Lane, who changed his name to the more English J. Cecil, staked out claims for himself and his sons and, when eligible, became a citizen. Following usual practice, they took liens for seed grain and paid twelve annual installments on principal and interest. One son, Walter, took up a particularly poor sand quarter, broke sixty acres, and abandoned the property to become a day laborer in Battleford, losing his land for taxes. All others had richer soil and fought through the first lean years successfully, excluding John Mayes, a boy of nineteen, who found that he had acquired a muskeg swamp. The farmers worked as teamsters during the winter months, returned to the land each spring, and—except for those who enlisted in the army during World War I—remained to fully improve their property. On the basis of twenty land patent reports, one finds that after three years the men had broken an average of forty-eight acres of land and were cropping an average of forty-two acres; that nearly all were able to build houses of logs and mud during their first summer on the land; and that at the beginning of their fourth year they owned houses, outbuildings, and fencing valued at an average of $617. Except for two men, one of whom kept a community fowl house, the heads of families also owned an average of five cattle, three horses, and three pigs, and between them the settlers had two oxen for heavy pulling.[24]

The settlers were eager to send their children to church and to school. They used the nearby common school at first—where they also were permitted to hold Baptist services—and in 1916 they opened their own. The first teacher, a Negro from Kansas, attended normal school classes in North Battleford to earn provincial accreditation, and she was succeeded by two other Negro teachers until the institution was integrated in 1923. Negroes continued to serve on the board of trustees of the Eldon district

ford], n.d.), pp. 18–19, 58; Robert Moon, *This is Saskatchewan* (Toronto, 1953), p. 163; interviews in North Battleford and Maidstone in August 1959, with Mr. C. Irwin McIntosh, Managing Editor of the *News-Optimist,* and with members of the Mayes and Lane families. I should like to thank Father A. E. Potter of Kitscoty, Alberta, for interviewing for me members of the Mayes family now living in Lloydminster.

24. Archives of Saskatchewan, University of Saskatchewan, Saskatoon: Canadian Department of the Interior, Land Patents Branch, Homestead Records, files no. 1169898, 1426250, 1890797, 1971295, 1977533, 1977535, 2043515, 2095066, 2099857, 2103158, 2155294, 2155296, 2190220, 2193187, 2398194, 2437569, 2538221, 2709992, 3213293, 5600808, and location chart of homesteaders on Eldon no. 471.

until 1954, although most black children attended schools, to which they were admitted without difficulty, in Maidstone or North Battleford.[25]

In Alberta the pattern was less encouraging. While a very few Negroes arrived as early as 1907, most came in 1909–10—also largely from Oklahoma—to take up land between Junkins (now Wildwood) and the northern shores of Chip Lake, on the railroad between sixty and ninety miles west of Edmonton. Other blacks settled south of Wabumun Lake near a bend of the northern Saskatchewan River. At Junkins the Negroes unsuccessfully tried to grow wheat, barley, and oats, with only shovels for breaking the land; and soon they moved into shacks and tents in the tiny village itself. There they hoped to grow peas for a cannery that was never established. During the war the younger blacks went to Edmonton to work, and more followed upon the agricultural depression of 1921. At one point the congregation of the Anglican mission church in Edmonton was largely Negro, and black men were common sights around the lakes west of the city well into the 1930s.[26]

The first Negroes moved to Breton, then known as Keystone, from Wabumun Lake late in 1909. When there were thirty-five Negro families in the area, they opened a school and a church. On the occasion of the Anglican missionary's first visit to "the nigger settlement" in 1915, he found nearly sixty "tremendously pleased and keen" blacks waiting to hear him, despite a snowstorm which, he thought, would have kept an English congregation away entirely. For some years the Negroes ran the school, church, and post office, until they began to leave in the 1930s, first for Leduc and then for Edmonton; ironically, in 1957 the Breton school would earn local notoriety by refusing to permit a Negro to teach white children. Of those blacks who had come by 1911, only one was still active in the community in 1960, when there were perhaps six Negro families left in the area.[27]

25. Archives of Saskatchewan, Legislative Library, Regina: Department of Education, Eldon School District, file no. 3613.

26. Interviews with residents in Wildwood, Breton, and Amber Valley, June–August, 1959; Glenbow Foundation: Transcript of interview by F. F. Parkinson with Tony Payne, March 1963; Department of the Interior, *Atlas of Canada,* rev. ed. (Toronto, 1915), p. 13 and plate 23; F. H. Eva Hasell, *Through Western Canada in a Caravan,* 2nd ed. (London, 1927), p. 75; Lewis G. Thomas, "Mission Church in Edmonton: An Anglican Experiment in the Canadian West," *Pacific Northwest Quarterly, 49* (1958), 57; Bickersteth, *Land of Open Doors,* p. 125; Archbishop's Western Canada Fund, *Occasional Paper,* no. 3 (1911), p. 3.

27. *Occasional Paper,* no. 18 (1915), pp. 7–8; Glenbow Foundation: Letter by James G. MacGregor on Negro settlements; interview with Mr. Charles King of Breton, August 1959; Land Titles Office, Edmonton: Tax Notification Records and Certificates of Title, nos. 1426250, 1616302, 2138539, 2174938, 2193187, 2193191, 2230831, 2398196, 2398220, 2398222.

Amber Valley was the only Negro settlement to survive both World War I and the Great Depression. Some three hundred Oklahoma blacks moved into the Pine Creek area, one hundred miles north of Edmonton and twenty miles to the east of Athabasca, beginning in 1910. Others took up grants at Poplar Ridge, Stocks, and Donatville. Leaving their families in Edmonton for the first winter, the men—led by Jefferson D. Edwards, a young man of twenty-two—accepted from one to five sections each. While a few were able to find abandoned claims on which improvements already had been made, most needed two years or more to harvest their first crop. During the winters they returned to Edmonton to work in a meat-packing plant. The settlers opened a school which served as their Methodist church as well. By 1920 the average holding at Amber Valley consisted of thirty-eight acres—virtually all in crops—three horses, two cattle, and houses and fences valued at $400, which although low was deemed sufficient by the local authorities. A number of blacks drifted into Edmonton in the 1920s in search of Anglican or Standard Holiness religious services, there to give rise to a local "blues" tradition, and to intermarry with whites or Sikhs; but the primal Negro community remained physically aloof and self-sustaining. In 1931, the opening of a post office marked official recognition of its permanency. Socially, the three hundred Negroes of Amber Valley were accepted into local women's organizations, the chamber of commerce, the agricultural society, and the public services; and Edwards, with his ten children and their twenty grandchildren, continued to dominate the valley to the 1960s.[28]

These Negro settlements failed to grow after 1911 partly because the Canadian government successfully frustrated attempts by reinforcement parties from Oklahoma to enter the west. Beginning in February, Winnipeg newspapers predicted that the Dominion government would move to exclude Negro immigrants. An unpleasant rape case involving a Negro reinforced the customary sexual mythology. Two Conservative members of the House of Commons from Essex County in Ontario, and the member for Saint John, asked Sir Wilfrid Laurier's Liberal Minister of the Interior, Frank Oliver, to explain governmental policy. Oliver, an Albertan, replied

28. Tax Notification Records and Certificates of Title, nos. 2500396/3001, 2843969/2418, 3153543/2450, and application no. 49660, in Department of Municipal Affairs file no. 1160 ES (1932); Department of Lands and Forests, Edmonton: map of township 66; telephone interviews with Mrs. Ruth Heslep, July, and Mrs. William Boyle and Reverend H. Wiggins, August 1959; Glenbow Foundation: transcripts of interviews by Parkinson with Edwards, Willis Bowen, Thomas Mapp, and Mrs. Nettie Murphy, March 1963; ibid., Rural preliminary list of Electors [Amber Valley], 1940; Ken Eric Liddell, "New Promised Land," *Saturday Night*, 65 (1950), 11; Ina Bruns, "Kind Hearts and Gentle People," *Montreal Family Herald* (June 25, 1959), pp. 10–11; *Edmonton Journal*, Jan. 19, March 11, 1963; Reverend W. J. O'Farrell, Boyle, Alberta, to the author, Sept, 14, 1965.

that he knew of no discrimination on grounds of race or color, although exclusion officers had been appointed to help administer a new Canadian immigration law, passed in 1910, which was "restricted, exclusive, and selective." If there was any latitude allowed local officials, he thought, it lay not with the proposed settler's color but with his destination: if Negroes wished to go onto the land, they could; if they wished to move into the cities, there would be the same presumption against them as against any city-bound immigrants. He acknowledged that there was "a strong sentiment" against Negroes, as settlers or citizens. George (later Sir George) E. Foster, then representing North York—and recently under attack by these same Liberals over his administration of the Union Trust Company, of which he was general manager—stingingly suggested that the law should be administered as it read, without presumptions or prejudices. The Ontario Conservatives seized the occasion to declare their affection for their Negro voters.

They also sought to embarrass the Liberal government by demonstrating that two Negroes who had passed difficult civil service examinations had been set to feeding chickens for the Department of Agriculture. Further, a bishop of the African Methodist Episcopal Church was ejected from the House, allegedly for attempting to assure that Negroes would have equal access to Canada, and the Ottawa press reported that Oliver intended to impose a head tax of $500 on each Negro arrival. Robert L. Borden, the leader of the Conservative opposition, declared that "No man should be excluded on account of his color, providing he was a good, honest, law-abiding citizen." Still, as the Conservative Member for Quebec's Lisgar—who wanted an all-white west—admitted, "negro immigration . . . is a question that no man in politics desires to touch." [29]

Laurier probably agreed, for the moment was particularly delicate. Only two months before, negotiations had ended with the United States on a reciprocal trade agreement long sought by the Canadians; and the Senate, which still had to ratify the agreement, might resent efforts to bar American citizens from Canada. Further, for the first time since 1884–85, Canadian commercial interests were beginning to talk of federation with one or more of the British West Indian colonies. In February, T. B. Macaulay, cofounder of the new Canadian-West Indian League, had persuaded the Bahaman House of Assembly to pass a resolution asking for an inquiry into the possibility of union.[30] Macaulay thought that a political merger would broaden Canada's outlook on "the colour question." Few

29. *Toronto Mail and Empire*, March 24, 1911; *Toronto Globe*, April 4, 27, May 2, 1911; House of Commons, *Debates, 1910–11, 5:* cols. 8125–28; *1911, 3:* cols. 4470–71, 5711–13; *4:* cols. 5941–48.

30. For a detailed analysis of this and other discussions of a federation, see Robin W. Winks, *Canadian-West Indian Union: A Forty-Year Minuet* (London, 1968).

wished to offend all black men at such a moment; although the Governor of the Bahamas, Sir William Grey-Wilson, did so when he visited Toronto, by suggesting that if the Bahamas joined the confederation, "the question of color" in politics could be resolved by putting the qualification for the vote so high that "the ignorant blacks" would be shut out. Nor was the Governor without his covert worries, for in conversation afterwards he added (and a reporter caught) the remark that he wished to assure Canadians that "the white woman in the midst of negroes" enjoyed absolute security under the colonial system. Even if union with the West Indies was not to be taken seriously, closer ties were of some concern, especially to Maritime businessmen, since in 1910 a Royal Commission had recommended strengthening trade relations. While the West Indian discussion urged delicacy upon those who would speak of race, its result also was to convince observers that in general "an influx of . . . diversified tinges of Negro, Spanish, French and British [blood] in greater or less degree into our Parliament would [not] be either acceptable or advantageous." Presumably, many Negroes could be turned back at the border by a strict application of standing regulations on health, literacy, and financial support.[31]

But the Negro migrants would not wait, and in March of 1911 the government had to take cognizance of the fact. On the twenty-first a party of two hundred blacks arrived at the border station at Emerson, Manitoba, opposite Pembina in North Dakota, and requested admission to press on to Amber Valley, to which relatives had preceded them. The Canadian officials subjected them to the most rigorous examination possible and found, contrary to expectations, that they could not stop a single member of the group. Not one had less than $300 (or $100 more than the law required), all were in excellent health, and all had documentary proof of good moral standing. They seemed to presage a wave of healthy, moral, and prosperous black men. The Secretary of the Edmonton Board of Trade, aware of those already passing through the city, now demanded that all Negroes be barred from entry; and a member of the government of Alberta (who refused to give his name) suggested through the press that the Dominion should apply a head tax on Negroes at once.[32]

Realization that normal application of the regulation might not be sufficient to block Negro entry led to a renewal of demands for remedial

31. CO 42/947: file of April 14, 1911, "Union of Bahamas with Canada"; CO 23/267: file of Dec. 15, 1911; *Toronto News,* Oct. 26, 1911; *Toronto Globe,* Oct. 27, 1911; L. A. M. Lovekin, "Canada and the British West Indies," *Canadian Magazine, 53* (1919), 293-96.

32. *Toronto Mail and Empire,* March 24, 1911; *Toronto Globe,* April 4, 27, May 2, 1911.

legislation. The Winnipeg Board of Trade joined in the clamor for a head tax. Falsely stating that many of the blacks had been unable to pass the physical examination at the frontier, the board resolved that those Negroes who had taken land in Canada had "not proved themselves satisfactory as farmers, thrifty as settlers, or desirable [as] neighbors," despite the obvious fact that most of them had been in the Dominion less than eighteen months and had yet to harvest their first crop. The Member for Lanark North predicted that Negroes would swarm by the tens of thousands and told the government officials that they must "preserve for the sons of Canada the lands they proposed to give to niggers." A false report that five hundred more blacks had arrived from Clearview, Oklahoma, during the last week of March led the Member for Grey East to suggest that seventeen thousand blacks had entered Canada during the previous year —an absurd confusion with the census total for 1901, as was pointed out in the House. Mindful of his Negro voters, the Member for Pictou deplored any color line, however; and Oliver again insisted that the law did not permit discrimination while reminding Parliament that it could change the law if it wished. Foster now remarked that since the government had blocked West and East Indians, both from within the Empire, there was little reason not to apply the same restrictions to American Negroes.[33]

The Dominion government wavered. Relations with the United States were going sour by the end of April, as ill-chosen remarks by President William Howard Taft fanned the fear that reciprocity was a prelude to annexation. The Conservatives were pointing to a series of scandals, one of them involving Frank Oliver, as evidence that the Liberals should be turned out. Negroes in western Ontario were writing to the Department of the Interior to protest against alleged rejections, most of which had not yet taken place (although in April forty Negroes were turned back at the border at White Rock, British Columbia, because the medical officer professed to find them all suffering from tuberculosis), and black voters, necessary to marginal Liberal seats in three Ontario constituencies, were threatening to desert the party entirely.

The press was full of advice, conjecture, and public opinion. From Kansas City a Canadian woman wrote that Jim Crow was fully justified: "Your towns will soon be as unsafe for women as the towns in the South are." A "Colored Canadian" responded by asking whether Canadians

33. *Toronto Globe,* March 28, April 18, May 30, June 1, 1911; *New York Tribune,* March 22, 1911; *Toronto Mail and Empire,* April 27, 1911; *The Crisis, 1* (1911), 9; NA, Foreign Affairs, Record Group 7, State Decimal Files, 842.5511: text of resolution.encl. in John E. Jones to Philander C. Knox, April 24, 1911; House of Commons, *Debates, 1910–11, 4:* cols. 6525–28.

were so cowardly as to fear inferior beings. When Toronto's *Mail and Empire* urged a total ban on Negro immigrants, since "Canada wants no negro question . . . no race riots," a Maryland Negro was had been living in Ontario asked, "Why should there be race riots if we hold true to British law?" The *Toronto Globe* suggested that the influx of Negroes would soon end in any case, for not only was the government opposed to them but so were the churches. By May news of Canadian concern had been picked up in the West Indies, where Jamaica's *Kingston Gleaner* said that the color problem would keep West Indians from wishing to live in Canada. In faraway Australia, the Melbourne press quoted Lord Milner to extol the advantages of being British and white, and warned Canadians not to let the side down.[34]

Throughout March and April the American Consul-General at Winnipeg, John E. Jones, labored to help the Negro immigrants. He intervened at the border on behalf of a band of a hundred blacks from Weletka, Oklahoma, after an attorney for the Chicago-Great Western Railroad Company forwarded information to the State Department suggesting that Canadian immigration agents intended to apply special regulations to all future Negro settlers. The American Consul-General in Ottawa, John G. Foster, replied that there were no such regulations, although in the meantime a Winnipeg newspaper reported that Canadian officials had left for Emerson to block the entry of another one hundred and sixty-five American Negroes and that the railway company was appealing to Washington and to Jones (who had fallen ill), to see to it that they were given the same treatment as all Americans.

Upon investigation in April, Jones learned that the Commissioner of Immigration for Western Canada had offered a fee to the medical inspector at Emerson for every Negro he rejected. A special medical officer was on the way from Ottawa to examine the black settlers already in Canada, he added, and he thought that after sufficient time had passed to make it possible for the Canadians to find that the climate was too severe for Negroes, the Dominion government would issue a proclamation under the Immigration Act of 1910 to prohibit entry. While admitting that feeling was running high against all black men, the Consul-General warned that any measures taken to prevent Negro entrance would be an unfriendly act.

The American Secretary of State, Philander C. Knox, concerned over

34. *Toronto Globe,* April 26, 27, 30, 1911; *Mail and Empire,* April 6, 28, 1911; *The Chautauquan, 63* (1911), 119–20; Schomburg Collection, John Edward Bruce Papers: A. Goldsmith, n.d., to Bruce, no. 1399; *Melbourne Age,* April 5, 1911; *Melbourne Argus,* May 27, 1911. I should like to thank Professor John D. Legge of Monash University, Clayton, Victoria, for searching out copies of these editorials.

the already precarious Canadian-American relationship, summoned Jones to Washington at the end of April. Immigration authorities in Winnipeg had prepared a memorandum, as Jones had anticipated, suggesting that Negroes might be barred "on the ground that [they] could not become adapted to the rigorous northern climate and consequently might become a public charge." A member of the American Bureau of Citizenship also had drawn up a memorandum suggesting that, in view of American exclusion of Asians, the United States could not consistently protest the expected Canadian ruling. Further, under Sifton, Canadians had blocked Americans of Italian origin. Knox advised Jones not to warn the Negroes until Canada seemed certain to act, while recognizing that there was little the United States could do.

The Canadian immigration authorities pressed forward in their efforts to block Negro settlers. In May, the Dominion Commissioner of Immigration in Winnipeg, J. Bruce Walker, gave Jones a confidential statement promising that the necessary order-in-council would be forthcoming at the next session of Parliament. Meanwhile, the Canadian government "was doing all in its power through a policy of persuasion, to keep negroes out of Western Canada." When delivering his note, Walker told Jones that "it was his purpose to bar [blacks] from Canada, upon the broad ground of being undesirables." A Canadian agent hurried to Oklahoma to talk with parties of prospective immigrants, "pointing out the difficulties of the climate and the general prejudice which was sweeping over Canada against the negro." He suggested that the Rock Island and Southern Pacific railroads were exaggerating the attractions of the north in order to get the Negroes' land cheaply—although at the same time other Canadian agents were describing those attractions to white Americans. Jones noted that two more carloads of settlers destined for the Edmonton area were due to arrive shortly, and he feared that they would be turned back at the border by health inspectors. He then took the precaution of sending a Negro doctor from the United States into the Negro settlements in western Canada so that he would have his own check on the Dominion's medical reports.[35]

Although Consul-General Jones was prepared to stand firm in defense of equal rights for all Americans, the State Department did not wish to make an issue of Negro immigration in the face of deteriorating Canadian-American relations. When Halvor Steenerson, a Representative from

35. *New York Tribune,* March 22, 1911; State Decimal Files, 842.5511: Herrick to Knox, encl. A. L. Craig to Herrick, both March 20, Foster to Knox, tel., March 21, 30, and Jones to Knox, April 22, all 1911; ibid.: Bureau of Citizenship memo., April 25, attached to Jones to Knox, April 22, 1911; ibid., 842.5511/7, box 8868: Jones to Knox, May 22, 1911.

Minnesota and Chairman of the House Committee on the Militia, protested in May that one of his constituents had been turned back at the Canadian border because she was a Negro, Knox disingenuously replied that there was no law against entry of Negroes into Canada because the climate was too severe for them, and not until July did he give Steenerson access to Jones's memoranda so that he might fully understand the situation. In June, however, Knox did write to the Governor of Oklahoma, enclosing extracts from Jones's reports, to ask that potential settlers from the state be warned. There the matter rested for the year; when, in September 1911, as Canadians wallowed in an orgy of anti-Americanism, the Laurier ministry fell, taking the reciprocity treaty down with him, one source for constraint in the relationship with Canada was removed.[36]

During the next year, the color line became more definite. In February the Great Northern Railway sent notices to its employees that Negroes would not be admitted to Canada under any circumstances and that ticket sales between Saint Paul and the border should be discouraged. In March the Superintendent of Immigration, W. D. Scott, publicly asked American Negroes not to come to western Canada since opportunities for them were better in a warmer climate. By June the Canadians appeared to be applying their restrictions to visitors as well, for a Negro doctor from Wewoka, Oklahoma, wrote to Knox that a party which had wanted merely to visit with earlier settlers had been turned back at the Alberta border. Knox inquired through his consul in Ottawa, who replied that Scott feared many visitors would attempt to remain permanently, so all Negro movement across the frontier was being discouraged.[37]

The situation remained unchanged until the outbreak of World War I. Frank M. Nye, a Representative from Minnesota, denounced the discriminatory policy, as did other Congressmen who objected to the misleading character of the Dominion's advertising campaign, which still made no reference to Negro exclusion. In Winnipeg, Jones gathered data showing how Canadian immigration officials worked to attract American farmers, and in Vancouver a group of Negroes organized a Negro Christian Alliance, with a barber, Milton P. Fuller, as their president, to combat discrimination. But with the beginning of war in Europe, all parties were

36. State Decimal Files, 842.5511: Steenerson to Knox, May 19, and reply, May 25, and memoranda, May 20, July 3 (twice), Huntington Wilson, Acting Secretary of State, to Charles Nagel, Secretary of Commerce and Labor, and Wilbur J. Carr to Jones, both June 9, with memoranda, May 25, June 3, and Knox to Lee Cruce, Governor of Oklahoma, June 3—all 1911.

37. Ibid.: J. J. Chandler to Knox, June 25, and replies, July 2, 27, 1912, Cass to Foster, July 2, encl. memo., July 1, memo., July 24, Horace M. Sanford to Knox, July 17, encl. Scott to Foster, July 11, all 1912: *The Crisis, 3* (1912), 145; *4* (1912), 148–49.

compelled to agree that in order to prevent enemy infiltration the Canadians had the right to set up any limitations on their border they chose, and nothing more was heard of the issue. The Dominion government retained the power to prohibit entry "to any nationality or race" if "such immigrants are deemed unsuitable having regard to the climatic, industrial, social, educational, labour or other conditions" of Canada, or "because of their probable inability to become readily assimilated." By 1914 the Oklahoma Negroes were seeking out opportunities in America's northern cities, and their interest in Canada waned. Those already in Canada preferred to forget their chilly reception and get on with the business of building their communities. Nearly everyone had forgotten them by 1929, when an acting Deputy Minister for Immigration would report, mistakenly, that none of the original black settlers remained in the West. In the meantime World War I reminded Canadian Negroes of the extent of prejudice against them.[38]

The nadir for the Negro in Canada came at the moment when the nation as a whole at last felt itself to be emerging as an identifiable culture on the world scene. Having rebuffed the United States by rejecting a reciprocity treaty that Canadians had been seeking for fifty-five years, having made abundantly clear that Indian, Negro, and Oriental immigrants were not wanted, and having rallied to the defense of God, Country, and Empire, Canada now stood at Armageddon. The moment was an emotional one—and a magnificent one. For the greatest efforts of patriotism, of commitment to long-voiced if not oft-defended ideals, and of physical sacrifice were drawn from the Canadian people, at Vimy Ridge, at Passchendaele, and at home. Amidst this rededication to idealism, men such as Newton W. Rowell, president of the Privy Counsel in the Canadian Union government of 1917, expressed the hope that Canada and the United States might be the only victorious nations not to press for territorial rewards at the end of a war that would truly have been fought to save democracy.

The Negro stood outside this new drama. Much of the nation seemed to surge forward between 1914 and 1916, before nearly foundering on the rock of conscription that once again divided English- and French-speaking Canadians. But that Negroes generally were not included in the

38. State Decimal File 842.5511: Nye to Knox, Aug. 21, encl. Robert Lee to Nye, Aug. 15, Jones to Knox, Aug. 30, Wilson to Nye, Sept. 3, Alvey A. Adee to F. W. Mandell, Oct. 1, 1912; *Journals of the Legislative Assembly of the Province of Saskatchewan, 1931*, pp. 29, 27; *The Immigration Act and Regulations* (Ottawa, 1921), par. 38; *The Crisis, 3* (1912), 184; *12* (1916), 243; Greaves, "Negro in Canada," p. 58. A search of the Nye Papers in the Minnesota Historical Society has produced nothing relevant.

patriotic and military institutions upon which the surge rose was made painfully evident to the blacks.

The most important of these institutions was the army. Two months after the outbreak of war, the first contingent of Canadian troops arrived in Britain. An initial call for volunteers was expanded to a quarter of a million in 1915 and to half a million in 1916, most of whom were sent to the Western Front. A few Negroes were among these troops, for individual blacks were permitted to enlist in such local regiments as would accept them. One of John Ware's sons was killed in action, and in 1918 James Grant, a Negro from St. Catharines, received the Military Cross for taking a field gun through a critical salient while under heavy shelling.[39]

Nonetheless, three months after the war began, Arthur Alexander, spokesman for those Negroes who remained in the Buxton area, wrote to the Minister of Militia and Defence, Colonel Sam Hughes, asking why black men were not permitted to enlist in the army. Hughes replied briskly that the selection of recruits was in the hands of the local commanding officers and that their work was not interfered with from headquarters. The following year, however, Hughes saw the need for a more positive statement about Negroes as soldiers, for increasing evidence flowed into his office that able-bodied men were being turned away solely because of their color. After all, such had been the case during the Boer War, when some enlistment officers had disliked the idea of black men carrying arms against whites, especially in South Africa. Now from Pictou County, Saint John, and Edmonton came letters indicating that recruiting officers assumed there would be a separate Negro battalion.[40]

Hughes and the regular militia men were at odds over what to do with Negro volunteers. Hughes's advisers did not favor an all-Negro unit since at least three thousand black volunteers would be needed to keep a regiment in the field for twelve months. The minister, Sir Sam, told the recruiting officers that he had no time for their racial sensibilities: "I will not . . . lend myself to the fad of giving [Negroes] a regiment to themselves any more than I intend to have a regiment of one-eyed men or men with yellow moustaches or red hair." Almost as if in reply, the commander

39. *The Crisis, 15* (1918), 248; *16* (1918), 134; Glenbow Foundation: separation allowance papers of Sapper William James Ware, and declaration by Charlotte Lewis; *Toronto Globe,* Jan. 1, 1916.

40. Public Archives Record Centre, Ottawa, General Headquarters Papers, 297-1-21 "Enlistment of Coloured Men in the Canadian Militia": Alexander to Hughes, [Nov. 5], and reply, Nov. 20, 1914, George Morton to Hughes, Sept. 7, Loring Christie to W. G. Gwatkin, Sept. 29, and reply, Sept. 30, J. F. Tupper to Hughes, Nov. 11, and Beverley R. Armstrong to W. E. Hodgkins, Nov. 18, all 1915; TPL, Abbott-Hubbard Collection: Anderson R. Abbott MS on Shadd family volunteer.

of the 104th Overseas Battalion wrote that he had rejected nineteen Negro volunteers from Saint John: "I have been fortunate to have secured a very fine class of recruits, and I did not think it was fair to these men that they should have to mingle with negroes." One of the blacks objected, however, and on November 29, 1915, the Militia Council resoundingly repeated an order that had first gone out on October 19, that "colored men are to be permitted to enlist in any battalion." [41]

Having often ignored the orders of his superiors, Hughes discovered that amidst the confusions of war his subordinates could find ways of ignoring him. Very few Negroes were accepted for military service, although the commander of the 106th Overseas Battalion based on Halifax, thinking that "coloured men should do their share in the Empire's Defence," was willing to accept some. However, as he wrote to the Militia Council as soon as news arrived from Ottawa that Negroes were to be taken into his battalion, several whites who were on the verge of enlisting refused to do so. "Neither my men nor myself, would care to sleep alongside [Negroes], or to eat with them, especially in warm weather," he confessed. Accordingly, he asked the local Negro minister, Reverend William A. White, to raise a separate platoon of blacks. In the same week confirmation of the desire for segregation came from the other side of the continent, when the Militia council received word that the color line in British Columbia was "very sharply drawn as compared with Eastern Canada" and that Negroes could not be enlisted with white men. Both officers asked, however, for authority to raise separate Negro units. [42]

In Ottawa the right hand did not know what the left should do. On December 22 the Department of Militia and Defence issued a memorandum to all adjutants-general: "The fiat has gone forth: There is to be no coloured line; coloured battalions are not to be raised; coloured men are to be allowed to enlist in any battalion of the C.E.F." (Canadian Expeditionary Force). But since some commanding officers objected, all should remember that it would "be humiliating to the coloured men themselves to serve in a battalion where they were not wanted." Hughes, who apparently did not see this directive, had contradicted it three weeks earlier. An energetic young Negro journalist, J. R. B. Whitney, who at the beginning of the year had launched the weekly *Toronto Canadian Observer* as the official Negro organ in Canada, had written to the minister to ask

41. *Saint John Globe,* Nov. 20, 1915; General Headquarters Papers, 297-1-21: George W. Fowler to 6th Division Headquarters, Nov. 25, Hodgins to same, Nov. 29, John T. Richards to Hughes, Nov. 21, and reply, Nov. 25, 1915.

42. General Headquarters Papers, 297-1-21: W. H. Allan to Hodgins, Dec. 14, and District Officer Commanding, Victoria, to Hodgins, Dec. 15, 1915.

whether he might raise a colored unit, and Hughes had replied with the sweeping remark that there was nothing in the world to stop him.[43]

Whitney—apparently obtaining some letterheads of the Canadian Northern Railway through its secretary, a close friend—wrote to various officers of the militia, solicited the leave of a Negro sergeant to help recruit other black men, and advertised for volunteers in his newspaper. Appealing to black pride with headlines proclaiming that "Germans Dread Colored Soldiers in the Battlefield," Whitney hoped to find a hundred and fifty men in Ontario who were prepared to go. At this juncture he learned that the Canadian army would not accept them.

Perhaps Whitney should have anticipated the army's response, for on December 13, after he had received permission from Hughes to begin recruiting but before he had actually done so, Whitney celebrated the first anniversary of his paper by inviting the president of the Canadian Bank of Commerce, Sir Edmund Walker, to address a gathering of black leaders. A man of wide-ranging interests, Sir Edmund was well informed on Negro history, and in his speech he indulged in ritual condemnations of slavery, praise for the Underground Railroad and the fugitive slaves, and urgings of race pride. He also chose to "speak frankly," as he said, and he told his audience that Negroes should not hope "to jump to the front in one or two or three generations," since they were the closest of all people to aboriginal man. "The white man's scale is immeasurably greater than the black man's. That is a thing that the colored race should remember with pride," he concluded somewhat obscurely. The point of Walker's statement was lost on the audience, which responded only to his offhand remark that he wished the Negro race were increasing in numbers in Ontario, since Negroes were faithful, hard-working, and good laborers. Walker made no reference to social equality, and his entire exposition, based on the environmental theories then fashionable, suggested that, while he found no inherent inferiority in the Negro other than his proximity to primitive man, he nonetheless found blacks seriously retarded.[44]

In March 1916, Acting Minister of Militia and Defence, A. Edward Kemp, unguardedly stated in Parliament that he was not aware of any effort to organize a unit of Negroes. Whitney immediately wrote to Kemp to correct him. A reply came from the acting adjutant-general of the second military district, of which Toronto was a part, revealing for the first time that no commanding officer in the area had been found who was

43. General Headquarters Papers, 297-1-21: Memorandum to all Adjutants-General, Dec. 22, 1915, and Whitney to Hughes, April 18, 1916, encl. copy, Hughes to Whitney, Dec. 3, 1915.
44. *Canadian Observer, 3* (1915), 1, 7–8; ibid., *3* (1916), 1; *Toronto Globe,* Dec. 14, 1915; *Toronto Financial Post,* Nov. 28, 1942.

willing to accept a Negro platoon under his command. The same officer had personally authorized such recruiting in February, only to withdraw that authorization in March. Whitney, believing that Hugh's letter overrode any others, had continued to solicit enlistments, and now appealed to Hughes for help—whereupon the irascible Colonel Sam fired off a peremptory telegram to Toronto demanding to know who had issued orders countermanding his letter. Whitney unwisely wrote Toronto suggesting that he would publish the entire correspondence in his newspaper and "cause a stir." In the interim a memorandum, written on April 13, nearly a month after Toronto had withdrawn authorization to recruit and three weeks before Hughes had demanded information, was transmitted to the Minister, although not to Whitney.

This memorandum, penned by the Chief of the General Staff at Ottawa, Major-General W. G. Gwatkin, became the basis for recruiting Negroes into a construction battalion rather than into the Canadian Expeditionary Force. "Nothing is to be gained by blinking facts," Gwatkin wrote. "The civilized negro is vain and imitative; in Canada he is not impelled to enlist by a high sense of duty; in the trenches he is not likely to make a good fighter; and the average white man will not associate with him on terms of equality." Further, "In France, in the firing line, there is no place for a black battalion, C.E.F. It would be eyed askance; it would crowd out a white battalion; and it would be difficult to re-inforce." No white officer would accept an all-black platoon. The only course open was to form one or more labor battalions, especially of Nova Scotian Negroes, and to ask the British Government if it might be able to use blacks on special duty, perhaps in Egypt. Until then, individual Negroes could continue to enlist in white battalions at the discretion of the commanding officers.[45]

But as 1916 wore on, Canadian volunteers were falling well short of the year-end goal of half a million. The need for more men was acute, especially as enlistment figures fell from thirty thousand to six thousand a month; and recruiting officers reached out to find men where they could. In Nova Scotia, contrary to regulations, they enlisted black Bermudans as officers' servants and such Negro seamen as deserted from West Indian schooners. In Edmonton Reverend C. W. Washington of St. Mark's Church of the First Born offered to raise an all-Negro battalion, somewhat ir-

45. House of Commons, *Debates, 1916, 3*, 2114–15; General Headquarters Papers, 597-1-21: Whitney to Kemp, March 29, to Hughes, April 18, to Leonard T. Trump, March 24, Hughes to [Francis] Logie [Armstrong], tel., May 3, Trump to Whitney, Feb. 18, March 15, Hodgins to E. A. Stanton, Feb. 5, and Gwatkin, memo., April 13, War Office to Duke Connaught, Governor General, secret, May 11, all 1916.

responsibly telling the lieutenant-governor, R. G. Brett, that there were ten thousand able-bodied Negroes within a radius of a hundred miles of the city, while admitting to a friend that no more than four hundred could be found. When Brett endorsed the proposal, the commander of the military district more realistically replied that no such body of men existed and that, in any case, he had no authority to raise a combat force. Rather, Negroes might be welcomed into some French-Canadian units; and because of "their great capacity" for manual work, they could be taken into a construction battalion—"labor" having been rejected as pejorative under the circumstances—which would be trained in the Maritime Provinces.[46]

The No. 2 (Negro) Construction Battalion, with white officers, received authorization on July 5, 1916. D. H. Sutherland, of River John, Nova Scotia, a railroad contractor, was given command of the unit. Except among the Negro coalminers of Cape Breton Island, who were not eligible to enlist, recruiting was carried out in all Canadian Negro centers. Some five hundred men joined in Nova Scotia; three hundred and fifty enlisted in Ontario, with a detachment of sixty—presumably largely Whitney's men —from Toronto and a hundred from Windsor; and smaller groups were raised elsewhere. At first, headquarters for the battalion was at Pictou, but the Negroes were then transferred to Truro. In March 1917, the battalion embarked from Halifax for Liverpool, crossing the Atlantic during one of the worst weeks of unrestricted submarine warfare; and after a brief period in England, the men were ordered to France. Already there before them was the South African Labour Corps, also made up of volunteer blacks.

In France, the black construction battalion was attached to the Canadian Forestry Corps, a labor unit that included Indians as well as Russian, Norwegian, and Irish Canadians. Most of the men were engaged in logging, milling, and shipping until the end of the war. (Later sixty-six Negroes, who enlisted after the Negro unit had gone overseas, were placed in the Eighty-Fifth Battalion.) Following the armistice, the Negro laborers were taken to the general base at Etaples and then, in December 1918, dispatched to England.[47]

46. General Headquarters Papers, 597-1-21: W. W. Scott to E. F. Fiset, Sept. 30, Hodgins to all General Officers Commanding, Oct. 4, Sir G. M. Bullock, Commander-in-Chief, Bermuda, to Hodgins, Aug. 18, Oct. 4, 20, J. Munton to E. A. Cruikshank, March 1, Brett to Cruikshank, March 13, Cruikshank to Hodgins, March 11, and Hodgins, memo., March 21, all 1916.
47. Ibid.: J. P. O'Leary, Secretary, The Citizens' Recruiting Committee, to Adjutant-General, Aug. 4, 1916; *Windsor Daily Star,* May 23, 1943; Edmonton Public Library, clipping file, from *Brooks Bulletin,* undated, on Ware family; M. S. Hunt, ed., *Nova Scotia's Part in the Great War* (Halifax, 1920), pp. 148–53; *The Clarion, 3*

There were no racial incidents of record during the war, but anti-Negro tensions combined with impatience over the slow pace of demobilization to produce an unfortunate riot in Liverpool in June of 1919. Members of the construction battalion were barracked near white Canadian and British troops while waiting to be taken back to North America. During exercises a group of whites blocked the line of march of the parading Negroes, and the encounter turned into a general brawl. In Ottawa the Member from Trois Rivières, Jacques Bureau, asked whether any steps might be taken to deal with these black Canadian undesirables when they returned. While Kemp, now Sir Edward and Minister of Overseas Military Forces for Canada in the United Kingdom, again showed his ignorance of the situation by replying that if there were any Negroes in the Canadian army at all, they were scattered throughout the forces, he promised that Canadian Negro soldiers "would be treated exactly the same as other Canadian citizens."

A second incident occurred later in the year, when whites in Truro, resentful over the retention of the Negro camp there, fell upon a number of soldiers and beat them badly. Blacks were blocked from seeking revenge only by the intervention of their white officers. By the end of the year all of the Negroes had been demobilized, however, and the head-quarters in Truro was virtually abandoned.[48]

On the home front Negroes had participated in the war, largely through their own patriotic clubs. The Good Government Club of Windsor, a black society, raised $700 to give to the national Patriotic Fund, while others gave volunteer labor—when it was accepted—in hospitals and on depleted farms. In Vancouver, Negro women of the Garvey Movement organized a branch of the Universal Black Cross Nurses, which received the commen-dation of Lord Byng of Vimy. West Indians denied access to the Over-seas Comforts Clubs organized a Home Service Association, while Negro societies in Toronto, Montreal, and Halifax were active in soliciting funds and distributing propaganda leaflets, usually on their own but on occasion in cooperation with larger white fraternal organizations. Ironically, Can-ada's white soldiers marched into battle in uniforms, the buttons for which were manufactured by the only Montreal company that extensively em-ployed West Indian labor after 1911.

(1948), 1; C. W. Bird and J. B. Davies, *The Canadian Forestry Corps: Its Inception, Development and Achievements* (London, 1919), p. 50; Richard Symonds, tape-recorded reminiscences made by Reverend Charles L. Coleman of Halifax in the presence of the author, April 1965.

48. Symonds, tape recordings: Deacon Symonds was an eye-witness to the riot in Liverpool; General Headquarters Papers, C-251, file 72, no. ii, "Reinforcements: Colored Labor": cipher tels., Nov. 20, 22, 26, 29, 30, Dec. 4, 1918; House of Com-mons, *Debates, 1919, 4:* col. 3741; interview with A. E. Nickerson, March 1961.

At the war's end the Canadian prime minister, now Sir Robert Borden, virtually recognized—though only privately—that his countrymen were not prepared to grant equality to substantial numbers of black men. In November 1918, the Canadian Parliamentary Under-Secretary for External Affairs, Francis Keefer, reminded Borden of the possibility of uniting with the British West Indies, a step that would make the acquisition of Newfoundland and Bermuda probable as well. Borden replied on New Year's Day, 1919, by summarizing the advantages and disadvantages of union. While he thought that the sense of responsibility Canadians would gain from administering territories "largely inhabited by backward races," and the accompanying training (and expansion) of the civil service, would be beneficial to the nation, he thought the greatest hindrance would be "the difficulty of dealing with the coloured population who would probably . . . desire and perhaps insist upon representation in Parliament." As T. B. Macaulay observed later that year, to allow the "heterogeneous and unassimilated population of [British Guiana] equal votes with the people of Ontario in controlling the destinies of Canada would strain our faith in democracy." The Dominion did not want a Negro population even "as a Christmas gift from *Santa Claus,*" wrote a perceptive Jamaican. Instead, what the Negroes got at the end of the war was the Ku Klux Klan.[49]

The Ku Klux Klan entered Canada in the 1920s. The original Klan, founded in Tennessee in 1866 and having derived its name from the Greek *kuklos,* meaning band or circle, may have had a few followers in the united counties of Leeds and Grenville in Ontario; but if so, they were not active. After the first Klan virtually had ceased to function, a more virulent and all-embracing hate group was organized in Georgia in 1915. The new Klan acquired considerable power in Oklahoma, Texas, Colorado, Indiana, and elsewhere following World War I; and although there were relatively few Negroes in Canada against whom the white race needed protection, an increasing number of Jews and Roman Catholics provided equal if not quite so readily identifiable dangers in the eyes of the Klan. Moving into Washington and Oregon on an antiforeign, anti-Bolshevik, anti-Catholic basis in 1922–23, the Klan encouraged naturalized ex-

49. *Toronto Globe,* Oct. 14, 1916; PAC, Robert Borden Papers, *319:* Keefer to Borden, and reply, 35998–99 (portions from these letters appear in James Eayrs, *Northern Approaches: Canada and the Search for Peace* [Toronto, 1961], pp. 91–93); David Lloyd George, *Memoirs of the Peace Conference* (New Haven, Conn., 1939), 2, 367–68; *West India Committee Circular, 33* (1918), 303; Macaulay, "Canada and the West Indies: The Case for Commercial Union," ibid., *34* (1919), 157; Louis Meikle, *Confederation for the British West Indies versus Annexation to the United States of America* (London, 1912), pp. 113–16; *Canadian Observer, 3* (1916), 1; Winks, *Canadian-West Indian Union,* p. 43.

Canadians, in particular, to join the Riders of the Red Robe, a subsidiary organization created by the Klan to accommodate "pure" foreigners of Anglo-Saxon stock. The Klan then sought out bases in Alberta, Manitoba, Saskatchewan, British Columbia, and Ontario, feeding on anti-Semitism and on the fear of Negro and southern European immigrants.[50]

The Klan was a simple-minded but dangerous organization at which Canadians laughed. There was much to laugh at. The KKK motto, *Non silba sed anthar,* must have confused any who thought they had Latin, and the reported titles of the Eleven Terrors—or officers—Klaliff, Klokard, Kludd, Kligrapp, Klobee, Kladd, Klarago, Klexter, and three Klokann, would have horrified any respecter of the English language. The journal of the movement, *The Kourier Magazine,* which was distributed in Canada from its Atlanta base, was a simple-minded, vicious mixture of pseudo-Christian piety, racist sloganeering, and one hundred percent North Americanism. Its articles, "Human Corpses Eaten by Reds" or "Negro Bucks Paw and Hug Young White Girls," were supplemented by accounts of Klan activities in each state, fully as dull as the pages of the average university alumni magazine. The journal's attempts at acknowledged humor (Klan Kwick Kuts) were of an even simpler mentality ("K.K.K. means Kick Kommunism Kold"). A second Klan organ, *The American Standard,* published in New York in 1924–25, was a semimonthly of a particularly latrine nature. It, too, was sold in Canada, and apparently more widely, if one may judge from references to it in the Canadian press, for it may have seemed more relevant to those who wished to keep Canada clean, in that it gave far more space to Jews and to papal plots. A series of pamphlets ("Jew Movies Urging Sex Vice") and of articles ("Jesuit Hypnotism Uncovered," "Jewish Corruption in 'Jazz,'" "Columbus Day, A Papal Fraud") spoke to at least some Canadians, and an Appreciative Reader in Toronto wrote to thank God that the citizens of Canada had such an eye-opening magazine to help them. Get the papists off the school boards, he advised, and "Canada will support you to a man and woman." [51]

Such words do move some people to action. The attorney-general of Ontario warned the Klan to stay out, and Canadians rather self-righteously suggested that the KKK was the direct result of lax administration of the laws in the United States. The *Toronto Globe* and *Montreal Gazette* affirmed that the entire course of Canadian history had trained people to

50. Gerald Stevens, *The United Counties of Leeds and Grenville* (Brockville, Ont., [1961]), p. 22; Eckard V. Toy, Jr., "The Ku Klux Klan in Tillamook, Oregon," *Pacific Northwest Quarterly,* 53 (1962), 60–64; Gerald M. Craig, "The Canadian Setting," in Albert Rose, ed., *A People and Its Faith: Essays on Jews and Reform Judaism in a Changing Canada* (Toronto, 1959), p. 11.

51. See *The Kourier Magazine, 1–9* (1924–33), passim; and *The American Standard, 1–2* (1924–25), especially 2 (1925), 382.

tolerance. But in 1924 a series of incendiary fires struck Roman Catholic churches, including the cathedral in Quebec, and public opinion ascribed them to the Klan. In 1925, as the Klan passed its peak in the United States, two Americans and a Canadian organized the Ku Klux Klan of Kanada, although Klaverns already existed openly in Vancouver and, rumor had it, in Ontario. When St. Mary's Roman Catholic Church in Barrie was bombed, police were able to show that a member of "the invisible empire" was involved, although Hiram Evans, the Klan leader in the United States, denied any connection with the Toronto-based group. The Royal Canadian Mounted Police began to infiltrate Klan meetings, and within months the Ontario Klavern closed.[52]

In Saskatchewan the Ku Klux Klan had a substantial following.[53] How substantial is impossible to tell, but many people, fearful of the rising tide of southern European immigrants, turned to the Klan for an answer. In Moose Jaw, a railroad center particularly affected by the influx, Protestant ministers—who were given free memberships—rallied to the new source of protection, organized there by the former Cyclops of South Bend, "Pat" Emmons. A special train ran from Regina to Moose Jaw to carry prospective members to rallies, and eight thousand people attended the founding meeting. Throughout 1927, Emmons, Lewis A. Scott, and Finlay Hugh, all Klan missionaries, flitted about the then-prosperous province burning crosses, selling memberships at $13.00 each, and incongruously preaching Canadianism. At the end of the year, however, Emmons made off with the Klan's funds.

Two new figures, "Doctor" J. H. Hawkins, who had been expelled from the Klavern in Ontario, and J. J. Maloney, an itinerant racist preacher, arrived to reorganize the Klan on a province-wide basis during the summer of 1928. Traveling tirelessly in the cause, they offered a wide-ranging platform: "The Klan believes in Protestantism, racial purity, Gentile

52. *The Living Age, 327* (1925), 128; "Canada's 'Keep-Out' to Klanism," *The Literary Digest, 76* (1923), 20–21; A. D. Monk, "Knights of the Knightshirt," *The Canadian Magazine, 66* (1926), 31; *London* (Ont.) *Dawn of Tomorrow,* Aug. 9, 29, 1924, Oct. 24, 1925; *Vancouver Sun,* Aug. 28, 1965; David M. Chalmers, *Hooded Americanism: The First Century of the Ku Klux Klan, 1865–1965* (Garden City, N. Y., 1965), pp. 279–80.

53. Most of the following account is taken from "An Observer," "The Ku Klux Klan in Saskatchewan," *Queen's Quarterly, 35* (1928), 595, 597, and John Patrick Kyba, "The Saskatchewan General Election of 1929" (M.A. thesis, Univ. of Saskatchewan, 1964), which draws upon the James G. Gardiner Papers. I am grateful to Mr. Kyba for letting me read his thesis. Subsequent references to Saskatchewan newspapers other than the *Moose Jaw Times-Herald* are drawn from Mr. Kyba's work. See also, Moon, *This is Saskatchewan,* pp. 44–47, and Morrison Finley Smeltzer, "Saskatchewan Opinion on Immigration from 1925–1939" (M.A. thesis, Univ. of Saskatchewan, 1950).

economic freedom, just laws and liberty, separation of church and state, pure patriotism, restrictive and selective immigration, freedom of speech and press, law and order, higher moral standards, freedom from mob violence, and one public school." Those immigrants who could not be assimilated must be blocked at the borders. Immigration policy in Ottawa was dictated by Roman Catholics, and because of Mussolini's antichurch activities in Italy, the Vatican was planning to move to Canada. Hawkins assured his listeners that, "The Klan in Saskatchewan has no connection with the Klan in the States. Neither has the Klan in Saskatchewan any right to bear the blame for what the Klan in the States might be doing." At Regina, he appealed to the older settlers' fear of being displaced: "The balance of power has passed out of your hands absolutely." Twenty thousand adherents and one hundred and nineteen local Klaverns were the rewards for such tactics.

Given such growth, the Klan leaders could not avoid becoming involved in provincial politics. The Liberal premier, James G. Gardiner, attacked the Klan, even though a number of its members were Liberals, and Hawkins responded by throwing his support to the Conservatives. Gardiner had anticipated such a move, for he wrote to William Lyon Mackenzie King, the prime minister in Ottawa, to ask his advice. King replied that Gardiner must expose the Klan quickly before it had time to spread. Gardiner then revealed that the grand wizard in Saskatchewan, the Klan secretary, and Hawkins had attended the Conservative party convention in Saskatoon in March of 1928; and he linked the name of the party leader, Dr. J. T. M. Anderson, to the Klan. He also ascribed a Conservative victory in a Moose Jaw by-election to Klan activities. An October by-election in Arm River, near Regina, gave the Liberals another test case— one which they may have manufactured, for Anderson rather successfully charged Gardiner with having created the appearance of a link that did not exist. In the meantime the federal government deported Hawkins and brought Emmons back to stand trial for fraud. Although his case was dismissed, he had ample opportunity to swear that it was Anderson who had tried to draw the Klan into politics.

During the election campaign of 1928 Anderson consistently refused to denounce the Klan, for although not a member he accepted its support. The Liberals defended themselves badly on the more substantial issues while the Conservatives ran a tight and intelligent campaign; and by exploiting the fear of aliens, sectarianism in the public schools, the need to make greater use of the province's natural resources, and an unfortunate series of scandals within the Liberal machine, the Conservatives raised their representation from four to twenty-four seats. The Liberals fell from fifty-two seats to twenty-six, throwing the balance of power to five

Progressives and six independents. In June 1929, a Liberal candidate in Prince Albert, C. S. Davis, charged the Conservative nominee, John Diefenbaker, with being hand in glove with the Klan, and won the seat by an eighty-seven vote margin in the city. Gardiner held on briefly, but in September of 1929 he was brought down. Anderson formed a coalition government, ending twenty-four years of Liberal rule.

Once in office, however, Anderson seems not to have turned to the Klan at all. Only in Moose Jaw did the KKK continue to enjoy respectability. There the *Times-Herald* chipped away at it with persistent attacks, compiling a seventeen-page list of members. The Klan helped to finance a ward of the Moose Jaw Hospital, where it affixed a plaque that read, in part, "Confederation . . . Our Public Schools, Law and Order, Separation of Church and State, Freedom of Speech and Press, White Supremacy." Soon the plaque was the only memorial to the Klan left, and in time it was quietly taken down and lost. As Saskatchewan—and Alberta, where a small klavern failed to interest the rising farmer's party—became aware of the fact that its Klan leaders had come almost solely to make money, since they were allowed to keep all the initiation fees they collected, and not from a sincere desire to resolve the province's vexing separate schools problem, the farmers turned to another means of combating nuns, priests, and crucifixes in the classrooms.[54]

By the end of the decade Klan attention had turned back to Ontario once again. On February 28, 1930, the Klan paraded openly through Oakville and burned a cross on main street, to protest the impending marriage of a white girl to a man they insisted was a Negro (although he was in fact an Indian). A spokesman for the Klan claimed Salvation Army support. The Crown Attorney of Ontario, pointing out that the girl had been living with the Negro, if he was such, thought it a little late to talk of racial purity, and charged four of the Klan leaders under an old law that prohibited going abroad at night masked. One was convicted and fined; upon appeal, the higher court described the light penalty as a travesty of justice and imposed a sentence of three months in prison. Virtually all Canadian newspapers condemned the Klan's "offensive buffoonery," suggested that it was simply a "scheme to sell cotton nightgowns to boobs," and helped to make all Klan members appear ridiculous. The glare of publicity, the prompt provincial action, and a continuing rumor that the Klan was an American conspiracy to set Canadians against each other,

54. *Regina Morning Leader*, May 23, 1927; *Moose Jaw Times-Herald*, May 26, 1928; *Saskatoon Daily Star*, June 2, 1928; *Saskatoon Star-Phoenix*, Oct. 19, 1928; *Canadian Annual Review, 1927–28* (Toronto, [1928]), p. 503; Saskatchewan Legislative Assembly, *Sessional Papers, 1928–29*, pp. 64–72; Gary William David Abrams, *Prince Albert: The First Century, 1866–1966* (Saskatoon, 1966), pp. 278–79.

put an end to Klan activities in Ontario, at least until the 1960s. Prejudice, the press opined, had been defeated.[55]

But by what index was one to read prejudice? Consider the formless-ness of the racial barrier. In London the mayor supported Negroes in bringing suit against a restaurant that refused to serve them; in Dresden, fifty miles away, they could not eat with whites. In Windsor Negroes were not admitted to the boy scout troops or to the YMCA and so organized their own; in Toronto they joined both freely. In many small towns, Negro musicians were welcomed into the life of the community; in Owen Sound they had to establish their own orchestra. In Sherbrooke a Negro was a jockey; in Windsor blacks could not ride and interracial boxing was forbidden. In 1926 the Canadian Northern Railway began to lay off its Negro waiters, cooks, and parlor-car men; the Canadian Pacific Railway retained North American Negroes while discharging West Indians. In 1924 the Edmonton City Commissioner barred Negroes from all public parks and swimming pools—and was overruled by the city council; in Colchester, Ontario, in 1930, police patrolled the parks and beaches to keep blacks from using them. In Saint John all restaurants and theaters closed their doors to Negroes in 1915; two years later the chief theaters of Hamilton also did so. In Halifax, Fredericton, and Colchester, Negroes could not be buried in Anglican churchyards; in Toronto and Windsor they could, and in Saint John a Negro was sexton. In Bathurst, New Brunswick, the citizenry falsely spread the word that a bylaw required all Negroes to be out of town by sundown; while in Pictou County, by convention, Negroes were not permitted to live in Stellarton, Westville, Trenton, or Pictou itself, although they could buy lots in New Glasgow. In Truro, a white vigilance committee ordered blacks off the streets at night. In Dundas a Negro was the town's tax collector, and Windsor and Niagara Falls, Ontario, and Kamloops, British Columbia, elected black aldermen; in Halifax and Owen Sound blacks were told not to run for office. In Toronto the fashionable Knox Presbyterian Church turned its pulpit over to a black Arkansan for a summer month of 1923; Presby-terian churches in Halifax and Saint John would not admit Negroes to services. In Saint John, Edmonton, and Victoria, Negroes could find no white barber to cut their hair; in Vancouver, Winnipeg, and Montreal, they could. When royalty visited Hamilton a Negro, William Mallory, was one of five marshals for the day; in Halifax, blacks were relegated to the rear of the welcoming procession. Sir Adam Beck, long a friend of the Negro in London, hired one as a clerk at the Ontario Hydro-Electric

55. *Dawn of Tomorrow*, March 24, 1930; *The Canadian Forum, 10* (1930), 233; *Hamilton Spectator*, April 7, 1965; *Toronto Globe*, March 3, 1930.

Power Commission, of which he was chairman, and was attacked for doing so by North Hamilton's member of Parliament. When a Negro was accused of rape in Ontario in 1927, the presiding judge at the trial congratulated the people of Chatham for not lynching the culprit. In 1929, when the World Baptist Conference was held in Toronto, Negro delegates were denied hotel rooms. As late as 1957, while Springhill, Nova Scotia, honored a Negro, Maurice Ruddick, as one of the survivors in that community's worst coalmine collapse, blacks could not join the local branch of the Canadian Legion. As one confused youth observed, in Canada he was "half free and half slave," having British justice and no job. In the United States the Negro was somewhat more sure—sure of where he could and could not go, of when to be meek and when to be strong. In Canada he was uncertain.[56]

More often than not, uncertainty produced inaction and disunity. How were individual Negroes to respond to cries for Negro racial pride, for activism, for organization? If touched by prejudice, they might well shrink from militancy, hoping to attract no more; they might equally well respond with cries to moral arms. If not touched at all, or able to convince themselves that no prejudice existed, or that if seen it arose from causes that were not racial, they might find political or social activism irrelevant or disruptive. If a West Indian, one could view the American-descended Negroes as outsiders, and if a Torontonian, one called Nova Scotian arrivals "herring-chokers" and avoided them. There were so many rationalizations for inaction, so many paths open to division rather than unity. There was so much willingness to hide behind the comforting thought that, even if prejudice were present in one's community "things" were worse "over there"—if one lived in Amherst, things were worse in Truro,

56. *Hamilton Spectator,* March 11, 1911; *The Crisis, 15* (1917), 91; *18* (1919), 36; *35* (1927), 204; *Chicago Defender,* Nov. 16, 1912; *Windsor Progress* (1954), pp. 14, 18, 21; *Montreal Daily Star,* May 19, 20, 1928; *Saint Paul Western Appeal, 13* (1897), 1; *Toronto Globe,* Jan. 10, 1916; Fred Landon Collection: Harry Logan to Landon, Sept. 19, 1919; Mrs. W. R. Ward, Oxford Historical Society, Woodstock, Ont., to author, June 28, 1961; LC, Carter G. Woodson Papers, *5:* John G. Smith to Woodson, Jan. 8, Feb. 24, 1917; General Headquarters Papers, 297-1-21: K. L. Hamilton to Duke of Connaught, Dec. 29, 1915, W. Stuart Edwards to Stanton, Jan. 31, 1916; *Amherstburg Echo,* Aug. 15, 1930; *Dawn of Tomorrow,* July 31, 28, Aug. 4, Sept. 15, 1923, Jan. 19, May 10, July 19, Aug. 9, 1924, March 7, 14, August 22, 1925, Sept. 4, 1926, Feb. 19, March 12, 1927; *The Labour Gazette, 27* (1927), 17–28; *Victoria Daily Colonist,* Sept. 13, Nov. 4, 5, 1890, March 1, 1895, Sept. 15, 1950; George E. Haynes, *Negro New-Comers in Detroit, Michigan* (New York, 1918),. p. 8; Greaves, "Negro in Canada," pp. 61, 64; "Hero: Second Class," *Ebony, 14* (1959), 70, 72, 74, 76; Leonard Lerner, *Miracle at Springhill* (New York, 1960), pp. 8–9, 49–50; H. D. Beach and R. A. Lucas, eds., National Academy of Sciences Disaster Study No. 13, *Individual and Group Behavior in a Coal Mine Disaster* (Washington, 1960), pp. 55–56, 115–18. I should like to thank Mr. E. J. Doucet, Executive Director, Town of Bathurst, for searching the municipal records for me.

if in Saint John, they were worse in Halifax, if in Hamilton they were worse in Chatham, and if in Chatham they were worse in the American South. "Things" also had been worse "back then"—back when Negroes were slaves, could not vote or own property, when they were fugitives and not free men. "Back then and over there" was a narcotic to inaction, especially when prejudice was individual, occasional, uninstitutionalized, and without legal backing.

Chatham was a case in point. In January 1891, some members of the Chatham Literary Association, a Negro club, organized the Kent County Civil Rights League to combat a rising tide of racial insults. In May a band of armed whites attempted to force an aged Negro couple from their land, only to be driven off themselves by gunfire. The League approved such decisive action. It also protested against the segregated schools of Chatham—to no avail. A few months later a police constable in nearby Raleigh attempted to arrest one George Freeman, who had kept a thirteen-year-old white girl in his hovel and forced her to bear his child. Beaten off with an ax, the constable sought help from the Chatham police who, upon appearing in Raleigh, were attacked by Negroes wielding guns and meat cleavers. Two policemen escaped with wounds; one was killed in the melee. As soon as the news reached Chatham, ten sleighs loaded with armed men set out in pursuit of any Raleigh Negro who could be found; and the chief of police, although cautioned by a lawyer standing at his side, declared that he would "get the murderers, dead or alive, if we have to burn their shack and every miserable wretch in it." The whites of Chatham lined the streets for the dead constable's funeral, thronged the inquest—at which seven Negroes ultimately were charged— and battered upon the courthouse walls in their eagerness to see the prisoners. Five hundred whites encircled the jail, threatening to lynch the Freeman family. Most of the Negroes of Chatham offered their assistance to the authorities to help hold back the mob, bringing charges of Uncle Tomism upon their heads from Buxton's blacks. During the furor four large barns near Chatham burned to the ground; to each was nailed a message attacking "white trash" and warning that the Negroes of the area were tired of mistreatment. Yet, a white detective forestalled an enlarged racial contretemps by proving that one of the white owners had fired his own barn for the insurance, destroying the others as a blind; and despite the anti-Negro fever, a few weeks after the Freeman trial the Chatham school board agreed to admit Negroes to the common schools.[57]

57. OPA, Dept. of Grass Lands Records: Willis Leeper to J. M. Gibson, Nov. 4, 1887; *Detroit Plaindealer*, May 23, 1890, Feb. 13, March 13, May 1, July 3, 24, Sept. 4, 11, 1891, Dec. 16, 1892, Feb. 3, April 14, 1893; *Toronto Globe*, Jan. 25, 28, Feb. 1, 1893; Mallory, *Old Plantation Days*, 3rd ed. ([Hamilton, Ont., 1902?]), p. 19; Victor Speer, ed., *Memoirs of a Great Detective: Incidents in the Life of John Wilson Murray* (New York, 1905), pp. 381–85.

Nor did all Negroes have to struggle to protect their property, or to get their children into the schools. In 1906, Perry H. Chase of Chatham was a man of wealth, as was Sylvester Groyer of Harrow, who owned forty-four acres of land on which he grew corn and tobacco. John Highgate of Dover Center owned a hundred acres and a prize stud; Richard Lucas of Windsor kept chickens on fifty acres; James L. and Robert Dunn of Windsor owned a thriving varnish works; Edwin Howard, also of Windsor, held land worth $4,000; and Delos R. Davis of Amherstburg, who was a product of Theodosia Lyons' missionary school, became in 1910 the first Negro to be appointed King's Council in Canada. In Chatham, Negroes owned four stores and two restaurants, in Dresden a café, in Windsor a variety of businesses. Two Negroes were lawyers, two were postmen, one taught in a white school, one had helped organize the Marine Cook's and Steward's Union in 1902, one was a county constable in Colchester—and one introduced candied popcorn to Canada. Clearly Negroes were not entirely without opportunities.[58]

The three Negroes who best epitomized the opportunities open to some blacks within the province were Wilson Ruffin Abbott, his son, Anderson Ruffin, and the father of the latter's son-in-law, William Peyton Hubbard, all Toronto businessmen involved in local politics. Wilson Abbot was born of a Scotch-Irish father and a free Negro mother in Richmond, Virginia, in 1801. Although apprenticed as a carpenter, he left home at fifteen to work as a steward on a Mississippi River steamer. Seriously injured aboard the vessel, he was nursed back to health by Ellen Toyer, the maid of a Boston lady traveler. Wilson and Ellen married and opened a grocery store in Mobile, Alabama, where they became prosperous enough to attract the anger of local whites, who drove them from town. After a brief sojourn in New York, the Abbotts moved to Toronto in 1835; and after a false start as a tobacconist, Wilson became a thriving real estate broker. By 1871 he owned forty-two houses, five vacant lots, and a warehouse, largely in Toronto, but also in Hamilton and Owen Sound; and he was able to purchase freedom for fugitive slaves, to keep his wife's sister as a well-paid housekeeper, and to engage extensively in community affairs.

58. D. D. Buck, *The Progression of the Race in the United States and Canada* (Chicago, 1907), pp. 113, 172, 183, 185, 192–93, 210, 211–12, 254, 283–84, 286, 289, 324–25, 326, 339, 354, 365, 385–86, 391–95, 404, 436, 444, 452–55, 457, 459, 463, 471–76, 482–91, 531; Fort Malden Museum, F.C.B. Falls Papers: will of Edmund Brooks, June 26, 1873, [W. E. B.] DuBois to Davis, n.d.; *Detroit Plaindealer*, Oct. 16, 1891; *The Crisis, 1* (1911), 8; *6* (1913), 116; *7* (1914), 112, 115; *8* (1914), 222; *Toronto Globe & Mail*, Feb. 24, 1948; *Toronto Star*, Sept. 21, 1957; *Windsor Progress* (1954), p. 18; Charlotte Brontë Perry, *The Long Road, 1: The History of the Coloured Canadian in Windsor, Ontario, 1867–1967* (Windsor, 1967), pp. 10, 19, 25, 33–34, 95.

Wilson Abbott committed himself entirely to Canada, never returning to the United States. During the uprising of 1837 he served in defense of the Crown; the following year he helped found the Colored Wesleyan Methodist Church of Toronto, partially because he hoped that such institutions—although separate—would create a sense of permanence among Canada's Negroes. Mrs. Abbott organized the Queen Victoria Benevolent Society in 1840, to aid indigent black women, and gave much support to the British Methodist Episcopal Church. Wilson supported the Anti-Slavery Society of Canada, taught his four sons and five daughters to think of themselves as Canadians, was elected to the Toronto City Council from St. Patrick's Ward, and served as a member of the Reform Central Committee. Before his death in 1876 he had seen his second son, Anderson Ruffin, take a degree in medicine at the University of Toronto and become, in 1861, the first Canadian-born Negro to receive a license to practice.[59]

Anderson was of a more militant persuasion than his father. Born in Toronto in 1837, he studied at Toronto Academy, operated in conjunction with Knox's College—where Samuel Ringgold Ward was a classmate—and graduated from Oberlin College, Ohio's abolitionist center, before taking up medicine. In 1863 Abbott was appointed a surgeon in the Northern army. After the war he opened a practice in Chatham where he was president of the Wilberforce Educational Institute from 1873 until 1880, was a vocal opponent of the public segregated schools, became coroner for Kent County in 1874, and was associate editor of the British Methodist Episcopal Church's local organ, *The Messenger,*[60] as well as a writer for the *Planet.* After living in Dundas, where he was assistant editor of the local *Banner,* and briefly in Oakville, Abbott moved to Toronto in 1890, became a close friend of Hubbard, and encouraged his career in politics. In 1894 Abbott became surgeon-in-charge at the Provident Hospital and Training School in Chicago, the first such institution for Negroes in the United States. In time he would return to Toronto, to die there in 1913, survived by five children, including a daughter, Grace, who would marry Hubbard's son, Frederick.

Abbott, like his father before him, appears to have been accepted at all levels of Toronto society; he was widely viewed as the champion of those he called Afro-Americans. In 1901, on the occasion of the death of Queen Victoria, Abbott composed a poem—"Neath the Crown and Maple Leaf. (Afro-Canadian Elegy)," for *The Colored American Magazine*—

59. TPL, Abbott-Hubbard Collection: Mrs. Ellen Abbott, diary, 1843, passim; family album, with obituary notices; will of W. R. Abbott, March 1, 1871; MS biography of Abbott, by Anderson R. Abbott; *Toronto Globe,* Dec. 11, 1847; *Toronto Evening Telegram,* May 17, 1911; *DCB,* vol. 3 (forthcoming), *1871–1880.*
60. No file has been found for this period.

which reflected his sense of pride in being both black and Canadian. He was an active member of the York Pioneers Society, of the Grand Army of the Republic (traveling to Buffalo for annual meetings), and of the Anglican Church. A man of great intellectual curiosity, he prepared a variety of manuscripts—some of which became public talks—on medicine, Darwinism, poetry, history, and education; and he justified both the carrying of arms by Southern Negroes for their own protection and the creation of separate all-Negro military units. He noted the rising, if form-less, incidence of discrimination in Canadian churches, theaters, hotels, and restaurants, which he blamed on the "paste diamond" class who, being "shabby-genteel," had to resort to "brickfront" discrimination in their social customs as in their houses. He thought most colorphobia in Canada could be traced to American immigrants. As the result of a study he conducted in Chatham in the 1880s, he concluded that, while Negroes became mentally tired more quickly than whites, they were fully as able at most academic subjects. This would lead him, in 1906, to condemn the creation of a new all-Negro school in Saint John, to support the Niagara movement of W. E. B. DuBois in opposition to Booker T. Washington's manual training school, and to embark upon a general history of Negro activities in Canada in order to encourage racial pride.[61]

The historical figure to whom Anderson Abbott pointed with particular pride was William Hall, the third British North American, and the first black man, to win the Victoria Cross. Born in Hants County, Nova Scotia, in 1827, of Refugee Negro parentage, Hall went to sea in his 'teens and later joined the British Navy. He was decorated during the Crimean War for his exploits at the battles of Inkerman and Sebastopol. In 1857, when the Indian Mutiny broke out, Hall was among those who followed Sir Colin Campbell, a former lieutenant-governor of Nova Scotia, to the relief of the British garrison under Sir John Inglis, a native of Nova Scotia, at Lucknow. Hall volunteered to join a virtually suicidal gun crew in breaching the walls of the Shah Nejeef, a temple converted to a fort by the Sepoys. Continuing to sponge and load after all other members of the crew had fallen, he opened a gap in the wall of the fort and so per-mitted the British to enter.[62]

61. Abbott-Hubbard Collection: MS autobiography by Abbott; MS biography of Abbott, by Grace (Abbott) Hubbard, family album of marriage and birth notices; notes on the Civil War, drafts of his addresses to the GAR, copies of Abbott's news-paper articles, MSS on the future of the Negro, fugitive slaves, the Elgin settlement, Negro history, the Boer War, Negro mental capacity, and color prejudice; *Toronto Evening Telegram*, Dec. 30, 1913; *The Colored American*, 2 (1901), 336; Ullman, *Look to the North Star*, pp. 294–99.

62. The best accounts on Hall are by Mrs. Nellie Fox in *The Hants Journal* (Windsor), Nov. 15, 1961, and Charles Bruce Fergusson, "William Hall, V.C.,"

After Hall retired from the navy in 1876, he returned to Nova Scotia, where he became something of a legend, the subject of many essays similar to Abbott's. Unmarried, Hall lived with two sisters, farmed, and when asked to supply data for a biographical dictionary in 1899, tersely replied, "Recreation, shooting crows." Although he was given a carriage in the procession that honored the Duke of York on his visit to Halifax in 1901, he was buried in an unmarked grave when he died three years afterwards. The *Halifax Morning Chronicle,* no doubt meaning to praise him, concluded a memorial notice by remarking that he had been "a pickaninny, not unlike other pickaninnies" who nonetheless had become a "Brave Colored Hero." (In 1947 the Hantsport branch of the Canadian Legion would erect a monument to him, and the Negro branch of the Legion in Halifax would be named for him.) [63]

The other figure to whom Anderson Abbott looked with particular pride was his father's friend, William P. Hubbard. The light-skinned son of free Negro parents, Hubbard was born in Toronto in 1842. He worked as a livery boy in an uncle's stable and often drove for George Brown, who is said to have encouraged him in his first interest in public affairs. His father, Mosley, had built up some small capital while working as a carver at a hotel in Niagara Falls, and with this he had gone into market gardening. A Torontonian who was then much interested in helping American Negroes, Colonel Robert Wells, agreed to send William to school, where he learned to be a baker—and enough mathematics to take up real estate as a later career. After a long period of self-education in finance and the law, both arising from his work with property, Hubbard decided to run for alderman in a ward with no appreciable Negro population. Narrowly defeated in 1892, he won in 1894—also narrowly—and served in the post until 1903, when as chairman of the Island Committee he helped plan the city's parks; he was elected again in 1913. From 1904 until 1907 he was city comptroller, and during the mayor's absence acted as Toronto's chief officer. He died in 1935. When Dr. Robert E. Park, the distinguished sociologist, asked Hubbard whether he had encountered any prejudice, he said that he had not, having run for office as a Canadian who was expert in real estate rather than as a Negro in politics. (On the same principle his son, an authority on street railways,

[Nova Scotian] *Journal of Education, 17* (1967), 15–21. They are contradicted in some details by D. Mills, "William Hall, V.C.," *Acadiensis, 8* (1908), 32–34; [G. Earle Logan], "Canada's Third V.C.," *The Legionary, 8* (1933), 5, 11; and "F. M. P.," "Humble Hero: William Hall, Son of Slaves . . . ," *Crowsnest, 4* (1952), 16–17, 32.

63. *Who's Who, 1899: An Annual Biographical Dictionary* (London), p. 471; *Hantsport Advance,* Aug. 31, 1904; *Halifax Morning Chronicle,* Oct, 21, 1901, Aug. 25, Sept. 28, 1904, May 8, 1933, Nov. 10, 1947; *Halifax Herald,* Nov. 8, 1938.

would become Toronto's transportation commissioner from 1930 until 1939.) Abbott and Hubbard agreed that Toronto was the least prejudiced city in Canada, and on the basis of their own careers their generalizations would appear to be true. In 1914, when Negroes in Saint John were refused admission to theaters, black men at the western borders were told to return to Oklahoma, and Windsor bars were opening "jungle rooms" for Negro patrons, William Hubbard was honored by having his portrait hung in the Toronto city chambers.[64]

But such experiences were rare enough in Ontario, and for Canadian-born Negroes, especially after the introduction of two new elements to the central and eastern Canadian black population by the 1920s. These were urban American Negroes, largely from New York City, who had entered Quebec gradually rather than in groups, and West Indians in the Maritime Provinces. In 1867 the Pullman Palace Car Company had introduced Negro porters to its cars in the United States, and when new rail connections with Canada were completed in the 1880s and Pullman service from New England and New York to Montreal began, the black porters came with the trains. An American, William (later Sir William) Van Horne, General Manager of the Canadian Pacific Railroad, soon extended the porters' range. The Canadian Pacific system made Montreal its general employment center, while the Canadian National used the city to hire for its Central and Atlantic divisions. Negroes who wished to find work with the railroads therefore concentrated in Montreal, having made St. Antoine Street their own by 1900, and to a lesser extent in Toronto and Windsor. In the last city they were employed by the rising automotive industry in Detroit, which was hiring Negroes rapidly. Each spring an agent for the lines visited Negro colleges in the South and recruited porters in New York and Philadelphia. A number of Nova Scotian Negroes also moved into Montreal to be nearer the railroad centers, and other groups settled in Winnipeg, Calgary, and Vancouver to work on the transcontinental trains which, by the 1920s, were crossing the nation regularly in five nights and four days.

64. Accounts of Hubbard's life are contradictory. The longest, and least accurate, is Booker T. Washington, "A Notable Instance of the Negro in Politics," *The Outlook, 83* (May 5, 1906), 78-80, for Washington took his information from James Cleland Hamilton. Hubbard's own account would seem most acceptable. He wrote it for Park, and it appears in the Woodson Papers, *5:* Hubbard to Park, Feb. 12, 1906, with a copy in LC, Walter White Papers. See also Abbott-Hubbard Collection: "William P. Hubbard Deceased: Tributes from Toronto Press"; TPL, Scrap Books, Vol. 5 and 12, passim; *Crisis, 6* (1913), 66; "William P. Hubbard, A Civic-Minded Canadian," *The Negro History Bulletin, 4* (1941), 161–62, 167; and Toronto Transportation Commission, *Wheels of Progress: A Story of the Development of Toronto and Its Public Transportation Services,* 2nd ed. (Toronto, n.d.), p. 109.

The effect of those five nights and four days could be seen in the black community. The hours were long but certain, and physical mobility was high. The porter was thus cut loose from some of the forms of social control which normal communal life creates. While he saw more of Canada and had some conception of the nation as a whole, he remained conservative; and no more than other Negroes did he think, at this time, in terms of national black power movements. He enjoyed higher status among his fellows and a salary which, in 1928, was $95.00 a month after three years service, together with tips that might run as high as $35 on each round trip, which he made twice monthly. Precisely because of his mobility and the prestige other Negroes attached to his work, the black porter liked the stability of a home, even though he changed it almost yearly, and he provided for Montreal Negroes in particular a counterbalance of conservative lower-middle-class aspirations to set against the new "sporting crowd."

This group controlled the "sporting district" of Montreal, below St. Antoine and above Bonaventure streets, running under the mountain and parallel with the railway tracks. There Negro prostitution, gambling, and other illicit activities developed, especially in the 1920s as other blacks moved in from Harlem to escape Prohibition. Each summer the St. Antoine district grew, with temporary porters, redcaps, and the "flitting element" who came for the races. In 1897 the first Negro cabaret had opened its doors; by 1928 there were three. In 1922 the Nemderoloc Club ("coloredmen" spelled backwards) became the center for the sporting crowd and was the object of persistent police raids, winning the intense dislike of the stable Negro population. But neither porters nor "sports" were inclined to take out citizenship or to enter into the mainstream of Negro Canadian life.

Thus the Montreal Negro gained a reputation—on the whole a false one—for loose morals, transiency, and lack of interest in Canadian values. Unfortunately, there was sufficient truth in the stereotype to add to the burden of white inconsistency carried by Canadian Negroes during the 1920s. Educational, social, and sanitation standards were low in "the district," the death rate exceeded the city average, and public transport was poor. Perhaps forty percent of the Negro men were married to white women (as against a national figure of seven percent). Private home ownership ended, and with it the stability that property implies, as trust companies became the absentee owners of the district—owners who often wished to see the properties deteriorate in order to justify selling the land to industry. With no expectation of resale, few structures were improved, and the vicious spiral downward to the slums was rapid. Generational conflict was common, for while many of the black arrivals were rural, their children soon embraced urban values. Often women were the breadwinners, leaving children unsupervised at home. Common-law marriages were frequent, especially with French or Indian partners, and sexual relations were casual: one Mary Smofsky, who fainted on the street, was taken by taxi to the room of a Negro porter, became his common-law wife, bore his child, and was deserted by him. She never learned his name, knowing him only as "Sweetness." Although not typical of contemporary Canadian Negro culture, the Negro nightclubs—which began to resound to jazz music at eleven o'clock six nights a week, to end at five A.M. with a rousing "God Save the King"—were taken as such by whites who lived nearby.[65]

The second group of black newcomers, the West Indians, began to arrive during World War I. Cut off from Britain by the conflict, they landed at Halifax and Saint John. Largely Jamaicans, many were British subjects from the Bahamas, British Guiana, Bermuda, and St. Vincent as well. Hundreds worked in the coalmines around Sydney, Nova Scotia, where they prospered. One, Isaac Phills from St. Vincent, who came in 1916, worked for the steel mill for forty-five years and raised a family that included four college graduates. Other West Indians went to the shipyards of Halifax and Collingwood; and in time the majority moved on to Montreal, Toronto, and other urban centers, pushing the scale of Negro urbanization up to eleven percent above the national average. While they retained much of their interisland sense of competition, they tended to band together in Canada and to hold themselves superior to other black men. They referred to the Maritime Negroes as "Canadians" and "coloured" and to the blacks in Quebec and Ontario as "Americans"; they were to be called "West Indians" only. Forming clubs of their own, attending Anglican churches, turning out to the cricket pitch for their sport, opposing integration, demanding freer West Indian immigration, and supporting Back-to-Africa movements, they wanted to see the Negro districts remain distinct. The West Indians thus found little in common with the Negroes of Montreal who had arrived before them.[66]

Still, despite irregularly applied urges to discriminate, despite sexual stereotype and literary myth, despite the vulnerability of the leaderless

65. *Detroit Plaindealer*, Dec. 13, 1889; *The Southern Workman, 52* (1923), 534; *Toronto Globe*, Nov. 23, 1925; *Montreal Star*, Aug. 6, 1927, June 20, 1928; Wilfred E. Israel, "The Montreal Negro Community" (M.A. thesis, McGill Univ., 1928), pp. 28, 46, 73–83, 119, 124–39; Herbert Brown Ames, *"The City below the Hill": A Sociological Study of a Portion of the City of Montreal, Canada* (Montreal, 1897), p. 67; Greaves, "Negro in Canada," pp. 49–50. The death rate appears by wards in City of Montreal, *Reports of the Department of Health* (1925–30).

66. *Halifax Evening Mail*, July 11, 1928; Greaves, pp. 45–46; "The Remarkable Phills Family of Sydney," DOSCO *World, 3* ([1961]), 2–4.

and fragmented Negroes, despite unwanted immigration, war, the Ku Klux Klan, and the presence of a class of Negroes many whites would have found objectionable whatever the color of their skins, most Canadians kept their heads. Between 1880 and 1930 contacts between Europeans and Asians in India sank to their lowest level; in South Africa the corner was turned toward what, in 1947, would become *apartheid;* and in Australia, New Zealand, and the West Indies consciousness of unalterable racial differences had long since reached the legislative threshold. Canada stood upon that threshold—and crossed it with discriminatory immigration laws—but it did not join the American drive toward giving legal sanctions to segregation or discrimination in places of entertainment, in transport, in churches, or in employment. In Canada there would be no law—as there was in 1930 in the city of Birmingham, Alabama—forbidding Negroes and whites to play dominoes together.

How, then, might Canadian Negroes hope to combat what Anderson R. Abbott described as the hollowness of local pretensions whenever racial questions were raised? How might one answer Rapier's question, put in 1857, "What signifies a man's liking a place if he cannot make some money?" when, in 1930, Negro wages in Detroit were twice as high as in Toronto? The very lack of Negro unity in Canada, the failure to produce leaders recognized by blacks throughout the nation or even within a province, may be explained by this absence of any consistent pattern in white-Negro relations in Canada. The racial barriers shifted, gave way, and stood firm without consistency, predictability, or even credibility. The Negroes themselves were mobile, carrying with them expectations of finding or of not finding prejudice. They were so different—rural blacks from small towns in Nova Scotia, prosperous farmers from Ontario, longtime residents of Vancouver Island, sophisticated New York newcomers to Montreal, activist West Indians who were not, they insisted, Negroes at all—and the cultural matrix of each Canadian community was so changed, under the impact of immigration, war, and depression, that one could not know whether discrimination, when it did appear, was based on social or economic priorities. Indeed, when Canadian Negroes encountered a wall, they could not know whether it arose from aesthetic, class, or social bias, whether it was real or imagined.

To combat indecision and confusion, as much as discrimination itself, a group of militant Negroes led by James Jenkins of London and J. W. Montgomery of Toronto founded the Canadian League (later, Association) for the Advancement of Colored People in 1924, following upon the similar association founded in the United States in 1909. The Association's first board of directors included three distinguished whites, Sir Adam Beck; Fred Landon, a friend of Jenkins who, as London's librarian from 1916 until 1923, had been working on the history of the antislavery movement in Canada, a project he had completed in 1919 as a graduate thesis for Ulrich B. Phillips, the University of Michigan's historian of the South; and A. E. Silverwood, a prominent London dairyman who employed Negroes. By 1926 the Association had organized branches in Toronto, Brantford, Niagara Falls, and Dresden. It formed an advisory council of three whites after Beck's death in 1925: William Renwick Riddell, the leading student of slavery in Canada, Professor J. A. Dale of the Department of Social Service at the University of Toronto, and W. Sherwood Fox, then dean and later principal of the University of Western Ontario in London. In 1927 the League held its first general conference, also in London, at which delegates agreed for the first time that Canadian Negroes should organize all of the institutional resources at their command—in politics, in the schools, in the churches, through the press, and in business—on a nation-wide scale in order to combat the rising anti-Negro prejudice. Here, the Negro spokesmen thought, would lie their sources of strength: in the churches, in the schools, in the press, in voluntary societies—in unity.[67]

67. PAC, Laurier Papers, *314*, 84611–13: B. B. B. Johnson to Laurier, April 18, and reply, April 23, 1904; *Dawn of Tomorrow,* Aug. 9, 1924, March 7, Aug. 29, Oct. 24, 1925, Jan. 16, June 26, 1926, March 12, 1927; *London Free Press,* Sept. 3, 1924; *Toronto Globe,* July 28, 1925; Fred Landon to the author, April 24, 1965; obituary of Fred Landon, *The University of Western Ontario News* (London), *5* (1969), [1–3]; Frederick H. Armstrong, "Fred Landon, 1880–1969," *Ontario History, 62* (1970), 1–4; Hilary Bates, " A Bibliography of Fred Landon," ibid., pp. 5–16.

11. Source of Strength?—The Church

Traditionally, oppressed peoples have turned within themselves to four major sources of strength. Through the voice from the muezzin, from within the pulpit, and out of the Torah they have listened for the word that they are the truly beloved of God. Ethnic presses have reinforced this belief in the secular world, enjoining all who can read *Le Canadien, Timarit, Correio Português,* or *Neith,* to unite through a common language, condition, or color. Through voluntary organizations immigrant ministers have attempted to exert an influence in the arena of politics, to help themselves, to draw attention to themselves, and to protect themselves. Through education they have sought the power of knowledge. In Canada, the Negro thought himself an immigrant and responded as an immigrant, establishing schools, fighting for unsegregated education, founding newspapers and journals, initiating benevolent societies and Associations for the Advancement of Colored People, and supporting activities and institutions which, for want of a more precise term, historians have called "the Negro church." [1] Religion lay at the center of the black experience: time and again the Negro was carried to the Brink of Bunyan's River to hear the last words of Mr. Despondency, "Farewell Night, welcome Day." Yet few crossed the River singing.

If there was no Negro church as such, either in British North America or in the United States, there were a series of churches that sheltered and sustained Negroes. While these churches usually were fragments of Protestantism, they frequently cut themselves off from the larger body, and tended to be theologically stagnant. Many reinforced the stereotype so beloved by white Christians—that of the noble black ready to bear suffering for the Lord because, in the end, the Lord has the whole wide world in his hands—for the Negro's churches often lacked intellectual conviction while possessing an abundance of emotion and faith. They

1. The concept of the "Negro church" was introduced by Carter G. Woodson in *The History of the Negro Church* (Washington, D.C., 1921). In 1933, Benjamin E. Mays and Joseph W. Nicholson, in *The Negro's Church* (New York), drew an important distinction. The best recent analysis is Joseph R. Washington, Jr., *Black Religion: The Negro and Christianity in the United States* (Boston, 1964), which rejects Woodson's definitions. See also Gary T. Marx, "Religion: Opiate or Inspiration of Civil Rights Militancy among Negroes?" *American Sociological Review, 32* (1967), 64–72.

represented theological and social positions taken, not argued; and because of this inflexibility, they were ultimately sources of strength for the Negro only as reminders to him that he must stand like a rock. This stockade mentality was useful—even good—in meeting the daily problems of lives cluttered with more problems than most; but such churches were unlikely to help tear down the barriers which, in the end, helped to justify them. They taught by example, even when they preached otherwise by precept, that passive acceptance of the world was somehow more Christian than were resistance and change. In contrast to individual preachers, seldom did a Negro church ask its brethren, in the bowels of Christ, to beseech the white world that it might be mistaken.

The Negro churches did perform very real functions, of course, and within the context of nineteenth-century social, racial, and religious thought, functions that had practical benefits within the Negro community. Until the 1780s there had been few separate black church organizations, and they were first established, as were the Prince Hall Masonic Lodges, because of a sharp and rapid decline in free Negro social mobility. The Negro church groups therefore evolved to fill a social as well as a spiritual need; for as whites denied Negroes access to the pulpit and to the priesthood, black men blazed their own segregated paths toward high office. These leaders and the churches they led came to accept segregation, to encourage the idea of racial solidarity, and to provide one means for social accommodation between the races; in some instances, through borrowings from extra-Biblical sources, they also developed a black Christ. Simultaneously, Negro fraternal and benevolent societies arose within the churches and followed the same paths. The result, naturally enough, was a conservative leadership with a vested interest in all-Negro institutions. In British North America, the movement toward all-Negro congregations came somewhat later than in the United States; and accordingly, the realization that a separate Negro hierarchy is not entirely to the good also has come more slowly.

In British North America, as everywhere, the rôle played by the Christian church in helping the Negro and the white come to terms with each other was an ambivalent one. Individually, many Negroes attended white congregations, especially before 1840, and few churches were officially segregated, although special galleries for Negroes had become more common with the passage of time. But on the whole, most congregations would appear to have preferred that Negroes worship elsewhere, and not necessarily for reasons of race. The newly arrived Negroes were socially less adept, they enjoyed a more enthusiastic sermon and song, and sometimes they seemed doctrinally unsound. When the number of Negroes in Canada West rose until they became, as in Chatham, a third of the population, whites felt they could see many nonracial reasons for encouraging separation. Well before, in Nova Scotia, whites had cooperated to give the Negroes church buildings of their own, both because they thought that blacks preferred life that way and because they wished to be able to fórget the Negro. White Christians often remembered to be as subtle as a serpent while forgetting to be as harmless as a dove.

In truth the Negroes did appear to prefer churches of their own. The reasons are obvious enough. They appreciated rather different types of services, they wanted preachers who spoke to them in a language and perhaps with an accent they might readily understand, and they knew they could not compete with whites at the collection plate or in the millinery shop. Further, a quite natural path to leadership among Negroes was through the church; and those who wished to be preachers— whether for God or for themselves—saw quickly enough that they much improved their chances for success and tightened the circle of their followers if they narrowed the range of competition. Few churches at the time were prepared to see Negroes become bishops, deacons, or priests; many fellowshipped with slaveholding congregations, as Linton had argued. The pressures upon fugitive slaves who joined such groups would have been intolerable.

As a result, the first organized Negro institution in a Canadian community usually was a church, followed by a temperance society and a school. These three institutions were to be found wherever there were Negroes, and they emphasized the pious, the puritan,[2] and the practical. The ultimate effect of these churches and their related services was beneficial in terms of compassion, patience, and resignation. But these qualities delayed the formation of other, more secular—certainly more

2. On the puritanical side, consider the following representative entries from the Minute Book of the Sandwich Baptist Church (Canadian Baptist Historical Association, McMaster University Library, Hamilton, Ont.):

> Jan. 18, 1868—Sister Mary Bedd called to question for dancing she acnoleg her rongs it was move and sect we for to for give her for dancing it was caried.
> Dec. 4, 1869— . . . it was moved an sect the the curch send a comitie to see Br George Brown for getting in in toxication an report next meting. . . .
> Feb. 5, 1870— . . . the Curch has a charg against mary Bedd for dansing Bro Marshall an sis mary an Bro Whiticar the Curch recieved their acklagments this case is dun for ever. . . .
> April 14, 1871— . . . on the case of Sis Jackson an Sis White Sister Jackson took the first an Secont stepps an got no satisfaction on Slandering her with out a cause Sister White call Sister Jackson a hore an Bitch Sis White says Sis Jackson cum to my an said I want you to get your witnesses to prove she got them stains on my Close she went to the Bush an I went down their she said if you com hear I will whip your ass well she sed ass. . . .

activist—voluntary associations. If in the wake of the church followed an
abolition society or a land association, each in its way activist, it invariably arose from within the congregation, the leadership was usually
the same, and the result was a series of interlocking directorates.

In the long run the influence of such leadership was not progressive.
Too often the interlocking directorate produced a single Negro whom
whites treated as the sole local spokesman for the entire black community. In time, whites felt that they were in sufficient contact with
Negro needs if they were in contact with the single spokesman, a man
who might well be falling out of step with his followers, and who might
well be tempted not to lead along any paths that would lose him white
support. Although the Negroes were quick to advertise their quarrels,
whites continued to funnel their aid and their sympathy through single
individuals—a Stephen Blucke, a Joseph Leonard, a Josiah Henson, a
Mifflin Wistar Gibbs, a William P. Hubbard. The slowness with which
Negro leadership—and therefore Negro goals and techniques—changed,
was owing as much to the whites' desire to have an identifiable Negro
figurehead as to the natural conservatism of the Negroes' churches.

Within this spectrum all Negro churches and churchmen were activist
on one issue: the condemnation of slavery as a moral evil. Richard
Preston, the Negro Baptist leader in Nova Scotia, had organized through
his church in 1842 an Anglo-African Mutual Improvement and Aid
Association and had suggested that its first committee should be devoted
to Political Action. Preston also organized a Negro Abolition Society in
1846. Still, the Negro meeting was not held until the whites had initiated
a society of their own; and Preston's association of Baptist churches
served to take Negro Baptists in Nova Scotia outside the mainstream of
general Baptist development in the province just as the sect was beginning
to experience an intellectual flowering not seen among members of the
faith in other Maritime colonies. During this period Negro and white
Baptists matured via separate paths, and in the Maritimes the Negro
church was relatively more backward at the end of the nineteenth century
than at the beginning.[3]

By the twentieth century the Baptist faith was overwhelmingly pre-
ponderant among Negroes in Canada. Indeed, although Baptism was introduced by whites, the Negro congregation often was the larger, at least
at first—as in Toronto, when the First Baptist Church was formed under

3. *Constitution and By-Laws of the Anglo-African Mutual Improvement and
Aid Association of Nova Scotia* ([Halifax, ca. 1842]); *Halifax Novascotian*, Aug. 24,
Nov. 23, 30, 1846; Acadia University, Wolfville, N.S., Maritime Baptist Historical
Collection: "A Sketch of the History of the Baptists in the City and County of
Halifax," pp. 2–3, 11.

the aegis of a West Indian from New York, Washington or William Christian, in 1826. The steady drift of Negroes toward the Baptist church [4] became a flood with the arrival of many Baptist fugitive slaves, the organization of American-based Baptist aid societies, and the creation of a racially self-conscious association of all-Negro Baptist churches in Canada West and Michigan. By 1931, the United Church of Canada (which had absorbed some, but by no means all, Negro Methodists) held less than twenty-two percent of all Negro communicants; the prestigious Anglican church commanded but seventeen and a half percent, mostly of Loyalist and West Indian background; and the Baptists dominated with over forty-one percent.[5]

At first the Negro-initiated Baptist churches in Upper Canada [6] were interracial, as at Colchester after 1830, at Niagara in 1831, and in Toronto until 1829, but few remained so past the early 1840s. In part, the impetus for segregation came from the whites who, when numerous enough, formed churches of their own; equally strong was the desire of the fugitive slaves to restrict membership to blacks lest the pharoahs from

4. The drift is attested to by Leavitt, *Leeds and Grenville*, p. 114; SPG, *Report for the Year 1840* . . . (London, 1840), pp. lxv–lxvi; *SPG Papers* (microfilm), *38, 52,* March 8, 1828; Charles M. Johnston, ed., *The Valley of the Six Nations: A Collection of Documents on the Indian Lands of the Grand River* (Toronto, 1964), pp. 265–68; *Canadian Baptist Magazine, 1* (1837), 165; *Amherstburg Echo,* Nov. 23, 1934; *London Free Press,* Feb. 6, 1948; and *Windsor Daily Star,* Aug. 11, 1950.

5. Daniel G. Hill, "Negroes in Toronto, 1793–1865," *Ontario History, 55* (1963), 77; John Ross Robertson, *Landmarks of Toronto: A Collection of Historical Sketches of the Old Town of York from 1792–1837 and of Toronto from 1837–1904* (Toronto, 1904), p. 471; *The Canadian Baptist, 86* (1940), 4; OPA, John M. Elson, "First Baptist Church Dedication, Toronto (Negro): Historical Links," MS, p. 2; Dominion Bureau of Statistics, Census Monograph No. 4, *Racial Origins and Nativity of the Canadian People* (Ottawa, 1937), p. 285, analyzing the census data of 1931. In contrast, only 8.7 percent of English and Dutch stock were Baptists, and over thirty years later only 3.3 percent of the entire Canadian population were adherents to Baptism (*Canada Year Book 1965* [Ottawa, 1965], p. 179).

6. On the history of Negro Baptists in Canada, see MacKerrow, *Coloured Baptists of Nova Scotia,* and Oliver, *Colored Baptists of Nova Scotia,* previously cited; [Dorothy Shadd Shreve, et al.], *Pathfinders of Liberty and Truth: A Century with the Amherstburg Regular Missionary Baptist Association* (n.p., [1940]); Wilfred Sheffield, "Background and Development of Negro Baptists in Ontario" (B. Th. thesis, McMaster Univ., 1952); James W. Johanson, "The Amherstburg Baptist Association, 1841–1861, including a Survey of the Civil War Period," MS (1962) held by the Canadian Baptist Historical Association; James K. Lewis, "Pioneer Coloured Baptist Life in Upper Canada," *Canadian Baptist Home Missions Digest, 6* (1963–64), 243–72; and Lewis, "Religious Nature of the Early Baptist Negro Migration to Canada and the Amherstburg Baptist Association," *Ontario History, 58* (1966), 117–22, 243–72. The abbreviated record that follows draws heavily on these accounts.

whom they had fled infiltrate them. Accordingly, in October of 1841 delegates from the Amherstburg, Sandwich, and Detroit Baptist churches met at the Amherstburg home of John Liberty, resolved that they were unable to "enjoy the Privileges we Wish as Christians with the White Churches in Canada," and organized an international association drawing upon all black Baptist groups from Niagara west and London south to the Detroit area. By 1861 the Amherstburg Association, under the direction of Madison J. Lightfoot, Anthony Binga, and William C. Monro grew from forty-seven founding members and seven churches to over a thousand members in nearly twenty churches, all but five in Canada West.[7]

Disagreement over how best to meet the challenge of slavery was at the root of the new foundation, and the Association thrived only so long as slavery continued in the United States. In 1843 delegates to the annual convention resolved that no Negro should unite with any faith that supported slavery elsewhere; in 1845 they agreed to pray monthly for the end of all human bondage; seven years later the members concluded that any baptism performed by a slaveholding minister (as a heretic) had been invalid. In 1855 fellowshipping was forbidden to anyone who, in turn, fellowshipped with any organization that attempted to apologize for (even while condemning) the slave system. Each church was asked to hold monthly antislavery rallies. To these meetings were added monthly temperance discussions, condemnation of secret societies, and attacks on Freemasons and Odd Fellows, both bodies that refused Negro members. In the midst of the Civil War, the Association pledged its aid to the American Union "by all means in our power, not inconsistent with British subjects," and when the war was over it spoke of future mission work among Southern Negroes.

Clearly the Association could not accomplish such purposes alone. In 1849 it entered into a relationship with the American Baptist Free Mission Society, the schismatic group from the American Baptist Missionary Union, and accepted *The American Baptist* as its organ. But in 1851–52, anti-Dawn members protested the presence of Free Mission agents within Amherstburg missionary territory, and on the grounds that white abolitionists were "teaching a strange religion" and that white men could not understand Negro needs, the Association refused its members entrée to Free Mission pulpits. The church at Dawn thereupon followed the American connection outside the Association, and a few like-minded congrega-

7. *London Free Press,* Oct. 27, 1956; Alvin McCurdy Papers, Amherstburg (in the possession of the family): Record book of Amherstburgh [*sic*] Baptist Church, 1841–77, p. 1; F. H. Armstrong, "Toronto in 1834," *The Canadian Geographer, 10* (1966), 180; Johanson, "Amherstburg Baptist Association," pp. 3–6, quoting the *Association Minutes* (Detroit, Mich., 1856), pp. 7, 12, 20, 33, 145, 171.

tions formed the Canadian Anti-Slavery Baptist Association in order to return church control to the province and to encourage fellowshipping with antislavery church groups. On the initiative of these Anti-Slavery Baptists, the rift within the Canadian church was healed in 1856–57 under the revised banner of The Amherstburg Antislavery Regular Baptist Association. The new organization permitted Free Mission workers access to Dresden as earnest of their good intentions in 1860. At the end of the war only five Negro Baptist churches in Canada West remained outside the Association. Thus, antislavery sentiment temporarily triumphed over other, more divisive, controversies, although once the Civil War had ended the common cement of such a cause would be effective no longer.[8]

The Association was slower to deal with the problem of education. Although it advocated Sabbath schools and Bible classes in 1842, no action was taken. In 1855 a succinct resolution, "That we admire education in the highest degree, and recommend our ministers to seek to become educated," reflected the growing sensitivity to criticism of their often illiterate and begging preachers, although without funds little could be done. To obtain money, the Association directed each church to pay a per capita tax of one penny a week and to appoint a home missionary to "collect his salary from the people as he travels." The result was disastrous: the money was not raised, begging increased, and some members accused the church of being a "nickel-starter and penny-finisher." In 1856 Israel Campbell reported that he had traveled 2,550 miles for the Association, had preached 106 sermons, had visited 212 families, had attended twenty-four prayer meetings and six church meetings, and had baptized thirteen new adherents. The Association sent him $2.50.[9]

The Amherstburg Association did attempt to work with white organizations. The Long Point Baptist Association, a conference of white Baptist churches that overlapped geographically with the Negro group, fellowshipped for a time, until controversies about land in Colchester, the refusal of the Long Point Association's member church at St. Thomas to accept Negroes, and the quite obvious anti-American sentiments of the

8. Johanson, pp. 6–38, quoting the *Association Minutes,* pp. 5, 6, 32–33, 44–49, 69, 78, 85, 99, 116, 124–27, 133, 143–47, 169–71, 184–85, 188, 191, 195, 197, 206, 221, 224, 238, 252, 275; *St. Catharines Post,* Aug. 24, 1858; McCurdy Papers: Amherstburgh Baptist Church, Minutes, April 30, 1853.

9. McCurdy Papers: Amherstburgh Baptist Church, Minutes, Feb. 9, 1856; J. G. Kohl (trans. Mrs. Percy Sinnett), *Travels in Canada, and Through the States of New York and Pennsylvania* (London, 1861), 2, 93–11; Howe, *Refugees from Slavery,* p. 89; Daniel Williams, "Some Pages from Collingwood's Story," Huron Institute, *Papers and Records,* 2 (1914), 30; *Windsor Herald,* May 16, 1856; *Woodstock* (Ont.) *Evening Sentinel Review,* Aug. 17, 1894; *London* (Ont.) *Dawn of Tomorrow,* Nov. 14, 1925.

white association—which increasingly would not recognize churches that sprang from American congregations—led to a sharp clash. In 1843 the Long Point conference withdrew its recognition from the "African Churches"; three years later the Negro Baptists circulated a letter identifying Long Point as the "yoke of Antichristian bondage," an "Arch-Necromancer of the infernal region of malignity and impetuosity," and a group of "base and ignominious" defrauders. Not until 1853 would the Negro churches again agree to send observers to meetings of the white organization (by then called the Western Association). Finally, in a belated gesture of approval in 1859, an elder of the Western Association preached at an Amherstburg annual meeting.

But the Negro churches remained divisive, schismatic, petty feudatories based upon isolated and impoverished followings. In the 1850s, for example, there were two Negro Baptist churches in Sandwich, the "Brick Church Brethren" and the "Frame Church Brethren," each with fewer than twenty-five adherents, one following the Anti-Slavery and the other the Amherstburg Association. In 1864 Samuel Gridley Howe noted that each group, however small, demanded a meeting-house of its own: "They do not wait for the first one to become full; for none of them do become full. . . . They expend an undue and unreasonable part of their time and substance in building churches; and their zeal leads them to go begging for aid in the work." A tendency toward litigiousness, insistence on a narrow doctrinal "soundness," and divided and unstable leadership slowed Negro progress, seemed to confirm white prejudices, and undermined any possibility of black power within the wider Baptist church, itself divided by evangelical and credal controversies.

The spirit of the Amherstburg Regular Missionary Baptist Association, although not the title, continues to the present time. In 1880 the Anti-Slavery Regular Baptist body was dissolved, partially as a result of a postwar decline in church membership. Two years later a Women's Home Missionary Society marked the emergence of women into positions of leadership for the first time. Chief among them was to be Mary Branton, who was born in Chatham in 1860 and who, after training as a missionary in Canada, withdrew from the Amherstburg church to go to Africa under the sponsorship of the Second Baptist Church of Detroit. She married John Tule, a Bantu missionary, and with him founded the Mary Branton Tule School in South Africa; both there and later in Liberia she gained considerable local fame for her work. But at home the Baptist church grew poorer yet, more begging ministries were encouraged, and the ablest and most ambitious Negro preachers left for nearby American cities. Between 1869 and 1901 a few congregations united to reduce the number of uneconomic church units, and after 1904 membership began to increase again. In 1909 the National Baptist Convention of the United States offered to incorporate the reformed Amherstburg Association. In the midst of the general wave of anti-Americanism in Canada occasioned by the debates over the projected reciprocity treaty of 1911, the Canadians declined. The Association did accept an invitation to unite with the Wolverine Convention in Michigan in 1920, however, only to break away after five years because too many of its ministers were leaving for churches on the American side of the border. In 1932 the truncated Association agreed to work cooperatively with the white Baptist Convention of Ontario and Quebec, which undertook to provide financial aid to individual congregations, and six of the Negro churches joined the convention itself. In 1939, for the first time in many years, the Amherstburg Association did not operate at a deficit. There were then ten member churches with four hundred and ten adherents.[10]

To the east, in Nova Scotia and New Brunswick, the separatist rationale for Negro Baptist churches also continued. As we have seen, at the Granville Mountain meeting in 1854 Richard Preston established the African United Baptist Association, which has persisted deep into the twentieth century.[11] At first there was no rigid separation of the races within the predominantly Negro congregations, although by the 1890s the presence of interracial churches at Tracadie, Waverly, and on the Musguodoboit Road were the subject of some comment.[12] Preston's successor in 1861 was a white man with whom he had worked for twenty years, James Thomas. Assisted by his young son John, Thomas was responsible for a substantial religious awakening at Beech Hill in 1868, when he immersed forty-seven of the newly faithful in a single ceremony. But in 1869 Thomas took the Preston church out of the Association, and until his death ten years later the Baptists remained badly split. Spiritual leadership passed from the Preston to the older Cornwallis Street church in Halifax, and the faith grew in fitful leaps during successive revivals in 1879, 1888, 1890, and 1893. In 1840 there had been seven Negro

10. Shreve, et al., *Pathfinders,* pp. 29–41; Sheffield, "Negro Baptists," pp. 52–55; *Toronto Globe & Mail,* Aug. 15, 1952; Program, Baptist Convention of Ontario and Quebec, *Centennial Home Mission Board, 1851–1951.*

11. See Chapter 5, supra pp. 138–39.

12. MacKerrow, pp. 49–58, 66-71, 92–94; Oliver, pp. 31–41, 71–72. The appointment of a white minister to a black church in 1871, the ordination of a Negro to serve an all-white congregation in Ontario in 1953, and the decision of Myles Estabrook, a white Amherst businessman, to become a deacon in the African Methodist Episcopal Church in Springhill, Nova Scotia, in 1959, also attracted much attention (for example, *see Amherstburg Echo,* Nov. 23, 1934; *Toronto Star,* Feb. 6, 1953; *Midland Free Press,* Feb. 14, 1954; *London Free Press,* Aug. 22, and *Amherst Daily News,* Aug. 29, 1959; *Halifax Chronicle-Herald,* Jan. 15, 1960; personal interview with reverends John Davidson and Myles Estabrook, Amherst, February 1961).

Baptist churches in Nova Scotia with 273 members; in 1897, following another awakening, there were twenty-two churches and 2,440 members; and in 1953, the semi-official history of the Association referred to a "constituency" of ten thousand. In 1911 ninety percent of Nova Scotia's Negroes were said to be Baptists, and in 1961 well over ten percent of the province's Baptists were Negroes, although the movement from countryside to town had reduced the number of active churches to eighteen.[13]

Maritime Negro Baptism also suffered from a steady drain of preachers to the United States. Typical was Cornwallis Street's Reverend A. W. Jordan, who had been born in Truro and had studied in America. He provided energetic leadership for some years, tried to work with whites, and cooperated with the Baptist Home Mission Board, only to leave for Indiana in 1891, when some Negroes attacked his growing involvement with the board. Reverend Wilton R. Boone, who came from Massachusetts, returned there because he found the customs of the country too different to accept. A future President of Livingstone College in North Carolina was among those baptized at Beech Hill in 1868. In Yarmouth County the Salmon River Church, renamed Greenville, lost most of its members to the Boston States, and six other churches reported substantial losses during the "great exodus" between 1870 and 1900, when fifteen churches fell to an average membership of ten. The rapid turnover in pastors hampered the development of any continuous program and left to a few families the spiritual responsibility—and the power, such as it was: in twenty-five years there were ten changes in ministers at the Cornwallis Street church alone.[14]

Thus, a few families rose to prominence, created an aristocracy of the faith, and often held the church to more than ordinarily frozen and conservative theological and social positions. The same family names occur repeatedly within the local church histories; for long after other forms of upward mobility had been found in Ontario and the West, the ministry remained the only means of access to the Negro aristocracy in the prov-

13. MacKerrow, pp. 31–106; Oliver, pp. 30–38; *The Maritime Baptist*, 65 (1960), 1–2; *New Glasgow Chronicle*, April 11, 1959; *Lunenburg Progress-Enterprise*, Aug. 19, 1964; M. Allen Gibson, *Along the King's Highway* (Lunenburg, N.S., 1964), pp. 58–62. The estimate for 1911 appears in E. R. Fitch, *The Baptists of Canada: A History of their Progress and Achievements* (Toronto, 1911), pp. 65–66; that for 1961 may be adduced from Dominion Bureau of Statistics, *1961 Census of Canada*, series 1.2., *Population: Religious Denominations*, Bulletin 6 (Ottawa, 1962), pp. 41–43.

14. Cornwalis Street Baptist Church Library: African Association of Nova Scotia, District Keyman's Report of Missionary and Extension Fund, Dec. 31, 1960; *Halifax Mail-Star*, March 23, 1957; James M. Cameron, *The Churches of New Glasgow Nova Scotia* (New Glasgow, [1965?]), p. 24; MacKerrow, pp. 72–80, 83–89; Oliver, pp. 36–37, 75–77.

ince. Preston had left each church in the charge of an elder, who was a pastor with full powers except over baptism, marriage, and the administration of the Lord's Supper; and several of these had retained control for decades, as for example did Brother David Dize, a West Indian who died in Yarmouth County in his one hundred and tenth year. By the 1930s most churches were led by ministers of advanced years, and there were only a handful of young men to whom the congregations might turn. To bridge this gap between generations, the Home Mission Board, with the approval of the African convention of 1938, appealed for funds from white Baptist churches so that an able Negro licentiate, Donald Thomas, might go to Acadia University. Yet the pattern was not broken, for Thomas was appointed pastor of the Second Church of New Glasgow in 1946, and he has remained in that post to the present time. Indeed, most of the names associated with the original Cornwallis Street church of 1832 still may be found in Nova Scotia; and in 1953 a list of fifty-one members of the Victoria Road church in Dartmouth showed only nineteen surnames, dominated by six names that extended back well into the nineteenth century. In 1955, when nearly every committee of the interracial United Baptist Convention of the Maritime Provinces included a Negro member, the same names recurred. While at least four preachers were West Indians and one was an African, church closures, the steady drift of the young to the United States and to Ontario, and the white preference for working with well-recognized old families, helped to keep the chief Negro churches in the hands of a few.[15]

The first thirty years of the twentieth century were the worst for the Negro Baptists of Nova Scotia. Membership remained static and small despite general population growth, preachers continued to come and go, and in 1904 the African United Baptist Association was at its lowest ebb financially. The early leaders were gone, for Reverend George R. Neal, who had brought the Preston church back into the fold in 1880, and Reverend George Carvey, who had helped to reorganize the Africville church, both died in 1893. Temperance, not civil rights, held the attention of the newer leaders, who threw their energies behind an unsuccessful plebiscite in 1898, on the introduction of prohibition into the province. Too many tiny churches were added, for the preachers again were reduced to begging their way around the Maritimes. Poverty was basic: in 1902 Reverend Wellington Naey States, who began his ministry in 1899 and

15. Oliver, pp. 1–14, 34–38, 53–57; MacKerrow, pp. 58–59, 77–80, 92–94; J. Murray Armstrong, ed., *The Year Book of the United Baptist Convention of the Maritime Provinces of Canada, 1955* (Saint John, N.B., 1955), pp. 5, 372; Harry A. Renfree, ed., *The Year Book . . . 1959* ([Saint John, N.B., 1959]), p. 370. I should like to thank Reverend Thomas for loaning me a number of his papers.

under whose guidance the Fundy church had grown substantially, became the Association's first missionary, on a salary of $20.00 a month. The church taxed each member twenty-five cents annually to support his work, but even this sum proved to be too much to collect until a Society of Gleaners was organized to extract funds more systematically.

The Association continued to function, although the more forward-looking Negro leaders saw that it was outliving its usefulness. Reverend Peter E. MacKerrow, Clerk of the Association, argued at the annual conference in 1885 that union with the white Maritime Baptist Association would be a progressive step, "both Christian and expedient"; and in the following year he unsuccessfully moved to end the Negro organization. He was a West Indian by birth, "a stranger," and he could be ignored in such matters.

The Negro Baptists did not ignore the need for social work, however. A lawyer, James R. Johnston, who had been an early Negro student at Dalhousie University, worked to break down rural prejudice against post-secondary school education. After succeeding MacKerrow as Clerk, Johnston sought to found a normal and industrial school to be patterned after Hampton Institute in Virginia. With the help of Reverend Moses B. Puryear, who came from Harrisburg, Pennsylvania, in 1909, Johnston convinced the church and civic leaders of Halifax of the need for such a school by 1914. The ladies of the church, who had been denied office until 1891, organized themselves informally into a group known as the Women at the Well to support the institute; through a new Workers' Missionary Society, organized in 1917, they promoted other social work.

World War I then intervened in a dramatic way. In November 1917, a Negro teacher arrived from Philadelphia to open the new school. Three weeks later, on December 7, two vessels, *Imo* and *Mont Blanc* (the latter a munitioneer carrying half a million pounds of trinitrotoluol and twenty-three hundred tons of picric acid), collided at the Narrows of Halifax harbor, directly opposite the low ground overlooking Bedford Basin where the straggling Negro settlement of Africville lay. Nearly two thousand Canadians, black and white, lost their lives in the resulting explosion, which sent shock-waves sweeping across the city to destroy docks, schools, railway station, and homes, until it was partially absorbed by the upward sweep of the walls of the Citadel. Although the new Negro school was in the path of the fire, it was unoccupied.[16]

During the interwar years the three chief leaders of the Nova Scotian Negroes were members of the Baptist church hierarchy. The most effective

16. Oliver, pp. 34–41, 44–45; F. McKelvey Bell, *A Romance of the Halifax Disaster* (Halifax, 1918); *Halifax Morning Chronicle,* June 7, 1921; *Statutes of Nova Scotia* . . . (Halifax, 1915), pp. 298–99.

of these, James A. R. Kinney, had been born in Yarmouth in 1878. The first Negro graduate of the Maritime Business College, he initially worked from within the Cornwallis Street church, where he was openly critical of nonactivists and was the chief spokesman for black racial pride. In 1921 Kinney withdrew from the church to devote his time to the Nova Scotia Home for Colored Children, which opened in June after he had persuaded the provincial government to purchase two hundred and eleven acres for a farm and to provide funds for a building. Drawing upon much the same group that had supported the proposed industrial school, Kinney was an officer, and for most of the time the superintendent, of the Negro home until his death in 1940, three years after he reunited with the church.

The Nova Scotia Home for Colored Children was the focus for a growing controversy within the Negro community. Kinney and those who followed him were activists of the Booker T. Washington persuasion: they would help themselves, as the founders of Elgin and Wilberforce had wished to do, while living apart from whites until they were able, through education, to compete upon equal terms. A smaller group felt that even such a step as this was too secular and criticized Kinney for insisting that the home should be interdenominational. Another group argued, as one member remarked in 1918 after hearing Kinney give a public address on "The Negro and His Accomplishments," that self-praise and self-segregation were ill-calculated to break down racial barriers. Certainly the white community was relieved to be able to retain unmixed orphans' homes, and at first the Negro asylum provided a valuable safety valve. But the Negro home continued into the 1960s, well after Negroes should have been prepared to demand full admission to other state-supported institutions of a similar nature. Despite denials that the province encouraged segregation, so long as the Protestant-based Home for Colored Children existed, no Negro was admitted to other public or private homes. Race, not religion, was the criterion for placement of abandoned or orphaned children; for an attendant in a Roman Catholic orphanage in Halifax suggested that a Negro child of Roman Catholic faith nonetheless would be placed "among his own kind, where he would be happiest." Not until 1965 would a substantial group of Nova Scotian Negroes determine to integrate their orphanage.[17]

17. *Minutes of the 65th Meeting of the African United Baptist Association of Nova Scotia* . . . (Halifax, 1918), pp. 8–13; *103rd Meeting, 1956* (1957), p. 10; *104th Meeting, 1957* (1957), p. 22; Oliver, pp. 42–49, 72–76; J. Clay Coleman, *The Jim Crow Car; or, Denouncement of Injustice Meted Out to the Black Race* (Toronto, 1898), pp. vii–viii; United Baptist Convention of the Maritime Provinces, *Annual Reports of Executive Boards and Committees . . . 1960* (Wolfville, N.S.,

Within the Negro church, two men were chiefly responsible for guiding Baptists through the depression. Reverend States, who was born in Wolfville in 1877, had been an orphan himself from his ninth year and had run away to sea at fourteen. After studying at Horton Academy, the leading Baptist school in Nova Scotia, he became a preacher and missionary from 1906 in New Glasgow, where he helped organize a competing convention, the Nova Scotia Northern Association. States was an active, inordinately handsome man who was one of the most effective evangelists the church had known; and after his death in 1927 his five children rose to prominence in Negro circles.

Most successful of all was a Virginia-born minister, William A. White. After completing his studies at Acadia University, he worked for the church in Truro for twelve years. White served as chaplain to the Number Two (Negro) Construction Battalion during World War I, through which he came to know most of the province's Negro families; and in 1919 he was called to Cornwallis Street, where he fostered the image of the Mother Church of Negro Baptism in Nova Scotia. He pioneered with radio services in the 1930s, and seeing that during the depression Negroes were being discharged from their jobs ahead of whites, he lauched a Five Year Programme to raise $2,500 annually to establish vocational schools within the churches. In 1936, a few weeks before White's death, Acadia University awarded him a Doctorate of Divinity—making him the first Canadian Negro to be so honored—for he was the universally recognized leader of the province's Negroes regardless of faith or heritage.[18]

White's mantle was taken up by Reverend William P. Oliver. Also born in Wolfville, Oliver took B.A. and B.D. degrees at Acadia University. Upon White's death, he was asked to take over the Cornwallis Street church. He too was a chaplain—for Colored Personnel during World War II— and in 1948 he introduced Negro voices to the Canadian Broadcasting Commission's trans-Canadian programs. He promoted credit unions, adult education, and closer contacts with Negro universities and colleges in the United States; and in 1949, with a grant from the Canadian Association for Adult Education, he visited Hampton and Tuskegee institutes, met several leading American Negro educators, and returned from the United States convinced that separate, vocationally oriented education remained the Negro's best hope. Under Oliver the church grew: conversions from

n.d.), p. 7; R. Ernest Estabrooks, *The History of the United Baptist Church at Middle Sackville 1863* [*sic* for 1763]—*1953* (n.p., 1953), p. [11]; personal interviews in Halifax, Dartmouth, and Preston, March 1961 and April 1965.

18. Gordon P. Barss, "'African' Churches in Nova Scotia," *The Maritime Baptist* (Jan. 16, 1946), p. 3; James M. Carlson, *About New Glasgow* (New Glasgow, N.S., 1962), pp. 63–64; Oliver, pp. 44–46. At an earlier date, McMaster University conferred an honorary degree on John Hope, the Negro President of Atlanta University.

the United Church increased, and at Cherrybrook in 1951 he baptized sixty-five persons in the largest such ceremony known to black Canadians.

For his time, Oliver's leadership was excellent. He nudged industry, service institutions, and the government toward granting his people more nearly equal opportunities for employment. He spoke out against discrimination in the job market, persuaded Halifax's hospitals to admit Negro girls to nurse's training in 1945, and in 1952 the city employed Negro school teachers for the first time, largely through his efforts. Oliver argued that the Negro shared responsibility for his own degradation, for the vicious cycle of unemployment arose from the black man's lack of marketable skills. He did not talk of social justice, of integration, or of civil rights often; rather, he spoke of the need for unlocking doors to education, from which all other bounties would flow.[19]

But the common *koine* of the 1940s, however well-spoken and successfully applied, would not remain the voice of the 1960s. In 1964 Reverend Oliver left his pastorate to become a field representative for the provincial department of education, to work among rural Negroes within the context he always had taught. He, too, received an honorary doctorate, from King's College, Halifax, and in his address on that occasion he stressed gradualism, Christian patience, and self-reliance. While the man who succeeded him at the Mother Church, Reverend Charles L. Coleman— who had been active in protest movements in Harlem—turned his sermons more and more to activist urgings, Oliver spoke out against those who would offer substitutes "for the love of Christ." [20] While the man who succeeded him as chief officer of the Nova Scotia Association for the Advancement of Colored People, H. A. J. Wedderburn—a Jamaican science teacher—mentioned the possibility of sit-ins at city hall, Oliver cautioned his people against following these new outsiders who did not understand local needs or customs. After all, it was Oliver who, in a quiet and often painfully slow way, had fought most persistently and over the greater length of time for Negro rights, lecturing on racial discrimination throughout the province, turning the Cornwallis Street church into the headquarters of the secular as well as of the religious wellsprings of Nova Scotian Negro thought. The changing of the guard in 1964–65 was in the

19. Oliver, pp. 70–78; personal interviews with reverends William Oliver and Charles L. Coleman, March 1965.

20. Oliver, "The University in Society," typescript, Nov. 20, 1964, pp. 1–11; *Halifax Mail-Star*, Aug. 18, 1965. I am grateful to Reverend Oliver for granting me interviews in 1961 and 1965, and for giving me a copy of his university address, as well as other related materials, and to Reverend Coleman for talking with me at length in 1965 and for providing access to the records of the Cornwallis Street Baptist Church and of the Nova Scotia Association for the Advancement of Colored People.

classic mold: the man who once had been in the vanguard had, by restricting himself to concepts now associated with an earlier time, fallen out of step with many members of the younger generation, to be replaced first by a man who followed a different drummer toward the Christian activism of a Martin Luther King—and, by the end of the decade, by visitations from Black Panther leaders. The church's discovery of the secular world was slow; Oliver had lived effectively in both worlds for his time; Coleman Burnley ("Rocky") Jones of Truro, and others, would reverse the order of priorities, setting their youth fellowships to reading *The Fire Next Time*. The result was also a classic one: a divided and still poverty-stricken Negro community.[21]

The Nova Scotian dilemma was a common one for North American Negroes at mid-century. A separate Canadian path, a separate Baptist church, even a separate historical experience had not led in any fundamental way to any different personal crisis for the Negro: he still had to decide whether, in the 1960s, he would continue to follow Christ or whether he should now seek out Black Power. If he chose the former course, as most Negroes in Canada did, then which Christ must he follow: He who turned the other cheek or He who drove the money changers from the temple? The story is an old one—even a trite one—and it is in that judgment that its significance lies: this source of Negro strength, at least, was continental; and if the Negro church was at times a source of weakness, that too was continental. That different Canadian path, that different Baptist church, that different historical experience had not led the Negro in Canada away from the continental problem.

All Canadian Negroes were not Baptists, and the nature of the personal crisis differed at least a little within other sects. There were isolated Christian Union and Colored Zion churches, and there were a few Negro Roman Catholics—the first Negro Catholic priest and bishop in the United States was educated in the Sulpician Seminary in Montreal in 1849, and the blacks of Tracadie and Tuskett, the latter in Digby County, were Catholics. From time to time there would be Negroes who were "non-practicing Mormons." Pentecostal churches claimed several Negro adherents in Fredericton, Montreal, Windsor, and Edmonton; and briefly in Toronto Negroes opened a Christadelphian meeting house. In the 1890s a former slave, William Allan, was a Quaker minister to several communities in Ontario. Although members of the First Church of Christ, Scientist, in Toronto were active

21. Oliver, "Racial Discrimination," mimeographed article in Library of Cornwallis Street Baptist Church, annotated in his hand; Cornwallis Street Baptist Annual Church Meeting, *Reports and Statements of Accounts for the Year 1964* ([Halifax, 1965]), pp. 2, 6, 22; Cornwallis Street Baptist Church Sunday program notes, 1964–65.

in fostering education among Negro youth in the 1930s, and one Negro became a well-regarded Christian Science practitioner, the Christian Science movement, with its emphasis on the Bible as a series of complex allegories, was removed from the usual direction taken by nonrevivalistic Negroes. Despite its failure to ordain a Negro until 1957, the Presbyterian church, as well as the Congregational and Anglican churches—the latter especially in New Brunswick or among West Indians—retained substantial smatterings of black members.[22]

Also active in Canada was the movement launched in Sayville, New York in 1917, by one George Baker, better known as Father Divine. One attraction of his teachings was that he did not speak in racial terms, and after 1926 the movement included numerous whites. During the depression Father Divine's Kingdom Peace Missions provided food and spiritual sustenance for the confused and world-weary, who addressed him as God, avidly read his semiweekly newspaper, *The "Spoken Word,"* and flocked to his "heavens," where one could buy a meal for ten cents. By the 1930s there were eleven heavens in Canada, nine of them in British Columbia; and Father Divine visited Toronto to encourage his eastern followers. In 1937 a Canadian student of the Science of Prayer accepted Divine's invitation to fly to New York in his personal airplane—piloted by Flying Determination Angel—only to announce, after an "independent investigation," that the movement was "an absolute fake." This setback was compensated for in 1946, when Divine married Edna Rose Ritchings, a white from Vancouver, who had gone to his Peace Mission in Montreal five years before, when she was seventeen. Divine's followers contended that she knew of his divinity when she was "a tiny body" in British Columbia and that he recognized her as his Sweet Angel, a reincarnation of his first wife, when she was seven. As Sweet Angel, Miss Ritchings had gone on to Father Divine's Philadelphia headquarters, where she helped the Rosebuds (young girls who wore uniforms marked with the letter *V* for Virtue, Victory, and Virginity) in their choir work, before she became the "Spot-

22. Israel, "Montreal Negro Community," pp. 151–59, 163–65; Sheffield, "Negro Baptists," p. 52; Perry, *Long Road, 1*, 132–38; Albert S. Foley, *God's Men of Color: The Colored Catholic Priests of the United States, 1854–1954* (New York, 1955), pp. 2–3, 45, 105–06, 301; Jessie M. Walton, *From the Auction Block of Slavery to the Rostrum of Quaker Ministry: The Life of William Allan, the Negro Missionary Preacher of the Society of Friends* (Aurora, Ont., 1938), pp. 3–8; *Ebony, 3* (1947), 34–38; *Toronto Star*, May 6, 1957; *The Anglican, 1* (1958), 7; *Montreal Gazette*, Nov. 2, 1961; *Toronto Globe & Mail*, Jan. 27, 1962; *The Christian Science Journal, 63* (1945), 40, through *75* (1957), 49.

Joseph Kelly Johnson, *Christian Science: A Case Study of a Religion as a Form of Adjustment Behavior* (Saint Louis, Mo., 1938), pp. 9–12, cites several reasons why Christian Science might have proved attractive to Negroes in the 1930s. Despite its title, the Africa Union First Colored Methodist Protestant Church, U.S.A. and Canada, seems to have had no following in the Dominion. See also p. 415, n. 3, *infra*.

less Virgin Bride" of "God Almighty personified." This allegedly celibate marriage with Mother Divine led the American press to comment rather wildly that such marriages were commonplace in Canada, and increased Canadian interest in Father Divine's activities. Those who entered his Kingdom did not smoke, drink, curse, dance, use makeup, go to movies, have sexual relations, or refer to people by their race. If some of these restrictions were pathological, the most severe of them undoubtedly were ignored, and all agreed that those Negroes who embraced his tenets were industrious, sober, God-fearing, trustworthy, and clean—thus providing precisely the code of behavior that white, middle-class Canadians insisted Negroes should embrace.[23]

Perhaps the most interesting and certainly the most militant of the Canadian Negroes' religious expressions was The African Orthodox Church, the single parish of which was formed in Sydney, Nova Scotia, in 1921. Founded by a West Indian from Antigua, George A. McGuire, the African Orthodox sect was an offshoot of Methodism that would find its principal strength in the West Indies, East Africa, and New York. Archbishop McGuire, a former follower of the back-to-Africa teachings of Marcus Garvey, sent Reverend William Ernest Robertson to Sydney to minister to the needs of postwar West Indians working in the steel mill there; and while a few Canadian-born blacks were admitted to the church, it rose and later declined upon the basis of the West Indian population. Incorporated in the province in 1928, the church grew under the guidance of a Tobagan Garveyite, Archdeacon Dixon Egbert Philips, until his return to the island in 1936. In 1940 Reverend George A. Francis, a Cuban-born and New York-educated Negro, arrived to keep the Parish of St. Philip's alive, and it continues under his leadership to the present time. Another militant quasi-Methodist group, the High African American M. E. Church of Canada, was organized in 1906 by a minister from Philadelphia, but it did not survive the 1920s.[24]

Only the more orthodox Methodists contested the Baptists for sub-

---

23. John Hoshor, *God in a Rolls Royce: The Rise of Father Divine, Madman, Menace, or Messiah* (New York, 1936), pp. 207–08; *The "Spoken Word," 1* (1935), back cover; *2* (1936), 32; *3* (1937), 24, listing missions; Ian S Bain, *Father Divine (A False Christ)* (Toronto, 1937), pp. 3–5; *Toronto Star*, Nov. 24, 1938; Sara Harris, *Father Divine: Holy Husband* (Garden City, N.Y., 1953), pp. 243–62; "Life with Father," *Ebony, 6* (1950), 52–54, 56–60.

24. Israel, "Montreal Negro Community," pp. 160–63; A. C. Terry-Thompson, *The History of the African Orthodox Church* (New York, 1956), pp. 99–101; and Gavin White, "Patriarch McGuire and the Episcopal Church," *Historical Magazine of the Protestant Episcopal Church, 38* (1969), 109–41, provide background. I should like to thank Reverend White of London, and Reverend Francis of Sydney, for supplying me with information on the church. That the Canadian church was initially founded as a subterfuge to hide Garveyite activities is argued in PRO, CO/Gambia,

stantial Negro followings. Black Methodists went further toward self-segregation than the Baptists had done, for rather than establishing separate associations within the larger church, they ultimately founded quite distinct sects, three of which were active in British North America: The African Methodist Episcopal Church, usually known as the AME; the British Methodist Episcopal Church, or BME; and the African Methodist Episcopal Zion Church, or AMEZ group. Each of these drew Negro Methodists away from the white chapels until relatively few remained within the parent body.

Both the AME and the AMEZ church organizations were brought to British North America by the early fugitive slaves. By 1826 there were enough Methodists in the western portion of Upper Canada to form two circuits, the Thames and the Amherstburg; and in the latter all save one of the predominantly Negro meetings broke away to organize churches of their own. At first they continued to be served by white circuit riders, but many of these were Scots-Irish and none too friendly to black men. In 1828 the entire body of Canadian Methodists parted from their brethren in the United States; and to many of the fugitives who arrived thereafter, the church must have seemed more foreign than the Baptist faith, which was still international in its organization at this time. As the presiding elder of the Methodist Episcopal Church in the Canadas and northwestern New York observed before the separation, Methodism was unable to hold Negroes, and by the 1860s several of their once-thriving churches were down to a handful of members.[25]

The African Methodist Episcopal Church was founded in 1816 in Philadelphia by Richard Allen and fifteen other Negroes, largely in response to the growing racial exclusiveness of the parent church in the United States and also from a desire to create bishoprics which Negroes

Confidential Minute Papers, no. 727: E. Urban Lewis to W. G. Armstrong, Sept. 24, encl. in Armstrong to FO, Oct. 6, 1924. I wish to thank Professor George Shepperson of the University of Edinburgh for drawing my attention to the church and for supplying this documentation. On Garvey, see infra, pp. 414–16.

25. *Anti-Slavery Reporter,* 4 (1856), 229; Drew, *North-Side View,* pp. 28, 173, 294, 342; Fort Malden Museum, Fugitive Slave File: reminiscences of Peter Stokes, March 8, 1944; *York Colonial Advocate,* Aug. 2, 1832; *Hamilton Free Press,* March 1, 1832; *Toronto Christian Guardian,* April 13, 1842; *Hamilton Herald,* May 22, 1903; *Hamilton Spectator,* May 14, 1938; Toronto Star, Aug. 11, 1943; John Carroll, *Case, and His Contemporaries; or, The Canadian Itinerants' Memorial: Constituting a Biographical History of Methodism in Canada . . .* (Toronto, 1871), *3,* 129–30; Hugh A. Stevenson, "Toronto Society, 1840–1863: Infant Canadianism and the Influence of Race, Nationality, Religion [,] Wealth, Education and Organized Societies" (unpubl. paper, Univ. of Toronto, 1962), pp. 59–64. I wish to thank Mr. Stevenson for giving me a copy of his paper. The Z in *AMEZ* is given the British pronunciation.

might fill. The AME organization entered Upper Canada in the 1820s, and in 1832 an itinerant pastor was appointed. A missionary went to St. Catharines in 1837, and within two years AME churches opened in Malden, Hamilton, Brantford, and Toronto.[26]

The BME Church was a logical progression. The African Methodists organized an Upper Canadian Conference in 1840; and in 1852 the area was reorganized into a Canadian, Ohio, and Indiana conference, with a Negro-Hindu bishop, William Paul Quinn, in charge. Following an AME annual meeting four years later, a number of the Canadian churches determined to withdraw in order to found an entirely new sect, the British Methodist Episcopal Church, in which Reverend Willis Nazrey of the AME Church had agreed to act as bishop. The impulse behind this separatist movement came from fugitives who felt that they would be safer from the effects of the Fugitive Slave Act if they became British citizens and were protected by an entirely Canadian-based organization. Further, a number of the fugitives had taken Negro Canadian wives, who objected to the designation "African." Since the chief bishop of the AME Church, Daniel Alexander Payne, shared these reservations, he helped launch the new sect. The AME Church in Canada dissolved, Nazrey moved to Canada West, and the BME absorbed most of the former AME congregations.[27]

Two into one made three: the break was not a clean one, and some churches preferred to remain within the AME group, both organizations existing side by side. Nazrey encouraged this attachment by serving both until 1864. In any case, the BME Church operated only in the Canadas at first, and AME churches in the Maritime Provinces continued under that

26. Hiram Walker Museum, Negro papers: AME Church Settlement, Sandwich, list of trustees, lots, and plans; *The History of the County of Brant, Ontario* . . . (Toronto, 1883), p. 333; *Toronto Star*, Oct. 31, 1956; Papers of Winston H. H. Clarke, St. Catharines: "The B.M.E. Church of Niagara Falls, Ontario" and "Origin of the British Methodist Episcopal Church of Canada in St. Catharines," typescripts. I wish to thank Reverend Clarke for loaning me his sermons, addresses, and circular letters. *Toronto and Early Canada: A Catalogue of the Toronto and Early Canadian Picture Collection in the Toronto Public Library* (Toronto, 1964), p. 8, dates the Toronto church from 1838, while George A. Singleton, *The Romance of African Methodism: A Study of the African Methodist Episcopal Church* (New York, 1952), p. 31, cites 1839.

27. AME Church in the Province of Canada, *Minutes of the Sixteenth Annual Conference* (Chatham, 1865); J. C. Coleman, "The African Methodist Episcopal Church," in J. Castell Hopkins, ed., *Canada: An Encyclopaedia of the Country* (Toronto, 1898), 4, 135–36; L. L. Berry, *A Century of Missions of the African Methodist Episcopal Church, 1840–1940* (New York, 1942), pp. 47–48, 63–64; Singleton, *Romance of African Methodism*, pp. 31–32, 107–08; Dwight W. Culver, *Negro Segregation in the Methodist Church* (New Haven, Conn., 1953), pp. 44–45; Walton, *Life of William Allan*, pp. 16–20. These accounts are not entirely compatible.

banner. Public confusion sometimes arose when an itinerant preacher solicited money that ultimately went to an unaffiliated church; and following Nazrey's death in Chatham in 1875, when he was succeeded by Richard Randolph Disney, a Maryland-born Negro who had served under him, Negro church members on both sides of the border began to discuss reunification. In 1876 the small Independent Methodist Episcopal Church organization, the creation of Reverend Alfred M. Green, united with the AME Church. A disagreement between AME and BME groups over property in Chatham underscored the problems arising from separation; and the fact that in the West Indies a local court had refused to recognize the validity of marriages performed by BME missionaries was embarrassing. At the request of the BME Church, the governor general in Council declared such clergymen competent to read marriage lines in Canada while giving it as the opinion that the BME organization was a branch of the AME Church of the United States. Disney, and AME Bishop Henry M. Turner, agreed that reunion was desirable, and in 1884 the two groups again became one, although against Payne's protests. Disney thus became bishop over an odd episcopal district consisting of the Demerara, South America, Bermuda, Nova Scotia, and Ontario conferences. This reunion generally was a beneficial one to Canadian members, if not to the churches, for in time three Canadians became bishops within the larger body, and one, Charles Spencer Smith, who was born in Canada West in 1852 and who was to serve as a Reconstruction member of Alabama's House of Representatives, was responsible early in the twentieth century for moving the AME Church away from a literal interpretation of the Bible. During these years the smaller Colored Wesleyan Methodist Church—organized in 1838 by Wilson R. Abbott and others—which also had embraced fugitive slaves, fell into complete decline, closing its last church door in 1891; its followers took up Baptist or BME affiliations.[28]

Union meant continued disunity, for several of the former BME churches had enjoyed their short-lived independence too much to forfeit

28. Daniel Alexander Payne, *Recollections of Sixty Years* (Nashville, Tenn., 1888), pp. 131–33, 260–61, 300–01, 318–20; John T. Jenifer, *Centennial Retrospect History of the African Methodist Episcopal Church* (Nashville, Tenn., [ca. 1916]), pp. 371–75; Windsor Public Library: Negro file, AME and BME churches; Clarke Papers: "Address of Bishop Nazrey, Delivered at St. Catharines B.M.E. Church, General Conference, August 24, 1860"; BME Church of Canada, *Seventieth Anniversary and General Conference* (Toronto, 1926), unpaged, with historical sketch; *The Crisis*, 20 (1920), 90–92; *Voice of Missions*, 29 (1921), 22; *Amherstburg Echo*, Nov. 23, 1934; *Collingwood Enterprise-Bulletin*, Aug. 14, 1947; R. R. Wright, *The Bishops of the African Methodist Episcopal Church* ([Nashville, Tenn.], 1963), pp. 28, 83, 160–61, 214; TPL, Abbott-Hubbard Collection: MS history of Colored Wesleyan Methodist Church [by Abbott, ca. 1893].

it merely because the Fugitive Slave Act posed no further threat. Seventeen congregations continued under the British rubric, while in Drummondville a Negro town councillor, Burr Plato, organized an eighteenth. The BME Church attempted, unsuccessfully, to shift its attention toward the Maritime Provinces, and in 1913 the church was incorporated to operate throughout Canada. In 1921 the AME group sent out eight missionaries to BME members, as well as to other nonjuring Negro Methodist churches, with some success; and by 1960 there were only eight BME churches left. In 1925, when the Methodist churches throughout the Dominion merged with the Congregational and most of the Presbyterian churches to form the United Church of Canada, the BME and AME sects remained outside —largely because they represented uncompromisable or conservative positions on doctrinal issues, but also because the Negro ministers did not wish to be displaced and because the merger had been difficult enough to effect without raising, amidst white churches, the question of interracial worship. The single exception was the Union Church of Montreal begun in 1907, an all-Negro congregation of American origin which was carried into the United Church of Canada and placed under the vigorous guidance of a West Indian-born Congregationalist, Reverend Charles H. Este. For the rest, the United Church agreed in 1926, to "recognize them as our brothers in Christ" without absorbing them; and the United Church of Canada would, by the 1950s, be the most vigorous of all the major church groups in promoting equal rights for blacks.[29]

There was no real change within the black BME leadership on any major secular problem between the 1880s and the early 1950s. During the 1920s Reverend Richard Ball—Canadian-born son of a Virginian fugitive slave and a leading member of BME churches in London, St. Catharines, and Winnipeg—argued that the Negro ministry was a legitimate form of black aristocracy, attacked any activist Negro ideology that would undermine BME loyalty to British institutions, and blocked further efforts at union with the AME Church. In 1949 Carl H. Woodbeck, the chief traveling church worker for the BME, opposed merger with the United Church, then under discussion again, on the ground that union would mean fewer opportunities for black men; and two successive general superinten-

29. *The United Church Record and Missionary Review, 11* (1935), 12; M. Morris and Annette Jackson, "The Union United Church: A Concise History," *Protestant Church News,* Sept. 15, 1936; *St. Thomas* (Ont.) *Times-Journal,* April 20, *Montreal Gazette,* June 5, both 1965; Melba (Morris) Croft, *Tall Tales and Legends of the Georgian Bay* (Owen Sound, Ont.), *1* (1961), 26; *Souvenir Programme, 1926–1965, 40th Anniversary Banquet Honoring Reverend Charles Este . . .* (Montreal, 1965); Perry, *Long Road, 1,* 115; Campbell, *Story of Hamilton,* p. 159. See also *The United Church Observer* for the 1950s and 1960s. I should like to thank Reverend Este for sending me letters and news clippings relating to his career and to the Delisle Street Church.

dents, Reverends Thomas Henry Jackson and F. O. Stewart, appear to have agreed. In 1950 the head of the church's public relations department announced plans for an all-Negro college in London, Ontario, where $50,000 was to be spent to renovate the old Wilberforce Institute building. Yet, BME churches continued to be physically poor; ministerial salaries were penurious; and in many instances it was not the church that supported the secular organizations, but rather the reverse.[30]

The African Methodist Episcopal Zion Church followed the same pattern as the larger AME and BME organizations. A Canada and Michigan Conference was organized from a scattering of small churches in 1876, with Thomas Henry Lomax serving as bishop and missionary in Ontario. A previous attempt in 1860 had failed, despite the moral support of Hiram Wilson, and the new Conference proved to be short lived. After a brief period of growth centered on the Maritime Provinces, the AMEZ group closed its Halifax church in 1905 and retreated to Windsor, Ontario, which could be served from the sect's Detroit headquarters. Even this church was abandoned in 1953, as its members sought out United Church of Canada or BME affiliation.[31]

For Canadians, the fact that the AME and AMEZ Churches—the latter strongest in Nova Scotia—were centered in the United States was a mixed blessing. If Negro leaders in Canada wished to move up in either organization, they had to leave the Dominion, depriving Canadian churches of their more ambitious workers and destroying any possibility for continuity of leadership except at the most local level. Still, the two sects also benefited from the occasional northward flow of Negro talent within the church, and the international relationship did not invariably mean denuding the smaller and poorer Canadian congregations. All of the churches no doubt felt that they gained something from the visit of Bishop Alexander Walters of the AMEZ Church to Canada in 1899 to speak on the work of the Afro-American Council, an 1898 revival of the old National Convention movement which was then under the dominance of Booker T. Washington. Specific congregations gained when American Negro college graduates were sent north to preach, as was increasingly common from the 1930s on. And the Michigan Conference of the AME Church gained

---

30. "Let My People Go," *Saturday Night*, 65 (1949), 25; *Toronto Star*, Sept. 15, 1950; *Toronto Globe & Mail*, Sept. 28, 1957; Canadian League for Advancement of Colored People, *Annual Financial Statement for Year 1931* (n.p., n.d.), not paged; *The Canadian Negro, 1* (Aug. 1953), 1; Alexander Walters, *My Life and Work* (New York, 1917), pp. 93–94, 247.

31. "Letters of Hiram Wilson to Miss Hannah Gray," *JNH, 14* (1929), 346; J. W. Hood, *One Hundred Years of the African Methodist Episcopal Zion Church* (Charlotte, N.C., 1896); W. J. Walls, "The A.M.E. Zion Church in Canada," MS sent to me by Bishop Walls in 1965.

much from having Reverend W. C. Perry of Windsor, a particularly artic-ulate Negro spokesman, as one of its presiding elders in the 1940s.[32]

By the 1960s the Negro Methodist Churches in Canada were sharing the same dilemma with their Baptist brethren, and they responded no less slowly. In 1957 the basically white Baptist Federation of Canada resolved to support the Ministerial Association of Little Rock, Arkansas, in its attempts to give constructive leadership in race relations in the United States; yet except for requesting changes in the Dominion's immigration laws, so that Negro churches might expand, the Negro associations in Canada remained silent. In 1958 the Negroes resolved to take notice of how "African nations and darker races" were rising, but in 1965 they refused to condone picketing as the means to any end. Assuredly, the Negro churches in Canada were not silent because they were big business, as was the case in the United States; yet as collective entities they were indeed silent.[33]

For all that these churches—Baptist, Methodist, and other—did give the Negro in succor and inspiration, on the whole they were ineffective in meeting the major problems—partially because they did not see those problems in terms of future goals so much as in terms of immediate needs,

32. *Official Minutes of the 46th Session of the New England Annual Conference of the A.M.E. Zion Church* (n.p., 1891), p. 44; Louis M. Rountree, comp., *An Index to Biographical Sketches and Publications of the Bishops of the A.M.E. Zion Church,* revised and enlarged ed. (Salisbury, N.C., 1963), pp. 11–12; *The Crisis, 3* (1911), 12; *10* (1920), 90; Bruce Papers: Edward E. Cooper to Walters, May 31, Cooper to Bruce, June 26, 30, and James D. Corrothers to Bruce, June 28—all 1899; *Toronto Telegram,* April 22, 1924; *Saint John Telegraph,* May 30, 1945, Aug. 14, 20, 23, 1948, April 10, Aug. 10, 21, 1959; *London Free Press,* May 16, 1946, Aug. 16, 1947; *Saint John Times-Globe,* Oct. 25, 1954, Aug. 25, Nov. 22, 1958, July 30, Aug. 8, 1959; [G. A. Burbidge, M. D. Morrison, D. A. Frame], *Historical Sketches of St. Andrew's Church, Halifax, Nova Scotia, United Church of Canada* ([Halifax], 1949), p. 10; *Souvenir Program: St. Phillip A.M.E. Church, Saint John, N.B., 1859–1959* ([Saint John, 1959]), on work of Reverend Arthur Scotland of Amherst.

33. *Minutes and Reports of the Annual Meeting of the Council of the Baptist Federation of Canada . . . 1957* (Toronto, n.d.), pp. 24–25; *Minutes of the 105th Meeting of the African United Baptist Association . . . Truro, 1958* ([Halifax, 1961?]), p. 8; N. S. Sanford, "The Highland A.M.E. Church," *The Canadian Conference, African Methodist Episcopal Church, 75th Annual Conference Diamond Jubilee* (Amherst, N.S., [1958]), p. [9]; *Saint John Telegraph,* Aug. 20, 1958; *The Canadian Negro, 1* (1953), 1; *St. Thomas Times-Journal,* April 20, 1965; interviews with church members in Windsor, Chatham, London, and Dresden, Ont.; Amherst, N.S.; Saint John and Sackville, N.B.; and Victoria and Vancouver, B.C., in February, June, and July 1961; December 1964; and August 1969. It should be noted that individual pastors continued to speak out: Oliver and Coleman, Eustace Meade of the Zion United Baptist Church in Truro, and George A. Coates of Amherst, who worked with the local Colored Improvement Association formed by John A. Davidson, are examples.

and partially because their solutions too often arose from the oldest method of all: solving a problem by failure. "Slowly, by Thy hand unfurled / Down upon the weary world / Falls the darkness. O how still / Is the working of Thy will" sang the more sedately pious. Perhaps, ignorant of or at least ignoring the terrible implication contained in their words, they found peace—that of a God bringing destruction through His subjects' loving acceptance. Indeed, as Melville's Pip saw, God did go a-blackberrying amongst their worlds. Begging ministers, poverty-stricken churches, and a narrow anti-intellectualism contributed to a sense of separation from the Christian community as a whole; Negro associations and separate Negro sects heightened the sense of distance on both sides of the color barrier; illiterate preachers who, in the words of that most activist Negro, Samuel Ringgold Ward, indulged in "religious burlesque"—all these hurt the Negro in his slow climb toward acceptance. But Christian resignation, misunderstood, did more harm. Too often did the Sandwich Baptist Church choose *Matthew* 18 : 4 as the text with which to open its business meetings; too many had fallen asleep in Christ.[34]

34. Mrs. J. C. Currie, "Reminiscences," *Niagara Historical Society Papers,* no. 20 (1911), p. 33; *Halifax Novascotian,* Nov. 23, 1846; *Voice of the Fugitive,* Dec. 1, 1851: Ward to Bibb; Sandwich Baptist Church, Minute Book, passim.

12. Source of Strength?—The Schools

If one could not cross over the River singing while asleep in Christ, one could turn to another, sometimes similar, source of strength—the school. "I come from the Town of Stupidity," wrote Bunyan, "it lieth about four degrees beyond the City of Destruction." The Negro sensed how near to that city he was as long as he was ignorant. If God would not lift up His people, He would give them knowledge, and—seizing it—they would lift up themselves. In 1790 David George exhorted his Nova Scotian brethren to pray and to learn: God, and their own knowledge, would help them, for the white man would not. In 1966 Reverend William P. Oliver also counseled prayer and education for his fellow Nova Scotians. The Negro leadership chose consistently to break into the vicious circle of discrimination through improved education. Here too, then, the Canadian Negro's response to the web of inabilities in which he found himself enmeshed followed the continental norm.

While nineteenth-century Negro leaders asked for equality of educational opportunity, generally they were prepared to accept the notion that separate education could be equal education. In the United States, Booker T. Washington emphasized a vocational training that often encouraged separation, so that the Negro need not compete directly with whites. Negroes in Canada embraced both the program and the assumptions that underlay it, accepting the separate but equal formula into the 1950s, long after Negroes in the United States, and especially in the North, had discarded the idea that a man who is kept separate can consider himself equal in dignity and therefore in opportunity to those who keep him separate. In short, the Canadian Negro was a generation behind his American counterpart in his efforts to move away from the City of Destruction.

Explanations for this willingness to accept separate and often inferior education are easy to find. Not only was the pattern of discrimination against Negroes uneven throughout Canada; only two provinces, Ontario and Nova Scotia, made separate schools the nineteenth-century practice rather than the exception. To generate even province-wide concern over this form of discrimination was difficult in Ontario, and in Nova Scotia Negroes convinced themselves that they would have greater rather than less opportunity through a separate school system. Across Canada Negroes were ill-organized and broken into groups which gave as much attention to internecine feuds as to the good fight in unity against the sources of discrimination. Even when, in the present century, elements within the Canadian labor movement began to take an interest in the Negro and his rights, attention turned to job and housing equality rather than to the problem of the schools. Not until after the Supreme Court of the United States moved against separate education, in *Brown v. The Topeka School Board* in 1954, did either whites or Negroes in Canada appear to be aware of the far-reaching rôle played by the school in the more generalized problems of race relations.

Indeed, most white Canadians would not have learned that there were Negroes in Canada at all had they relied upon their formal schooling. Textbooks forgot that black men existed after 1865, and only a few Canadian books gave even passing reference to the influx of fugitive slaves in the 1850s. Most did not mention Canada's own history of slavery, and none referred to Negroes—or to separate schools—after discussing the American Civil War. C. D. Owen's 1842 text for use in Nova Scotian schools contained a single reference to the long Negro involvement with the province: blacks "are perpetually begging and receiving charity," he wrote, "yet in general they are neither prosperous nor useful." In the twentieth century those few books which purported to discuss social problems for a school-age audience were imported from the United States, and readers not unnaturally assumed that the racial problems revealed in such books were unique to the Republic.[1]

Canada has had much experience with the separate school as an institution. Protestant school boards warred within themselves over what a Protestant school was (in 1874 Newfoundland established a straight denominational system as a result); while Separate (or Roman Catholic) schools required constant legislation, and the legislation required constant revision. With such ready machinery at hand, a legislature could easily establish a provision for yet another form of separation based on race rather than on religion, and two provinces did so.

Between these two extremes of expressly prohibiting and expressly requiring segregated schools by law, lies the soft middle ground where the Negro may not be mentioned in any statute, or where legislation may permit individual school boards to establish separate schools, creating a form of local option on discrimination, the option to be exercised by either majority or minority. Where religious minorities are involved, the option usually is taken up by the minority itself; where racial minorities exist, the option usually is exploited by the majority. Informally segregated

1. [Owen], *History, Statistics, etc. of Nova Scotia,* p. 70. I have examined over fifty Canadian school history texts published between 1920 and 1960 and have not found one post-1865 reference to Canadian Negroes in them.

schools can arise under either of the two middle-ground positions, and once created, such schools may last until a legislature takes one of the two extreme positions. Such has been the Canadian experience.

The first record of a Negro receiving any education in Canada comes from the *Relation* of the Jesuits' Father Paul le Jeune who, as we have seen, reported in 1632 that as a teacher "the other day I had a little Savage on one side of me, and a little Negro or Moor on the other." Occasionally masters taught their slaves to read and write, and eighteenth-century advertisements for runaway slaves sometimes mention a Negro's literacy. But most Negroes were functionally illiterate, and nearly all of those aboard Clarkson's fleet, or on the *Asia,* signed their names with their mark.

If the Negroes could not do for themselves, God was expected to: most early Negro education came through the offices of one church group or another. The provinces did very little for their Negro inhabitants, aside from Governor Wentworth's early effort in Nova Scotia to obtain a provincial grant for a Sunday school that would teach more than scripture. This early failure of the provinces to provide better, or any, education for blacks is understandable. Despite the widely held belief in many rural quarters that privation builds character, there is no evidence outside the novels of Thomas Mann that suffering leads to godliness. Job, it will be remembered, had already developed his character while he was rich. Legislatures were unlikely to do anything extra for Negroes when an entire province was locked in the vice of poverty. If black education in Nova Scotia was mechanical, rooted in an increasingly outworn curriculum, badly taught in unattractive buildings by only semiliterate teachers, the white Nova Scotians often fared little better. The chief difference was that on many occasions the black Nova Scotians fared not at all.

Organized education for Negroes in Canada therefore began in 1796 when the Society for the Propagation of the Gospel sent Benjamin Gerrish Gray to Boydville, and later to Preston, to work among the Maroons. Before this time, what organized tutoring there was had come from within the black communities themselves, from preachers such as David George, Cato Perkins, and Moses Wilkinson, and in the rare instance from a secular leader like Stephen Blucke at Birchtown. Between 1800 and 1850 the SPG and the Associates of the Late Dr. Bray provided most of the schooling for Negroes in the Maritimes. In 1818 special classes were offered to Negroes and Indians in Halifax, and there were soon two or three schools for blacks in Granville. In 1820, at the request of the lieutenant-governor of New Brunswick, the schools in Saint John extended instruction to colored children "in a separate branch of the institution." Two years later a local representative of the SPG wrote that Negro children were excluded from schools because white parents would not allow their children to mix with them.[2] Thus, as noted earlier,[3] the Anglican mission organizations, including Dr. Bray's Associates, did what they could—with modest provincial help after 1836—to meet the more rudimentary educational needs of the blacks, most of whom studied in all-Negro schools if they studied at all.

In New Brunswick and Prince Edward Island separate schools were not created by an act of the legislature, and where the Negro population was small, black children mixed readily with white. In St. Andrews in 1831 two colored students enrolled with eighty white children. On the island, Negroes attended the same schools, although most blacks gravitated to a single school in Charlottetown. This, the Old Bog School, was built in 1848 by the Colonial Church and School Society, and it was used for fifty years by the "coloured and also whites of the poorer class." But where concentrations of Negroes were comparatively heavy, as near Fredericton or in Saint John, local pressures continued to deprive the Negro of any schooling at all, or to force him into opening his own school. In 1848 the New Brunswick legislature provided a grant for a Negro day school at Loch Lomond, near Saint John, and forty pupils enrolled. Four years later a committee of whites and Negroes announced a subscription list to establish a permanent School for Colored Children in Saint John, with only temporary success.[4]

By the 1850s many Negroes in Canada West also attended separate schools as the result of a process of exclusion that had begun two decades before. In some cases they had wanted such schools, for most fugitive slaves were unable to do the regular work set by the Education Department,[5] and the curriculum was unlike that known even to free Negroes from New York or Ohio. A few of these schools had grown out of, or

2. SPG Papers (microfilm): George Best, report, Jan. 1, 1820, Robert Willis to Anthony Hamilton, Jan. 9, 1821, Nov. 10, 1823, and Willis, report, Oct. 8, 1822; MacKerrow, *Coloured Baptists*, pp. 57–58, 69; SPG Archives, Dr. Bray's Associates Minute Books: 7, April 20, 1858; James Bingay, *Public Education in Nova Scotia: A History and Commentary* (Kingston, Ont., 1919), p. 39.

3. See Chapter 5, supra, pp. 135–37.

4. SPG Papers: John Hasson to J. H. Markland, Treasurer, Jan. 1, 1831; *Saint John New Brunswick Courier*, Oct, 6, 1849, March 13, 1852; *Reports of the Visitors of Schools of Prince Edward Island for the Year, 1871* (Charlottetown, 1872); Charlottetown Public Library: T. E. MacNutt, "The Bog School," MS article; Benjamin Bremner, *Memories of Long Ago: Being a Series of Sketches Pertaining to Charlottetown in the Past* (Charlottetown, 1930), p. 11.

5. However, in most instances the same texts were used in the Negro schools, and if the King Street School in Amherstburg is representative, examination papers were also creditable. J should like to thank Mr. Alvin McCurdy of Amherstburg for allowing me to see his collection of old texts and examination papers.

remained a part of, the Christian mission systems of Dawn, Wilberforce, and Buxton, where at least a temporary separation of the races was assumed. Black leaders in the peninsula of Canada West preferred that their people should have their own schools, whether provincial or private, while the Negroes of Toronto and in Canada East were less willing to segregate themselves from the mainstream of Canada's developing educational systems. Voluntary self-help organizations among the Negroes and church-supported Negro schools encouraged the assumption held by many whites that Negroes could not attain equal standards and that they invariably preferred separation. Two examples were: the Wilberforce Lyceum Educating Society, founded in Cannonsburg, in Colchester Township, to "promote the furtherance of the true religion of God, politeness, and such other genius in our Society as will entitle us to mix more freely in the great crowd of her Majesty's subjects"; and the Wilberforce and Nazrey Educational Institute, the manual labor school established by the British Methodist Episcopal Church in Chatham in 1872, through union with Chatham's Wilberforce Educational Institute.[6]

At the height of the period when Negroes were denied admission to the public schools, their leadership was divided over whether separate schooling was in their interest. The division became apparent in 1850 when the separatist Elgin Association for the Social and Moral Improvement of the Coloured Population of Canada successfully sought incorporation by the provincial legislature. A member of the Association, Skeffington Conner, prepared the first petition, and several whites backed it because they believed segregation to be best for all. Counter-petitions against the Association came from other Negroes, and a group of petitioners from Niagara asked the Assembly to exempt Negroes from the provisions for separate schools, which were primarily intended to apply to Roman Catholics. By 1859, when a revised Provincial Association for the Education and Elevation of the Coloured People of Canada requested incorporation, the division among Negroes was public. Those of Kent County, led by J. D. Shadd, and of Hamilton, represented by Thomas J. White, opposed the bill because the Association would perpetuate separate education and would depend upon public solicitation for funds. But with "Provincial" struck from its title, the new organization was incorporated in

6. London, Ont., Grant African Methodist Episcopal Church: Prospectus of The Wilberforce and Nazrey Educational Institute, 1876; TPL: Prospectus of the Wilberforce Lyceum; *Toronto Globe,* July 1, 1851; *Chatham Daily News,* Feb. 11, 1949; *Statutes of Ontario, 1859* (Toronto), c. 124, May 4; J. George Hodgins, ed., *Documentary History of Education in Upper Canada from . . . 1791 to . . . 1876,* 28 vols. (1894–1910), 9 (Toronto, 1902), 2; and Hodgins, ed., *Historical and Other Papers and Documents Illustrative of the Educational System of Ontario, 1853–1868 . . .* (Toronto, 1911), 3, 109–11.

May, with an interracial board of trustees, including Wilson R. Abbott, Isaac N. Cary, and Joseph Mink. Discussion of Negro education thereafter was made more complex as the "begging question," until then limited to the churches, acquired a wider significance.[7]

Still, the great majority of Negroes paid taxes to support the common schools and they wished access to them. In 1840 the lieutenant-governor told them that they were entitled to admittance. In Toronto Negroes studied with whites, and in Brantford whites studied with Negroes: the black community had opened its own school in 1837, since Negro children were excluded from the public school; and as the level of instruction in the Negro school was recognized as superior to that offered in the common school, the whites enrolled with the blacks until both institutions were united. Nonetheless, in several communities Negroes found themselves directly barred from the common schools, and in October 1843, Negro residents of Hamilton petitioned the governor-general to confirm their right of access. Although they had paid their taxes, they were denied use of the schools even after an appeal to the local board of police for help. "[T]his kind of treatment is not in the United States," they wrote, incorrectly, "for the children of colour go to the Public Schools together with the white children," while in Hamilton, "We are called nigger when we go out in the street."

The governor-general, Lord Elgin, wrote to the Hamilton Board of Police, the very body the Negroes said had provided them with no relief, for an evaluation of the petition. Not surprisingly, the president of the board, George S. Tiffany, replied that a strong prejudice against blacks existed among the lower order of whites, and that if Negro children were admitted to the common schools, white parents would withdraw their children entirely. Tiffany responded with more vigor than the Negro petitioners themselves had been able to arouse, however, for he concluded that "The Board of Police are unanimous in their opinion, that whatever may be the state of feeling at present . . . , it would not be advisable to yield to it, but that the law ought to be enforced without distinction of colour. They think that if a firm stand be taken at first, the prejudice will soon give way." This was done, and the school in Hamilton remained unsegregated.

There were 2,610 schools in Canada West by 1844, giving instruction to nearly ninety-seven thousand pupils, and the problems of maintaining equal education for a few hundred Negro students received low priority

7. *The Friend of Man,* March 7, 1838: William Raymond to Editor; Hodgins, *Documentary History: 7,* 124. For an analysis of how the educational system worked, see Herbert Thomas John Coleman, *Public Education in Upper Canada* (New York, 1907).

compared to the many more pressing issues that confronted a sprawling frontier educational system. Thus, for example, unofficial segregation was firmly entrenched in Amherstburg by 1846. In January of that year Isaac J. Rice wrote to the provincial Superintendent of Education, Egerton Ryerson, on behalf of the Negro ratepayers of the community. The local school trustees, Rice said, declared that rather than send their offspring "to School with niggers they will cut their children's heads off and throw them into the road side ditch." Despite many entreaties, the Negroes could not gain admittance to the schools, and the town superintendent, Reverend Robert Peden, had failed to help them. In reply to Ryerson, Peden acknowledged that the complaint was "not without some reasons. The prejudice in this part of the Country is exceedingly strong against the Coloured people." Yet he had not been quite as remiss as the Negroes thought, for he had warned the exclusive white schools that, there being no black school, they could be deprived of the government's allowance for their teachers if they denied admission to Negroes. The town council informed Peden that the law did not give him the power to withhold the government's grant, and while Peden did not admit to this, he encouraged the Negroes to establish a separate school of their own. Ryerson supported Peden, informed the Negroes that they were within their rights, and urged them to prove that British institutions "deprive no human being of any benefit which they can confer, on account of the colour of his skin." But he suggested no remedial action and provided no new machinery by which Rice could achieve his ends; and since the town then replaced Peden as superintendent, the Negroes had lost their champion. They remained barred from public instruction and were forced to found a private school of their own.[8]

The provincial legislature passed a Separate School Act in 1850 that permitted any group of five Negro families to ask local public school trustees to establish such a school for them.[9] While the act was intended to be permissive and in keeping with the Canadian principle of individual choice in supporting schools, its effect was to give whites a weapon by which they forced Negroes to apply for separate institutions. Within the act's first year, the Negroes of Simcoe asked Ryerson to admit their children to the common schools; and although he replied that it was a

8. OPA, Education Department Papers, Incoming Correspondence [hereafter, Ryerson Papers]: petition, Oct. 15, Robert Murray to Tiffany, Oct, 19, and reply, Nov. 9, 1843; Hodgins, *Documentary History: 6,* 294–96: Rice to Ryerson, Jan. 23, Peden to Ryerson, Feb. 23, Ryerson to both, March 5, 1846; *10,* 110, 294; *12,* 234, 237; *14,* 133, 135, 137–40, 143–44; Harriett Chatters, "Negro Education in Kent County, Ontario, up to 1890" (M.A. thesis, Howard Univ., 1956), pp. 1–2, 26–28, 34–36, 56–61.

9. For the bill see 12 Vict., c. 83, ss. 69–71, 13 and 14 Vict., c. 48, s. 19, and 16 Vict., c. 185, s. 4.

"deplorable calamity" that children of a group so depressed in the United States would also be abused in Canada, he was unwilling or unable to help the petitioners.

Ryerson considered himself to be a genuine friend of the Negro, a view with which the much-revered Thomas Clarkson agreed, and in 1847 Ryerson acknowledged the special nature of the problem of equal schooling for black children. He suggested that Negroes be given separate school privileges because of the intensity of the prejudice directed against them in some quarters. In submitting to the legislature the provision for the establishment of Schools for Coloured Children, he reported that although he had "exerted all the power I possessed, and employed all the persuasion I could command . . . the prejudices and feelings of the people are stronger than law." With "extreme pain and regret" he turned to segregation, especially for the Western District, where he had found not one Negro child admitted to the schools of the incorporated towns. Yet, to another group of petitioners he argued that "good sense, and Christian and British feeling" should be sufficient to prevent discrimination. When he urged Negroes who were denied access to public schools to prosecute for damages, few did so, from fear, ignorance of the law, lack of funds, or weary indifference.[10]

The first and possibly the most important court action involving attempts to segregate Negro pupils was that of *Washington* v. *Trustees of Charlotteville* in 1855. Here, after three trials, a Negro plaintiff in Simcoe won a verdict for damages and costs in an action against school trustees for barring his child from the local school. But since the defendants in fact had no property that could be sold, the plaintiff had to pay the court costs himself, and he was forced to sell his farm in order to do so. Under such circumstances, damage suits were unlikely. Still, the legal principle won by the plaintiff's perseverance was an important one, for the trustees of Charlotteville had attempted to establish a de facto separate school by a grotesquely gerrymandered school district. Successful, long-term gerrymandering would be a sure path to continuing segregation in many Northern cities in the United States, and by striking down this device at the outset, the court assured the Negroes of at least one measure of protection.[11]

10. OPA, Hodgins Papers: W. H. Draper to Ryerson and reply, April 5, 12, 1847; Ryerson Papers: Simcoe petition, Dec. 12, and Letters Outward, Book F, p. 243, reply, Dec. 17, 1851; Letter Book G, pp. 409–10: Ryerson to Dennis Hill, Nov. 30, 1852; *Chatham Gleaner*, Jan. 9, 1848; Hodgins, *Documentary History: 7*, 210–11; *8, 91.*

11. Ryerson Papers: J. G. Hanton to Ryerson, May 25, 1855. *Washington* v. *The Trustees of School No. 14, in the Township of Charlotteville* may be found in *Report of Cases decided in the Court of Queen's Bench,* 2nd ed. (Toronto, 1874), *11, 569–73.*

Any other protection that arose from the decision in *Washington* v. *Trustees of Charlotteville* was largely illusory. When attacking the gerrymandered district, the chief justice, John Beverley Robinson, pointed out that there was no separate Negro school in the township in any case, and that the effect of attempts to run a school district line that would exclude the plaintiff's land therefore was to deprive him of schooling entirely. It was simply because there was no other institution that the plaintiff must be given access to the common school, Robinson ruled. Thus, by 1859 school administrators agreed that where no separate school was established for Negroes, they had the right to attend the common school; while if in fact a separate school had been established for them, all Negroes could be compelled to attend that school, including those who were not party to the petition from which the black school originated. Therefore separate schools were initiated or given formal status, where previously they had been informal results of social pressure—in Niagara, St. Catharines, Dresden, Simcoe, Chatham, Buxton, Sandwich, Gosfield, Malden, and Anderdon; and in Colchester there were four such schools, these perhaps the best of the lot.[12]

Ryerson also supported more active separation by 1859, when a new act respecting separate schools provided that twelve or more heads of families, Protestant or Negro, could open their own institutions and receive apportionments from the common school fund. He argued that boards of school trustees could establish any kind of schools they felt "best adapted to the social condition of their respective communities," and he told one inquirer that if public feeling against Negroes were very strong, the expedient path should be followed to the separate school. The effect of Ryerson's advice, and of the interpretation generally given to Robinson's decision, was to create local option on separate Negro schools; and while in theory such schools were to be established only in response to requests from Negroes, school trustees were in a position to force such requests. One group of Negro petitioners asked, Was it possible for any twelve heads of families to request a separate school and thus make attendance binding upon those who did not request such schools? The answer appeared to be yes.[13]

12. *Annual Report of the Normal, Model and Common Schools in Upper Canada for the Year 1862* . . . (Toronto, 1863), App., p. 135; *1863*, App., p. 147; *1864*, App., p. 56; Janet Carnochan, *History of Niagara (In Part)* (Toronto, 1914), pp. 132, 176, 189, 206; *Kitchener-Waterloo Record*, Nov. 19, 1965. The *Report of the Royal Commission on Education in Ontario, 1950* (Toronto, [1951]), Sess. paper no. 43, p. 535, incorrectly states that there never were more than three such schools.

13. Ryerson Papers: drafts, Ryerson to William Horton, Feb. 21, and to A. R. Green, March 10, 1859; *Voice of the Fugitive*, Sept. 10, 1851; *Annual Report of the Normal, Model and Common Schools in Upper Canada for the Year 1850* . . .

As prejudice against Negroes mounted throughout the 1850s, it was reflected in the school situation. Where separate schools did not exist, Negro children were seated on separate benches. The separate schools for Negroes lacked competent teachers and attendance was irregular. Some schools met only three months in the year. Most had no library. In some districts, school taxes were collected from Negro residents to support the common school from which their children were barred—although after 1853 this was clearly illegal—while in other districts Negroes were omitted from the tax rolls, and in yet others the taxes were collected and then returned. The education so received could hardly have been regarded as equal. In Windsor one Negro petitioner pointed out that a coop, sixteen feet by twenty-four feet, was used for thirty-five Negro pupils, while the white school remained unfilled.[14]

In some localities Negroes persisted in their attempts to gain admittance to the common schools, and education for both races suffered. In 1862 a long-term trustee from Harwich, near Chatham, resigned in anger because the local school, once fifty pupils strong, had declined to two whites and seven blacks as the white parents removed their children in the face of Negro enrollment. Indeed, as soon as the first Negro family began sending their children to Harwich school, the whites themselves voted to establish a separate school for Negroes. Since the community could not support two teachers, the whites proposed to build a second school adjacent to the first, so that one teacher could move between them. In Chatham itself the municipal council altered a school section in order to cut off the portion where Negroes lived. From nearby Raleigh Plains came word that the local school was "likely to be entirely ruined on account of the Colored people some five or six who persist in sending their children to it." The secretary of the Malden school district told Ryerson that the whites "want to keep [the Negroes] seperate [*sic*] to themselves." In 1862 the school authorities in London, despite vigorous opposition from Negroes led by Alfred T. Jones, voted to establish segregated schools "when financially practicable." The *Toronto Leader,* a conservative daily, praised this decision and with staggering originality asked, "Where is the

---

(Toronto, 1851), App., p. 182; *1857,* App., p. 202; *1865,* App., p. 51. The Act for 1859 is 22 Vict., c. 65.

14. 16 Vict., c. 185, s. 4; Ryerson Papers: petition from Dresden, Jan. 13, and from Amherstburg, Aug. 9, James Douglas, Secretary of Schools, West Flamboro, to Ryerson, Feb. 3, James G. McLaren to Douglas, n.d., and Samuel Atkins to Ryerson, Dec. 29—all 1856; petition from Malden to Ryerson, Feb. 26, J. G. Currie to Ryerson, June 4, 1857, Lightfoot to Ryerson, Oct. 5, 1858, Horton to Ryerson, Feb. 16, C. Harris, Green, and Thomas Jones to Ryerson, March 2, 1859, and Robert Burns to Ryerson, Jan. 30, 1860.

white man or woman in this city who would wish to see his daughter married to a black man?" [15]

Such racial bias easily overrode religious solidarity. If most Negroes were Baptists and Methodists, so too were the whites who wished to exclude them. All of the separate Negro schools were Protestant, and when in 1861 the Ursuline nuns of Chatham thought to establish a school to which Catholic Negroes might be admitted, as Father Antoine Manseau had hoped to do in Tracadie in 1812, white Catholics (except in Windsor) objected. Earlier, in 1852, the Bishop of Toronto had protested what he considered to be better treatment to Negroes than to Catholics in Chatham, obviously a shocking state of affairs. Most private schools for Negroes received no support from the province, and while most of the private Negro schools also were denominational—as with Alfred Whipper's in Chatham, or Mary E. Bibb's in Windsor, or Mary Ann Shadd's in Sandwich—pupils seem not to have been asked about their parents' religion.[16]

Voices of protest continued, of course. Henry Bibb condemned the separate school system, and Samuel Gridley Howe, noting how Negro children were forced to play apart from whites, denounced Ryerson for encouraging "caste schools." In 1864 when the Teachers' Association of Canada West held its fourth annual convention in Toronto, the entire question of the propriety of separate schools for Negroes was placed before the delegates, and after Archibald McCallum of Hamilton, one of the Association's founders, roundly attacked all forms of discrimination and maintained that he had found Negro children equal in intelligence to whites, the assemblage adopted a resolution opposing segregation. Initially, this was to little avail, and not until 1869 was an integrated school organized in previously segregated Amherstburgh. Within six years it was

15. Ryerson Papers: School Trustees of School No. 6, Malden, to Ryerson, Dec. 29, 1856; P. Andrew, Raleigh Plains, to Ryerson, Feb. 2, 1859, D. Campbell, Harwich, to Ryerson, March 14, petition from Harwich to Ryerson, March 17, M. Severs, and V. White to Ryerson, March 18—all 1862; *Toronto Leader*, Jan. 5, 1863; C. B. Edward, "London Public Schools, 1848–1871," The London and Middlesex Historical Society, *Transactions, 5* (1914), 20–21.

16. Mother M. Mercedes, "The History of the Ursulines in Ontario" (M.A. thesis, Univ. of Western Ontario, 1937), pp. 38–40; Chatters, "Negro Education in Kent County," p. 44; Hodgins, *Documentary History: 10, 178–81;* Mother M. St. Paul, *From Desenzano to "The Pines"* . . . (Toronto, 1941), pp. 163–64; Perry, *Long Road, 1,* 26–27; Angus Anthony Johnston, *A History of the Catholic Church in Eastern Nova Scotia* (Antigonish, N.S., 1960), *1,* 125, 249, 269–70, 367, 373, 379, 486; Luke Schrepfer, *Pioneer Monks in Nova Scotia* ([Tracadie], 1947), pp. 102–03; *Memoir of Father Vincent de Paul, Religious of La Trappe* (Charlottetown, P.E.I., 1896), trans. A.M. Pope, pp. 34–36; Joseph-Octave Plessis, "Journal de deux voyages apostoliques dans le golfe Saint-Laurent . . . ," *Le Foyer Canadien*, vol. 3 (1865).

closed and the Teachers' Association's resolution remained ignored or unknown throughout the peninsula.[17]

Over the years the courts did more to shape the segregated schools than any teachers, however forthright in their opposition, were able to do. Four cases in particular gave legal form to the social substance. The most crucial of these was *Hill* v. *Camden*.[18] In November 1852, Dennis Hill of Dawn Mills—whom Samuel Ringgold Ward had called "one of the best educated yeomen in Canada"—wrote to Ryerson that he had used every possible means to get his son admitted to the common school and had failed. He owned three hundred acres of land—all taxed, with eighty under cultivation—and he was not a poor man. Ryerson offered him no direct relief, and in the following year Hill again demanded that the school trustees grant his children, now two of school age, admittance. The nearest separate Negro school, opened under a Camden bylaw in 1852, was over four miles away. When the case at last reached the Court of Queen's Bench, Robinson ruled that the legislature no doubt intended that if a separate school were established for colored people, attendance at that school would be compulsory. Separate schools obviously were established because whites felt their children's morals would be harmed by association with Negroes recently escaped from slavery. "It can hardly be supposed that the Legislature authorized such separate schools under the idea that it would be more beneficial or agreeable to the coloured people," he admitted, and once a separate school was established, the legislature had not intended to leave any choice to the Negroes. Since the original bill had argued that separate schools were a temporary expedient to be used only until local prejudices and ignorance were overcome, Robinson's ruling was ill-calculated to further the spirit of the act. But during the decade that spirit was changing.

In *Simmons* v. *Chatham* [19] in 1861, Robinson did quash another at-

17. *Voice of the Fugitive*, Jan. 1, April 23, 1852; Windsor Public Library: unpubl. address of James Dougall on occasion of laying cornerstone of Windsor Central School, Nov., 1871; Drew, *North-Side View of Slavery*, pp. 94–96, 147–48, 234–35, 313, 341–43, 348–49; Hodgins, *Documentary History: 9*, 64; Howe, *Refugees from Slavery*, pp. 50, 52–53; Landon, "Fugitive Slaves in Ontario," pp. [6–8]; Edwin C. Guillet, *In the Course of Education: Centennial History of the Ontario Educational Association, 1861–1960* (Toronto, 1960), p. 31.

18. On *Re Dennis Hill* v. *The School Trustees of Camden & Zone*, see Ryerson Papers: Hill to Ryerson, Nov, 22, 1852; *Queen's Bench* (1874), *9*, 573–79; Frances G. Carter, ed., *Judicial Decisions on Denominational Schools* (Toronto, 1962), pp. 132–35, with excerpts of the decision; H. W. Arthurs, "Civil Liberties—Public Schools—Segregation of Negro Students," *The Canadian Bar Review, 41* (1963), 453–57; and Ward, *Autobiography*, p. 194.

19. *In the Matter of Simmons and the Corporation of the Township of Chatham* appears in *Queen's Bench, 21* (1862), 75–79.

tempt to gerrymander a school district. In response to a petition from a
Negro minority, Chatham had established two schools. The boundaries
of the school districts were defined by reference to the presence or absence
of Negroes. Thus all blacks were excluded from the public school and
were assigned to a separate school whether they lived near it or not.
Robinson remarked that Chatham's by-law provided no school section
limits that could be "known at any point of time" on a map and found
the action illegal.

Three years later, through *In re Stewart and Sandwich East*,[20] Chief
Justice William Henry Draper ruled that if a separate school had been
established for Negroes, and was then allowed to fall into disuse, Negroes
must be admitted to the still-functioning common school. The creation of
a separate school suspended but did not annul privileges conferred by
the Common School Act, he argued, and if the separate school ceased to
function the rights revived. Thus, by these two decisions, the Court of
Queen's Bench did assure that segregationists would have to be active
rather than passive if they wished to maintain separate school systems.

The modern problem of pupil placement arose in two other cases. In
1871, *In re Hutchison and St. Catharines*[21] gave Justice Joseph Curran
Morrison of the Court of Queen's Bench an opportunity to strike down
the contention that a municipality might rely upon its broad general powers
to establish "any kind or description of schools." St. Catharines had
founded a separate Negro school in 1846, before the act making such
schools legal had been passed, and the justice found this procedure highly
irregular even though the school had been established through the means
the law later prescribed. He denied the Negro plaintiff access to the common school, however, on the ground that there was no room in the school
for his children; since his admission initially had been refused by the
school trustees because of his color, they were nonetheless ordered to
pay court costs. In *Dunn v. Windsor*[22] in 1884 Justice Thomas Ferguson
of the chancery division of Ontario's courts denied an application by a
Negro parent for a writ of mandamus to compel the Windsor public
schools to admit his child, for the superintendent of schools—who was
also a doctor—had filed an affidavit stating that the school in question was
full and that to admit the Negro would be unsanitary. The plaintiff had

20. *In re George Stewart and the Trustees of School Section No. 8 of the Township of Sandwich East, in the County of Essex,* appears in *Queen's Bench, 23* (1864),
634–38. See also Carter, *Denominational Schools,* pp. 149–52.

21. *In re Hutchison and The Board of School Trustees of St. Catharines* appears
in *Queen's Bench, 31* (1872), 274–79, and excerpts in Carter, pp. 135–38.

22. *Dunn v. The Board of Education of the Town of Windsor,* in *The Ontario
Reports . . . , 6* (Toronto, 1885), 125–28; Alvin McCurdy Papers: Scrapbooks, pp.
16, 154.

not proved that admission was denied solely on the ground of color, Ferguson ruled, and in effect, prior consent from the administrator of any school was necessary before a pupil might be transferred from one building to another.

But the courts could not rule where separate schools were not formally involved. A cause célèbre in Essex County in the late 1870s, known as "The Thornton Case," [23] revealed how social pressure and the whites' belief that race mixing was contrary to God's way might effectively achieve the same ends. One Reuben H. R. Thornton charged that twelve Negro families in Colchester Township were unable to send their children to any school; and at the request of the governor-general, the Earl of Dufferin, the county inspector of schools submitted a detailed report which revealed that the whites had been struggling for several years to keep the Negroes out of the common schools, although all save one of the former Negro schools had closed. In 1875 the township council had arranged to accommodate the Negroes in schools of their own once again, schools which were not formally designated as separate. A small settlement of Negroes, as well as a few scattered families, were not provided for, and they were not allowed to attend any of the three common schools. Earlier the township had been divided into four sections, three of which were laid out for whites and—despite *Simmons* v. *Chatham*—the fourth for all Negroes in the concession. One of the three white school districts had also been reorganized in 1875 and lots were enumerated, with those owned by blacks omitted, so in the one district they were no longer assessed for school rates. Two white rate-payers refused to pay their own taxes because of this exemption, and in time one of the replevin suits arising from their action was heard before Queen's Bench. Although judgment was given against the school trustees, the Negroes continued to attend their four exclusive (not separate) schools, since the few whites who lived in predominately black sections sent their children to the nearest white school. The inspector concluded his report with the observation that, "Everyone is willing that the Blacks should have their children well taught if only it can be done without their associating with the children of the whites." In the meantime, however, Thornton had left for New York, where he had inherited property, and no one continued his protest against this informal and effective pattern of discrimination.

23. Rhodes House, Anti-Slavery Collection, G83, Letters from Canada: memo. in shorthand signed by Thornton, and James Bell to Alexander Marling, Provincial Secretary, June 27, R. L. Brodie, Acting Assistant Provincial Secretary of State, Aug. 9, and H. Langevin to E. G. P. Littleton, Secretary to the Governor-General, Aug. 12—all encl. in Dufferin to Sir Michael Hicks Beach, Aug. 20, 1878; *Annual Report of the Normal, Model, High and Public Schools of Ontario for the Year 1872 . . .* (Toronto, 1874), App., p. 99.

Slowly some of the discriminatory schools fell into disuse, and in accordance with the decision *In re Stewart* v. *Sandwich East,* Negroes were admitted to the common schools increasingly throughout the latter part of the nineteenth century. In 1868 a missionary for the Colonial and Continental Church Society found the schools "rigidly, though . . . illegally closed against coloured children," and in 1875 there still were Coloured Separate Schools in Chatham, Sandwich, and Anderdon; an unofficial separate school in Hamilton remained open until about 1895. But while an attempt to get an antidiscrimination motion past Chatham's Board of Public School Trustees failed in 1881, two years later the school board bowed to the persistent request from Chatham's Negroes that their children be admitted to the common schools, and in 1891 Chatham's last separate Negro school closed. Soon afterwards, the separate school closed in Sandwich, and in 1917 Amherstburg shut down its Negro school. Nonetheless, the act of 1859 remained on the books in Ontario until 1964.[24]

The pattern of development was similar in Nova Scotia, although the issue of segregated schools became the subject of full-scale debate in the legislature, as it did not in Ontario, well before the turn of the century. By Nova Scotian law, the school commissioners of any municipality could establish separate institutions if necessary and if the government approved. Few separate state schools had been maintained for Negroes under this law because residential segregation was more widespread than in Ontario, and the majority of Negroes therefore went to schools which were exclusively for their own use. However, Halifax did open three separate schools for Negroes. These schools were not filled, and they were supported by the province with an annual grant of $1,100, while the white schools were overcrowded and, on occasion, less well-financed. Many Negroes were satisfied with this situation and wished to have separate schools maintained for them, but others contended that, even though the black schools were equal in quality to the common schools, by virtue of separation Negro children "had not been treated the same as the white people." Early in 1884, therefore, Negroes submitted to the government two petitions against the separate schools. One came from Pictou, where

24. McCurdy Papers: Public School Daily [attendance] Register, King Street School, 5 vols. (1879–1903), especially *1* and *3; Board of Education Office, Chatham: Minutes of the Board of Public School Trustees, Jan. 3, Feb. 7, April 3, 1888; [Ontario] *Journal of Education, 21* (1868), 151; Windsor Public Library, Scrapbooks: Amherstburg Churches and Schools, *12, 50, 54; Mission to the Coloured Population* (1869), pp. 12–16; *Hamilton Spectator,* Nov. 15, 1947; Edwin C. Guillet, *The Pioneer Farmer and Backwoodsman* (Toronto, 1963), *1,* 183–84; J. George Hodgins, ed., *The Establishment of Schools and Colleges in Ontario, 1792–1910* (Toronto, 1910), *1,* 300. In 1970, Toronto's Black Heritage Association opened a new Black School at Thorncliffe Park. See *Toronto Contrast,* April 17, June 20, 1970.

Negroes were not in fact separated, and the second originated in Halifax. The first petition became a political football. It was championed by Pictou County's conservative member of the assembly, Robert Hockin, who wished to strike down the "barbarous law" upon which separate schools were based. While he had several Negro constituents, they were not affected by the law, and to explain his interest in it one must turn to his involvement in one of the late nineteenth-century's more heated political feuds: Hockin hoped to embarrass the inept Liberal government of William T. Pipes. The chief defender of segregated schools was William S. Fielding, managing editor of the *Halifax Morning Chronicle*, minister without portfolio in the Pipes cabinet, and M.L.A. from Halifax County. Exactly four months later Fielding was to become Premier himself, a position he held until 1896, and under him Negroes were unlikely to see separate schools abolished.

Fielding recited virtually every argument known to man against mixing the races. Laws were made "for the greatest good of the greatest number." In theory colored children were entitled to admission to public schools, but prejudice was too deep to be uprooted quickly. School boards should be given time in which to find solutions. The schools of Halifax would be destroyed if integration were forced upon the white community. Parents would send their children to private schools rather than permit racial mixing. There were rowdy children in the white schools who could not be trusted to treat the Negroes kindly. It was "questionable whether any honorable gentleman would like to have his children occupy a position at a school desk with colored children," said another member from Halifax, although personally he had "nothing to say against the colored people."

Hockin had the better of the argument and the worse of the vote. He charged Fielding with phrase-mongering and remarked that if legislation was to be governed by such trite concepts as "the greatest good of the greatest number," then the House should remember the fundamental principle of all law—that there is no boundary to the liberty of a subject save where the subject trespasses on the liberty of another, and that Nova Scotian whites were trespassing on the liberty of Nova Scotian blacks. Hockin was supported by Jason Mack—a barrister from Queens—and by a number of apparently silent partners, for when the division was taken, his motion failed narrowly, 15 to 17. Five Liberals supported the motion, including one member of the Executive Council; and five of Hockin's fellow Liberal-Conservatives opposed it.[25]

This and subsequent votes on the question of revising the acts relating

---

25. PANS, "Assembly Petitions: Education, 1858–1869": Feb. 19, 1859 and March 22, 1860; *Journal and Proceedings of the House of Assembly of the Province of Nova Scotia, 1884*, pp. 65–66; *Halifax Morning Chronicle*, April 1, 1884.

to public instruction must be viewed in terms of the very special situation then prevailing in Nova Scotian politics. The upper house, the Legislative Council, had obstructed the House of Assembly for years, and by 1884 efforts were well forward in the Assembly to abolish the Council entirely. The latter's most vocal leader, Thomas F. Morrison, was an inveterate Liberal partisan who had used the upper chamber to block virtually every attempt at legislation by the Conservative administration of 1878 to 1882. The Council in general and Morrison in particular therefore were targets for Conservative attack, and the public education bill was one means by which both might be reached. Between March 28 and April 10, when the Negro had his few days in the Assembly, the House was conducting its most heated and lengthy debate of the period, in which the opposition mounted a strong challenge to the government over a railway bill, a debate the ministry survived by a majority of seven. Partisanship was evident throughout these proceedings, and while Hockin and Mack no doubt were genuinely concerned over discrimination, they also enjoyed whipping up an anti-Pipes tempest when they could.[26]

The Council took up this "Color Line" debate on April 2. Of nineteen members present, eight spoke to the question after Loran E. Baker, a Liberal from Yarmouth, moved that all reference to color be struck from the education bill. On the day before the Council entertained the question, a delegation of Negroes once again had called upon the school authorities to ask for their rights, and Baker unguardedly accepted their contention that nowhere else on the continent was there such a segregationist statute on the books. In seconding Baker's motion, Dr. Daniel Parker, a Conservative, also mistakenly argued that no other province permitted separate Negro schools. He maintained that among the lower classes Negroes were as clean and as able as whites and that the blacks were seeking a better education and not social equality. Five of the twelve school commissioners, he confided, were known to favor the amendment.

Morrison replied at length and offensively, jesuitically charging Parker with having insulted the Council by implying that it had proscribed Negro children from Nova Scotian schools, when it was the commissioners who had made the decisions to exercise the permissive clause, not the legislature. In any case, Negroes did not wish to mix with whites, so the entire debate was only a stratagem by which a few men hoped to harm the government. A member suggested that the Negroes should be permitted to continue to "enjoy this privilege" of a separate school and that any Negro who could pass his examinations at the end of the seventh grade should be permitted to go on to a higher school wherever he wished. The colored

26. *Halifax Morning Chronicle*, April 5, 1884; J. Murray Beck, *The Government of Nova Scotia* (Toronto, 1957), p. 235.

schools should offer a different, more practical, program of studies best suited to Negro abilities, with sewing for girls and industrial drawing for boys. In the Council too the amendment was then lost, seven to eight.

Samuel Creelman, a former schoolteacher from Truro, substituted an amendment that was passed, however. It affirmed that colored pupils could not be arbitrarily excluded from instruction in the section or ward in which they lived. The government could continue to establish separate schools for sexes and for colors, but if no Negro school existed, admission to the public school was guaranteed. In effect, this amendment strengthened segregated schools in those areas where Negroes were numerous enough to justify the creation of a separate school for them, while preventing segregation in fringe areas where only a few Negro families lived. The Council accepted Creelman's compromise—a compromise which did not in fact meet any of Hockin's original points—and after a brief debate on April 10, the Assembly also accepted the new amendment by a vote of sixteen to ten. Hockin was absent; Mack reluctantly accepted the amendment for not going far enough; Fielding opposed it for having gone too far. The Council passed the bill on April 19, and in its revised form the new education act remained on Nova Scotia's books until 1918.[27]

The twentieth century brought no quick changes to the segregated schools of Nova Scotia. The Education Act of 1918 provided that the Council of Public Instruction could entertain recommendations from any school inspectors to establish separate buildings for different sexes or races of pupils in any part of the province, provided that Negro pupils were not excluded from instruction in the section in which they lived. Negroes were not admitted to the provincial training school in Truro, and only the Home for Colored Children attempted to help orphans or the mentally retarded in any way. Between 1918 and 1954, when the racial reference was dropped from the statute, the Negro schools continued to fare badly, and the most blind of school inspectors could not have pretended that separate education was equal education.[28]

The annual reports of the Superintendent of Education attest to the general uncertainty of the Negro schools and their pupils: uncertainty whether they would open or not, uncertainty whether a teacher might be

27. *Halifax Morning Chronicle,* April 10, 12, 17, 19, 1884; *Journal and Proceedings of the House of Assembly, 1884,* p. 85; *Official Report of the Debates and Proceedings of the Legislative Council . . . of the Province of Nova Scotia, 1884,* pp. 41–53; *The Revised Statutes of Nova Scotia, Fifth Series* (Halifax, 1884), p. 219; *The Revised Statutes of Nova Scotia, 1900* (Halifax), *1,* 373.

28. *The Revised Statutes of Nova Scotia, 1923* (Halifax), *1,* 498–500; *Annual Reports of the Board of Management of the Nova Scotia Training School . . . and the Annual Reports of the Psychiatrist, 1929–31* (Halifax, 1930–32), passim.

found, uncertainty as to the legal status of their property. All children near Annapolis and Digby, for example, had access to schools in 1918 except for the Negro section of Fundy, where there had been no school for ten years, even though there were twenty children of school age. At Joggins whites and Negroes used the same building, with the latter given access to the school only one-third of the time. In 1927 black ratepayers of Five Mile Plains refused to pay school taxes, and the Canadian Gypsum Company, a major employer of Negroes, offered $200 provided the community would contribute an equal sum, which it did. In 1912 and again in 1919 there was no school for Negroes in Guysborough County because no teacher could be found who would accept the salary. In 1920 the Negroes of Greenville in Yarmouth County failed to find a teacher; and the Beechville school remained closed for at least eight years. Six other schools also closed because black teachers were unobtainable.

During none of this time was Nova Scotia prosperous: after 1929 it was poverty-striken, and common schools suffered with separate schools for want of teachers, equipment, and transportation. The Negroes of Guysborough raised funds themselves, through concerts and benefit suppers (together with a grant from the Department of Education), for a school opened there in 1932. In seven localities, including Maroon Hill, Negro schools operated only during the summer. In Annapolis and Digby only one of four colored schools could find a licensed instructor. By 1934 all one hundred and forty-two schools in Annapolis County and the District of Digby were functioning again, but six were open less than full time—including both of the Negro schools. Not until 1936 did the Negroes of Guysborough County's Birchtown receive any schooling at all. In 1940 the one uninsurable school in the province was the dilapidated building for Negroes near Tracadie, also in Guysborough County. Conditions thus remained unchanged until World War II.[29]

The same currents of opinion that brought change in other areas of Negro activity between the 1930s and the 1960s influenced education, of course. Environmentalist theories increasingly displaced notions of inherent and hereditary racial inferiority or superiority. While the conventional

29. The School Inspectors' reports appear in full from 1879, in the *Journal and Proceedings of the House of Assembly of the Province of Nova Scotia*—usually as an appendix published in the year following the date of the report—and in the *Journal and Proceedings of the Legislative Council of the Province of Nova Scotia*— also as an appendix, most frequently number 5 or 8. This and the following paragraphs are drawn from *Assembly, 1918, 1,* 66–69; *Council: 1895–96,* p. 78; *1910–1911,* pp. 74–75; *1912,* pp. 58, 65; *1915,* p. 66; *1916,* p. 73; *1919,* p. 72; *1920,* p. 63; *1926,* pp. 59, 63, 66–67; *1927,* p. 65; *1928,* pp. 44, 47; *1931,* p. 41; *1932,* pp. 34, 37, 68; *1934,* pp. 38–40, 74; *1935,* p. 34; *1936,* p. 79; and *1940,* p. 83.

wisdom of the 1930s concluded, as did Harry Ambrose Tanser in a widely read study of the mental capacity of Kent County Negroes, that intelligence tests scientifically proved the black to be inferior,[30] a growing number of Canadians were prepared to explain this inferiority by reference to the institutions that shaped the Negro environment. One such institution was the school, and the separate schools of Nova Scotia and Ontario came under renewed and enlarged attack. More and more, although still relatively few, Negroes were successfully completing university courses, including postgraduate work. By the early 1950s it was no longer good Christianity, good politics, good international affairs, good image-building, good human relations, or even good sense to discriminate openly against Negroes, especially in a nation which so prided itself on its moral superiority to the United States.

Given these changing circumstances, separate schools would not survive. All but those of Colchester had closed in Ontario by 1900, in any case, although the permissive legislation had remained part of the provincial law code. More separate schools existed in Nova Scotia, where most were exclusive to Negroes by virtue of residence rather than separate by force of law. In Alberta too a single Negro school lasted into the 1960s —at Amber Valley, where the isolated all-Negro settlement maintained school through the first ten grades. Only in Nova Scotia did Negroes continue to have cause for genuine complaint. There Reverend Oliver and others did not deviate from their conviction that more and better education was the solution to the Nova Scotian Negro's problems, for education would make job discrimination impossible or clearly open to proof. Slowly, such men convinced the Negroes of this and persuaded the province that it owed the entire Negro community better educational facilities.

Until the war, adult education was ignored in Nova Scotia, but in 1946 the government opened a Division of Adult Education within its educational department. A white Dalhousie graduate, Guy Henson, was appointed director. Sensing that a program imposed from the outside would not succeed, Henson enlisted Oliver's aid. They began by adding a course in home economics at three Negro schools and in the Home for

30. Tanser's *The Settlement of Negroes in Kent County, Ontario, and a Study of the Mental Capacity of their Descendents* (Chatam, 1939), was a doctoral dissertation written under Edward L. Thorndike at Columbia University at a time when Thorndike's now-rejected conception of an I.Q. test was just beginning to come under attack. See my "The Canadian Negro: A Historical Assessment," *JNH, 53* (1968), 283–300; *54* (1969), 1–18; Clarence J. Karier, *Man, Society, and Education: A History of American Educational Ideas* (Glenview, Ill., 1967), pp. 170–76; and Tanser's "Intelligence of Negroes of Mixed Blood in Canada," *The Journal of Negro Education, 10* (1941), 650–52. Tanser also wrote "Josiah Henson, the Moses of His People," *Journal of Negro Education, 12* (1943), 630–32.

Colored Children; and two years later the province, with the support of the Canadian Association for Adult Education and at the urging of the Nova Scotia Association for the Advancement of Colored People, initiated adult education programs in eight Negro communities. Between 1945 and 1950 the government built five new schools in Negro areas, and two hundred and fifty Negroes were drawn into the adult education groups associated with these and other schools. By 1956 perhaps seventy-five percent of the adult Negroes in the province could take courses in community recreation, "shop," agriculture, health, and elementary education.[31]

Much of this activity was busy work, for no one in Nova Scotia seems to have developed a clear and long-range program for the elevation of the Negro. In 1950 the adult education branch of the provincial government still was encouraging Negroes to plant high bush blueberries so that they might better continue to provide fruit for the Halifax market. The 1950s were perhaps a bit late to apply the philosophy of Booker T. Washington: to make hewers of wood and drawers of water more efficient at their hewing and drawing was strangely out-of-step with the more vigorous developments elsewhere in North America. Nonetheless, Nova Scotia's hesitant and often outdated approach to Negro education was, in part, only a reflection of the province's general economic depression: in 1962, not one Maritime city was among the twenty-five communities with the highest income in Canada.

But Reverend Oliver had returned from his study tour of the United States in 1949 with several ideas, partially arising from a talk with the famed Negro educator, Mary McLeod Bethune. One proposal was to build teacherages, or dormitory apartments, near the more remote Negro schools. Although teacherages were common throughout the American West, in Nova Scotia instructors were still expected to board with local families, never a desirable solution in an impoverished community. In 1954 the NSAACP, local churches, the Halifax County school board, and the provincial government provided funds so that the registrar of Virginia's Hampton Institute, Dr. William M. Cooper, might study the situation.

After discussion with municipal leaders throughout the province, Cooper selected the New Road settlement as most in need of help. New Road had been more than normally deprived of qualified teachers, and over a hundred pupils there had never been to a school of any kind. Accordingly, in 1956, a province-wide appeal was made for funds to build a teacherage

---

31. *Journal and Proceedings of the House of Assembly: 1947,* p. 33; *1948,* pp. 213–14; *1949,* p. 196; *1950,* pp. 39–40, 166–67; *1951,* p. 117; *1953,* p. 84, 102; *1954,* pp. 8–9; *1956,* pp. 78–79; Gwendolyn V. Shand, "Adult Education among the Negroes of Nova Scotia," [Nova Scotian] *Journal of Education,* 5th ser., *10* (1961), 11–21.

at New Road. A total of $2,200 was provided, and by 1958 New Road had its teacherage, eight teachers, a Home and School Association, and two hundred and eighty students. Through the Hampton Institute an experienced American Negro teacher who held an advanced degree, Frizzell Jones, became principal, and another American Negro was added to the staff to help with retarded children.[32]

What labor to produce so little! Nothing more painfully illustrates the plight of the Negro in Nova Scotia than the homely tale of the New Road teacherage. In their poverty-striken community, New Road taxpayers could not support a school themselves, nor did many residents really see the need for a school at first, locked as they were in the vicious circle of their own illiteracy and lack of opportunity. The sum needed was so small, a single small-time philanthropist could have provided it as an afterthought to a day's shopping. The province might have provided the money but did not. The municipality of Halifax might have provided the money but would not. When at last New Road was singled out for improvement, seven years were needed to do the work of weeks. When a local leader, Reverend Oliver, saw the need, everyone hesitated until a presumed outside expert might give his own approval. A province of one of the richest nations on earth could not find either the money or the will to act in the face of a manifest need for education on the part of a substantial number of its citizens. When at last action was taken, public charity, the nineteenth century's solution to the eighteenth century's problems, was the means. That Nova Scotia considered itself to be an impoverished province may be accepted, but one suspects that all of the impoverishment was not financial.

No group of Canadian Negroes has been more closely and cautiously studied over the years than that in Nova Scotia. Annual conferences with Negro leaders from twenty or more different communities have been held in Halifax since 1951. The Division of Adult Education has sponsored two close examinations of the problem of Negro housing in Halifax; the municipality has financed both a sociological survey and an inquiry into possibilities for Negro resettlement; academicians based at Acadia and Dalhousie universities have conducted separate investigations at Five Mile Plains and in Guysborough County; two Dalhousie-based sociologists have studied the effects of urban relocation upon Africville; and a body of scholars from Columbia, Cornell, and Harvard universities have covered

32. Shand, "The New Road Teacherage," *Canadian Welfare, 34* (1958), 60–65. Other examples of private philanthropy include a tutoring team from St. Mary's University and the Independent Order of the Daughters of the Empire's decision to provide $1,000 annually for Negro schooling (*Halifax Mail-Star*, April 26, 1965; *New Glasgow News*, June 3, 1965; *Canada Week, 1* [April 29, 1964], 6).

the entirety of Digby County in a series of interviews. Negro groups set up self-study units. The Maritime School of Social Work granted numerous master's degrees based on theses about the Negro problem in Halifax. Reverend Oliver also submitted lengthy reports and recommendations to the province. And yet, for all of this remarkable industry, for all of the data gathered, the informants interviewed, the cards filed, the computers programmed, little of moment emerged. The studies seem to have been acted upon slowly if at all, and recommendations made in 1955 with respect to Africville required thirteen years to put into effect.[33] The Nova Scotian Negro seemed in 1969 very little better off than in 1959, or, for that matter, than in 1949; where he had risen he had done so through his own sporadic efforts, more often secular than religious, or because of a general improvement in the condition of the province. By 1970 the Negro in Nova Scotia—one tenth the population of the province—was one of the most overstudied underprivileged minorities in Canada.

One area in which the province had the undoubted power to act was that of the separate school, however. In 1940 public attention once again had focused on the reality of de facto segregated schools, for Negro children were barred from the schools in Lower Sackville. Mrs. Pleasah Lavinia Caldwell, a Nova Scotian white who had taught in western Canada for five years, responded by organizing her own black school, which she called "Maroon Hill." For eleven years this "kitchen school" provided the only instruction available to many Negro children. In 1959 school buses in Hammond's Plains still were stopping only in the white section of the community, thus effectively cutting off the more indolent or apathetic Negro students there from further formal education.[34]

Yet, the walls came tumbling down in most quarters with little effort, for by 1950 few Canadians can have wanted to share with the United States the institution of the segregated school. Custom, inertia, and widespread ignorance of the laws, rather than the active will of white segregationists, had permitted the clauses to remain on the books. Once attention was given to them, in the context of a more general Canadian interest

33. The chief of the studies are *The Condition of the Negroes of Halifax City, Nova Scotia* (Halifax, 1962), published by the Institute of Public Affairs at Dalhousie University; Albert Rose, *Report of a Visit to Halifax with Particular Reference to Africville* (mimeographed, 1963); Donald Clairmont and Dennis W. Magill, *Urban Relocation of Africville Residents* (research proposal, mimeographed, 1968); and Charles C. Hughes, *People of Cove and Woodlot: Communities from the Viewpoint of Social Psychiatry* (New York, 1960).

34. *Toronto Globe & Mail*, Nov. 28, 1949; *Time Magazine* (Canadian ed.), *55* (1950), 12; *The Canadian Negro, 1* (1953), 1; *Halifax Chronicle-Herald*, Dec. 8, 1958, Oct. 26, 1959; Pearleen Oliver, *Colored Baptists*, p. 76.

in civil rights, the legal foundations for de facto segregation were removed in Ontario and put in course of removal in Nova Scotia.

Nonetheless it took fifteen years. In 1951 a Royal Commission on Education in Ontario had strongly recommended repeal of the pertinent clauses, which had been retained virtually intact in the Revised Statutes of the previous year. In 1952 a minister of the United Church of Canada in Markham asked the provincial legislature to abolish separate schools for Negroes, and several delegations from Kent County opposed the motion—often contradictorily—arguing that such schools no longer existed in any case. In 1957 the United Church asked the government to repeal the offending sections of the Common Schools Act, and renewed protests from Kent County, and from Essex County as well, blocked legislative action. In the latter county the Negroes of North Colchester wished to preserve their separate schools, arguing that their children were not prepared to compete with whites. A more militant body of Negroes in Amherstburg, led by Alvin McCurdy, descendant of manumitted slaves from Kentucky and Virginia, and one of the family which had helped to found Malden and Gilgal and to provide leadership for Amherstburg, worked to persuade their Colchester brethren that separate education was not equal. Since the Negro school board had a vested interest in maintaining its functions, however, McCurdy was unsuccessful both then and in 1959 when the United Church, this time through its official organ, *The Observer,* protested against the separate school clauses.[35]

The successful drive against the school law, now one hundred and fourteen years old, began in February 1964, when a newly elected member of the lower house in Ontario, Leonard A. Braithwaite, chose the subject for his maiden speech. Braithwaite, a Liberal from Etobicoke, a suburb of Toronto, was the first Negro ever to be elected to a provincial legislature in Canada; and while he made it clear that he did not take civil rights as his special province, he felt it fitting that such should be the object of his first effort. In response, the Minister of Education announced that all references to separate schools for Negroes would be removed from the statutes. By this time the North Colchester school board had begun agitating for improvement in the physical condition of its school, and a hastily organized group, the South Essex Citizen's Advancement Association, protested retention of the school at all. In November, with the knowledge that the permissive legislation soon would be struck from the books, the board met, barred the press, and issued a joint statement with the Associa-

35. See the McCurdy Papers, held by Alvin McCurdy in Amherstburg, to which the author was given access; Perry, *Long Road, 1,* 102–03; and Landon, "Amherstburg," p. 9.

tion, in which they agreed on a procedure and a timetable for moving the Negro children, by bus, into other schools. In September 1965, the last segregated school in Ontario closed its doors.[36]

Not surprisingly, change came more slowly to Nova Scotia, and perhaps with cause. The Negroes of Nova Scotia on the whole were less progressive, less aggressive, and less ambitious than their Ontario counterparts. The majority remained rural, the impacted ghetto was unknown to them, and the most ardent civil rights advocates would have been hard put to argue that immediate integration of the Negro children of New Road, in particular, was to their advantage. But as Reverend Oliver argued, one must begin sometime, and somewhere. There were seven Negro school districts (and three other exclusively Negro schools) in the province in 1960, and the premier, then Robert Lorne Stanfield, began with West Hants when, in that year, he personally and successfully moved the abolishment of the three segregated school districts there. Still, at mid-decade, three such districts remained at Beechville, Hammond's Plains, and Lucasville, all in Halifax County. Two of the de facto Negro schools had also been breached by being opened to white children, and while the permissive legislation remained in force, both it and the remaining separate schools in Nova Scotia appeared to be on the road to extinction, especially as Hammond's Plains fell into sharp decline as the demand for barrels, made by Negro coopers in the area, fell off when orchardists and potato growers turned to other types of containers.[37]

In addition to continuing to press against their segregated schooling, Negro leaders remained faithful to their belief that education was the most important weapon in the battle against discrimination. As in the past, the Negroes' churches often were the initiators of adult education programs and of informal schools, and on Sundays the church buildings were increasingly used for various forms of instruction, usually domestic or religious in nature, although sometimes simply remedial. In August 1949, the growing African United Baptist Association of Nova Scotia, meeting

36. *Revised Statutes of Ontario, 1950* . . . , *4*, 643–80: c. 356, pt. 1, s. 2; *Report of the Royal Commission on Education in Ontario*, pp. 534, 536; *Toronto Star*, April 17, 1952; *Canadian Labour Reports, 12* (1957), 3; *Toronto Globe & Mail*, Jan. 19, 1959; *Kitchener-Waterloo Record*, March 13, Nov. 19, 1964; *Canada Week, 1* (March 23, 1964), 2–3; Windsor Public Library: scrapbooks on local Negro activities; Perry, *1*, 71–72, 86, 102–03, 145; *Journal of the Legislative Assembly of the Province of Ontario . . . Session 1951, 75*, 15; *Session 1964, 98*, 19, 97, 105, 136, 156, 160, 168.

37. *Revised Statutes of Nova Scotia, 1954* . . . (Halifax, 1955); *Halifax Chronicle-Herald*, Feb. 25, 1960; *Canada Week, 1* (May 11, 1964), 2; *Toronto Daily Star*, July 21, 1965; John Connor and M. V. Marshall, *Three-Five Mile Plains Study: Socio-Economic Indicators* (Wolfville, N.S., 1965), pp. 2, 4–7, 14, 21, 28, 31–35, 47–52, 56–58. As of 1969, only one all-Negro school remained, in Beechville.

in Dartmouth, established an Urban and Rural Life Committee which stressed three needs above all others. "First," the delegates resolved, ". . . it is important for people to own property, because of the sense of security and responsibility derived. Secondly, people must have the opportunity to use their abilities freely in their efforts to secure a livelihood. There must be unlimited job opportunities. Thirdly, people must be trained and educated in order to function successfully." The Committee saw this education as central to its purpose: Negroes had to be shown "how important it is to look right and to act right if they wish to be received rightly." Reverend Oliver, speaking for the Committee, insisted that much discrimination was rooted in problems of social standing or class rather than in race, problems which could be overcome only through employment and consequent status which, in turn, would follow from intensified education at all levels.[38]

Educational problems for Negroes were not restricted to the primary and secondary levels, of course, but on the whole those students who entered universities encountered little prejudice in Canada. Canadian participation in the Colombo Plan, membership in the Commonwealth of Nations, and a close economic relationship between the Dominion and the West Indies, brought thousands of black-skinned university students to Canadian institutions following the Second World War. While relatively few Canadian Negroes attended universities, those who did found that the presence of African, West Indian, and Asian students had created a sophisticated and, on the whole, nondiscriminatory student body and faculty—except for McGill University, which was charged with applying racial restrictions in the 1920s, 1930s, and again after the war. Those problems that did exist within the university communities were incidental rather than central to the institution: barbers who would not cut Negroes' hair, landladies who would not let rooms to black men, donors of scholarships who insisted that they must go only to whites, and fraternities or sororities that would not initiate Negroes. Qualified blacks had been admitted on a basis of equality to the University of Toronto and to Queen's University before the American Civil War, and by the end of the nineteenth century Negroes had studied in most of the Maritime universities, so even those problems that arose within the broader communities that surrounded the universities were basically minor ones, for the presence of black faces was not usual. In the 1960s, an increasingly heavy influx of

38. Oliver, *Urban and Rural Life Committee of the African United Baptist Association of Nova Scotia* (mimeographed, n.p., n.d.), a general statement of activities and scope. See also Oliver, "The Negro in Nova Scotia," *Journal of Education, 13* (1964), 18–21; and Basil Deakin, "Problem of Education," *Atlantic Advocate, 55* (1965), 63–65.

West Indian students, and the rise of demands among Negroes in the United States for Black Studies programs, created a new tension that would become evident in Canadian universities. It culminated in a racially centered riot at Sir George Williams University in Montreal in 1969—the university which was named for the man who had thought, in the previous century, that Canada would face no black confrontations.[39]

Nor did a pattern of discrimination develop with respect to Negro teachers. Most instructors in all-Negro schools during the nineteenth century were Negroes themselves, and when the schools were abandoned or closed, they had no difficulty finding employment elsewhere, usually in other Negro schools. In the twentieth century, as more Negroes attended teacher training colleges, and as the North American teacher shortage grew worse, especially after 1945, black teachers encountered little difficulty in finding employment. Isolated incidents did occur, in which racial bias was said to have played a rôle; and in the 1950s and 1960s dismissals near Victoria, British Columbia, in Drumheller and Breton, Alberta, in Wawota, Saskatchewan, and in Dartmouth, Nova Scotia, were given considerable publicity by the local press. Upon investigation, however, only two of these cases were shown to have a racial basis. Not unnaturally, Negro spokesmen tended to charge school boards with discrimination rather than appear to be unwilling to support a member of their own community; but unlike the problem of separate Negro schools, the issue of continued Negro teacher employment arose in most instances from questions of ability rather than of race.[40]

Nonetheless, on the whole, the school was no more effective as an institution that the church was in breaking down the barriers that separated black from white. Most Negroes dropped out of public schools, especially in Nova Scotia, by the end of the sixth or seventh grade. In 1960 those Negroes who remained in school in Halifax were older for each grade— on the average—than the white children, and a third or more of the city's Negroes had intelligence quotients in the low-normal range and below.

39. See, for recent examples, *Dalhousie Gazette* (Halifax), Feb 3, 1960; *Toronto Telegram,* Sept. 7, Nov. 11, *Calgary Herald,* Sept. 8, 9, *Vancouver Sun,* Sept. 13, Oct. 6, and *McGill Daily* (Montreal), Sept 29—all 1961, and *Toronto Daily Star,* April 30, 1965, on fraternities. On the alleged discriminatory policies of the Ontario College of Physicians and Surgeons, an accrediting body, see *Toronto Daily Star* for Aug. 26, 31, and Sept. 14—all 1965, and Greaves, *Negro in Canada,* pp. 69–70. See also James H. Whitelaw, "Ethnic Groups and the University" (unpubl. paper, Sir George Williams Univ., 1970), pp. 1–9.

40. See, for example, *Edmonton Journal,* Sept 6, 1957; *Calgary Albertan,* June 15, 16, 1961; *Halifax Mail-Star,* March 31, April 7, 23; *Regina Leader Post,* May 8; and *Owen Sound Sun-Times,* June 17—all 1965. I examined files, including correspondence relating to the dismissals and written work presented by the teachers involved in two of these instances, and am convinced that the dismissals did not arise from racial prejudice.

The Nova Scotian Negro was, by all objective standards, proving to be inferior in educability to whites.

This did not mean, of course, that the Negro was in fact inferior. On the contrary, as a team of Canadian social investigators pointed out in 1962, race did not determine the lower Negro standards in Halifax. Inadequate educational achievement arose from "the need for money, the belief that education would be of little help to [Negroes] in seeking employment, crowded living quarters, lack of intellectual stimulation among their peers, friends quitting school early, inferior educational facilities (under Africville's previously segregated school program at least), lack of a normal family pattern," and other class differentials.[41] The future remained gloomy, for although the repressive conditions at work were not inherent, they were real and massive, and the Negro continued to be caught up in the old, old story of frustration. The vicious cycle of poverty, ignorance, and unemployment had lasted far too long for anyone save the most idealistic to expect the Nova Scotian Negro to assimilate to the normative values of Nova Scotian society quickly or easily—or for the Nova Scotian white, however much he might be prepared to concede the Negro's inherent equality, to think of Negroes as equal in fact as well as in potential. For Negroes were not likely to become equal in fact until the slow curative power of that equal education of which the Negro leadership had so often spoken could work its way. It would not be this generation that would be liberated, but the next.

The time had come for concerted, secular action, for an attack by the province and the municipality as well as by the Negroes themselves on the problems of unemployment, substandard housing, and the resulting stultification of the educational environment. What was needed was a combination of voluntary associations and of governmental agencies interacting at all levels with the Negro communities throughout Canada and with other minority groups, and drawing upon the dominant white culture for actual support rather than for mere tolerant acquiescence. Within such associations and such agencies, and through the social communication generated by their activities, would lie yet another, and more promising, source of released strength. To create such an awareness of community should have been the task of a third traditional tool of any wronged minority, the press.[42]

41. *Conditions of the Negroes of Halifax City*, p. 19. This study was prepared in draft by Mrs. E. D. Wangenheim, who kindly gave me access to a portion of her material before publication and who talked with me at length about the report itself. Portions of the final statement are reprinted as "Socio-Economic Condition of Negroes in Halifax," in Laskin, *Social Problems: A Canadian Profile*, pp. 153–61.

42. A slightly different version of this chapter, with fuller documentation, has appeared as "Negro School Segregation in Ontario and Nova Scotia," *CHR, 50* (1969), 164–91.

13. Source of Strength?—The Press

Wherever published, the Negro newspaper has faced particular problems, and these problems have been compounded in Canada. Parochial in outlook, such papers could not expect to hold a readership beyond a quite limited area unless they tried to unite all Negroes behind activist protests and reportorial enumeration of grievances. Except for the banner of anti-slavery, however, there were no causes to be held aloft by Canada's fragmented blacks: any editor who championed colonization would be attacked by anti-emigrationists; any who counseled begging in order to stay in business would lose those who saw solicitation as degrading. The papers reflected the divisive moments and uncertain goals of the Negroes themselves; and while words of protest are often ennobling, tones of grievance are too often merely negative and enfeebling. Just as small-town weeklies have done, Negro newspapers turned more and more to highly local social news and columnists in order to hold their readers, thus increasing their parochialism. While many weekly newspapers could survive and, in some instances, grow fat in the nineteenth century by serving a geographically defined advertising base, the Negro communities had few businessmen who needed to, or who could afford to, advertise. White businessmen seldom supported such papers, since they competed with the more widely circulated journals that constituted the natural vehicle for reaching the wider audience, and since most literate Negroes read the white newspapers as well. And while most ethnic newspapers might survive on language alone, offering the only material that newly arrived immigrants could read, the Negro papers were in direct competition with the nonethnic press, and were read merely as supplements to the metropolitan dailies which by the mid-1850's had become a necessity in the Canadas.[1] In 1970 there were some two hundred ethnic publications in Canada, one with a continuous life of eighty years, thirty-five in the Ukrainian language

1. Negro readers usually abandon their newspapers in moments of crisis, for they recognize that the large metropolitan dailies will provide greater news coverage whenever a Negro-oriented story impinges sufficiently upon the white community. Thus, during interracial rioting in Watts, a suburb of Los Angeles, in August of 1965, the influence of the two local Negro newspapers, the *Sentinel* and the *Herald,* was minimal. They were overwhelmed by California's mass press, and both became mirrors of public opinion among blacks rather than leaders of that opinion. See Frederic C. Coonradt, *The Negro News Media and the Los Angeles Riots* (Los Angeles, 1965), passim.

alone. In Canada's history there were twenty-three Black publications, with only three surviving 1970. The average life of the publications had been less than two and a half years.

That Negro periodicals survived for even two years plus in British North America testified to the growing literacy of the Negroes. Although not one of these papers was financially successful, they did provide the Negro with another potential source of strength. They rallied Negro opinion on local issues, kept Negro voters in line, attracted modest political advertising in election years, bolstered the churches with an ardent Protestant fundamentalism, and joined the chorus that insisted on education. Before the Civil War they provided information on the growing abolitionist movement in the United States, reprinting copious extracts from other antislavery and Northern journals, and into the early twentieth century they were forthright in their attacks upon the more obvious forms of discrimination. They survived, if barely and briefly, on the quite legitimate fear of the Negro that other newspapers either would ignore him entirely or would associate him exclusively with crime reports.[2]

All failed. Negro communities were too transient, readerships too small, levels of education too low, advertisers too few, subscribers too faithless, the competition from other English-language newspapers too great for survival. Some of the papers were well-edited; indeed, *Provincial Freeman,* published between 1853 and 1858, was as good as any weekly paper in Canada West; and *The Clarion,* edited in New Glasgow, Nova Scotia, between 1947 and 1956, was as creditable as any within its county. Negro newspapers did not fail for lack of literary quality, although such lack was evident in some, but rather for want of business ability. And by the time such ability was available, in the years following World War II, the metropolitan press had discovered the Negro and often was giving greater, more effective, and certainly more immediate attention to instances of discrimination than any weekly paper could hope to do. Negro apathy did not destroy the Negro press in Toronto; a rising awareness within the rooms of the *Toronto Star* and *Telegram* of the newsworthy nature of discriminatory practices brought Negro readers to these papers and, in 1961, helped put an end to the last of the older Toronto Negro journals.[3]

2. While the metropolitan newspapers were giving space to Negro social news by the late 1950s, the small-town weeklies still were not. An examination of the *Maidstone Mirror* for 1958–64, of *The Galiano Islander* (later *The Gulf Islander*) for 1958–62, and of *Driftwood,* published from 1960 to 1962 at Ganges, on Saltspring Island—all from communities with proportionately representative Negro populations —revealed no Negro news as such.

3. See Emma Lou Thornbrough, "American Negro Newspapers, 1880–1914," *Business History Review, 40* (1966), 467–90.

Competition from Negro newspapers in the United States also stifled Canadian Negro efforts. The first black newspaper, *Freedom's Journal,* published in New York City in 1827, was edited by John Browne Russwurm, a Jamaican-born mulatto who went to school in Lower Canada, and by Samuel Cornish, who later edited three other antislavery sheets; as noted earlier, they sent agents throughout the Northern states and into British North America to solicit advertisements and subscriptions. Although this effort expired within two years, the pattern set by Russwurm and Cornish was followed by dozens of American-based Negro newspapers for the following century and a half. Prior to the Civil War, American editors often hired fugitives on a commission basis to peddle copies of their papers to the growing British North American settlements, and Benjamin Lundy's *Genius of Universal Emancipation,* Garrison's *Liberator,* and *The Friend of Man*—issued by the New York State Anti-Slavery Society in Utica from 1836 until 1841, under the editorship of William Goodell—circulated quite widely west and north of Toronto. Following the war, with the flowering of an independent Negro press, the larger Northern dailies and weeklies also sought out Canadian readers. The *Boston Colored American, Pittsburgh Courier, Chicago Defender, Saint Paul Broadax,* and *San Francisco Elevator* mailed copies into Canada, and in 1912 the *Detroit Informer* introduced a column on "Our Canadian Cousins" which dealt with the area from Toronto west, while retaining a separate "Across the River" section on Windsor.[4] Canadian Negroes often worked for Detroit-based enterprises, and one of the four editors of the *Detroit Plaindealer* was William H. Stowers, who had been born in Canada West. Not surprisingly, therefore, there were no post-Civil War Negro newspapers in Windsor; for the *Plaindealer,* founded in 1883, the *Informer,* the *Leader* (especially after 1910), the sensational *Michigan Chronicle,* which began in 1937, and after 1944 the *Sun* provided the south shore of the Detroit River with all of the Negro news it could absorb.[5]

By the early twentieth century the Negro press in the United States was big business, and in many instances the more successful newspapers even from cities well removed from the border were able to expand into the Canadian market. By 1899 there were three Negro dailies and one hundred and thirty-six weeklies in the United States; at that time there were none in Canada. By 1921 there were four hundred and ninety-two Negro journals in the United States and again none in Canada. Eleven years later many of the poverty-stricken American efforts had vanished or united with larger newspapers, but there still were over two hundred

4. March 16; San Francisco *Elevator,* May 14, 1869. A file of *The Informer* may be consulted at LC.

5. I. Garland Penn, *The Afro-American Press and Its Editors* (Springfield, Mass., 1891), p. 162. Files of these newspapers may be found in the Detroit Public Library.

and fifty Negro periodicals in the United States and only one in Canada. Few of these publications gave more than the most cursory and apparently accidental attention to Canadian Negro news, however, and most Negroes within the Dominion must have continued to turn to the larger Canadian metropolitan dailies or to local white weekly papers. By 1950 at least 2,700 Negro newspapers had been founded in the United States since *Freedom's Journal* was first published, while there had been thirteen in Canada, the first dating from 1851; many of the American papers had been dailies, while none of the Canadian efforts appeared more often than weekly, and monthly publication was usual, so that news was stale long before it was read. Yet, only two of the editors recognized that, by virtue of infrequent performance, their natural competition was with magazines. Most held to the format of the newspaper when, in fact, they were less than newspapers—outlets for opinion, publications of Negro short stories and poetry,[6] exhortations to be up and doing, and advertising media.[7]

The Canadian newspapers faced special problems as well. In the United States the Negro often remained loyal to his newspapers even as his educational level rose, while in Canada most blacks did not wish to be identified with the unsophisticated and unfashionable Negro efforts. The Canadian tendency to denote ethnic identity in terms of language gave rise to a vigorous Ethnic Press Federation, which no Negro newspaper could or would join.[8] No Canadian Negro newspapers affiliated with either the Afro-American Press Association or the Canadian Press Association. None submitted its records to the Audit Bureau of Circulation. Only one was a subscriber to the Associated Negro Press, founded in 1919. Most papers cost too much in a land where black wages were often half those the Negro could earn in the United States: when a daily newspaper could

6. Blacks in Canada publish in "white" journals as well, of course. The poetess Anna M. Henderson, for example, has written for *Canadian Poetry Magazine, 2* (1937); *4* (1939); and *Atlantic Advocate, 50* (March, 1960), as well as publishing a collection of her work. Her poems also appear in Ethel H. Bennett, comp., *New Harvesting: Contemporary Canadian Poetry, 1918–1938* (Toronto, 1938), pp. 54, 194. Austin C. Clarke, a Barbadian by birth, often writes for the better literary journals and is a novelist and editor of stature. Mervyn Procope is another serious poet who does not restrict himself to a black audience, as his *Energy = Mercy Squared* (Toronto, [1966]) shows; nor does Raymond Spence, author of *Nothing Black but a Cadillac*. Clarke is clearly the best established black writer in Canada, however.

7. See Frederick G. Detweiler, *The Negro Press in the United States* (Chicago, 1922), p. 1; Maxwell Roy Brooks, "A Sociological Interpretation of the Negro Newspaper" (M.A. thesis, Ohio State Univ., 1937), p. 18; Armistead Scott Pride, "A Register and History of Negro Newspapers in the United States: 1827–1850" (Ph.D. diss., Northwestern Univ., 1950), pp. 3, 5, 53.

8. Canada Ethnic Press Federation, *Fact File* [1964] (Winnipeg, 1963), no pagination, with insertion.

be purchased for five cents, a price twice that for a four-page monthly sheet must have seemed extravagant to many. Canadian postal increases in 1914 and again in 1921 tended to weigh against weekly papers and in favor of dailies, and all Negro newspapers then and since suffered from the postal rates (except for the period 1882–98, when newspapers in Canada were mailed post free) and, also in common with all Canadian newspapers, from increasing newsprint costs.

Following World War II, competition from American Negro magazines was to be added to the disadvantages of Canadian journalism. From 1947 —the second year of its publication—the Chicago-based *Ebony,* modeled on another American invader, *Life,* contained frequent references to Canada and had readers ranging across the Dominion. One also finds Canadian Negro news in such journals as *Crisis,* the organ of the National Association for the Advancement of Colored People, *Negro World,* the National Urban League's *Opportunity,* and *Common Sense Historical Reviews.* The last was a hodgepodge of misprinted, misstated, and mis-spelled materials, poetry, and blank pages, published in Chicago from 1942 until 1955 by Ira O. Guy, and consistent only in its attachment to the African Methodist Episcopal Church. A British Negro monthly, *Bronze,* published between 1954 and 1955, also gave attention to Canada, as did *Muhammad Speaks,* the Black Muslim journal, beginning in 1970.[9]

The earliest Canadian Negro newspapers were written for and often by fugitive slaves. The first, *The British American,* appeared in Toronto in March of 1845 and survived less than a month.[10] The best, *The Provincial Freeman,* was launched in March 1853, in Windsor, Canada West.[11] The

9. *Ebony,* for example, gave attention to Canadian developments in thirteen is-sues between 1947 and 1959. The writer asked each surviving publication for Ca-nadian circulation figures in 1965, but none could supply them.

10. While I have found no copy of this newspaper, its existence is attested to by the *Hamilon Bee* of February 4 and March 25, 1845, copies of which are in the Fred Landon Collection.

11. A bound volume of *The Provincial Freeman* for March 24, 1853, to Sep-tember 15, 1857, may be found in the Library of the University of Pennsylvania in Philadelphia. The paper has been microfilmed. There is a photostatic copy of the issue for November 18, 1854, in the Smith College Library, and TPL holds an origi-nal of the same issue. In March 1855, the newspaper's title was changed to *The Provincial Freeman and Weekly Advertiser.* On its history, see Alexander L. Murray, "The Provincial Freeman: A New Source for the History of the Negro in Canada and the United States," *JNH, 44* (1959), 123–35, or the same article, somewhat shortened and with an altered title, in *Ontario History, 51* (1959), 25–31; and Edith G. Firth, ed., *Early Toronto Newspapers, 1793–1867* . . . (Toronto, 1961), pp. 24, 27. *The Canada Directory for 1857–58* (Montreal, 1857), p. 1040, gives "J. D. Shadd" as publisher, printer, and proprietor, and shows that the *Freeman* was issued until November of 1857, and perhaps later, although no copies have been found past September.

redoubtable Samuel Ringgold Ward was its owner and editor, and Mary Ann Shadd, then author of an 1852 pamphlet, *Notes on Canada West,*[12] was listed as publishing agent. The first issue was meant to be an advertisement for a fuller newspaper to come. It was well-printed and well-edited, and its promoters were to make it the most vigorous Negro newspaper Canada would see, striking out at slavery, drunkenness, begging ministers, segregated black settlements, and all that might make the black man subservient.[13] Regular publication would begin in London or Toronto, Ward promised, as soon as cash subscriptions made this possible. His name, the caution with which the enterprise was launched, and the fully competitive format all promised well for the future, as did Ward's commonsense observation that "the colored people are precisely like any other people, especially are they like any other ignorant people." He guaranteed that a committee on publication drawn from Windsor, Buxton, Chatham, London, Hamilton, and St. Catharines would assure province-wide news coverage.[14]

The paper did not appear again, however, until March of 1854, a year later, and this time in Toronto. In the summer of 1855 the editors moved to Chatham, taking their printing press with them, and there they became the official printers to the Chatham Town Council. In the meantime, Ward had left for Britain and the controversial William P. Newman had become nominal editor. Mary Ann Shadd was the true editor, however, as the paper's agent in Philadelphia, William Still, recognized; Daniel Alexander Payne, hearing her give two lectures in Chicago in December of 1855, also referred to her as the editor and financier of the *Freeman.* In the spring of 1856 H. Ford Douglass, Isaac (or Israel) D. Shadd, and Mary openly assumed a shared editorial responsibility.[15]

Vigorous, honest, and outspoken, but with little gift for eloquence, Mary Shadd saw the newspaper as the most effective medium for her message. That message in itself was simple, and it differed markedly from what Henry Bibb and others were writing at the time in the competitive Negro sheet, *Voice of the Fugitive.* As the title of the latter implied, Bibb's paper was meant to appeal to those fugitive slaves who thought of themselves as living a life in exile, awaiting the time when they might return to a United States cleansed of slavery. Mary Ann Shadd would have none of this sense of impermanence; it would slow the efforts of Negroes in Canada who should be getting on with the daily business of making a life for

12. I have been unable to locate this publication.

13. For the rôle of *The Provincial Freeman* in Canada West's communitarian controversy, see Chapters 7 and 8, supra, pp. 202–03, 206–08, 221, 225–26, 261, 266–68.

14. March 24, 1853; *Toronto Globe,* April 3, 1854.

15. *London* (Ont.) *Free Press,* Aug. 6, 1959; Payne, *Recollections,* pp. 126–27.

themselves. She did not consider herself an exile and she attacked the *Voice* for encouraging such an attitude. Home, she made clear, was now Canada West. Worried by the constant quarrelling within the Negro leadership, and by the unwillingness of different black groups to work together in harmony because of too many centripetal forces operating from the United States, she warned the Negroes that they must become British. She found their "caucuses, conventions, [and] resolutions" fruitless, since "the pretended leaders of the people" always had to return to them, "like a dog to his vomit," for more support.

Ultimately *The Provincial Freeman* was too fractious for its small audience. Poverty-striken, unlettered fugitives could not read the paper, and of those Negroes in Canada who could, many were alienated by the free-wheeling way in which its editors lay about themselves. The newspaper supported the Conservative party after 1856, likening the reform party of George Brown, toward which many black leaders increasingly looked, to the Locofocos in the United States: *"Clear Grit,* Reform and Radical," said the paper, "are words that belong to the vocabulary of Yankeedom." Involved with the True Band of Amherstburg, accepting money from a missionary society while simultaneously disclaiming it, and attacking the Refugee Home Society, the American Missionary Association, Josiah Henson, and Hiram Wilson with equal fervor, Mary Shadd served meat strong even for the time, and few cared to digest it. In 1858, when John Brown held his meetings in Chatham, he used the *Freeman's* offices on one occasion; by the beginning of 1859, and most probably earlier, the newspaper had stopped publishing.[16]

The *Voice of the Fugitive* had preceded and also predeceased its competitor.[17] Published in Sandwich and Windsor by Henry Bibb between 1851 and 1853, the *Voice* probably reached more Negroes than the *Freeman* did, and it was quoted widely in the Northern abolitionist press. Born in Shelby County, Kentucky, in 1815, Bibb had escaped from slavery five times. On the second of these occasions, in 1838, and on the last, apparently in 1842 when he went to live in Detroit, he traveled in the Canadas. Until 1849 he was active in the antislavery cause in the border area and in Ohio and New York; he then moved to Canada West where he began a campaign against Negrophobia. At first he, Ward, and Mary

16. *Provincial Freeman,* March 23, 1853, March 25, 1854, June 4, 1856, Jan. 31, April 11, May 2, 1857; Lauriston, *Romantic Kent,* p. 298; Ward, Autobiography, pp. 126–43, 227–28.

17. A file of the *Voice of the Fugitive* for Jan 1, 1851 to Dec. 16, 1852, is in the Burton Historical Collection of the Detroit Public Library. The file has been microfilmed. Issues for Jan. 1, 15, 21, March 21, 26, and Nov. 5, 1851, are in the library of the University of Western Ontario. Robert W. S. Mackay, *A Supplement to the Canada Directory . . . to April, 1853* (Montreal, 1853), p. 361, suggests that the paper was published into 1853.

Shadd were in agreement on most issues, and early in 1852 Bibb's *Voice* joined theirs in condemning the growing number of "begging agents." But Bibb's intimate involvement in the Refugee Home Society, and the fact that he was the recording secretary of the Sandwich Convention, of which Josiah Henson was president, introduced elements of strain between them. Bibb broke any slender ties that remained when he revealed that Mary had received support from the American Missionary Association while teaching in Windsor. These quarrels, proximity to Detroit and its better newspapers, and a loss of interest on Bibb's part led to the demise of the *Voice of the Fugitive* in 1853.[18]

Two other Negro-oriented newspapers struggled for survival in Canada West between 1856 and 1860. The first of these, *The Voice of the Bondsman,* was issued at Stratford by J. J. E. Linton, the Presbyterian abolitionist from Scotland who most persistently attacked fellowshipping with slaveholders. Linton had written for *The Provincial Freeman* until the end of 1856, when he decided that a louder voice was needed for his analysis of the church problem. In November he distributed his five thousand free copies of a first number, and the following month he gave away seven thousand copies of a second issue, only to abandon his efforts in the new year when he found that this particular antislavery message attracted only a miniscule following.[19]

Four years later Reverend A. R. Green of the new British Methodist Episcopal Church launched *The True Royalist and Weekly Intelligencer* in Windsor. Wishing to stress the British loyalties of the BME congregations, he obtained Bishop Nazrey's permission to begin his paper and solicited support from Rowland Wingfield, leader of Anderdon's black community, only to abandon the effort after some ten numbers were published in Windsor and Detroit over thirteen months in 1860 and 1861. In time Green broke with the BME Church and moved to Washington, and Wingfield left for Guelph. *The True Royalist,* while intended for Negroes, contained little news that was racial, rather discussing dissension within the church and preaching political conservatism and obedience to the Queen.

The depression of 1857 and the Civil War ended all Negro newspapers in the Canadas. With the rapid movement of the fugitive slaves back to the United States following the war, no audience existed for any further

18. Bibb, *Narrative of the Life and Adventures,* pp. 13, 21, 46–62, 74–77, 82, 84–89, 134, 150, 169–72, 174–91, 195–96; Silas Farmer, *The History of Detroit and Michigan, or The Metropolis Illustrated* (Detroit, 1884), pp. 346–47; Pease, and Pease, *Black Utopia,* pp. 82, 111–12, 116–19; Murray, "Canada and the Anglo-American Anti-Slavery Movement," pp. 337, 410, 418–19, 424–27, 435–36.

19. *Toronto Globe,* July 23, 1856, and *Voice of the Bondsman* (Dec. 1856), one copy of which is in the Library of the University of Western Ontario. On Linton, see supra, pp. 221–23, 261–62.

enterprises of this kind. Not until 1881 did a Negro found another newspaper in Canada, and then the new effort was a four-page monthly which, despite declarations of political independence, seems to have been intended largely to keep the Negro population of Hamilton firmly within the conservative camp. This paper, *The British Lion,* was edited by Charles A. Johnson, and it appeared sporadically until 1892 and possibly a little later, enjoying Canada's brief period of free mailing privileges for news sheets, without having any apparent effect outside its immediate, political and "African" circle.[20]

The most interesting and certainly the most intellectually ambitious effort toward a Negro publication in Canada was a short-lived monthly, *Neith,* a "Magazine of Literature, Science, Art, Philosophy, Jurisprudence, Criticism, History, Reform, Economics," edited in Saint John, New Brunswick, by A. B. Walker.[21] A barrister and an orator of considerable talent, Walker was also a Negro separatist and early advocate of black power. Born in British Columbia, he took a law degree in the United States and toured the South lecturing on "the philosophy of race development from a Canadian standpoint." In 1889 he delivered a well-received address at the Wheat Street Baptist Church in Atlanta, an address which was a black version of Russell Conwell's celebrated "Acres of Diamonds" speech. He urged all Negroes to make "periodical visits to Great Britain and Ireland," the centers of civilization, where there was no racial prejudice, and he felt that all should emulate the virtues of English gentlemen, who are "a chosen people who cling to [God's] Right Hand." In Galt, Ontario, he boasted of his "pure Abyssinian lineage" which he could trace back fifty-eight thousand years and which was free of the slavery which had overtaken less intelligent lines.[22]

20. Two copies of *The True Royalist*—those for May 20, 1860 and June 21, 1861—have survived and are in the Fort Malden Museum. On Wingfield, see *Amherstburg Courier,* June 2 1849. See also Morrison, *Garden Gateway,* p. 50. Despite searching the Hamilton Public Library and other Ontario and Negro-related archives in general, and despite several private inquiries and advertisements, the author has been unable to locate a single copy of *The British Lion.* It is cited, and its political affiliation is given, in *The Canadian Newspaper Directory . . .* (Montreal, 1892), p. 87, and in *N.W. Ayer & Son's American Newspaper Annual* (Philadelphia, 1883), p. 614, and subsequently from 1884 (but it is dropped from the 1890 edition). It also appears in *Geo. P. Rowell & Co's American Newspaper Directory . . .* (New York, 1885), *17,* 716, and subsequently in 1886 and 1888, although not in 1890. While *The Desbarat's Newspaper Directory 1904–1905* (Montreal, n.d.), p. 123, listed the *Lion,* it almost certainly had ceased publication much earlier. On Johnson, see *Hamilton Spectator,* Dec. 29, 1892.

21. NBM holds a broken file of *Neith.*

22. Walker, *The Negro Problem; or, The Philosophy of Race Development from a Canadian Standpoint* ([Atlanta, 1890?]), p. 3; W. G. MacFarlane, *New Brunswick*

Walker moved to Saint John in 1890, living at first with a tailor while soliciting funds for Negro training schools in the British West Indies.[23] As the only Negro barrister in the Maritimes, he quickly became an intermediary between Negro voters and the Conservative Party. He delivered the black vote to Sir Charles Tupper, who in 1896 briefly became the federal prime minister, and apparently he expected to be elevated to the position of Queen's counsel for his efforts. Tupper clearly never made any such promise, but two of the city's members of Parliament and the provincial minister of justice may have done so; for in August of that year, shortly after Tupper's defeat at the hands of Sir Wilfrid Laurier's Liberal Party, Walker wrote to Laurier that as "a coloredman . . . the Ministry did not care one snap of the finger whether my claims or rights were considered or not." For eighteen years, he confessed, he had bowed down and worshipped Conservative idols, and the only reward that Negroes had received was the appointment of one day-laborer in the Saint John Post Office. He could not expect a Liberal cabinet to grant him the honor his own party had refused him, he concluded, and he was prepared to emigrate to the United States.

Sir Oliver Mowat, the newly designated minister of justice in Laurier's cabinet, advised the prime minister to tell Walker that when a new list of Queen's counsels was prepared, his name would be considered without regard to race. This promise pleased the black barrister, and he replied in tones so fulsome that Laurier appears not to have taken up the correspondence again. Even in an age of political hyperbole, Laurier cannot have cared to be likened unto

> a mighty host of mighty leaders in civilization—leaders in jurisprudence, leaders in divinity, leaders in philosophy, leaders in poetry, leaders in romance, and leaders in oratory—such as, Domat, Montesquieu, Pothier, Gambetta; Massillon; Descartes, Melebranche [sic], Compte; Lamartine, Hugo; Balzac, Dumas, Zola; Molière and Fenelon— . . . most spelndid [sic] and magnificent galaxy . . . whose exalted brilliancy and learning and probity have made you the first statesman in the Dominion.

In any case, Laurier soon was persuaded by his minister for the interior, Clifford Sifton, to give thought to barring Negro entry into Canada, and Walker never became a Queen's counsel.[24]

Bibliography: The Books and Writers of the Province (Saint John, 1895), p. 82; Hamilton Public Library, Scrap Books, 91: no. 90.

23. *McAlpine's Saint John City Directory for 1890–91* . . . (Saint John, N.B., 1890), pp. 196, 396, 672, 695.

24. PAC, Laurier Papers, *17*, 6207–10, 6212–14: Walker to Laurier, Aug. 3, 28, and Mowat to Laurier, Aug. 11, all 1896.

Walker did become a journalist, however, for in 1903 he launched
Neith. A substantial monthly magazine which sold for ten cents a copy,
it was well-edited and intelligently conceived. Roughly half of each issue
of sixty-two pages was devoted to Negro materials in order, as Walker
wrote, "to set people thinking, to extirpate erroneous ideas, to advance
the spirit of freedom, to stir up a feeling of brothership among all men,
and to spread Christian civilization throughout Africa." While Walker
was a Conservative again, as his editorials on labor unions and politics
showed, he was ahead of his times in many ways. He argued that South
African natives should be sent to Tuskegee and to the Ontario Agricultural College to study farming, he attacked Thomas Dixon, Jr.'s racist
novel, *The Leopard's Spots,* praised Theodore Roosevelt for appointing
Negroes to office, and informed any unlikely female "Georgia cracker"
readers he might have that a "single drop" of Negro blood would give
them "a pretty face and figure." Walker also used words not frequently
found in Canadian journals of the time—declaring southern Negroes less
prone to rape than southern whites—and he described a lynching in
horrific terms. He opposed the industrial training program advocated by
Booker T. Washington, who was a deluded man: "All that the oily-
tongued, two-faced wise acres have had to do has been to command him
to dig and sweat and bleed, and he has immediately lifted his hat and
made an obeisance, and, without even a sigh or a frown, set to digging
and sweating and bleeding." [25]

In response to Washington, Walker advocated colonization in Africa,
where Canadian, West Indian, and American Negroes might live under
British rule in an interracial colony of their own and "worship the God
and the Christ of the English." By "fraternal suasion" such a colony could
absorb all of Africa in twenty-five years, creating a British and Christian
"empire of dazzling glory and power." In time, Walker concluded, the
Negro race would overtake all others, if ten thousand "clever Negroes,
Puritanic Negroes, trained Negroes" would now come forward to carry
the black man's burden to Africa. He claimed to have talked with Sir
John A. Macdonald, the much-revered father of the Canadian Confederation, about colonization during a private interview in Ottawa. Since Macdonald had died in 1891, he could not deny the meeting, in which Walker
said he took down in shorthand notes Macdonald's conclusion that emigration was "the only correct way to solve the Negro Problem, and lift
the Negro race up to the level of the Anglo-Saxon." However, Walker
did not press his colonization plans, and while he traveled throughout the
Maritimes to solicit advertisements for *Neith,* he used neither the alleged

25. *Neith, 1* (1903), 1, 17, 18.

interview with Macdonald nor his general interest in Africa as an excuse to launch an emigration scheme of his own. Indeed, Walker's own plans remained vague to the end.[26]

For *Neith* that end came quickly. The first number was attacked by *The New Freeman,* a Roman Catholic newspaper published in Saint John, for being anti-Catholic, for praising the immoral literature of Emile Zola, and for the "exaggerated thought and extravagant language" to which it found the Negro race addicted. Other papers thought Walker disloyal; and accordingly in his second number he protested that *Neith* was "not a Negro magazine, nor a Caucasian magazine, but a Canadian magazine inspired with Canadian principles of Liberty and Equity. . . . That we discuss the Negro a good deal is not because we belong to the Negro type of the genus homo, but because the Negro is downtrodden, and because we are Canadian, and, also, because the Canadian people, white and black, believe in fair play." In response to the *Freeman,* Walker added, somewhat irrelevantly, "We live in Canada, and not in Mississippi." Nonetheless, Walker did not stand firm, for he increased his advertising content, cut back on his forthright editorials, reduced Negro material, and gave increasing space to articles by his son George on literature, including highly favorable reviews of the novels of H. Rider Haggard, no believer in African equality. "Neith shall be British to the very core," Walker promised. By January 1904, *Neith* had twice fallen behind on an already revised publication schedule, and although its editor bravely inscribed "No Surrender, is our slogan" across his journal, the Ethiopian divinity of thunder and tempest sank without a trace. Walker remained in Saint John until 1905, turning back to his advocacy of African colonization, and then left, apparently for Boston.[27]

The demise of *Neith* was unfortunately representative. Had Walker established his journal in Ontario, where there was a larger and somewhat more prosperous Negro audience, and had he been willing to be uncompromisingly Negro as an editor, rather than tempering his own convictions and binding his often muscular prose with basically irrelevant political and religious hesitations, he might have succeeded. For Walker was clearly a man of exceptional intelligence, dedication, and energy, and for all of its short life, *Neith* introduced into Canadian journalism a magazine fully the equal of most monthly literary periodicals of the time

26. *Neith, 1* (1903), 17, 21–25, 180–81.

27. Ibid., pp. 1–3, 25, 46, 53–58, 63–64, 70–72, 98–100, 108–10, 131–33; *Neith* (1904), pp. 199, 211–16; *Saint John New Freeman,* March 7, April 11, 1903 (consulted in the office of the *New Freeman*); *Liberia and West Africa, 7* (1905), 2; *Saint John Daily Telegraph,* Feb. 10, 1905.

and to Negro journalism as a whole a publication superior to most. No other Canadian Negro journal was to be so competently edited, even though at least one was to win substantially greater success.

The Dawn of Tomorrow, founded in London, Ontario in 1923, and published there until 1966, was to be a marginal exception to the story of persistent Canadian failure. Its owner and editor was James F. Jenkins, who was born in Georgia, educated at the University of Atlanta, and who came to London in 1904 when he was twenty years old. An eight-page weekly, *Dawn* drew heavily upon the Associated Negro Press in Chicago for most of its news, and it was at once attacked by white Canadians for disloyalty and by black Canadians for its persistent use of the word *Negro* as taken from its American sources, rather than *coloured,* as many preferred to be called. Until the depression, circulation ran between four and five thousand copies of each issue. In 1926 the paper dropped to twice-monthly publication, and Jenkins's death in 1931 further cut into sales; but his widow continued to edit it in his name, largely as a memorial, until 1938 when it virtually ceased publication. Thereafter *Dawn* appeared occasionally—twice in 1939, for example—with paraphrased reprints of Jenkins's old editorials. In 1947 Mrs. Jenkins, now remarried, attempted to build circulation once again and in 1950 claimed to have reached the former level of five thousand copies. *Dawn* continues to be listed in the standard directories, although since 1947 and perhaps earlier it had been distributed to most readers free of charge as an advertising sheet, and it had ceased to function as a genuine newspaper.[28]

Dawn's first editor began with several advantages. London was the chief metropolitan center for the Negro concentration between Toronto and Windsor, and postal and other communications turned upon the city. Jenkins was a man of education who, at the time of his death, had become an associate judge of the Juvenile Court in London. The newspaper was the official voice of the Canadian League for the Advancement of Colored People, and it was able to use syndicated Negro news. A professional and scholarly quarterly, *The Journal of Negro History,* which had begun publication in Washington in 1915, allowed Jenkins to reprint extracts from its pages. Most important, Jenkins received the support of several influential members within the community at large. Fred Landon, then the city's public librarian and a former newspaper

28. *Dawn of Tomorrow,* July 14, Aug. 11, 1923, July 12, 1924, May 1, 1926, April, 1935; n.s., *4* (1947), 1; *London Free Press,* July 16, 1923, May 6, 8, July 30, 1931, Sept. 15, 1950; *Ayer & Son's American Newspaper Annual* (1925), p. 1203, and in each issue from 1926–66, showing circulation figures as reported by the publisher, and shifting publication dates and subscription lists. At various times *Ayer & Son's* states that *Dawn* was first issued in 1921 or 1922 (see 1966 ed., p. 1196).

man who had taken a deep personal interest in Negro history, wrote for *The Dawn of Tomorrow* and advised on editorial problems; and William Renwick Riddell, the jurist and authority on the slave period of Canadian history, also contributed material. A number of substantial advertisers, an intelligent assistant editor, Robert Paris Edwards—who was based in Toronto—and a network of apparently dependable social correspondents from as far away as Edmonton, Montreal, and New Glasgow, as well as from Ontario's communities, gave the initial issues a prosperous look. The result was a middle-class, nonsensational, somewhat dull publication, which contained nothing of interest to children, rather too much news from the United States, and copious social and religious notes.[29]

The attachment to the Canadian League for the Advancement of Colored People injected a tone of militancy into *Dawn's* editorial pages, however, a tone which except for *Neith* had been absent from Canadian Negro journalism since the days of *The Provincial Freeman*. While race sensitivity had not developed to the point that advertisements for "Mammy's Wash-day Smile," a cleaning agent, would be rejected, race consciousness was clear enough. Readers were reminded that Negro labor had built the seven wonders of the world and that, as a commodity, labor gave the black man power; they were encouraged to think of the Chinese and of all non-Caucasian peoples as being natural allies of the League, and they were told to emulate specific successful Negroes—usually Americans —such as the singers Marian Anderson and Roland Hayes. In order to assure continued loyalty to "One King, one flag, and one Empire," Jenkins advocated mass Negro colonization of Canada. In 1923, in the face of Canadian opposition to Negro immigrants, the editor asked for two million Negroes of "the better class," and suggested that black Canadians should visit the American South to attract settlers, "men who are real men." Noting that Negro ministers, in particular, opposed such growth for fear that prejudice would increase among whites, Jenkins warned against churches that did not have the courage of their convictions, while cautioning his readers not to turn to the opposite extreme of black racism, as Marcus Garvey then was suggesting, adopting the "foolish, grotesque and idolatrous" notion that God was black. Jenkins frequently wrote on "the Joy of Being Black," on the necessity to vote as a solid bloc, and on one hundred percent Canadianism.[30]

29. Landon to author, April 14, 1965; *JNH, 16* (1931), 343; *Dawn of Tomorrow,* July 14, Oct. 20, 27, 1923, Sept. 20, 1924, Feb 26, 1929, Aug. 29, 1931.

30. *Dawn of Tomorrow,* Aug. 4, 18, 25, Sept. 1, Oct. 13, 20, Nov. 3, 1923, Jan. 26, Feb. 23, April 26, May 10, Sept. 20, 1924, May 16, Oct. 16, Oct. 24, 1925, Feb. 26, 1929; Canadian League for the Advancement of Colored People, *Report for 1932 and Appeal for 1933* ([London, n.d.]).

Under Jenkins's editorship, *The Dawn of Tomorrow* attacked the quiescent Negro churches of Ontario in particular. Complaining that the only source of leadership in Canada lay with the ministry, since there were few Negro physicians, lawyers, or teachers, he accused the churchmen of having no social sense, of failing "to stand by their guns and proclaim the message of human Brotherhood." There were too many congregations, he thought, thus keeping all impoverished. Hopeful of AME and BME entry into the United Church of Canada, between 1925 and 1929 Jenkins asked for conferences with white Methodist, Presbyterian, and Congregational spokesmen, and he accused the Reverend H. D. Wright, General Superintendent of the BME Church, of obstructionism. Jenkins, a member of the BME church in London, broke with his pastor over the question of union, and Wright felt the editor's charges were sufficiently serious to warrant a special church meeting, called in Brantford in February 1929, in which Jenkins was denounced for false reporting. The BME Church had not declared itself with respect to ecumenicism at all, the special committee concluded, unwittingly confirming Jenkins's own contention that BME leadership was doing nothing to make wider church union possible. Someday, he wrote, there would have to be a movement larger, better directed, and more courageous than the church had proved to be, for it had failed to improve the Negro's condition in Canada. For praise he singled out the Toronto Negro Business League, founded in 1924; for he almost alone among Negro newspaper editors in Canada insisted that secular institutions were needed to solve secular problems.[31]

Other Negro-related newspapers were even more ephemeral and less effective. Between 1934 and 1941, *The Free Lance,* self-styled "Canada's Greatest Negro Weekly," appeared in Montreal. In 1935 there were two other quite brief ventures into Negro-related journalism, *The Outcome,* also in Montreal, and *The Canadian Tribune,* a white working-class paper published in the Negro district of Toronto which, before it grew silent in 1946, had turned well to the left politically. *The Free Lance* was significant largely for its dedication to the idea of "Afro-Canadianism," a concept much modified in two racially aware successors, *The Canadian Negro,* which began in Toronto in 1953, and *Africa Speaks,* a slightly later Toronto monthly. For a few months of World War II *The Afro-Beacon* came out of Toronto to exhort Negroes to help in the defense of Canada, just as J. R. B. Whitney's short-lived *Canadian Observer* had urged Negroes to enlist during World War I. In 1966 a Negro journalist in Halifax, Denfield Grant, launched a monthly, *Coppertone,* which did not survive the first two issues; and in 1965 a group of young Toronto Negroes who wished to stress their sense of identification with West

31. *Dawn of Tomorrow,* Jan. 19, 1924, Jan. 31, June 27, Oct. 3, Aug. 29, 1925, Feb. 26, 1929.

Indian and black African students and workers in the city began to mimeograph *Ebo Voice,* an occasional publication not seen after the end of the year. This was the same year in which the Negro Citizenship Association of Montreal initiated a quarterly, *Expression,* under the editorship of Messrs. Carl Taylor and Donald McPhie. In April 1967 the monthly *West Indian News Observer* was begun in Toronto, to die in January of 1969. *Cotopaxi,* speaking for "The Third World of the Americas," began late in 1968 under Jan Carew, a novelist from Guyana, but did not continue after its first excellent number, and Carew left for the United States in 1970. *Progress,* an annual publication edited by Walter Perry in conjunction with the emancipation celebrations held in Windsor, Ontario, could therefore declare itself to be "the oldest international colored publication in the world," even though it was little more than a souvenir for the yearly holiday and, while it sold well, was not a newspaper except by self-nomination.[32] However, the *News Observer* was reborn in Toronto in February 1969 as a tabloid, *Contrast,* under the editorial guidance of a Jamaican, Olivia Grange-Walker, and of A. W. Hamilton. While stating that it was "Serving the Black Community Coast to Coast," the twice-monthly journal appealed largely to West Indian readers. With *Contrast,* a Black—as distinct from Negro—press was launched.

During World War II the Negro press in North America grew, for the general concern with reform associated with the defeat of Nazi Germany gave American Negro newspapers ample opportunity to speak out on racial issues. As the *Amsterdam News*—published daily in New York City—trumpeted, *v* was for *vassal* as well as for *victory.* But no Negro newspaper was printed in Canada during the war except for *The Dawn of Tomorrow,* which was virtually moribund. Following the war Mrs. Carrie Best, wife of a Canadian National Railway porter, published *The Clarion* in New Glasgow, Nova Scotia; and it and *The Canadian Negro* showed a renewed activism in the advocacy of civil rights.[33]

32. *The Free Lance* and *Outcome* are attested to in *The United Church and Missionary Review, 11* (1935), 12i, 12n, and the former's circulation is given as five thousand for 1940, in André Beaulieu and Jean Hamelin, eds., *Les journaux du Quebec de 1764 à 1964* (Quebec, 1965), p. 94. Despite advertizing, I was unable to locate copies of these, the *Afro-Beacon,* or the Canadian *Black Worker.* A broken run of the *Canadian Tribune* for 1940–46 may be read in TPL. Files of *Coppertone, Expression,* and *West Indian News Observer* are in the National Library of Canada, Ottawa, and of *Ebo Voice, Expression, Contrast,* and *Cotopaxi* in the Yale University Library. All are absent from *McKim's Directory of Canadian Publications . . .* (Montreal). A broken file of *Progress* may be found in the Windsor Public Library; and the Yale library holds several numbers, a gift to me from its editor, for which I wish to express my appreciation. On the *Observer,* see supra, Chapter 10, pp. 315–17. I have seen only three issues of *Uhuru,* a Montreal tabloid begun in mid-1969.

33. A file of *The Canadian Negro,* lacking only Vol. 4, no. 4, is in TPL. There is a single copy of the newspaper in the James Weldon Johnson Collection in the

This last newspaper, issued weekly in Toronto from June 1953 until December 1956, was particularly promising at first. Launched by the Canadian Negro Publishing Association, which declared itself to be a nonprofit organization, and edited by Roy Greenidge and Donald Carty, *The Canadian Negro* began within the general Canadian mold for such papers. Denouncing sensationalism, it emphasized social and church news, sporting events, and hortatory articles dealing with racial history. It advocated the study of Canadian Negro history in the schools, protested against the retention of Little Black Sambo in the classroom, and took "Long Live the Queen!" as a motto. Joe Louis, a former heavyweight boxing champion of the world, gave it modest financial support, and for the first year issues appeared on time. In the following year Greenidge withdrew, and late in 1954 the circulation manager, John E. White, son of Reverend W. A. White of Nova Scotia, took over as editor. White introduced several new features, increased the number of articles on the racial issue in the United States, and injected more activist content into the paper. *The Canadian Negro* became increasingly anti-American—naïvely attributing discrimination in Dresden, Ontario, to "the desire of a few business men to lure American Tourist Trade their way"—and attacked *Maclean's Magazine* for publishing an accurate if derogatory article about the New Road Settlement in Nova Scotia. Although *Maclean's* had wished to draw attention to the need for reform, *The Canadian Negro* intemperately branded the Canadian author of the article, Edna Staebler, as a southerner who "would do anything for a buck" and who wished to protect Canadian womanhood from black men. "How rotten can one woman get?," White wrote, ordering this "babe" to take heed of the injunction, *"Yankee, go home!"*

This absurd attack was symptomatic of *The Canadian Negro*'s problems. Issues were appearing a month late, replete with misprints. Historical articles were increasingly slanted to attack whites in general and the United States in particular. Negro jazz artists were chastised for distorting old Negro spirituals. The editor was an apologist for the Mau Mau uprising in Kenya, lashed out at William Faulkner for his view of Negro life, and quarrelled with other black groups, especially (and paradoxically) the Universal Negro Improvement Association of Toronto. The paper seemed to be moving politically toward the left and socially toward a narrow black racialism.[34]

Bienecke Library at Yale University, and one copy in the Schomburgh Collection. Scattered copies of *The Clarion* may be found in the New Glasgow and Truro public libraries, and the Yale University Library (these the gift of Mrs. Best); one issue is in the Schomburgh, and Mrs. William P. Oliver of Halifax holds a virtually complete file. See also *Directory of Pictou County Towns, 1951* . . . (New Glasgow, [1951]), p. 89.

34. *The Canadian Negro: 1* (June 1953), 1, 3, (Sept.), 4, (Nov.), 1, 4; *2* (Feb.

On the whole such charges lost rather than gained readers among the generally conservative Canadian Negroes. Members of the National Unity Association of Dresden, led by P. L. Shadd, complained that there was too much emphasis on race in the journal and suggested that Negroes in Canada preferred to read the *Baltimore Afro-American.* The same group, as well as others, protested against the word *Negro,* preferring to be known as *Afro-Canadians* or as *coloured.* In Toronto sold only in Negro barbershops, and elsewhere largely through poorly compensated "stringers" and "runners" (usually the same person doubling in both activities), the paper could not broaden its audience, and by devoting itself to a series of fruitless protests—against retention of John Buchan's *Prester John* on library shelves, against a cartoon strip called "Joe and Asbestos" then appearing in the *Toronto Telegram,* against the sale of an ashtray that caricatured the Negro, against Aunt Jemima Pancake Mix—it needlessly dissipated its energies. By treating Negro religious movements humorously, the editor lost his more pious readers; by sponsoring dances in which West Indian and Canadian blacks were to mix together, the newspaper attracted the hostility of those who considered the former foreigners; and by denouncing the *Toronto Telegram* and the *Globe & Mail,* which were advocating a gradual approach to racial problems, *The Canadian Negro* drove away many of its urban readers.

The *Globe* intimated that Communists were financing the paper, and white social workers repeated the hints. Black Canadians themselves decided that the newspaper's cause was "of a foreign nature," whether Communist, West Indian, or even American. In September 1956, the editor confessed that the paper could not meet its bills, and he appealed to his subscribers—two hundred of whom had continued to receive the paper without paying for it—and to his advertisers, who were decreasing in number, to help find funds to keep the venture afloat. If each of the eight thousand Negroes in Toronto would contribute thirty cents to the newspaper, it could continue. By the end of the year *The Canadian Negro*'s voice was stifled.[35]

Donald Carty, one of the original editors of *The Canadian Negro,* had previously served as the western regional agent for *The Clarion,* a paper which showed that one could espouse activism without anti-Americanism. Mrs. Best began her paper as a church bulletin in July 1946; it quickly grew, since there was no other voice of "colored Nova Scotians" (as

---

1953 [*sic* for 1954]), 2 (May 1954), 2–3, (June), 2–3, (Nov.) 1–4; *3* (March 1955), 1–2, (May), 1–2, (Oct.), 1–2, 6, (Dec.), 2; *4* (May 1956), 2, (June), 1–2, (Sept.), 1, 3. Stamps on the TPL copies show the extent to which the paper was running behind its datelines.

35. *The Canadian Negro: 1* (Aug. 1953), 2–4, (Sept.), 1, (Nov.), 1, 3; *2* (Dec. 1954), 3–4; *3* (Jan. 1955), 2–3, (Nov.), 1, 4, (Dec.), 1–2; *4* (March 1956), 1–2, 4 (Sept.), 1–2, (Nov.), 1 (Dec.), 1–2.

the paper's motto read), and the following June the sheet became a four-page outlet for twice-monthly news. A. E. Waddell, a prosperous Halifax Negro physician, was chairman of the enterprise. Notable features of the newspaper were articles by Mrs. Best on the Negro communities of the area, based upon personal visits in which she tested the degree of discrimination in restaurants and theaters. She soon found that New Glasgow, from which the paper was issued, was "the center of Jim-crowism in Canada"—for she was refused service herself—and that Truro, where the paper was printed at first, was not much better. On the other hand, she matched her condemnation of discrimination by reports on Sydney and Moncton which praised both for their equal treatment of blacks (as a reward to the latter, she shifted her printing contract there).

Mrs. Best, finding the provincial civil rights society inadequate, advocated a national association for the advancement of colored people, and in 1949 she sought out a national circulation for her paper under a new masthead, *The Negro Citizen.* This proved too ambitious; in 1950 she had to double her subscription costs, and soon afterwards the paper began a slow decline—again under its former name—with the last issue appearing in 1956. *The Clarion* gave much space to American Negro news without attacking the United States, added a women's page, ran social notes from Toronto east, and provided thoughtful essays on sports and race by her son Calbert, until his work took him to Ottawa where, in 1960–62, he was national president of the Civil Service Association of Canada and, by 1970, an Assistant Deputy Minister for Manpower and Immigration.

Africa Speaks, edited by Carl H. Woodbeck, followed almost immediately. Primarily an advertising medium, it was distributed free of charge, particularly to students, and it was styled the "Big Brother to Colored Education" and "The Voice of the Colored Man in Canada," for Woodbeck used his pages to raise money for students, over the years providing $5,000 in this way. Correspondents in Toronto, St. Catharines, and Owen Sound—and on occasion elsewhere—filled the columns with news of accidents, trips, engagements, weddings, and births. When there was little news, poetry of an inspirational nature and filler quotations from Walter Duranty, Edward R. Murrow, and the Bible closed the gaps. Content was consistently conservative, praising Dwight Eisenhower, George Washington Carver, and the newspaper's advertisers. On occasion *Africa Speaks* did rise above the parochial nature of its contents, devoting considerable space to events in Africa, discussing West Indian attempts at federation in 1959 and 1960, and encouraging Canadian Negroes to travel in order to see for themselves how the new nations were developing. The newspaper also was more than ordinarily eclectic in its sources of religious inspiration, giving equal space to the Baptist and Methodist faiths and quoting often and at length from Mary Baker Eddy's textbook of the Christian Science movement, *Science and Health with Key to the Scriptures.* Woodbeck, who was not a Christian Scientist, nonetheless avoided death notices; he also refused to use the word *Negro,* deleting it even when referring to organizations whose name included the term. But even with the somewhat broader base represented by the often more affluent student, and despite (or perhaps because of) the desire to reach all black men, Woodbeck's newspaper was unable to stay afloat for long. *Africa Speaks* fell off schedule by 1960, and after late 1961 until 1966 it was only published occasionally, issues returning briefly to a monthly sequence in 1967.[36]

Each of these publications reveals the fluidity and the transiency of the Negro communities. *The Clarion* was filled with news of Nova Scotian Negroes who had gone to Montreal, usually to work for the railroad, and with references to others who had sought out wider opportunities in Boston. In a representative issue,[37] it referred to the death of a Truro-born woman in Montreal, the move of a Negro woman from Quebec City to Long Island, the attendance of a New York family at a funeral in Quebec province, the visit of a Montreal man with his parents in New Glasgow, the return of an Amherst resident from Quebec, the wedding of the daughter of a Sydney Negro now resident in Toronto, a New Waterford man, the wedding of an Oxford, Nova Scotia, girl in Saint John, and the visit of a former Dartmouth resident who had moved to Sarnia. *The Canadian Negro* and *Africa Speaks* similarly attested to such mobility.

The newspapers also reflected basically middle-class and accommodationist values. The *Clarion* urged Negroes to "keep climbing." *The Canadian Negro* asked its readers to show a sense of "higher responsibility." *Africa Speaks* reminded its audience that time is money and concluded that "Black Power is Not: The Image and Likeness of God Is." All insisted that the white man would admit the Negro to an equal station in life when the Negro proved his worth. None suggested that the white man might, even then, be selfish, inflexible, un-Christian, or racist. Conformity to the work and success ethic that was basic to North American society, together with insistence upon unity, honesty, patience, and courtesy before elders and superiors, lay behind virtually every editorial.[38]

In the long run, none of these newspapers proved to be a genuine source

36. These generalizations are based upon an examination of a file of vols. 7 and 8 of *Africa Speaks,* for April 1959 to September 1961, and vols. 11–13 for 1966–68, which are in my possession.

37. Feb. 28, 1948. On *The Clarion,* see Jan. 15, Aug. 1, 1947, July 15, Aug. 15, 1948, Jan. 26, 1949, and *The Negro Citizen,* May 4, 1949. I wish to thank Mrs. Best for giving me a file of her paper for 1946–50.

38. See, for example, *Dawn of Tomorrow,* Sept. 20, 1924; *Opportunity, 17* (1939), 241–42: "First Negro Milkman is a Big Success"; *Africa Speaks, 12* (Dec. 1967), 1; Detweiler, *The Negro Press,* pp. 79–100.

of strength. But unlike the churches and the schools, which directed toward different goals might well have served the Negro communities rather better than they did, the persistent failure of such papers may be taken as a sign more good than bad. The disappearance of any ethnic journalism is an indication that the group concerned no longer needs, or will no longer support, an institution that will continue to cut it off from the broader community. In the nineteenth century such newspapers were necessary, for the fugitive slave had quite different motivations and needed quite different reading matter than did the well-established white Canadian groups. In all probability those Negroes who were descendants of Canadian slaves, Loyalists, Black Pioneers, and Maroons did not read *The Provincial Freeman* or the *Voice of the Fugitive*. Indeed, the latter declared itself to be for the displaced group alone, and the former was, in terms of content, clearly intended to be read by the alienated American rather than by the Canadian Negro of the 1850s. That until the twentieth century no Negro publication was begun in the Maritime Provinces, where the fugitive population was small and numerically inferior to earlier Negro settlers, is a clear indication that only those who shared the exile mentality of the fugitive felt the need for a separate and clearly unequal news medium. In the present century only *The Dawn of Tomorrow* made any attempt to carry nationwide Negro news, and those attempts were ineffective. Except for the short-lived *Neith* and *Clarion*, all Canadian Negro publications were issued from the exile or fugitive heartland of Ontario and Quebec.[39] There was no need for a national journal, if the various Canadian Negro groups continued to be both geographically separate, as they were, and historically and spiritually apart, as they increasingly became. One could not expect a national newspaper to emerge when no national sense of common identity, unity, or purpose had emerged among the Negroes. In life the newspapers mirrored rather than led opinion, and in their disappearance they also reflected Negro attitudes.

The Negro newspapers in Canada did reflect one of the most obvious of Negro inconsistencies, however, and it was because of that inconsistency that they grew at all. Negroes repeatedly insisted that newspapers should be free of racial bias, indeed, of racial awareness. They complained that the white dailies did not give sufficient space to Negro social news—the complaint was justified—and that too often the only stories in which Negroes were identified as such were those dealing with crime. Racial designations were irrelevant, the Negroes insisted. Yet, both within their own newspapers and repeatedly in conversation, Negroes insisted that

39. The mimeographed quarterly newsletter of the British Columbia Association for the Advancement of Colored People, issued in Vancouver from 1963, is not a publication. Nor is the newsletter of Toronto's Jamaican-Canadian Association.

black men should be identified by race when they achieved some success, however minor that success might be. They did not ask for color-blind newspapers, they asked for value-free newspapers. *The Dawn of Tomorrow* spoke of "another victory for the Colored race" whenever a Negro did well at any given task—whether running one hundred yards faster than other men or being designated trash collector of the year in Hamilton, Ontario—while it spoke only of individual responsibility whenever a Negro failed. The strength that such reporting gave to the Negro was not sure, and when white newspapers began to accord the Negro equal treatment, incorporating news—favorable and unfavorable—without reference to race, black newspapers lost much of their reason for existence.

The other raison d'être for Negro newspapers was not, in fact, one connected with news but with secular exhortation, a function transferred in time to other institutions. Ward, Bibb, Walker, and Jenkins had used their sheets to remind the Negro of the constant necessity for action. The pre-Civil War newspapers were overtly abolitionist, and their editors were active in antislavery work. Walker had worked on behalf of colonizationists, and Jenkins made his paper the official voice of the Canadian League for the Advancement of Colored People. But to survive as newspapers, such enterprises needed to speak for the entirety of the Negro community, not just for one activist group. The League withdrew its support from *Dawn* upon Jenkins's death partially because the newspaper had begun to embrace too many positions at once. Thus, Negro newspapers in Canada failed to remain for long the voice of any one organization, and an important function—to exhort, to proclaim, to chart paths for action—was taken over by a wide assortment of voluntary organizations, social clubs, and cooperatives, and by the newsletters these groups issued to fellow insiders.

On the whole the Canadian newspapers, short-lived as they were, may have contributed to the Negro's sense of racial pride, although they did not contribute effectively to Negro protest, since most remained politically conservative. Pious, practical advice, ranging from recipes to insistence upon the need for education, placed the Negro editors within the non-militant mainstream represented by the Negro church leaders. The papers had performed a temporarily useful supplemental function while generally avoiding controversial themes. They carried more advertising matter than news, and the advertisements often were of a dubious nature, emphasizing hairpieces, cosmetics, and funerals parlors, together with references to butchers, dairies, restaurants, plumbers, and laundries that would accept Negro trade. In the small and closed Negro communities within the larger cities, such advertising was scarcely needed, since an effective grapevine kept the Negroes informed of where they would be welcomed.[40]

In content the Canadian newspapers differed from their American counterparts in only one important respect. Seldom were they sensational. They almost never contained advertisements for tobacco or alcohol, they did not use lurid headlines, and any sexual content that a story might legitimately have was played down. The newspapers would have been acceptable in any Christian Negro home. Whether such content contributed to the low sales or sustained such sales as there were cannot be guessed. But this moral content of the Canadian Negro press sets it apart from the continental norm, although well within the national ethos of the time.

Negro churches, schools, and the press had proved they were not genuine sources of strength. While functional they often were not relevant. The traditional instruments through which other ethnic communities had achieved accommodation with the Canadian norm had proved ineffective. A fourth—and perhaps last—source of strength lay in associations with activist goals, in voluntarism itself.[41]

40. A typical 1959 issue of *Africa Speaks* consisted of four pages of print with sixteen columns in all, eight of which were taken up with advertizing. A representative 1953 issue of *The Canadian Negro* gave four columns to paid material. The *Clarion*, in a 1948 number of six pages and thirty columns, gave ten columns to advertizing matter. The 1966 issue of *Progress*, with forty-four pages in all, ran over thirty-one pages of advertizements.

41. Negroes also edited nonethnic newspapers in Canada, as Anderson R. Abbott and Alfred S. Shadd did. A Montreal-born Negro, Felix R. Fraser, became editor of the *Regina Weekly Mirror*, a tabloid, early in the 1960s, and sold it in 1962 (see *Canada Month*, 2 [1962], 49).

14. Self-Help and a New Awakening, 1930–1970

In August of 1932 "De Lawd" came to Canada. Born near London, Canada West in September 1864, Richard B. Harrison was—to thousands of North Americans, black and white—the figure of God in *The Green Pastures,* Marc Connelly's Pulitzer Prize-winning play of 1930. Formerly a newsboy in London, a bellhop in Detroit, and a Shakespearian reader on the Great Western Lyceum Bureau's circuit, Harrison had been plucked from the headship of the Department of Dramatic Art at a Negro agricultural and technical college in North Carolina to play his new rôle. The son of a fugitive slave from Missouri and a free Negro from Kentucky, Harrison was no longer a Canadian, but he remembered Canada well and returned to it frequently. He had what other blacks in London had wanted: relative wealth, a secure position in society, and fame. He had left Canada to find all three. In 1932 he returned to exhibit all three and to sing of those greener pastures.[1]

Also in August of 1932 a young black man from Jamaica who was a medalist of McGill University, was hired as a clerk by the chief of the Canadian National Parks Branch office in Ottawa, J. B. Harkin. To Harkin's surprise, several of the branch's employees informed him that they would not walk through the same door with a Negro. In the face of much vocal opposition, "Bunny" Harkin kept the Negro on, only to find that, when the time came, his superiors would not approve a promotion, on the ground that honoring a black man would result in white resignations.[2]

These two homely events—the visit of a successful Negro to his birthplace and the ultimate discharge of a young Negro for want of oppor-

1. *London* (Ont.) *Free Press*, Aug. 20, 1932, Aug. 10, 1936; *Crisis, 9* (1915), 116–17; Hazel McDaniel Teabeau, "Daniel L. Haynes, Distinguished Catholic Actor: A Glimpse of Him and Richard B. Harrison," *The Chronicle* (St. Louis), *5* (1932), 79, 87; Edith J. R. Isaacs, *The Negro in the American Theatre* (New York, 1947), pp. 86–88. Shelton Brooks, who composed "Dark Town Strutters' Ball," was born in Amherstburg (see Vivian M. Robbins, *Musical Buxton* [Toronto, 1969]), while Godfrey Cambridge, a leading black cinema actor, was born in Sydney, Nova Scotia (*Contrast,* June 20, 1970).

2. J. B. Harkin Papers, in the possession of Miss Dora Barber, Ottawa: typescript, testimonial of Albert Berga on Harkin, 1955; interview with Miss Barber, who was Harkin's private secretary.

tunity—embody the Canadian Negro's problem of the 1930s. To find opportunity, he often had to go to the land of segregation. To combat discrimination, he stood alone, without effective national organizations, social cohesion, dynamic church leadership, full education, protective legislation, or a medium for making known achievements or grievances.

Several Negroes were beginning to conclude that all-black associations often perpetuated social distance, that the types of organized movements to which they would do better to contribute were interracial, drawing in men of good will such as Commissioner Harkin. Some black leaders now spoke of national rather than local activities. Some saw that political leverage was essential to an assertion of equality. Some thought they might find allies in the radical wing of the labor movement, among other ethnic groups that felt the sting of discrimination, through legislators who wished to take positive action to narrow the channels for discrimination, and in the desire of many Canadians to dissociate themselves from social offenses they regarded as peculiarly American. As Canada changed during the Great Depression and World War II, Negroes found allies with power and persuasive abilities in the press, in politics, and in the broken privacy of once inward-looking Negro organizations—groups now hesitantly moving toward restrained forms of activism. Despite continued division in the ranks, Negroes slowly came to find a source of strength in publicity, in pressure, and in voluntarism—in the initiatives of self-help movements.

Voluntary associations have a way of becoming both coercive and divisive, however, especially if they base their appeal on a single principle that demands universal acceptance. Such was particularly the case with the Canadian branch of one of the 1920s' earliest and most notable black self-help efforts, Marcus Garvey's Universal Negro Improvement Association. Begun in Jamaica in 1914 by an explosive and charismatic leader of rural Maroon extraction, the UNIA transferred its headquarters to Harlem in 1916 and spun off a subsidiary organization for the Dominion, The West Indies Trading Association of Canada.

The first such unit of the Garveyite movement opened in Montreal in 1919. Its organizers successfully challenged an older, ineffective group, the Colored Political and Protection Association—to which largely Canadian-born Negroes belonged—and they more slowly eroded away the membership of a tiny Association of Universal Loyal Negroes which drew mainly upon American-born blacks. In 1921–23, when some Canadian Negroes left for the United States because of Canada's relatively more severe farm depression, Garvey's West Indian Association temporarily became the chief instrument of protest in Nova Scotia and Quebec.[3]

3. Daniel G. Hill, "Negroes in Toronto: A Sociological Study of a Minority Group" (Ph.D. diss., Univ. of Toronto, 1960), pp. 42–43; Edmund David Cronon,

Nonetheless, in Canada the force of Garvey's movement was blunted from the outset. His insistence on racial purity was unlikely to appeal to non-West Indian Negroes, since considerable intermixing with Canadian Indians and whites had gone on over the years. The pseudo-religious overtones of the UNIA, and the secular preachings of its African Orthodox Church, were uncongenial to many in Canada, while Garvey's attacks on the nonracial teachings of Father Divine alienated others. As time passed Garvey increasingly singled out the light-skinned Negro rather than the white man as the enemy, and he gave ever greater emphasis to the Back-to-Africa gospel, an idea never widely attractive to Canadian blacks. Furthermore, Garvey overlooked the Dominion during his 1920 International Convention, staged in Harlem, although he tried to repair this omission for the 1921 meeting by inviting a special Canadian delegation.[4]

Annual conventions of the UNIA met in Canada each year during Garvey's wanderings in the wilderness. Deported from the United States in 1927 for using the mails to defraud, he traveled in Jamaica and Britain to revitalize his movement and then set out for Canada in September 1928, perhaps hoping to use Montreal as a base in his attempts to regain full control of the association he had founded, since the Canadian branches had remained loyal to him while many of the American ones had not. Much encouraged by the fact that the prime minister, William Lyon Mackenzie King—who sailed for Montreal on the same ship—was courteous to him and his second wife, Amy Jacques, Garvey appealed from Canada to his loyal followers in the United States to support a new continental movement. However, when he also advised Garveyites to vote en bloc against Herbert Hoover in the forthcoming American election, the American consul in Montreal protested such "interference" in American politics to

---

Black Moses: The Story of Marcus Garvey and the Universal Negro Improvement Association (Madison, Wisc., 1955), pp. 5, 16, 19, 25, 44–46, 150; Israel, "Montreal Negro Community," pp. 87, 94–98, 111–12, 204–09, with Garvey handbills and programs for 1928 attached. I should like to thank Amy Jacques Garvey, of Kingston, Jamaica, for sending me clippings and a partial set of *The Black Man* magazine, published in New York and later in London between 1933 and 1938; Thomas W. Harvey, President General of the Universal Negro Improvement Association in Philadelphia, for giving me a set of *Negro World*, published between 1918 and 1933; and Professor Cronon, of the University of Wisconsin, for loaning me his complete file of *The Black Man.* I have not had access to the Garvey materials found in Harlem in 1970. The Loyal Negroes' Association was a church as well. It published a Manifesto of loyalty to British institutions.

4. London (Ont.) *Dawn of Tomorrow,* Aug. 25, 1923; *United Church Record and Missionary Review, 11* (1935), 12h; Columbia Univ., Alexander Gumby Collection: "The Rise and Fall of Marcus Garvey," scrapbook with undesignated and undated clippings on Garvey's activities, including Quebec; *Negro World,* June 30, Dec. 29, 1928; Morris Goldman, "The Garvey Movement, 1916–1927" (M.A. thesis, New School for Social Research, 1953), pp. 40–41.

the Canadian authorities, who summarily deported Garvey before he could move on to speaking engagements in Ontario.[5]

When Garvey presided over another of his International Conventions of the Negro Peoples of the World, this time in Toronto in 1936, he alienated yet more Canadian followers by indiscriminate attacks on ex-Prime Minister R. B. Bennett, W. E. B. DuBois, Richard B. Harrison, and parliamentary government. The following year he returned to Toronto to lead a Regional Conference of the American and Canadian Branches of the UNIA and to open a School of African Philosophy, actually three weeks of seminars conducted by Garvey himself, from which ten students graduated. He promised to teach forty-two subjects and to award degrees up to the Doctorate of African Philosophy, a correspondence course requiring fifteen years to complete at $25 a year. But no one finished the course, for three years later Garvey was dead.

Those Garvey left behind were divided in their counsels. In Sydney and Glace Bay, Nova Scotia, where West Indian Garveyite purists dominated, efforts went forward to complete the first of his proposed Five Year Plans. In Toronto, some blacks had begun to shrink from his demand that if one could not get an eye for an eye from the white man "to-day, get it to-morrow, but get it any way you can, get it anyhow!" There in 1937 Garvey had warned his followers that they were too religious, for God had "made man once, and was through making him," and He could not be held responsible for the black man's position. Hearkening back to the fugitive slave, Garvey had insisted that Negroes were only sojourners in Canada, and whenever he spoke he invoked the "Negro spirit"—while the Canadian chairmen of his public meetings invariably and sometimes pointedly referred to "coloured people." None of Garvey's positions was popular with Canadian-born Negroes; and as they denounced his movement, West Indians charged them with Uncle Tomism. While a loyalist Garveyite lawyer, B. J. Spencer Pitt, held the Toronto chapter of the UNIA together into the 1940s, and while a branch office in Vancouver survived to the end of the decade, Garvey's brand of racially proud activism made little impact on black Canadians. Its appeal was limited, for the most part, to West Indians, who in 1967 revived the UNIA and hailed Garvey as the chief spokesman of "The West Indian Nation in Exile."[6]

5. NA, State Department Files, Consular Despatches, Montreal: F. Frost to Frank B. Kellogg, Nov. 8, 1928; *New York Times,* Nov. 1, 1928; *New York Amsterdam News,* Nov. 7, 1928; Amy Jacques Garvey, *Garvey and Garveyism* (Kingston, Jam., 1963), pp. 183–84; Garvey, "Canada's Election," *The Black Man, 1* (1935), 2.

6. Howard University: files of newspaper clippings relating to Garvey, with numerous references to his work in Canada; Garvey, "My Visit to Canada, the British West Indies and British Guiana" and "The School of African Philosophy," *The Black Man, 2* (1937), 4–6; "Speech of Marcus Garvey at Bethel Church, at

Other West Indians started a Commonwealth Co-Operative Buying Club, out of which would grow the Toronto United Negro Association and an allied credit union. This organization strove from the outset for a broad base, was conservative in its racial philosophy, and assumed that the black man was in Canada to stay. Together with similar clubs in Hamilton, Niagara Falls, and Windsor, these societies tried to combine West Indian, "Canadian," and "American" groups.

During the 1920s Negro Canadians also formed a variety of self-help societies at the local level. In Montreal, for example, there was a Little Mothers League which worked to make Negro girls "proficient . . . in household duties." A Porters' Mutual Benefit Association, organized in 1917 by Thomas M. O'Brien, became a predominantly Negro providential club; and the Phyllis Wheatley Art Club, formed in 1922 by Mrs. Lillian Rutherford, gave young Negro women a sense of purpose long after it was transmuted, in the mid-1930s, into the Negro Theatre Guide of Montreal. The Women's Club, the oldest Negro organization in the city, having been formed in 1902, and the Woman's Charitable Benevolent Association, organized in 1919, were close-knit and effective bodies in the 1920s and 1930s, purchasing graves in the city's cemeteries for destitute Negroes, sponsoring bake sales, dramatic skits, and art groups. As the UNIA's literary and debating clubs—The Gamma League and the Dunbar Society —lapsed in the 1920s, the Excelsior Debating & Dramatic Club was formed by Reverend Charles Este, West Indian pastor of the black United congregation of Montreal, which invited non-West Indian members. Este also launched a Negro Community Centre between 1926 and 1928, and it continues to thrive to the present time. Montreal was merely representative: roughly the same pattern of quiet, quasi-segregationist, increasingly broad voluntarism could be found in Toronto during those years.[7]

There were, however, organizations that were both more enduring and more activist in their intent, if on a modest scale. Most were based upon

---

Halifax: A Straight Talk to the People," ibid., *3* (1938), 8–11; *Dawn of Tomorrow*, March 14, 1925; *Toronto Star*, Aug. 26, 1936, Aug. 6, 1953; *Toronto Telegram*, Aug. 6, 1948; Mary White Ovington, *Portraits in Color* (New York, 1927), p. 24; Caribbean Conference Committee, *West Indian Nation in Exile* (Montreal, 1967), pp. [6–8]; *Uhuru*, Aug. 3, 1970.

7. *Montreal Daily Star*, May 4, 1928; D. P. Sykes, "Racial Uplift," *The United Church Record and Missionary Review*, *11* (1935), 12g–h, o, p; *The Clarion*, *3* (1948), 1; Hill, "Negroes in Toronto: A Sociological Study," pp. 349–55; Ruth Körner, *Kanada: Junge Welt* (Vienna, 1954), p. 171. Dates on the Montreal center are contradictory. See *Saturday Night*, Aug. 22, p. 2; Mrs. H. Lambek, "Development of Racial Preferences and Self-Consciousness as a Member of a Race" (M.A. thesis, McGill Univ., 1949), p. 5; and Sykes, "Racial Uplift," p. 12g, for 1926, 1927, and 1928, respectively. *Souvenir Programme, 1926–1965, 40th Anniversary Banquet Honoring Reverend Charles Este . . .* (Montreal, 1965), supports 1928.

American models, although they lacked direct American affiliation, a separation consistently maintained into the 1960s. Just as the National Urban League—founded in New York City in 1910 as the National League for Urban Conditions among Negroes—made no effort to extend its activities into Canada, so too in the 1960s there were no Canadian chapters of the Congress of Racial Equality (CORE); and most of the seventy-five Canadian subscribers to *The Southern Patriot,* organ of the Southern Conference Educational Fund, could be explained by the fact that its editor was a Canadian.[8] The one exception to this purely local pattern would be the Niagara Movement, which after 1909 led to the National Association for the Advancement of Colored People.

Formed by W. E. B. DuBois, black intellectual and opponent of the work ethic of Booker T. Washington, the Niagara Movement began in 1905 when delegates from thirteen states and the District of Columbia met in Fort Erie, Ontario, after futile efforts to find accommodation in Buffalo. No Canadians were invited. From the movement, after much discussion and dissention, emerged the NAACP. But its journal, *The Crisis,* paid little attention to Canada, and even after 1924, when Sir Adam Beck and Fred Landon organized the Canadian equivalent of the American body— independent and without branch affiliation but patterned directly upon it— the magazine seldom found occasion to mention the Dominion.

Formally chartered in January of 1925, this tiny and isolated League for the Advancement of Colored People sponsored Jenkins' newspaper, *The Dawn of Tomorrow,* encouraged Judge Riddell in his continuing research into Negro history, and sought to increase job opportunities for blacks in the London area. Despite its title, the League was not even a provincial, much less a national organization, having affiliates only in Dresden and, temporarily, in Windsor and Hamilton; and while locally it did much good by helping Negroes to continue their education, or by working with the London Juvenile Court, it tended to become a charity organization for the distribution of mid-winter food baskets. The League gave the major portion of the funds it collected to the Beth Emanuel Congregation (thus countenancing the trend toward segregated black churches), and except for a vigorous protest in 1944 against the use of Victory Loan posters that depicted all Negroes as redcaps, it did not press for fundamental changes in public attitudes. Still, under the chairmanship of A. E. Silverwood, and with support from W. Sherwood Fox, the League demonstrated to Londoners that some members of the local establishment frowned upon discriminatory

8. Marie Simmons, CORE, to author, Nov. 21, 1966; Carl Braden, SCEF, Nov. 16, and Joy Fenston, ed., *Southern Patriot,* to author, Dec. 25, 1966; John A. Morsell, NAACP, to author, Nov. 28, 1966; Langlois Sirois, Comité pour la Défense des Droits de l'homme, to author, March 23, 1967; *Canadian Labour Reports, 12* (1957), 3.

activities. Riddell and Landon were also active contributors to the Association for the Study of Negro Life and History, organized by Carter G. Woodson in Chicago in 1915; and Sir Edmund Walker of Toronto became a life member of the latter association, although here too the impact of such activities was limited.[9]

Nonetheless, such organizations were more forward-looking than their equivalents in the Maritime Provinces. In New Brunswick there were no activist clubs of any kind, although both Fredericton and Saint John had their inevitable self-segregated social organizations, under a variety of rapidly changing titles. Significantly, a Nova Scotia Association for the Advancement of Colored People was not established until March of 1945. In the Maritimes, most Negroes remained content to meet within their churches, to seek out improved education, and to let all-black branches of the Canadian Legion and Prince Hall Masonic Lodges serve their social needs.[10]

This was so even though—or perhaps because—discrimination remained most persistent within the Maritime Provinces. When a Negro purchased a house in Trenton, Nova Scotia, in October 1937, a mob of a hundred whites stoned the owner and broke into his home. After being dispersed by Royal Canadian Mounted Police, the mob returned the following night —now four hundred strong—and destroyed the house and its contents. The RCMP would not act unless requested to do so by the mayor, who refused, and the mob moved on to attack two other Negro homes. The

9. LC, Booker T. Washington Papers: C. W. Anderson to Washington, July 14, 1905; J. Max Barber, "The Niagara Movement at Harpers Ferry," *The Voice of the Negro*, 3 (1906), 403; Elliot M. Rudwick, *W. E. B. DuBois: A Study in Minority Group Leadership* (Philadelphia, 1960), pp. 94–119; Warren Baker, "North of the Border," *Negro Digest*, 1 (1943), 39–41; *Dawn of Tomorrow*, June 26, 1926; Fred Landon Collection: clippings relating to CLACP; *London Free Press*, Aug. 12, 1924, Aug. 7, 1934; *Toronto Star*, May 8, 1944; *Tenth Annual Appeal of the Executive Board, The Canadian League for the Advancement of Colored People* (London, 1934), which incorporates an annual report and financial statement; *Fourteenth Annual Appeal* (1938); *Fifteenth* (1939); *Sixteenth* (1940); ASNLH, *Official Souvenir Program, Twenty-fourth Annual Convention* (New Orleans, La., 1939), p. 6.

10. *The Statutes of Nova Scotia* . . . (Halifax, 1945), pp. 463–65: chap. 97, 9 Geo. VI; Cornwallis Street Baptist Church Library, Halifax: misc. flyers on founding of NSAACP; *Crisis*, 29 (1924), 32–33; *Toronto Star*, Feb. 21, 1945; *Hamilton Spectator*, Dec. 12, 1951. On the Negro Masons in Canada, see Reginald V. Harris, "Negro Freemasonry," mimeograph, in two parts, 1946, and "The Story of Equity Lodge No. 106, Halifax," 1957 (both in Halifax), for which I should like to thank Mr. Harris; *Minutes of Proceedings of the Fifteenth Annual Session of the Widow's Son Grand Lodge* . . . (Hamilton, Ont., 1871), passim; *Proceedings of the Semi-Annual and Annual Session of the Grand Lodge of A. F. & A. Masons of Ontario* . . . (Windsor, 1874), both of which contain confused general histories; and Edward Nelson Parker, "Negro Secret Societies," *Social Forces*, 23 (1944), 208–12.

only arrest was of a New Glasgow black, who was convicted of assault on a woman during the riot; and the original Negro purchaser abandoned efforts to occupy his property. While there were no other racial incidents of this dimension in the Maritimes, evidence of discrimination was persistent, job opportunities for black men were few, and the segregated schools continued to reinforce the racist assumptions of many rural Nova Scotians. Truro, to the province's Negroes, had become "Little Mississippi," and Africville, to the province's whites, remained "Nigger Town." Tiny Elm Hill, in New Brunswick, was a squalid satrapy from which a black postmaster delivered up the local vote upon demand, despite the efforts of two active leaders, Lemuel MacIntyre and Josephine Eastman, and Negroes continued to be dismissed as "the happiest, most carefree" people in the province.[11]

Still, as in the decades before World War I, no clear pattern of discrimination emerged in the 1930s or early 1940s. Incidents were frequent in Toronto, Hamilton, Windsor, and Winnipeg. Only one hotel in Montreal could be depended upon not to turn Negroes away in 1941. An Edmonton hospital admitted to drawing the color line; many dance pavilions, skating rinks, and restaurants made it clear that they did not welcome blacks; and several pubs in Saskatchewan and British Columbia insisted that Negroes sit in corners reserved for them. In April 1940, a mob of three hundred Canadian soldiers stormed the home of a Negro bandleader in Calgary, attacking whites found on the premises for loving "nigger joints." Yet there also was change: most notably, the press reported individual incidents with great frequency and an air of increasing disapproval. When a border city newspaper defended segregated accommodations, most of the press of Ontario rebuked it. When a Toronto skating rink turned away a Negro youth, students from the University of Toronto organized a picket line. When in 1940 a Vancouver Negro proved that a beer parlor had refused to serve him, the local court fined the offender. And as Negroes moved into the polyglot Salter-Jarvis area of Winnipeg, or into working-class districts of outer Montreal in growing—if still small—numbers, they encountered relatively little discrimination from their Indian, Chinese, Italian, Ukrainian, and central European neighbors.[12]

The change was punctuated, and perhaps hastened, by World War II. On

11. *Saint John Telegraph-Journal*, Oct. 11, 1937; *Halifax Chronicle*, Oct. 27–30, 1937; *Toronto Star*, Oct. 29, 1937, Nov. 14, 21, 23, Dec. 4, 1945, Jan. 29, 1947; *Toronto Globe*, Oct. 6, 30, 1942; *Toronto Globe & Mail*, Feb. 23, 1947; Hamilton Public Library: folder, "Negroes in Canada"; *Hamilton Spectator*, April 15, 1954, Dec. 7, 1957; Legislative Library of New Brunswick, Fredericton: folder, "New Brunswick Parade Continued," item 69.

12. Hill, "Negroes in Toronto: A Sociological Study," printed abstract; L. H. Glassco, "The Winnipeg Multi-Service Project," in Institute of Public Affairs,

both the war and the home fronts, the Negro's position improved. Initially, the Canadian army rejected black volunteers, although seldom openly on grounds of race; and the Royal Canadian Air Force was reported to have refused to accept qualified black applicants. Army officers had to be British subjects, and when West Indian students applied for the university officers' training plan, they found that some recruiters interpreted "British subject" to mean "white." Nonetheless, as the war continued, blacks were accepted as equals into both the regular army and the officer corps, the majority (among whom would be the first premier of independent Barbados, Errol Barrow) receiving their training virtually without incident, at Summerside, Prince Edward Island, and—after 1955—at unsegregated Gagetown, in New Brunswick. By 1941 the Canadian Army was said to have attracted "many" American Negro volunteers who found the northern services less discriminatory than those of the United States; and when five Negro brothers from Saint John enlisted in the air force, the press across Canada dutifully took notice of a new national "first." Some evidence of continued separation of the races remained to the end of the war, notably in the Colored War Veterans branches (in Montreal and Halifax) of the Canadian Legion, and in the commissioning of a Chaplain to Colored Personnel for the Halifax area, Reverend William P. Oliver. Further, the Home Service Association now broadened its base, opened a community house in Toronto, and engaged in social work, providing counseling, recreational opportunities, and educational outlets for those who remained at home as well as for returning servicemen.[13]

Dalhousie University, *1964 Human Rights Conference*, no. 42 (1965), pp. 6–16; Lambek, "Development of Racial Preferences," pp. 2–4; D. L. C. Rennie, "The Ethnic Division of Labour in Montreal from 1931–1951" (M.A. thesis, McGill Univ., 1953), pp. 14, 23; Louise Macfarlane, et al., "Pontville, A Substandard Working-Class Suburb" (M.A. thesis, McGill Univ., 1954), p. 41; Norbert Lacoste, *Les Charactérisques sociales de la population du grand Montreal: Étude de sociologie urbaine* (Louvain, Belgium, 1958), pp. 129, 133; *Toronto Star*, April 27, 1935, Oct. 10, 1936, Nov. 24, 1938; *Star Weekly Magazine*, Jan. 15, 1938; *Toronto Globe*, April 8, 1940; *Montreal Witness*, Feb. 26, 1936; *Dawn of Tomorrow*, 4 (1947), 1; *Montreal Standard*, May 29, 1943; TPL, Picture Collection: five files of clippings and advertisements; *The Negro Motorist Green Book* (New York, 1941), p. 48. The 1951 edition of this book shows two hotels in Montreal that would accept Negroes, and *The Green Guide for Travel and Vacations* (New York, 1962), as the publication became, listed thirty-one hotels and motels in Ontario and Quebec.

13. Austin C. Clarke, "A Black Man Talks about Race Prejudice in White Canada," in Laskin, *Social Problems*, pp. 147–52; *Time* (Canadian ed.), April 14, 1967, p. 14; *London Free Press*, April 20, 1940; *Toronto Star*, Oct. 23, 1941, Jan. 26, 1943, April 8, 1944; *Toronto Globe*, Aug. 21, 1942; *Saint John Times*, Sept. 9, 1943; *Saint John Telegraph*, July 31, 1944; *United Church Record*, 11 (1935), 12i; Perry, *Long Road*, 1, 21, 56, 77, 182–85; Frank G. Weil, "The Negro in the Armed

An area of Canada that had seen very few Negroes was introduced, as a result of wartime needs, to many hundreds of such servicemen: the far Northwest. So that the northwest frontier's air bases might be connected by highway transport, and in order to open a supplementary supply route to Alaska against possible closure of the inner passage by the advancing Japanese, in February of 1942 authorization was given for construction of a road from Dawson Creek, British Columbia, to Big Delta, Alaska. Nearly a third of the laborers involved were black. In Edmonton, one of the major staging bases, there was opposition to the arrival of so large a number of American Negroes, until the servicemen proved to be segregated, busy, and five hundred miles away; and there were no racial incidents arising from the Alcan project. In seven and a half months, seven regiments—including the 93rd, the 95th, and the 97th all-Negro construction units—completed the greatest engineering project in the Americas since the opening of the Panama Canal. First on the scene, via Skagway, were the 18th (white) and the 93rd. At first the local Indians called members of the latter "Midnight Men." And since nearly all of the Negro laborers had been recruited in the deep South and hurried north without acclimatization, they suffered seriously from the cold. By the completion of the highway in October 1943, however, the Negro regiments were working fully at pace with, and on occasion ahead of, the white contingents, one black unit completing a bridge for which engineers had allowed two weeks, in three and a half days of round-the-clock work. When the lead bulldozers of two spearheads moving from the north and the south symbolically met, one was driven by a Negro corporal from Philadelphia— Refines Sims, Jr.—and the other by a white Texan.[14]

The black laborer who stayed at home also won a number of modest, if largely symbolic, victories. Until 1942 Canada's national employment agency, the National Selective Service, accepted racial restrictions from prospective employers. When Negro university graduates protested through

Forces," *Social Forces, 26* (1947), 98; Isabel LeBourdais, "Canada's First Community House for Negroes Represents a Forward Step in Social Service," *Saturday Night, 39* (July 25, 1942), pp. 1, 4–5.

14. Office of the Chief Military Historian, Washington, D.C.: Historical MS File 3-1.1/DB/VI/C1/, "The Alaskan Highway (Control Division Report No. 175) Text," pp. 1, 18–22, 46; also "History of the Whitehorse Sector of the Alcan Highway," restricted typescript (June 1943), pp. 4, 6, 14; "A History of the Ninety-Third Engineer Regiment (G–5) to 1 Jan. 1943" undated typescript, pp. 1–3, 6, 7; ". . . for 1943," p. 1; Freeman C. Bishop, et al., "The Alaska Highway," undated typescript, pp. 6, 10, 15—all held by the Historical Record Section, Analysis Branch, Dept. of War, Washington, D.C., and examined there. See also Harold Griffin, *Alaska and the Canadian Northwest: Our New Frontier* (New York, 1944), pp. 100, 109–10, 119–21. I should like to thank Dr. Stetson Conn for making available to me the official army records relating to the construction of the highway.

the *Toronto Globe & Mail* that the agency could find them only inferior work, the *Globe,* joined by the *Winnipeg Free Press* and the Canadian Jewish Congress, applied pressure upon the Service and won from them the promise that questions relating to race would not be permitted in the future. Buxton also came into the news again when its men took charge of all maintenance work on a major portion of Canadian National Railway track. Shortly after, Negro railway porters organized into trade unions and began agitation for federal and provincial antidiscrimination bills in the areas of employment and accommodation. Further, the rapid growth of the black populations of Detroit and Ypsilanti (the latter trebling during the war) increased the already high Negro interchange between Windsor and Michigan, opening new job opportunities to Canadian residents and making them aware of the erosion of the more obvious racial barriers in the American North. The Canadian Negro's experience was broadened, as substantial numbers of West Indians left Cape Breton for Montreal and Toronto, bringing tales of the Maritime situation. At the war's end, a Joint Labour Committee to Combat Racial Intolerance was formed in Winnipeg, initially to help Ukrainians and Jews but soon including Negroes; and shortly similar committees were functioning in Toronto, Montreal, Vancouver, Calgary, Windsor, Hamilton, Halifax, and Sydney. Thus, the total impact of World War II was an educational one for white and black, bettering the status of the Negro worker—in and out of uniform—throughout Canada and the North.[15]

The most important change brought to Negro Canadians by World War II was the new militancy in the organized black labor unions, a militancy dating from the end of the earlier war. In the summer of 1918 the black porters of the Canadian National Railway's transcontinental run had organized an Order of Sleeping Car Porters and had applied to the Trades and Labour Congress of Canada for a charter. The Congress had preferred that the porters became part of one of the existing, and larger, railway labor groups and had rejected the application. When the Negro porters had previously applied to the Brotherhood of Railway Workers, however, they were informed that the Brotherhood's constitution restricted membership to whites. Under pressure, the Brotherhood had promised to take up the question at its next annual convention, during which the president of the union unsuccessfully sought to have the racial qualification

15. NA, R.G. 212, Labor and Transportation, Committee for Congested Production Areas, 1943–45: Central File, Detroit-Willow Run, boxes 22, 24, 47, 48; D. MacLennan, "Racial Discrimination in Canada," *Canadian Forum, 23* (1943), 1964–65; *Globe & Mail,* Oct. 28, 1943; *Ebony, 2* (1946), 24–27; Harold H. Potter, "Negroes in Canada," *Race, 3* (1961), 40; *Montreal Star,* Oct. 16, 1957; E. L. Homewood, "The Preacher was a Bootblack," *United Church Observer,* n.s., *21* (1959), 8–10, 21.

struck. As a compromise, the Brotherhood agreed to charter the proposed order as an auxiliary organization, and in January 1919, the predominantly black union of sleeping-car porters, with J. A. Robinson as its president, was recognized. At the next general convention of the Brotherhood, the racial clause was removed and the new order given full status.

This, the first time a Canadian union had abolished racial restrictions upon membership, gave the order the leverage it needed to begin organizing the porters on the competing Canadian Pacific Railway. Almost immediately the CPR responded by discharging thirty-six porters without giving cause; seven of the dismissed Negroes demanded a formal hearing under the Industrial Disputes Investigation Act of 1907. Early in 1920 a three-man board took evidence. Race was not mentioned by any parties to the dispute, the porters insisting that they had been fired because of their union activities. The CPR preferred to negotiate with its porters through a company-initiated welfare committee, and it refused to recognize the bargaining rights of the porters' grievance committee, chaired by one of the dismissed workers. The final decision ran two to one against those dismissed, and the defeat thus hastened general organization among CPR porters.[16]

Until World War II further progress by the porters' union had been limited to absorbing the benefits of labor battles fought in the United States. In 1925 a new Brotherhood of Sleeping Car Porters was organized, drawing upon the Canadian initiative, in New York City. There, in 1937, the union negotiated a sweeping new contract with the Pullman Company covering wages, hours, and working conditions for all porters, attendants, and maids in the Pullman service in Canada and the United States. In the meantime, the Canadian railroads had reclassified work categories in order to limit blacks, except for those already otherwise employed, to being porters only. Thus clustered into a single activity and bolstered by an international union, the Canadian porter aristocracy took an even firmer hold upon black economic leadership in Montreal and the other rail centers.

During World War II, membership in the union grew rapidly, moving on the CPR alone from 153 in 1942 to 620 the following year. Between 1939 and 1942, A. Philip Randolph, International President of the Brotherhood, traveled regularly in Canada as an organizer; and in 1948 the union won recognition there. By the end of the war porters' wages had

16. W. E. Greening, *It was Never Easy, 1908–1958: A History of the Canadian Brotherhood of Railway, Transport and General Workers* (Ottawa, 1961), pp. 58–60; Brailsford R. Brazeal, *The Brotherhood of Sleeping Car Porters: Its Origin and Development* (New York, 1946), pp. 200–01, 223; Hill, "Negroes in Toronto: A Sociological Study," pp. 113–14; *The Labour Gazette*, 20 (1920), 239–49.

climbed to $187 monthly, with an average of $50 extra from tips, and the work month had fallen to sixteen days on the road. Of 585 porters on the CNR, nearly all were black, and 118 were now West Indian—quite often, they were the source of the greater sense of activism. Many others were from southern colleges, especially Morris Brown and Fisk, although these porters usually were limited to summer work. Still, promotion from the ranks of porter remained closed to Negroes, and as rail traffic fell into general decline in the 1950s, so too would the porter aristocracy.[17]

A new phase of militancy had begun as a result of the war, however, and in Canada the men most responsible for it were Stanley Grizzle and A. R. Blanchette. Born in the West Indies in 1910, Blanchette had come to the United States in 1928 and had completed three years of education at Howard University, until the depression forced him to abandon his plans to become a doctor. A summer job with his uncle, J. A. Robinson, carried him into the order. In 1942 Randolph established a Winnipeg division of the Brotherhood, and Blanchette was elected secretary. Seven years later the union transferred him to Montreal as International Field Organizer, and from 1952 Blanchette represented the Brotherhood at all meetings with nonoperating railway union groups. Porters on the Northern Alberta Railway were organized, membership reached a thousand, and by the late 1950s Blanchette become a vocal member of the Committee for Human Rights of the Canadian Labour Congress, speaking on behalf of both the union and blacks in general.

In Toronto, Negro porters were ably led by Canadian-born Stanley G. Grizzle, who served with particular effectiveness as president of the Toronto CPR Division and on the Committee for Human Rights. In 1938 he helped form the Young Men's Negro Association of Toronto; in the 1950s he organized deputations to meet with the provincial and federal governments to discuss antidiscrimination legislation, appeared often on radio and television, and plunged into the controversial area of immigration policy as spokesman (together with Donald Moore, President of Toronto's new Negro Citizens' Association) for the first delegation of Canadian blacks to meet—on April 27, 1954—with members of the federal cabinet in order to discuss discrimination against West Indian applicants. In 1959 Grizzle became the first Negro to seek a seat in the Ontario legislature, as

17. *Regional Conference . . . Brotherhood of Sleeping Car Porters . . .* (Montreal, 1945), passim; Frank Collins Correspondence, held by Mr. Collins, Burnaby, B.C., 1942–48, with statements and attachments, passim; *The Clarion, 2* (Feb. 15, 1947), [4]; McKenzie Porter, "Three Thousand Nights on Wheels," *Maclean's* (March 15, 1949), pp. 16–17, 32–34; Byron Fisher, "I Am a Canadian Negro," *Canadian Railway Employees' Monthly, 38* (1952), 366–67. I should like to thank Mr. Collins for granting me access to his files on the Brotherhood, and also on the B.C. Association for the Advancement of Colored People.

a CCF (Co-operative Commonwealth Federation) candidate, and although defeated he attracted nearly ten thousand votes.[18]

In the meantime, the union ceased to conceal its militancy. In 1949 and again in 1954 Randolph returned to Canada, visiting CPR locals and denouncing communism. The union's voice, *The Black Worker,* began to give substantial space to Canadian activities after his first visits, and Blanchette, Grizzle, and a Negro porter and preacher in Hamilton, John Christie Holland, who in 1954 won that city's Distinguished Citizenship Award, became internationally known in the movement. Canadian immigration authorities were denounced as "villains" for their discrimination against West Indians. *The Black Worker* accused Minister of Citizenship and Immigration Walter E. Harris of "Fascistic racialism" for his defense of a restrictive immigration policy on the grounds that natives of tropical areas were "apt to break down in health" and would find it hard to succeed in the "highly competitive Canadian economy." In 1955 the union won for sleeping-car porters the right of promotion to conductor, and in 1957 to other positions. The Brotherhood organized provincial committees to combat discrimination; its women's auxiliaries sponsored Negro History Weeks; affiliation with the Trades and Labour Congress was tightened; and union officials intensified their campaign for federal and provincial fair employment practices acts.[19]

But union organization was not enough to give the Negro equality of opportunity, since only a small and sometimes aloof segment of black Canada was touched directly by the Brotherhood. Some unions discriminated against Negroes. Only the Barbers' Union professed to give unqualified support to antidiscrimination laws. Changes were necessary elsewhere, changes which could parallel those brought by the increasingly aggressive and publicity-wise porters, changes which would be reflected

18. *Labor* (Washington, June 24, 1961), p. 2; *The Black Worker* (May 15, 1957), pp. 1, 3; *Montreal Star,* June 23, 1952; Grizzle, *Discrimination: Our Achilles Heel?* (Ottawa, 1951), passim; Grizzle, "How it Feels to be a Negro in Canada," *The* [Toronto] *Star Weekly Magazine* (April 9, 1960), pp. 10–12; "Autobiographical Sketch of Stanley George Grizzle," MS in possession of Mr. Grizzle, passim. I am grateful to Messrs. Blanchette and Grizzle for sending me manuscripts, clippings, and other materials relating to their work.

19. *The Black Worker,* 7 (Jan. 1952), 6; *23* [sic] (July 1952), 7, (Feb. 1953), 7, (April 1953), 7, (May 1953), 5, 7, (June 1953), 3, 7, (Aug. 1953), 1, (Nov. 1953), 2; *26* [sic] (June 1955), 1, 4–5, 8; *24* (Jan. 1957), 1, (March 1957), 7, (June 1957), 1; *28* (April 1957), 1, 3, 6; (Feb. 15, 1958), p. 5, (March 15, 1958), p. 2, (April 15, 1958), p. 5; Ontario Northland Railway, *The Quarterly* (March 1952), p. 1; *Labour Gazette* (Sept. 15, 1954), pp. 1265–74. On Holland, see *The Substance of Addresses Delivered before the Lincoln Fellowship of Hamilton, Canada . . . 1956* ([Hamilton, Ont.], 1956), p. 15; and Jessie L. Beattie, *John Christie Holland: Man of the Year* (Toronto, 1956), passim.

in—and also be effected by—new legislation. For World War II had also brought an awareness, in provincial and federal legislative bodies, of the necessity to recognize that, while civil liberties ultimately must rest on enlightened public opinion, the opinion of some can be led toward the light because of the law itself. At the end of the war, many Canadian Negroes were said to have decided that the United States, despite the overt discrimination to be found there, might well be more desirable to live in than Canada. For Canada seemed to prefer "tubercular Europeans" to healthy blacks; made the Negro feel that he was "dodging through a plantation without touching a tree" because he could not know whether a hotel, restaurant, or barber might snub him; and had fewer job opportunities, partially because of the larger and increasingly self-contained Negro market across the border.[20]

Ontario was the first province to respond to the winds of change when, in the midst of the war, it passed the Racial Discrimination Act of 1944. This act prohibited the publication or display of any symbol, sign, or notice that expressed racial or religious discrimination. Then, early in 1950, fifty organizations—three of them Negro—submitted a brief to the provincial premier asking for the enactment of more sweeping protections. The province responded by outlawing discrimination in collective agreements and declaring restrictive covenants in land sales null and void. The following session gave Ontario the distinction of being the first jurisdiction in the Dominion to pass a Fair Employment Practices Act. A Fair Accommodation Practices Act, initially limited to public places, followed four years later. In 1958 the legislature also established an Anti-Discrimination Commission charged with publicizing human rights activities throughout the province. Changed to the Human Rights Commission in 1961, this body's powers were broadened then and the next year, after the consolidation of all fair practices statutes into a Human Rights Code, to include administration of the law. In 1965 the code was amended to cover private apartment buildings with three or more self-contained units,

20. Grizzle, "How it Feels," p. 10; Porter, "Three Thousand Nights," p. 34; Rose D. Parry, "The Negro in Canada," *Crisis*, 54 (1947), 272; [Charles Coleman], "The Negro in Nova Scotia," *CCF Comment* (Halifax), 1 (Dec. 1964), 10–11, 15; Canadian Labour Congress Joint Advisory Committee on Human Relations, MS files, Workman's Circle Center, Montreal: "Maritime Trip Correspondence," interview, Halifax, n.d.; *Canadian Labour Reports*, 11 (April 1956), 3–6. I am grateful to Mr. Sidney Blum, Secretary of the Committee, for giving me access to his files for the period 1950–60. They are cited here under the stipulation that names on the documents not be used. Hereafter the file will be cited as "CLC." Notes taken from this material have not been deposited with the Schomburg Collection. See Blum's *Education, Equality and Brotherhood* (Montreal, [1959]), passim.

to apply to the provincial government itself, and to protect prospective lessees of office and other commercial space from discrimination.[21]

Other provinces followed Ontario's lead. Fair Employment Practices acts were passed in Manitoba (1953), Nova Scotia (1955), New Brunswick, Saskatchewan, and British Columbia (1956), and Quebec (1964). Saskatchewan had already enacted a Bill of Rights in 1947, and in 1956 added a Fair Accommodation Practices Act. Nova Scotia, New Brunswick (1959) and British Columbia followed (1961), and Nova Scotia passed a code of human rights in 1963, as did Alberta in 1965. The federal government also responded with a fair employment bill in 1953 and two months later took firm action to investigate the act's first infringement, directed against a Negro stenographer.

Enforcement of the acts differed from province to province, with Ontario again proving to be most vigorous. The Human Rights Commission of five members, responsible to the Minister of Labour, investigated nearly a thousand cases between 1962 and 1967. (Nova Scotia's Department of Labor, responsible for that province's Human Rights Act, investigated ten cases in 1963–65, a Human Rights Commission not being established until 1967.) Unlike the commissions established in the United States, the Ontario body had both investigative and adjudicative functions and could seek on-the-spot settlements, preventing lengthy investigations and subsequent judgmental activities which were likely to make it difficult for either party in a dispute to accept an embarrassing and public defeat or compromise. Under the able direction of Missouri-born and Toronto-trained Negro sociologist, Daniel G. Hill, the Commission also investigated some two thousand complaints that occurred outside its formal jurisdiction. Further, the Commission engaged in a fruitful research and educational program, making Ontario's residents aware of their rights, distributing over a million pieces of literature, working with a variety of ethnic organizations—including a growing number of Negro businessmen's clubs, and African and West Indian student associations—and individual religious leaders, and opened branch offices, beginning in 1965. One effect of such activity was the signing, in June of 1966 by the members of the Ontario Association of Real Estate Boards (who represented eighty per-

21. *Journals of the Legislative Assembly of the Province of Ontario,* 1944: pp. 35, 49, 52–53; ibid., 1950; pp. 16, 60, 95, 100; ibid., 1951: pp. 6, 15, 57, 165, 173–75, 212, 254–55, 267–70, 274; ibid., 1954: pp. 103, 119, 137, 153, 166; *Statutes of the Province of Ontario,* chap. 51, 1944, pp. 231–32, chap. 78, 1950, chap. 24, 1951, pp. 169–72, chap. 28, 1954, pp. 157–59, chap. 28, 1961, p. 95 and chap. 93, 1962, pp. 567–73, 975; *Revised Statutes of Ontario* (Toronto), *4,* chaps. 328, 203; ibid., *1960, 2,* chaps. 131–32, 139; *3,* chap. 270; *A Brief to the Premier of Ontario* (n.p., 1950), passim.

cent of those registered to sell such property) of an agreement not to permit discrimination in listings.[22]

The most controversial enactment was neither so practical nor so effective as these provincial bills, which were building human rights piecemeal and one jurisdiction at a time. In September 1958, the federal prime minister, John Diefenbaker, introduced in the House of Commons a bill to recognize and protect "human rights and fundamental freedoms." Noble in purpose but vague in content, this bill was pressed forward by the prime minister with great persuasiveness and vigor. He had shown a consistent record of opposition to ethnic discrimination since the 1940s; and it was Diefenbaker who, at the Commonwealth prime minister's conference in London in 1961, would speak out most openly against apartheid in South Africa. He felt that Canada would not have sufficiently demonstrated its commitment to the postwar values of libertarianism and to the Charter of the United Nations without passage of a Bill of Rights. After long and acrimonious debate—largely over whether such a bill was needed, and secondarily over whether it should be entrenched within the constitution (the British North America Act) by formal amendment, or left as a statutory bill that might be overridden, repealed, or amended later by another session of Parliament—the Bill of Rights became public law in 1960 under the second rubric.

The decision not to incorporate the bill in the constitution was a pragmatic one: the BNA Act contained no amending procedure, and the Canadian Parliament would have had to go to the Imperial Parliament in London. Furthermore, the provinces (and Quebec in particular) were in dispute with the federal government over this method of amendment, and

22. Marshall Pollock, "Human Rights Legislation in Ontario," *Race, 9* (1967), 193–203; *Time* (Canadian ed.), May 9, 1969, pp. 15–16; *Labour Gazette, 63* (1963), 877–78; Vivien Mahood, "Toward Better Race Relations," *Food for Thought, 10* (April 1950), 24–25; Frank H. Hall, "Fair Employment Practices—A Good Beginning," in Michael Starr, et al., *Equality of Opportunity in Employment* (Ottawa, 1959), pp. 12–14; *Toronto Globe & Mail,* May 19, 1950, Feb. 18, 1961; *Fredericton Daily Gleaner,* Jan. 11, 1960, July 24, 1965; *Toronto Daily Star,* Feb. 15, Nov. 8, 1961; *Vancouver Sun,* Feb. 4, 1961; *Halifax Mail-Star,* March 30, 1965; *Calgary Herald,* April 5, 1965; *Quebec Le Soleil,* Oct. 1, 1965; *Windsor Star,* Nov. 2, 1965; *Canada Week, 1* (March 5, 1965), p. 3; *Human Rights Review, 19* (Feb. 1967), 1. The work of the Ontario Commissioner may be contrasted with Quebec's reluctance to move on FEP and FAP acts in W. F. Charness, "Racial Discrimination in Employment: Canada's First Case," *Expression, 1* (iv/1966), 26–34; "Her Majesty, the Queen vs. Hilton of Canada Limited (Queen Elizabeth Hotel)," ibid., pp. 6–25; and George P. Springate, "Housing and Public Accommodations for the Montreal Negro," ibid. (ii/1965), pp. 13–23. For a convenient summary, see Robert William Kerr, *Legislation against Discrimination in Canada* ([Fredericton], 1969).

the government feared that there would be no agreement between them, thus delaying the bill indefinitely. The act was thus a declaration of rights rather than a means of providing positive legal protection for those rights. It employed the fiction that these rights had "already existed" in Canada, which clearly was not the case, and that specifically to enact such rights would be to suggest that they had not existed previously. The result was a bill which contained much moral suasion and little practical force, and its functional effectiveness would fall to the courts to determine.[23]

The courts in Canada had changed more slowly than the legislative bodies. In 1964 the Supreme Court of Canada, in *Robertson & Rosetanni v. R.,* would interpret the new Bill of Rights so cautiously as to reveal that it contained no real guarantees, the justices ruling that the bill could not affect legislation existing before it was passed. This decision was consistent with the court's tendency to interpret civil liberties in terms of purely legalistic, and often quite narrow, principles rather than in terms of the broader intent of an act. Moreover, an open "sociological jurisprudence" was unlikely to arise in Canada, as it did in the United States (in particular during the period of the Warren Court), because common law operates upon "the people" differently, and because the British North America Act distributes law-making power between the national and provincial legislatures in a manner roughly the reverse of the American pattern. Unlike the Constitution of the United States, the BNA Act contains no Bill of Rights, no list of areas of potential legislation that are to be regarded as beyond the reach of either national or local power. Civil liberties in Canada are subject to control and denial by both the national legislature and the provincial bodies, and so long as the national parliament did not legislate

23. On the bill, see Walter Surma Tarnopolsky, "The Canadian Bill of Rights" (Ll. M. thesis, Univ. of London, 1962), and Frank R. Scott, *The Canadian Constitution and Human Rights* (Toronto, 1959). D. A. Schmeiser, *Civil Liberties in Canada* (Oxford, 1964), and Donald V. Smiley, "The Case Against the Canadian Charter of Human Rights," *Canadian Journal of Political Science, 2* (1969), 277–91, defend lack of entrenchment for the bill; three arguments critical of this position are Edward McWhinney, "The Bill of Rights, the Supreme Court, and Civil Liberties in Canada," in John T. Saywell, ed., *Canadian Annual Review for 1960* (Toronto, 1961), pp. 261–72; an essay review of Schmeiser's book by R. Dale Gibson in *La Revue du barreau Canadien, 43* (1965), 385–89; and A. Alan Borovey, *Human Rights and Social Equality—The Tactics of Combat* ([Toronto, 1954]). Schmeiser appears to have changed his views somewhat after the Robertson case: see *Brandon Sun,* April 1, and *Prince Albert Herald,* Nov. 16, 1966. For Quebec opinion of the bill, see *Montreal La Presse,* Feb. 4, Feb. 8, *Gazette,* Feb. 10, *Sherbrooke La Tribune,* Feb. 8, *Quebec Le Soleil,* Feb. 9—all 1960. Note then the Nova Scotian bill establishing a Committee on Human Rights applied to apartments with more than *four* units. See *Statutes of Nova Scotia* (Halifax, 1962), pp. 36–45.

(as, until 1960, it had not done), provincial legislation stood valid. Canadian lawyers had little occasion to speak of "civil rights," a French legal term (*droits civils*) which does not carry precisely the same meaning as "civil liberties." In any event, neither subject had been much discussed in the nineteenth century: in 1900 the library of the prestigious Osgoode Hall Law School in Toronto contained not a single title on either.[24]

It is not surprising, then, that turn-of-the-century court decisions involving discrimination against Negroes had reflected conservative and limited conceptions of the law. In 1899, in *Johnson* v. *Sparrow et al.,* the Superior Court of Montreal had found that no place of public entertainment could "make any regulation excluding negroes", but in 1921, in *Loew's Montreal Theatres Ltd.* v. *Reynolds,* a higher court found that one could. The first case arose when a Negro bought two orchestra seats for a concert at the Montreal Academy of Music and was prevented from using them by ushers who offered alternate seating. The plaintiff claimed damages for breach of contract; the defendant denied that blacks ever had been seated. Nearly a dozen Negro witnesses swore that they had been admitted at earlier times, and Justice J. S. Archibald, recounting the history of slavery and citing *Somerset* v. *Stewart* as precedent, awarded the plaintiff $50, a decision which stood upon appeal before the higher court, though on the sole ground of breach of contract. A similar decision was reached in Toronto soon after: a light-skinned Negro woman purchased a ticket for her son at a skating rink; the boy—who was much darker—was refused admittance when he appeared, and his mother sought damages in the divisional court. The company agreed to pay twenty-five cents, the price of the ticket, and the judge dismissed the action with the opinion that no other damages beyond the ticket could be shown.

However, for all practical purposes the *Johnson* decision was reversed in 1921. In January 1919, one Sol Reynolds, a member of the Coloured Political and Protective Association of Montreal, tried to sit with friends in the orchestra seats of Loew's Theatre and was removed to the balcony. Reynolds sued, and the Superior Court granted him only $10 damages because, the judge noted, the plaintiff had known that he would not be seated and had purchased a ticket in order to present a test case. The Court of Appeals reversed this judgment, noting that Reynolds had not been in evening dress, as were all the other ticket holders, and that "when a coloured man . . . wants to take a seat in a part of the House which he

24. See Bora Laskin, "Our Civil Liberies: The Rôle of the Supreme Court," *Queen's Quarterly, 61* (1955), 455–71; and William George Eakins, comp., *A Subject-Index to the Books in the Library of the Law School of Upper Canada at Osgoode Hall, Toronto Jan. 1st, 1900* (Toronto, 1900), passim. Slavery in Canada is referred to on pp. 218, 293.

knows is by the rule of the manager prohibited to a coloured person, he cannot complain if he is refused admission." In a forthright dissent, one member of the court, H.-G. Carroll, argued that black men must be recognized as having the same rights as whites. The reality, he suggested, was that the Negro had the same rights as anyone else until he tried to exercise them, and then he might be legally restrained.[25]

This view was sustained over the next two decades. In July 1923, a Negro watchmaker from Kitchener was refused service in a restaurant while visiting London, Ontario. His suit, in *Franklin* v. *Evans,* to "establish . . . what he believes to be a right as a Canadian citizen," was dismissed the following year because the restaurant had no monopoly on service—the plaintiff was free to seek a meal elsewhere. In July 1936, two Negroes in the company of a white man were refused service in a tavern attached to Montreal's Forum, although the plaintiff held a season-ticket to the hockey matches played in the building and had previously been served in the tavern. In *Christie and Another* v. *York Corporation,* the Superior Court found illegal the bylaw by which the defendant said it might refuse service to Negroes. Upon appeal, the higher court, with one dissent, overturned this decision, ruling that "in the absence of any specific law, a merchant . . . is free to carry on his business in the manner that he conceives to be best." Upon further appeal to the Supreme Court of Canada, the Chief Justice, Sir Lyman P. Duff, ruled for the majority that the doctrine of freedom of commerce gave a tavern-keeper the right to refuse to sell beer to a Negro solely on the ground of color. The plaintiff had been refused service without commotion, and if he had been humiliated, as he claimed, it was because he persisted in demanding service and called the police, "which was entirely unwarranted." In dissent, one justice contended that the holder of the permit to sell liquor under the province's laws was not an ordinary trader but held a quasi-monopoly, since the plaintiff could not reasonably have sought service elsewhere. Nonetheless, the notion of freedom of commerce was upheld, and it would remain supreme in Quebec into the 1960s, freedom of contract running counter and superior to the principle of equality before the law.[26]

25. *Les Rapports judiciaires de Québec . . . Cour Superiéure (en Révision) . . . ,* 15 (Montreal, 1899), 104–12; *Les Rapports judiciaires de Québec . . . Cour du banc de la reine, 8* (Montreal, 1899), 379–84; ibid., *30* (1921), 459–67; *Montreal Gazette,* March 5, 1919; *Crisis, 18* (1919), 36.

26. *The Ontario Law Reports . . . 1923–1924, 55* (Toronto, 1924), 349–52; *Québec . . . Cour Superiéure . . . , 75* (1957), 136–38; *Cour du banc du roi, 65* (1938)́, 104–39; *Dominion Law Reports, 1* (Toronto, 1940), 81–92. For commentary on the case, see Scott, *Canadian Constitution,* pp. 36–38, and Bora Laskin, "Tavern Refusing to Serve Negro—Discrimination," *The Canadian Law Review, 18* (1940), 314–16.

There were no rapid changes in the legal quarter, unlike in other spheres of Negro interest, during World War II. Indeed, in 1946 in Nova Scotia, *R. v. Desmond* saw a decision in line with those of the 1920s. In November 1946, a Negro resident of Halifax, Viola Desmond, purchased a balcony ticket for a theater in New Glasgow and then sat elsewhere. When the manager threatened to remove her, she offered to pay the difference in price; a police officer carried her from the theater and she spent the night in jail. In court the next day she was found guilty—although without representation by counsel—of violation of a provincial statute requiring payment of an entertainment tax of one cent. Fined $20 and costs, she failed to file notice of appeal within the required ten days, and when she later did so—the delay being explained on the ground of having been injured during the arrest—the province's higher court, being under no legal obligation to accept the case, did not.[27]

Here and there a court decision suggested that the principle of equality stood above a narrowly defined freedom of contract; in 1949 the Supreme Court of Canada ruled restrictive covenants illegal, and as provincial legislatures passed FEP and FAP acts, the courts were moved to uphold them in a series of cases in the late 1950s and early 1960s. Still, as the *Vancouver Daily Province* noted with respect to the nullification of that city's covenants, ways would be found to get around the decision since, one owner explained, people liked to restrict themselves to their own kind: "We exclude aliens, Asiatics and Negroes and we discourage Jews." In 1960 much doubt was expressed in professional legal circles about the efficacy of the new federal Bill of Rights; and in 1962, in *R. v. Gonzales,* the Court of Appeal of British Columbia made plain the problems involved.

An Indian, convicted of possessing liquor off a reserve, which was contrary to the Indian Act of 1952, appealed on the bases of the principle of "equality before the law" and the new Bill of Rights. Two justices dismissed the appeal on the ground that "equality before the law" did not mean that there need be the same laws for everyone; the third member of the court, in a concurring opinion, argued that the Bill of Rights did not repeal the Indian Act, having no greater force than any other legislation. As an early spokesman for the original Bill of Rights now remarked, it stood revealed as a "botched up document."

Following the *Robertson & Rosetanni* decision in the Supreme Court two years later, one Negro asserted that it had become impossibly "difficult to fight an enemy who smiles." Clearly, World War II had brought some changes for the Canadian Negro, had accelerated some, and had revealed

27. J. B. Milner, "Civil Liberties . . . Abuse of Legal Process," *The Canadian Law Review, 25* (1947), 915–24; *Toronto Star,* Nov. 30, 1946, May 17, 1947; *Saturday Night* (Dec. 7, 1946), p. 5; *The Clarion, 2* (Jan. 15, 1943), 2.

the need for some. Yet twenty years later many blacks felt they still were "creeping about the plantation dodging the trees." [28]

By the end of World War II activist black men in Canada wanted, above all other changes, two forms of legislative recognition of their equality. Canadian-born Negroes had placed much emphasis upon the need for a pyramid of strictly enforced civil rights laws: provincial fair employment and fair accommodation acts and a federal bill of rights. These they had received by 1960. West Indians, on the whole not yet citizens, were more concerned about a liberalization of Canada's restrictive immigration policy, both in order to help other West Indians to come to Canada and because they considered the operative law of 1910 a personal affront. Both groups had numerous allies; indeed, only because both goals coincided with the desires of other ethnic groups did the black reformers win. Indians, Eskimaux, Ukrainians, and others were no less eager to see legislation on civil rights, and Greeks, Italians, Hungarians, Chinese, and South Asians were no less vocal in their protests against the immigration policy.[29]

Canadian immigration policy was never as restrictive as that of Australia or New Zealand, and it was only marginally more offensive to black men than the policy pursued by the United States for half of the twentieth century. Yet Canada faced a special problem. Not only as a member of the Commonwealth of Nations which, after 1931, began to work out numerous and often surprisingly effective means of communication between former dependencies of Great Britain, but also as the senior member (after the United Kingdom) of that association of states, Canada thought of itself as a pacesetter in the long process of evolutionary

28. *The Clarion, 3* (July 31, 1948), 5; *Toronto Star,* Feb. 23, 1940; *Toronto Globe & Mail,* June 10, 12, 1948, Jan. 11, 1949; *Montreal Star,* Nov. 20, 22, 1950; *Daily Province,* Nov. 20, Dec. 25, 1950; *Montreal Gazette,* July 17, 1965; *Toronto Telegram,* Aug. 13, 1965; *Prince Albert Herald,* Nov. 16, 1965; Files of the BCAACP, in the possession of Frank Collins, Burnaby: "Survey of Racial Discrimination in Vancouver Beer Parlours," Nov. 1951; John T. Saywell, ed., *Canadian Annual Review for 1962* (Toronto, 1963), pp. 283–84.

29. Except where otherwise documented, the following paragraphs are drawn from David C. Corbett, *Canada's Immigration Policy: A Critique* (Toronto, 1957); Corbett, "Canada's Immigration Policy, 1957–1962," *International Journal, 18* (1963), 166–80; George A. Rawlyk, "Canada's Immigration Policy, 1945–1962," *Dalhousie Review, 42* (1962), 287–300; Michael Barkway, "Turning Point for Immigration?" *Behind the Headlines, 17* (Nov. 1957), whole no.; Mabel F. Timlin, "Recent Changes in Government Attitudes toward Immigration," RSC, *Transactions,* 3rd ser., vol. 49, sec. 2 (1955), pp. 95–105; and Timlin, "Canadian Immigration Policy: An Analysis," *International Migration, 3* (1965), 52–73. The 1910 act is chap. 93 in *The Revised Statutes of Canada, 1927* . . . (Ottawa, 1927), *2,* 2065–111.

government. Several of the steps toward the Commonwealth idea had first been taken by Canadians, or as a result of Canadian insistence, Canadian pressure, or—as in the instance of the Durham Report in 1839—a crisis arising from Canadian events. With good reason Canadians sometimes called their country the First Dominion, in chronology and in leadership. Also with reason, West Indians, South Asians, and—after World War II, with the independence of India, Pakistan, Ceylon, Ghana, and Malaya in rapid succession—the nationals of other Commonwealth members, asked what the Commonwealth relationship meant if they were virtually barred from admittance to that First Dominion.

Canadians pointed out that the Statute of Westminster, by which the Commonwealth became a reality, explicitly stated that each member nation was "sovereign and equal" and that, as such, the Dominion had no less right to bar entry to nationals of other foreign nations—whatever special relationship existed—than those nations had to bar Canadians. As William Lyon Mackenzie King stated in the House of Commons in 1947, "Canada is perfectly within her rights in selecting the persons whom we regard as desirable future citizens. It is not a 'fundamental human right' of any alien to enter Canada. It is a privilege." [30] Read from Jamaica this may have seemed arrogant, but it was unquestionably true.

What seemed increasingly offensive to West Indians, however, as the world moved rapidly away from the certitudes of the 1930s and 1940s, was King's assertion that the people of Canada did not wish, as a result of mass immigration, "to make a fundamental alteration in the character of our population." Although King was speaking of Orientals, this formulation became the writ to which postwar ministers of immigration returned. The writ was, in all probability, set more firmly by King's secretary, John W. Pickersgill, who in 1954 become Canada's second Minister of Citizenship and Immigration. From 1947 until 1957, under Pickersgill (and his predecessor Walter Harris), policy adhered to this statement.

Canada's was not, in fact, an ungenerous immigration policy. From 1947 to 1954 Canada admitted 165,697 displaced persons, largely victims of the war. In 1956 Pickersgill dropped all immigration barriers so that thousands of refugees from the Hungarian uprising of that year could find new homes in Canada, and only the unwillingness of Ontario to absorb as many as could come led to a closure of this rescue mission. Despite what King said, by 1957 it was apparent to most observers that the character of the Canadian population was changing, for a third group—neither British nor French so much as indiscriminately continental European—was evident in all statistics. By 1969 twenty-seven percent of all Canadians were of neither French nor British background. Nonetheless, all continentals did

30. Canada, *House of Commons Debates, 1947:* May 1, pp. 352, 365.

not think of themselves as a single group; and most ethnic groups, although often keeping to themselves, tended to use as their basis for integration the social, and particularly the economic, patterns of the predominant old-line Canadians into whose environment they moved. Those Italians who settled in Ontario sought to learn English, as did German Mennonites who prudently reported themselves in census returns as Dutch. European Jews who settled in Montreal found French useful to learn. However, while the balance between the two languages, French and English, was tilted more toward the latter, the mass immigration did not substantially disturb the key indices—language and religion—traditionally used by Canadians to determine the sense of who they were.[31]

Under such circumstances Negroes had no real place. Their language was English, except for a small number of Haitians who came to live in Montreal.[32] The West Indian inclination was to gravitate toward English-speaking Canadians, and largely toward the old stock Charter groups, since the New Canadians, as immigrants were called, were likely to speak English far less well than the blacks and yet were also likely to look down upon them. Furthermore, Europeans often thought of Negroes as rivals for jobs which, given the steadily rising Canadian unemployment figures of the 1950s, were scarce. The old-line Canadians, while certainly not racist in the sense of white South Africans, firmly believed that men of the tropics could not assimilate readily, could not take the long Canadian winter, or would not be accepted by the new European residents, whose skills seemed higher and more desirable.

Many pressures were at work on the ministers of citizenship and immigration, and on the whole these much-abused figures moved ahead of the people rather than behind them. Virtually all commentators in newspapers, from the pulpit, and within the universities, agreed that Canadians did not want large-scale Oriental or African migrations to the Dominion. In a democracy, the ministers properly gave the people what they wanted: in Canada a Gallup Poll taken in 1956 showed that nearly sixty percent of the respondents felt that immigration policy should make entry more difficult for some than for others. But the ministers were also alert to those winds of change sweeping through the United Nations, across Africa and Asia, and even up from the United States. Each recognized that on balance Canada's discriminatory policy was harmful in international

31. James Eayrs, *Canada in World Affairs: October 1955 to June 1957* (Toronto, 1959), p. 47; Learie (now Lord) Constantine, *Colour Bar* (London, 1954), p. 77; *Toronto Financial Post,* July 12, 1952; William Petersen, *The Politics of Population* (Garden City, N.Y., 1964), pp. 314–15, 319–21. According to the *Encyclopedia of Canada* (Toronto, 1926), *4, 388,* "Canada has never welcomed Negro immigration."

32. Lysiane Gagnon, "Les Haïtiens, ces immigres pas comine les autres," *Montreal La Presse,* Aug. 21, 1965. In 1969 there were about 4,000 Haitians in Canada.

relations. Each thought that in the long run economics and not race would determine the movement of peoples. Each also saw that even were the barriers lowered, at least marginally, there would be no sudden black rush toward Canada. The greater danger lay in a rush of Asians, and one could not lower the gates for West Indians (who would come) and for Africans (who probably would not in any great number) while barring Asians, and expect to be purged of charges of discrimination. Once again, the black man was excluded largely because he was unwittingly linked to a greater source of Canadian fear.

Thus ministers of immigration were expected to do nothing that would impair Canadian sovereignty, yet had to show Canada to be a democratic, humanitarian nation willing to help the distressed. Ministers must be conscious of world opinion, and especially so as Canada began to find a middle-power rôle to play in the polarized Cold War world—a rôle that was often thought to involve interpreting a "colored" nation such as India to a "white" nation such as the United States. They must also do nothing that would cost their party defeat at the polls—and by the 1950s at least twelve federal ridings could have turned upon ethnic issues. Employers wanted more immigrants, and some—especially in Quebec—were quick to use them as strikebreakers; the Canadian Labour Congress tended to oppose immigration from fear that wages would go down. Fundamentalist Protestant clergymen disliked Italians, Greeks, and Hungarians because they were likely to be Roman Catholics; many French Canadians insisted that the Catholic balance in the population must be preserved. Professional groups, such as the medical associations, were doubtful of the qualifications of the professional men among the new arrivals. Highly technical enterprises wanted immigrants with specialized skills, university degrees, and immediate competence in English or French; employers in the building trades, in construction work, and in heavy industry in general preferred more stalwart laborers in sheepskin jackets. While the nation needed immigrants and knew this, the nation fragmented into time-honored interest groups when the real question was raised: what kind of immigrants?

On the whole the immigration laws themselves answer this question. The basis for the initial postwar immigration was the Act of 1910, parliamentary revisions of that act in the interwar years, and Orders-in-Council. Numerous inconsistencies burdened the system, and in 1952 the government promulgated new regulations, which were proclaimed on June 1, 1953. During the debate on the bill, minister Harris hewed closely to the Liberal line as laid down by Mackenzie King in 1947, saying that Canada wanted "a good type of immigrant" and identifying this type with those who could become readily integrated. Accordingly, the provisions of the act of 1952 gave the minister the power to prohibit the entry of an immigrant because of "nationality, citizenship, ethnic group, occupation, class or geographical area of origin," because of "peculiar customs, habits, modes of life or methods of holding property" and, in addition to other provisos, because of "unsuitability having regard to the climatic, economic, social, industrial, educational, labour, health, or other conditions, or requirements existing [in Canada], temporarily or otherwise." The minister received great discretionary power under the act, which became the basis for the relatively flexible policy that characterized the remaining years of the Liberal government. Thus, Pickersgill admitted Hungarians without an extensive canvass of public opinion, while Harris, also without resort to polls, rejected West Indians.

Blacks protested in particular against the application of a "climatic" criterion to their suitability as immigrants. Even before the new regulations came into effect, they were challenged, for a Barbadan granddaughter of a Canadian citizen was rejected on these broad grounds. Joseph Noseworthy, CCF Member of Parliament for York South, wrote to Harris for clarification; the minister responded somewhat disingenuously that "experience" had shown that people from tropical countries were more apt to break down in health than those from temperate zones, and "generally speaking, persons from tropical or subtropical countries find it more difficult to succeed" in Canada. "It would be quite contrary to fact, however, to infer from this that coloured immigrants are debarred from Canada." Rather, "exceptional qualifications" would lead to favorable consideration. On April 24, 1953, Noseworthy read portions of this letter to the House of Commons. Blacks at once challenged the statement and pointed out that West Indians were being asked to offer "exceptional qualifications" to counteract a vague notion about climatic disabilities. Stanley G. Grizzle called the letter "illogical, unsound, undemocratic and un-Christian," and Noseworthy turned it against its author, since Harris had contended that the disabilities arising from climate were "a matter of record." What, Noseworthy asked, putting his questions on the order paper of the House— thus demanding a prepared reply from the Department—was the number of British West Indians living in Canada, how many had entered between 1947 and 1951, and what statistics existed comparing these West Indians' health records with other immigrants? In each case Harris's answer was that such information was not available.[33]

Nor did Harris improve matters by confessing that his letter had been

33. Canadian Institute of Public Opinion, Gallup Poll of Canada, release, Feb. 29, 1956; *The Canadian Negro, 1* (June 1953), 2, 4; *CCF Comment: 3* (June 1953), 9; *5* (vii/1955), 12; and *2* (ix/1952), passim; Canada, *House of Commons Debates, 1953:* April 24.

sent out by mistake, and that he had meant to reconsider the phrases—
drafted by someone else—before it was posted. He issued a public statement which, while stated negatively, suggested that West Indians could
become citizens—a remark that already had appeared in his letter. The
statement was somewhat irrelevant, as several black activists pointed out,
for applications for citizenship related to those already within Canada, and
there was no law that would suggest that Negroes were not accorded the
same treatment as whites when applying for citizenship, the real issue
being entry. In any event, from 1953, instructions sent to special inquiry
officers acting under the immigration regulations omitted reference to
climate.

Late in 1955 the Canadian government agreed to admit one hundred
female domestics each year from Jamaica and Barbados. By 1960 the
government increased the number to nearly three hundred. Under the
regulations some were able to have their fiancés and close relatives join
them, and the domestics could take out citizenship after five years. The
effect of this regulation, though it supplied upper-class homes in Montreal,
Toronto, and Ottawa with badly needed household help, could well have
been harmful to the West Indian community as a whole, for it brought into Canada a class of people calculated to foster white notions of superiority,
since West Indians were to be found largely in menial jobs. In fact, however, some of the domestics were relatively well-educated young women
who chose this means of gaining entry to Canada, even though the
majority were scarcely above the level of literacy. If Canadians were to
receive the West Indians with respect, the government would need to
conduct an educational (or what the 1970s would call a "sensitivity") program among the employers.[34]

A newly instituted Citizenship Branch of the immigration department,
charged with such education, attempted to fulfill this need. Staffed by
idealists who found any taint of discriminatory policy personally objectionable, and faced with the difficult job of discovering, analyzing, and then
disseminating a coherent "Canadianism" which generations of Canadians
themselves had been unable to find, the branch became a useful but
scarcely powerful propaganda voice in the federal government's effort to
educate Canadians to accept the equality of men. A number of brochures
attempted to explain in simple language the concept of a plural society,
and each ethnic group in Canada was dutifully mentioned in a compli-
mentary way. The branch also financed some of the research carried on by
the Institute of Public Affairs at Dalhousie University in Halifax. How-

34. Corbett, *Immigration*, p. 55; *Canadian Labour Reports, 11* (Jan. 1, 1956),
1–2; *MacDuff Ottawa Report* (Toronto), Aug. 24, 1959; *Toronto Telegram*, March
8, 1961.

ever, cooperation with voluntary home and school associations was not as close as it should have been, the old line Negro leadership in Canada tended to suspect a West Indian bias in the work of the branch, and the federal government did not supply funds adequate to the charge.[35]

Few West Indians who gained admission to Canada reported overt discrimination, although difficulties in finding adequate housing was commonplace. The experiences of a Trinidadian, Yvonne Bobb, who came to Canada for advanced work in library science despite having to serve a year as a domestic to gain admittance, were representative: on presenting herself to the YWCA in Toronto, she was referred to the British West Indian Club on the assumption that she would prefer to be with "her own kind." (A contemporary survey of Canadian YWCA secretaries found that nearly seventy-five percent thought marriage of white women to men of another race was distasteful, and they wished not to create contacts that might lead to interracial marriages.) Miss Bobb, who returned to a university position in Trinidad in 1966, concluded that blacks still had to leave the Dominion if they wished to progress in their work, that the problem of education against prejudice was great in Canada precisely because most Canadians thought there was no need for such education, and that the West Indian students and domestics would have to unite with African students if they wished to be heard.[36]

Nor did the plan for domestics work as well as white Canadians hoped. In 1959 there were five hundred West Indian women in Canada, drawn on a quota system from Jamaica, Barbados, Trinidad, British Guiana, St. Lucia, and St. Vincent. Regulations held that they must be single, between twenty-one and thirty-five years of age, must pay their own passage, and must remain as a domestic for one year. Insular, at first still divided by memories of island rivalries, often of rude peasant stock, and obliged to do the work that three would normally do in the West Indies, the women were confused and unhappy. Sent to seventeen different cities across Canada, the women concluded that Canadian policy was shaped by a preoccupation with their sex: that Canadians feared the black male and deliberately chose to separate the black women so that they could not find male companionship. The result was disgruntled, future-obsessed domestics who hoped to move into professional nursing, or to go to the United States

35. Interview with Miss Josephine Lynam of Ottawa, in Halifax, Feb. 17, 1960.
36. V. C. Phelan, "Organisation of Migration into Canada," *International Labour Review,* 65 (1952), 325; Bobb, "Are Canadians Really Tolerant?" *Chatelaine, 34* (Sept. 1959), 27, 64, 66; *Canadian Labour Reports, 11* (Aug. 1956), 3; Edbrooke Sidney Wyborn, "The Canadian Y.M.C.A. as an Agent of International Understanding" (D. Ed. diss., Columbia Univ. Teachers College, 1960), pp. 73–74; Violet P. King, "Canadian Adventure," *The* [YMCA] *Journal* (Toronto), Jan. 1959, pp. 8–10.

where they could become hairdressers or dressmakers; and many performed their duties badly because they regarded them as purely temporary. Those who tried to bring their fiancés to Canada, as they were permitted to do, found the regulations cumbersome and insulting; for the fiancé was supposed to marry them within thirty days of arrival or return to the West Indies, and a woman could be asked to prove that the man she sponsored was truly her fiancé by surrendering personal letters to substantiate the relationship.[37]

Students comprised a second group of temporary blacks in Canada. The number of students from the West Indies and Africa rose steadily in the years after World War II, and on the whole they were well-received by the white community. In Sackville, New Brunswick, where many attended Mount Allison University, they were admitted to all university functions on a basis of full equality, although by unspoken convention they did not attend Saturday night dances in the town. At first their failure rate at Canadian universities was high, and interisland competition was carried into the universities to the extent that Trinidadians and Barbadians would not work together; but by 1960 such divisive tendencies had been reduced to a minimum. The number of West Indian students in Canada grew from four hundred and fifty in 1955 to three thousand by 1965, with particularly large contingents at Queen's, McGill, Sir George Williams, Mount Allison, and Dalhousie universities, at Macdonald College and the School of Agriculture at Guelph (now the University of Guelph), and at the universities of British Columbia, Manitoba, and Toronto. Few attended French-speaking universities, although a handful of Haitians did so.[38]

Nonetheless, these students seldom added to the general strength of black Canadians. In Halifax they were unwilling to mix with the less educated Negroes of Africville or Cornwallis Street, and in Montreal black students at Loyola University drafted a resolution prohibiting West Indian domestics from attending student functions. Aware that they were present in Canada only temporarily, the students drew into organizations of their

37. Violet P. King, "Calypso in Canada," *Canadian Welfare, 34* (Nov. 1, 1958), 178–83; *Time* (Canadian ed.), Oct. 17, 1955, p. 35; George Lamming, "The West Indians: Our Loneliest Immigrants," *Macelan's Magazine* (Nov. 4, 1961), pp. 27, 52, 54–56; *Victoria Daily Colonist,* May 30, 1961; Frances Henry, "The West Indian Domestic Scheme in Canada," *Expression, 3* (ii/1968), 14–22.

38. Interviews with university officials at Dalhousie, Mount Allison, Sir George Williams, and Queen's universities; at the universities of British Columbia, Manitoba, and Toronto; and at United College, February–March 1960, June–July 1965. See also Fayne Bullen, "Relations between Canada and the West Indies (1600–1959)" (B.A. honours thesis, Mount Allison Univ., 1959), pp. 102–05, 115–16. The location of West Indian students may be ascertained from the *Location List* [of] *West Indian Students in Canada, 1961–62* (Montreal, [1961]), *et seq.,* issued by the Montreal Office of Commissioners for the West Indies, British Guiana, and British Honduras.

own, whether a West Indian Students' Club—which at McGill published a newspaper and fostered a self-contained social life—or the continental African Students Association of the United States and Canada.[39] As students, they were not permitted to work, and yet nearly all had to do so if they were to complete their education. This led to evasions of the law, to the necessity of taking work many felt demeaning and at lower than ordinary wages, and forced all who were confronted with clear discrimination in job applications to remain silent, since a formal complaint would also be an implicit confession of intent to break the law. Many West Indians felt they were exploited by employers who were well aware of the situation.[40]

The emerging West Indian leadership also had known discrimination in Canada. As a young man Sir Alexander Bustamante, the prime minister of Jamaica from 1962 until 1967, had lived briefly in Canada, which he had not liked; and the fact that Sir Grantley Herbert Adams, premier of Barbados and first prime minister of the short-lived West Indian Federation, was honored by both Mount Allison University and the University of Alberta may not have entirely canceled out his memory of being refused service in a Montreal hotel shortly after becoming Barbados's leader. When a white teacher who was married to the daughter of the accountant-general of Jamaica was discharged from his position in a private school at Shawnigan Lake near Victoria, British Columbia in 1954, on what appeared to be racial grounds, the Jamaican Parliament formally protested. In 1961 the Jamaican premier, Norman Manley, openly attacked the Canadian color bar, as he saw it; and two years later, while speaking at the University of New Brunswick, the new prime minister of Barbados, Earl Barrow, charged Canadians with discriminating against West Indians in trade as well as in immigration. Eric Williams, Prime Minister of Trinidad and Tobago, was even more forthright in his condemnation of the "color-bar." [41]

39. The association sponsored *The African Interpreter,* published in New York from 1943–44, the February, March, and April 1943, and spring 1944, issues of which contain news of African students in Canada. See also C. S. Bayne, "The Social Function of Resident Caribbean Associations (Montreal)," *Expression, 2* (ii/1967), 25–33.

40. One of the commonest forms of summer employment for West Indian (but not African) students was taxi driving. Since I also drove taxis while at university, I sought out such West Indians whenever I needed transport in the larger Canadian cities, and found that most were willing to discuss their grievances. The preceding paragraphs, therefore, are based largely upon a number of such informal talks.

41. Colin Rickard, *Caribbean Power* (London, 1963), p. 21; *Edmonton Journal,* Sept. 22–24, Oct. 2, 13, 18, 28, 30, Nov. 3, 4, 1954, Aug. 3, 1959; *Time* (Canadian ed.), Oct. 4, 1954, p. 26; *Toronto Daily Star,* July 7, 1961, May 26, 1965; *Atlantic Advocate, 54* (Nov. 1963), 71; Sheila Patterson, *Dark Strangers: A Sociological Study of the Absorption of a Recent West Indian Migrant Group in Brixton, South London* (London, 1963), p. 313.

For the most part few Canadians specifically cited race as their reason for wishing to block West Indian immigrants, but the arguments of the 1950s and 1960s echoed those of the 1920s. Writing for *Maclean's*, Canada's leading mass-circulating magazine, a former adjutant-general of the Canadian Army argued that no nation could survive a "process of dilution," for—to coin a phrase—oil and water would not mix. Writing for the prestigious journal of the Canadian Institute of International Affairs, an executive officer of the Ford Motor Company of Windsor stated that Canadians must expand their population as quickly as possible, and that it was "inevitable that economics will take precedence over race"; yet he concluded, in the face of his own evidence and argument, that in view of the fact that "civilization . . . in Canada" was "set on three foundations, one Western, one Christian and one industrial," Negroes would not adapt to Canada's needs by taking "the final and most important step of intermarriage." In 1965 religious fundamentalists in Saskatchewan, insisting that segregation was God-ordained, required all students at the Briercrest Bible Institute near Moose Jaw to sign a pledge not to engage in interracial dating. Three years later a right-wing weekly review from Ontario equated the mildest forms of black activism with race hatred. Interracial adoption schemes encountered much hostility. The traditional arguments from those who did not think of themselves as racists could still be heard.[42]

Happily, these voices were fewer by the 1960s, and Canadian policy underwent further change in 1962, the year of Great Britain's restrictive Commonwealth Immigration Act. Mrs. Ellen Fairclough, the second Progressive-Conservative minister of citizenship and immigration under Prime Minister Diefenbaker and the first woman cabinet minister in Canada, brought in new regulations which put stress upon education and skills. Each immigrant would be considered "entirely on his own merit, without regard to race, colour, national origin or the country from which he comes." West Indians hailed the new regulations as the vindication they had sought. Ironically, prior to the passage of the new act, many Canadians had viewed Mrs. Fairclough as a particularly discriminatory minister, and students at United College in Manitoba had hanged her in effigy. Much of the hostility to her, however, quite obviously arose because of her manner rather than her method. She was not lacking in courage, and as early as 1951, as a member of parliament from Hamilton West, she had introduced

42. Macklin, "Canada Doesn't Need More People," *Maclean's* (Oct. 27, 1956); Donald Gordon, "Canada's Immature Afro-Asian Romance," *Saturday Night, 76* (April 15, 1961), 15–16; Paul M. Roddick, "Canadian Immigration Policy: The Hard Facts," *International Journal, 11* (1956), 124, 127–28; *Lloydminster Times,* May 19, 1965; *Moose Jaw Times-Herald,* April 19, 1965; *Saint John Telegraph-Journal,* April 20, 1965; *On Target* (Flesherton, Ont.), June 10, 1968, p. 2; Margaret E. Edgar, ed., "Some Experiences in Inter-Racial Adoption," *Expression, 3* (i/1968), 13–22.

an antidiscrimination bill. Still, although she wished to give Canada a freer and more fully planned immigration policy, she could appear to be stiff-necked and offensive; and following the election of 1962, Diefenbaker moved her to the postmaster-generalship and brought in French Canadian ministers who were able to project a more benevolent image.

Thereafter West Indian migration increased rapidly. In 1946–50 there had been 947 black arrivals, or 0.22 percent of the total number of immigrants; for 1961–65 there were 11,835, or 2.37 percent of the total; and by 1966 blacks—largely West Indian—comprised over 3 percent of all immigration. In that year the Canadian government issued a White Paper on immigration which stated that there would be "no discrimination by reason of race, colour or religion." In 1967 immigration from Africa, the West Indies, and Brazil (substantially Negro by North American reasoning) rose past the ten thousand mark, or just below 5 percent of the total influx for the year; in 1969 the figure was 8 percent. Of the total black immigration, over seventy percent was from the West Indies. By 1968 —when Canada took 464 teachers, doctors, engineers, and journalists from the West Indies—the size and nature of the flow had created a backlash among some West Indian nationalists, who feared that the Dominion, hungry for skills, would denude the islands of its most highly educated stratum, a charge largely without foundation. Canadians were learning the realities of race.[43]

Perhaps the most important change brought by the 1960s lay not in regulations but in perspective. The removal of discriminatory bases for admission, the improvement of the immigration service itself, and increased use of the minister's discretionary powers—largely on the side of benevolence—were the most important of the changes. Symbolic proof was given to the Canadian contention that policy was no longer racially discriminatory when a recruiting office was opened in Tokyo, Japan—the one nonwhite nation where technical skills were beginning to be reasonably abundant.[44] However, as a leading student and critic of Canadian immigra-

43. Frank Rasky, "Ellen Fairclough: Saint or Sinner to New Canadians?" *Liberty,* *37* (May 1960), 17, 46, 48–51; *Montreal Star,* Oct. 13, 1951, Dec. 14, 1952, April 14, 18, 1953; *Toronto Telegram,* Dec. 7, 1961; John T. Saywell, ed., *Canadian Annual Review for 1961* (Toronto, 1962), pp. 225–27; *for 1962, pp. 204–05; for 1965,* p. 314; Wallace Collins, *Jamaican Migrant* (London, 1965), pp. 120–22; *Time* (Canadian ed.), July 15, 1966, p. 12; Rosaine Morin, *L'Immigration au Canada* (Montreal, 1966), p. 62; Anthony H. Richmond, *Post-War Immigrants in Canada* (Toronto, 1967), pp. 5, 16; *Canadian Immigration Policy, 1966* (Ottawa), p. 6; *Expression, Special Bulletin,* nos. 1 and 2 [1969], on "The Anderson Affair"; Kingston (Jam.) *Sunday Gleaner,* March 2, 1969; *Abeng National Weekly* (Kingston), Feb. 22, 1969, p. [4]; *Contrast,* Aug. 15, 1970.

44. *Canada Year Book 1962* (Ottawa, 1962), pp. 161–67; Blair Fraser, "The Built-in Lie Behind Our Search for Immigrants," *Mclean's, 78* (June 19, 1965), 12; B. B. Davison, *Commonwealth Immigrants* (London, 1964), passim. Immigration

tion policy pointed out in 1963, the most significant step lay in "placing . . . immigration policy in its proper context as part of foreign policy." In March of 1962, shortly before giving up her post, Mrs. Fairclough declared that "Canadians too realize that the winds of change are blowing. The maturity we show today can reap big dividends for future generations." It was in this spirit that subsequent ministers conducted themselves, and it was in the context of foreign affairs that many overseas observers interpreted the new policy. As the *Toronto Daily Star*—which had campaigned for many of the changes—noted when the regulations of 1962 came into effect, Canada had removed a major obstacle to improved standing in the Commonwealth, the United Nations, and the world.[45]

As the Dominion played an increasing rôle in world affairs in the 1960s, Canadians became more and more conscious of a basic fact of modern life: that nonwhites far outnumber whites and that African and Asian nations could soon outvote Europe and North America in the United Nations. Canadian newspapers between 1960 and 1965 showed a steady upward curve in African-related stories, both because of the inherent news value in the emergence of African states, and because of the new strains placed upon the Commonwealth by the rise of such nations.[46] The rapid march of apartheid in South Africa attracted much attention, and Canadian newspapers often pointed out the relevance of events in Africa and the West Indies to the local situation, occasionally straining to do so. The presence of a substantial number of Canadian signalers and supply personnel in the African United Nations Emergency Force that began service in the strife-

---

figures appear in the *Canada Year Books,* in the *Quarterly Immigration Bulletin* of the Department of Citizenship and Immigration, and in the *Annual Reports* of the Department. The last figures are drawn from Department of Manpower and Immigration, *1967 Immigration Statistics* (Ottawa, 1968), p. 5. But for hostile appraisals of the new regulations, see the Negro Citizenship Association's journal, *Expression,* 2 (ii/1967), 3–10.

45. Corbett, "Immigration Policy, 1957–1962," p. 179. There has been little suggestion of discrimination since 1962. When a score of Greek sailors who illegally entered Canada, and an American Negro, Harry Claude Hooper, were kept in Toronto's Don Jail for nearly two months, the New Democratic party demanded an investigation. A Toronto lawyer who carried out a meticulous examination of deportation procedures found administrative laxness and errors, but no evidence of discrimination. Hooper, three times deported, had deserted his Toronto wife, refused to answer questions, and was clearly an undesirable; and the lawyer, Joseph Sedgwick, concluded that to make him "the object of sentimental sympathy is ridiculous." See *Time* (Canadian ed.), April 16, 1965; Canada, *House of Commons Debates, 1965:* col. 1929; *Toronto Star,* Jan. 29, 1962.

46. See *Toronto Star,* July 15, 17, 19, 20, 27; *Fredericton Gleaner,* July 16, 20, 21–23, 27–29, Aug. 5; *Toronto Telegram,* July 26; *Kingston Whig-Standard,* July 31; *Montreal Star,* July 28, all 1965.

torn Congo in 1960, and the visit to Canada of the Congolese prime minister, Patrice Lumumba, who wished French-speaking technical advisers to come to Leopoldville, both underscored the opportunity for Canada to be of direct service to Africans. Canadians, Lumumba said, were "honest and sincere people," and he looked to them because they too had "emerged from the colonial status to freedom." Operation Crossroads, American-based but including Canadians, the Colombo Plan, the Canadian University Service Overseas (CUSO), a steady stream of African ministers of state to Ottawa, the work of the Canadian-based United Church Mission (largely Congregational in content) in Angola—these and dozens of other means for widening contacts with nonwhites brought the intolerable pressures of knowledge to bear against indifference.[47]

Canadian awareness of the problems arising from racial discrimination became apparent at the Commonwealth Prime Minister's Conferences of 1960 and 1961. Prior to the 1960s the Canadian position on racial discrimination in South Africa had been cautious and somewhat aloof. While the Canadian delegation to the United Nations supported general condemnatory resolutions aimed at eliminating discriminatory practices, Canada had abstained in November 1959, when the General Assembly entertained a resolution more specifically criticizing apartheid in South Africa. The Canadian press had supported the Diefenbaker government in not meddling in South African affairs, and when the Canadian Labour Congress submitted a brief to Diefenbaker asking for the exclusion of South Africa from the Commonwealth, the prime minister had declined to support such action. Then, during the spring of 1960, events in South Africa rather than pressures within Canada changed Diefenbaker's mind.

In March the South African police at Sharpeville panicked in the face of an unruly but not violent demonstration and killed sixty-seven black Africans. Canadians were reminded that their world was shrinking, as the national press pointed out how Sabre jets, built in Montreal and sold to the South African government, had strafed the crowd. Two weeks later a Canadian reporter for the *Toronto Daily Star* was arrested in Durban, held for questioning, and released only after Diefenbaker sent a strongly worded protest. Immediately following this incident, the Canadian House of Commons opened debate on apartheid, although since the prime minister asked not to be forced to raise the question at the forthcoming Prime Ministers' Conference in London, it brought forth no resolution. Nonetheless, opinion clearly was running against South Africa—in the Commons, in newspapers, and in the intellectual community. The president of the Canadian Historical Association, William L. Morton, then of the University of Manitoba,

---

47. I wish to thank my undergraduate bursary student, Reginald Ford, for surveying Canadian newspapers and journals for me on this subject.

probably spoke for most academicians when he observed that racial discrimination had become incompatible with membership in the Commonwealth. At a rally in Toronto, organized by a Committee of Concern for South Africa, nearly three thousand people cheered a telegram sent to Diefenbaker asking for South African expulsion from the Commonwealth; the Canadian Labour Congress voted to boycott South African goods; and the president of Mount Allison University compared South Africa to Nazi Germany in 1936.[48]

The Commonwealth prime ministers met on May 3. Diefenbaker's desire to avoid discussion of apartheid was dashed when the prime minister of Malaya issued a press statement, contrary to convention, criticizing South Africa's delegate, Foreign Minister Erik Louw. Although Ghana was informed that it could retain membership in the Commonwealth when it became a republic, South Africa was warned that should it take such a step—as it planned to do—it would have to apply to the then-members of the Commonwealth conference for continued membership. By the following year nonwhite members would heavily dominate the meeting, for a number of African states were moving rapidly toward independence.

During the ensuing year, Diefenbaker formally embraced the concept of a multiracial Commonwealth and, reversing his earlier stand, was instrumental to South Africa's withdrawal from the association. When the Commonwealth prime ministers again convened in London in March of 1961, in special meeting to consider South Africa's application for continued membership, Diefenbaker at first sought some formula by which South Africa might remain a member. The spokesmen for Malaya, Ghana, and Nigeria made it clear that they would not remain if South Africa were permitted to do so, and Julius Nyerere of Tanganyika—soon to be independent Tanzania—suggested that his nation would not join. Diefenbaker and Prime Minister Jawaharlal Nehru of India, wishing to avoid direct expulsion, proposed a general resolution condemning racial discrimination in terms that would be unacceptable to South Africa's Prime Minister H. F. Verwoerd, and that nation accordingly withdrew its application for continued membership and resigned from the Commonwealth.

Diefenbaker had achieved a considerable personal victory. Sincere in his opposition to discrimination, he also felt that the Commonwealth relationship should be sufficiently flexible to contain virtually all political philos-

48. Guy Courrier, "The African Background," *The Canadian Forum, 40* (1960), 176; Peter Calvocoressi, *South Africa and World Opinion* (London, 1961), p. 4; *Toronto Globe & Mail* (Overseas Edition), Aug. 10, 29, 1960; Peter Worthington, "The Human Side of the Congo," *Saturday Night, 75* (Dec. 24, 1960), 12–13; *Time* (Canadian ed.), Dec. 30, 1966, p. 10; Canada, *House of Commons Debates,* 3rd sess., 24th Parl., *3* (Ottawa, 1960): 2451, 3087–88, 4357.

ophies. The only white prime minister to support the African and Asian nations, he provided a means by which the majority goal of South African exclusion could be achieved without resort to a formal condemnatory resolution. In the words of the Canadian (and the African) press, Diefenbaker was a Canadian hero; when he returned to Ottawa he was hailed by the House and, that same evening, by a rally of Tories. In Africa and Asia the Canadian Prime Minister was heralded, at least temporarily, as "the white champion of the colored races." Logically enough, then, when a Commonwealth secretariat was established in 1964, a Canadian—Arnold Smith— became its first director, largely at African urging.[49]

Nor was Africa the only source of moral pressure, for there remained the old mirror for reflecting and distorting Canadian values, the United States. As the American Negro drive for civil rights intensified, Canadians looked across the border with concern—and some air of superiority. Three thousand Canadians wrote to the Governor of Alabama in 1958 to urge clemency for a fifty-five year old Negro illiterate sentenced to death for stealing goods valued at $1.93. Canadians followed the efforts of the Reverend Martin Luther King in Montgomery and Atlanta, shuddered at Little Rock and again at Selma, walked to school with the lonely black children of New Orleans, looked on horrified at the conflagration in Watts in the summer of 1965, and wept a few lives later over Dr. King's murder. Television and radio brought American events into Canadian living rooms and schools, and Canadians responded by sending money to the NAACP and to Coretta King (and the Ku Klux Klan); by joining with freedom-riders to Jackson, Mississippi, in 1961; by marching on Montgomery and later on Washington; and by picketing the American consulate-general in Toronto. Black Americans also brought racial awareness directly to Canada, as members of the Washington-based Non-Violent Action Group addressed students at the University of Toronto, to which Canadians responded by organizing a Friends of Students Non-Violent Co-Ordinating Committee. The customary self-satisfied editorials of the 1950s were gone from the Canada of the mid-1960s; for every editorial intoning that one would "find no racial discrimination" in Canada, there were ten that invoked motes and beams, glass houses, and first stones.[50]

49. Richard A. Preston, *Canada in World Affairs, 1959 to 1961* (Toronto, 1965), pp. 200–05; *Edmonton Journal*, Dec. 8, 1959; *Montreal La Presse* and *Fredericton Daily Gleaner*, Jan. 29, 1960; *Halifax Chronicle-Herald*, Jan. 30, 1960, Nov. 11, 1961; *Montreal Star*, March 23, 1960; *Maclean's* (Feb. 13, May 21, 1960), both p. 4; *Toronto Globe & Mail*, May 3, 1960; *Time* (Canadian ed.), May 9, 1960, p. 11; *Kingston* (Jam.) *Gleaner*, May 10, 1960; William L. Morton, *The Canadian Identity* (Madison, Wisc., 1961), p. 56; Canada, *House of Commons Debates*, 4th sess., 24th Parl., *3* (Ottawa, 1961): 2451–52, 2619–21, 3011, 3079–87.

50. Preston, *Canada in World Affairs*, pp. 205–07; *New York Times*, Sept. 14,

Perhaps overreaction was to be expected, therefore, when in August 1965, the spectre of the Ku Klux Klan again appeared in Canada. The site was Amherstburg, where some three hundred Negroes lived side by side with four hundred whites. Five days of incidents threw the town into turmoil, providing an example of how concentrated newspaper coverage can embarrass an entire community into action. Very possibly, the Negroes of Ontario learned something of the uses and abuses of exaggeration from the tragi-comic events of Amherstburg, when the scenario of racial confrontation moved through its initial stages.

The chain of events began when the proprietor of a model-car raceway threw three Negro teenagers off his premises. Two returned and were arrested by the Amherstburg police for causing a disturbance; one allegedly was kept in jail for seven hours before charges were brought against him. Almost immediately afterwards, three other Negro boys came running home to say that a shot had been fired over their heads. The young daughter of a Negro double amputee reported that a voice, speaking in a broad southern accent, had said "nigger beware, the Klan is coming," over the telephone to her; and Ralph McCurdy, a town councillor, received a similar call. Two signs were painted on the black Baptist Church, and the markers on the approach highways denoting the name of the town were altered with spray paint to read, "Amherstburg . . . Home of KKK." At night a cross burned away on the town's main intersection without anyone admitting to having seen who placed it there.

Members of the predominantly Negro South Essex Citizens Advancement Society met under President George McCurdy and proposed a mass march upon the raceway, although after deliberation they agreed to send a small delegation to see the proprietor. In the meantime, the chief of police denied that anything more than teenage vandalism was involved. Professor Howard McCurdy of the University of Windsor, a brother of George and Ralph, cautioned the Negroes of Amherstburg not to overreact to what might well be pranks, and the mayor declared that an investigation had

1958; Peter C. Newman, *Renegade in Power: The Diefenbaker Years* (Toronto, 1963) pp. 258–59; A. Cairns, "South Africa and the Commonwealth," *The Canadian Forum, 41* (April 1961), 4; *Antigonish* (N.S.) *Casket,* May 31, 1956; *Toronto Telegram,* Feb. 8, 1961, April 8, 1968; *Vancouver Province,* Jan. 23, 1961; *Toronto Globe & Mail,* Feb. 17, March 6, 7, 14–18, 21, 1961; *Ottawa Citizen,* March 22, 1961; *Montreal Star,* March 27, 1961; *Vancouver Sun,* Feb. 8, March 24, 1961; *Calgary Herald,* April 15, 1961; *Ridgetown* (Ont.) *Dominion,* March 23, 1961; *Montreal Gazette,* Nov. 30, 1961; *Saturday Night* (April 29, 1961), p. 236; *MacDuff Ottawa Report,* March 27, 1961; "Canadian Team for Tanzania," *Canadian Army Journal, 19* (1965), 23–31; Peyton V. Lyon, *Canada in World Affairs, 1961–1963* (Toronto, 1968), pp. 290–302; interview with Mr. Arnold Smith in May 1965, in London.

shown that the shots thought to have been fired over the heads of the Negro children were discharged some distance away by a police officer in pursuit of a thief. The provincial attorney-general's office ordered an immediate investigation by the Ontario Provincial Police, who reported they could find no evidence of Klan activity; and the director of the Ontario Human Rights Commission, Dr. Hill, arrived to confer with local leaders. He, too, thought that pranksters rather than the Klan were involved, although George McCurdy continued to insist otherwise. On the evening of August 11 the *Toronto Telegram* lent credence to McCurdy's contention by printing a statement allegedly made by Robert Shelton, the Imperial Wizard of the Klan in the United States. The Klan, Shelton was quoted as saying, had shown substantial growth in Canada during the last few months.

Objectively it is difficult to know what to make of the incidents at Amherstburg. No other newspaper followed up Shelton's statement, and even the inflammatory *Telegram* did not contend that there was any direct connection between the Klan and the burning cross in Ontario. The Negro participants were highly contradictory, at least as reported in the press, for first one and then another was said to have received telephone calls, and the small boys over whose head a shot was fired could not recall whether they were walking down the street of the town or gathering rubbish from the dump at the time. The cross burned on various street corners and, at last, in the forecourt of a gasoline station. The town and provincial police, the attorney-general's office, and Dr. Hill could find no evidence of Klan activity. The confusion seemed to affect everyone—even the chief of police could not seem to remember consistently how long he had held his office— as the headlines moved across Canada. From St. John's, Newfoundland, to Victoria, British Columbia, the fiery cross in Amherstburg was front-page news.

Hill more than anyone else was responsible for the benefits that were to flow from the confusion. The blacks confronted Hill, himself a Negro, with sweeping charges of Klan activities, police incompetence, and widespread discrimination. Refusing to condone infringements on the civil liberties of others in a frantic search either to turn up the culprits or to whitewash the police, Hill and an investigative assistant quietly took statements while letting the pressure of newspaper opinion continue to build. The *Amherstburg Echo,* a weekly, appeared with the offer of an anonymous $100 reward for the arrest and conviction of those responsible for racial incidents. Hill did not comment when a reporter from the *Windsor Star* contacted Imperial Wizard Shelton again, to learn that he denied the *Telegram*'s story and that he insisted there were no members of the Klan in Canada. Even so, as

George McCurdy insisted, "A report like this is not silly until it has been proved silly."

For Negroes throughout Canada, the events at Amherstburg had a special meaning, and their more activist spokesmen were quick to point it out. It was in the same Baptist church, built in 1849 and now defaced by alleged Klan scribblings, that Mrs. Stowe's Eliza was reunited with her husband in *Uncle Tom's Cabin.* Here, at nearby Fort Malden, and at Windsor, were the chief memorials to the fugitive slave years. Here the myths of racial harmony and good will had grown, and now the glare of publicity and the unsubstantiated claims made by some of the Negro leaders endangered much of the genuine good will that did exist. When one Negro protested that blacks were barred from a bathing beach nearby, she soon had to admit that the beach was entirely private, behind a home, and that anyone—white or Negro—was quite properly asked to leave as a trespasser. Both the *Toronto Daily Star* and the *Windsor Star,* newspapers which had been among the Negroes' champions, warned against the dangers of exaggeration, lest "a once friendly community . . . be torn apart."

Amherstburg also provided a special opportunity. No arrests were made. The raceway reopened to an interracial clientele. The town appointed a committee to investigate further; and Dr. Hill, who agreed to act as temporary chairman, pursued his quiet course. The premier and the attorney-general condemned racial prejudice; the metropolitan dailies kept a wary eye on the community for other incidents, offering rewards up to $500; and the investigative committee became a permanent citizens' committee to establish a program for ensuring equal employment opportunities locally, broadening its investigation to include discrimination in housing, public accommodation, and law enforcement. George McCurdy declared his satisfaction at the turn of events; and in October—when four major Amherstburg businesses advised the mayor that they would hire qualified Negro personnel—the chief officer turned the publicity full circle, concluding that his town was, after all, one of the "most enlightened communities in Canada." An unspoken suspicion remained that some Negroes had knowingly exaggerated and used a vicious non-Klan prank as leverage for major review of the local scene, and even the National Committee on Human Rights, within the Canadian Labour Congress, said as much. The final report on the series of incidents contented itself with a sweeping condemnation of discrimination, prejudice, and ethnic-centered humor.[51]

51. For examples, see *Windsor Star,* Oct. 6, 1961; *Toronto Globe & Mail,* Jan. 24, May 1, 1961, Jan. 22, 23, 1962, April 12, May 10, 24, 29, 1965; *Toronto Telegram,* June 1, Sept. 18, 1961; *Toronto Daily Star,* Feb. 10, May 15, 19, Aug. 25, Nov. 3, 1961, Jan. 22, 23, 1962, May 26, Aug. 3, Nov. 20, 1965; *Toronto Financial Post,* June

The Amherstburg incident drove home a fundamental lesson to black Canadians: in publicity lay protection. For in the 1960s white Canadians could not permit pejorative comparisons with the United States. On the whole, Canadians were prepared to do what seemed right by racial relations—even if they had to be embarrassed into doing so. Verbal not physical violence might suffice.

Two other cases—in Nova Scotia's Halifax and in Ontario's Dresden— also wrought changes in the 1960s, far more slowly but in the face of more entrenched racial barriers. In 1960 wages and salaries in Halifax were lower than for any other major city in Canada except St. John's; most of the Negroes were part of an ill-paid, unskilled labor force in which the median earnings of heads of families were less than $1,800 a year. Among the blacks there was a high proportion of female labor with median earnings of $800 annually. Unemployment was double that of whites. Negroes lived in two blighted areas, along Creighton and Maynard streets and in Africville, the latter crowded up against the municipal rubbish dump which lay between the railway tracks and Bedford Basin. Of 134 Negro families on Creighton and Maynard streets, 85 percent lived in inadequate housing and 66 percent shared eating, sleeping, or bathroom facilities. Respiratory illnesses and skin diseases ran disproportionately high. Only 6 percent of the Negroes had graduated from high school. Nearly all of the thirty Negroes who had earned university degrees between 1960 and 1964 had left the province. Still, Negroes were not segregated, and while they continued to support Negro chapters of the Masons and Odd Fellows, they were admitted to white churches and, in turn, 5 percent of the congregation at the Cornwallis Street Baptist Church was white. For this mid-city area some investigators were cautiously optimistic.

Objective data did not lead investigators to encouraging conclusions about Africville, however. Throughout the 1950s there was little in-migration, 92 percent of the adult population of Africville having been born in

3, 1961, Aug. 7, 1965; *Vancouver Province*, June 16, 1961; *Vancouver Sun*, Jan. 7, 21, Feb. 11, 20, April 5, May 5, 19, 20, June 2, 6, 13, 15, 30, 1961, May 22, Sept. 21, Oct. 5, 1965 (in particular, the columns by Jack Wasserman); *Saskatoon Western Producer*, Aug. 8, 19, 1965; *Kitchener-Waterloo Record*, Aug. 26, 1965; *Picton* (Ont.) *Gazette*, May 5, 1965; *Kamloops Sentinel*, July 23, 1965; *Sarnia Observer*, June 26, 1965; *Montreal Star*, June 2, Sept. 19, 1961, Jan. 22, 1962, Aug. 31, 1965; *Fredericton Gleaner*, Aug. 16, 24, 1965; *Montreal Le Devoir*, Sept. 2, 1965; *Montreal Metro Express*, Aug. 19, 1965; *Quebec Le Soleil*, May 24, 1961; *Canada Week*, July 30, 1965; *London Free Press*, Sept. 15, 1958; *Ingersoll* (Ont.) *Tribune*, April 28, 1965; *Hamilton Spectator*, Aug. 18, 1965; *Brockville* (Ont.) *Recorder and Times*, Aug. 16, 1965; *Halifax Mail-Star*, Oct. 12, 1965; *Montreal Gazette*, Nov. 3, 1961; *Regina Leader Post*, April 30, 1965; *Ebony, 20* (May 1965), 17; *Lethbridge* (Alta.) *Herald*, June 15, *Victoria Colonist*, June 14, 30, *Calgary Herald*, July 3, Nov. 9, *Regina Commonwealth*, Aug. 2, all 1961.

Nova Scotia. The proportion of Negroes under twenty years of age was much larger than for other ethnic groups, and there was a striking excess of females. Virtually all residents tested low on I.Q. examinations. Almost none held regular jobs, there was no school nearby, and all of Africville's houses were judged inadequate. There was no sense of racial pride, and Africville's children professed to dislike other blacks.[52]

Earlier, Nova Scotian whites had shrugged Africville off with the retort that Negroes lived in worse slums in the United States. In 1945 the Halifax Civic Planning Commission had stated that Africville should be razed; not until nine years later, when money was less tight, did the city consider what it might do. The answer, for the most part, appeared to be nothing, for Africville was to be viewed in the context of larger hopes for urban renewal. "Africville," wrote the designer of Halifax's redevelopment program in 1957, "stands as an indictment of society and not of its inhabitants." Smarting under the growing attention the Canadian press outside the Maritimes gave to Africville—newspapers as far away as Prince George, British Columbia, denounced the slum as a blot on Canada's record in race relations—the city fathers continued to debate what to do.

While discussion continued, the inhabitants of Africville fell even further below the provincial norm in wages, housing, and sanitation. Residents were caught scavenging at the adjacent city dump; and one—who said that he was looking for breakfast for his family—was arrested. By 1960 the area was overrun by rats, and although the Negroes asked to be connected to a source of fresh water, Africville continued to be served by a contaminated well. By 1961, Africville's Negroes had been the subject of several intensive studies by sociologists, town planners, and welfare officers; and as one black remarked, they could not see that any good had come from all of the information scholars had gathered. Indeed, one suspected that the city had found a way to sweep Africville under the rug of scholarly inquiry and recommendation.[53]

52. On the events at Amherstburg, and for examples of news opinion, see: for August 11, the *Telegram, Oshawa Times, Guelph Mercury, Toronto Daily Star, Toronto Globe & Mail, St. John's Telegram, Windsor Star,* and *Amherst* (N.S.) *Daily News & Sentinel;* for Aug. 12, the *Star, Winnipeg Free Press, Montreal Matin, Truro News,* and *Barrie Examiner;* for Aug. 13, the *Daily Star, Star, Le Nouvelliste* of Trois Rivières, *Globe & Mail,* both news and columnists; for Aug. 14, the *Star, Daily Star, Telegram, Calgary Albertan,* and *Quebec Le Soleil;* for Aug. 16, columnists John Lindblad and W. L. Clark, and news item, in the *Star;* and for subsequent developments, *Amherstburg Echo,* Aug. 19, *Star,* Aug. 25, 31, Sept. 21, Oct. 2, 26, *Peterboro Review Weekly,* Aug. 26, all 1965; and National Committee on Human Rights, *Report of Activities . . . ,* Oct. 15, 1965, p. 4.

53. Mrs. Betty Wangenheim permitted me to read portions of her draft report, "The Negroes of Halifax County," and I was able to read pages 1–20 and 77–150, together with the appendixes, of her final statement as well. Some of the conclu-

Yet, in 1963 the Halifax Advisory Committee on Human Rights asked the City Council to engage a researcher to survey the local scene so that he might say whether "a study in depth is indicated." Accordingly, the city invited Dr. Albert Rose, Professor of Social Work at the University of Toronto, to make such an assessment. Dr. Rose wasted no time: eleven days after he completed his visit to Africville he submitted a terse statement and a set of recommendations. Africville already was "one of the most intensively studied communities in North America," he wrote, and *"no further research in depth is required or is likely to be helpful. . . .* The time has come . . . for the City and the people of Halifax to cease the study and the debate and to formulate and promulgate clearly, a policy and a program of social action with respect to Africville." Pointing out that the community's leaders "readily admit that Africville is a slum, that it should be cleared and that it would long since have been cleared if its inhabitants were of a different racial background," Dr. Rose urged undeliberate speed. Nor should narrow fears be permitted further to stay the necessary measures: "These negotiations must not be diverted or subverted by the argument frequently heard by this investigator, that one or more features of a possible settlement will set a precedent. Africville will not, we trust, occur again, and its solution will not become a precedent." [54]

---

sions she has drawn from her "sociograms" are questionable, I believe, but I can see no reason not to accept her statistics or first-hand quotations from informants. See in particular pp. 1–4, 7, 10–15, 18, 20, 77, 80, 88, 93, 100, 110, 113, 121, 130, 143–49. Statistically valuable is G. Brand, "Survey of Negro Population of Halifax County . . . ," unpubl. MS, Halifax, 1964. I have also drawn upon the following M.A. theses, all submitted to the Maritime School of Social Work, Halifax, in 1959: Catherine Frew, "The Health of Colored Families in Halifax"; Marion Sheridan, "Housing as a Factor in the Life of the Colored Family" (St. Xavier Univ.); Sister Lydia Tyszko, "Family Life and Family Stability of Negroes in Halifax"; Phyllis McClellan, "The Coloured Community" (St. Xavier Univ.); also H. Marjorie Yeadon, "Stress of Adolescence in a Coloured Community" (Mount Allison Univ.). The last quotation comes from Jean Beverly Ross, "The Effects of Racial Attitudes and Prejudices on the Colored People of Halifax" (Mount Allison Univ.), pp. 131–33. See also Claribei Gesner, "The Negro in Nova Scotia," *Canadian Scene*, no. 654 (Aug. 21, 1964); and H. A. J. Weddenburn, "From Slavery to the Ghetto: The Story of the Negro in the Maritimes," unpubl. paper presented to the N.B. Human Rights Commission (1968).

54. Civic Planning Commission, *The Master Plan for the City of Halifax* (Halifax, 1945), pp. 55–56; Gordon Stephenson, *A Redevelopment Study of Halifax, Nova Scotia* (Toronto, 1957), pp. 27–28, and *Supplementary Volume*, p. 17; H. S. Coblentz, *Halifax Region Housing Survey . . .* ([Halifax], 1963), p. 27; *City of Halifax, Central Business District Draft Development Plan* ([Halifax], 1964); *Halifax Mail-Star*, Aug. 20, 1954, Feb. 17, 1960, April 14, 30, June 5, Aug. 6, 1965; *Toronto Globe & Mail*, Sept. 12, 1959; *Halifax Chronicle-Herald*, Nov. 7, 1960; *Montreal Star*, Nov. 5, 1962; *New York Times*, June 14, 1964; *Toronto Telegram*,

The central block to quick action lay in finding a formula for properly compensating Africville's property holders. The city wished to pay those who could prove ownership—between twelve and twenty-five of the eighty families involved—enough to make a down payment on older houses in the mid-city area; some of the homes in that area, as a fire in 1965 showed, did not meet modern building codes. Negroes who did not hold acceptable deeds were to be compensated $500, in recognition of the equity they held in the general community. But the Negroes felt that once Africville was cleared, the site would be used for industrial development and land values would soar; they wished to be compensated on the basis of the values they projected. Viewed from a bookkeeper's perspective, the city's proposal was fair enough; viewed by the Negroes who felt they were to be dispossessed, the sum seemed woefully inadequate.

While Rose did not attempt to supply a solution to the knotty problem of compensation, he recommended that the city move immediately to an equitable solution, so that clearance of the land might begin the following April and be completed by the end of 1966. He also urged the city to view its financial offer as a minimum base for negotiating with individual families, since variations in family size, marital status, and available employment should be recognized. Further, he thought, the Halifax Housing Authority should admit families relocated from Africville into each housing project as it was completed, in a ratio of one in every five families so accommodated, to avoid creating a new ghetto within the city's center. The city should also supply free legal aid to help Africville residents purchase homes.

Although the city accepted several of Rose's recommendations, the performance was not an encouraging one. Arguments over compensation continued to slow progress and divided the Negro community. In 1965 the Halifax City Council showed itself almost pathologically sensitive to criticism: when the city's welfare director allegedly remarked that the city should have provided proper water and sewage facilities to Africville long before relocation took effect, the council demanded that he resign. The Negroes regarded the mayor as opposed to their interests on racial grounds: and rather than decreasing, interracial tension appeared to grow. Maritimers have never been known to move more rapidly simply because out-

April 8, 1965; *Toronto Daily Star,* June 16, 1965; *Prince George Citizen,* May 28, 1965; *Maclean's, 80* (Nov., 1967), 1; Institute of Public Affairs, *Condition of the Negroes,* passim; J. A. Oliver, "Final Report on the Problem of Unemployment for the Negro," unpubl. MS, Halifax, 1969; Morris Davis and H. D. Beach, "A Personality Study of Negroes in Halifax, Nova Scotia," mimeographed interim report, 1961; both passim, and Morris Davis, "Results of Personality Tests Given to Negroes in the Northern and Southern United States and in Halifax, Canada," *Phylon, 25* (1964), 262–68.

siders thought they should, and if some outsiders thought that twenty years was a rather long time to effect the removal of Africville, perhaps in the context of local problems and mores it was rapid enough. By January of 1967, when the last building fell to the bulldozers, Africville was more than a designation on the city's old maps, however—it was a word to which militant black Nova Scotians now rallied, the place which had led two sociologists to conclude that Nova Scotian society was "traditionally racist." [55]

The situation was no better at New Road. There was less public concern, however, since this all-Negro settlement was concealed from view, laying well out into the county rather than on the city line, as Africville did. There some eighteen hundred Negroes lived apart in the largest all-black community in the Dominion. In the midst of a barren area from which all the wood cover had been removed and along the sides of a lake that had been fished out, the Negroes of New Road (or Preston North) drifted from one seasonal job to another. New Road felt a sense of pride, however. Many residents claimed descendance from Governor Wentworth because of his Maroon mistress, and the community held an annual Emancipation Day celebration apart from the Halifax blacks. When in 1956 an Ontario-based white researcher revealed in a nationally circulated magazine something of the moral and economic plight faced by the residents of New Road, they erupted in anger over her efforts. In nearby Dartmouth, however, this *Maclean's* article produced a more positive effect; within hours the magazine was sold out, and the town, once proud to say that it contained no slums, was jolted out of its complacency. The local *Free Press,* pointing out that most whites did not know of the conditions at New Road, began a campaign to draw attention to problems there, a campaign which continued over the next decade. As the wife of the *Free Press*'s editor noted, Nova Scotians were "honestly convinced they are beyond reproach and that the negroes are all happy children at heart." To awaken any group to the need to combat discrimination was "like battling with feathers." [56] By 1965 the

55. See Donald H. Clairmont and Dennis W. Magill, "Poverty among Nova Scotian Blacks," unpubl. MS, Halifax, 1969. Messrs. Clairmont and Magill are engaged in a general study of "Africville: The Life and Death of a Canadian Black Community." I am grateful to them for letting me see their paper. I should also like to thank Miss Marjorie Whitelaw of Pictou, Nova Scotia, for loaning me her tape-recorded interviews with Africville residents.

56. Mrs. Keith Staebler, "Would You Change the Lives of These People?", *Macleans,* 69 (May 12, 1956), 30–31, 54, 56–58, 60, 62–63; *Free Press,* May 10, 1956;. Department of National Defence, Geographical Section, Map of Bedford Basin, no. 385e (1939), showing "New Road Negro Settlement"; William P. Oliver, "Brief Summary of Nova Scotia Negro Communities" (mimeograph, Halifax, 1964), pp. 2–3; Ruth Morton, July 12, 1956, and Ian Sclanders, May 16, 1957, to Mrs. Staebler, and Mrs. Staebler to author, April 15, 1965. I should like to thank Mrs.

battle had attracted national attention because of the work of such men as William P. Oliver, now more radical in his views, Burnley Jones, and a newcomer, Calvin Ruck—who had learned to speak out while growing up in the union town of Sydney and who organized a Black United Front self-help association among the residents. New Road would remain in the news into the next decade, as a source for Nova Scotian voluntarism.[57]

A more central area in which discrimination attracted national attention was Dresden, Ontario. Long the center of a substantial Negro population, Dresden was proud to be the home of Uncle Tom, and its merchants were pleased to serve white tourists who came on pilgrimages. Black tourists encountered some difficulties, largely in the community's restaurants; black residents were virtually barred. The Negro population was roughly 17 percent in 1949, and when Canadian Prime Minister Louis St. Laurent visited Dresden in 1950, he made a point of being photographed while holding a young black girl on his knee. In 1954, after Ontario had passed its Fair Accommodation Practices Act, two Negroes from Toronto—one the daughter of Stanley G. Grizzle—tested Dresden's cafés and found that two openly admitted that they could not be served. The *Toronto Telegram,* on the trail of news stories relating to discrimination, repeated the experiment with a photographer and two more Toronto Negroes, and they too were refused service.

With this Dresden suddenly found itself under a glare of publicity that spread across Canada, into the United States, and onto the pages of *The Times* of London. Unquestionably, the *Telegram* was precisely what the Progressive-Conservative Member for Lambton East in the provincial Parliament said it was—an outside agitator. So, too, was the fortnightly *Saturday Night* which, under the lively direction of B. K. Sandwell until 1951, had also pried into the Dresden story. Equally unquestionably, without such outside agitation the situation in Dresden would have remained unchanged. The National Unity Association, a black voluntary group based in Chatham, led by William J. Carter and Hugh Burnette, voice of Dresden's more activist Negroes, now found that they had substantial outside support. A public hearing was held on the complaints filed under the FAP Act, and the minister for labor ordered an inquiry. At the hearing, one owner admitted that he would refuse to serve Negroes and that he

Staebler, for loaning me her original notes taken at New Road, and letters written at the time to her husband. More recently, see Nancy Lubka, "Ferment in Nova Scotia," *Queen's Quarterly,* 76 (1969), 213–18.

57. Guysborough County continues to present a discouraging picture of unemployment, poor schools, and poverty—in 1965 the per capita income among blacks was $325. See Donald Clairmont, et al., *A Socio-Economic Study and Recommendations: Sunnyville, Lincolnville, and Upper Big Tracadie, Guysborough County, Nova Scotia* (Halifax, 1965).

would continue to break the law to protect his business. The decision was not to prosecute but to attempt further education through the Human Rights Commission. Shortly after, the two Dresden proprietors again refused service to Negroes.

Over the next ten years Dresden continued to attract publicity. The Human Rights Commission conducted frequent inquiries and bombarded the community with antiprejudice literature. As national magazines, the provincial and federal governments, Negro organizations, and the Canadian Broadcasting Commission maintained public pressure, blacks found themselves admitted, if somewhat sullenly, to the white establishments. By 1965 they could go where they pleased, and reckless charges that the Negro pressures had been generated by Communist influences had been forgotten.[58]

If the pressures had, in fact, initially been generated by the press and by the Human Rights Commission, public attention to discrimination was also giving rise to more effective Negro civil rights organizations. Out of the Community Credit Union of Halifax would come a reinvigorated Nova Scotia Association for the Advancement of Colored People (with branches as far afield as Yarmouth), from which, in turn, would stem the Black United Front, which in 1969 became the first citizens' group in Canada to receive a pledge of direct federal aid to promote a self-determination program. Out of the Montreal Negro Conservative League, a political body founded in the 1920s to support the Tory party, would belatedly come a unity association intent upon convincing Quebec of the need for provincial FAP and FEP laws. Out of Windsor's Guardian Club would come a new political activism. Out of the British Columbia Association for the Advancement of Colored People (formed in 1958 by Frank Collins) would come both a Unity Credit Union and a newsletter that put blacks on the West Coast into contact with those on the East for the first time. While these associations, and several others, continued to suffer from too much fragmentation (there were, for example, a Guyana Association, a Trinidad Association, and an Associacion des Haitiëns in Montreal in 1969), uncertain goals, and too little money, they were now far more vocal than in the past, for they finally had means of reaching the public. These means were augmented by a third approach which could focus attention on Negro vol-

58. *The Negro Citizen, 4* (May 4, 1949), 1; Gordon Donaldson, "I Lived through Race Hatred in a Canadian Town," [Canadian] *Liberty, 23* (Dec. 1966), 24–25, 64, 66, 69–70; Dale C. Thomson, *Louis St. Laurent: Canadian* (New York, 1968), facing p. 229; Grace J. Carter, "Dresden," *Ontario Hydro News, 39* (1952), 17; H. Gordon Green, "They Don't Talk in Dresden," *Family Herald* (Oct. 11, 1956), pp. 6–7; Ian Sclanders, "The Good Town that's Fighting a Bad Name," *Maclean's, 78* (May 15, 1965), 17, 53–57; Human Rights Commission of Ontario, Toronto Office: five folders of reports relating to discrimination in southern Ontario, passim.

untarism where necessary: the entry of Negroes into politics at a higher than purely local level.[59]

In the nineteenth century Negroes had been active in local politics, as aldermen, town councillors, and members of elective school boards, but none had risen higher in office than had City Comptroller Hubbard in Toronto. In the changing political climate of the post-World War II years, Ontario Negroes returned to such offices and entered provincial politics as well. James E. Watson, a graduate of the University of Toronto, was named city solicitor in Windsor in 1950. Dr. Roy Perry, a Negro dentist in Windsor and long an alderman and member of that city's Board of Control, contested the mayoralty in the 1950s and lost. In 1964, after serving a year on the town council, Dr. S. F. Monestime, a native of Haiti, won election as mayor of Mattawa, and his name was among those considered to be a possible Progressive-Conservative nominee in Nipissing. Most important, Leonard A. Braithwaite—a Canadian-born Negro who was a graduate of the University of Toronto, the Harvard School of Business Administration, and Osgoode Hall Law School—was elected Liberal member of the Ontario legislature from Etobicoke, an upper middle-class suburb of Toronto, in 1963.

The following year the Progressive-Conservative Party in Hamilton West chose another black lawyer, also a graduate of Osgoode Hall (and McMaster University), Lincoln Alexander, to contest the Liberal-held seat for the federal Parliament once occupied by Ellen Fairclough, who nominated him. Party spokesmen suggested that "Canadian indignation about events in the U.S. civil rights movement" had created "a whole new climate . . . for a Negro seeking public office" in Ontario. Alexander—who had failed to gain the nomination in 1963—campaigned vigorously in Halifax as well as Hamilton on behalf of his party; and while he made few references to his race, the press was inclined to see his nomination by the Conservatives as a conscious attempt to counter the Liberal Party's Braithwaite. When black activist organizations in the United States offered to supply money so that the election might be carried on racial terms, Alexander rejected outside help; nonetheless, many of his supporters clearly saw him as the cutting edge of a cause. "When he's elected we'll be showing the world what kind of a country Canada is," one remarked, and Alexander

59. *Toronto Daily Star*, Dec. 6, 1960; *Maclean's, 80* (Nov. 1967), 1; *New York Times*, Feb. 22, 1969; Martin O'Malley, "Black Pride? Well, Not Quite," *The Globe Magazine* (Feb. 15, 1969), pp. 15, 17; *N.S.A.A.C.P. Newsletter, 1* (March and May, 1955), whole number; *B.C.A.A.C.P. Annual Report for the Year 1963*, mimeographed, passim; *B.C.A.A.C.P. Quarterly, 1* (June and Dec., 1963), whole numbers, and *4* (April 1966), 8; *Annual Report of the Department of Education . . . 1960* (Halifax, 1961), pp. 53–54; Ronald Lebel, "So it Couldn't Happen in Montreal?", *The Globe Magazine* (Feb. 15, 1969), pp. 20, 22; *Contrast*, May 1, 1970.

often mentioned his personal fact-finding trip to Africa in 1960, from which had arisen the Hamilton Goodwill Africa Foundation. Alexander's loss to the Liberal incumbent by two thousand votes was inconclusive with respect to judging whether the color of his skin had been relevant.[60]

In any event, Alexander did not lose on the next occasion, for in 1968 he was elected by a narrow margin to the federal Parliament. As the first Negro in Parliament, Alexander attracted much publicity, and while he did not concentrate on civil rights issues, he became a national rallying point for Canadian blacks. In his maiden speech on September 20, which he devoted largely to praising Hamilton, Alexander paid homage to former Prime Minister Diefenbaker, who had been the first to encourage his interest in politics; stated that he was "not the spokesman for the negro," that honor not having been given to him—a clear reference to the fragmented nature of black politics in Canada; and, significantly, quoted from Frederick Douglass, "Power concedes nothing without a demand." Alexander, and Braithwaite, encouraged other Negroes to run for office, regardless of party. In 1965 Pierre-Elliott Trudeau, in time to be Canada's Liberal Prime Minister, denounced discrimination in Canada (and his Progressive-Conservative opponent suggested that he was a "professor" who had given "a lecture instead of discussing the important issues"). In both Nova Scotia and British Columbia in 1969 there were black candidates within the CCF, a party consistent in its stand on human rights.

Alexander was an active and accepted member of Parliament as well as an adroit politician. Appointed to two key committees—on Justice and Legal Affairs, and on Labour, Manpower and Immigration—he did his homework, spoke often in the House on immigration, relief for Biafra in the Nigerian Civil War, and urban renewal, and took a hard line against professional agitators and on the Official Languages Bill. In 1968–69 he addressed his colleagues ninety-four times, on forty-three different subjects, which placed him slightly above the House average, and he was substantially more active—and effective—than either of the other nonministerial members for Hamilton constituencies.[61]

60. *Negro Citizen*, [5] (May 15, 1950), 1; *Edmonton Journal*, March 9, 1950; *New York Times*, Nov. 30, 1958; *North Bay* (Ont.) *Nugget*, Aug. 31, Sept. 18, 28, 1965; *Toronto Telegram*, Dec. 6, 1960, Aug. 14, Sept. 29, Nov. 9, 1965; *Saint John Telegraph-Journal*, Nov. 27, 1963; *Toronto Daily Star*, Dec. 6, 1960, Oct. 1, 21, 1965; *Hamilton Spectator*, Oct. 13, 29, 1965; *Halifax Chronicle-Herald* and *Halifax Mail-Star*, both Oct. 21, 1965; *Montreal Le Devoir*, Oct. 2, 1965; *Moncton L'Evangeline*, Oct. 6, 1965; *Sydney Cape Breton Post*, Oct. 5, 1965; Lennox Brown, "Canada's First Negro MPP—The Man at the Door," *Ebo Voice*, *1* (ii/1965), 7; Perry, *Long Road*, *1*, 79. In 1955 a Negro was elected alderman in Sydney, Nova Scotia (*Toronto Star*, Dec. 7, 1955).

61. *Edmonton Journal*, Feb. 22, 1957; *London Free Press Weekend*, March 10, 1956; *Toronto Telegram*, June 12, 1947; *Amherstburg Echo*, July 13, 1950; *Detroit*

Appearing before the House was a new experience for a Negro in Canada; but there also existed traditional North American means of seeking out public approval—through athletics, public entertainment, and on occasion through literature. As in the United States, so too in Canada did individual Negroes win acceptance first in these intensely competitive activities. It was the quasi-athletic ability of John Ware, like the quasi-entertainment value of a stentorian Negro preacher, that attracted favorable attention to them; and race tended to be forgotten where team victory counted more. Early in the century Samuel Langford of Weymouth, Nova Scotia, won fame as a boxer, and Elbridge Eatman of Zealand Station, New Brunswick, reputedly held a number of world sprinting records. In 1933 the Negroes of Chatham organized a baseball team, the Colored All Stars, which won the provincial title in 1934. Despite the fact that hotels seldom would accept them, the team continued to tour the province to capacity crowds until the outbreak of World War II.

After the war American Negroes entered Canada to play professional football, and some, such as Johnny Bright and Rolland Miles, won widespread acceptance. Miles, in particular, felt secure enough to be outspokenly hostile to those white Canadians who said that there was no discrimination in Canada, and he admitted that he escaped it only because of his athletic success; Bright, in turn, would enter provincial politics in 1970. Other American imports, such as Herbert Trawick and Thomas Casey, also became Canadian citizens; and in 1955 Casey received Winnipeg's Citizen of the Year award. In 1961 four black athletes signed an open letter to the *Edmonton Journal* protesting against the anti-Negro and anti-Indian attitudes they found in Canada, although most team members reported virtually no evidence of discrimination directed against them when they sought out accommodations and off-season employment. This flow continued until 1965, when curbs were placed upon the number of non-Canadian trained football players that clubs might hire.[62]

Free Press, Aug. 2, 1967; *Toronto Star,* Sept. 2, 1942; *Montreal Gazette,* Oct. 29, 1965; *Windsor Guardian,* April 15, 1965; *Toronto Globe & Mail,* July 25, 1968; Canada, *House of Commons Debates,* 1968, *1,* 288–91. The figures on Alexander are calculated from the index to ibid., *1968–69,* vol. 113.

62. *Toronto Star,* May 14, 1938; *London* (Ont.) *Free Press,* May 17, 1947; Citizenship Branch, *Canadian Family Tree,* p. 109; NBM, Eatman Family File: Elbridge (Gus) Eatman; personal interview with Eatman, Saint John, Feb. 1960; E. L. Homewood, "Breaking the Race Barrier," *United Church Observer,* n.s., *18* (March 1, 1956), n.p.; *Toronto Telegram,* June 12, 1947; *Winnipeg Free Press Weekend,* March 10, 1956; *Winnipeg Free Press,* Feb. 23, 1960; *Edmonton Journal,* Feb. 22, 1957, July 20, 1959; *Calgary Herald,* Feb. 7, 1961; *Vancouver Pacific Tribune,* June 30, 1961; *Hamilton Spectator,* Sept. 25, 1965; Boonton Herndon, "Young Man, Go North!" *Sports Illustrated,* 12 (Oct. 26, 1969), 84–86, 89–90, 92–94; Tex Maule, "Getaway went Thataway," ibid., *13* (July 25, 1960), 59; Carl T. Rowan, "Negroes in Canada," *Ebony, 15* (August 1960), 98–100, 102, 104–06; The Sir George Williams

Negroes broke into prominence in other sports as well. In track and field Jessie Jones of Edmonton, Dr. Phillips Edwards of Montreal (one of the trainers of the 1956 Canadian Olympic team), and Harry Jerome, a Negro from Vancouver who ran on the Canadian Olympic teams of 1960, 1964, and 1968, moved readily into white circles; so too did Willie O'Ree, a native of Fredericton who became the first black player in the National Hockey League, working with the Boston Bruins between 1958–61, and for Canadian teams before and after. Canadians were quick to point out that in 1945, when Branch Rickey, President of the Brooklyn Dodgers, decided to introduce Negroes into major league baseball in the United States, it was to the Montreal Royals, a farm club of the Dodgers, to which he sent Jack Roosevelt Robinson and Johnny R. Wright. The former, as Jackie Robinson, thus prepared for his rôle as the first black baseball hero. Robinson found that Canadians regarded him "as a United States citizen who happened to have a colored skin"; and although he went to the Dodgers in 1947, he regarded Montreal as a "paradise." [63]

Another well-known American Negro shared this view. In 1945 the leading black writer in the United States, Richard Wright, preferring Paris but unable to reach it because of a lack of ocean transport, sought out Quebec as a refuge from the hectic pace of New York City. He thought the people "lovely," serene, and happily prepared to accept him at face value. He was not famous in Canada and was unknown on the Ile d'Orleans, a preindustrial haven afloat on the St. Lawrence. There he savored the financial independence that the mounting sales of *Black Boy* were giving him and sought out "a way of living with the earth" rather than, as in New York, "against the earth." Already having begun the inner search for a distinct black past that would eventually carry him to Africa, into exile in Paris, and give power to his later work, Wright found Quebec a "cultural island, static, self-sufficient, retaining the past intact." To Gertrude Stein he wrote of his impressions; and years later he wove the same impressions into his impassioned appeal, *White Man, Listen* (1958)

University *Georgian* (Montreal), March 14, 1960; *The Crisis* (Jan. 1951), p. 18; *Atlantic Advocate, 48* (1958), 76; ibid., *49* (1958), 68–69; "Ice Hockey's Willie O'Ree," *Ebony, 16* (April 1961), 49–50, 52; *Fredericton Daily Gleaner*, Jan. 20, April 7, 1961; *Fredericton Capital Free Press*, April 6, 1961. Langford died, blind, in New York. See *The Clarion, 3* (July 51 [*sic*], 1948), 1.

63. Gumby Collection, three scrapbooks on Jackie Robinson; *New York Times*, Oct. 24, 25, 1945, March 5, 17, Aug. 13, 1946, March 29, 1947; *Toronto Globe & Mail*, April 14, 1947; *Vancouver Sun*, Oct. 17, 1961; A. S. Young, *Negro Firsts in Sports* (Chicago, 1963), pp. 115–16; Carl T. Rowan and Jackie Robinson, *Wait Till Next Year* (New York, 1960), pp. 137–70. The two quotations are from Jackie Robinson and Charles Dexter, *Baseball Has Done It* (Philadelphia, 1964), p. 43, and A. S. Young, *Great Negro Baseball Stars and How They Made the Major Leagues* (New York, 1963), p. 36.

—an appeal deeply affected by his two-month sojourn among a people who, he believed, cherished an organic sense of what and where they were, and even why, a sense he felt the white man had taken away from the detribalized Negro in the United States. Wright's brief insight into Canada was a reflection of an earlier century's infatuation with the notion of the *beau sauvage*. In unity, in simplicity, in racial pride would lie the future generations' salvation.[64]

In the United States, Negro efforts to combat discrimination passed through at least four distinct phases. From the verbal protests and self-segregation of the nineteenth century to the more activist pressures exerted by the National Association for the Advancement of Colored People in the twentieth century may have seemed a long step; in retrospect it was less of a dramatic change than many thought. The NAACP at first worked—as the purely verbal groups had before—through the intermediating power structure of liberal whites, and sought to achieve reform by political persuasion and pressure. To abandon the white leadership and turn to nonviolent direct action, as Negroes did increasingly during the 1930s, was a giant step, and one which led inexorably if by many twistings and turnings to the revolutionary movements of the 1960s. These began with the Black Muslims and the breakaway Malcolm X, moved to the uncontrolled pillaging of Watts and the mass marches upon Washington and Montgomery, and at last to Black Panthers and voluntarism for vengeance. While the NAACP had urged group action and unity, it had not proposed mass action and violence. To be sure, neither did the responsible Negro leadership of the 1960s propose violence; but by turning to the mass—unstructured and shifting in its grievances, its goals, and its membership—they also created the mob; and to challenge and also to channel the potential strength of the mob, the youthful leadership of such organizations as SNCC and CORE began increasingly to speak of revolution.

In Canada, Negro efforts had been slower and more restrained. Such restraint was the product, in part, of scale: the Negroes were few, ethnically rather than economically divided among themselves, and spread across a

64. Yale University, Carl van Vechten Collection: Wright to Van Vechten, June 21, 1945, and postcard, n.d. [summer, 1945]; Yale University, American Literature Collection, Gertrude Stein Papers: Wright to Stein,. May 27, June 23, Oct. 29, 1945; Constance Webb to author, June 26, 1968; Thomas Knipp, ed., *Richard Wright: Letters to Joe C. Brown,* Kent State University Libraries, *Occasional Papers,* no. 1 (1968), pp. 14–15: Wright to Brown, Aug. 9, 1945; Wright, *White Man, Listen!* (Garden City, N.Y., 1957), pp. 106–09. Efforts to contact Wright's widow in Paris for possible additional papers have failed. I wish to thank the officials of the Canadian Broadcasting Commission in Toronto for showing me Joseph Schull's "The Concert," originally telecast in February 1958.

continent without massive concentration in any single area. As a result, discrimination was not massively concentrated either; and since individual acts of discrimination—unsupported by a legislative framework or by widespread social sanctions—provided a small and moving target, those Canadian blacks who did wish to pursue activist policies were forced into being individual grievance collectors—never attractive people. Such activists were unable to command representative followings because many blacks had not been touched directly by prejudice; and they were unable to hold such followings as they did attract because, with minor exceptions, overt discrimination presented no consistent configuration. Although there was discrimination in housing, in hotel accommodation, at golf clubs, and in employment, who were the authorities to attack in such cases? Had there been substantial and legal segregation in the schools, the Negroes could have moved as they did in Ontario, against the school boards. Had there been universal discrimination in transport, Negroes could have approached the railways or the federal government. But who, when a group is small, divided, and dispersed, can it approach to protest against a motel, a block of flats, or a dairy that would not admit or employ Negroes? In the days before the Human Rights Commission, the easiest solution lay in patience, avoidance, hoping for a change in ownership, and continued grievance collection until a clear pattern of discrimination—not only against Negroes but against potential allies, such as Jews—might be proven. And in a mobile society into which immigrants always moved, even if in reduced numbers after the 1920s, how was one to know that the motel that discriminated one summer would not pass into new ownership and not discriminate by the next summer?

The same phases of protest cannot, therefore, be found in Canada as in the United States; and where some of the phases arose, they did so much more slowly. American Negroes had passed beyond merely verbal protest early in the twentieth century; despite the creation of numerous voluntary associations intended to strengthen the Canadian Negroes' social and economic position, they did not emerge from the verbal phase of their activity until after World War II, when they began to see that the sources of strength upon which they had been depending were ineffective without greater unity. When the search for unity came, it was directed as much toward seeking out an alliance with other minority groups within a province as toward a national Negro alliance. At first, Canadian Negroes in Montreal learned that they could expect more support from radical Jewish groups than from West Indians. Most Canadian Negroes were too conservative to ally themselves with any truly radical or Marxist movements, and they preferred not to identify too closely in the west with Chinese or Japanese, and not at all with the latter by the late 1930s, as war loomed in the

Pacific. The old divisions continued even among the Canadian-born, as in New Brunswick, where before the war the old-line Loyalist Negroes of Kingsclear, near Fredericton, looked down upon the fugitive-line Negroes who lived nearer the city, and refused to let their daughters marry "niggers." Thus, outside Quebec and Ontario, the Negroes did not enter into their phase of nonviolent direct action until the 1960s, most of them scorning sit-ins, marches, and picketing to the present day; while the blacks of the heartland became activists only in shifting and temporary alliance with other groups, until such time as those groups became too radical or secular for comfort.

The Negroes' efforts to win full recognition of their rights never became, as they did in the United States, a central issue of sectional or intellectual controversy. Nor, perhaps fortunately, were they the subjects of faddists. Thus the healthy tensions created by dissent and counterdissent in America, tensions erupting into sometimes productive anger, were not present in Canada, where ethnic divisions and intellectual discourse centered upon the problem of the French- and English-speaking communities. For the most part the Negro was a peripheral member of the latter, receiving few benefits from the deliberations on biculturalism or bilingualism in Canada. As ethnic awareness among university and political activists was fragmented further, focus tended to fall upon the far greater problems of the Indians, the Esquimaux, or the Doukhobors; and while the last two groups were numerically inferior to the Negroes, they nonetheless received far more attention.

The problem was, in part, one of relative distance and the perception of that distance, morally speaking. Because Canadians were accustomed to compare their institutional growth with that of the United States, and because they liked to see their liberties under the monarchical system as both more stable and more far-reaching than those often highly qualified freedoms that Americans enjoyed, they naturally felt that the Canadian Negro was much advanced in a legal sense over his American counterpart. The Negroes, although far more alert to the relative decline of economic opportunities for them in Canada, also knew that freedom under the lion's paw had very real compensations. Negroes were not lynched, they need not step off the sidewalk to let a white man pass by, and they rode the same buses as everyone else did. That the job of making real those legally held liberties was not yet complete was obvious to all Negroes but hardly obvious to the generality of Canadians.

Because Canada had trumpeted abroad its love of liberty less than the United States had done, there was less need to make image and reality coincide. Because there was no large Negro ghetto, large-scale race riots were unlikely. Because Canadian Negroes could, if influenced more by economic necessity than by abstract equality, move to the United States—to riot or not to riot there—Canada had a vast safety valve. Because the natural Negro leadership—those few who went to university, the Negro preachers, the very few schoolteachers or editors, the occasional business-men—usually wanted nothing more than to be accepted as quiet Canadians, they were unlikely to organize militant, noisy, pushing protests. The news value of the peaceful Negro was slight, partially because his nuisance value was slight, and thus few people in positions of real or potential power, white or black, sought to complete that journey between internal image and reality.

In the United States, that journey was speeded by the Supreme Court, which blazed shortcuts between old trails. In Canada, the courts did not set the pace; and since judicial commitment often precedes legislative action, there was little action until after World War II. Only then, and at first at the provincial level, did governments begin to think in terms of active intervention on behalf of oppressed groups. And none of the interventive legislation was meant primarily to aid the Negro, although as a minority he shared in such benefits as were given.

"When we say that Canada is a land of freedom and equality, we either mean what we say or we do not. If we permit signs and notices to be put up in conspicuous places indicating that any particular group of people are denied the ordinary rights available to other people, then those who should be most indignant are not the people against whom the signs and notices are directed, but those whose basic principles of freedom, justice and equality have been insulted." So had the premier of Ontario spoken in 1944. Although his statement was little noted at the time, it marked the turning point at which a provincial leader committed himself to those principles which would emerge from the war years as the United Nations Charter of Liberties. Increasingly, the other provinces would recognize the need for positive as well as for prohibitory legislation, a recognition that would culminate in the moral expression of national rectitude found in the Canadian Bill of Rights.

It would be many years yet before subconscious assumptions about Negro inferiority would pass. Even in those communities and among those people who not only professed to harbor no prejudices but who, by their actions, seemed to have none, the old stereotypes still lived. In the late 1950s a Brantford researcher, writing to Fred Landon, confessed to having found that a distinguished local family had Negro blood. "Needless to say," confided the researcher, "I am not pursuing these leads." From Prince Edward Island came a letter to this writer speaking of the "delicate . . . subject" of certain white men in Charlottetown believed to be married to descendants of Negroes, and another curtain of delicate reprobation was drawn. In Fredericton, residents were angered in 1959 when national publicity was given to the notion that the deanery in that city had once been used as slave quarters. This, said the spokesman for the cathedral, was an offensive myth; and when two local antiquarians declared that slaves definitely had been kept in the deanery as well as at a homestead at Barker's Point, several townspeople protested against this reminder of a slave past, since, as one remarked without sense of contradiction, "the Negroes really had no history in any case, and all talk of slave quarters merely reminded them of the wrong kind of history." [65]

Balanced against these quiet and unaware expressions of the thought that "Negro blood" should still be relevant to social position may be set the equally obvious and more important fact that there had been much progress in changing anti-Negro attitudes in the public at large. Throughout Canada there were black professors, finance managers, mechanical engineers, schoolteachers, independent farmers, dentists, and the occasional physician, lawyer, and politician. Negroes had succeeded in climbing to the very top of the occupational class scale; and if one suspects that Prince Edward Island would not have leapt so quickly to apologize to a Negro who was denied accommodations in 1959 had he not been a physician, one is merely observing that class prejudices, as all know, cut across racial prejudices in northern society. In that year a Gallup Poll revealed that Canadians were less concerned about residential segregation than real estate dealers had thought: only 5 percent of those polled said that they definitely would move if a Negro purchased property next door, while 80 percent said that they definitely would not. The implication was that if a Negro could acquire a well-paying job, he would face no major opposition to his efforts to escape the ghetto. In a sense perhaps Reverend Oliver had been right in Halifax: the first necessity was education, leading to equal job opportunities. And equality of job opportunities lay—intransigently— just around the corner, over there, soon, soon.

During the years of change, as the Negro rose from his prewar nadir, he had begun to help himself. In response to continued instances of discrimination, blacks organized province-wide civil rights leagues and unity societies and allied themselves increasingly with the middle-of-the-road efforts of the Canadian Labour Congress and similar bodies to expose discrimina-

65. Third World Information Service, *Black Power and the Third World* (Thornhill, Ont. [1967]); Carl A. Taylor, "Some Reflections on 'Black Power'," *Expression*, 2 (ii/1966), 9–11; *Fredericton Daily Gleaner*, April 8, 9, 11, May 12, June 12, 16, 1959; Edward Weeks, "Fredericton, New Brunswick," *Ford Times, 50* (Aug. 1958), 43–47, apparently the article responsible for redirecting tourist attention to the alleged slave quarters; Esther Clark Wright, *The Saint John River* (Toronto, 1949), p. 191; Bernard R. Blishen, "The Construction and Use of an Occupational Class Scale," *Canadian Journal of Economics and Political Science, 24* (1958), 519–31.

tory practices through widespread publicity. By 1960, when the province of Ontario created its Human Rights Commission, the Negro was on the way to finding a rôle within the national drama, and many municipal as well as provincial governments were alert to their responsibilities in the area of civil rights. If a gap between image and reality remained, as it always would, at least machinery for bridging that gap had been created. The Negro in Canada was at last accepted, if not always as an equal, at least as a Canadian. He was on the high road from being a Canadian Negro to that status enjoyed by the charter members of Canadian society and marked by a structural difference that covered a nearly infinite number of new connotations—a Negro Canadian.[66]

66. As stated in the Preface, no historian can claim to bring the tale he tells down to the present, for events near to us lack perspective, and so do we. While the various strands of black self-help associations, of changing attitudes toward Negroes, and of related Negro activities have been summarized up until 1970, much additional work might reasonably be done on the decade of the 1960s, and in particular on West Indian participation in activist movements. Although this chapter carries its story to 1970, the author recognizes that his discussion of post-1960 events will undoubtedly require revisions as perspectives change and as sources now private become public. See, for example, "Canada's Negroes: An Untold Story," *U.S. News & World Report,* 68 (May 11, 1970), 46–50.

One rapidly changing problem is that of "hate literature." The Dominion's Negroes benefited in 1963 and thereafter from a growing Canadian concern over the spread of such literature, which was usually directed against Jews. To the growing arsenal of legislation was added, in 1967, a federal law that opened up once again the complex problem of freedom of speech versus license to incitement.

After World War II Adrien Arcand, founder of the National Unity Party in Quebec, and John Ross Taylor, head of an organization styling itself Natural Order, in Gooderham, Ontario, included the Negro among those to be indicted for mongrelizing Canada. From 1963 publications of the American Nazi Party began to flow into Toronto from Arlington, Virginia, and over a twenty-eight-month period many thousands of leaflets, directed against Jews, race-mixing, and Martin Luther King, were stuffed into automobiles, dropped from the roofs of buildings, and posted to the city. The National White Americans Party of Atlanta, Georgia, mailed similar pamphlets into Nova Scotia, and the National States Rights Party, launched in Kentucky in 1958 and then transferred to Birmingham, Alabama, sent its monthly journal, *The Thunderbolt,* into Canada.

In Toronto counterextremist groups, notably the N3 Fighters Against Racial Hatred, a predominantly but not exclusively Jewish movement ("N3" representing Newton's Third Law of Motion), clashed with the Canadian Nazi Party in a Toronto park on May 30, 1965. One result was a report, arising from a Special Committee under the chairmanship of the Dean of the McGill University Faculty of Law, Maxwell Cohen, which found the "hate" situation in Canada "serious enough to require action." "Group libel" was recognized in all provinces except Manitoba, the Canadian postal authorities issued prohibitory orders against the new American hate publications, and Negro groups submitted evidence on the literature directed against them, especially through the American Nazi Party's "Brotherhood Nigger-Talk Dictionary".

The federal law followed. But hate literature in Canada continues to exist: in the White Man's Mission, which used a post-office box in Toronto to urge nonblacks to awaken to the dangers around them; in the attack on a Negro bookstore in Toronto in 1970; and in the rise of a countervailing black hate literature directed against whites.

On this issue, see *Report to the Minister of Justice of the Special Committee on Hate Propaganda in Canada* (Ottawa, 1966), pages 1–6, 11–25, 253–56, 261, 319; "Provocation and Defence: Action against Racialists in Canada," *The Wiener Library Bulletin, 20* (1966), 18–20; Arcand's credo, *A Bas la haine* ([Montreal], 1965); Leo A. Ryan, "Canada East and West," *Censorship, 2* (1966), 32; and D[aniel] E. W[oodward], "Hate Literature," *Canada Month, 5* (1965), 5. I should like to thank Dean Cohen and Professor Mark R. MacGuigan, a member of the Committee and then of the University of Toronto, for sending me copies of the Report, and Professor MacGuigan, now of Osgoode Hall Law School, for sending me an advance copy of his article, "Hate Control and Freedom of Assembly: The Canadian Nazi Party in Toronto, 1965–1966." See also V. M. H. Rodriguey, "Fundamental Rights and Freedoms in Canada," Canadian Jewish Congress, *Information and Comment: Social and Economic Studies,* no. 32 (1968), whole number. Here, clearly, is one story that races beyond the historian's grasp.

15. The Black Tile in the Mosaic

One must draw conclusions both about Canada and about black Canadians. Several have been offered in the preceding chapters. While occasionally comparative, the purpose of this book has not been to demonstrate that in this or that particular, Canadian discrimination was more or less harsh than American, or to assess relative blame in a pathetic situation in which all, black and white, shared responsibility. Nor has the purpose of this description of large grievances and small triumphs, of comparable and incomparable conditions, of names, places, and resurrected indignities, been to show that Canadians were not pure. Few of their own historians have thought them so, any more than any people are faultless in matters of human relations. Since all Canadians were subject to many of the same continental forces as whites and blacks in the United States, one would expect to find similarities.

Indeed, many characteristics of American Negro life, and especially of the life of the black in the northern states, are to be found in Canada. As in the United States, so in Canada, the Negro family revoives around the mother as the enforcer of discipline in the home and as the most dependable breadwinner. In both countries, centuries of relative deprivation, of being taught by the dominant white society to think of themselves as second-class citizens, have led some Negroes into the familiar early stages of paranoia, when racial insults are detected where none are intended.[1] Much that Gunnar Myrdal, W. Lloyd Warner, John Dollard, C. Vann Woodward, Thomas F. Gossett, and other students of race in the United States have written about Negro-white contact applies with only slight modifications to Canada. When, for example, Myrdal suggested that the racial issues over which whites and Negroes felt most strongly could be placed on a rough scale of values, and when researchers applied his test to the rank order of discrimination in northern communities, one could see that save for a single important exception, Myrdal's analysis would apply to Canada as well.[2]

1. For one detailed example, see my paper, "The Canadian Negro: An Historical Assessment," mimeographed (University of London, Institute of Commonwealth Studies, Feb. 1965), pp. 2, 17. Also consult Davis and Beach, "A Personality Study of Negroes in Halifax," pp. 10–11, 40; and Marjorie Whitelaw, taped interviews with Nova Scotian Negroes, numbers 1 and 3.

2. On Dollard and Warner, see Ruth Danehower Wilson, "Note on Negro-White Relations in Canada," *Social Forces, 28* (1949), 77–78. On Myrdal, see his *An*

Myrdal argued that the highest bar the white raised against the Negro was over intermarriage and sexual intercourse involving white women. Next rose the question of general etiquette and social courtesies, including dancing, swimming, eating, and drinking together. Of less importance to whites was the preservation of discrimination in the use of public facilities, such as schools, churches, and transport. Political disenfranchisement stood lower in priorities, followed by discrimination in the law courts and in access to land, credit, jobs, and social welfare. Myrdal also found that the Negroes' own rank order was roughly parallel but inverse. These scales hold true for Canada, with the important exception of equality of access to job opportunities. Passing through longer and often more chronic stages of depression, faced with proportionately larger groups of immigrants to be absorbed, plagued with persistent unemployment, and less buoyed by ideological and messianic national purposes, Canadians had reason to place the power to grant or to withhold work higher in the order of discrimination. For this reason, among others, Canadians moved more slowly than Americans toward recognizing the need for legislation to assure equality of access to employment.

But Canadians are not Americans, and they have never been more conscious of this political fact—or more eager to make the contention express a cultural and social reality—than during the last decade. As a result, Canadian attitudes toward the United States also influenced Canadian attitudes toward Negroes; and as we have seen, until recently Canadians tended to view their neighbors in the midst of their racial dilemma with a certain air of moral superiority, as Canadians often have done when the United States has tripped over its own egalitarian rhetoric. When discrimination was manifest in Canada, many Canadians pointed the finger of blame at "American contamination," whether in 1860 or in 1960. The Negro thus played a rôle in the developing nature of the complex Canadian-American cultural relationship, a symbolic function in which he stood for the superiority of Canadian institutions in the minds of many Canadians. By the 1960s, however, some Canadians were aware that the Dominion's Negroes were the object of Canadian, not imported American, acts of discrimination, whatever the source of the body of ideas that originally encouraged prejudice may have been. And if a note of self-righteousness did creep into the Canadian monologue over freedom and equality, such a note was natural enough when the party being judged so patently was not listening.

American Dilemma: The Negro Problem and Modern Democracy (New York, 1944), *1*, 60–61; and W. S. M. Banks II, "The Rank Order of Sensitivity to Discriminations of Negroes in Columbus, Ohio," *American Sociological Review, 15* (1950), 529–34.

Another source of Canadian inaction lay in widespread ignorance of Canada's own Negro history. The poet Cowper, in celebrating Justice Mansfield's decision, thought that "Slaves cannot breathe in England: if their lungs / Receive our air, that moment they are free." This was adequate poetry but inaccurate current events, for Mansfield's decision freed no substantial body of slaves, even in England, and in Greater Britain Negroes remained enslaved for sixty years. Yet by the present century most Canadians appear to have assumed that slavery in British North America was struck down unilaterally by colonial assemblies which, in fact, lacked the power to move against such Imperial laws. A standard account of Ontario's history published in 1898 concluded that Canadians could "claim the proud distinction for their flag . . . that it has never floated over legalized slavery," a statement true only if one intrudes upon Canada's flag controversy.[3] The 1960s most extensively used tourists' guide to Canada credits the entire Negro population of Nova Scotia to men who came solely from the West Indies.[4] An intelligent survey of Canadian attitudes suggests that fugitive slaves accounted for most of the Maritime blacks, and one of Canada's students of race relations, in writing of discrimination against the Negro, states that since the eighteenth century there had been no slavery in Canada, a notion repeated as recently as 1968 in a scholarly collection of essays on Victorian Canada.[5] As a West Indian Negro noted in 1965, too many well-meaning Canadians assumed that race-consciousness was like a coat, to be "taken off and put on at will," a coat, moreover, that Canadians never had worn.[6] There is no accurate historical memory in Canada of British North America's own experience with the Negro, and until the 1960s there was little knowledge of the extent of discrimination practiced across Canada.[7]

The effect of this lack of historical awareness in Canada was threefold. Canadians commented freely and unencumbered by the facts, for what was

3. Thomas Conant, *Upper Canada Sketches* (Toronto, 1898), p. 127.
4. Robert S. Kane, *Canada A to Z* (Garden City, N.Y., 1964), p. 187.
5. Alistair Horne, *Canada and the Canadians* (Toronto, 1961), pp. 11, 39, 120; Charles W. Hobart, "Non-Whites in Canada: Indians, Eskimos, Negroes," in Laskin, *Social Problems: A Canadian Profile*, pp. 85–86; William L. Morton, ed., *The Shield of Achilles* (Toronto, 1968).
6. Ivan Burgess, "You Like Us in Private, Reject Us in Public," *Canadian Weekly* (Toronto), May 22, 1965, p. 7.
7. Two studies that provide documentation on prejudice are Franklin J. Henry, *Perception of Discrimination among Negroes and Japanese Canadians in Hamilton* (Hamilton, Ont., 1965); and Rudolf A. Helling, *The Position of Negroes, Chinese and Italians in the Social Structure of Windsor, Ontario* (Windsor, 1965); both reports were prepared for the Ontario Human Rights Commission. See also *Peterborough Examiner*, Nov. 24, 1965; and National Committee on Human Rights, *Documents on Discrimination in Canadian Housing*, rev. ed. (Montreal, 1960).

commonly accepted was apocrypha, and apocrypha is not easily pruned. Finding that their record was clean, and seen to be clean, they found much ill and little good in those who were so clearly unclean. And action on behalf of the Negro in Canada was slow to find direction or even expression among whites since so few were aware of any need for action. The editor of the *Montreal Witness,* who in 1848 wrote that "In Canada . . . we must necessarily, trace the prejudice of colour to the neighboring States," presumably saw no contradiction and found no racism in his thinking, when he added that if God made Negroes as they were, man should not condemn His work. The leader writer for the *Toronto Globe & Mail,* who in 1954 suggested that Canada might best prevent the rise of a "racial question" in the Dominion by extending aid to the West Indies so that there would be enough jobs in the islands to keep the black men home, presumably would not have thought himself prejudiced. Canada could, it seemed, avoid prejudice by avoiding blacks.[8]

If white Canadians followed a continental norm, the Canadian Negro did not, in fact, conform to that norm below the surface level. At each stage of his development, he seemed to be perhaps a generation behind his American counterparts; and on the whole he did not seem to have shown the cumulative pride, energy, enterprise, and courage that the catalog of individual acts of defiance would lead one to expect. In Canada Negroes continued to subscribe to Booker T. Washington's nonmilitant, essentially separatist, precepts long after W. E. B. DuBois had begun to move his fellow American Negroes toward militancy. Even today the majority of Negroes in Canada object to the word *Negro* and many wish to be styled *colored,* a term which most American Negroes have come to despise. Few Canadians prefer *Black,*[9] although the number clearly is increasing, as the first National Black Coalition meeting, in Toronto in 1969, attested.

There is, as yet, little Canadian Negro unity, for the black men of Nova Scotia and those of British Columbia have never been brought together in common cause through an organization or a leader. The Canadian Association for the Advancement of Colored People, which has little communi-

8. *Witness,* May 1, 1848; *Globe,* July 2, 1954. See also *Toronto Telegram,* July 25, 1956, Feb. 4, 1958; *Peterborough Examiner,* Sept. 13, 1956; *Pembroke Observer,* Sept. 8, 1958, Sept. 30, 1959; *Toronto Financial Post,* Sept. 12, 1958; *Cornwall Standard-Freeholder,* Oct. 5, 1959; *Toronto Daily Star,* May 13, 1960; *Montreal Gazette,* July 27, 1965; *Maclean's* (Dec. 6, 1958), pp. 46–48, (Jan. 7, 1961), p. 6, (April 17, 1965), p. 12; *Canada Month, 2* (1962), 31–32; Carl T. Rowan, "Negroes in Canada," *Ebony, 75* (1960), 98; M. Marchand, "Le Canada et le condition de ses citoyens nois," *La voix nationale, 39* (1965), 3–5.

9. See W. A. Domingo, "What Are We, Negroes or Colored People?" *The Messenger, 8* (1926), 180, 187; and H. C. Brearley, "Race as a Sociological Concept," *Sociology and Social Research, 23* (1939), 515.

cation with its American counterpart, is scarcely a national organization at all; and until quite recently the Nova Scotia Association for the Advancement of Colored People looked for guidance from the local Negro churches, and from the white-led Canadian Labour Congress, rather than to the Canadian Association. The National Black Coalition served to reveal the divisions that existed rather than to heal them, despite the efforts of its Chairman, Professor Howard McCurdy. (The West Indians also remained divided, as shown in 1970 when Montreal's Black Power newspaper, *Uhuru*, attacked Toronto's *Contrast* for supporting a Caribana festival which would reinforce white notions that blacks were fit only "to sing, dance and take life easy.") While each community has its own, often able, spokesman, those leaders are little known elsewhere. Not even those Negroes who have moved into the administrative echelons of a national organization, such as A. R. Blanchette of the Brotherhood of Sleeping Car Porters or Violet King of the Citizenship Branch of the federal government, have rallied the Negroes of Canada together. There has been no Canadian Martin Luther King, no national figure to whom Negroes can turn. This is a reflection of the general Canadian condition, however, for in a plural society there have been few, if any, figures upon whom whites might place the mantle of national hero.[10]

Nor is a national leader likely to emerge in black Canada in the near future, for as in the United States the secular leadership has been contradictory and divisive. Negroes protest newspaper articles that direct attention to the race of a Negro criminal, but when a Negro achieves distinction they wish the fact to be advertised in racial terms. They wage small battles—to get boxed dates labeled "nigger brand" removed from a Montreal department store, or to force Maritime merchants to give up Pancake Day, an annual celebration in which displays of Aunt Jemima figured prominently—and until the end of the 1960s they have ignored the larger campaign.[11] Where the Canadian Association for the Advancement of Colored People is disassociated from Negro churches, as in Vancouver, membership remains small and attendance at meetings even smaller. Where the associations are directly affiliated with a church, as in Nova Scotia, membership is larger and priorities of action differ, preventing effective national cooperation and circumscribing the expression of alternative secular methods. Black power appeals to the young but not to the middle-aged, and it is thought to be an American import. There are, of course, reasons why

10. See *Uhuru,* Aug. 3, and *Contrast,* June 1, Aug. 1, 1970; and Robin W. Winks, "In Search of a National Hero," *Dalhousie Review, 50* (1963). The Nova Scotia Association eventually became the Nova Scotian Association.

11. "Report on Activities for improved human relations in the labour field during the month of February 1959, Submitted by the Assistant Secretary to the National Committee on Human Rights of the Canadian Labour Congress," mimeographed, p. 2; *The Maritime Merchant, 68* (1960), 13–14.

the Negroes of Canada have not brought forward an effective national leadership of their own, quite apart from the general Canadian tendency towards regional fragmentation. Very few Negroes were of the middle class; and until the 1960s those few who became successful professional men tended to disperse into the wider Canadian community, achieving the assimilation they sought without carrying any or many of their brethren with them. This is especially true in Montreal and in the prairie provinces, in the latter because there are so few brethren to carry in any case. Until recently, regard for sweeping reform has been a concern of the middle class; the lower class, especially in Canada, has settled for improvement, for traditionally it is too poorly educated to plan for reform and too preoccupied with daily needs to carry it forward. At best, few Negroes in Canada have been above the lower middle class in social or economic standing, and class barriers have reinforced those of race.[12]

Then, too, each Negro community has been ill-informed of developments by, on behalf of, or against Negroes elsewhere. There has been no genuinely national newspaper in Canada to make these developments widely known, and all attempts to promote Negro news outlets have failed, with the possible exception of Toronto's *Contrast,* on which judgment would be premature. One result has been the "back then and over there" hypnosis by which Negroes have ignored the tasks near at home. In virtually every black community, I visited—and between 1960 and 1968 I visited them all—Negro spokesmen said that conditions were not as good as they might wish, but after all, life for them was much better than it had been for their fathers, and in any case, if one wished to see a community where conditions were much worse, one should go to place X. In Amherst place X was Truro; in Truro, Sydney; and in Sydney, Halifax. In Halifax urban Negroes thought conditions were far worse in small-town Amherst. In Dresden, the focus of national publicity over the refusal of restaurants to serve Negroes in the face of a court order, Negro spokesmen suggested that one should look to the Maritimes for the more burdensome restraints; and in the Maritimes one was reminded that after all things were much worse for the Negro down in the Boston States. Indeed, the whole of the United States constituted a last resort, a monolithic "over there" to which Canadian Negroes could point when asked whether they had encountered any prejudice. Perhaps they had forgotten their simple Christian's precept, that evil is to be resisted however large or small its apparent manifestation, since evil as such has no dimensions, being an unqualified condition.[13]

12. Stanley R. Mealing has noted that lower-class history is a serious omission from Canadian historiography; the present book, while not based on a class-oriented analysis, is largely about the lower class. See Mealing's "The Concept of Social Class and the Interpretation of Canadian History," *CHR, 46* (1965), 201–18.

13. See Hugh Garner, "Do Canadians Take Pride in Prejudice?" *Liberty* (Montreal), *36* (March 1960), 17, 44, 46, 49.

Today the Negro American may, on the whole, assume himself to be the product of a common historical experience of slavery, war, and reconstruction; and as he wages his civil rights campaigns, he does so with at least some sense of historical continuity and of ethnic unity. In Canada the Negro's position was different from the outset, and the Canadian Negro who emerged from the period of abolitionism and the Civil War differed even more markedly than before the war from the Negro American. That difference, rather than diminishing over the years, was accentuated. By the early 1960s, as English-speaking Canadians angered those who spoke French by demanding that they "talk white"—that is, speak only English—the black men of Canada had made the decision to talk white by identifying when possible with the predominant mores of the charter members of English-speaking Canadian society. Because Canadians thought of themselves in terms of language communities, the Negro automatically was part of that growing mass of Canadians who, whatever their ethnic origin, were carrying the nation toward a projected English-language base of 80 percent by 1981.[14]

The general Canadian response to environment,[15] to immigration, and to cultural pluralism has differed, then, in two important respects from the response in the United States; and as a result the Canadian Negro has come to occupy a rather different position in Canadian society than the Negro does in American society. The first difference arose from the tendency of many white Canadians, especially in the nineteenth century, to think of themselves as transplanted Europeans. While the Americans had consistently asked Crèvecoeur's question—"What then is the American, this new man?"—assuming that the American had become, in fact, a new man (although, to be sure, obscuring Crèvecoeur's original meaning), many Canadians continued to assert with equal vigor that they were representatives of European man and of European civilization. Given this feeling, the Negro in their midst was related by them to his origins, as the MacGregors, the O'Sullivans, or the Thomases related themselves to their Scots, Irish, and Welsh origins. To white Canadians the Negro was and is an African, even more to the degree than they are Europeans; and as such he is a sport, an exotic in a commonly shared and mutually alien environment. In short, although in the United States the Negro became an object of enslavement, discrimination, and even hatred, he came to be viewed (colonizationists aside) as a natural part of the new American landscape;.

14. Rosaire Morin, "L'immigration au Canada," *L'action nationale, 55* (1966), 785. On the "charter groups" and race, see John Porter, *The Vertical Mosaic: An Analysis of Social Class and Power in Canada* (Toronto, [1965]), pp. 60–103.

15. The following four paragraphs are taken, with minor changes, from the author's essay, "Abolitionism in Canada," in Duberman, *Anti-Slavery Vanguard,* pp. 339–42.

while in Canada the Negro who achieved a measure of equality nonetheless was deemed foreign to the landscape, equal but alien.

Related to the tendency of many Canadians to seek no new man in the New World was a second cultural response of white Canadians to their environment that influenced the Negro as well. One goal of newly arrived immigrants to the United States was to shed the old world and its ethnic badges of identity as quickly as possible. Immigrants to Canada were far less eager to be assimilated into some amorphous, anonymous North Americanism or even Canadianism. A bicultural society of English- and French-speaking settlers encouraged what was to become a plural society, in which each group (and most strikingly the French Canadian, Ukrainian, and Doukhobor) fought to guard its separate identity. Since most Canadians retained a justifiable pride in their own ethnic and past national heritages, they assumed that the Canadian Negro should do so too; it was natural that he should be left alone, a foreigner self-segregated to his own communities, a black tile in the mosaic of Canada. But while the white British North American should take pride in his national heritage, march as an Orangeman, thrill to the skirl of the pipes or to tales of Dollard des Ormeaux at the Long Sault, and read of Casimir Gzowski, the Canadian Negro had no national heritage to fall back on for self-identification. He was alone.

While the enslaved American Negro was, in a very real sense, also alone, he at least had the common unity of a shared North American experience, and following the Civil War this common unity was carried forward into new expressions of self-awareness, ethnic identification, and eventually of militant pride. The Canadian Negro, on the other hand, was divided, withdrawn, without a substantial body of shared historical experiences; and until the late 1960s Canadian Negroes remained stratified within by class lines virtually of their own creation. The descendants of the Negro slaves brought to Nova Scotia and the Canadas by the Loyalists at the end of the American Revolution thought of themselves as among the founders of the nation, and they felt they had relatively little in common with the descendants of the Black Refugees of the War of 1812 or the few true descendants of the Jamaican Maroons. The descendants of the fugitive slaves who fled to British North America during the ferment of abolitionism were viewed by the line of Loyalist blacks, free or slave, as outlanders; the fugitive line in Ontario, in turn, looked down upon the Nova Scotian Negroes who were aided in their escape by the British government, not having to fear the breath of pursuit from Simon Legree and Mrs. Stowe's mythical hounds, when Eliza carried the Negro race northward with her to freedom. The subsequent Negro migrations to Canada—those West Coast Negro businessmen who entered British Columbia, the dry land Negro farmers from Oklahoma who moved onto the Canadian plains in 1909–12, the

Harlem Negroes who sought out the gayer lights of Montreal during the period of America's experiment with prohibition, and the renewed post-World War II migration of West Indians—had even less in common with these earlier groups. Except, of course, for the color of their skins, and the common mistake of whites—liberals as well as conservatives—of viewing blacks as a monolith.

Widely dispersed nationally, if clustered locally, brought to Canada in separate waves of immigration which provided little common experience, and well aware that they would best avoid discrimination by drawing as little attention to themselves as possible, Canadian Negroes not only failed to unite, they viewed black unity as a too visible danger. Although abolitionism in the United States did not lead to Negro equality, it did provide a link between the progressive white community and the Negro leadership; and until recently, given good will, it remained a reservoir of fact and emotion upon which many engaged in the battle for Negro equality could draw. Abolitionism in British North America united neither whites nor Negroes, and after 1865 myths arising from the period when British North America had succored fugitive slaves served to help Canadians obscure their own need for subsequent legislation in the area of civil rights. Jean Genêt might well have been thinking of those who today barely hear the muffled voice that speaks of the real meaning of that period of Canadian abolitionism, when he wrote, in *The Blacks,*[16]

> In order that you may remain comfortably settled in your seats in the presence of the drama that is already unfolding here, in order that you may be assured that there is no danger of such a drama's worming its way into your precious lives, we shall even have the decency . . . to make communication impossible. We shall increase the distance that separates us . . . everything here . . . will take place in the delicate world of reprobation.

Many of the young, who read Baldwin, Genêt, Malcolm X, and Franz Fanon, would by 1970 reject the delicate world of reprobation, the NAACP—"for elderly Negroes, those 35 and up"—and accommodationist values, and would begin to speak of Black Power. That the turning point may have come in February of 1969 in the thoughtless, needless, and frustrated destruction of the twentieth century's symbol of quantification, the ultimate equality—Sir George Williams University's computer center—provides an ironic caesura to our story.[17] The conviction in Montreal of

16. (New York, [1960]). Portions of the preceding matter have also appeared in *JNH, 53* (1968), 283–300, and *54* (1969), 1–18, as "The Canadian Negro: A Historical Assessment," in two parts.

17. See "The Blacks of Canada—a Special Survey," *The Globe Magazine* (Toronto), Feb. 15, 1969, pp. 7–26; *Time* (Canadian ed.), Feb. 28, 1969, pp. 10–11; and

Trinidadians involved in the damage to the center would, in 1970, set off extensive Black Power rioting in Trinidad.

This has been, perhaps, a depressing story. It is also a petty one. The number of Negroes in Canada has never exceeded two or two and a half percent of the total population, and even in 1970, when some estimate the black population to have reached one hundred thousand, the percentage remains low.[18] Perhaps for this reason alone, the story has not warranted recounting before. But history is not, after all, democratic, and to dismiss the many thousands of Negroes who have walked across the Canadian stage since 1628—however silently—is to dismiss a human, interesting, and clearly visible segment of the wider Canadian story. Still, such an account must have greater justification than merely being human, interesting, and susceptible to research. Today no historian has the right to indulge himself in the luxury of research that has no point other than merely to unscramble a segment of the past, whether the participants in that segment of the larger human record were numerous or few. Perhaps some may draw from the account presented here, both explicitly and implicitly, conclusions the author believes to be valid and some suggestions he feels worthy of consideration within other contexts by other scholars.

That the story is a depressing one is, in itself, not surprising; but the sources of that depression were not entirely to be expected. That white Canadians held black Canadians in conditions of servitude, if not widely known could nonetheless have been anticipated, for neither white nor black in Canada has escaped many of the major dramas played upon the North American stage. More and more, as historians, social scientists, and social psychologists compare institutions, attitudes, and experiences in Canada and the United States, they find broad patterns of continental rather than national norms—allowing for the essentially regional deviations represented by, for example, the American South and French Canada. That British North Americans allowed the irrelevant institution of slavery itself to wither away, while racial prejudice followed in the nineteenth century upon the heavier influx of black fugitives, might also have been anticipated. Indeed, scholars already had filled in the outlines, and in some cases far more than the outlines, of such conclusions. Nonetheless, paradoxical surprises remain, some surprising because they reflect an unexpected continentalism and others because they depart from that continentalism in precisely those phases of the Negro's history where others have looked for the norm.[19]

Dorothy Eber, *Canada Meets Black Power: The Computer Centre Party* (Montreal, 1969), pt. 1.

18. Anastasia.Erland, "The New Blacks in Canada," *Saturday Night* (Jan. 1970), p. 18.

19. The Negro submission to the Royal Commission on Bilingualism and Bicultur-

Negroes in Canada were often responsible for their own plight, since they by no means made use of all the channels of opportunity or all the roads to progress and all the sources of strength open to them. As in the United States, Canadian Negro leaders strove for accommodation to the dominant white community. They accepted the dominance of that community and worked neither to undermine it nor to become equal to it but to find a guaranteed rôle to play within it. Time and again Negro leaders preached doctrines of postponement, tactics of resignation, and morals of subservience. Rather than insisting that the Negro stand as a man, equal if yet afraid, they insisted that he prepare himself, study and be diligent, and imitate the mores of the surrounding white society, in preparation for the day when he might assert that equality. As a group Canadian Negroes never asserted that equality, and for the most part those individual Negroes who chose to make such an assertion passed across one of three borders and out of the black community: across the color border into the white world, across the residential border into employment and housing conditions so disassociated from the rest of the Negroes as virtually to cut themselves off, or across the political border to the United States. The chief instruments of accommodation, employed even by activist Negro leaders, lay within the schools and the churches. The schools taught values that often divested the Negro of his own legitimate cultural heritage, and the churches too often stressed that final grand accommodation to come in the hereafter, diverting eyes from the immediate problems of the day. To lead the Negro toward white goals may have been laudable, to insist that the North American Negro wished nothing more than to share in the promise of North America through cultural assimilation may even have been sensible, given the few alternatives open to men of little power. Yet these men would always remain Negro in the eyes of white men, since in North America the admixture of even minute quantities of Negro "blood" placed one in such a racial category. In the nineteenth century Negroes ran from a heritage they might well have embraced.

Nor did the pattern change in the twentieth century. The Negro tended to work for and through white leaders of presumably greater power. Perhaps this was the wise way, the Christian way; certainly it was the way of nonviolence, as wise and Christian men will take. But unity need not lead to violence any more than protest need lead to destruction. Goals were defined in gradualist terms and often, by the Negroes themselves, in paternalistic terms: white man, give us funds for a new school house. White man, give us land. White man, we are poor (and you have made and keep

---

alism, "Negro Settlement in Canada, 1628–1965: A Survey," unpublished typescript prepared by Harold H. Potter and Daniel G. Hill (the cover reads D. H. Hill), reaches some conclusions which parallel those that follow and some which are opposed to them. Our respective manuscripts were exchanged in 1967.

us so), give us alms, funds, books, education, grace. In the long run this approach could not continue in the United States, where the Negro constituted over ten percent of the population and where in many southern states in the nineteenth century and in many northern cities in the twentieth century he was in the majority, numerically and occasionally politically, if not economically. How could such tactics be expected to work for the Negro in Canada?

If the Negro in Canada were to have any power, politically, economically, or socially, given his minor presence numerically, he would have had to unite with the far greater body of Negroes in the United States. He consciously would have had to identify himself with a continental norm, with America, with the Negro oppressed wherever the oppression occurred. He did not and, in fairness, he could not. When numerically most obvious, during the 1850s, many blacks had turned their backs upon the United States from which they had come. They could not have been expected openly to work in league with Negro abolitionists in the United States (even though a handful did so), since such activity would have been a denial of the British nationality they now professed to seek. No nation can tolerate a substantial number of recently arrived immigrants who devote their major activities to affairs in another country—often in ways that might embroil their adopted home in war with that country. The United States might tolerate Irish Fenians, for they represented a political power within the nation that required pampering for local reasons, or in terms of foreign policy; the Canadian and British governments could not have tolerated activist black Canadian residents who similarly devoted their chief energies to continued identification with another country. And in the late nineteenth century and during the twentieth century, as Canadians increasingly devoted themselves to insisting that they were not Americans, Negroes who had sought refuge in Canada from social conditions in the United States could hardly have been expected to embrace the country they had just left, nor could Negroes whose roots went back fully as far as the United Empire Loyalists' roots have been expected to embrace continentalism. The Negro in Canada could not change his own situation without more power, and he could not turn to his neighbors across the border for that power. He thus remained cut off from the broad Negro story unfolding on the continent.

This often meant, of course, that he did progress more rapidly, for he did not need to combat institutionalized segregation. Yet precisely because he had the more subtle battle to fight—that against uninstitutionalized, unorganized prejudice—his was in many ways the harder job. In the United States, white Americans would not admit Negroes to be equals in the face of all evidence that, environmental conditioning aside, they were equals. But in the United States white Americans could not ignore Negroes either: they could not be told to leave, for they were needed as a labor force. They could not be forgotten, hidden, or—ultimately—overridden. In Canada they were forgotten, hidden, and overridden: if they left, no one would miss them on the labor market; if they stayed, seldom did they count on that market either. White Canadians could afford to be indifferent to their fellow blacks, and for the most part they were. Prejudice in Canada was not the product of slavery, of fears for job security, of sexual myths, or of any other single factor; it was the product of indifference; the product of a society that was far more hierarchally minded than American society outside the South; the product of far more generalized and thus far less identifiable assumptions about race held widely in the Western world in the nineteenth century and in Canada perhaps longer because they were attacked later.

The story is not that simple, of course. For the Canadian society of which the Negro was a part—or was striving to become a part—was a fragment of a broadly North American society of mobility, affluence, and freedom. Canada did differ in profound ways from the United States; and consequently Canada's reception of the Negro, and the Negro's place in Canadian society, differed from the Negro's place in American society. These contrasts arose not from quantitative differences, real as these were, but from fundamental disjunctions between Canadian and United States mores arising out of their historical development.

One returns, then, to one of the many morally ambiguous ironies of the late 1960s. If the United States was to be likened to a melting pot, whether or not in fact the pot melted (as we now realize that it did not), Canada was to be likened to a mosaic—and, as a sociologist has observed, a vertical one at that. Thus, there was a social totem pole on which the Negro was to take his place, as in the United States; but unlike in the United States the other ethnic groups tended to assume that the Negro would take pride in that place as they took pride in the retention of their identifiable old world cultures. Yet, of all ethnic groups in Canada, the Negroes were the one that no longer had a cultural base to which they could return. They had wanted nothing more than to assimilate—in a society which did not value assimilation, indeed, in a society which persistently denied that there was a cultural norm against which assimilation could be measured. Against the reflected light of which color within the secular mosaic should the Negro cast his shadow? The Italian, the Irish, the French, the Ukrainian, the Scots, the English? For there was no clear form of Canadianism by which Negroes could show their loyalty.

Today, then, the black man in Canada finds himself a symbol of the basic Canadian dilemma. Should he follow outside leadership, the Black Panthers, Stokely Carmichael, Eldridge Cleaver? Should he follow Canadian leadership at the provincial level, as in the new and moderate Black

United Front of Nova Scotia? Should he—as an increasing number of West Indians were doing—turn to the new separatism of Black Power? Should he accept continentalism or reject it? Canada had fragmented him and set him apart from black America. Canada might now give cause to a younger generation to answer the fundamental question, were they Negro Canadians or Canadian Negroes? As one New—and Black—Canadian remarked, "I feel Canadian in the sense that Canada must be what I want it to be." [20] The historian cannot race ahead of the headlines, but possibly, in the 1970s, there was still a choice. The black tile in the mosaic appeared ready to test the pattern.

20. Mervyn Procope, quoted in Erland, "New Blacks," p. 21.

Appendix: How Many Negroes in Canada?

At no time have Negroes constituted more than five percent of the population of any one Canadian province, and consequently they have not been abundant enough, either relatively or absolutely, to threaten any large segment of the Canadian working class. They have posed no major problem relating to intermarriage, for although Negro males frequently were more numerous than females,[1] until recently both sexes have maintained a relatively stable statistical relationship with white Canadians. Nor have Negroes in Canada been sufficiently numerous, organized, or politically oriented to make up a voting bloc, to gain power, or to attract hatred because of their political potential.

But these generalizations have not always been true at all times and in all places. As we have seen, Irish immigrants arriving after the 1840s did fear the Negro as an economic threat, especially competing for jobs on railroad construction gangs; and in the 1850s the Negroes of Chatham, in Canada West, and in the twentieth century those of Halifax County, did exert very real—if minor—political influence through solidarity at the polls. Nonetheless, white Canadians had little reason to think of Negroes in terms of "black power," for they were neither numerous nor strong.

Indeed, we do not know for any decade just how many Negroes there were; nor do we know today. Neither the relatively exact statistics that one might expect of an official census, nor the inexact estimates that one asks of foreign travelers, newspapers, and school authorities, provide a firm basis for enumeration. Well-informed if unofficial estimates of Negro populations in the twentieth century at least double the numbers given in the official census reports,[2] for the reports appear, on occasion, to have been

1. This is particularly so with West Indian immigrants; from 1923, and especially from 1955, the female disproportion among landed West Indians increased. On the other hand, more Negro immigrants from the United States were males, and in the 1920s and 1930s considerable intermarriage between male Negro Americans and female West Indians resulted.

2. In 1930, Greaves ("Negro in Canada," pp. 33–34) noted that the 1861 census returns often underenumerated Negroes, and in 1961 Potter ("Negroes in Canada") remarked that statistics referred to avowed Negroes only and that, while the census of 1951 reported 18,000 Negroes, an estimate was made in 1957 of 23,500 (p. 39). The Canadian Citizenship Branch—in *Notes on the Canadian Family Tree* (Ottawa, 1960), p. 106—reported that, while the 1951 census listed 367 Negroes in Montreal,

administered poorly and, when administered well, to have used an inexact definition for the Negro segment of the nation. The result is that census data, informal guesses, and the more precise estimates of scholarly investigators cannot be reconciled. One may best illustrate the nature of the problem that enumeration presents to the researchers by citing examples.

The central government of Canada has taken decennial censuses regularly since 1871; and as early as 1666 France undertook an elaborate accounting for her colony. This census listed each person by name, residence, age, sex, marital status and occupation. It did not include racial origin, although slaves were enumerated; the majority of these were Indians rather than Negroes. Thereafter the French and then the British continued the census, and detailed reports were prepared throughout the first half of the nineteenth century in most of the provinces (see table on pp. 486–87). New problems present themselves in the use of even those census data based upon a uniform method of calculation after 1871. Most of these reports reveal racial origin, although race, national origin, language, and place of birth were occasionally used as though they represented approximations of the same thing.[3]

At no time was the national census clear as to what was meant by "Negro." When such a category was given as one of twenty-eight or more permissible areas of "national origin" in the census returns, there was no Negro nation; and since respondents were asked to name their own national origin, many Negroes appeared under "African" and "West Indies," while the American-born of fair skins in all probability listed what the questioners—after all—asked for but did not have in mind, by claiming the United States. For "origin" was not related to birthplace by the Canadian census so much as to ethnic background; a Canadian of four generations whose great grandparents had immigrated from Scotland in the 1830s was expected to reply "Scots." Ultimately "Negro" was dropped as a national origin, while being retained in questions relating to ethnic origin.

In other ways terminology is frustratingly vague. In 1861 the Nova Scotian census asked for reports on "origin" in such a way as to lead many Negroes quite properly to specify "native-born" if they wished; that 5,927

informed estimates for 1960 indicated 6,000. *Canadian Welfare, 39* (1963), 30–31, referred to 13,000 Negroes in Nova Scotia as half the Canadian total.

3. On the census, see Department of External Affairs, *Reference Papers*, no. 59, "The Census of 1961," (revised, Oct. 1964); R. H. Coats, "The Growth of Population in Canada," *Handbook of Canada* (Toronto, 1924), pp. 20–26; and as representative, the census returns for 1851, 1911, and 1961. Particularly revealing is the *Census of Canada, 1880–81,* 4 vols. (Ottawa, 1882–85), *1,* 205–301, where Negroes also appear as "Africans" and "Various." Census data through 1961 are conveniently if roughly summarized in the *Canada Year Book* (Ottawa, 1965), pp. 177, 209–11. See also the *Encyclopedia Canadiana* (Ottawa, 1957–58), *7,* 261–62.

SOME INDICATIVE CENSUS RETURNS [1]

	Date of Census	White Population [14]	Reported Negro Population
Nova Scotia	1767		101
	1817	84,913	2,760
	1827	123,878	not given [2]
	1851		
	1861	324,930 [14]	5,927
	1881		7,062
	1921		6,175 [18]
New Brunswick	1767	1,196	1 [3]
	1824	71,420	1,513 [2]
		72,663	
	1834	117,834	1,623
	1840	154,451	1,711
			1,633 [4]
	1851	191,626	836 [5]
			1,058
	1861	249,254	1,233 [5]
			1,584
Prince Edward Island	1881		165 [6]
Lower Canada, Canada East, Quebec [17]	1844		266 [7]
	1861 [8]		163
			190 [10]
Upper Canada, Canada West, Ontario [17]	1842		4,167
	1847		5,571 [15]
	1848		5,469
	1851		4,669
	1861 [8]		13,566 [9]
			11,223 [10]
	1871		13,435
	1881		12,097
	1891		not given
	1901		8,935
	1911		6,747
	1921		7,220
British Columbia	1870	10,124 [11]	462
Dominion of Canada	1871		21,496 [12]
	1881		21,394
	1891		not given
	1901		17,437
	1911		16,877 [13]
			16,194

SOME INDICATIVE CENSUS RETURNS (*Continued*)

Date of Census	White Population [14]	Reported Negro Population
1921		18,291
1931	11,422,000	20,559
1941		
1951		18,020
1961		32,127 [16]

1. Unless otherwise indicated, census data are taken from the *Censuses of Canada* from 1880–81 forward; from the *Canada Year Book;* from Hill, "Negroes in Toronto," p. 35, which summarizes data for Ontario from 1861 to 1911; or from [Canada, Department of Agriculture], *Censuses of Canada, 1665 to 1871* (Ottawa, 1876), pp. 71–376. These figures are indicative only, no attempt having been made to list all returns.

2. From [Robert] Montgomery Martin, *The British Colonial Library* . . . (10 vols., London, 1838–44), 6, *Nova Scotia* . . . , 21, 155–56; PANS, 446, Census Returns, 1827. The larger figure for the white population in 1824 in New Brunswick is taken from *Censuses of Canada, 1665 to 1871.*

3. Although New Brunswick was at this time part of Nova Scotia, these figures are distinct from those for Nova Scotia, above.

4. The smaller figure for Negroes is from James Holbrook, comp., *A Census of the Population of the Province of New Brunswick in the Year 1840* (Fredericton, n.d.), pp. 1–13.

5. The first figure applies to four of twelve counties only: Carleton, Kings, St. John, and York. In the census of 1840, Charlotte, Queens, and Westmorland counties had larger Negro populations than Carleton County did; and assuming that figures for these counties remained constant in proportion to the others, the smaller and larger figures cannot be reconciled. (See *Journal of the House of Assembly*, New Brunswick, *1852, 1862,* Appendixes.)

6. The summary in the *Census of Canada, 1880–81, 1,* 206–21, says there were 155 "Africans" in Prince Edward Island, but the listings total 165.

7. This figure is low, as there were 17,000 "servants," and while the bulk of these would not have been Negro, some would have been.

8. This census was taken in 1860 and 1861 and is especially unreliable since Negroes were moving into the Canadas in substantial numbers at the time the data were being compiled. On the higher Negro figure for Canada East, see Greaves, pp. 33–34.

9. This census gives the Indian population of Canada West as 10,400.

10. See Hill, p. 35, as opposed to *Censuses of Canada, 1665 to 1871,* p. 266.

11. This figure included Chinese.

12. This report did not include British Columbia or Prince Edward Island.

13. The smaller figure is cited by Hill, p. 35, while the larger is drawn from the census and is supported by Coats, "Growth of Population in Canada," p. 24.

14. The returns are frequently vague as to whether they report the number of Negroes as distinct from whites or the number of blacks within a total population. In several instances, I have subtracted the Negro figure from the total figure to arrive at the "white" total, although this total, in fact, may include Indians and other "non-

(*Table notes continued on page 488*)

preferred "colored" merely indicates that the Negro population must have been substantially larger.[4] In the 1862 census for Prince Edward Island, Negroes seem to have been subsumed under Micmac Indians, and many Negroes appear to have been listed as Indians in Canada West in 1861. In a 1929 study the Dominion Bureau of Statistics referred to "the coloured stocks" as all Chinese, Japanese, Hindu, Negro, and Indian residents of Canada taken together. And while the national census of 1931, for example, classed the issue of marriages between white and colored as Negro—following the North American norms that "Negro blood" darkens rather than the Latin norm that "white blood" whitens—in other censuses the respondents classified themselves, and many of those who could pass as white probably did so.[5]

Not only has terminology been imprecise; census-taking techniques have been inadequate until recent times. Research has thrown serious doubts on much of the census of 1861 for the united Canadas, and an examination of the census report for 1851 leads one to discount it as well. Numerous inconsistencies appear in other census returns. Also, as census-takers in the United States have observed, there is a tendency to underenumerate Negro males in any case for various complex reasons, several of which would have been operable in the Canadian censuses.[6]

Further, underenumeration of adults is more likely and passing as white much easier in fluid city conditions, and the Canadian Negro was increasingly urban. By 1960 the Canadian Citizenship Branch of the Department

4. *Report of the Secretary of the Board of Statistics of the Census of Nova Scotia, 1861* (Halifax, 1862), pp. 10, 114–15.

5. *Journal of the House of Assembly of Prince Edward Island* (Charlottetown, 1862), Appendix A; H. Harry Lewis, "Population of Quebec Province: Its Distribution and National Origins," *Economic Geography, 16* (1940), 59–68; *Origin, Birthplace, Nationality, and Language of the Canadian People* (Ottawa, 1929), pp. 13, 16; Greaves, p. 33.

6. John Langton, "The Census of 1861," *Transactions of the Literary & Historical Society of Quebec,* n.s., pt. 2 (1864), pp. 105–24; Carl Schott, *Landnahme und Kolonisation in Canada am Beispiel Südontarios* (Kiel, 1936), pp. 75–76; Daniel O. Price, "A Check on Underenumeration in the 1940 Census," *American Sociological Review, 12* (1947), 44–49.

white" groups. As an example, see *Report of the Secretary of the Board of Statistics of the Census of Nova Scotia, 1861,* pp. 10–15.

15. "Colored Population of Upper Canada, according to the Census of 1847," *African Repository,* pp. 10–13.

16. In 1961 there were 12,526 Eskimaux in Canada.

17. For additional data, consult Greaves, pp. 44–52.

18. For a listing of 1921 figures for all provinces and the Dominion, see Dominion Bureau of Statistics, *The Canada Year Book 1924* (Ottawa, 1925), pp. 108–10. The Year Books for 1930, 1945, 1948–49, and 1956 also provide full figures not incorporated here.

of Citizenship and Immigration estimated that there were 12,000 Negroes in Montreal and Toronto, although the preceding census had shown 1,908. In 1969 the black politician, Lincoln Alexander, said there were 20,000 Negroes in Toronto alone, and one Canadian magazine suggested in 1970 that there were 100,000 blacks in the Dominion. Without question many Negroes are passing as white in Canada today; and with good reason since, except in those nations where a minor portion of Negro "blood" defines one as Negro, they would be regarded not only "cosmetically" but racially as white.[7]

If census data are unreliable, one may expect to find that most unofficial observers in the nineteenth century were remarkably imprecise and that virtually none were disinterested. In 1837 a Montreal lawyer reported that he had heard there were ten thousand Negroes living at Wilberforce,[8] the refugee settlement in Canada West which could not have held more than two hundred at the time. When in 1861 the official census listed 11,413 Negroes in the Canadas, the Montreal *Gazette* asserted that there were ten times more Negroes in Montreal than the census-takers had found. In 1862 Samuel Gridley Howe, on the whole a careful man, estimated that there were fifteen to twenty thousand Negroes in Canada West alone;[9] and in 1901 a writer gave it as his opinion that "well-nigh 100,000" Negroes fled "to Canada." While contemporary observers tended to overestimate the Negro total, sometimes wildly, during times of comparative neglect of the Negro, or of Negro dispersion from his traditional Canadian centers of residence, observers tended to underestimate his numbers.[10]

Three different sets of figures, each set an estimate, seem to have become confused, first in press reports and later in secondary accounts. Several observers gave figures for "Canada," meaning the whole of the British North American Provinces—figures which other observers pre-

---

7. *New York Times,* Feb. 21, 1969; Erland, "New Blacks," p. 18. Adam Clayton Powell, Negro Congressman from New York, took his vacations as a child in exclusive Canadian resorts where his family passed as white (*Time* [New York], *75* [May 2, 1960], 17). On "passing," see E. W. Eckard, "How Many Negroes 'Pass'?" *American Journal of Sociology, 52* (1947), 498–500; John H. Burma, "The Measurement of Negro 'Passing,'" ibid., *52* (1946), pp. 18–22; and James E. Conyers and T. J. Kennedy, "Reported Knowledge Negro and White College Students have of Negroes Who have Passed as White," *The Journal of Negro Education, 33* (1964), 454–59. Eckard and Burma concluded that the popular conception of up to 30,000 Negroes "passing over" annually was mistaken and suggested 2,000–2,750 as more realistic. Conyers and Kennedy argued that more Negro females than males may "pass."

8. New-York Historical Society, Misc. MSS: Thomas Nye Journal, Dec. 12.

9. Pease and Pease, *Black Utopia,* p. 49. The *Gazette* may have inflated its estimate, since it favored white supremacy.

10. *Gazette,* quoted in *Toronto Leader,* Jan. 24, 1862; Howe, *Refugees from Slavery,* pp. 16–17; William Hannibal Thomas, *The American Negro . . .* (New York, 1901), p. 339.

sumed to have been meant to apply solely to Canada West or, at most, to the united Canadas, and upon which they built expanded figures that they thought more accurate for the whole. At other times, sources referred exclusively to the number of fugitive slaves to be found in the provinces, and those who were unaware of an earlier slave period in Canadian history assumed that the total Negro population was covered by the term *fugitive*. Booker T. Washington, for example, wrote that in 1850 the "number of coloured people" was 60–75,000, of which 15,000 were free-born. He apparently meant for readers to infer that between 1850 and 1860 up to 30,000 additional fugitives fled to Canada. And while later scholars, such as Fred Landon, attempted to arrive at reasonable estimates for the total Negro population, the popular press persistently misread what he and others had written: Landon estimated that between 1850 and 1860 from fifteen to twenty thousand Negroes, free and slave, entered the Canadas, bringing the total Negro population for the whole of the British North American provinces to nearly sixty thousand by 1860. The *London* (Ont.) *Free Press* was representative in reporting, on the basis of Landon's research, that sixty thousand Negro slaves escaped into the Canadas alone in the one decade of the 1850s.[11]

Again as we have seen, propagandists for the Underground Railway, and southerners who had reason to exaggerate their losses, inflated the figures relating to fugitives. The American Anti-Slavery Society estimated that fifteen hundred slaves escaped annually from the slave states from 1810 onwards.[12] An unnamed abolitionist clergyman, probably Hiram Wilson,[13] declared from Canada West in 1852 that five thousand fugitives had entered that province in the last two years, while in 1848 he estimated that when he first went to Upper Canada, in 1836, he had seen ten thousand Negroes and that the number had doubled since.[14] In 1855 an English traveler, Henry A. Murray, reported that up to two thousand fugitives escaped into

11. Washington, *Historical Development of the Negro, 2,* 240–44; Landon, "The Negro Migration to Canada after the Passing of the Fugitive Slave Act," *JNH, 5* (1920), 22; *Free Press,* Jan. 12, 1958. Arnold M. Rose (*The Negro's Morale: Group Identification and Protest* [Minneapolis, 1949], p. 15, n. 8) and John Bartlet Brebner (*Canada: A Modern History* [Ann Arbor, 1960], p. 227) accept Landon's figures; and Carter G. Woodson (*A Century of Negro Migration* [Washington, 1918], pp. 35–36) anticipated them.

12. American Anti-Slavery Society, *Twenty-Eighth Annual Report* (New York, 1859), p. 158. See also *New Orleans Commercial Bulletin,* Dec. 19, 1860.

13. The unnamed clergyman wrote on Feb. 2, 1852, that J. W. Loguen had been living in his house since the previous October; this can only have been Wilson.

14. *National Anti-Slavery Standard,* March 18, 1852, quoting the *Christian Register,* in which Wilson's letter appeared, and the *Boston Recorder,* Jan. 7, 1848, quoted in "Colored Population of Upper Canada, According to the Census of 1847," *The African Repository, and Colonial Journal, 25* (1849), 12.

"Canada" each year. Reverend J. B. Smith, a Freewill Baptist missionary who went to the Canadas in 1853, wrote that there were 32,000 Negroes there; the *National Anti-Slavery Standard* discovered there were 20,000 Negroes "in Canada" in 1850, and the following year John Scoble, the British antislavery advocate, said there were 30,000. *The Friend of Man* thought there were 10,000 by 1837; the *London Free Press* found 3,400 in 1839, but 40,000 in 1859; the *Liberator* detected 25,000 in 1852; and the *Buffalo Express* noted that a "recent census" had revealed 45,000 run-aways living in Canada West alone in 1860.[15] The *Markham* (C. W.) *Economist,* on the other hand, could find only 40,000 "slaves" in the province late the preceding year. The Anti-Slavery Society of Canada, which had some reason to know, gave the Negro population for Canada West in 1852 as 30,000; but the government of the province, which also had reason to know, enumerated only 4,669 Negroes in its census for 1851, and elsewhere in the same report referred to 8,000.[16]

Presumably there is less chance for error in local police returns, assessment rolls, and school records (even though some schools were segregated); and some of these kinds of data are worth close examination. The assessment rolls for Fort Malden, across the Detroit River from Michigan, none-theless show something of the problem of finding reliable figures. In 1822 there were, the roll shows, twelve Negroes in Fort Malden, in 1823 there were seven, by 1826 only two, but in 1827 there were thirteen; in 1831 there were twenty-five, but in 1832 there were forty-two and in 1833 only twenty-nine; by 1838 there were forty again.[17] Although one may take these figures to illustrate now mobile the black rate-payers were, those Negroes who were sufficiently established to be assessed were unlikely, in fact, to fluctuate in number quite so widely; one suspects that other factors —human error, variations in those who chose to classify themselves as Negro, changes in township boundary lines, subdivision of land among adult sons, and other changing bases for assessments—account for most of the apparent fluctuations while, at the same time, the statistics do illus-trate a substantial overall increase in numbers that one may accept. And

15. Murray, *Lands of the Slave and the Free: or, Cuba, The United States, and Canada* (London, 1855), p. 225; "Canadian Colonization," *The Freewill Baptist Quarterly, 1* (1853), 413; *Standard,* Sept. 5, 1850; *Voice of the Fugitive,* June 4, 18, Oct. 8, 1851, May 20, 1852; *Liberator,* July 30, 1852; *Friend of Man,* March 15, 1837; *Free Press,* Dec. 3, 1859; *Express,* quoted in *News of the Week,* July 12, 1890 (but on Sept. 5, 1896, the *Express* reduced its figure to 35,000).

16. *Economist,* Nov. 3, 1859 (clipping from Fred Landon Collection); Anti-Slavery Society of Canada, *First Annual Report,* p. 17; *Canada Census, 1851, 1,* 37, 317.

17. Assessment Rolls for the Township of Malden, 1822–1839, copied into an "Assessment Book" in possession of Alvin McCurdy of Amherstburg, Ont.

when in 1841 the governor-general asked the Chief of Police of Niagara to find out how many Negroes there were in his area, and he reported that there were five hundred, one may assume that, when given a specific charge in a limited space, a man presumably trained to standards of reasonable accuracy produced a report that may be reliable.[18]

Still, when one refers to pressures exerted by a Negro population, primary reference is usually made to adult male Negroes who could compete for labor, who would be sufficiently mobile to be observed within a community, and who made their presence felt in other ways. The number of Negro children, on the other hand, was significant largely in relation to pressures on schools and to latent fears of a potential increase in the Negro population. Census data are not always revealing about the age-spread of the Negro population; but one may conclude that the majority of those enumerated were children (although, in turn, children—especially in rural areas—no doubt were considerably underenumerated in these days before children's benefits were paid directly to parents by the state). The raw census data for the township of Sandwich in 1851, for example, shows 407 "people of colour." Of these, not over fifty were born in the Canadas; and of those so born, only eight were over twenty-one years old (and four of these were in a single family). Most of the enumerated Negro families had been in the Canadas five years or less, and therefore almost all of those listed as born in Canada were children.[19]

What is one to make of this welter of contradictory assertions? Clearly no one knew how many Negroes there were in Canada West, or in the British North American Provinces as a whole, and no one had any clear notion of how many fugitive slaves fled into the provinces after passage of the Fugitive Slave Bill in 1850. Census data were inadequate, and for several reasons Negroes were underenumerated; abolitionist newspapers were equally inadequate as judges, and for other reasons they overenumerated. (However, while census data may be of relatively little use in terms of total figures, one may learn much about patterns of segregated residence and ownership of property from several of the earlier returns, and the data have been used this way elsewhere in this study.) Travelers attempted to extrapolate from limited evidence, hearsay, and visits to single communities that were atypical. When the census for 1861 listed the Negro population of Toronto as 510, while the Anti-Slavery Society of Canada, with its headquarters in Toronto, found the city "filling-up" with fugitives, one can rely

18. PAC, G 20, *3:* Charles Richardson to Governor General's Secretary, July 12, 1841.

19. PAC, microfilm of raw census data for Sandwich, 1851, in three books. Amherstburg is lacking.

only on one's own judgment of the relative values to be given such evidence.[20]

However inadequate the official census data may be, certain conclusions nonetheless may now be drawn. From the formation of the Dominion of Canada forward, Negroes have never been more than 2 to 2.5 percent of the total officially recorded population of Canada, and generally much less. Although Canadians have given far more attention to their Indian population, in 1860 Negroes outnumbered Indians in Canada West, Nova Scotia, and New Brunswick; and although the Eskimo is thought to be particularly important to the Canadian self-image, from the 1850s Negroes consistently appear to have been more numerous.

The Negro concentrated in a few areas, especially in Nova Scotia and Canada West, and in those provinces he came to comprise between four and five percent of the population. Furthermore, even within Canada West he tended to cluster in a few communities, so that for those communities at least he seemed to loom large: in the 1850s Negroes made up nearly 20 percent of the total population of Chatham, 25 percent of Amherstburg's, and 33 percent of Colchester's. In 1817 Negroes were roughly eight percent of the population of Halifax, and in some of the smaller communities around Halifax they were substantially more than half the total.[21] Obviously, few Canadians at any time had occasion to give thought to the Negro except as an abstraction; but where the Negro was, he was in some numerical force, especially in the nineteenth century before his wider dispersal.

Beginning in 1865 the number of Negroes in Canada fell, first sharply and then slowly, until 1919–21 when the census of 1921 showed a population increase of 8.38 percent. This was followed by a clear if uneven increase to 1961, when the Negro population was reported to have grown from 18,291 to 32,127, the most rapid rise since the decade of the 1850s. This apparent rise led to widespread but ill-supported speculation in the Canadian population about the presumed attractions of Canada for black immigrants from the United States. In all probability the dramatic growth may be traced not to a sudden increase in immigration or in the Negro birthrate but to new methods of enumeration and to new Negro attitudes.

One may reasonably conclude that the total Negro population of the

20. Nicely representative of the confusion is the *Kitchener-Waterloo Record* for January 7, 1963, which reports under a Toronto dateline a Negro population in Nova Scotia of 9,000 and elsewhere in the issue, under a Halifax dateline, says 13,000.

21. Edwin C. Guillet, *The Pioneer Farmer and Backwoodsman* (Toronto, 1963), *I*, 240; *Halifax Acadian Recorder*, Feb. 7, 1818; *Halifax Evening Mail*, Aug. 6, 1924; PANS, *446:* Census Returns, 1827, pp. 12–15, 34–40.

British North American Provinces (including the West Coast) in 1860 was approximately 62,000, with nearly two-thirds of these in Canada West and perhaps two-thirds of the total having come—whether as fugitives or as free men—from the United States between 1840 and 1860. One may also conclude that in the 1960s there were at least 40,000 blacks in Canada, including students from the West Indies and Africa.[22] As noted, Lincoln Alexander, Canada's only black member of the Federal Parliament, put the figure at 60,000 in 1969. The editors of Toronto's Negro paper, *Contrast,* asserted that there were 40,000 to 45,000 blacks in that city alone in 1970. If these figures are accepted—and the last three in particular are open to dispute since they depart substantially from the official census returns—the Negro population of the Canadas has declined from an unofficial high of approximately four percent in the 1860s to something slightly more than one-half of one percent for the entire nation in the 1960s.[23]

Nonetheless, while one must accept the fact of decline itself, the total number in each decade represented by the decline may be accounted for by the province of Ontario alone. The decrease in Negro population was most marked in the province where earlier the increase also had been most marked, and in all probability both fluctuations were exaggerated. The Negro total for all other provinces remained relatively stable until the end of World War I, when Negro movement out of the Maritime Provinces began to contribute to a substantial increase in Quebec and the West. In short, while no doubt there was exodus from Canada West beginning in 1865, there appears to have been no equivalent movement to the United States from any of the other provinces at any time.[24]

Rather, in Canada as in the United States the Negro has tended to move steadily toward the city. Even as the total Negro populations of Nova Scotia, Canada East, or Canada West declined, the Negro populations of

22. In 1961–62 there were 1,318 nationals of the West Indies officially known to be in Canada, with approximately another 150 believed to be. See Office of Commissioner for the West Indies, British Guiana, and British Honduras, *Location List West Indian Students in Canada, 1961–62* (Montreal [1962]).

23. Several volumes, which need not be cited here, give the Negro percentage for Canada as two, but this arises from an obvious typographical error in Angel Rosenblatt, *La Población indígena de América, desde 1492 hasta la actualidad* (Buenos Aires, 1945), p. x, which reported 20,559 Negroes in Canada in 1940, in a total population of 11,422,000, as 1.80 percent rather than .18. This error was copied over into Frank Tannenbaum, *Slave and Citizen: The Negro in the Americas,* in both its original and reprint editions (New York, 1946, 1963); and from Tannenbaum, in turn, *The Negro Year Book . . . 1941–1946* (Nashville, 1947), p. 198, derived its figures—figures quoted since in many publications. See also *Contrast,* Aug. 15, 1970.

24. This appendix is meant to be illustrative of the problem of enumeration, and it is not a full statistical summary of population movements, trends in intermarriage, and related matters, which are mentioned in their proper places in the text.

Halifax County, Montreal, and Toronto either increased or held steady. At the time of the early censuses in the eighteenth century, 25 percent of all blacks were resident in Montreal and Quebec. In 1911, virtually half the total Negro return for Canada came from seven cities: Toronto, Montreal, Windsor, Halifax, Saint John, Sydney, and Winnipeg. By 1941, 63 percent of all blacks were urban dwellers,[25] and the trend has continued.

Since the census report for 1921 revealed the first modern increase in Canada's Negro population, this postwar assessment—coming as it did in the most anti-Negro decade in the Dominion's history—is especially useful for what it reveals about Negro life in relation to other ethnic groups. The statistics gave little support to racist dogma. Negro fertility ran 21.9 per 100; the English figure was 21.6. (But the infant mortality rate was the fourth highest of all ethnic groups: 15.9.) The Negro illiteracy rate above the tenth year was 8.4 percent, only fifteenth of forty-one groups studied, while the French rate was little better: 7.9 percent. There was an eight percent Negro male surplus over females; the figure for the Scots was six percent. The total number of Negroes who were Canadian-born—74.8 percent—was higher than the total for the English group—68.3 percent—and was exceeded by only four of the forty-one categories.

Thus, the Negro in Canada was not a newcomer and he had lived more or less side by side with the dominant groups—the French, English, and Scots—for some time. Of the remainder among the blacks, 16.9 percent had been born in the United States. Negroes were not noticeably youthful: 21.9 percent were under ten years of age, while the national average was 24.8 percent. Intermarriage was not yet common: only 7.1 percent of the Negroes (a figure identical to that for the Chinese) had intermarried; of those who did so, 54.2 percent intermarried with "British stock." Two figures that were damaging to the Negro, however, and which were to be quoted frequently, dealt with crime: of those in the ten- to twenty-year age group, 602 Negroes (based on per 100,000 of population) were in reformatories, while of those over twenty-one, 415 per 100,000 were in penitentiaries: the second highest and the highest ethnic figures, respectively.[26]

One other source of statistics is almost impossible to reconcile with the

25. Paul Veyret, *La Population du Canada* (Paris, 1953), p. 70. In 1961, nearly all of Alberta's officially enumerated 1,307 Negroes were in cities, except for Amber Valley. See Hugo L. P. Stibbe, "The Distribution of Ethnic Groups in Alberta, Canada, According to the 1961 Census" (M.A. thesis, Univ. of Alberta, 1966), pp. 94–96. See also Norman Pearson, *Town of Amherst Nova Scotia Urban Renewal Study* (n.p., 1965), p. 29; and Lillian Thomson, *Saint John,* p. 46, Maurice Gill, *Montreal,* pp. 69–71, and Wilson Head, *Toronto,* pp. 75–78—volumes in D. E. Woodsworth, et al., *Urban Need in Canada 1965: A Case Report on the Problems of Families in Four Canadian Cities,* 4 vols. (Ottawa, 1965).

26. *Origin, Birthplace, Nationality and Language of the Canadian People,* passim.

above, earlier, or subsequent data: immigration reports. These data also
suffer from imprecise definitions, for black immigration to Canada was reported most often in terms of arrivals from the United States and via ocean
ports. These two categories are not genuinely helpful, for numerous American Negroes undoubtedly entered through the ports of Halifax, Saint John,
Montreal, and Vancouver, just as West Indians and Africans may have
crossed into Canada from the American border rather than entering by sea.
Other data do refer to West Indians as distinct from Negroes, the latter
word apparently being reserved for Americans; but in 1926 the ethnic
totals were dropped, as was the West Indian designation, temporarily. And
immigration reports could be contradictory: although the 1922 report
showed that no Negroes had entered Canada the previous year, this was
corrected in the report of 1923.[27]

A comparison of census returns, birthrate estimates, and immigration
reports for the period 1911 to 1951 shows that one body of data was in
error, or that a considerable number of Negroes "passed over" each decade
into "white" classifications—not primarily through intermarriage, since the
intermarriage rate was low, but presumably through electing to consider
themselves white. This conclusion would also help to account for the
obvious movement throughout the period from Ontario into other provinces
(except Nova Scotia), and for the movement out of Nova Scotia into
Quebec in the second half of the period. In Ontario and Nova Scotia the
Negro communities were more readily recognizable, and if one had made
the decision to "pass," moving to one of the other provinces was an initial
step. By 1961 however, a growth in Negro self-awareness and pride may
help to explain the sharp increase in the reported Negro population, for
many who formerly would have chosen to "pass" may now have chosen to
assert their heritage. In the previous decades a modestly advancing immigration, largely from the West Indies, also contributed measurably to the increase.

If neither the estimates of interested observers nor the reports of disinterested statisticians are to be accepted for this study, one may yet conclude that the Negro, although never numerous, has on the whole been
more numerous than Canadians have thought. His influence in Canadian
history has been of long duration and, at times, of marked importance.
Even more, one may demonstrate that the Canadian experience has been
of significance for the Negro and that the interaction between the black,
the white Canadian, and their shared environment has revealed much of
general interest and importance about Canadian ethnic and racial attitudes.

27. See *Annual Reports of the Department of Immigration and Colonization* . . .
(Ottawa, 1919–27); the Department's successor's reports, printed separately and in
the *Sessional Papers;* and the excellent discussion in Greaves, pp. 44–52.

A Note on Sources

This book arises largely from manuscript materials. That is true of most books by most historians, and usually the fact would not be worthy of special comment. Negro, or Black, history manuscript materials present unusual problems, however. Manuscripts left by Negroes are fewer in number, more difficult to find, and less self-consciously revealing, than manuscripts arising from more traditional sources. The reasons for this comparative dearth are obvious enough, even though until recently few historians seem to have remarked upon the ways in which an anti- or at least non-Negro bias might be reflected in many aspects of North American social history. In historiography, as in chess, the white is always the first to move—or has been until recently.

As slaves, blacks often were illiterate; even when free, they were the least likely of all newcomers to North America to leave behind a written record. They had left no one in Africa to whom they would write of their new experiences; they were not organized in the New World in ways conducive to communication on paper; and they often lacked the skills required to prepare the historian's cherished manuscript, to be produced in time in some neatly catalogued archive. They also were highly itinerant, and frequently not in control of their own movements, so that the little they had by way of a historical record was swept aside, left behind, or burned to keep a body warm during the winter. Furthermore, they were not organized institutionally, so that until the mid-nineteenth century there were very few religious groups, schools, mutual aid societies, fraternal organizations, or other self-venerating institutions to preserve a collective record. Accordingly, Negro records are few, scattered, and require much time and effort to find, assess, and relate.

The assessment of those records that have survived poses another problem. One need not recite here the many arguments about the special nature of Black history, for a flood of monographs has appeared in recent years to attest to the angry shoals upon which anyone who casts himself adrift from traditional historiography may run aground. Obviously, much of the documentation relating to the Negro in North America comes from sources which are "white"; thus we often must view black activities and responses —even Negro thought—through sources which, while contemporary, are at one remove from our subject matter. To note that one must also view ancient Greek thought through modern eyes is not to vitiate the conclusion that by its nature much white-authored history will be biased history. It does not follow, however, that all white observers have got their sums wrong. In any event, the historian works with what he has, and while black observers are to be preferred in many instances, this is not invariably so; and even were it so, surely it is not beyond the empathy of man to compensate at least somewhat for the bias inherent in any observation that moves across ethnic, cultural, or religious chasms. Two superb books —David Brion Davis's *The Problem of Slavery in Western Culture* (Ithaca, N.Y., 1966), and Winthrop Jordan's *White Over Black* (Chapel Hill, N.C., 1969)—have been criticized by some scholars on the ground that they are less about what the Negro did than about what the Negro had visited upon him. If this is so, it does not challenge the validity of telling the latter story, and I cannot hope, in this more modest effort, to escape such criticisms.

In any event, this book says something about both subjects. I have sought out black sources carefully, and feel that I have demonstrated that vast quantities of material do exist, if not always in the customary places. Such sources are not used in preference to white sources, as a substitute or supplement to them, nor in token integration, but as parallel sources of equal and different validity.

As drafts of this work were revised, the documentation was substantially reduced. Anyone interested in additional references to a specific point in the text may consult the author's original notes or one of the earlier drafts of the manuscript, now in the Schomburg Collection of the New York Public Library. The documentation is relatively full as presented here, however, and the following essay will deal with contemporary or original source materials only. The footnotes will lead the reader to the more important of the secondary works, as well as printed documents, which are not discussed here.

Most of the books, pamphlets, and articles cited in the notes were consulted at the British Museum, the Library of Congress, the Public Archives of Canada, or one of the Canadian provincial archives. All major collections of Negro Americana (as the term once had it) known to me were consulted. These include the five leading collections: the Schomburg, the James Weldon Johnson in the Yale University Library, and the holdings of Fisk, Hampton, and Howard universities. Lesser collections in the Boston Athenaeum, the Brookline (Mass.), Chicago, and Providence public libraries, the State Historical Society of Wisconsin, the Confederate Memorial Library in Richmond, Tuskegee Institute, Lincoln University, and the universities of Atlanta, California, and Vermont, were examined, as were special collections of antislavery pamphlets at Cornell University and

Oberlin College. I also consulted over a hundred theses and dissertations. Those drawn upon are cited in full in the footnotes. For a basic list, one may consult Earle H. West, comp., *A Bibliography of Doctoral Research on the Negro, 1933–1966* ([Ann Arbor, Mich.], 1969).

The only partial bibliography on *The Negro in Canada* appeared as this work neared completion. Subtitled *A Select List of Primary and Secondary Sources for the Study of Negro Community in Canada from the Earliest Times to the Present Days,* and prepared by Sushil Kumar Jain, it is available from the University of Saskatchewan library (Regina, 1967). The list is highly selective and uncritical. *A Bibliography of Antislavery in America,* prepared by Dwight Lowell Dumond (Ann Arbor, Mich., 1961), is the most important guide to antislavery literature and other printed sources. It does not entirely replace two earlier, and excellent finding aids: W. E. Burghardt DuBois, *A Select Bibliography of the American Negro* (Atlanta, Ga., 1905), the only one of several such bibliographies consistently to include Canadian citations; and the references in Mary S. Locke, *Anti-Slavery in America, from the Introduction of African Slaves to the Prohibition of the Slave Trade (1619–1808)* (Boston, 1901). These and other bibliographies include a number of highly general histories of slavery which make passing reference to Canada—histories not cited in the present volume. (A representative example is Frank Hoyt Wood, *Ursprung und Entwicklung der Sklaverei* [Leipzig, Germ., 1900], which discusses Canada on pages 7 to 16.) Anyone wishing to compile a definitive bibliography on Canadian Negroes must therefore consult the standard finding aids as well as the raw notes to the present study, for not all relevant secondary titles are incorporated in the printed footnotes of this book.

OFFICIAL PAPERS

Official papers tend to survive, private papers tend not to. Most official papers, at least until recently, will tell far more of the Negro as a person acted upon rather than as actor. For these reasons, the papers of official bodies—and especially of governments—were of relatively less use in this study than in most books which attempt to examine some facet of the Canadian-American relationship. Nonetheless, the official papers were indispensable, especially for a record of the Black Pioneers, the migration to Sierra Leone, the Maroons, and the Refugees.

The Public Archives of Canada, a uniquely well-run and organized depository, contains many basic collections of importance. Among these are the Canadian "G" series, consisting of dispatches and ancillary records relating to the office of the governor-general. Of this record group's twenty-three numbered subseries, the most valuable were G1, Despatches from the Colonial Office, G12, Letter Books of Despatches to the Colonial

Office, and G20, Civil Secretary's Correspondence. The "C" series, British Military Records, provided much information, especially on the War of 1812 and the rebellion of 1837. Particularly fruitful were C1, C35, C801, and C1049. The Minutes of the Executive Council, Upper Canada Land Petitions, State Papers of Upper Canada, transcripts of Letters Patent, transcripts of Treasury letters to the Naval and Military Departments for 1815–21, the raw censuses of Canada, the internal correspondence for Quebec, and several miscellaneous volumes of petitions, also added pieces to the mosaic. The Public Archives Record Centre, a storage depot for the archives, contained the important General Headquarters Papers relating to World War I.

The Public Archives of Nova Scotia, in Halifax, provide equally important data. Beginning with the voluminous Akins Collection (to which belong most PANS volumes bearing a number in the footnotes), successive archivists have drawn together an exceptional range of material. Among the official papers are volumes of unpassed bills, the letter books of the surveyor-general for 1784 to 1824, letters of the lieutenant governor to the Colonial Office, accounts on the final settlement of the Jamaican Maroons in Nova Scotia, a variety of petitions, deeds, and bills of sale, a loose collection of land papers, a bound series of Crown Land Papers, raw census returns, Council Minutes; the Minute Books of Proceedings of the Port Roseway Associates, official documents on Old Township and Loyalist settlements, French documents relating to Acadia, and a number of miscellaneous volumes (on occasion with incorrect binder's titles, as when a volume labeled 1815–18 is found to contain a letter for 1836).

The line between official and unofficial papers is a thin one, of course, and often impossible to draw. Several of the collections used in the New Brunswick Museum in Saint John were of this kind. They include the order books of the York County Militia, the records of the Provincial Chasseurs, extracts from King's County wills, miscellaneous records of the York County registry office, the record book of the Pennfield settlement, and a variety of marriage and death certificates. A wide range of papers pertaining to Crown lands in Ontario, together with the papers of the Education Department (often referred to as the Ryerson Papers) of Canada West, are among the most valuable sources in the Ontario Provincial Archives in Toronto. Deeds, petitions, location tickets, and the papers of the Toronto City Council for the 1840s (supplemented by minutes of town meetings held by the Toronto Public Library), also proved useful. The History Branch of Ontario's Department of Lands and Forests holds a substantial number of survey records that were relevant. In Windsor, the registry office provided lists of property holders, plans for lots, and lists of burials which helped plot the patterns of black settlement in Essex County.

To the West, the Archives of Saskatchewan and those of British Columbia proved especially useful. At the former's Saskatoon branch, a wide range of homestead records have been microfilmed, while the Regina branch holds films of the provincial Department of Education's district files. The British Columbia archives, in Victoria, also hold many official land records, as well as the correspondence of the Commissioner of Lands and Works. The Land Titles Office, in Edmonton, Alberta, and the provincial Department of Lands and Forests, also in Edmonton, provided maps, tax records, and certificates of title.

American official records were of great value, since the majority of Negroes in Canada arrived via the United States. The National Archives in Washington holds such diverse collections as the papers of the Continental Congress, the George Washington papers, the Interior Department's records on the slave trade and Negro colonization, the Harper's Ferry Select Committee files, the records of the Labor and Transportation Committee for Congested Production Areas (1943–45), the State Department's Decimal Files for the first four decades of the present century, and dispatches from twenty-one American consulates in Canada, as well as from American consuls in Nassau, Bahamas; Kingston, Jamaica; and Aux Cayes, Haiti.

The most important repositories of official and public papers proved to be in Britain, however. The Public Record Office is an overburdened, ever-richer storehouse for the colonial, imperial, or diplomatic historian, and many of its volumes were central to this study. These include eighteen CO series: 2, 23, 42, 44, 45, 60, 188, 217, 218, 219, 220, 267, 270, 296, 305, 398, 410, and 537; together with FO series 5, 35, 115, and 414. Each of these series may run to hundreds of volumes, as in CO42, which consists of over 600 volumes, 131 of which proved to contain relevant material. HO45, confidential extradition prints, the Confidential Minute Papers on The Gambia, Admiralty series 1, WO series 1 and 61 (the latter the Jeffery Amherst Papers), the Chatham Papers, and the Headquarters Papers of the British Army in America also were of use. The Public Archives of Canada holds microfilms of the CO series, and PANS holds copies of CO188 and 217–20, although for maximum effectiveness one must still consult the originals. To these official documents should be added Additional Manuscripts 15,485 in the British Museum, on exports and imports of North America, 1768–69.

PRIVATE PAPERS

In the end, however, private papers proved to be of the greatest utility. On subjects of race personal statements are likely to be franker, more frequent, and ultimately more unconsciously revealing than the cautious records of governments can be. If one includes among private papers those of unofficial corporate bodies, such as the Society for the Propagation of the Gospel, of the many antislavery societies in Britain, Canada, and the United States, and of self-help societies, one inevitably will find a more open, accurate, and fuller expression of opinion and reflection of events than any official records might provide. Unfortunately, the number of collections consulted makes a full critical discussion here impractical.

In the United States, all paths lead to the Library of Congress. There I drew upon single volumes of papers relating to Sir Guy Carleton and Sir William Johnson; two boxes and sixteen volumes of materials (the Edward Vernon and Charles Wager collection) on the slave trade prior to 1773; Arthur Hamer's manuscript bibliography on the trade, compiled at Magdalen College in 1799; collections of papers relating to James Gillispie Birney, John Brown, Edward Everett, Augustus John Foster, Hugh Gaine, Joshua Giddings, Marcus Gunn, Mrs. Basil Hall, Julia Ward Howe, Samuel Gridley Howe, John Mitchell, Wendell Phillips, F. W. Pickens and M. L. Bondam, James Redpath, Franklin B. Sanborn, William H. Seward, John Sherman, Elizabeth Cady Stanton, B. F. Stevens, Mary Church Terrell, Booker T. Washington, Theodore Dwight Weld, Walter White, Elizur Wright, Frances Wright, the Western Anti-Slavery Society for 1845–57, and the Edith Rossiter Bevan Autograph Collection. Most valuable of all was the Carter G. Woodson Collection of Negro Papers, the minutes of the American Anti-Slavery Society, and papers of Benjamin, Lewis, and Arthur Tappan. (Several of the letters from Thomas Clarkson and John Scoble to the Tappans have been reprinted in Anne Heloise Abel and Frank J. Klingberg, eds., "The Tappan Papers," *JNH*, 7 [1927], 128–329, 389–554 and simultaneously in their *A Side Light on Anglo-American Relations, 1839–1858* [Washington].)

Boston is the chief center for research on abolitionism. In the Massachusetts Historical Society one may consult the papers of John A. Andrew, John Brown, George Ellis, Edward Everett, Thomas Wentworth Higginson, Amos A. Lawrence, Edmund Quincy, and Amasa Walker—all drawn upon chiefly for unravelling the story of Josiah Henson—as well as the Francis Parkman Papers. The Boston Public Library holds the papers of William Lloyd Garrison, the original manuscript of Josiah Henson's narrative as written by Samual A. Eliot, and Lydia Maria Child, Samuel May, Jr., Amos A. Phelps, and Maria Weston Papers. Across the river in Cambridge, at Harvard's Houghton Library, one may contest wills against the awkwardly organized Charles Sumner Papers, which include correspondence with Clarkson, Eliot, Ellis, Scoble, and Walker, as well as George Thompson and Hiram Wilson. The Ralph Waldo Emerson and William H. Siebert Collections, the latter consisting of forty-five volumes of clippings and notes (three on Canada), and the Houghton theatre collection, with its several relevant playbills, add to the attractions of this most elegant library. One is then drawn further west, to the Sanborn Papers and the typescript volumes of John S. Keyes and Adams Tolman, at the Concord Free Public Library; the Stephen and Abby K. Foster Papers at the American Antiquarian Society in Worcester; and the Sophia Smith and W. L. Garrison II collections in the Smith College Library in Northampton.

New York is no less rich. The New-York Historical Society provided some Thomas Clarkson papers and an excellent copy of John Clarkson's diary, papers of Frederick Douglass, Granville Sharp, Gerrit Smith, and John Taylor, Thomas Nye's journal, a single Charles Stuart letter in the manuscripts of Reverend Francis Hawks, a miscellaneous collection on Canada and settlement, correspondence on the slave trade and slavery, and the records of the Society for Promoting Manumission of Slaves. (Other Frederick Douglass papers were consulted in the Douglass Memorial Home in Washington in 1961.) Down the island, at the New York Public Library, are papers of James Miller McKim and William Lloyd Garrison, and of Maria Trumbull Church, Horace Greeley, and Gideon Welles, all of which proved to be of little relevance, and—in the Schomburgh Collection in Harlem—the John Edward Bruce Papers, a single Henson manuscript, and the Alexander Crummell Collection (useful on Samuel Ringgold Ward). At Columbia University one finds the papers of George Plimpton, of Sydney Howard Gay (in fifty badly sorted boxes), the papers of the Toronto Emigration Office, the John Bartlet Brebner, James T. Shotwell and William J. Wilgus collections—all with materials of relevance—and the L. S. Alexander Gumby Collection of Negroiana, 140 volumes and 25 boxes of clippings on black activities collected from 1910 until 1950, so organized that one may readily find materials on Douglass, Marcus Garvey, Jackie Robinson, and related subjects. The New York Geographical Society library has manuscript maps which denote black settlements in the Maritime Provinces, and playbills and programmes for Tom Shows are in the New York Library for the Performing Arts.

In New York one moves north, most fruitfully to the Syracuse University Library, where a singular private collection was mined. The Gerrit Smith Miller Papers contain voluminous correspondence to Smith from John Brown, Jr., Anthony Burns, Thomas Clarkson, James C. Fuller, Thomas Henning, Benjamin Lundy, Samuel J. May, Jr., Joshua R. Giddings, Isaac J. Rice, John Scoble, Joseph Sturge, George Thompson, Samuel Ward, and Hiram Wilson, as well as subject matter volumes, as for example on the Jerry Rescue. Nearby, the Syracuse Historical Society holds a file on J. W. Loguen and the Syracuse Public Library has a useful collection of genealogical materials. In Rochester, the university preserves the large

William Henry Seward collection, and the Samuel D. Porter holdings on the Underground Railroad. In Auburn one may examine a variety of artifacts, some Canadian, in the Harriet Tubman Memorial Home; and at Cornell University, in Ithaca, the College Papers, an extensive autograph collection, and the Samuel J. May antislavery pamphlet file proved of use.

The State Historical Society of Pennsylvania, in Philadelphia, is yet another of America's superlative state archives. Here the Simon Gratz Collection yielded several interesting items. William Still's letter book, and the journal of the Pennsylvania Anti-Slavery Society Underground Railroad, were disappointing. The minutes of the Pennsylvania Abolition Society, John Brown papers (which produced some Redpath material), and the Robert Vaux, James Buchanan, American Negro History Society, and British Naval Prisoners' correspondence were marginal. Nearby Swarthmore College holds some Elihu Burritt materials.

Other collections were more widely distributed and I researched them as the opportunity arose, usually while on other business. The William L. Clements Library at the University of Michigan houses the large collections of James G. Birney, Theodore Dwight Weld, and Angelina and Sarah Grimké. About one-third of the most important manuscripts were edited by Dwight L. Dumond in 1938, as the *Letters of James Gillispie Birney, 1831–1857* (2 vols., New York). Scoble, Stuart, Sturge, Walker, Wilson, and Henry Bibb are included. Far more extensive are the papers of Sir Henry Clinton (260 volumes) and Lord Shelburne (179 volumes), which are well organized, and which contain John Graves Simcoe and Sir John Wentworth letters. In Detroit, the Detroit Historical Society holds reference files of local Negro materials; and the Detroit Public Library, in its Burton Historical Collection, has numerous scrapbooks, manuscript histories, and related local items, including much on Windsor, Ontario.

At the Ohio State Historical Society in Columbus one may use the papers of John Brown, Joshua Giddings, Benjamin Lundy, and Wilbur H. Siebert, the last consisting of 129 boxes of source materials and notes on the Underground Railroad and five boxes on the Loyalists, especially in Shelburne. At the Rutherford B. Hayes Library in Fremont, Ohio, are letters from or to Harriet Beecher Stowe, John Greenleaf Whittier, and Henry Wilson, as well as Hayes's diary. Elizur Wright's papers are in the library of Case Western Reserve University in Cleveland; while Oberlin College, in its miscellaneous correspondence, treasurer's letters, and the Henry Cowles manuscripts, throws light on the early fugitive slave settlements in Canada West.

At Yale, the James Weldon Johnson Collection, in the Beinecke Library, yielded up several fugitive items and journal files, as well as the original Constitution of Vancouver Island's Confederate League. The Carl van Vechten collection, and the papers of Ulrich B. Phillips and Gertrude Stein, also proved of some use. In Hartford, the Connecticut Historical Society holds the papers of abolitionist Calvin W. Philleo, and the diaries of John J. E. Linton's correspondent, Reverend W. W. Patton, for 1835–89, but unfortunately with 1862–71 lacking. The New Britain Public Library has several diaries of Elihu Burritt that make minor reference to his Canadian journeys. Thomas Clarkson letters are to be found in a variety of places: at Atlanta, Duke, and Howard universities; in the Henry Huntington Library in San Marino, California (and of course in several collections in Britain, to be mentioned shortly). Equally dispersed are the materials of Harriet Beecher Stowe—in some sixty libraries, most of which were circularized with a questionnaire rather than visited—those of Samuel Gridley Howe, in eight libraries, and the papers of John Brown, as noted above. Brown papers are also in the Fisk and Princeton university libraries, the Chicago Historical Society (together with Zebina Eastman papers), and the Kansas State Historical Society. This last institution, in Topeka, also provided Benjamin "Pap" Singleton's scrapbook, while Fisk University sent Xerox copies of relevant letters from the American Missionary Association archives. Howard University has a copy of John Clarkson's diary, Joel E. Spingarn's materials on the NAACP, clippings on Marcus Garvey, and a revealing collection of John H. Rapier papers.

Finally, a scattering of private papers elsewhere were consulted. At Berea College, in Kentucky, Gerrit Smith and Lewis Tappan papers provided no new information. The Slavery-Abolition manuscripts in the University of Virginia's Alderman Library, in Charlottesville, gave up a single document, as did the Robert Trelawny Collection in the Maine Historical Society in Portland, and the Oliver Johnson papers in the Vermont Historical Society in Montpelier. The Oakland (Calif.) Art Gallery holds the will of one mulatto migrant to Canada. The Halvor Steenerson Papers, in the Minnesota Historical Society, were searched for me, without success; and I used a microfilm of the Wickett-Wiswall Collection of Elijah Lovejoy Papers at Texas Technological College. The Office of the Chief Military Historian, in Washington, D.C., made available within its Historical Record Section a variety of manuscript files on the building of the Alaskan Highway.

Papers in Canada were also dispersed across the continent. Again, the most valuable collections were in the Public Archives of Canada. There one may contend with the large and tightly organized papers of Sir John A. Macdonald, Sir Wilfrid Laurier, Robert Borden—all prime ministers— as well as of George Brown, the chief abolitionist, of Sir Alexander Tilloch Galt, Sir Clifford Sifton, and of lesser officials. The Louis-Hippolyte Lafontaine Papers were of great use on the French period, as were the extensive transcriptions from the Archives de la Marine (Serié B) and Archives des colonies (Serié B, C, E, F) in Paris, the general correspondence of Intendant Giles Hocquart, Fonds Français from the Bibliothèque Nationale, and a variety of transcripts from the Archives Nationale. The papers of James Murray, a number of Carleton transcripts, the Ward Chipman, William King and William Dummer Powell papers, the diary of Alexander McNeilledge, the Reynolds Family papers, plans of the Elgin settlement with contemporary maps, and the journal of Mgr. J. O. Plessis were of substantial use. The PAC also holds microfilms of the annual reports, occasional papers, and minute books of the Colonial and Continental Church Society, the originals of which are at McGill University, at the Methodist Missionary Society chambers in London, and in the British Museum. With the exception of the last, it was the microfilm I used. George Julien's "Coon" of Laurier is in the National Gallery of Art, also in Ottawa.

In Toronto, the Ontario Provincial Archives provided the papers of William Canniff, J. George Hodgins, Mrs. Edmund George O'Brien, James R. Roaf, the Robinson and Russell families, John Graves Simcoe, Thomas Smith, D. E. Stevenson, Bishop John Strachan, and a typescript by John M. Elson. The University of Toronto added the John Carleton papers; while the Toronto Public Library, always pleasant and efficient, drew from its midden the diary of Elizabeth Russell, the papers of Peter Russell, Robert Baldwin, William Jarvis, and David William Smith, the Hubbard-Abbott Collection, the manuscript autobiography of Thomas H. Scott, Mrs. Amelia Harris's scrapbooks, and a variety of broadsides, playbills, prospecti, and clippings. All save the Smith papers proved of immense value. The pamphlet and newspaper holdings of the Victoria University (Toronto) Archives were of great use. A Bengough sketch satirizing blacks hangs in the William Lyon Mackenzie House.

Elsewhere in Ontario, the obvious centers of research were Windsor, London, and Hamilton. The first provides, in its public library, files on the AME and BME churches, on black activities in the area, and on Amherstburg's churches and schools. Several private individuals made available to me family letters, genealogical charts, marginally annotated books, and maps, while the Hiram Walker Historical Museum also possesses maps, miscellaneous Negro papers, and lists of black settlers. Nearby, in the Amherstburg Public Library, the tiny Boyle Collection attested to the presence of the early missionaries, while the museum of the Fort Malden National Historical Park offered the account book of David McLaren Kemp, an undertaker who was racially conscious, the F. C. B. Fall and Farney papers, assessment rolls, Amherstburg deeds, and miscellaneous fugitive slave and genealogy files.

The second city, London, provides unpublished local histories in both the public library and at the University of Western Ontario, while the Hamilton Public Library holds a number of Negro-related scrapbooks and G. C. Porter's manuscript history of the area. McMaster University, in Hamilton, houses the Canadian Baptist Historical Association collection. This includes James W. Johanson's manuscript history of the Amherstburg Association, 1841–61, the minute book of the Sandwich Baptist Church, and the minutes of the Western Regular Baptist Association.

Local libraries in Ontario, the province to which the majority of fugitive slaves fled, cannot be ignored. The Barrie and Orillia public libraries, the Simcoe County Surrogate Court Office (in Barrie), the Norfolk, Lennox and Addington, and Oxford historical societies, as well as those of Lundy's Lane and Thunder Bay (the latter in Port Arthur), and the Chatham-Kent Museum in Chatham, all hold relevant manuscripts. The last also has books from William King's library; and Uncle Tom's Cabin Museum, near Dresden, displays playbills and artifacts relating to Henson. The office of the Board of Education in Chatham, in the minutes of the Board of Public School Trustees, and the Grant African Methodist Episcopal Church in London, through its church records, helped fill in lacunae in the local story.

The Maritime archives were of slightly less importance. The Public Archives of Nova Scotia holds individual files on several early settlers, transcripts from the Carleton papers, the diaries of Simeon Perkins (now available in carefully edited form), a copy of the first volume of John Clarkson's diary, an Etter family genealogy, several Ward Chipman papers, and typescript local histories. Unfortunately, the papers of William S. Fielding remain closed to researchers. Also in Halifax, the public library, in its local history collection, and the provincial library, in its newspaper holdings, proved of great help. The Cambridge Maritime Military Library has compiled a file on William Hall, V.C. The libraries of Saint Francis Xavier University in Antigonish and Acadia University in Wolfville, the last incorporating the Maritime Baptist Historical Collection, also yielded scarce pamphlets and journals; and the Colchester Registry Office, in Truro, has a relevant registry book. The office of the *Halifax Chronicle-Herald* holds clippings on the singer, Portia White. I am particularly grateful to Marjory Whitelaw of Pictou, who loaned me seven reels of taped reminiscences of, and conversations with, Blacks living in Nova Scotia in the 1960s.

In New Brunswick, the provincial museum in Saint John provided papers and files on the Eastman, Hazen, Mayes, Odell, Thompson, and Whetsel families, and some surviving Chipman papers, together with numerous scrapbooks. In Fredericton, the University of New Brunswick, the legislative library, and the Rectory office of Christ's Church, hold local registers, wills, and minutes. The Saint John Public library has several files on local Negro activities. The Woodstock Public Library has a small collection of petitions. The Charlottetown, P.E.I., Public Library offered typescript local histories which attest to early Negro arrivals.

In Quebec, Negro-related private materials were less frequent than one would expect. The Chateau de Ramezay, in Montreal, has a manuscript record on slavery in New France, while the Archives du Palais de Justice attest to sales, births, marriages, baptisms, deaths, and burials. The McCord Museum of McGill University, in the Porteous Manuscripts, and the McGill University Library in its local history materials, were of some value. The provincial archives in Quebec hold the manuscript second volume to Marcel Trudel's study, wills and other actuarial records, and transcripts of the Ordres du Roi. The Brome County Historical Society in Knowlton offers local manuscripts and files. The single most valuable collection in the province, however, is one not generally open to the public: the records of the Canadian Labour Congress's Joint Advisory Committee on Human Relations, originally kept at the Workman's Circle Center in Montreal. Extensive and highly revealing, these records tell of annual trips into the Maritime Provinces, as well as within Quebec, to note and combat instances of overt discrimination. These, together with folders on discrimination in the Toronto office of the Human Rights Commission, provided the single greatest non-newspaper source of data on the 1950s and early 1960s. The collection includes mimeographed reports on activities, normally issued eleven times a year, files of local union newspapers, newsletters of municipal employee groups, and carbons of correspondence with representatives in the field. In the end, relatively little of this material was incorporated into the present study since the decision was made to limit it largely to the years before 1960.

Across western Canada private collections helped tell the story of Negro settlement, although interviews proved to be the most valuable source for the prairie and mountain provinces since most settlement was within the memory of living men. The Archives of British Columbia hold the reminiscences of John Sebastian Helmcken, the diaries and account books of Wellington D. Moses, the diary, correspondence, and record books of Edward Cridge, the diaries of Reverend Ebenezer Robson and of Augustus F. Pemberton, the South Saanich Public School Visitor's Journal, transcripts relating to the Colonial Missionary Society, several questionnaires directed to early pioneers, and letters written by J. S. Matthews concerning early black settlers. The Vancouver City Archives, in the Vancouver Public Library, has other Matthews correspondence and local clipping files, and Victoria's City Hall gave me documents signed by Mifflin Wistar

Gibbs, which I will deposit with the Yale University Library. The University of British Columbia and Victoria University, in Victoria, hold scarce pamphlets. The Central Saanich Baptist Church records, in that church, attest to other Negro settlers, while the Nanaimo Archives has a single document on the Stark family. Interviews on Saltspring Island, as well as in Vancouver, proved of great importance.

On the prairies, private papers were less useful. The Glenbow Foundation Archives, in Calgary, holds typescripts and taped interviews with Nettie Ware and seven other black settlers, related papers, and letters on the settlements. The Edmonton Public Library has a clipping file on the Ware family, and the Rutherford Library at the University of Alberta, in Edmonton, has several manuscript local histories. So, too, does the Saskatchewan Legislative Library, the University of Saskatchewan, and the North Battleford and Moose Jaw public libraries. Again, interviews in Amber Valley, Breton, Wildwood, Lloydminster, and Calgary, Alberta, and in Maidstone and Battleford, Saskatchewan, proved of greater value.

In Great Britain records are voluminous, cherished, yet nonetheless not so well cared for as in North America. Most collections in the British Museum take on a semiofficial character, as with the Bright, Clarkson, Chatham, Cobden, Haldimand, Layard, Liverpool, Peel, and Sturge papers. The BM reading room is unparalleled, of course, for yielding up rare pamphlets, such as the annual reports of the Sierra Leone Company or the Elgin Association; odd copies of the *Nova Scotia Packet* for 1786, almanacks, and other printed primary sources. The Archives of the Hudson's Bay Company, at London's Beaver House, provided many references to Negroes in the fur trade. Somerset House on the Strand, through its wills; the College of Arms, in its modest Joseph Brant file; the West India Committee Library, in the minutes of that body for the nineteenth century; the visitor's register in the Lambeth Palace Library; and the Estlin Papers in Dr. Williams Library—all in London, also proved helpful. University College, London, houses the papers of Lord Brougham, which fortunately include a full, annotated index to that collection's fifty thousand letters.

Of particular value for this study were the various archives and libraries of the London-based missionary societies. The Society for the Propagation of the Gospel was exceptionally important. It holds the account and minute books of the Associates of Dr. Bray, the Canadian Papers of that group, abstracts of proceedings, the journals and reports of the SPG, and special West African and Nova Scotian files, together with the Houseal correspondence and many pamphlets. The original SPG letters from Nova Scotia are contained in a file box labeled "Dr. Bray's Associates, Canadian Papers." While most of this material is now on microfilm at the PAC, the film is unusually difficult to use, and one is well advised to consult the originals if at all possible. The Muniment Room of the Methodist Missionary Society holds twenty boxes of letters from the Canadian colonies to London, of which six were pertinent. (All are on microfilm in the United Church of Canada Archives at Victoria University, Toronto.) The Society for the Propagation of Christian Knowledge preserves annual reports and lists of votes for grants of money; the Church Missionary Society held relevant journals; and Friends' House contains letters to and from Philadelphia that proved relevant, as well as the journals of John Candler and his wife.

The other great classification of records in Britain upon which I drew were those of antislavery groups. By far the most important is the large antislavery collection at Rhodes House, Oxford. This consists of most of the papers of the British and Foreign Anti-Slavery Society (and the Anti-Slavery and Aborigines Protection Society), which are systematically transferred from the latter body's headquarters at Denison House, in London, to Rhodes House, every ten years. (The Society retains a small research library, the Thomas Binns Collection of pamphlets, some reports of the Sierra Leone Company, and a modern file on Sierra Leone for the period of independence.) Rhodes House holds the early minute books, memorials and petitions, correspondence, and files of the printed *Annual Reports* and of the *British and Foreign Anti-Slavery Reporter,* from 1840. These papers were acquired in 1951. To them have been added manuscripts on the South African Labour Corps of World War I, which grew from an offshoot of the Society—the Committee for the Welfare of Africans in Europe—and manuscripts relating to Indians in Canada. The antislavery papers have been edited and microfilmed, with an introduction by Howard R. Temperley, the author of a forthcoming study on the Anglo-American antislavery connection which I have read in manuscript.

Elsewhere in the United Kingdom one finds a variety of lesser collections. The Earl Fitzwilliam Papers, in the Sheffield Central Library Archives, and other Fitzwilliam Papers in the Northamptonshire Record Office at Delapre Abbey, were relevant to the story of Sir John Wentworth. The Southampton Civic Record Office has made available the papers of George S. Smyth. Wilberforce House, at Kingston upon Hull, the Ipswich Central Library, and the East Suffolk and Ipswich Record Office in Ipswich hold papers of the ubiquitous Thomas Clarkson. Other Clarkson letters are in the hands of Thomas Hodgkin, of Oxford, who was kind enough to grant me access to them at his home in Ilmington; and in the Granville Sharp papers, at Hardwicke Court, Gloucester, which Lieutenant-Colonel A. Lloyd-Baker, their owner, made available. The John Rylands Library in Manchester has some George Thompson materials and the Crawford Muniments, containing letters written by Earl ᴾalcarres. The Royal Archivist at Windsor Castle consulted the appointments book of

Queen Victoria for me, while the Greenwich Naval Library microfilmed the log of the *Sandown,* which touches upon the *Asia.* The National Library of Scotland, in Edinburgh, has the Edward Ellice Papers, while the papers of the Earl of Dalhousie, in the Scottish Record Office, contain correspondence with Bathurst for the Refugee period. The County Archives of the East Riding of Yorkshire, in Beverley, holds one such letter. There are Simcoe Papers in the National Library of Wales in Aberystwyth and in the Devon Record Office, Exeter. A petition from Hitchin, Herts., relating to the fugitive slaves in Canada, listed by Charles O. Paullin and Frederic L. Paxson in their 1914 *Guide to the Manuscripts in London Archives for the History of the United States since 1783* (Washington), as being in the House of Lords Papers, could not be traced.

Some records that one would like to consult are apparently gone forever. We know that the papers of Reverend Daniel Cock, as well as most of those of Benjamin Lundy, were destroyed by fire. None of the original records of the Anti-Slavery Society of Canada have been preserved outside the George Brown papers. The papers of Sam Hughes appear not to have survived in any quantity. Materials relating to T. B. Macaulay are said to exist in a garage in suburban Montreal although efforts to gain access to them failed. While the widows of both Marcus Garvey and Richard Wright sent me various printed materials, they were unable to make available any manuscript collections. No references to the Fort Erie meeting survive in the papers of W. E. B. DuBois, now in the hands of Herbert Aptheker, who kindly searched them for me. One could also wish that registers of marriage had been kept in Ontario prior to 1867, but they were not, and thus only Anglican and Roman Catholic interracial marriages could be documented for Canada West.

Archives in other lands proved of marginal utility. In Bermuda, the Bahamas, and Jamaica, local archives, public libraries, and churches yielded records relating to the period when *Canadian-West Indian Union* was under desultory discussion. This documentation is cited in my recent short monograph, subtitled *A Forty-Year Minuet* (London, 1968). The Jamaican Institute, the public library of Montego Bay, and the University of the West Indies hold rare printed materials on the Maroon Wars. The Sierra Leone Archives, in Freetown, contain John Clarkson's draft diary, while the library of the University of Sierra Leone has the diaries of George Ross. In Freetown I interviewed some members of the Sierra Leone Settlers' Descendents League. In Bathurst, The Gambia, I passed an exciting week in anticipation while working through the archives—then totally unorganized and strewn about a small shed—to find only two documents relating to the Nova Scotians, duplicated elsewhere. By chance, the diary of Thomas Haweis, in the Mitchell Library, Sydney, Australia, while being searched for another purpose, helped to confirm one aspect of the

Nova Scotian migration. In Paris, visits to the Bibliothèque Nationale, the Archives Nationale, and related archives confirmed that the transcripts (many handwritten) in the PAC and in Quebec were full and accurate.

Finally, one must note other papers which remain in private hands but which nonetheless were made available to me, in addition to those mentioned above. Fred Landon's private collection, to which that devoted scholar gave all interested historians ready access, proved to be of great value, especially on the 1840s and 1850s. Consulted in Professor Landon's home in London, Ontario, these materials have been transfered since his death in 1969 to the University of Western Ontario. Of only slightly less value were the records kept in the Cornwallis Street Baptist Church in Halifax. These include the reports of the African Association of Nova Scotia, and also of the Nova Scotia Association for the Advancement of Colored People together with extensive church records. Other churches in British Columbia, Alberta, Ontario, and Nova Scotia also opened up their records. The documents of the Negro Community Centre in Montreal, made selectively available by Stanley Cylke, and those of the Canadian Labour Congress, discussed above, were particularly useful. So, too, was the private collection of Mr. Alvin McCurdy of Amherstburg, who has drawn together many local records on the Negro community along the Detroit River. At the Harvard School of Public Health I was given unrestricted access to the original research transcripts of the "Stirling County" project, which includes raw data on Negro residents in Digby County, Nova Scotia.

I advertized for individuals to come forward with materials, and a number did so. In this way files, letters, and clippings were made available on Matthew Henson, by Herbert M. Frisby of Baltimore; on John Ware, by Nettie Ware of Kirkaldy, Alberta; on Henry Vandusen, an early black settler, by Glen Ladd of Dresden; on J. B. Harkin, by Miss Dora Barber of Ottawa; on Negro Freemasonry in Canada, by Reginald V. Harris of Halifax; and on the Brotherhood of Sleeping Car Porters and the British Columbia Association for the Advancement of Colored People, by Frank Collins of Burnaby. Mrs. Keith Staebler loaned her notes on New Road and her letters to her husband, written at the time; the Reverend William P. Oliver, Bishop W. J. Walls, and Reverends Charles Este and Winston H. H. Clarke, as well as Messrs. Stanley G. Grizzle and Daniel G. Hill, all made personal items available. Cecil Harmsworth King kindly permitted the author to examine his copy of John Clarkson's diary in his office at the *London Daily Mirror*. (This diary has since gone to the University of Illinois.) Many others wrote letters of reminiscence, provided references, sent clippings from local newsapers, and simply offered encouragement in response to my appeals printed in a variety of journals.

Printed Materials

The chief depositories for rare and scarce published materials have been indicated above. A wide variety of printed sources, especially annual reports of societies and government agencies, is cited in the notes. These range from *The Jesuit Relations and Allied Documents* (Cleveland, 1897), edited by Reuben Gold Thwaites, through the annual reports of the Education Department of Nova Scotia. Wherever possible the originals of printed materials have been consulted, as with the *Relation* of 1632, by Paul le Jeune, which is in the John Carter Brown Library in Providence. Of particular value were the annual reports of the Canadian League for the Advancement of Colored People, of the United Baptist Convention of the Maritime Provinces, of the Elgin Association (of which only numbers 3, 4, 6–7, and 10–11 appear to have survived, although number 2 is quoted in the *Voice of the Fugitive* for November 5, 1851, and number 5 in Benjamin's Drew's work), and of the British Columbia Association for the Advancement of Colored People. Some reports that one expected to be of value—those of the Upper Canada Committee of the Society for the Propagation of the Gospel in Foreign Parts, for example—proved of little use, while others that one ordinarily would pass over (the Proceedings of the *Semi-Annual and Annual Session of the Grand Lodge of A.F. and A. Masons of Ontario . . .*) were found to contain Negro-related records. A wide range of almanacs, maps, novels, artifacts (as with Negro berry baskets preserved in the Citadel Museum in Halifax), and "association items" (i.e. inscribed books belonging to John Scoble, or locks of Thomas Clarkson's hair) helped to demonstrate a relationship, an activity, or an attitude.

Other contemporary materials are less difficult to find. The British, Canadian, and provincial *Hansard's,* for example, provide most of the evidence on the legislative record. The published accounts by fugitive slaves, such as William Wells Brown, Lewis Clarke, Frederick Douglass, Josiah Henson, J. W. Loguen, Austin Steward, or Samuel Ringgold Ward, and the contemporary works of Benjamin Drew, Levi Coffin, Samuel Gridley Howe, John J. E. Linton, Harriet Beecher Stowe, Charles Stuart, Joseph Sturge, and others, are all central to this study. The value of most of these is indicated at the appropriate places in the notes.

Newspapers and Magazines

While newspapers are a particularly valuable source for the historian, they also present special problems. Full files of any except the major metropolitan papers are not likely to have survived and if one wishes to consult an entire run of a single newspaper, issues often must be pieced together from a variety of locations. Viewed as a source of data, a single issue of a single paper has its values; viewed, as in this study, as a source of public opinion, and as a molder of that opinion as well, longer and coherent runs of a paper are essential. Before accepting a news item, the historian must do what he can to verify its version against other types of sources or, failing such sources, against another newspaper. The researcher must know of the newspaper's ownership, the politics of its management and of its editors, the extent to which it may be dependent upon advertising revenue for survival, and the nature of its readership. Obviously, news concerning Negro activities that appears in a Negro newspaper differs from news that appears in an anti-Negro paper. Equally obviously, the estimate given to the size of an abolitionist meeting by the antislavery *Toronto Globe* is to be set off against an estimate provided by the anti-abolitionist *Toronto Leader,* although not necessarily equally. The editorial opinions of Toronto's *Christian Guardian* will spring from different sources than the opinions expressed by a secular press. And one must view distinctions within their time, for most nineteenth-century newspapers in North America, even if overtly secular, employed biblical and racial rhetoric on their editorial pages.

Apart from the problem of interpretation there is, when dealing with the press of the last century and a half, the added problem of quantity. The nineteenth century was a time of thriving local newspapers, and for a full understanding of what Canadians read about black men (or about events which would have given rise to thoughts about black men, as reporting on the Civil War and Reconstruction in the United States did), one might reasonably be expected to examine many dozens of titles. In the twentieth century, with the growth of massive Sunday newspapers, of supplements, and of advertising, the researcher must contend with a bulk beyond the capacity of any one person. Yet these newspapers demand examination, for on their editorial pages, in their news items, among the social notes, through those letters to the editor which they chose to print, and even in the products they advertized, one may find frequent suggestions of racial awareness. A full content analysis of the Canadian press on this subject would be a lengthy study in itself (and very possibly not worthwhile).

Accordingly, I narrowed the range of research in two ways. Leaving myself thirty-two newspapers which I examined personally and—to the extent that complete files were available—on an issue-by-issue basis, I chose forty-five other newspapers, largely weeklies, which both I and bursary assistants examined on the basis of specific known events, or in the light of a bulking of Negro-related news items in the initial twenty-three papers. These thus came to comprise a "control" group. Further, since it quickly became apparent that no single researcher could keep abreast of press opinion and news items in the decade of the 1960s (during which time this investigation was made) while carrying out other research as well, I sought professional help. From 1960 to 1968 the Canadian Press Clipping Service of Toronto supplied weekly sets of material drawn from the entire spectrum of the Canadian press, including all items referring to Negroes—whether in the United States or Canada—and to discrimination, against whatever group. The specific newspapers drawn upon, 210 titles in all, are indicated seriatim in the footnotes. A full list would be superfluous here, as well as unduly cumbersome, especially since masthead titles often changed two or three times. These clippings have also been given to the Schomburg Collection.

Certain newspapers were of particular help. Fortunately, many are now available on microfilm from the Canadian Library Association; and the Public Archives of Canada, which has runs of all those on film, will loan its microfilm holdings. The Ontario Public Archives provides many others. In this way one could examine, for example, the *Amherstburg Echo* for 1888–1949, the *Charlottetown Islander* for 1853–65, the *Chatham Journal* for 1841–44, the *Chatham Planet* for 1850–58, *The Christian Guardian* for 1837–39, the *Fredericton New Brunswick Royal Gazette* for 1786–1816, the *Halifax Acadian Recorder* for 1813–1919, the *Halifax Herald* for 1897–1938, the *Halifax Journal* for 1796–1817, the *Halifax Morning Chronicle* for 1884–1969, the *Halifax Novascotian* for 1841–47, the *Halifax Royal Gazette* for 1752–1824, the *Hamilton Spectator* for 1916–47, the *London Free Press* for 1859–1969, the *Montreal Gazette* for 1840–1969, the *Montreal Witness* for 1846–54, the *Quebec Gazette* for 1768–94, the *Saint John Globe* for 1847–1912, the *Saint John New Brunswick Courier* for 1849–52, the *Saint John Royal Gazette* for 1784–1800, the *Toronto Globe* for 1850–1969 (in later years the *Globe & Mail*), the *Toronto Financial Post* for 1942–69, the *Toronto Mail and Empire* for 1911–28, the *Toronto Star* for 1930–65, the *Toronto Telegram* for 1924–69, the *Vancouver Province* for 1935–69, the *Victoria Colonist* for 1859–1969, the *Victoria Daily Evening Express* for 1863–65, and the *York Upper Canada Gazette* for 1793–1838. The *Maidstone Mirror* for 1943–53 is on microfilm in the Saskatchewan archives. Joseph Howe's personal copies of *The Nova Scotia Chronicle and Weekly Advertiser*, together with the *Nova Scotia Gazette and Weekly Chronicle*, both from Halifax, are in the PANS. For background on many of these papers at mid-nineteenth century, see Helen Elliot, comp., *Fate, Hope and Editorials: Contemporary Accounts and Opinions in the Newspapers, 1862–1873, Microfilmed by the CLA/ACB Microfilm Project* (Ottawa, 1967).

Another approach was to examine, in so far as possible, all of the press of a single key community. For this purpose Windsor was chosen, and extant files of the *Windsor Herald, Daily Star,* and *Daily Record,* were consulted. For Halifax, in addition to the papers cited above, the *Nova Scotia Packet, Weekly Chronicle, Mail-Star, Herald,* and *Evening Mail* were used.

Particularly important, of course, were the abolitionist newspapers. In Canada these were the *Voice of the Fugitive,* published in Windsor from 1851 to 1852 (with a file in the Burton Historical Collection of the Detroit Public Library); *The Provincial Freeman,* from Chatham, 1853–ca. 1857 (the originals of which are in the University of Pennsylvania Library), the short-lived *Voice of the Bondsman,* from Stratford (with a single 1856 copy surviving in the library of the University of Western Ontario), and *The True Royalist,* of Hamilton (of which two copies may be found in the Fort Malden Museum). In the United States there were far more such newspapers, and they have survived longer. Those that were searched (although there is much duplicated content among them) were the *National Anti-Slavery Standard* from New York, 1840–70 (New York Public Library), *The Friend of Man,* 1836–38 (on film), Garrison's Boston-based *Liberator,* 1831–65, *The Oberlin Evangelist* for 1848–53 only, *The Anti-Slavery Record,* New York, 1835–37, *Anti-Slavery Examiner,* New York, 1836–45, *American and Foreign Anti-Slavery Reporter,* New York, 1840–46, *Anti-Slavery Lecturer,* from Utica, N.Y., 1839, *The Emancipator,* New York, 1834–49, and the *National Anti-Slavery Bazaar,* Boston, 1845–50 (all at Yale); *The Genius of Universal Emancipation,* Benjamin Lundy's parapetetic newspaper, 1821–39 (The Johns Hopkins University Library); and *Frederick Douglass' Paper,* for 1853, and the Salem, Ohio, *Anti-Slavery Bugle,* 1845–60 (both LC). Also consulted was the *New York Herald* for 1854–71, which is not cited in the footnotes since it was drawn upon heavily in a previous book by the author, and since most of its news items on Negro activities in Canada were reprinted from other sources. Of the greatest value was the *British and Foreign Anti-Slavery Reporter* to which 'and Aborigines Friend' was later added, published in London 1840–1966 (Yale University Library, 1840–57, 1859–67, and 1857–59 on microfilm).

American and Canadian Negro newspapers were a chief source of information and opinion. All Canadian Negro newspapers and magazines, as discussed in Chapter 13, were researched on an issue-for-issue basis. Locations of files are discussed in the notes to that chapter. Of some sixty-three American Negro newspapers available on microfilm by 1968, eighteen were used. Those that proved to be helpful were the *St. Paul Appeal* and *St. Paul Broad Axe* (not to be confused with the *Chicago Broad Ax,* which was also consulted), *The Elevator,* from San Francisco, in which Mifflin Wistar Gibb's articles appeared, New York's *Amsterdam News,* the *Pittsburg Courier,* the *Detroit Plaindealer,* and the *Cleveland Gazette.*

Several newspapers were used at the office of the papers themselves, on occasion with the aid of an informal index compiled locally for in-house purposes. That this method of approach was useful may be shown by the *Saint John Telegraph*. Two important items relating to the Refugee Negroes of the 1820s, drawn from reminiscences of early settlers in Nova Scotia, appeared in issues in 1875 and 1884. *The New Freeman*, a Roman Catholic newspaper, also of Saint John, and read in that paper's library, first revealed in its issues for 1903 the controversy with *Neith* magazine, as related in Chapter 13. The *Toronto Star*'s clipping file proved of great use as well. Regrettably, two files of newspapers that might well have enriched the story told here were not found: The *Truro News,* of which only a post-1949 run survives in that paper's office, following upon a fire in that year; and the *Dresden Times,* published weekly from 1872 into the 1890s.

Magazines, like newspapers, are organs of opinion. The number of articles on Negro-related subjects, as well as their content, is one index to the degree of interest in the "Negro problem." Articles on race relations in the United States, appearing in contemporary Canadian periodicals— *Atlantic Advocate, Commentary, Canadian Forum, Canada Week, Maclean's, Saturday Night*—reveal much about the use of the Negro as a metaphor in the relations between the two countries. Articles in welfare-oriented journals, such as *Canadian Labour Reports*, the *Journals of Education* for both Ontario and Nova Scotia, *Canadian Welfare, L'Action nationale, The Labour Gazette, The Journal of the Y.M.C.A., The Anglican,* or *The United Church Record and Missionary Review*, increasingly contain Negro-related materials. American journals, especially in the nineteenth century, had occasion to report on the progress of the fugitives in Canada and, later, on race relations in the Dominion. Thus, *Atlantic Monthly, The Chautauquan, The Literary Digest, The Living Age,* the *New York Times Magazine, The North American Review, Outlook, Scribner's* and *The Southern Workman,* all contain relevant matter. So, too, do religious periodicals in both countries: *Acadia Bulletin, American Missionary, The* [Canadian] *Baptist Magazine and Missionary Register, Canadian Christian, Canadian Evangelist, Freewill Baptist Quarterly, Gospel Tribune and Christian Communionist, The Maritime Baptist, The United Church Observer,* the *Upper Canada Baptist Missionary Magazine,* and several others. The most important British publications were the *American Baptist Free Mission Society* (seen in the American Antiquarian Society), *Arminian Magazine, Baptist Annual Register, The Colonial Protestant, Free Church of Scotland Monthly,* and *Herald of Peace.* British and Canadian popular periodicals were of substantial help. These include the *Acadiensis, The Anglo-American Magazine, Canadian Antiquarian, Canadian Illustrated News, Canadian Magazine, The European Magazine, Excelsior, Le Foyer Canadien, The Imperial Magazine, Knox College Monthly, London Review, Lowery's Claim, The Maple Leaf, Numismatic Journal, The Tourist: A Literary and Anti-Slavery Journal,* and *The University Magazine.* Special interest publications were often of value: *Canadian Cigar and Tobacco Journal, Canada-West Indies Magazine, McDuff Ottawa Report, The Maritime Merchant, West India Commercial Circular,* or the New York organ of the Ku Klux Klan, the *American Standard.*

The publications of and for Canadian and American Negroes were carefully searched. Among these were those magazines discussed in Chapter 13, together with *The African Interpreter, African Repository and Colonial Journal, The Afro-American Magazine, The AME Church Review, Amherstburg Quarterly Mission Journal, The Black Man, The Black Worker, Bronze American, Challenge, The Colored American Magazine, The Colored Harvest, Crisis, Ebony, The Freedmen's Advocate, The Informer, The Messenger, Negro Digest* (now *Black World*), *Negro World, Pine and Palm, The "Spoken Word,"* and *The Street Speaker.*

Most of the above were consulted at the Library of Congress, the Yale University Library, the British Museum, or the Schomburg Collection. Exceptions are the Canadian religious periodicals, read in the New York Public Library, at Acadia University, McMaster University, the Union Theological Seminary (New York City), the American Baptist Historical Society (Rochester, New York), or the Southwestern Baptist Theological Seminary (Fort Worth). Four earlier journals were consulted at the Harvard library: *American Baptist Magazine and Missionary Intelligencer, Massachusetts Baptist Magazine, Massachusetts Missionary Magazine* (all published in Boston), and *Vermont Baptist Missionary Magazine* (Rutland).

These early journals gave way to others, of a secular nature, in the twentieth century. Again, as in the 1920s so in the 1960s, Canadian fiction in magazines and books reflected continental norms, and the black man was set to play the same rôles in Canadian as in American fiction. Negroes began to appear with regularity in Canadian novels, still as stock figures but now supporting other stereotypes. Mazo de la Roche wrote her poorest book, *Morning at Jalna* (1961), about pro-Southern Canadians during the Civil War; Ernest Buckler, a highly regarded Maritime novelist, was to prove unexpectedly graceless when he attempted to hint at prejudice in Nova Scotia's classrooms in his 1959 short story, "Long, Long after School" (*Atlantic Advocate, 52* [1959], 42–44); and even Gabrielle Roy and Ethel Wilson, fastidious writers both, could not bring black men to life in *Street of Riches* (1957) or *The Innocent Traveller* (1949), respectively. Still, Canadian fiction comprises yet another source in which one may explore racial attitudes, and I have attempted to read all that touches upon the black experience.

Some of this fiction is discussed briefly above, on pages 295 and 393, note 6. A full analysis would require control over techniques of literary criticism not available to me. One may note the frequent use of the Negro for sexual imagery in poetry (for example Karl Shapiro's "Nigger," who was but a "penis as loaded and supple and limp as the slaver's whip"); he appears often in the work of Leonard Cohen, Raymond Souster, Louis Dudek, and Irving Layton, and on the poetry pages of such "little magazines" as *Evidence, Exchange, Limbo,* and *Prism.* Just as Canadian smut sheets such as *Tab* and *Flash* lost few opportunities to report on allegedly undesirable Negroes, so did liberal and often very able writers give black men prominence in order to satirize the Establishment. In this, Mordecai Richler was especially consistent, as well as cutting, in a succession of novels: *The Apprenticeship of Duddy Kravitz* (1959), *The Incomparable Atuk* (1963), and *Cocksure* (1968). It was left to an uncommonly disabled little magazine, *Edge* ([ii/1964], p. 71), to suggest a new ritualistic rôle for the black man, since ". . . the sexual revolution and the Negro revolt give promise that men may yet come to love each other truly, i.e. erotically." To the rural rustic behind the barn the Negro remained the subject of graffiti, while to the self-nominated intellectual he provided a litmus-paper test for Freedom, Now, of the desire to infuse meanings with symbols rather than symbols with meanings. Since the Negro—always covertly and frequently overtly—had become part of the general cultural baggage for the Canadian of the 1960s, a far wider range of materials than ever before became the source for a study of racial attitudes in Canada. Thus, even individual library copies of Morley Callaghan's moving novel of human weakness, *The Loved and the Lost* (1951)—which describes the fascination of a white girl for Black culture—become sources because, through the marginal notations penciled in by angry readers, they reveal responses to black-white relationships. Few references to these, or to most of the journals mentioned above, have been incorporated into the footnotes, however, since the notes already are extensive, the magazine items highly repetitive of data found elsewhere, and the study of public opinions more rightly the province of the social scientist than of the humanist.

Still, not all knowledge arises from the printed word. Interviews with many dozens of Canadian Blacks, from Cape Breton Island to Vancouver Island, helped to provide a background of attitudes, recollections, regrets, and pleasures for the post-1865 years. Seldom was I refused the gift of time, attention, and of being taken seriously; often this gift was accompanied by a willingness to bring out faded photographs, wedding invitations, and family Bibles, the visual evidence of a past that was thought worth remembering. Such items are not "documents" to add to the piling of note upon note—no more than the casual conversation with a black laborer, a sidewalk artist, or a school custodian may be—but they provide above all the interest and the pleasure to sustain the more traditional search for evidence. There are many thousands of Negroes in Canada to whom I was not able to talk, and this study is the weaker for that. It is nonetheless much the stronger for the help of those with whom I could talk, for the fact that no one appeared to feel that the end result would lack "relevance" to the continuing black experience.

These contacts often took place at the scenes of events described in this book, for no archive can provide a substitute for traversing the ground of history itself. One must see for oneself precisely where William King's house stood, or William Peyton Hubbard was buried, or John Clarkson spoke to the assembled Nova Scotians. To see the Cockpit Country of Jamaica; to view Freetown from the heights above Fourah Bay; to write upon a table in Kingston upon Hull where Wilberforce wrote—in short, to experience the place, the sight, and occasionally the sound of history is to remind oneself that the historian must always use that slight gift of intuition which makes the leaps of faith he takes between evidence and conclusion possible. It is in such places and moments as these, as well as in the continuing chase within the confines of an archive, that the historian must ever seek his pleasure and his sole reward.

Index

In the index, as well as the text, hyphens appear in French-Canadian names when their owners generally used them, and otherwise not. Place names in Canada, but not all place names elsewhere, are indexed. Only those footnotes which contain substantive discussion of a point are included in the index. The maps are omitted, as is the Note on Sources, except for pages 512 and 519–20.